I0796583

UPSTATE NOW

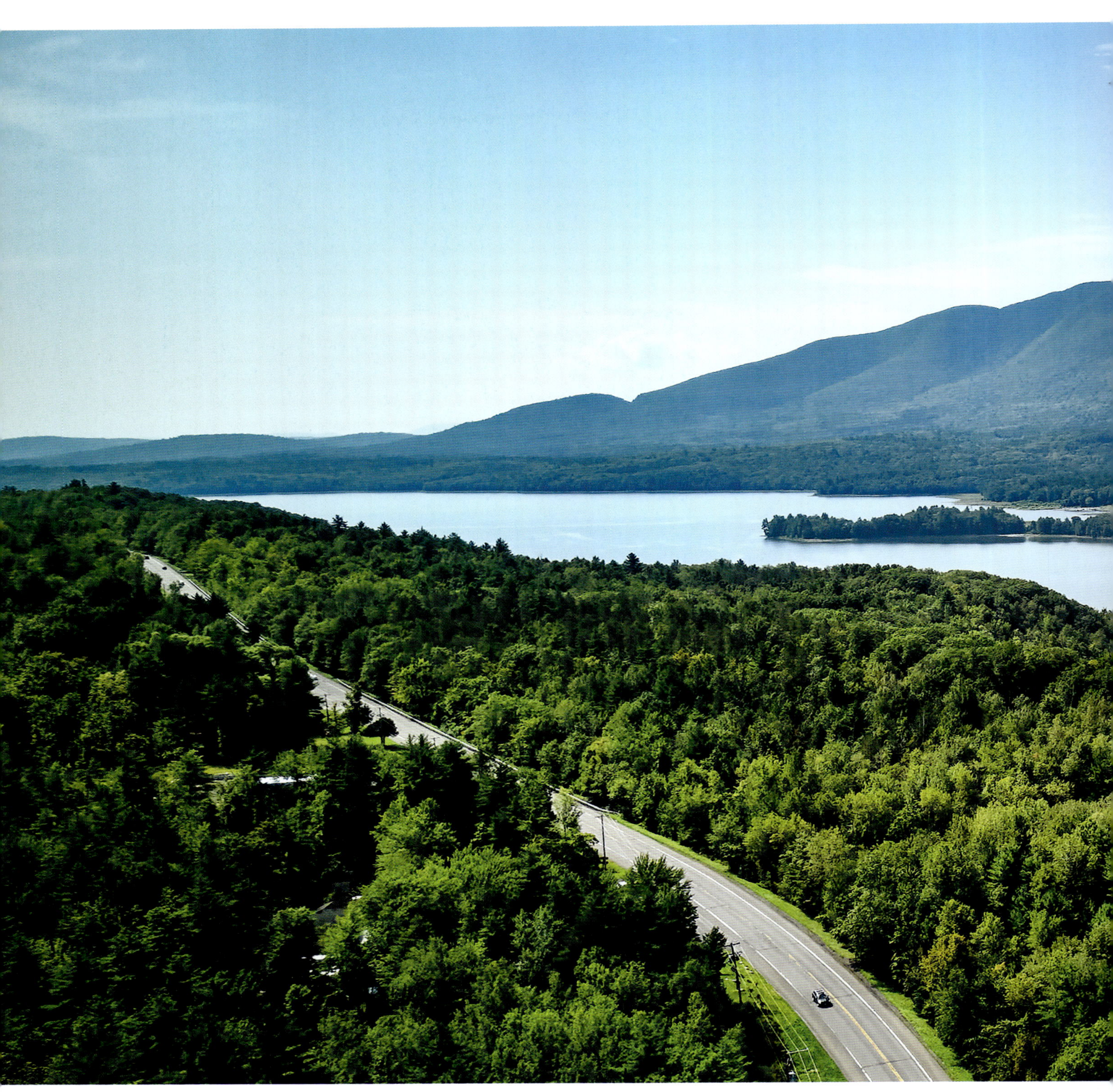

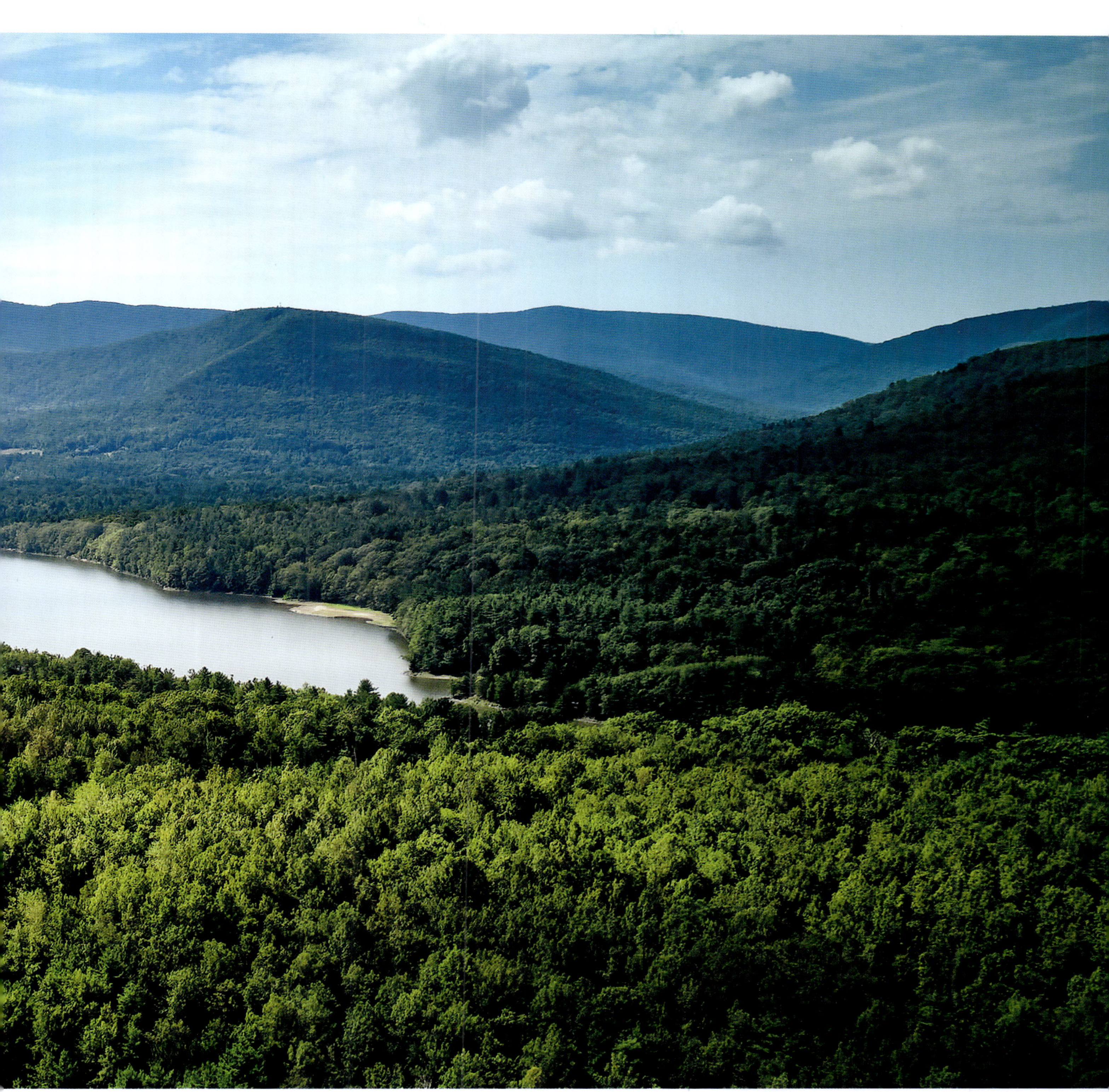

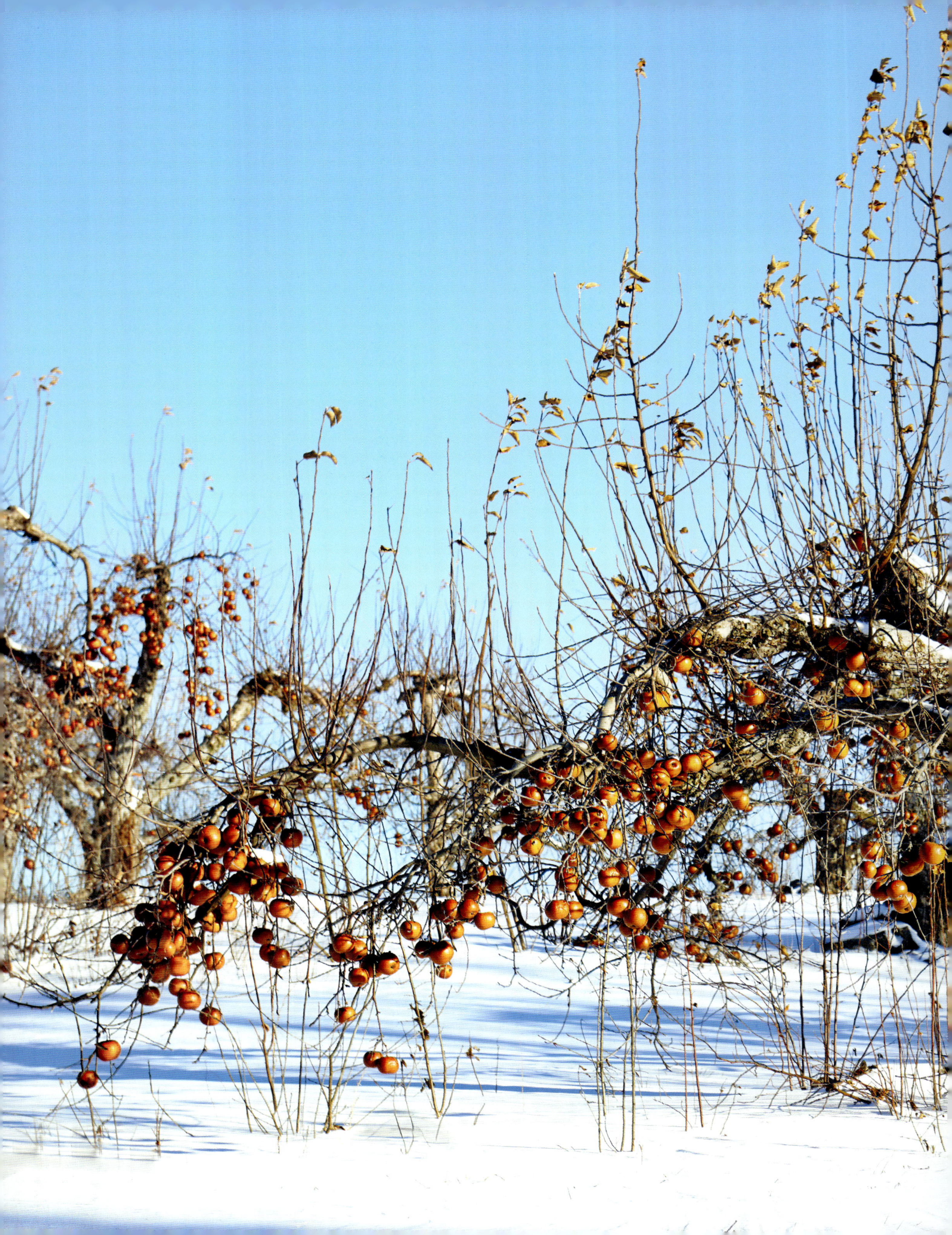

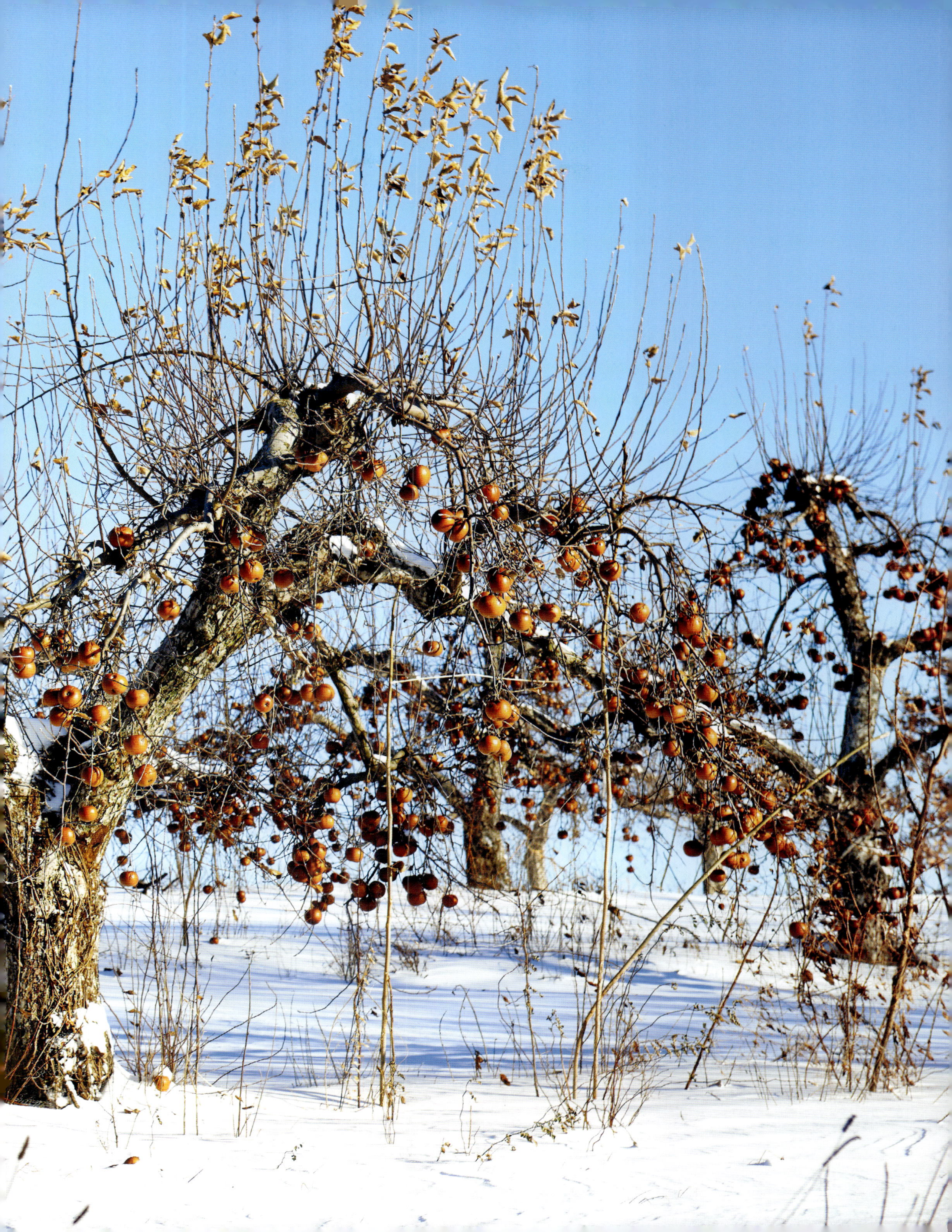

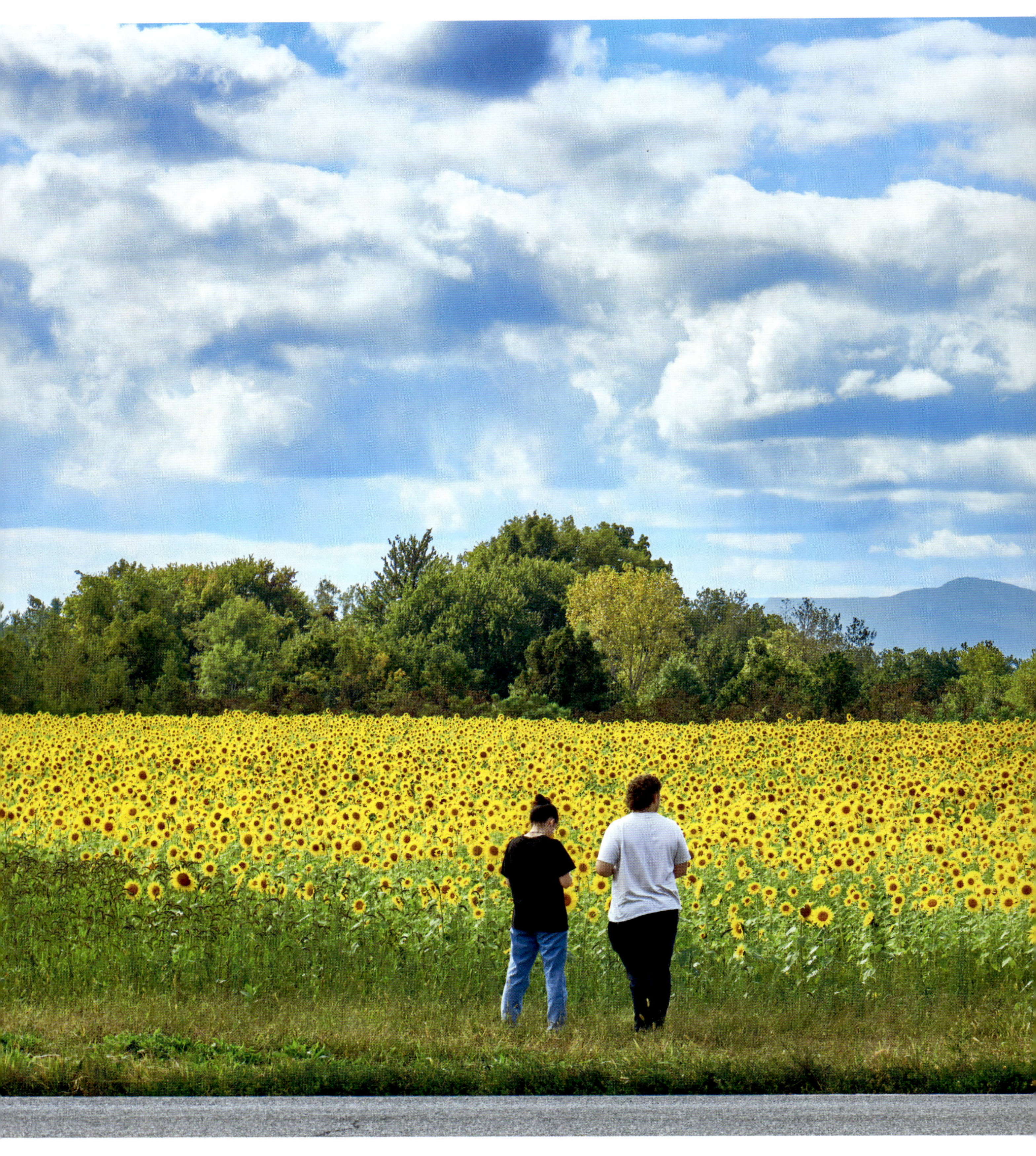

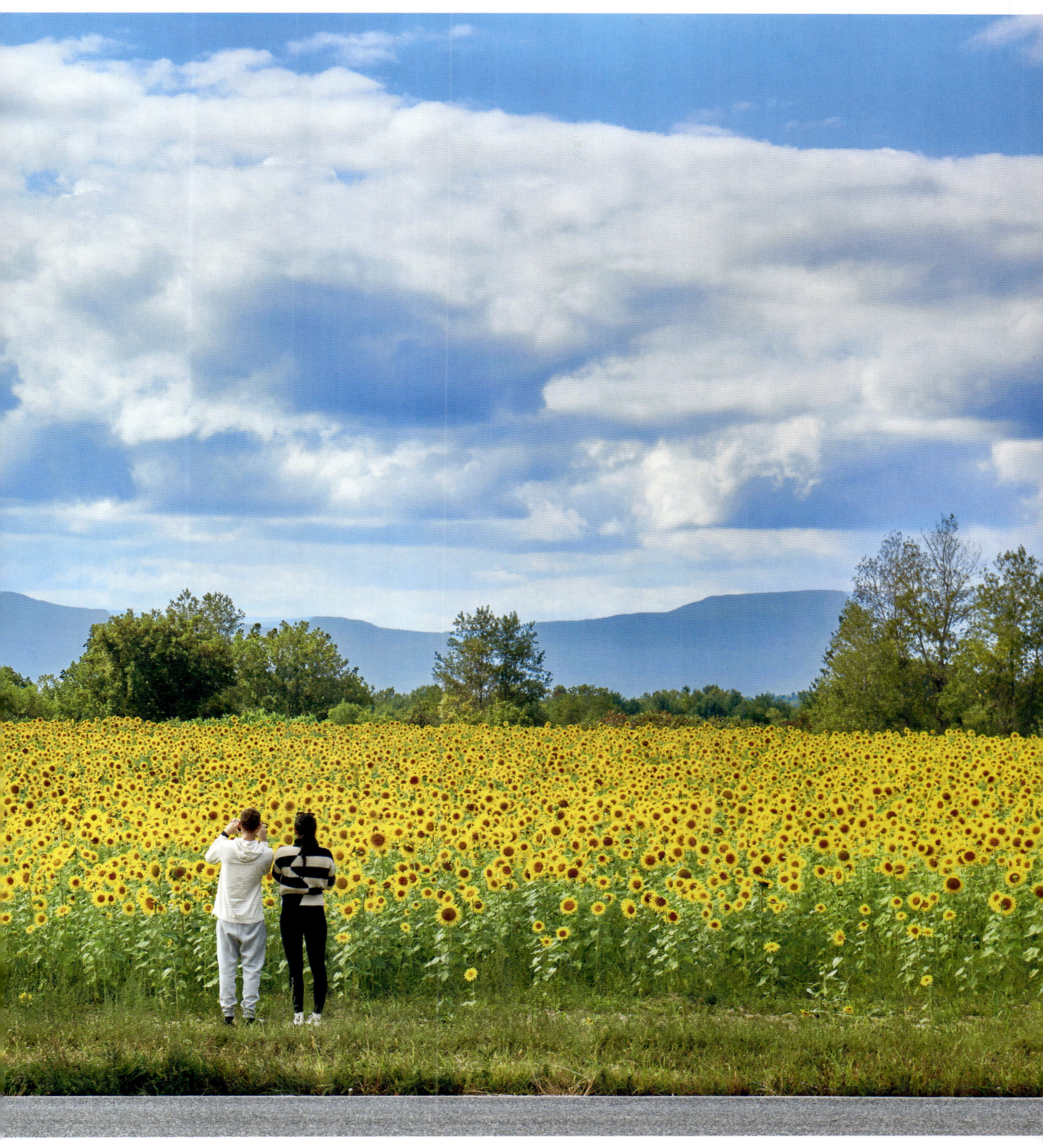

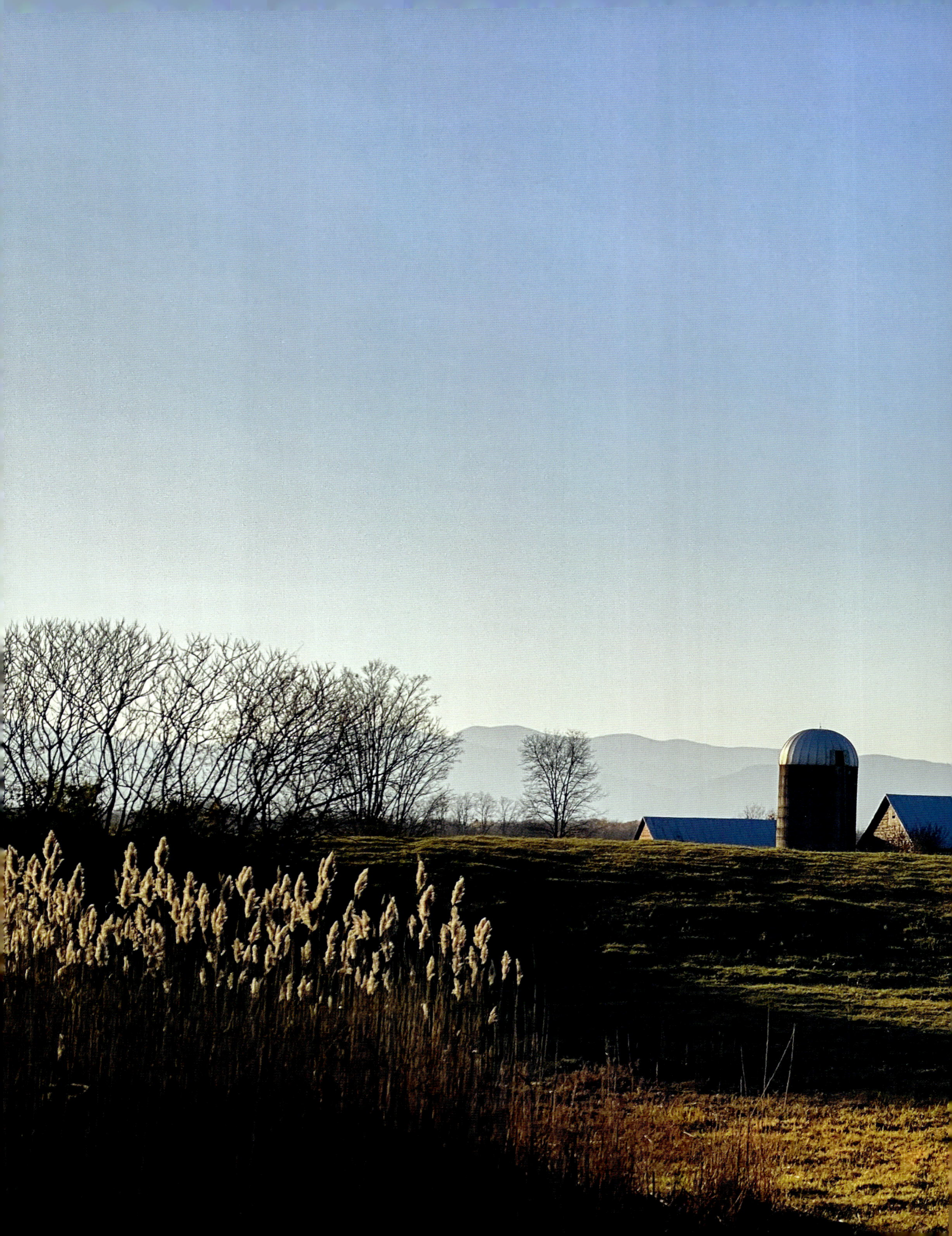

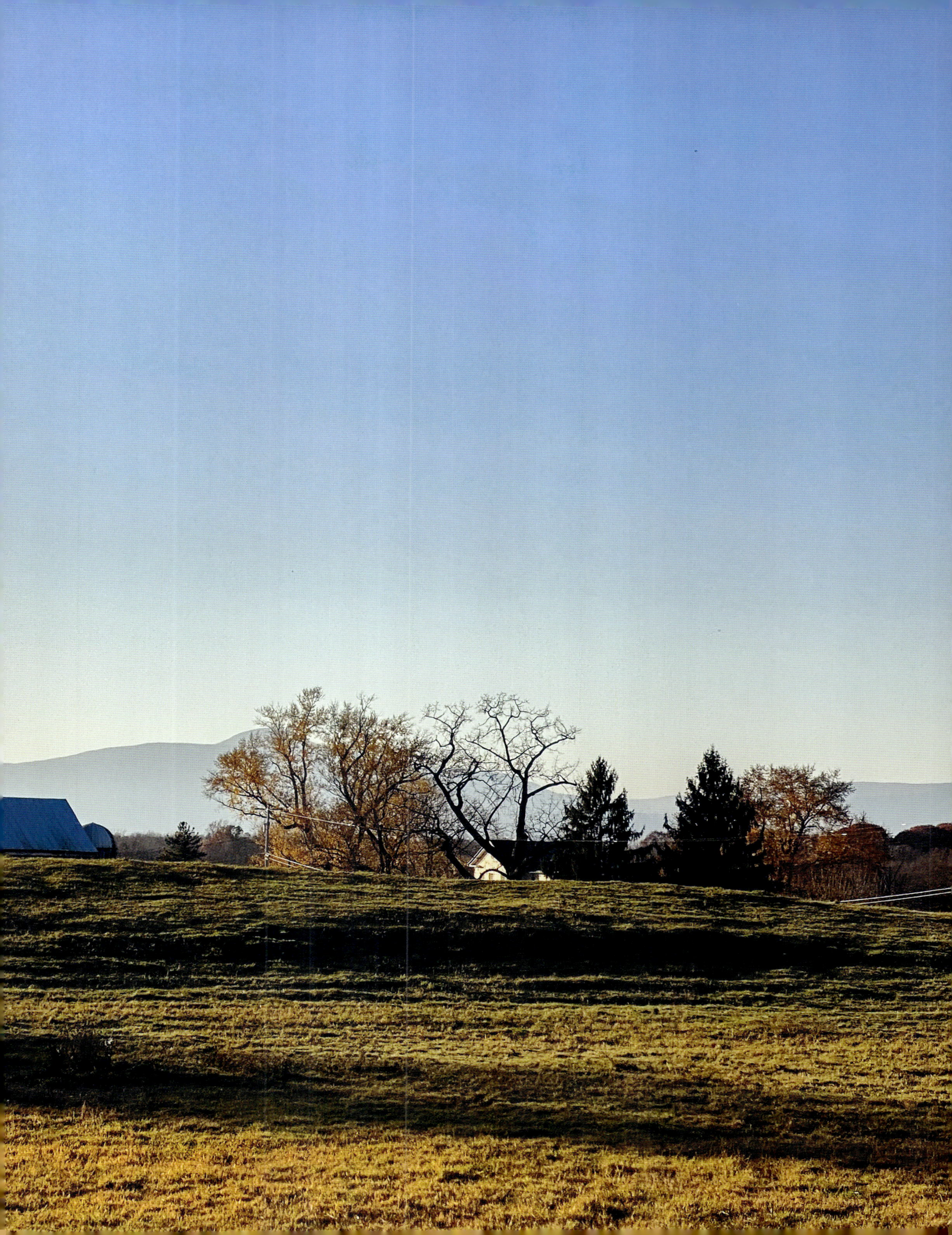

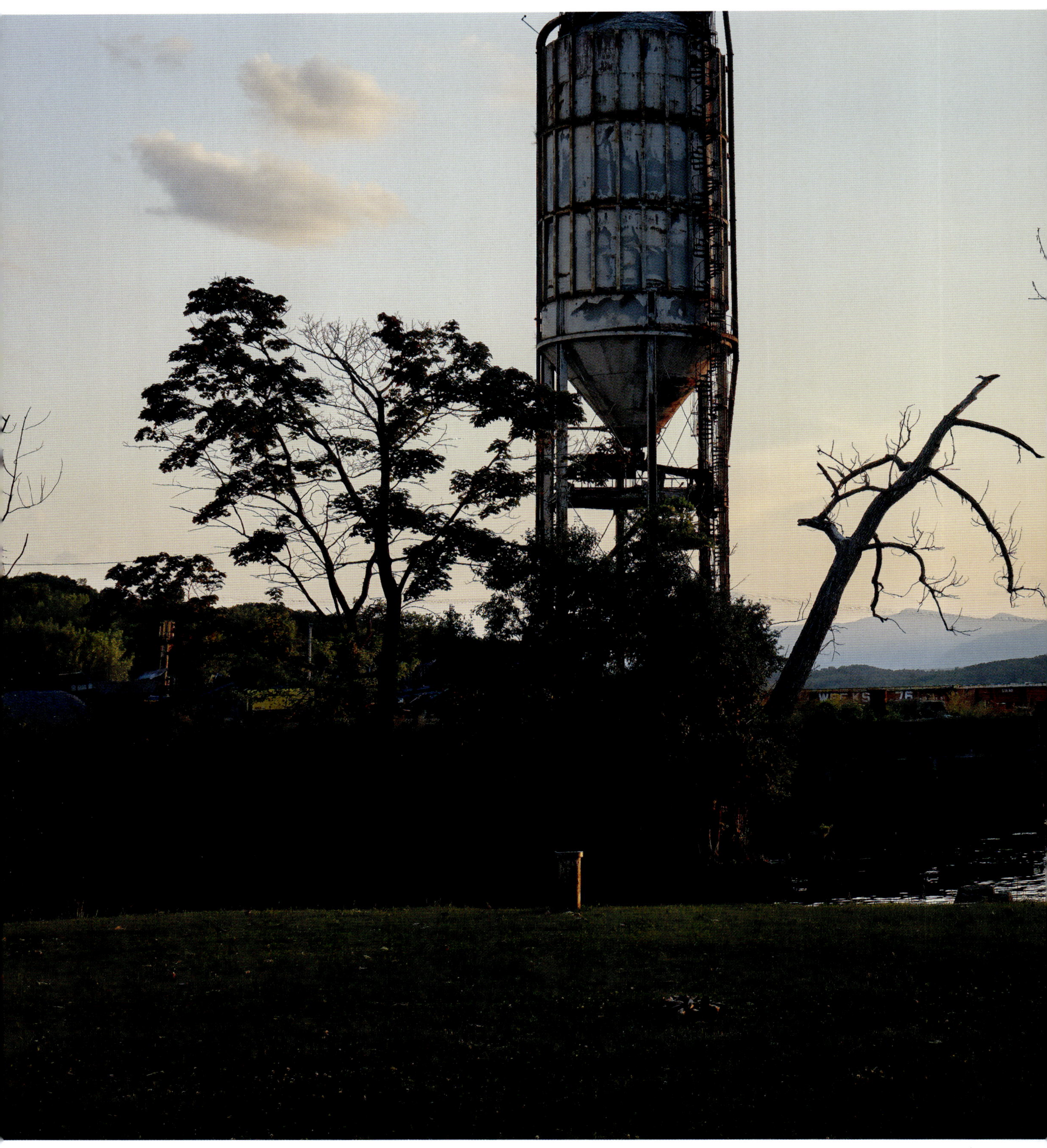

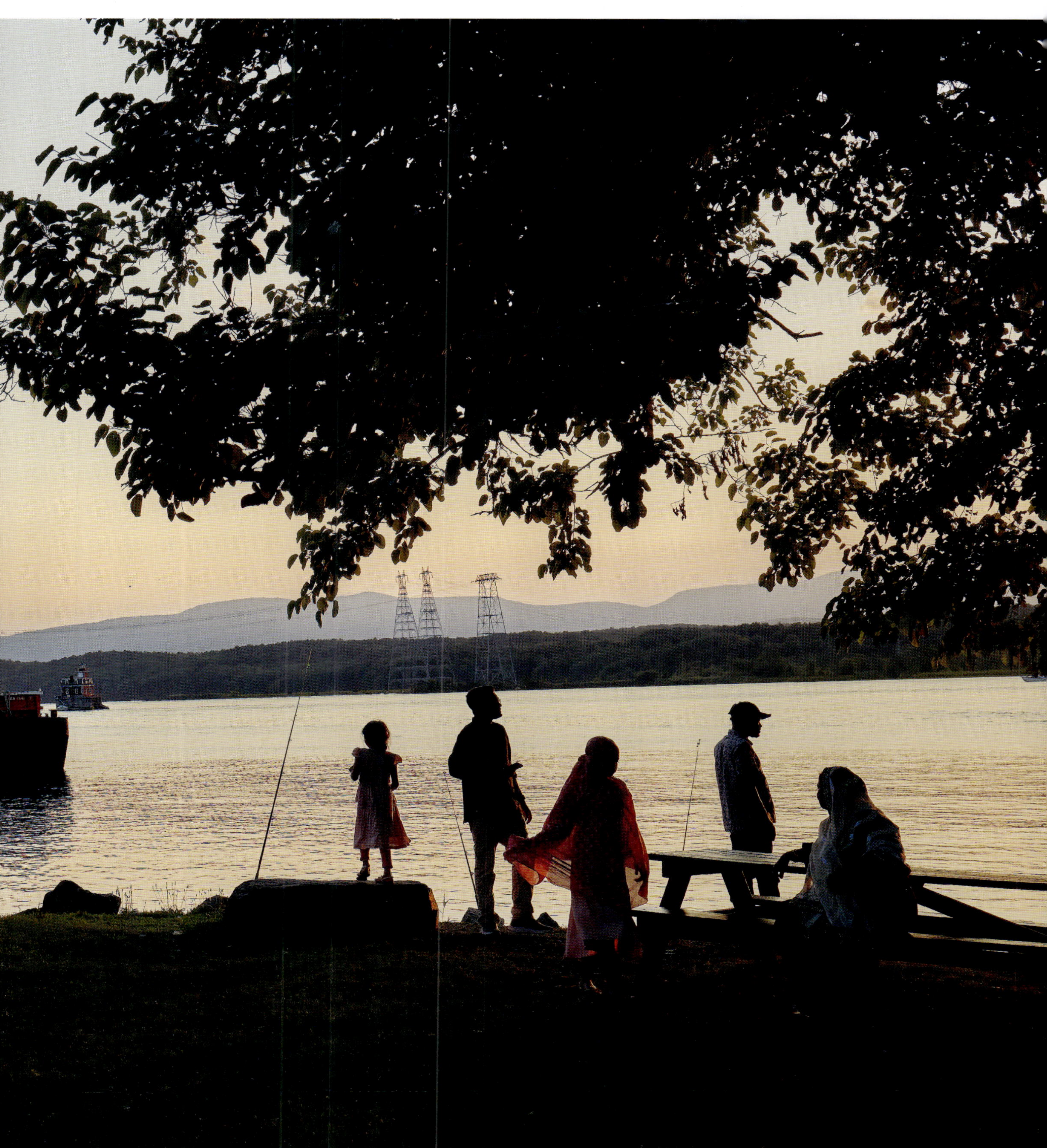

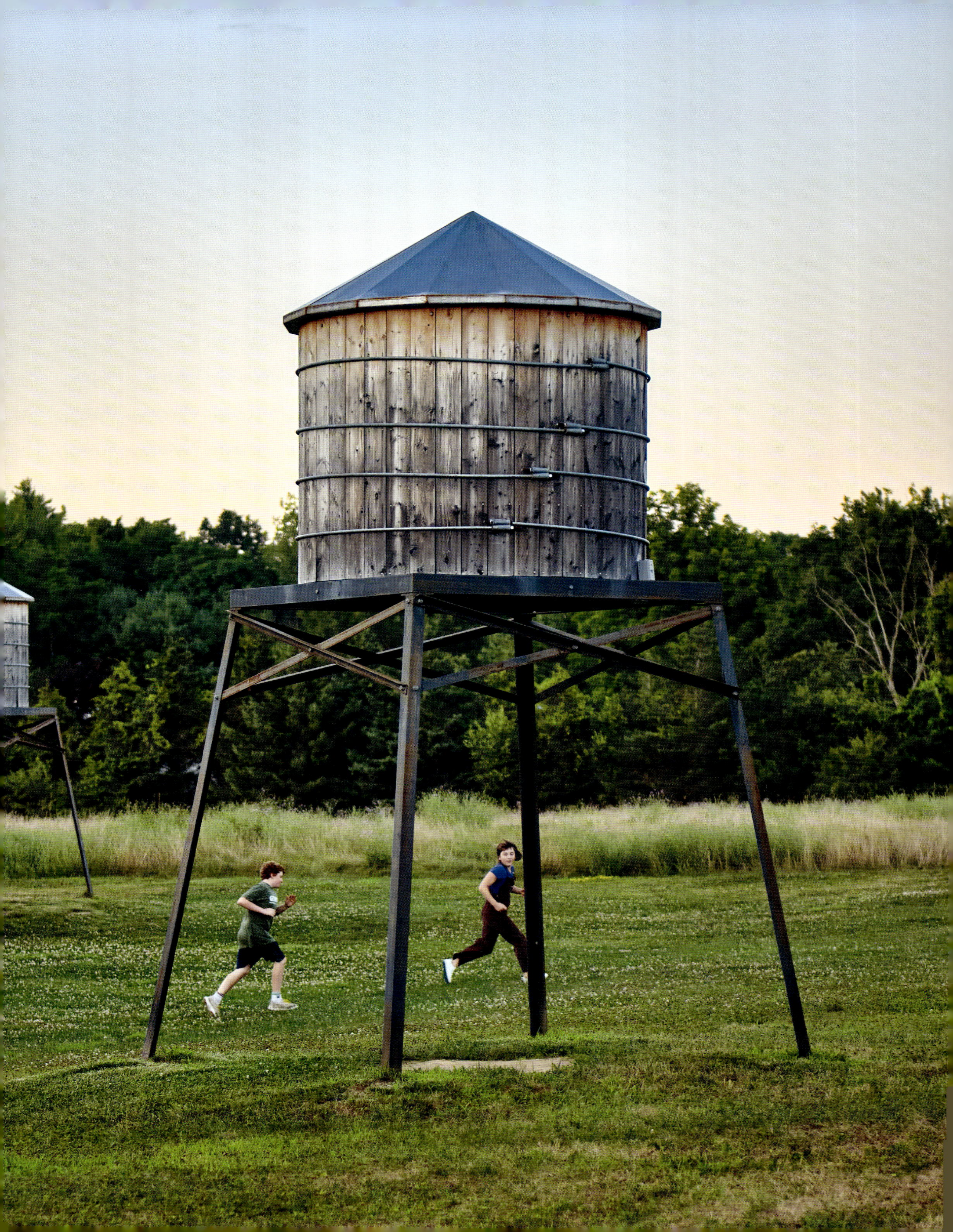

UPSTATE NOW

Art, Design, and Rural Life in the Hudson Valley and Catskills

Michel Arnaud with Jane Creech

PA PRESS

PRINCETON ARCHITECTURAL PRESS · NEW YORK

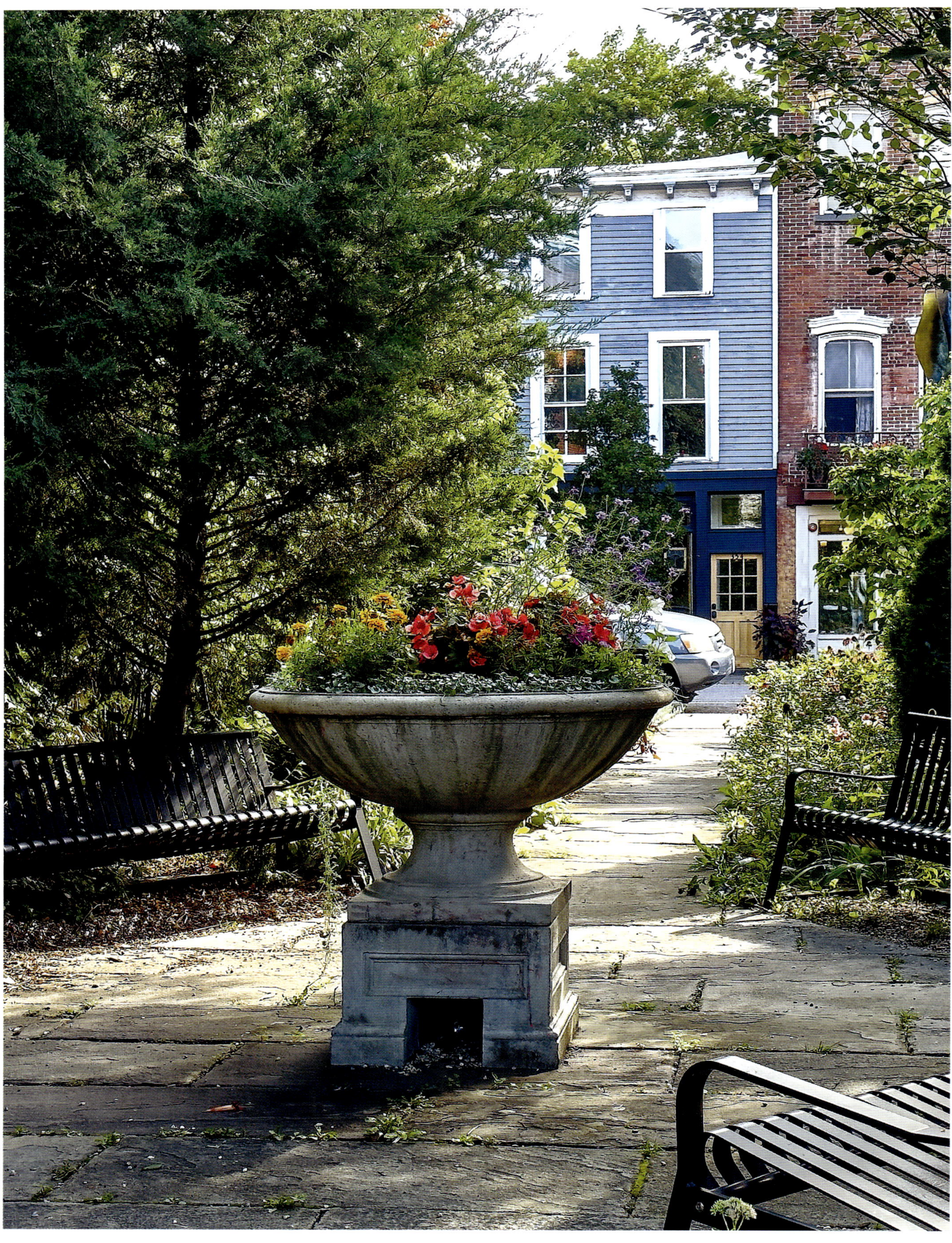

CONTENTS

pages 2–3:
Looking over the Ashokan Reservoir toward Ashokan High Point, the highest elevation in Ulster County, part of the Catskill Mountains.

pages 4–5:
An apple tree caught in an early October snow in East Chatham, New York.

pages 6–7:
MX Morningstar Farm's field of sunflowers planted alongside Route 9H.

pages 8–9:
A farm near Germantown, New York. At one time, the Hudson Valley was the breadbasket of America.

pages 10–11:
Fishermen and their families on the banks of the Hudson River at sunset.

page 12:
Children are welcome at Art Omi, where they often play among the artworks displayed in the Sculpture & Architecture Park, including Iván Navarro's water tower–like work *This Land Is Your Land* (2014).

page 14:
Leggio Park was created on the corner of Main Street and Factory Street, which connects to Water Street. It offers a quiet respite and a green space in downtown Catskill.

opposite:
The Metro-North train on the Harlem Line passes through the hamlet of Wassaic toward its end point nearby.

Published by
Princeton Architectural Press
A division of Chronicle Books LLC
70 West 36th Street
New York, NY 10018
papress.com

Printed and bound in China
28 27 26 25 4 3 2 1 First edition

Editor: Jennifer N. Thompson
Designer: Paul Wagner

Library of Congress Cataloging-in-Publication Data
Names: Arnaud, Michel, author, photographer. | Creech, Jane, author.
Title: Upstate now : art, design, and rural life in the Hudson Valley and Catskills / Michel Arnaud with Jane Creech.
Description: First edition. | New York : Princeton Architectural Press, [2025] | Includes bibliographical references. | Summary: "Place, community, and living a creative life alongside the Hudson River and in the Catskill Mountains"—Provided by publisher.
Identifiers: LCCN 2024056480 | ISBN 9781797231587 (hardcover) | ISBN 9781797231594 (ebook)
Subjects: LCSH: Community life—New York (State)—Upstate New York. | Upstate New York (N.Y.)—Pictorial works.
Classification: LCC F126.8 .A76 2025 | DDC 974.7/100222—dc23/eng/20250206
LC record available at https://lccn.loc.gov/2024056480

To Kate & Will

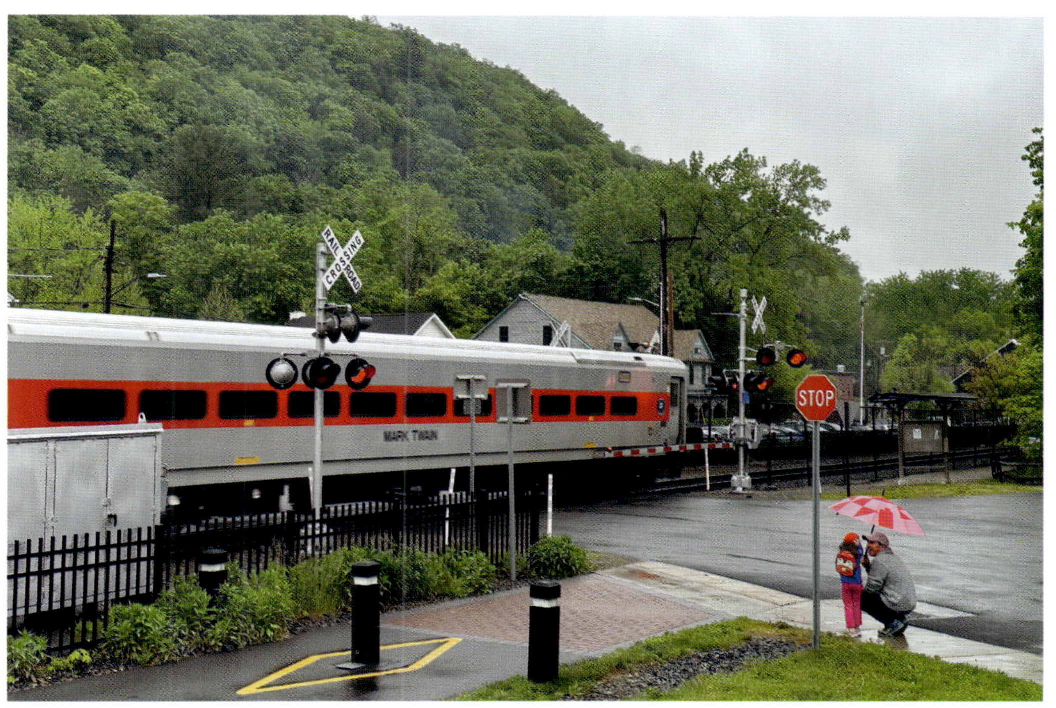

FOREWORD

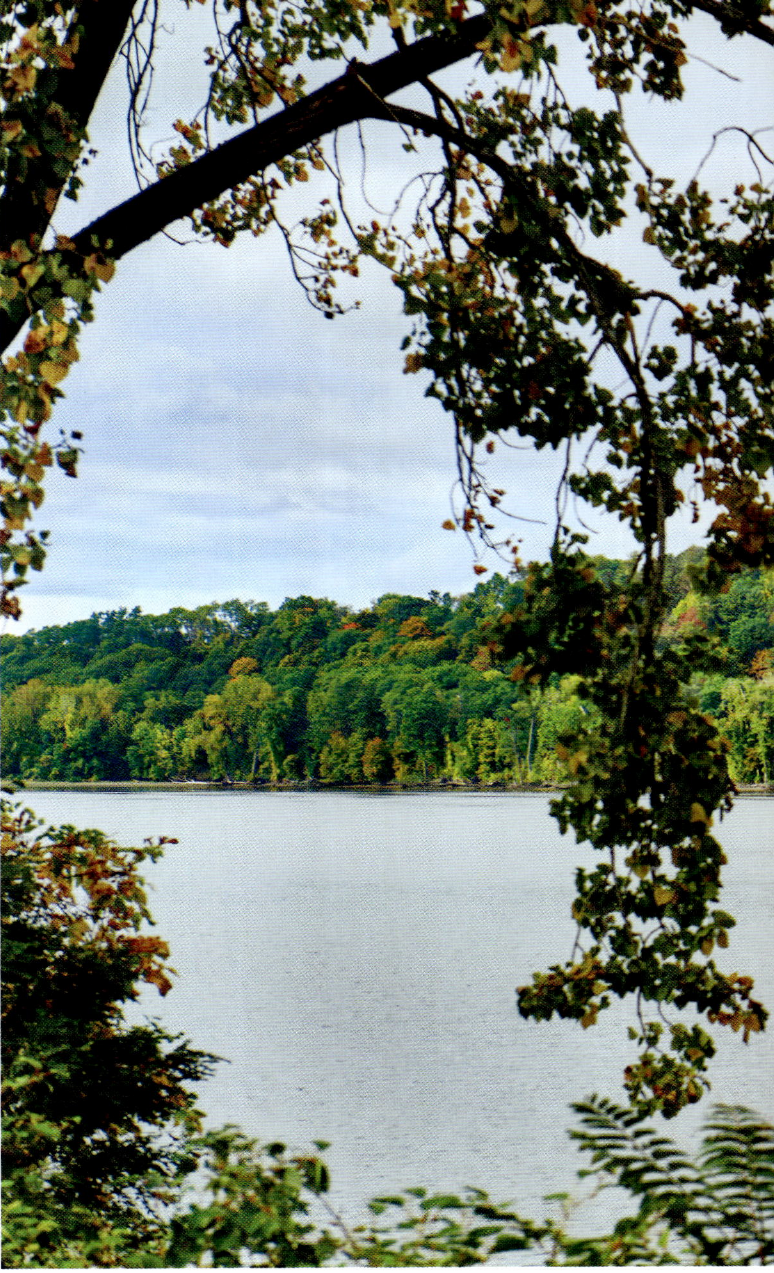

The Hudson River has its source in the Adirondack Mountains, running more than three hundred miles through the Catskill Mountains on the west and the Taconic Mountains to the east. The Hudson flows both to New York City—where it meets the Atlantic Ocean in New York Harbor—and also away from it. Ocean tides affect a majority of its navigable length, making it appear to flow northward at times. The indigenous Lenape people called it Muhheakunnuk, "The River That Runs Both Ways," before Henry Hudson claimed it for the Dutch.

It is this mixture of waters that makes the Hudson's ecosystem so unique. Saline water from the Atlantic Ocean mixes with the Hudson's freshwater all the way up to Troy, 153 miles north of the Battery in Manhattan. In my fifty years of living alongside the Hudson, I have found it impossible to talk about the river without mentioning this fact, as impossible as writing about the Hudson Valley without mentioning "city people." New York City is—and has always been—an inextricable part of the Hudson Valley.

There is no denying that many communities in the Hudson Valley are in trouble. Dying farms, decaying factories, schools shuttering, emergency services staffed by elderly volunteers—they can all make it feel like this beautiful place is on an inexorable downward spiral.

For centuries, city people, starved of space, have ebbed into the Hudson Valley, yearning for the simple life, with liquid capital and daydreams of an Arcadian future. It's easy to know a newcomer from a "local" thanks to the region's complex history of colonialism, as many of the Hudson Valley's town names are famously difficult to pronounce.

I grew up in one of these small towns, where I came to believe that there were two options at adulthood: stay or leave. My mother co-owned a gift shop in a neighboring, more "cosmopolitan" town, through which flowed the spectrum of city people who ensorcelled me with the possibility of a future outside the Hudson Valley. As I approached my senior year at Ichabod Crane High School, I knew exactly what I was going to do: leave. And I knew exactly where I was going: the city.

I had internalized the idea that city people were better than locals, that only they could rescue our troubled Arcadia. I believed that to be successful I had to leave and return as one of them. I vowed to return as a city person, the type that keeps a weekend country home to escape to when New York City is too hot or too crowded or too noisy. Or when there's a global pandemic.

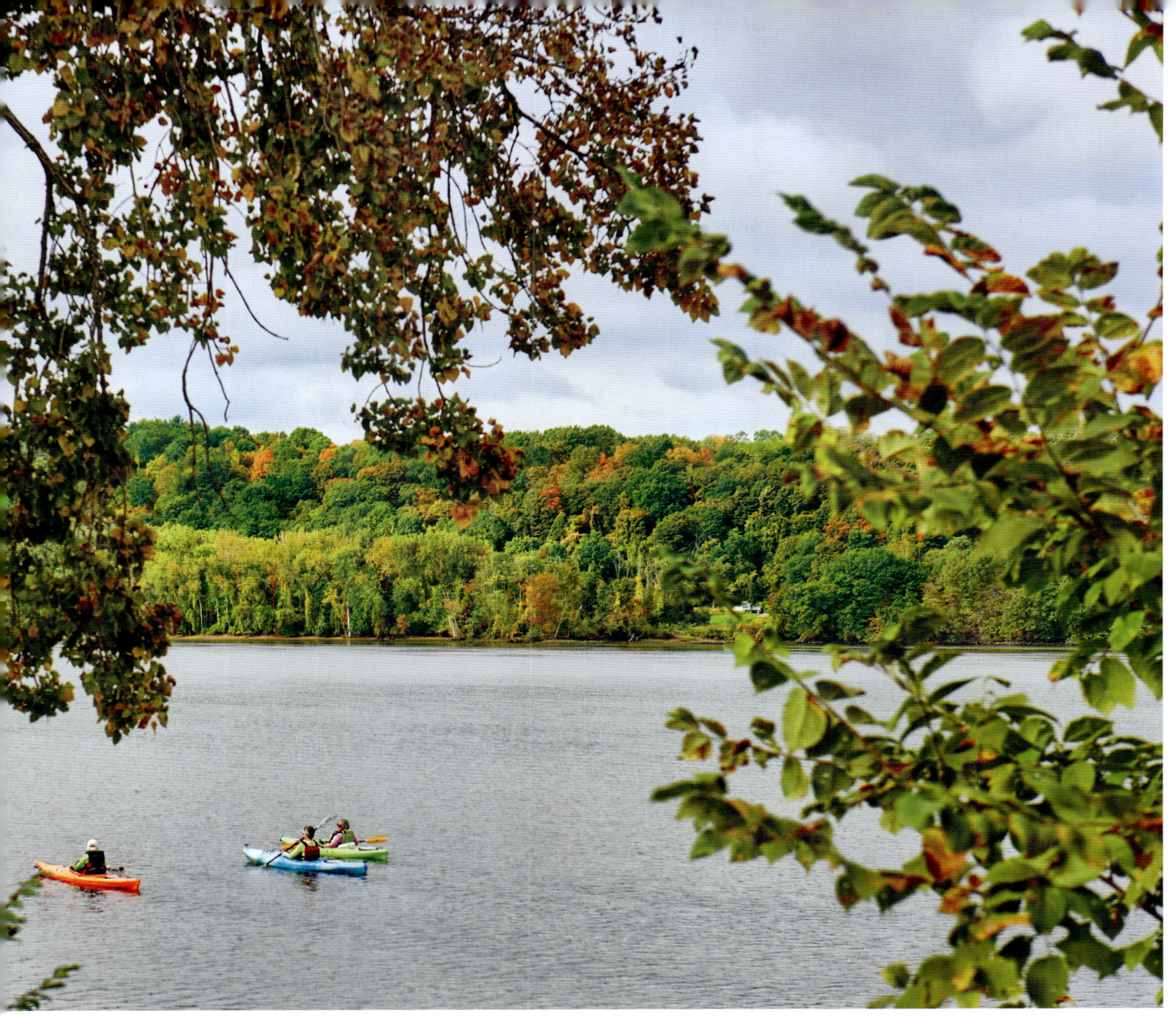

And it was with this mindset that I found myself again in Valatie, first as a weekender to buy a country home with my husband in 2008, and then for good in 2020 with our child and cat in tow. That's when I noticed something: Much like the Hudson River's brackish mixture of ocean and fresh waters, the flow of people to and away from New York City and into the Hudson Valley creates communities unlike anywhere else in the world.

There are two ways to approach the future, through collaboration or through conflict. We can walk through life pigeonholing everyone we meet into "city person" or "local," a sort of lazy discord in which we all lose. Or we can focus on our shared humanity and what is best for the place we love. We can ebb and flow, listen and be curious, have patience and collaborate with kindness and compassion. It's the formula showcased by so many of the stories in this book, proof that beautiful communities can grow from oppositional binaries.

Ann Sublett

Three kayakers launched along the Hudson at the hamlet of Stuyvesant Landing, near where Henry Hudson landed his ship, *Half Moon*, in 1609.

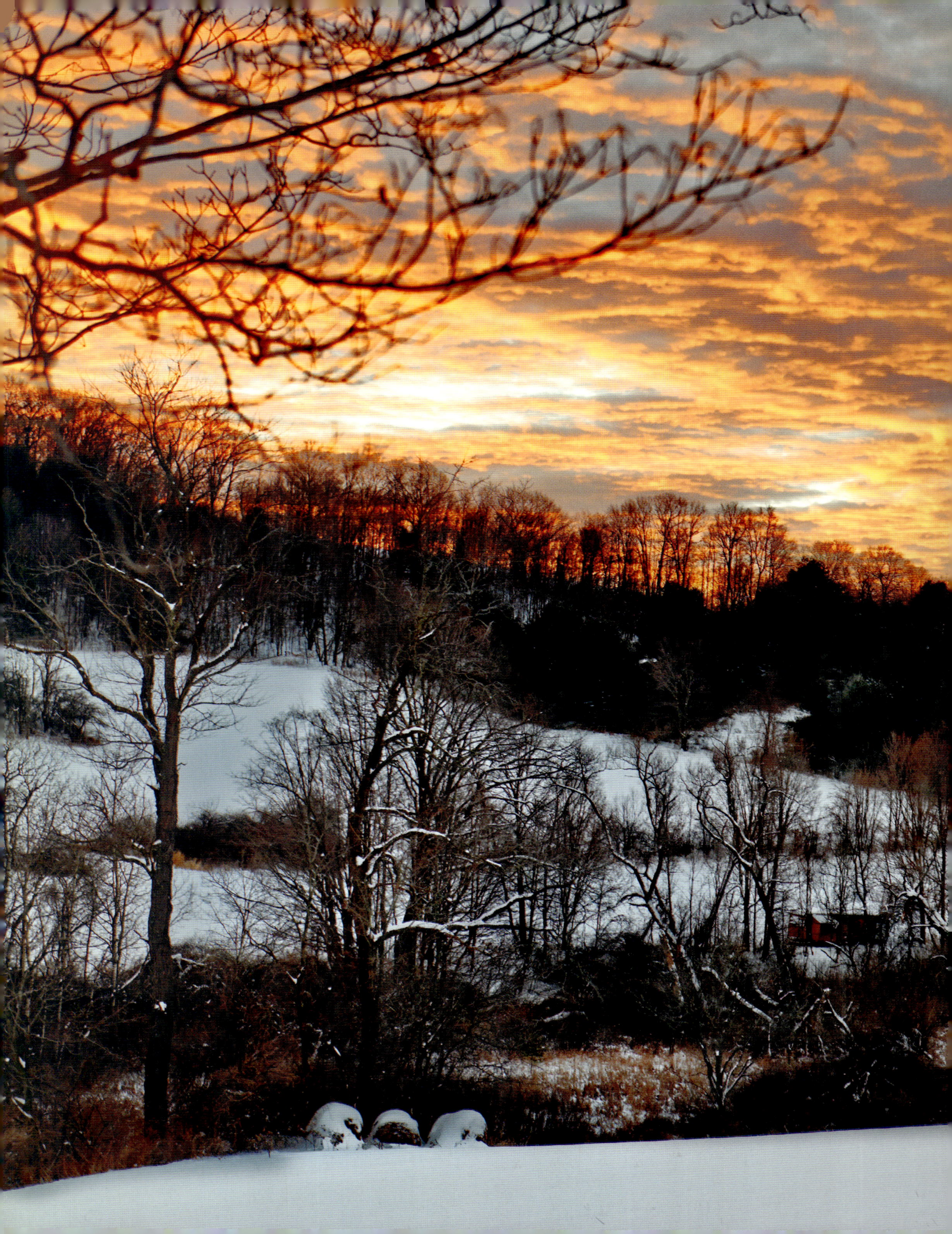

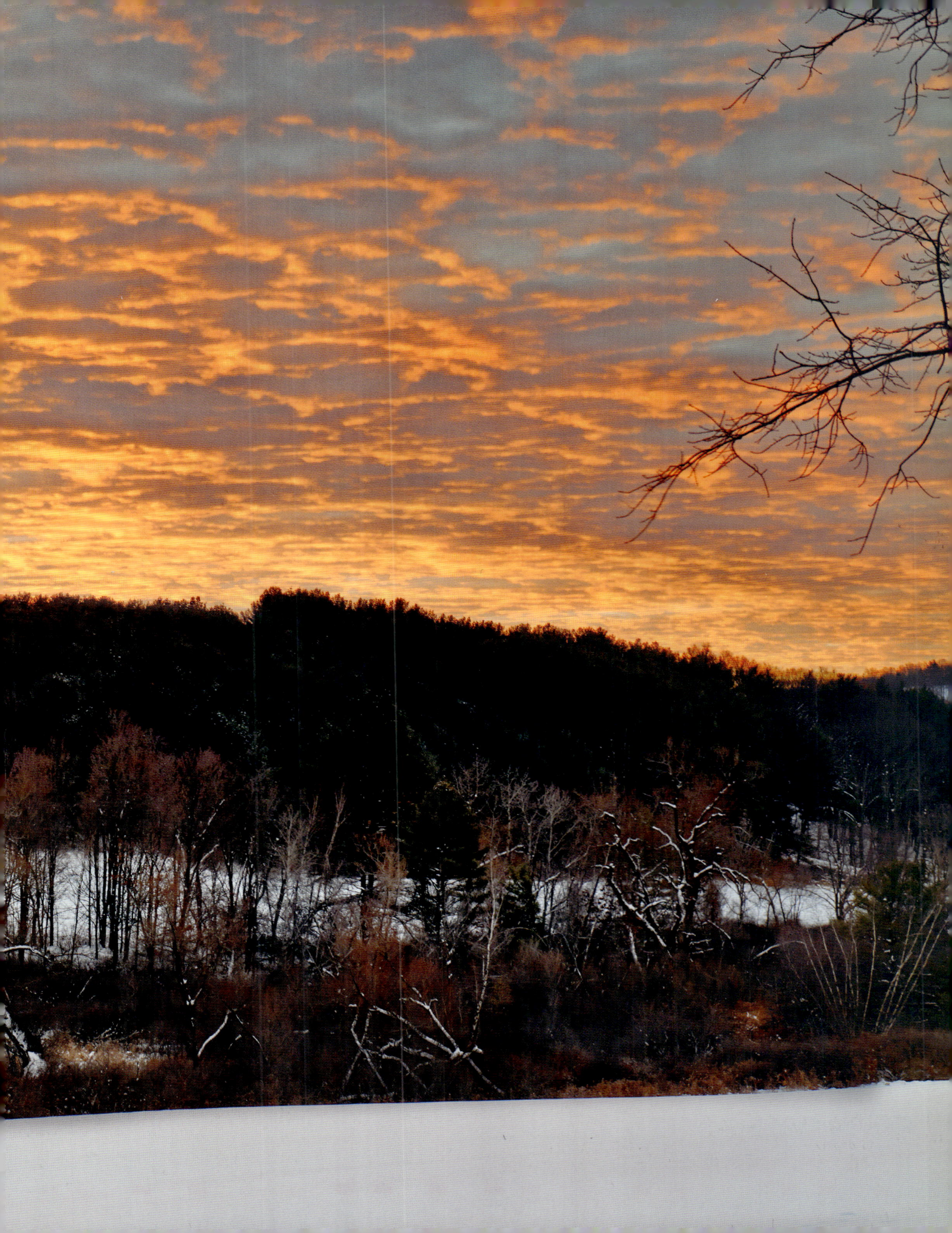

INTRODUCTION: LIVE/WORK

This book is perhaps my most personal project because it is about a place where I have lived for over thirty years. As a photographer on assignment for *English Vogue*, *Harper's Bazaar*, *House & Garden*, and *Town & Country*, among others, I traveled all over the world and was on the road more than I was home. In 1992, Liz Tilberis, editor in chief of *Harper's Bazaar*, asked if I would consider moving from London to New York City to help in the relaunch of the magazine. My wife Linda, a born-and-bred New Yorker and color forecaster for the fashion industry, agreed—with the caveat that we find a place outside the city where we would spend weekends and holidays.

We spent a year visiting friends out on Long Island, on the Massachusetts coast, and around New York State. Then, we took a trip to Columbia County, about two hours north of New York City. We fell in love with the area. The rolling hills of the Taconic valley, the majestic Catskill mountain range, and the landscapes sometimes reminiscent of the English countryside had such a strong draw. We loved the slower lifestyle. We loved the roadside farm stands selling seasonal vegetables, fresh eggs, flowers, or honey, often presented on wooden crates or an old cart. Many of these businesses practiced the honor system of payment, where customers tally their purchases and leave a payment in a cash box. To me, that practice reflects a sense of trust within the community, a feeling long lost in Europe. And of course, we loved the closeness to New York City.

Linda and I set out to look for a house. Not finding anything that fit our style and needs, we decided to buy land and build a house on Mercer Mountain, up a 2-mile dirt road, at an elevation of 1,811 feet, and with a 75-mile view of the valley and the Catskills. While I continued to travel and go back and forth to the city for work, Linda immersed herself in the community and her painting studio. Her subject matter was the landscape. She also worked on events for arts organizations such as Olana, the historic home of Hudson River Valley School painter Frederic Church, and the Shaker Museum in Chatham, New York, dedicated to preserving the work of the early American utopian society, and she wrote two cookbooks. In 2009, Linda was diagnosed with cancer. We were devastated. She died at home almost a year later. In the depth of my grief, the one thing I knew was that I wanted to stay upstate and try to rebuild my life. Yet most of my work life was in the city. I kept the house on the mountain and started working in the city again.

Fast-forward to 2019, when my wife, Jane; my young son, Will; and I moved upstate permanently, six months before the COVID pandemic began in 2020. The global health crisis brought a shift in population. Many people decided to leave New York City for upstate New York. The *New York Times* reported at the time that upstate cities such as Hudson and Kingston had 9.7 percent and 5.2 percent increases in population, respectively. Of course, this was not the first time that a crisis drew people to live upstate; the 9/11 terrorist attack on the World Trade Center also brought new residents to the countryside. But we saw the shift writ large during the pandemic as houses were bought in cash-only bidding wars taking place in the owner's driveway. Housing inventory in the area reached an all-time low. The tiny towns and small villages that are strung like pearls on a thread along the Hudson, and dotted in the woods and pastures of the Catskills, made room for more people.

Unlike the Hamptons, where there is one highway in and one highway out with the geography bound by water, populations upstate are spread out, down country roads or in village neighborhoods. Solitude and privacy are possible. The obligation to make appearances or attend social functions doesn't seem to exist upstate. The lack of the "scene" that engulfed out east on Long Island hasn't quite taken root up north.

Or has it? Since the pandemic and the rise of the population, activities have increased. At the same time, there are families upstate who have lived here for a long time—six or seven generations in one neck of the woods or on a family farm. Architecture and homes from the early colonial days still stand. Revolutionary War veterans are buried in the local cemeteries. The question then becomes, how does a place balance the space between the two ideals—heritage and future? How does a place and a people with a deep history and connection to the land and each other mix with new people and new establishments? It is the underlying story of America.

When we made the decision to tell the story of upstate New York, Jane and I first looked for examples of projects that were new. However, in conversations with homeowners and business-owners, we realized that the stories that were most compelling included people who had been in business for over twenty years. They were folks who were rethinking, adjusting, and tinkering with their business and life plans. Those were stories of creativity and resilience. We also found that newcomers shared these same characteristics but were at the exciting moment of starting something.

This book showcases that mix of projects and places. Some places are iconic upstate institutions, other places are a riff on those ideas, and still others are completely fresh or off the beaten path. I found that there's not one aesthetic that defines upstate; however, one aspect that nearly everyone we interviewed mentioned was their desire to be close to nature, to enjoy the magnificence of the landscape and ever-changing skies.

It is also worth noting that when artists, architects, and photographers gather and build community in a place, we should pay attention. The Hudson Valley and the Catskills have been a site of artistic practice, movements, colonies, and residencies since people arrived in this place. Early crafts such as basket weaving are among the artifacts of the First Nations peoples who lived in the region. Today, those traditions continue as new galleries open to showcase artists living upstate and to bring in art from around the world for the benefit of our community. For me, I've sought to present the projects and people shown here as I find them. I shoot with natural light; I didn't photograph any of the images with artificial lighting. I used a tripod and camera as well as my iPhone to capture these images. I looked for shots that tell the story as unadorned as possible.

While in many ways this book was born from loss and change, moments of growth, joy, and renewal abound. One of my favorite seasons is fall, with its splendid foliage of bold and vibrant colors—gold, orange, vermilion, red, and crimson that grab you attention instantly. "Leaf-peeping" season is a busy time upstate; hotels are full, streets are closed for festivals, and farm stands are overflowing. Fall is a moment of abundance and fulfillment before the quiet of winter. Over the years, I have also developed a great fondness for the subtle charm of spring, with its delicate shades of green that unfold slowly to the richer, deeper greens of the coming summer. The colors of spring offer a quiet beauty as a reward for the patient observer, much like many of the stories you will find on the pages of this book.

I urge you to make your own journey upstate. If you are local, I hope that this book will inspire you to explore your surroundings, as we did. If you are coming from somewhere else, as many travelers do, on an Amtrak train riding along the edge of the great Hudson River, make sure you get a seat at the window on the left side of the compartment for the best views of the Catskill Mountains.

Michel Arnaud
2024

previous
A view from our house of the Doyle Farm in East Chatham, New York.

overleaf
The herb garden in the center of the first Shaker settlement, located in Albany, New York.

1. A Sense of Place

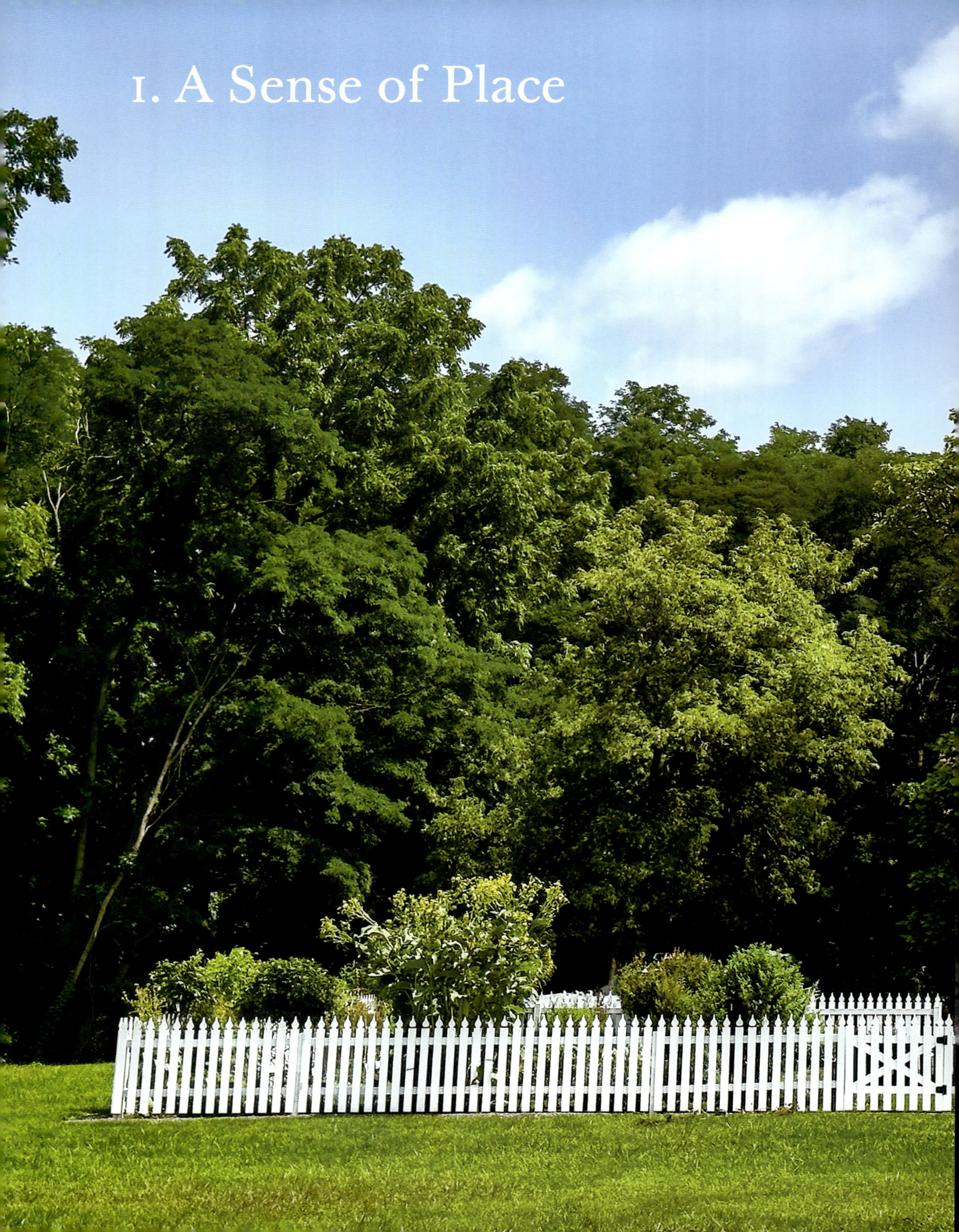

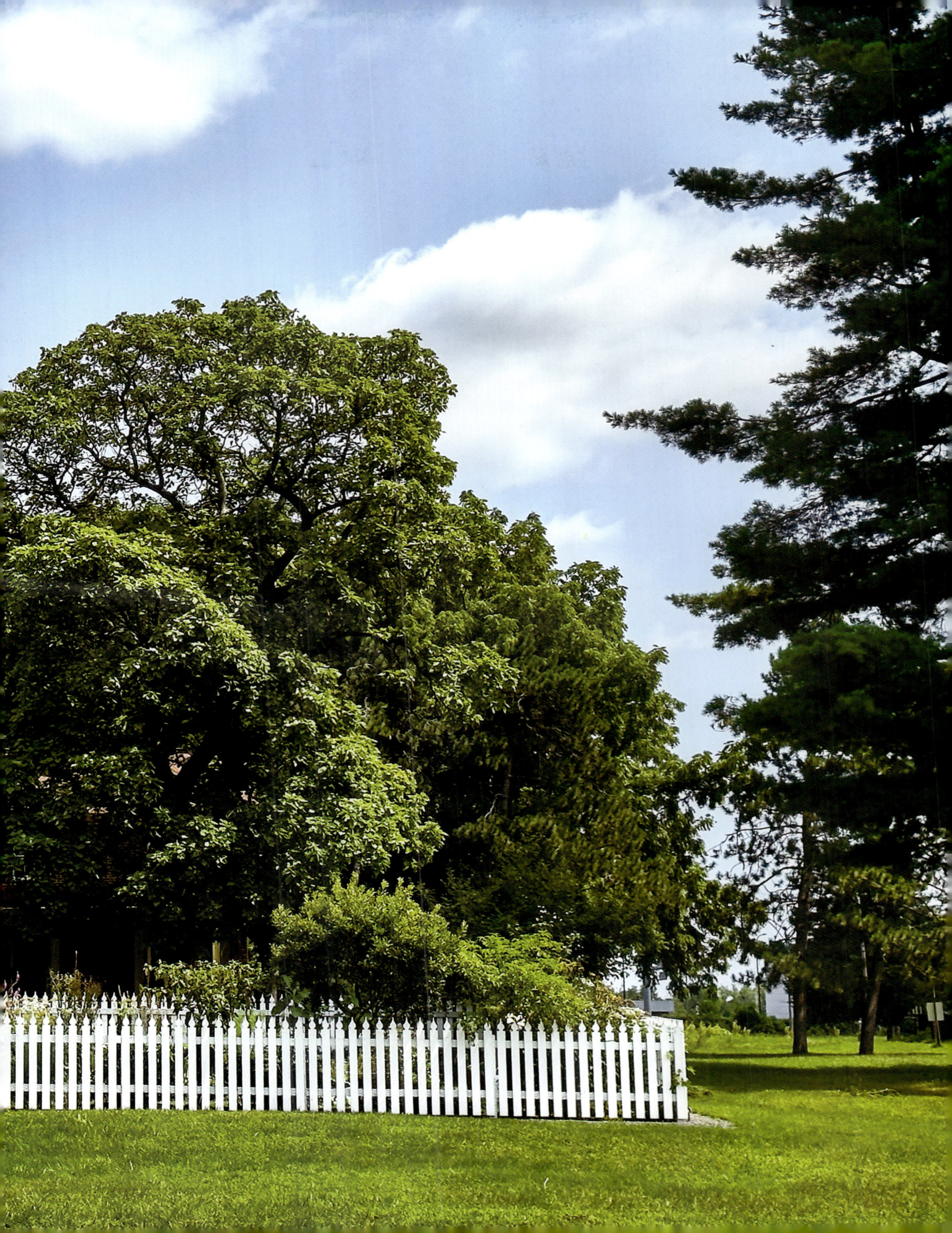

Watervliet Shaker Settlement, Church Family Site

Albany, New York

Near the Albany International Airport are the remaining buildings of the first Shaker (or United Society of Believers in the Second Coming of Christ) settlement in the United States. These days Shakers are mostly associated with the functional simplicity of their aesthetics and designs—think the ubiquitous Shaker pegs—rather than as a religious organization and Utopian communal society.

Escaping religious persecution in England, Ann Lee landed in New York City in 1774 along with her small group of followers, including her husband and brother. They went to work, earning money to purchase land upstate, where the group moved in 1777. The surviving settlement location is in an area first called Niskayuna and later Watervliet. Its twenty-six acres and eight buildings are known as the Church Family Site and are managed by the Shaker Heritage Society. A meeting house, barns, a drying house, and a washhouse, among other structures, make up this historic district owned by the city of Albany.

Tucked away in a nondescript commercial zone, this place is a respite from both car and air traffic close by. With an extensive herbal garden that functions as an educational exhibit at its center, the property seems close to paradise on Earth. At the heart of the Shaker ethos was hard work, perseverance, and equality among the sexes and races. Here, evidence of these ideals still exists, if only in the buildings they erected and the land they cleared and prepared for farming.

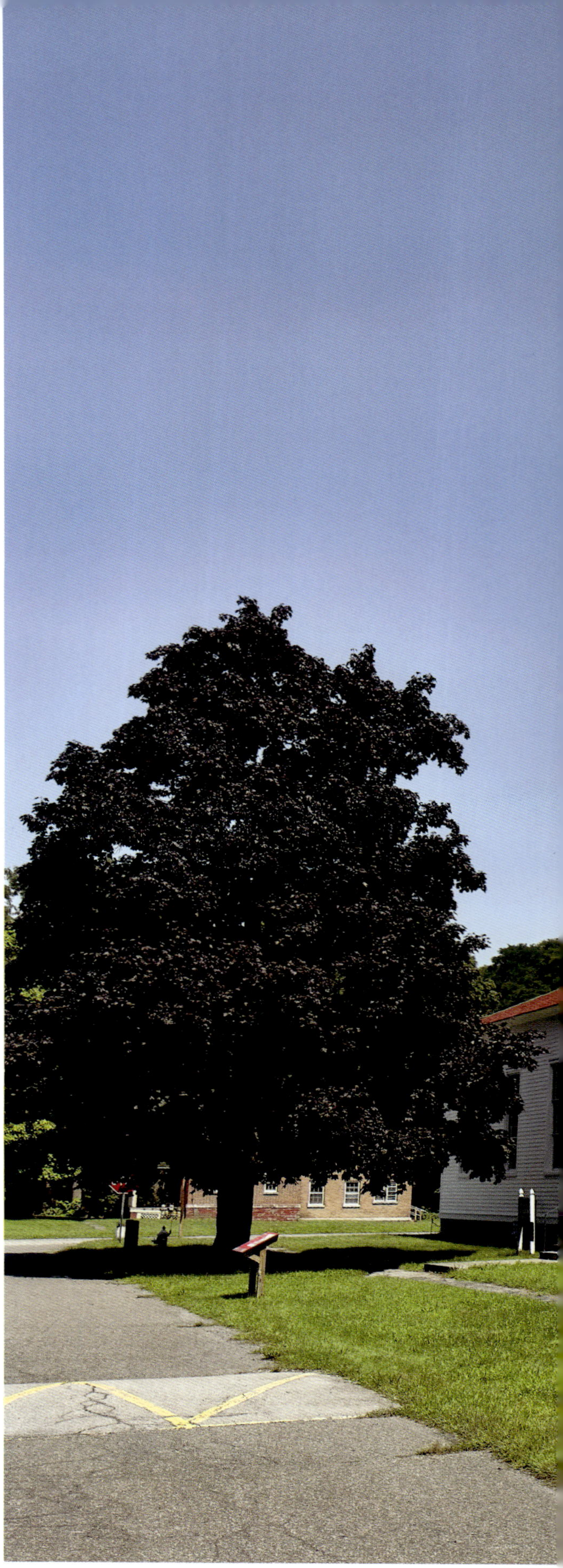

The meeting house of the Shaker Church Family Site, built in 1848.

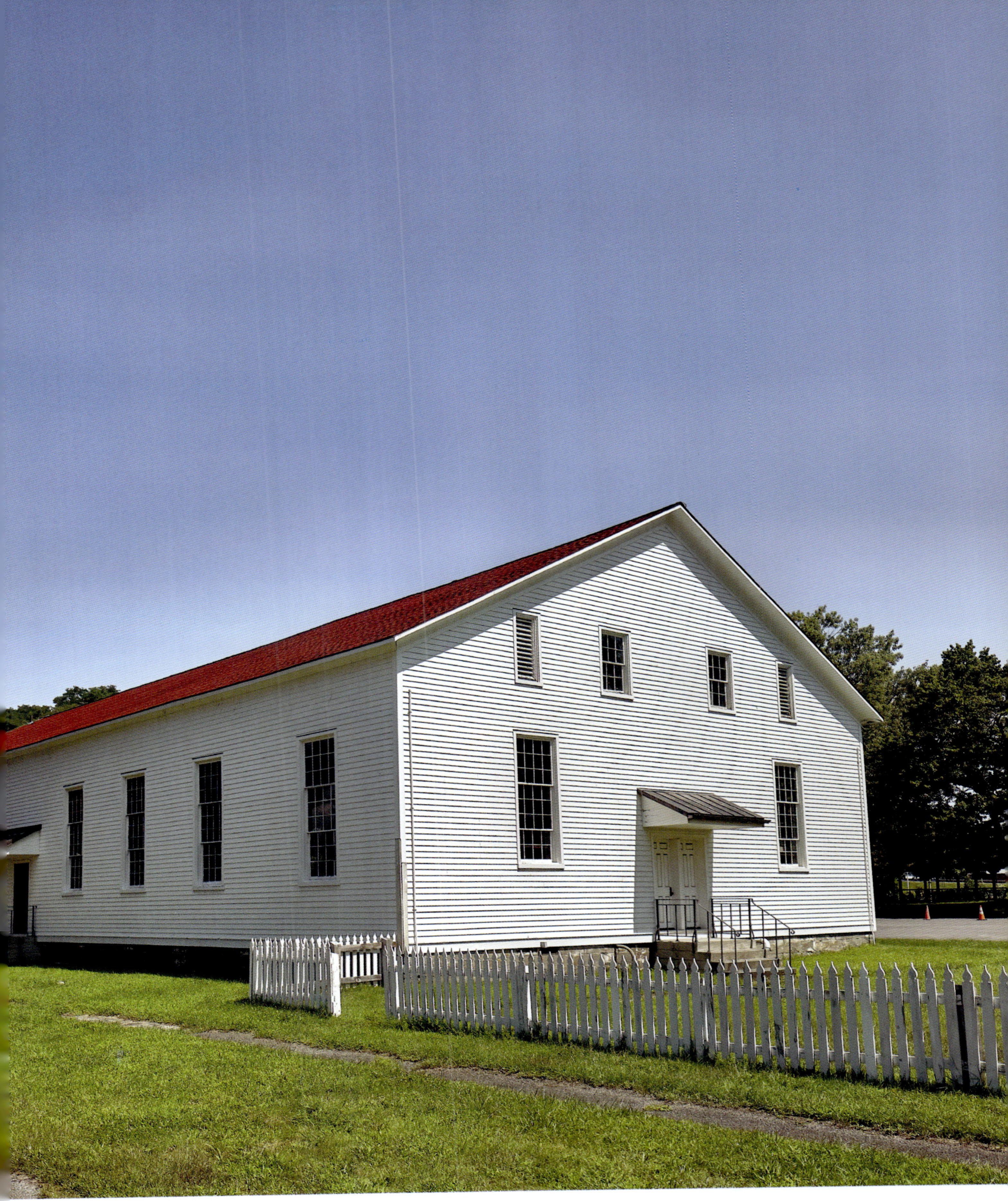

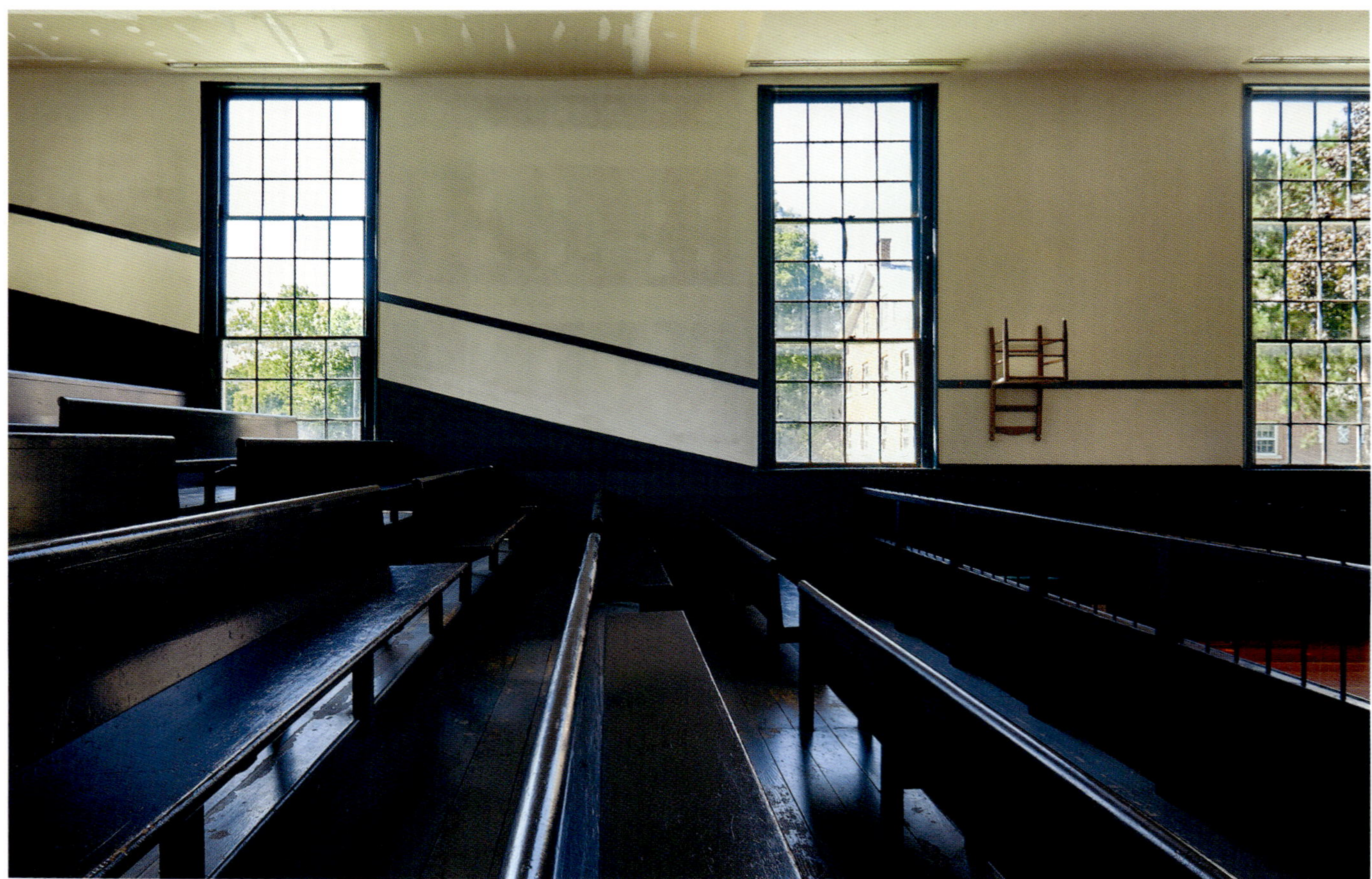

The Shakers were people of their time and welcomed new technology, including radios and cars. They were inventive. One example, the first, more efficient "finish flat" broom that was designed by a Shaker brother in Albany, is still used today. The site is an open and welcoming place. Visitors can walk freely on the grounds and explore the buildings to see how they were constructed. The Shaker Heritage Society has invited contemporary artists to make on-site art installations, continuing a connection with visionaries.

Ann Lee died at the age of forty-eight in Watervliet, the place where she began making her American dream, and is buried in the cemetery close by. At the height of the Shaker movement in the 1840s, up to 150 people lived in this settlement, and there were Shaker villages in Massachusetts, Maine, Kentucky, and Ohio—some of which are preserved as historic places. Today the Shaker Heritage Society hopes to bring more people to the Church Family Site to learn about the Shakers' influence.

above
The interior of the meeting house's meeting room includes built-in benches at one end of the large room. The open space left room for group dances. Thirty-six pane windows bring natural light inside.

opposite, top
Examples of Shaker-made chairs, ladder-back and cloth-tape-back chairs, are hung on the Shaker peg system. Chairs were hung upside down to minimize dust on the cloth-tape seats.

opposite, bottom
A stalk of sorghum (also known as broom corn), which is the plant used to make brooms, hangs against the plaster walls of the meeting room.

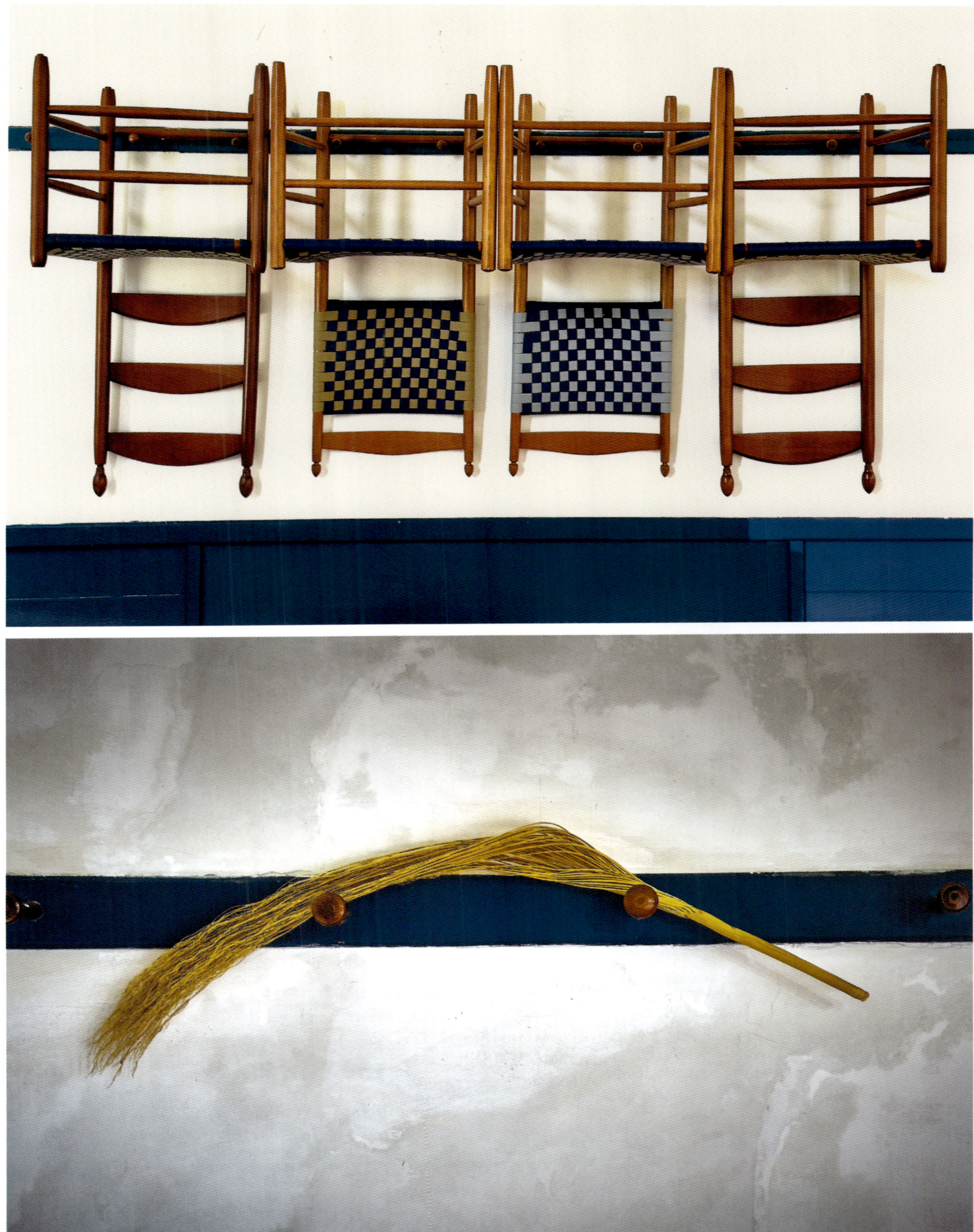

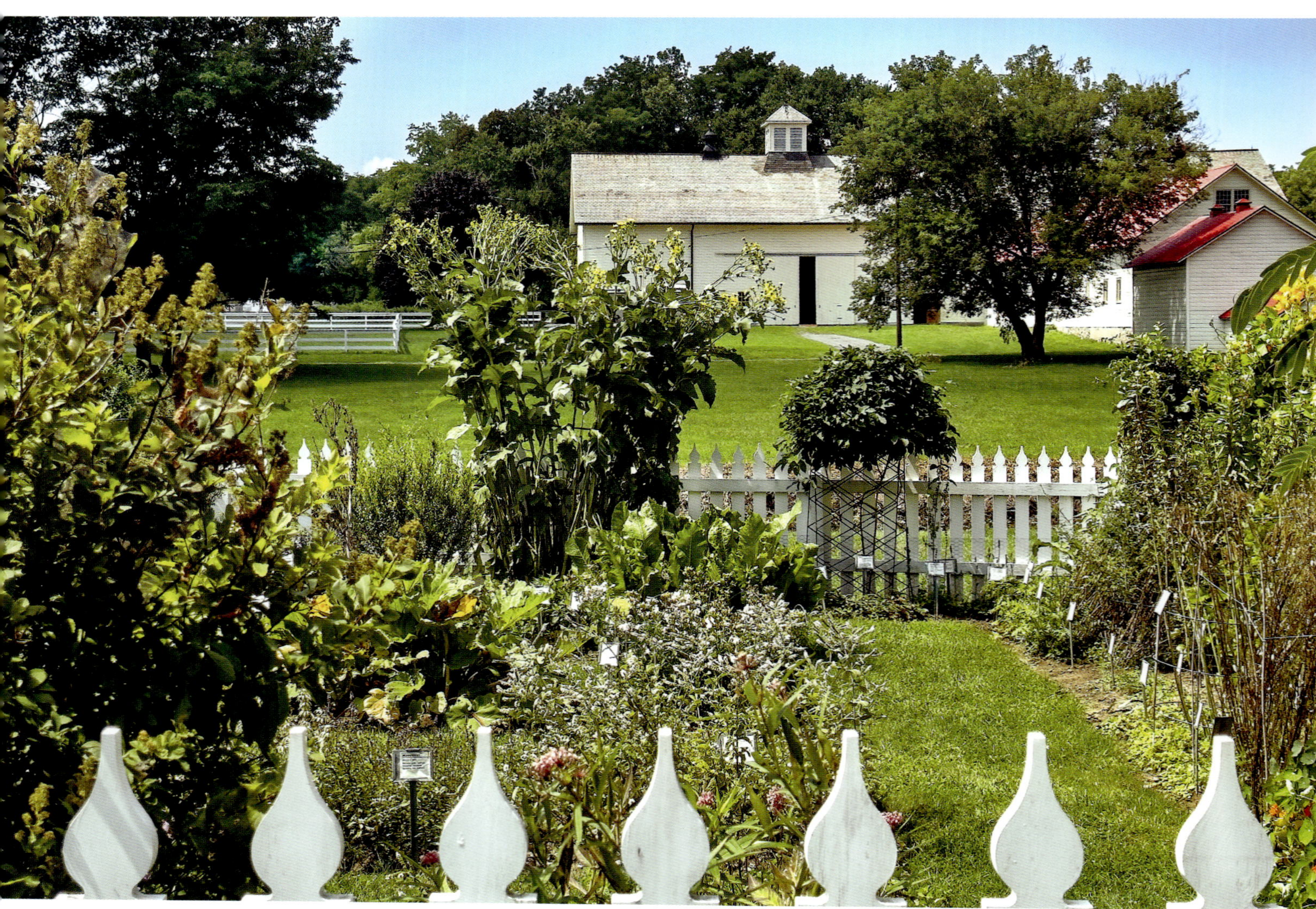

above
The Shakers were active and thoughtful gardeners. Not only did they recognize the medicinal qualities of plants in the healing process, but they also created a business selling the seeds in the United States and internationally. The Shaker Heritage Society created the garden at the site in 1990 as an educational exhibition. The garden is a volunteer-run program and is surrounded by a white picket fence of Shaker design.

opposite
Milkweed is one of the plants grown in the garden.

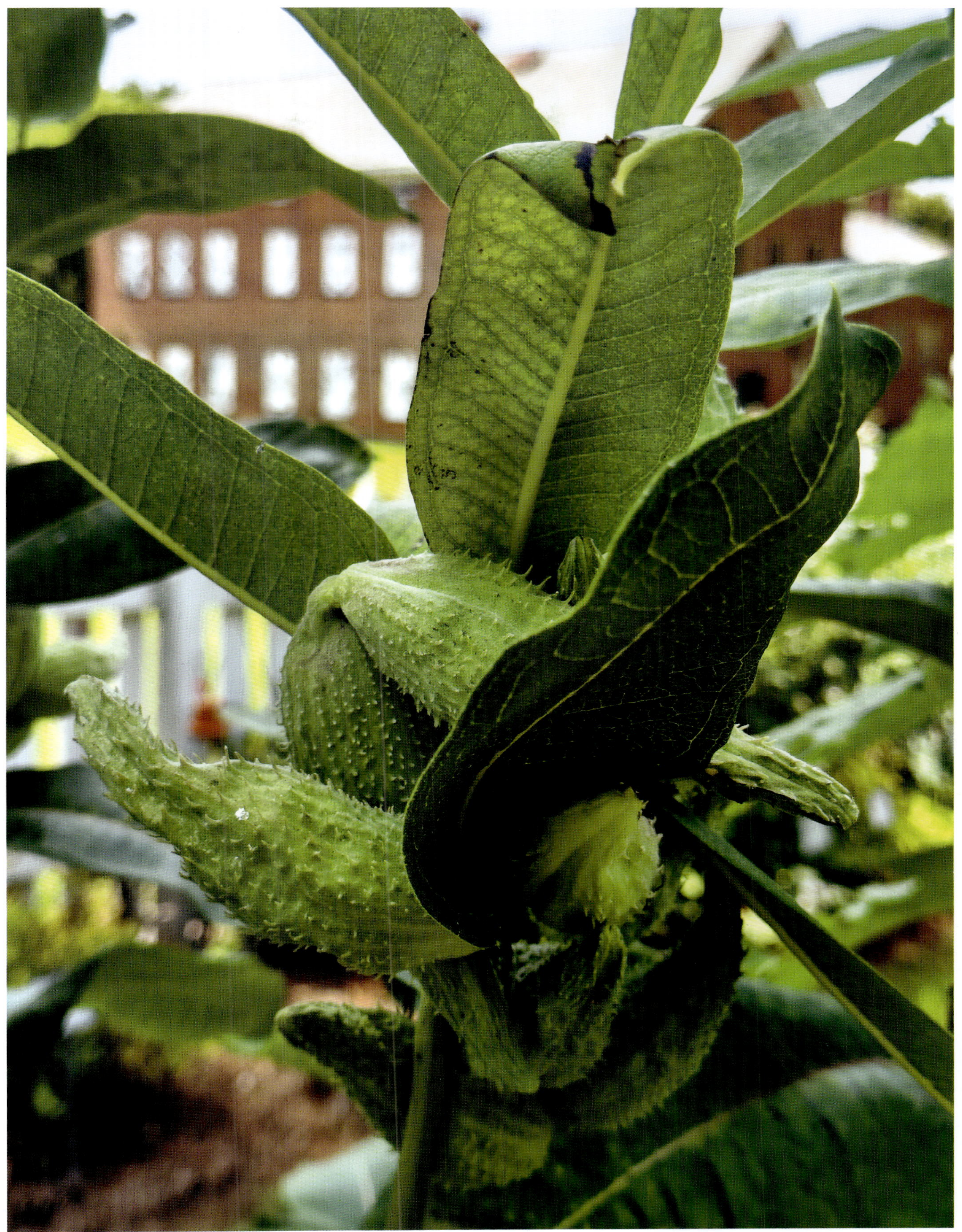

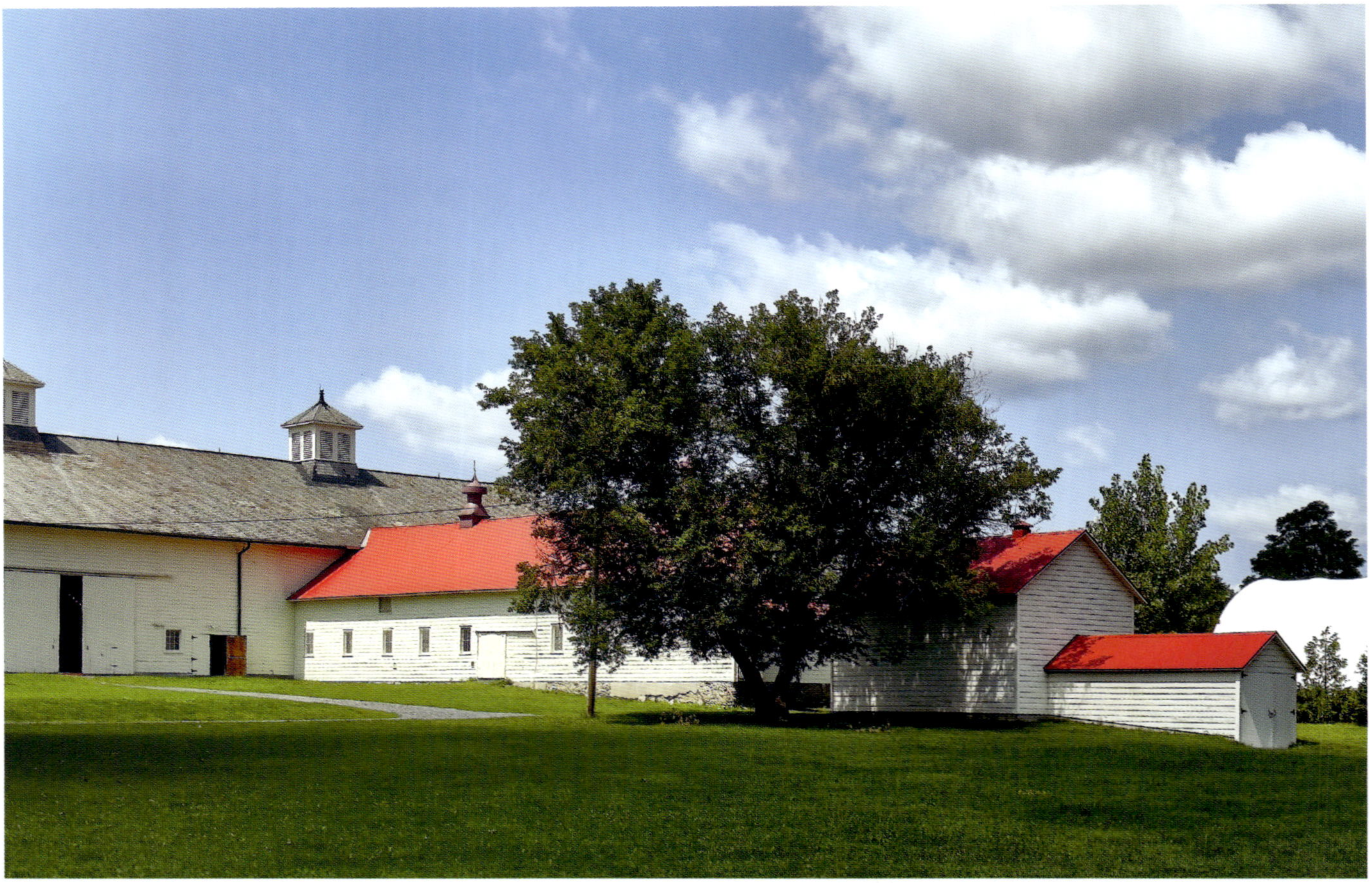

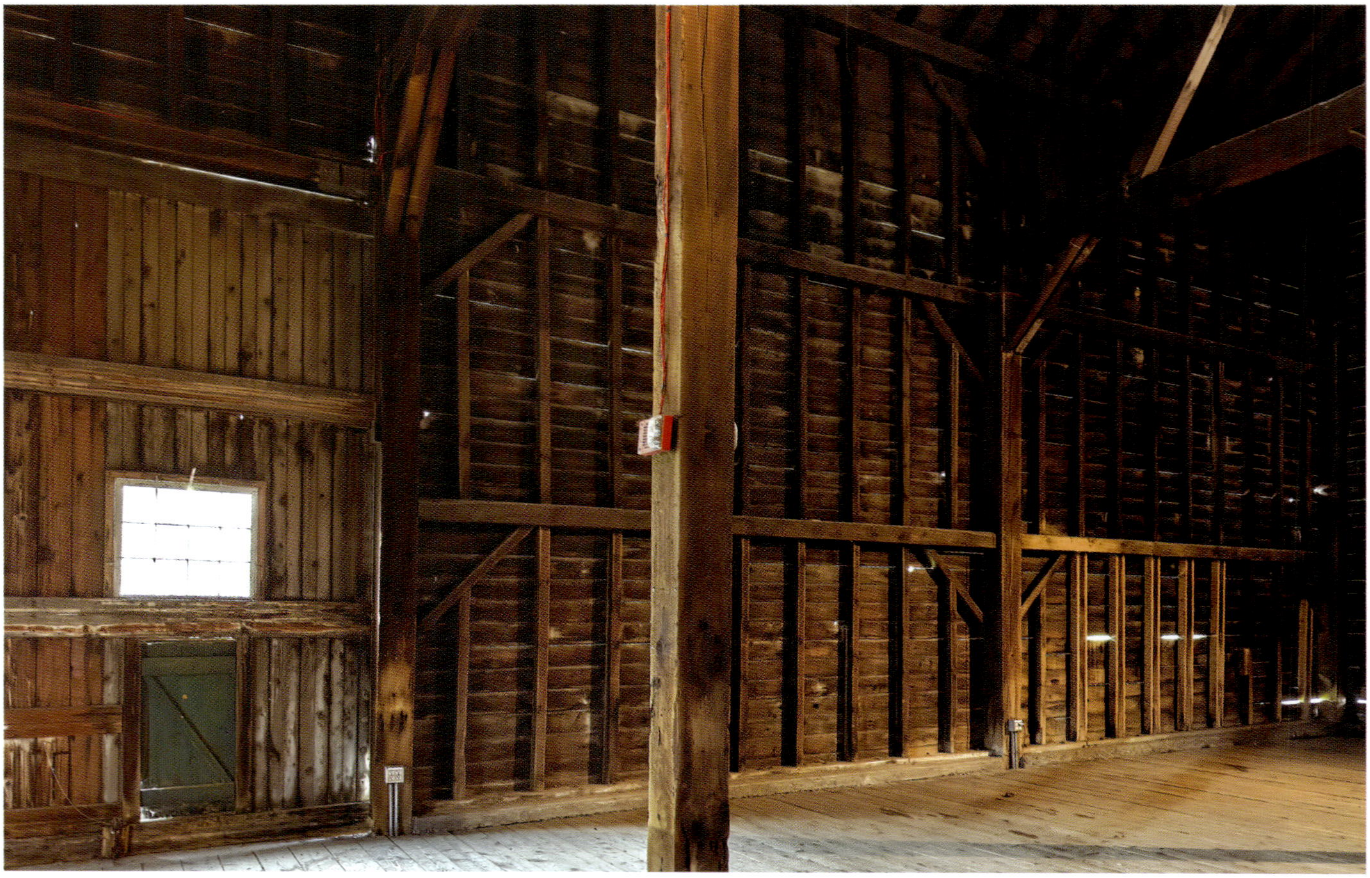

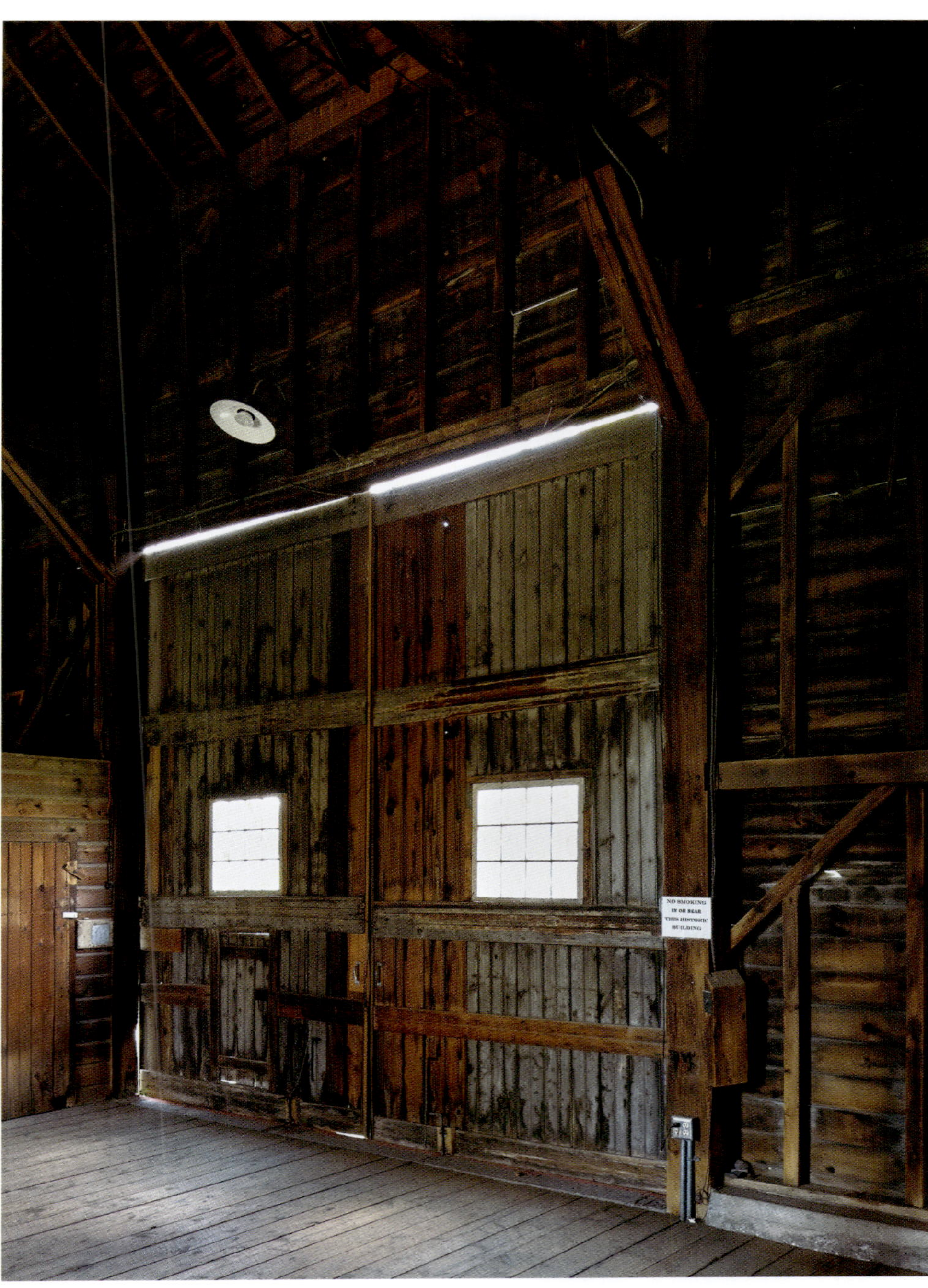

opposite, top
The Shaker barn was built in 1915 under the supervision of one of the Shaker elders, who planned the layout of the connected series of agricultural buildings, including a hay barn, cow barn, and manure shed.

opposite, bottom
The hay barn, with its tall ceiling and exposed timber structure, is impressive. These days, it is used for community events and weddings.

above
Huge sliding doors allowed for wagons filled with hay to enter the barn and be unloaded.

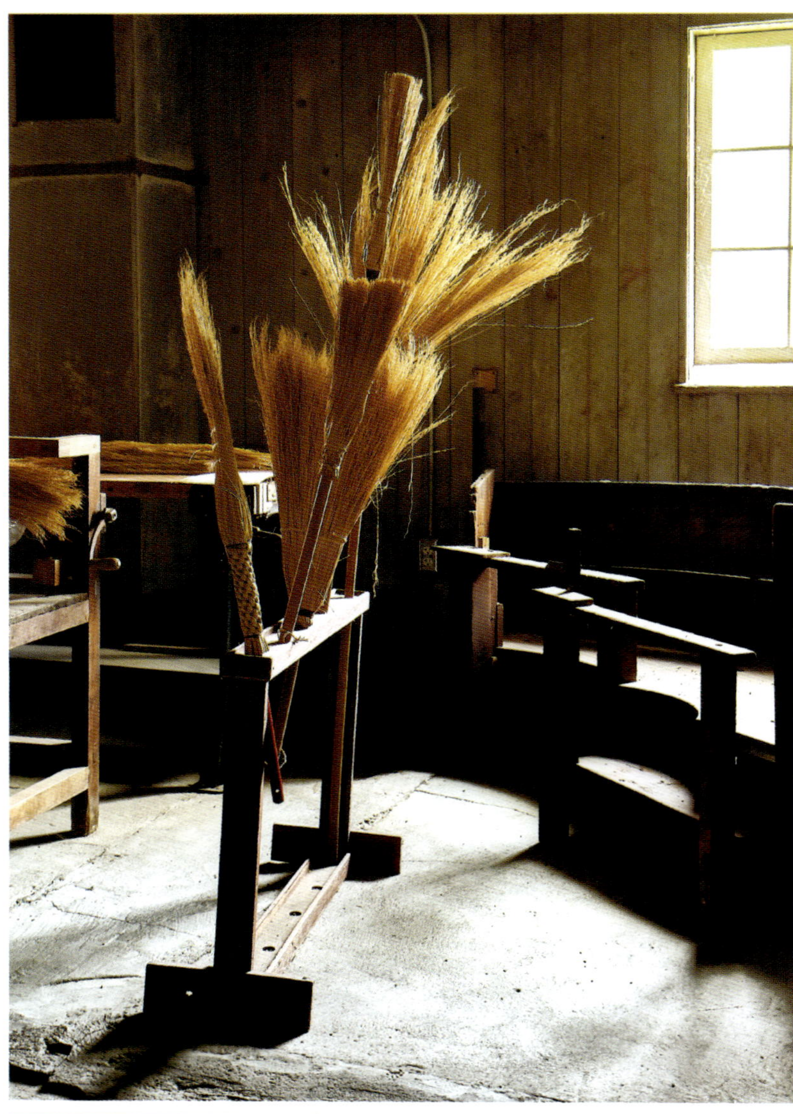

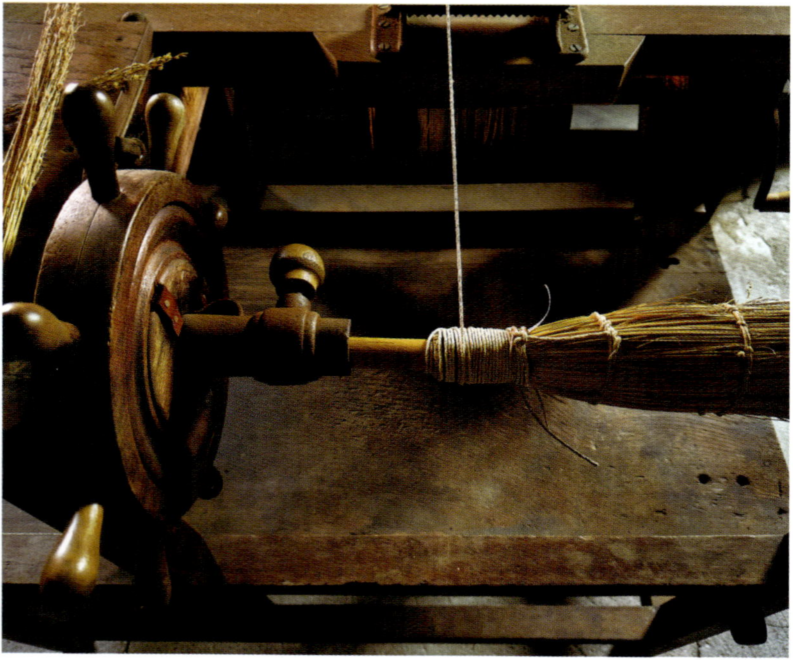

left
Brooms are shown in various stages of completion to demonstrate the process. Handmade brooms created in the Shaker tradition are still sold by artisans in the Northeast.

opposite
Shakers also made the wooden tools, including vices and holders, as well as the brooms themselves.

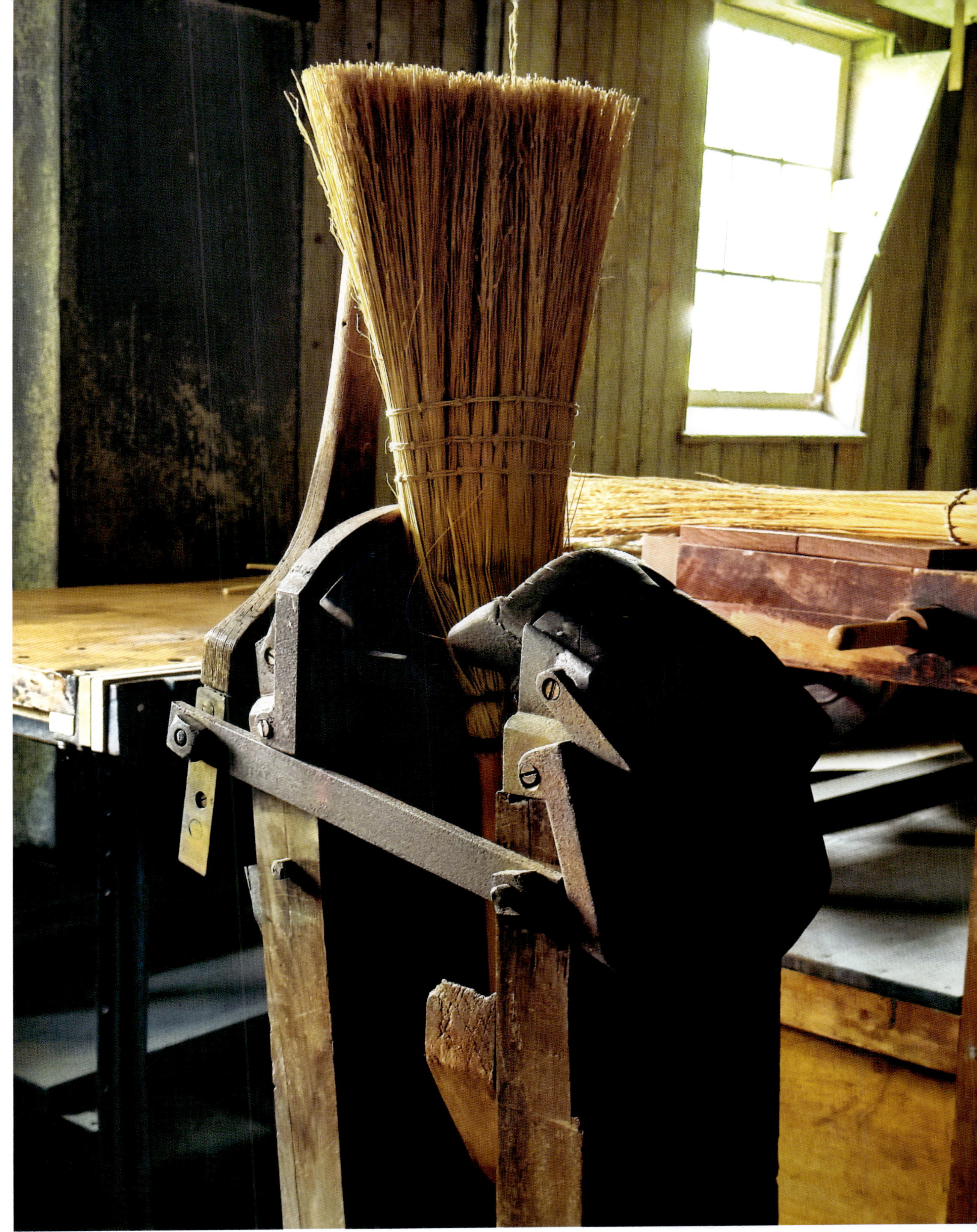

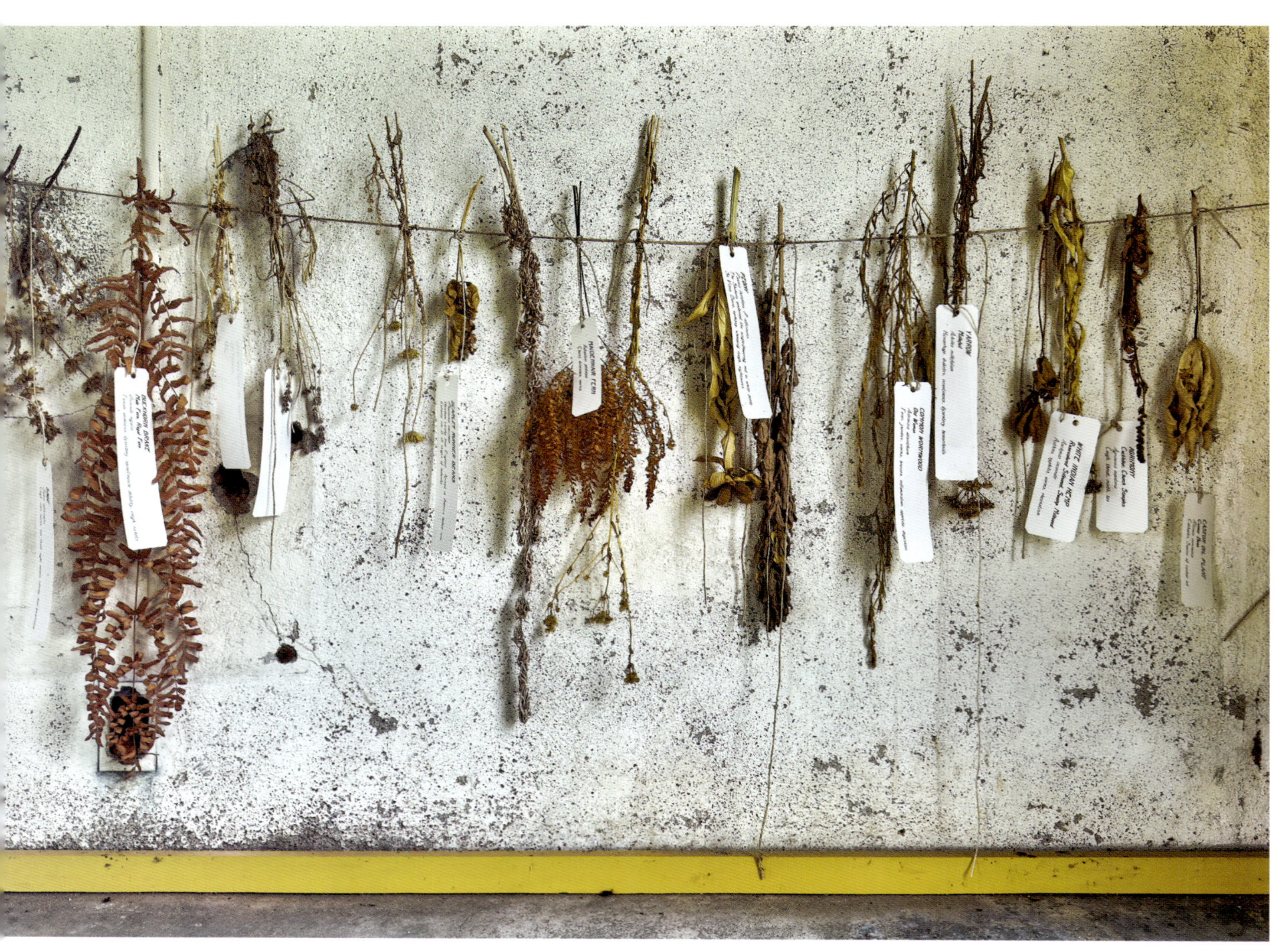

above and opposite
Artist Julie Whitney Barnes completed an installation titled *Planting Utopia* in and on one of the Shaker buildings. She used herbs grown on-site in the garden as inspiration for her paintings. The work was influenced by the Shaker practice of making spirit drawings. Herbs that Julia gathered and labeled hang below one of her Blue Cyanotype paintings.

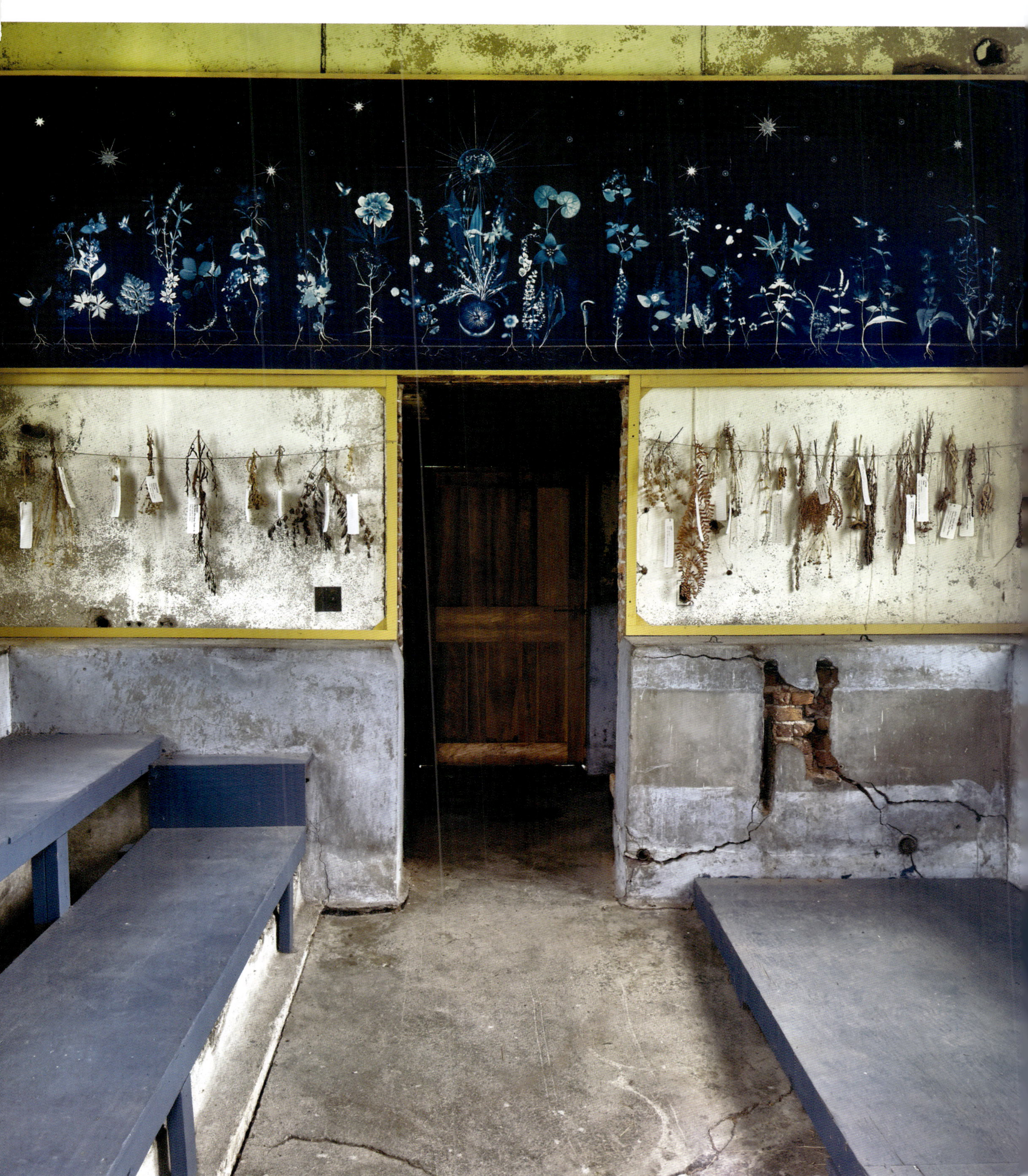

The Iroquois Museum

Howes Cave, New York

The Iroquois Museum is a beehive of activity. Staff, volunteers, and vendors are setting up for the "Roots, Rhythm, and Ale" party. It includes events, demonstrations, and exhibitions that draw the community to the site. Inside, the long narrow space is also filled with visual activity. The first-floor main space is split between anthropological finds and a contemporary art gallery. The downstairs area has an interactive children's museum with a live turtle pond.

Rising above the hubbub is the singular dignified building, elegant in its simplicity, poetic in its connection to the past, and optimistic in its vision of the present and future. Designed by modernist architect Charles Trent Arnold, the Iroquois Museum opened in 1992. The elongated design was inspired by the traditional longhouse—a one-room open-plan shelter where multigeneration families lived together in groups. Nearby materials such as trees and bark were used to make the longhouse. The museum's design also uses natural materials, in this case, single wood shakes as siding. Inside the longhouse, holes were made in the roof to release the smoke from fires, lit for warmth and cooking. Skylights replace these vents in the current structure.

The Iroquois Museum was built on forty-five acres in a valley of the Catskill Mountains' Schoharie County. Nature trails lead visitors through the grounds. The museum acknowledges that it is located on ancestorial homelands of the Kanien'kehá:ka (Mohawk) people. The Haudenosaunee (Iroquois) Confederacy is made up of the people of Six Nations members: the Mohawk, Oneida, Onondaga, Cayuga, Seneca, and Tuscarora. The name *Iroquois* originated from French explorers in the 1600s. *Haudenosaunee* translates to "People of the Longhouse." The museum's mission is to honor and respect the traditions of the Haudenosaunee people by collecting and exhibiting contemporary Iroquois nation artists' work from 1960 to the present. In addition, the museum has a collection of Iroquois artifacts that have been discovered in Schoharie County.

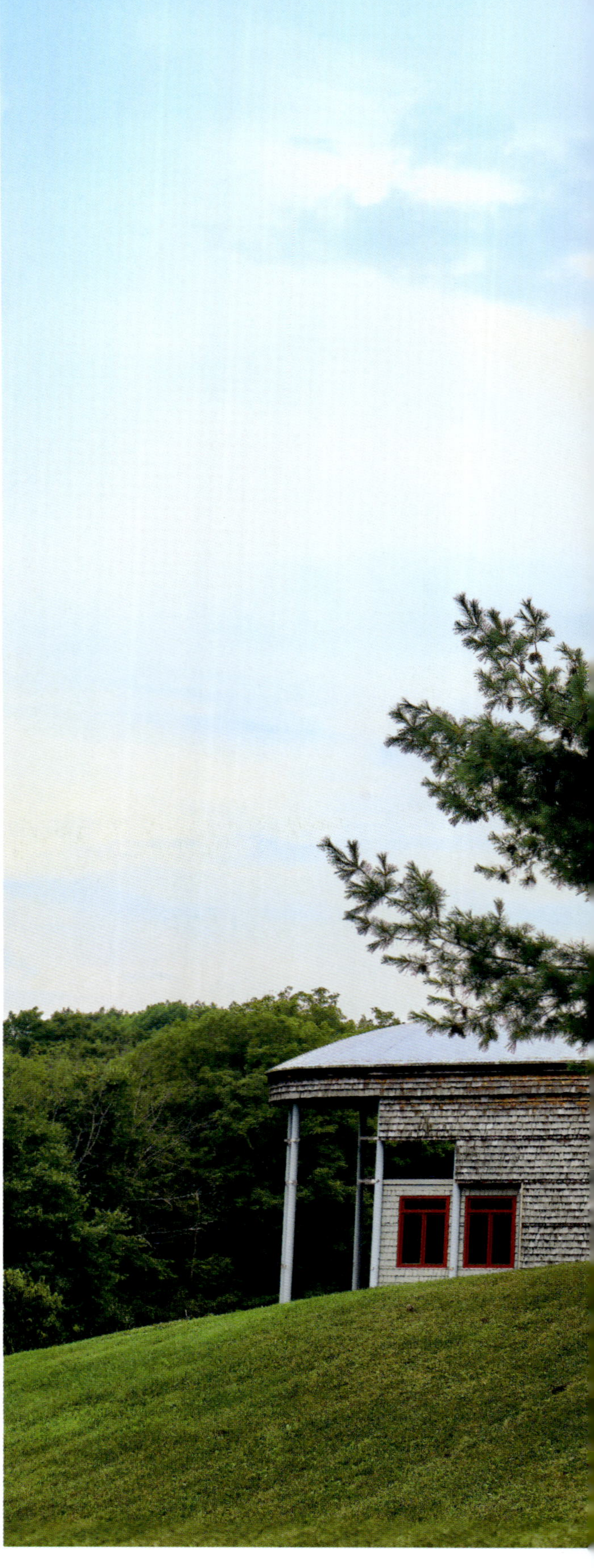

A pine tree stands alongside the Iroquois Museum.

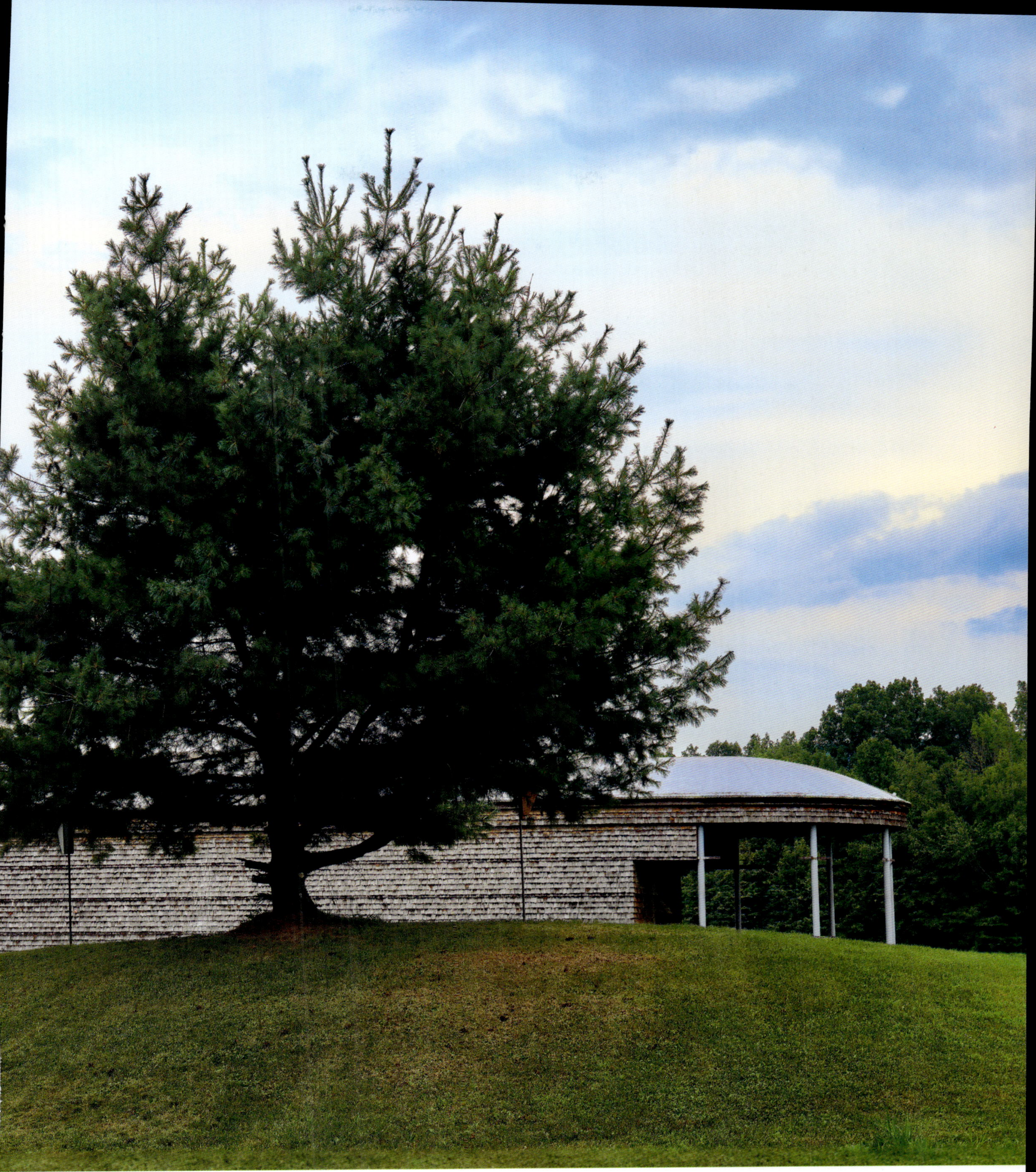

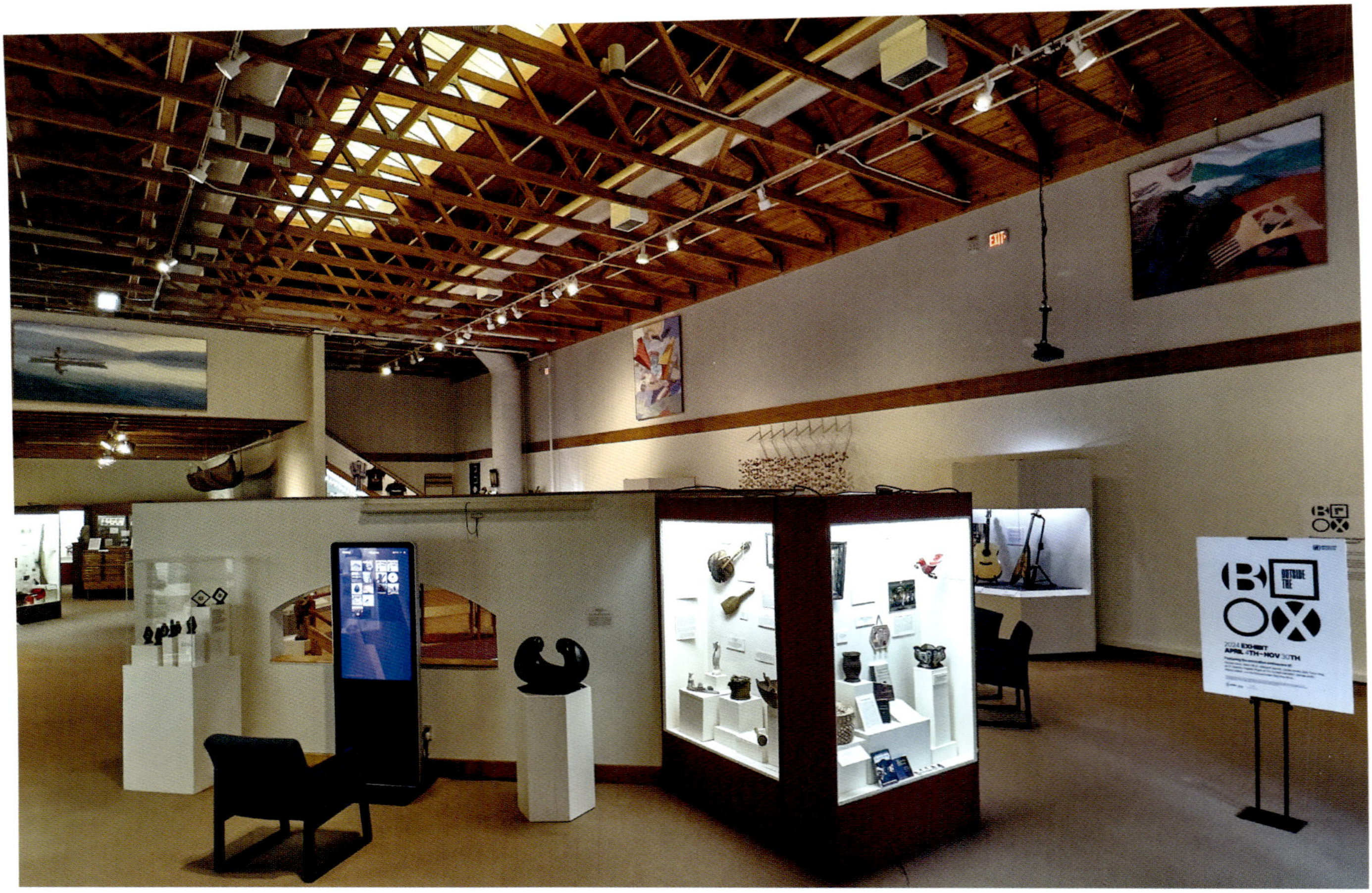

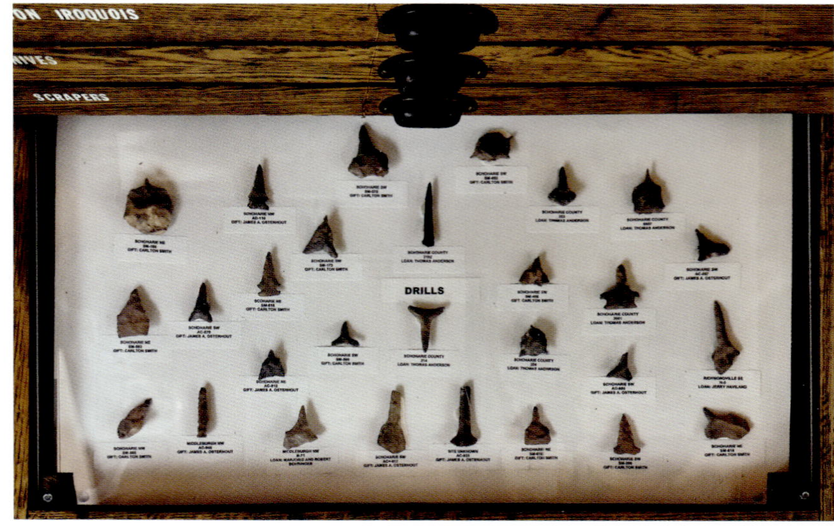

top
The interior of the main-floor gallery is divided. Exhibitions on the left include cultural items and documents. The space on the right is used for rotating exhibitions. Above the wood rafters, the skylights reference the “smoke holes” of the traditional longhouse and allow natural light into the space.

bottom
A flat file case holds a selection of the museum’s collection of gifted or loaned early tools, many of which were made using a “hammer stone” to form the shape for the tool’s use, such as drills, knives, and points for arrows. Labels indicate the date and place of origin if known. These tools are categorized as early technologies.

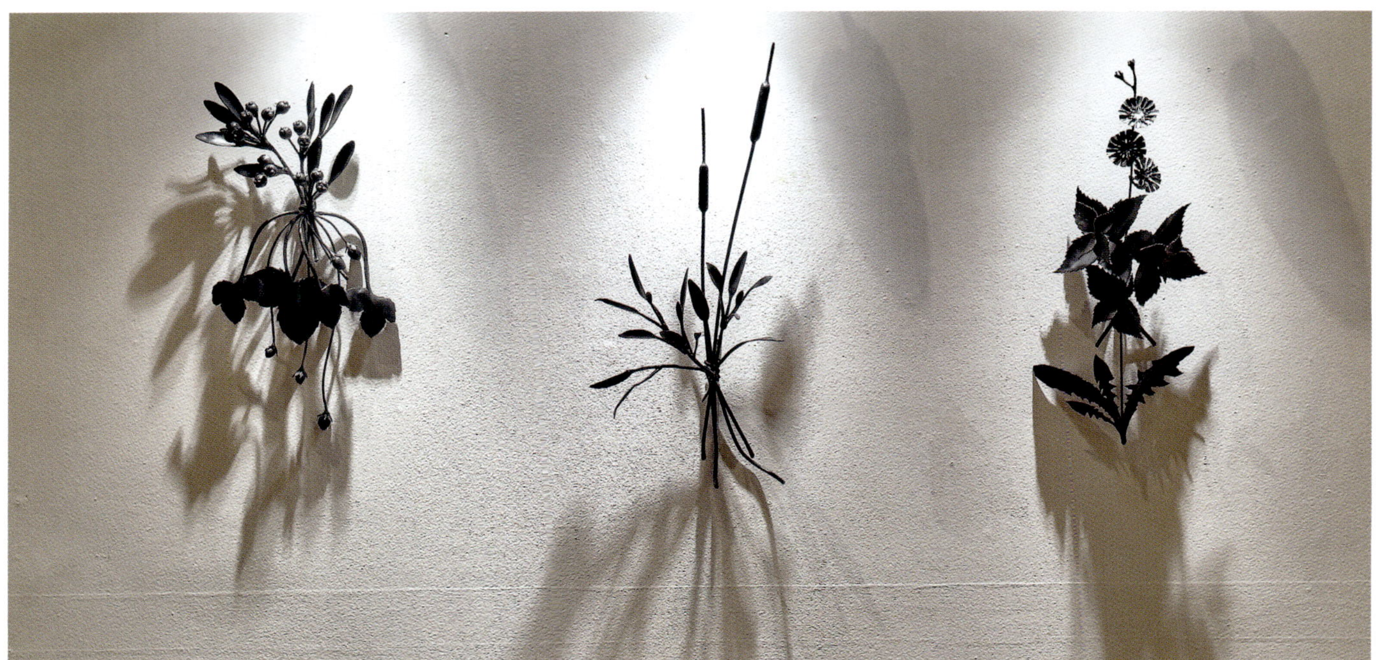

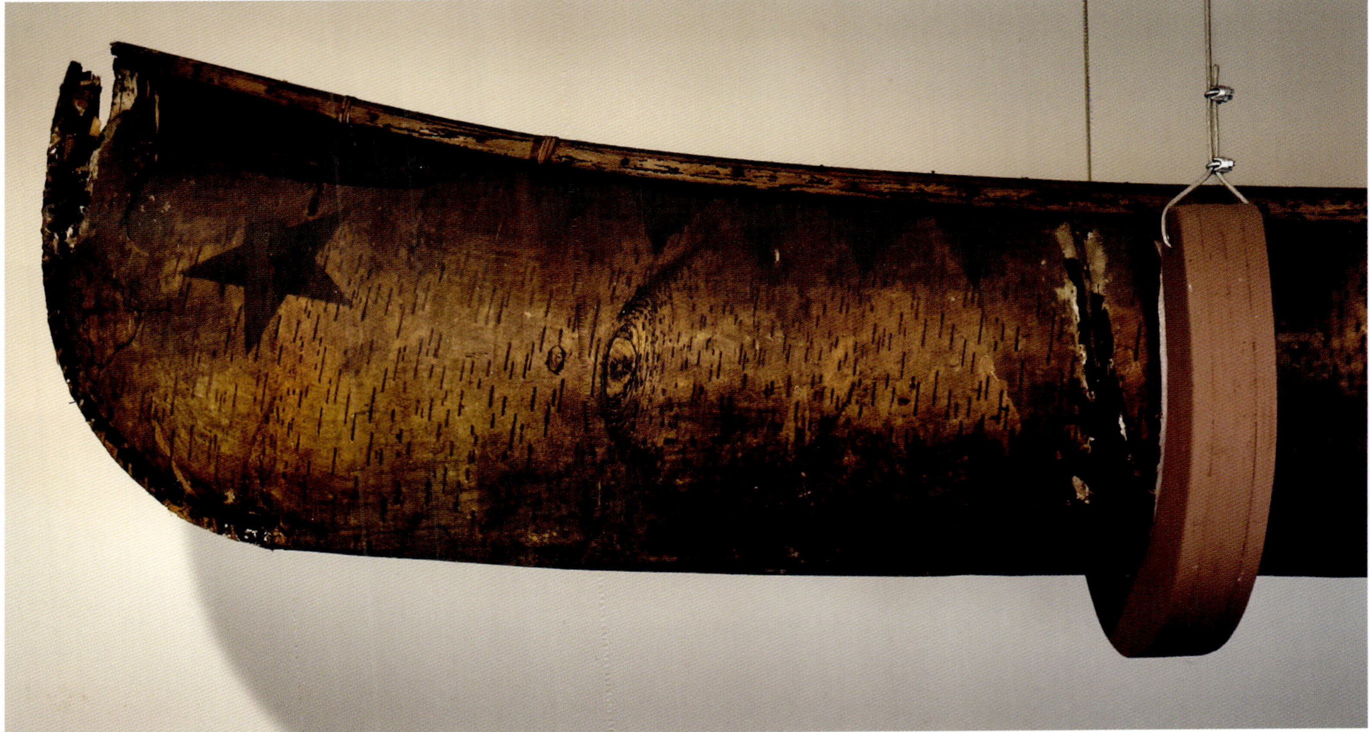

top
From April to November 2024, the work of metalsmith Margaret Jacobs, a member of the Akwesasne Mohawk tribe, was shown in the Iroquois Museum's exhibition "Outside the Box." Her pieces made from steel are titled, from left to right, *Bouquets for a New Era: Blueberry and Strawberry* (2024), *Bouquets for a New Era: Sage and Cattail* (2024), and *Bouquets for a New Era: Mint and Chicory* (2024).

bottom
A 1907 birch bark canoe with a star on the front hangs above the cabinets of artifacts.

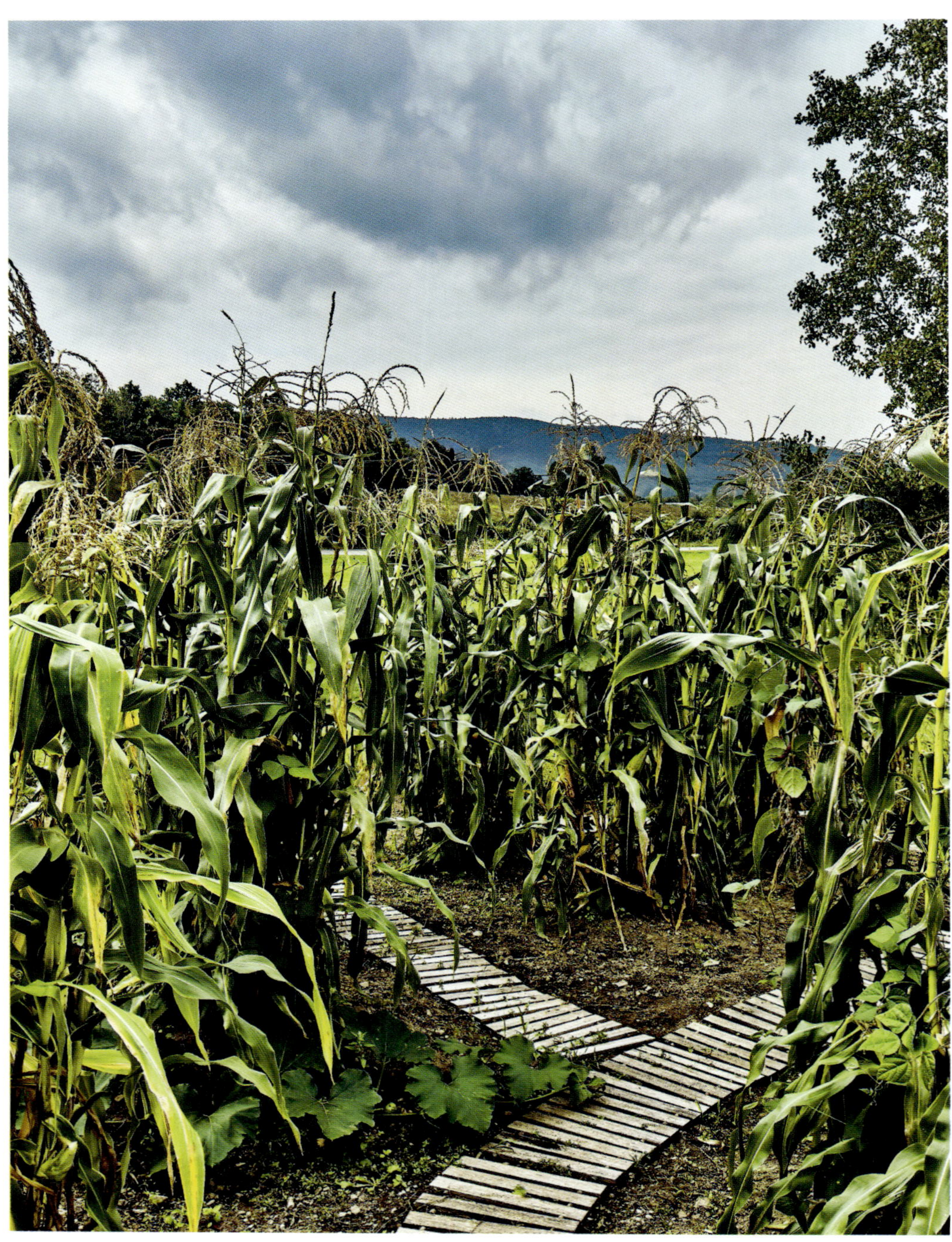

above and opposite, top
A garden of corn, beans, and squash, known as the Three Sisters in the Haudenosaunee culture, is planted in front of the museum's entrance. Additional medicinal plantings are also grown here as part of an educational exhibit.

opposite, bottom
Longhouses had slabs of bark attached to timber frames. The layers of wood shingle shakes siding pay homage to the original design using modern building materials.

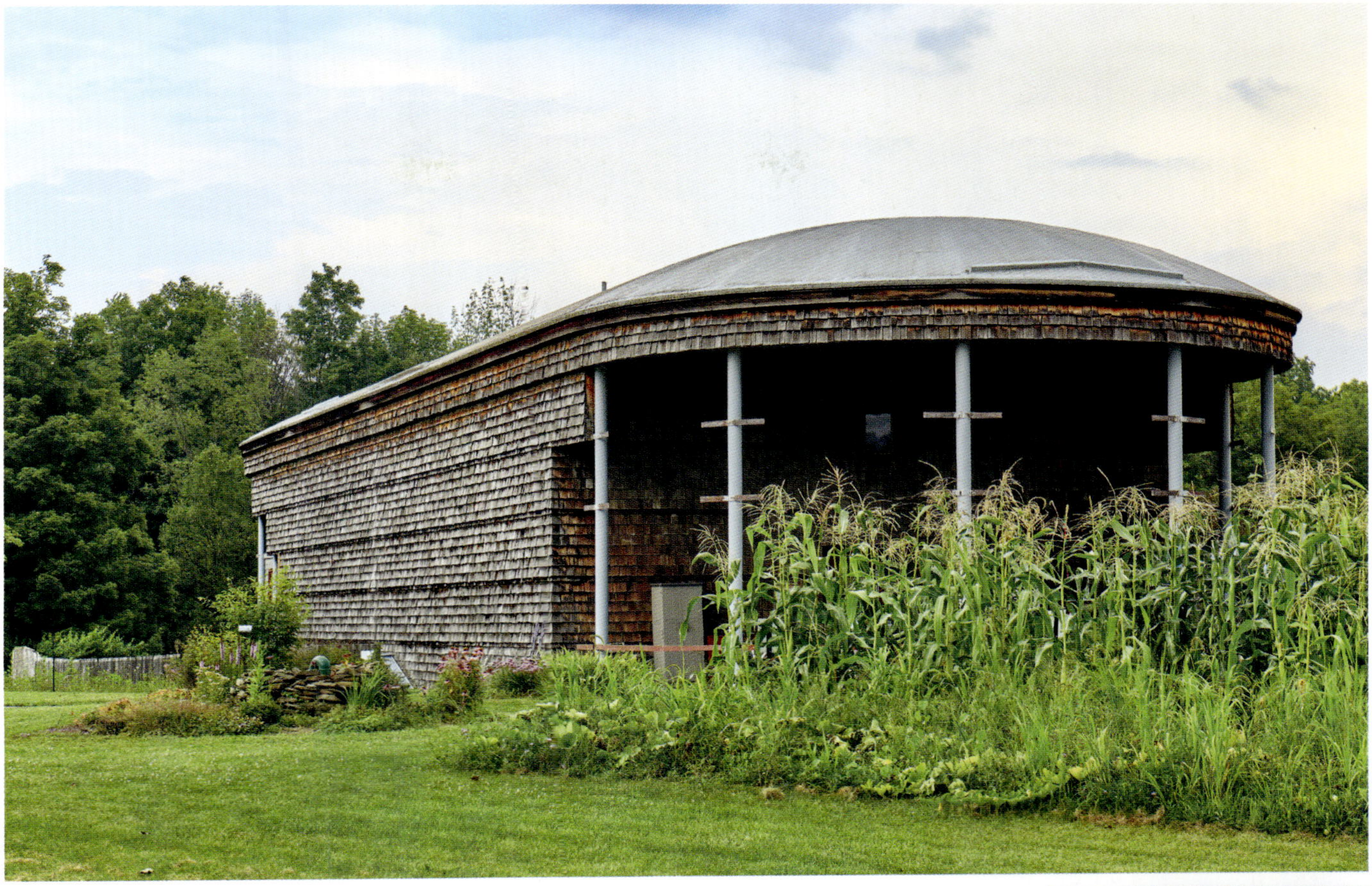

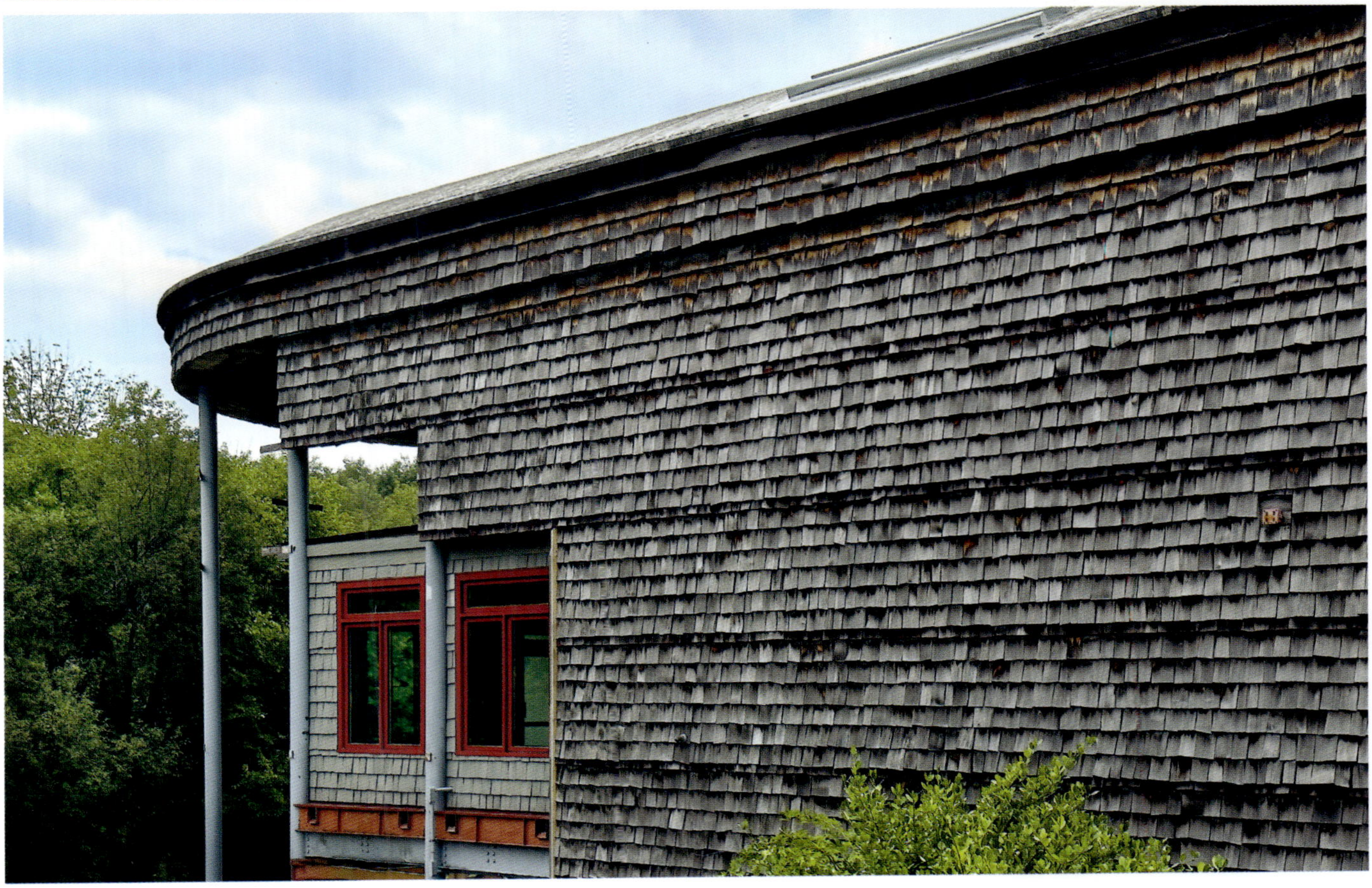

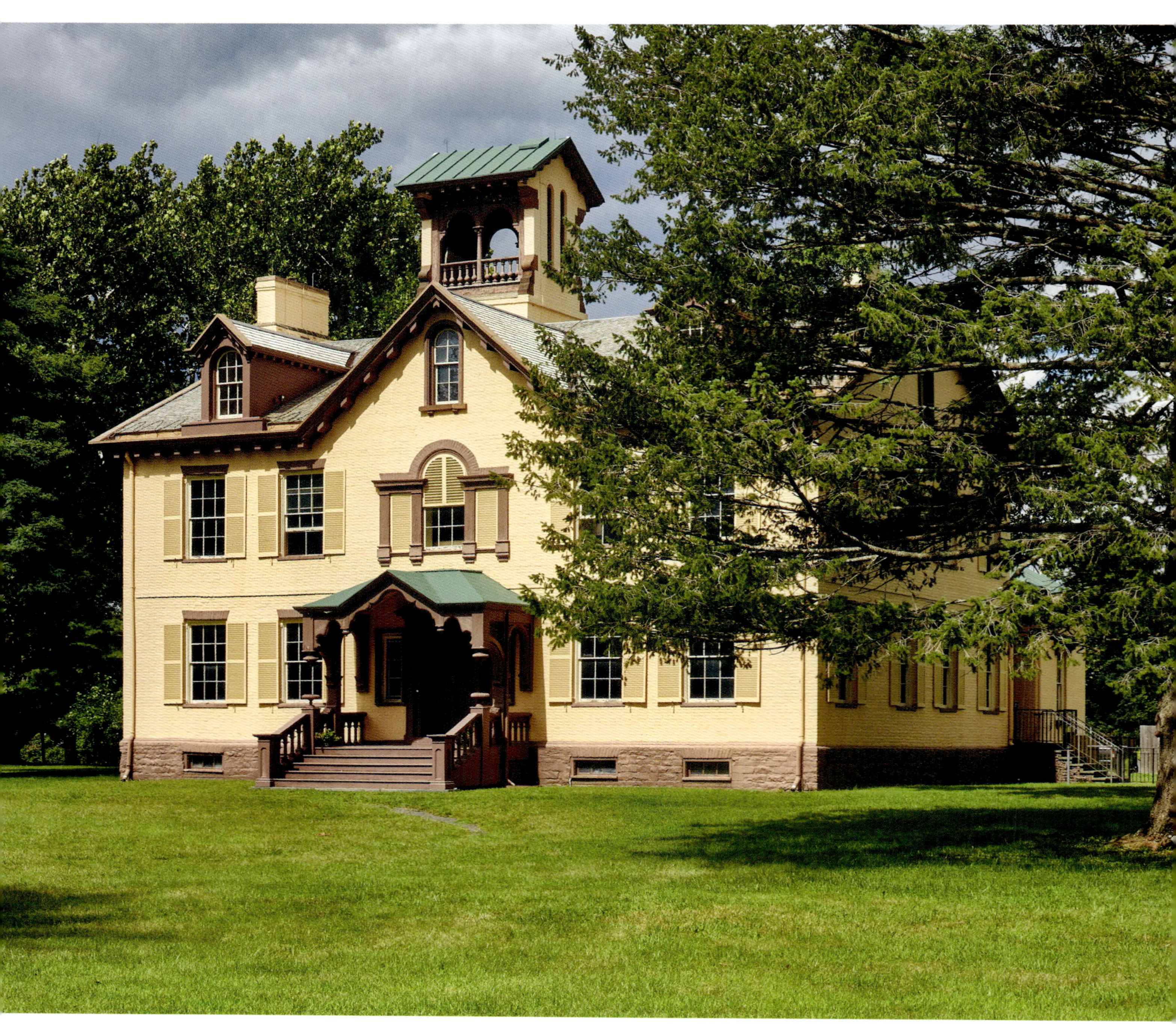

While Martin Van Buren added the black locust trees along the front semicircular drive, only one tree is believed to have survived from the time of his residence there. The remaining trees were planted in 2002. The drive meets a front Italianate portico that was added during the 1841 renovation and a split Dutch door, a feature that dates to the first owners of the eighteenth-century house.

Lindenwald, Martin Van Buren National Historic Site

Kinderhook, New York

A large light ochre–colored house set back off Old Post Road in Kinderhook, New York, was first known as Kleinrood. The brick Georgian-style house was built in 1797 for Peter Van Ness, a wealthy landholder and judge. In 1839, while in his second year of serving as the eighth president of the United States, Martin Van Buren purchased the 220-acre property from one of Van Ness's sons.

How did a boy who grew up in a roadside tavern and on a farm come to be the president? In his early years in a young America, Martin Van Buren's upward trajectory seemed improbable. However, Old Post Road in Kinderhook, where his father's farm and inn were located, went to Albany and in time so did Van Buren. His roles in state government and politics eventually took him to Washington, DC, serving in the cabinet of Andrew Jackson, notably as secretary of state and vice president. Van Buren was president from 1837 to 1841. A widower—his young wife Hannah died in 1819—Van Buren and his four sons, now young men, went to live in the White House. Four years later, he lost his reelection campaign.

Van Buren and three of his sons returned home to Kinderhook, where they renovated, redecorated, and renamed their new home Lindenwald after the linden trees on the estate's lands. A New York City architect, Richard Upjohn, was brought in by Van Buren's youngest son, Smith Thompson Van Buren, to design an addition to the house. The renovation took place between 1849 and 1850. On the first floor, Upjohn's plan added a bedroom, an indoor bath and toilet, and a hallway with an additional entrance; downstairs, a full basement housed servant quarters, the kitchen, and the laundry; and in the back of the house, Upjohn added a six-story tower. Van Buren's son Abraham and his Southern-born wife, Angelica Singleton Van Buren, influenced his decorative interior choices. Perhaps Van Buren's sophisticated tastes resulted from his time spent as secretary of state and envoy to Great Britain. According to his letters, Van Buren was quite proud of his work in the house and on the grounds. He lived at Lindenwald until his death in 1862. Afterward, the home was sold and resold over the years, and used mainly as a private residence.

The property was acquired by the National Park Service in 1974. Extensive work, research, and scholarship were utilized to furnish and restore the building to reflect the time of the president's life there. Criteria for collecting furnishings and interior details were set. Only displaying furnishings original to the house would not give an impression of how the Van Burens lived there, as many of the furnishings had been given away, taken, or sold. For example, an accordion dining room table that extends to allow for more guests, now on display, is a replica of the original table that was documented as owned by Van Buren. Some of the furnishings are "period appropriate." Today, Lindenwald is open as a historic house museum.

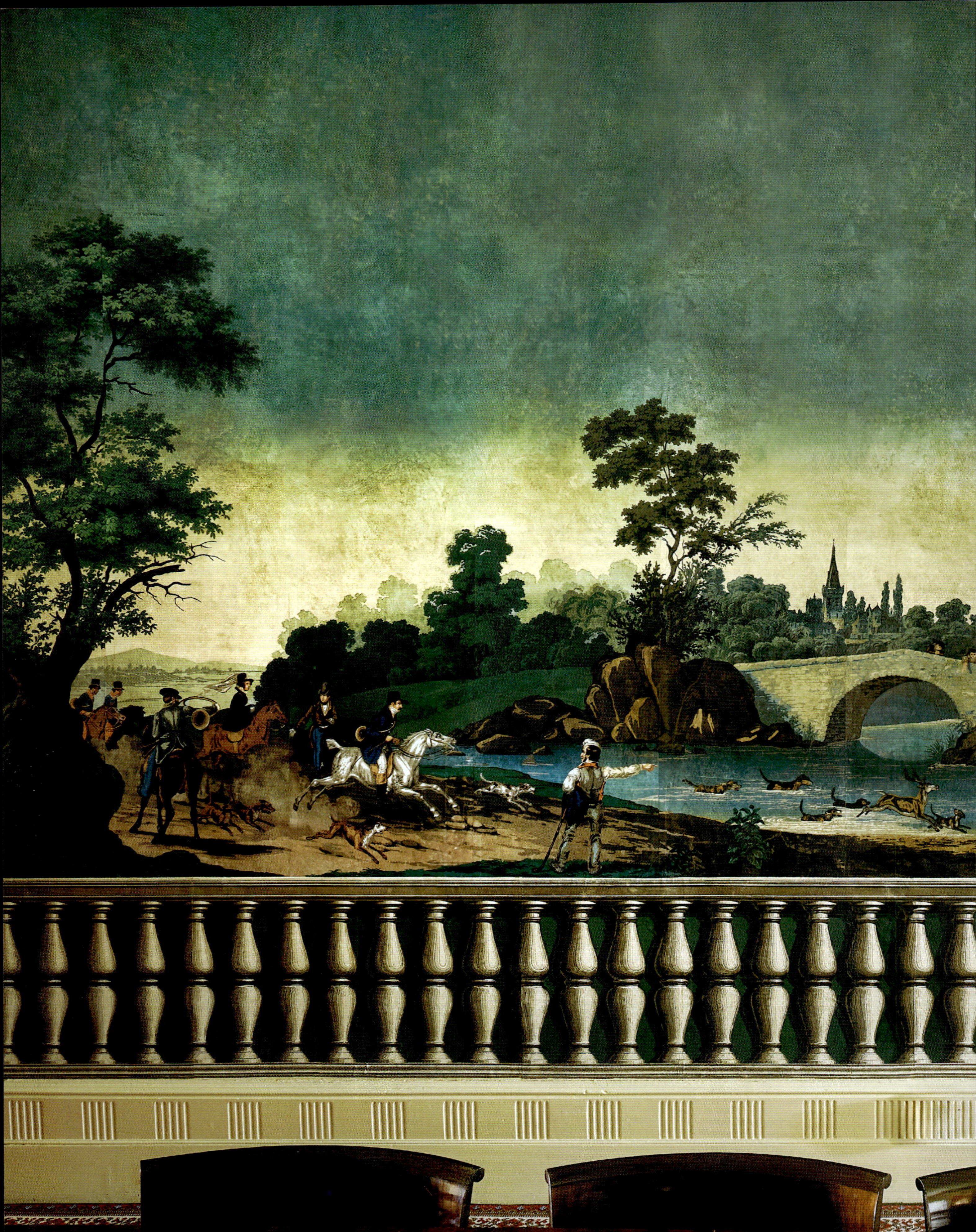

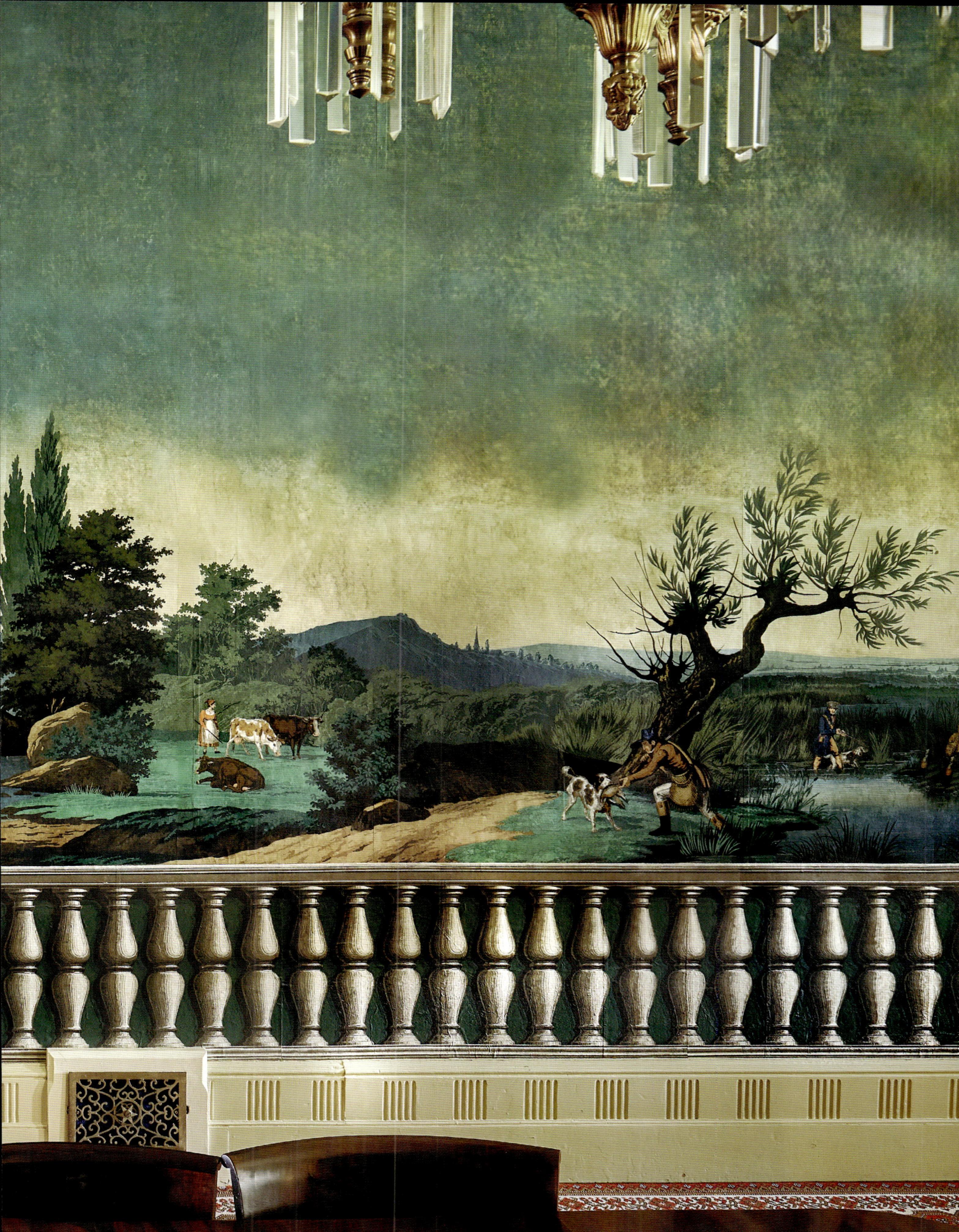

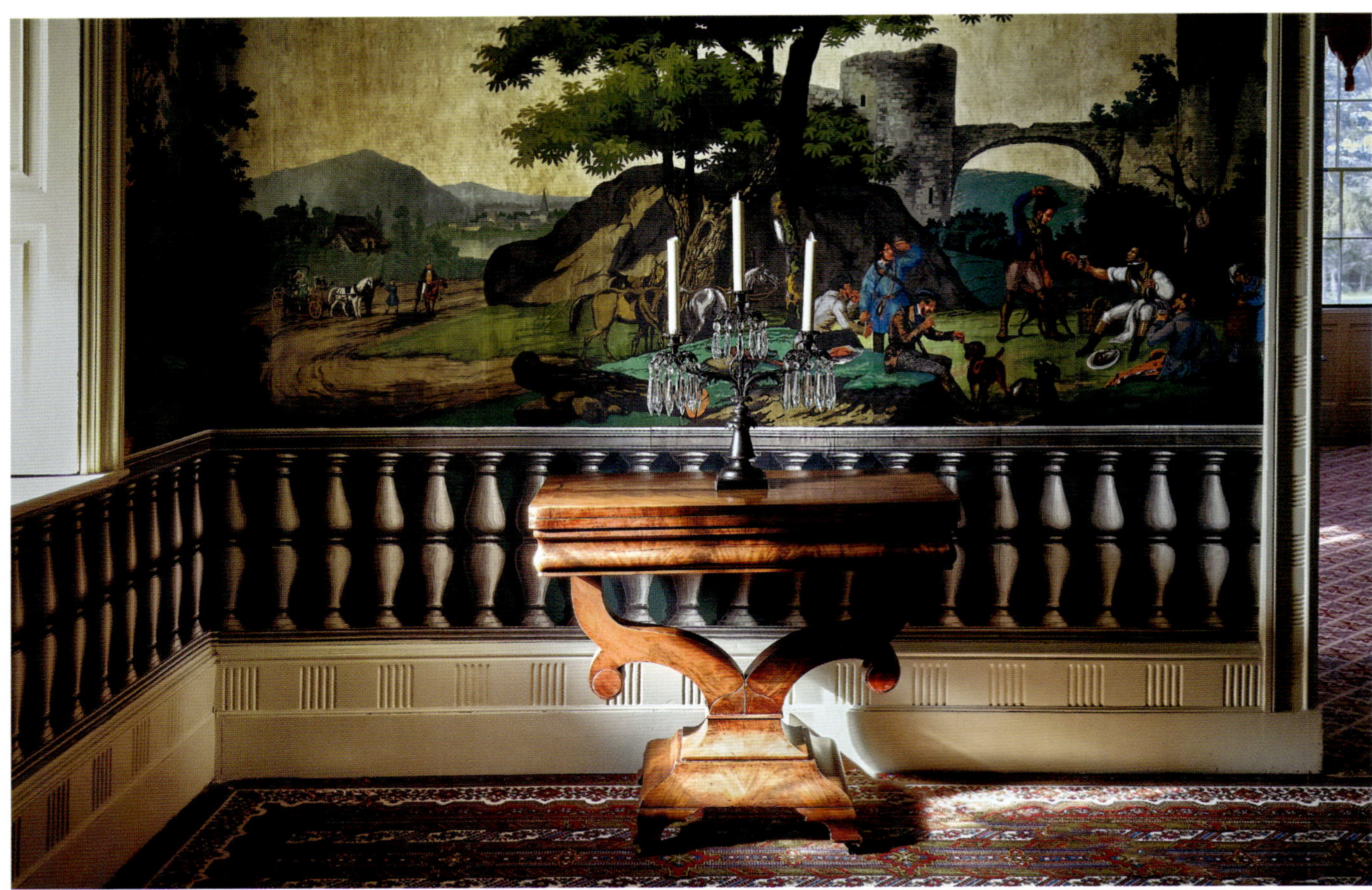

previous
The pièce de résistance of the interior design is the splendid French scenic wallpaper installed in the main hall dining room in 1841. Van Buren chose the paper made by the famous wall-covering company Zuber. What influenced his decision to install *Le Paysage à Chasses*, or *The Hunting Landscape*, is still uncertain. The wallpaper was made using 1,253 wood-blocks and 142 colors. The company still manufactures this pattern.

above
Large sections of the wallpaper survived into the twentieth century but not without damage. In 1981, as part of the restoration of the house, the original remaining paper was removed, repaired, and reinstalled in the dining room. A new balustrade pattern, installed below the dado, was reproduced by the House of Scalamandré. Restoration of the historic paper is ongoing, especially as the climate changes.

opposite
New wallpaper of the same scene was ordered from Zuber, replacing missing pieces at either end of the long room to replicate the room as it was in Van Buren's time.

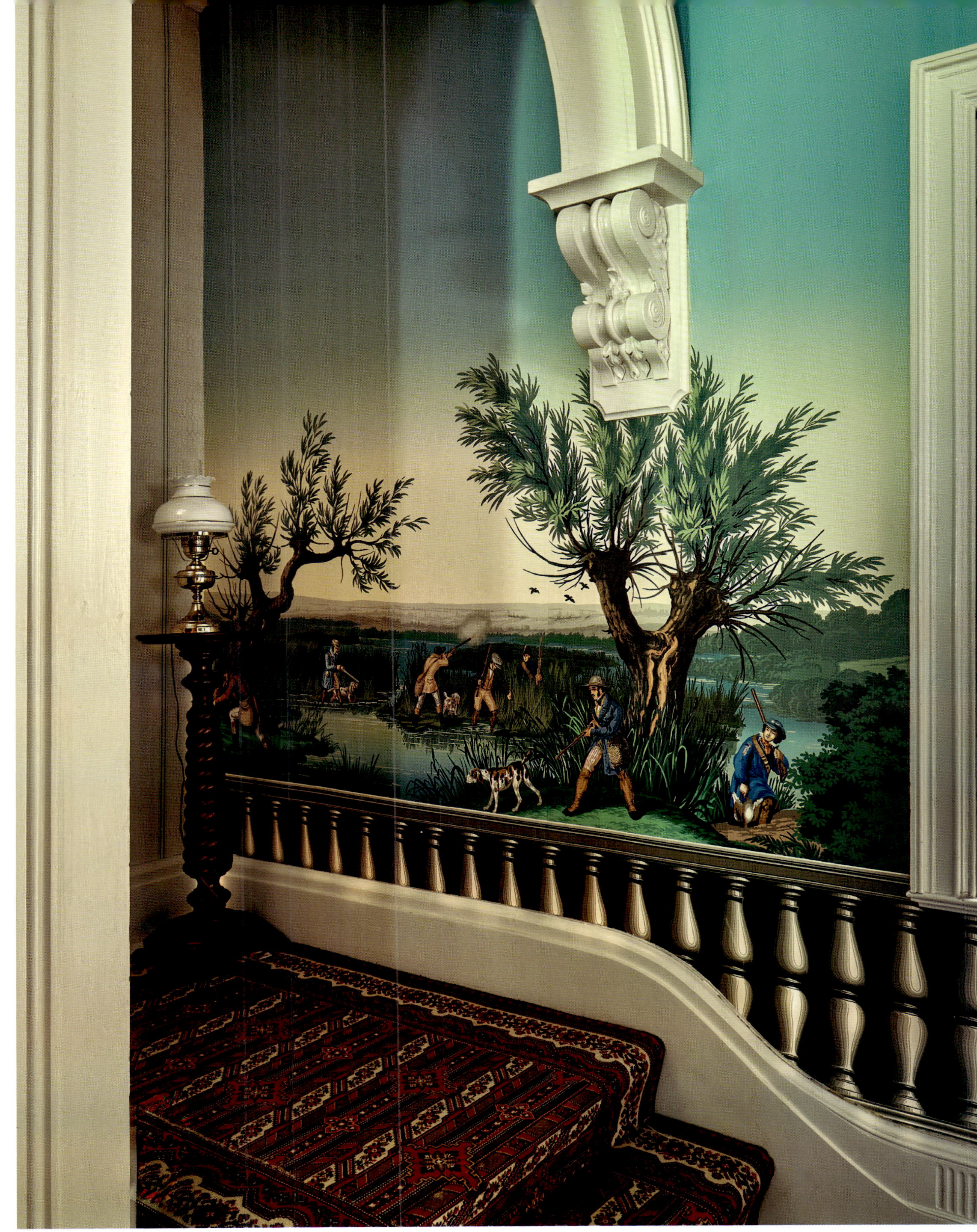

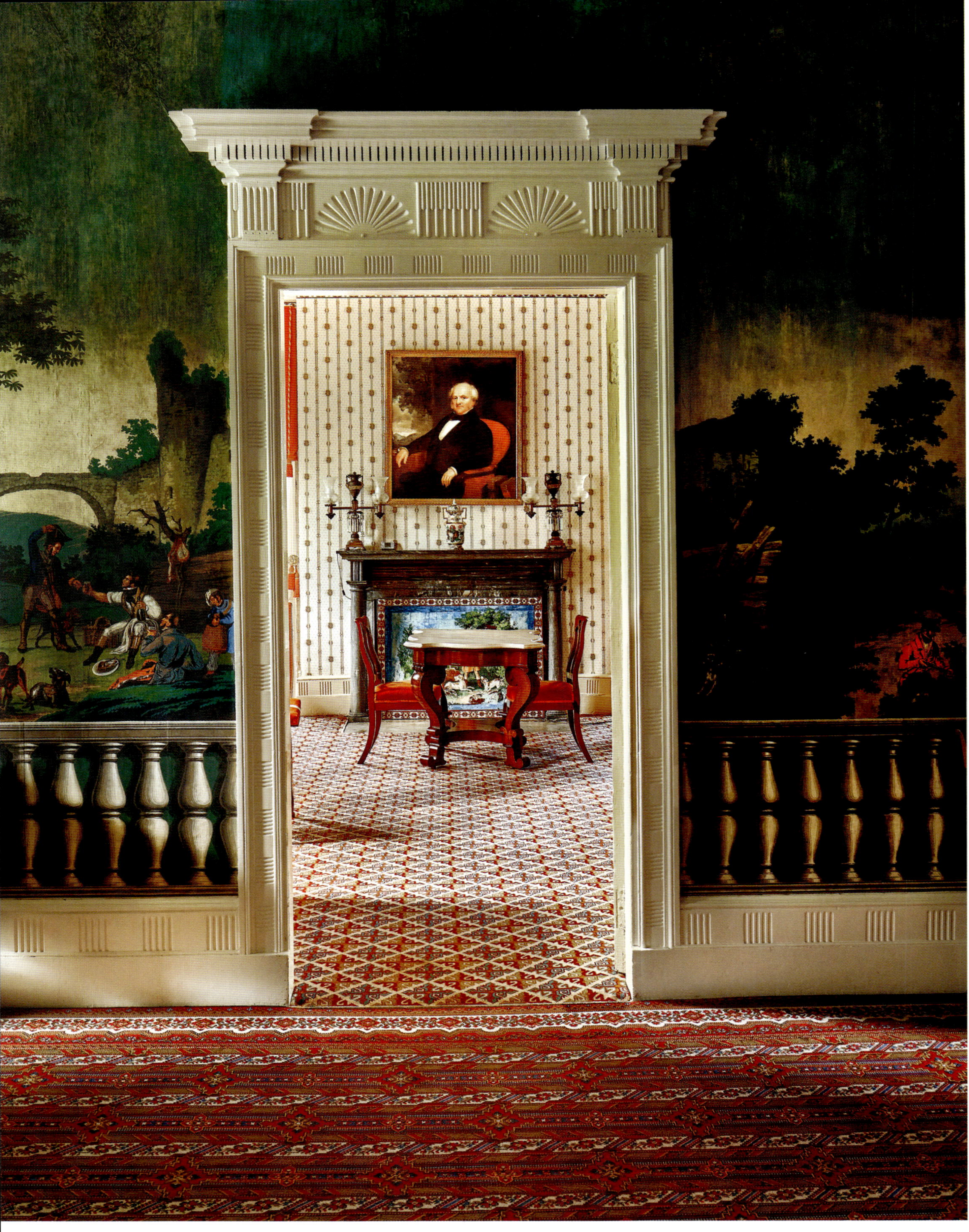

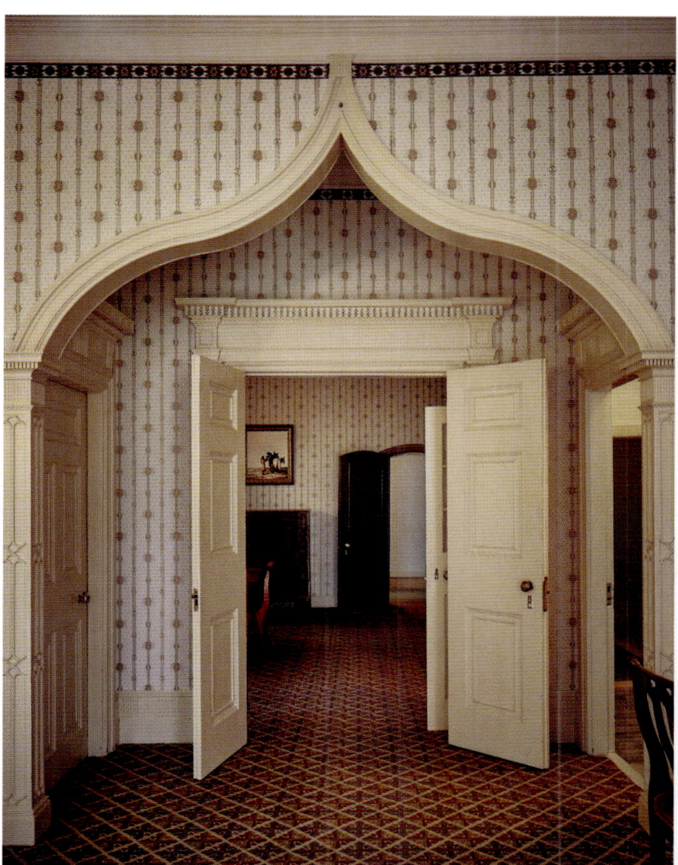

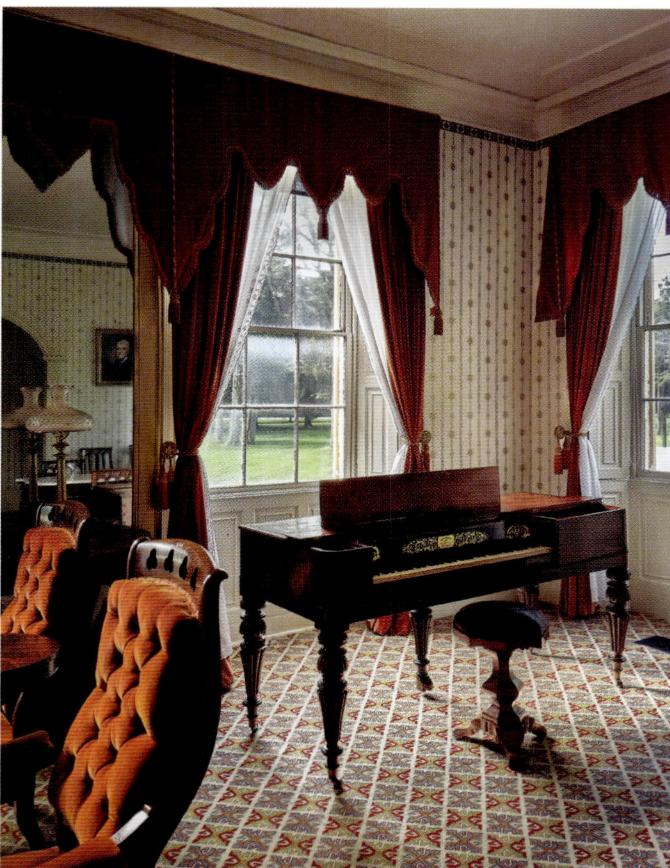

opposite
From the dining room, a view looking into the front formal parlor or drawing room frames a portrait of Van Buren. Remnants of carpeting and wallpaper in other rooms survived as well, providing helpful clues in re-creating the interior design of the president's house during the period he lived there. The upholstered chairs and a card table also date to the Van Buren residency.

top left
A Gothic-style ogee archway leads into the breakfast room, where the family took their meals. The majority of wood trim work is painted a creamy white.

top right
The formal front parlor faced the Old Post Road. According to the Martin Van Buren National Historic Site's report on the historical furnishings, Van Buren installed the gilt mirror between the two windows. A piano whose ownership is uncertain was moved from the main hall to the parlor. The window drapery and valances were also restored in the house.

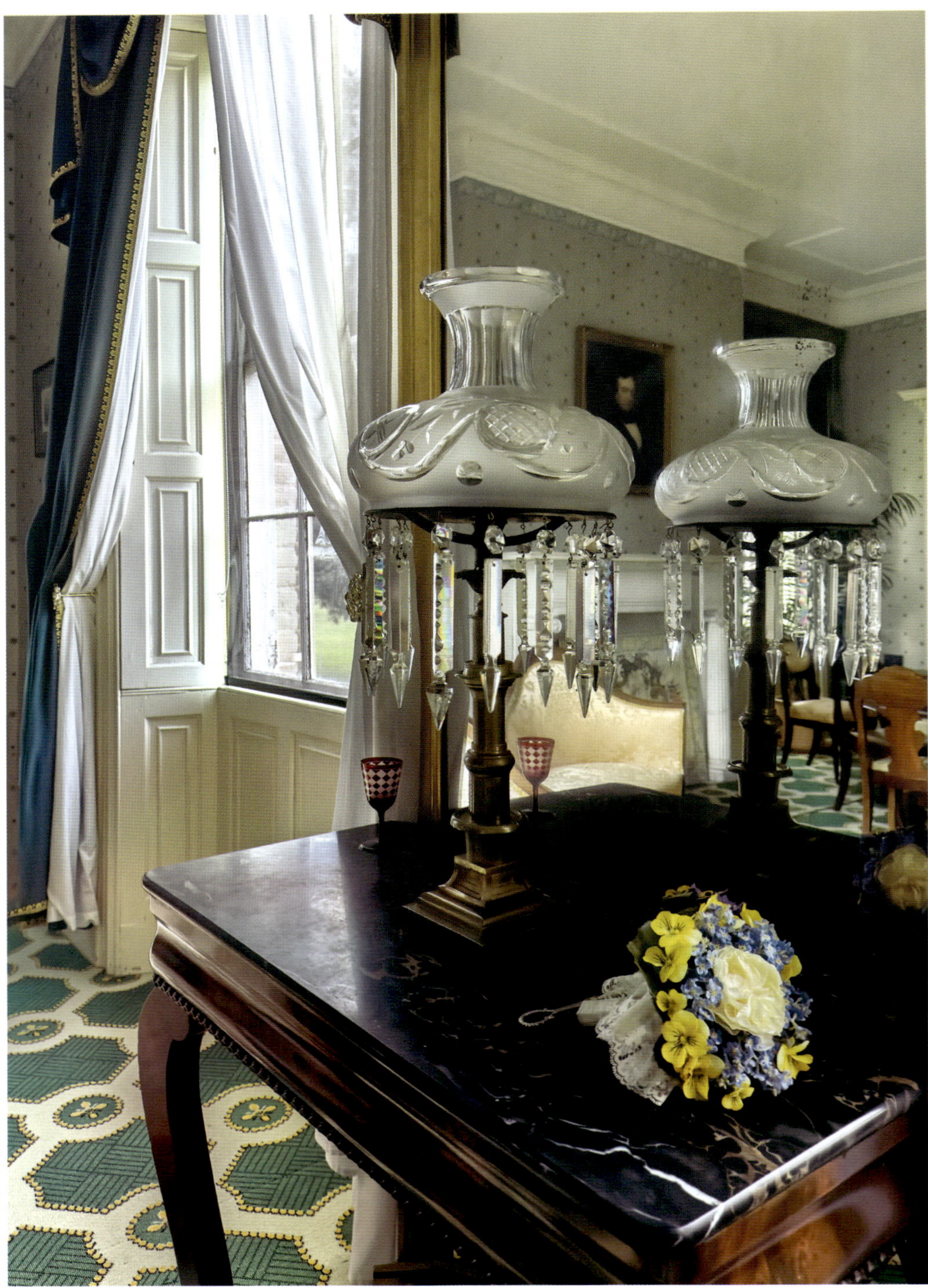

above
A marble-top table was placed in front of a large gold-framed mirror. Decorative accessories such as this glass lamp were like ones in other Van Buren residences.

opposite
The green sitting room served as a family gathering place. Tables were placed throughout, along with a sofa covered in a pinkish damask fabric. As images of this room taken in 1925 show, the carpet installed during Van Buren's time survived. Reproductions of fireboards from Zuber were placed against the fireplaces' openings in most of the rooms in the house. A portrait of the president's son John Van Buren is hung over the marble mantel.

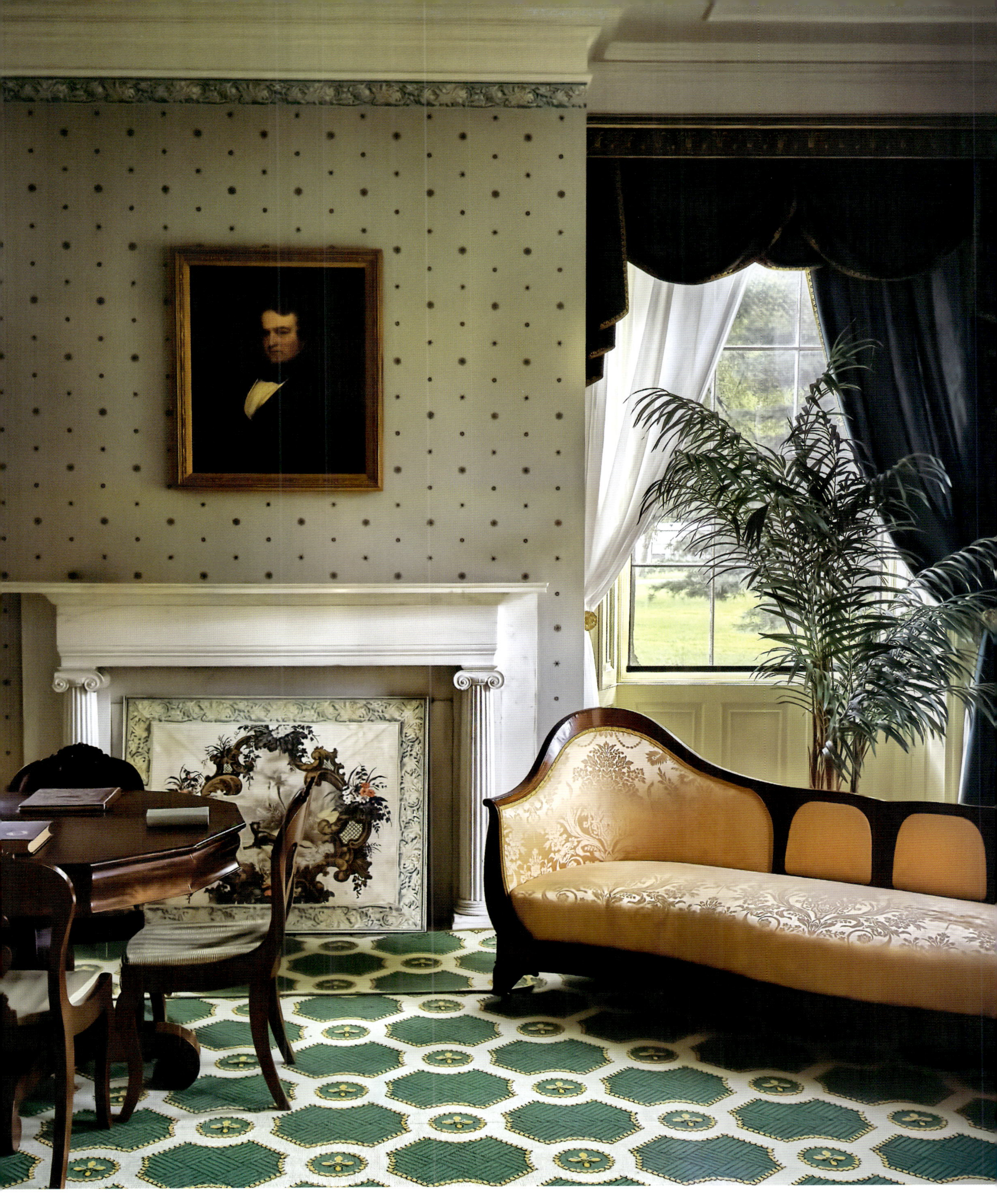

Librarium

East Chatham, New York

From bookstores on main street to tiny free libraries and large book barns, the vintage and used book "ecosystem" in upstate New York is alive and well. At one time, a map of the Hudson Valley Book Trail detailed at least seventeen different locations of independent booksellers that offered discount prices on books of all types, and now there's an Instagram account that does the same. Many of these shops are located off the beaten path and have long histories of passion and dedication to the printed word.

Sharon S. Lips started out as a graphic designer, but she always loved books and worked in bookstores. In 1979, after a conversation with her father, Richard Socky, a General Electric engineer and lifelong book collector, she decided to open a used bookstore named Librarium, a Latin word for "bookcase." He offered to help her get started by donating his book collection. Her mother, Ella, a real estate agent, found the perfect colonial-style farmhouse located near the hamlet of East Chatham. Sharon and her husband, Pieter, moved from Saranac Lake to set up the shop out of the old kitchen attached to the house. A barn on higher ground in the backyard was fitted with shelves. Nowadays, the barn houses an estimated 40,000 used books.

While Sharon does have collectible and rare books in stock, she calls herself as a generalist. She carries something for everyone, from kids' books to art books to fiction. To keep her stock fresh, she gathers books from estates. After her father retired, he too opened a bookstore, Kings Way Books and Antiques on Cape Cod, which he ran for twenty years. After his shop closed, his extra inventory went into the barn's loft.

In 1991, a few years before Amazon started, the *New York Times* reported that there were over "several hundred used bookstores within a 125-mile distance to Manhattan." As book buying shifted to the internet, Sharon saw a 90 percent drop in her walk-in traffic, but over the years she has built her business back to 50 percent online and 50 percent from the shop.

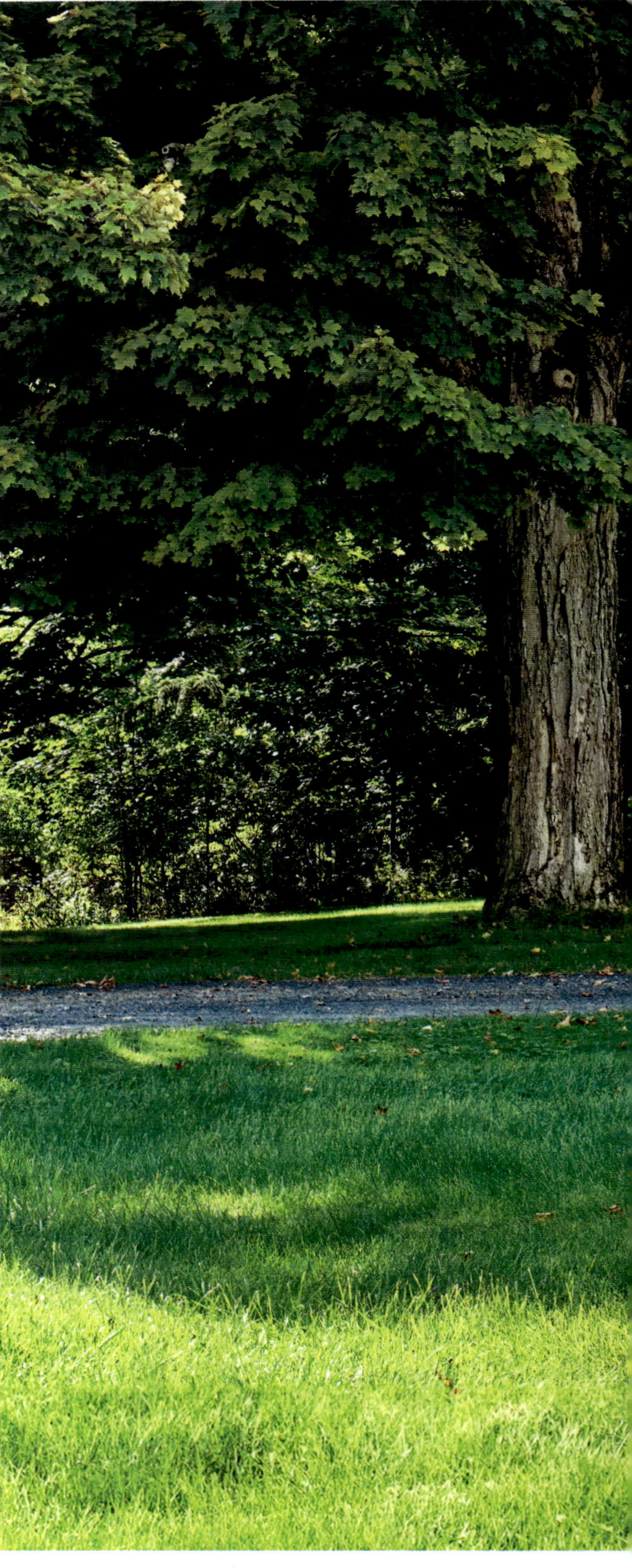

Librarium has been in business for over thirty years. Maple trees shade the front lawn where chairs are set up for readers.

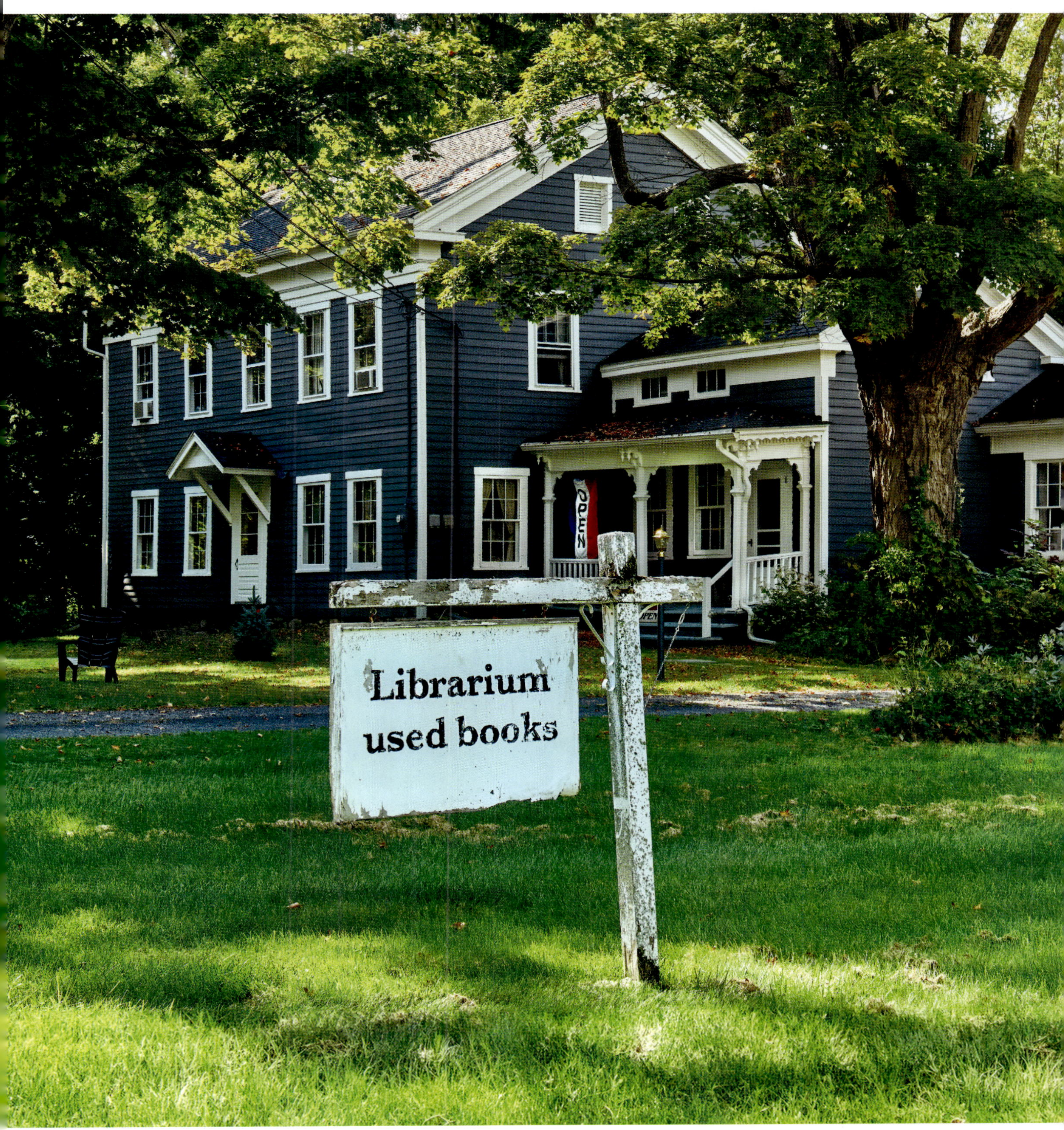
Librarium
used books
OPEN

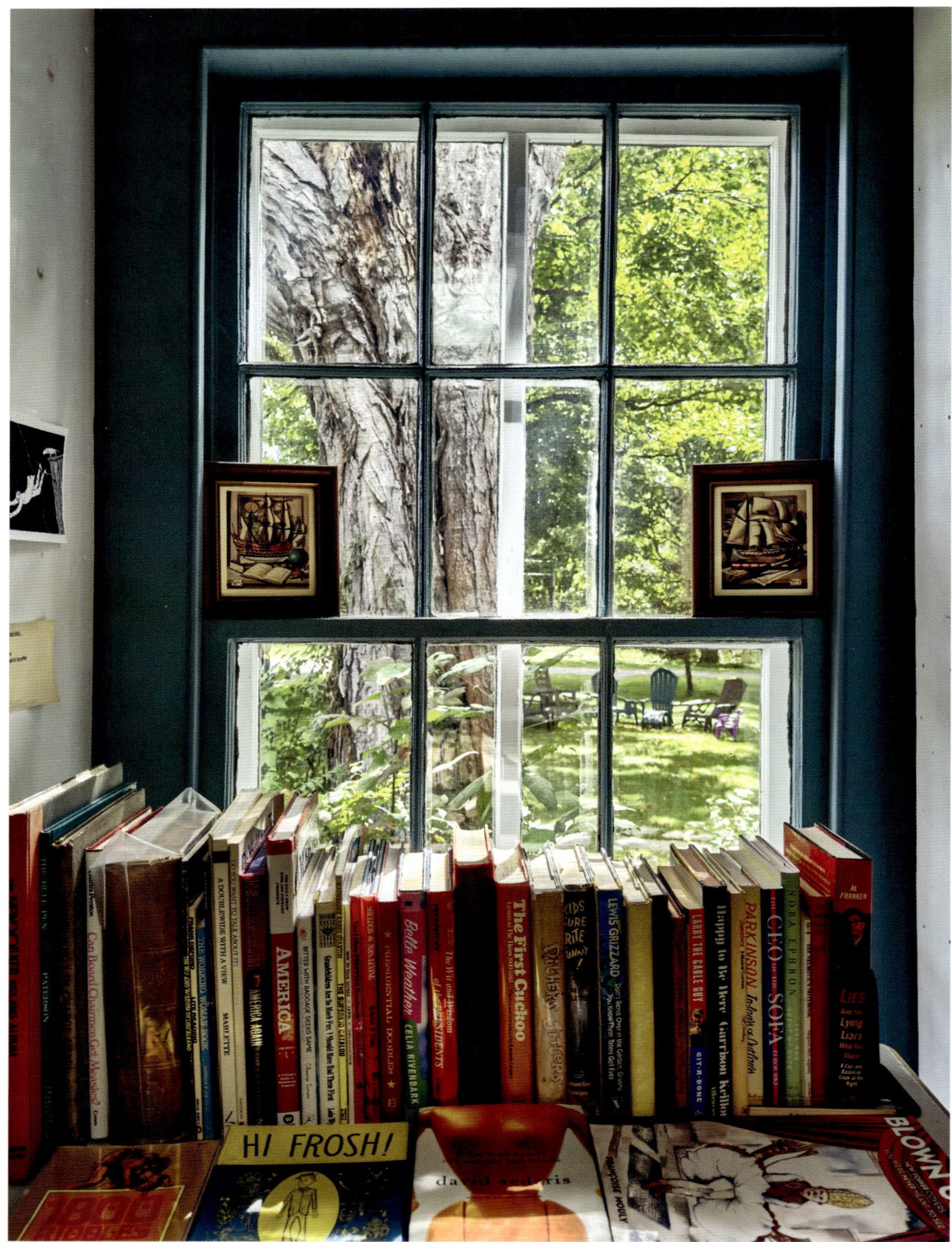

above
Librarium means "bookcase" in Latin, and this shop has plenty, all packed to the brim with all kinds of books. In fact, every single surface in the shop seems to have a book on it. Windows to the outside world keep things in perspective. Sharon says she stocks every form of written word, from poetry to dissertations.

opposite
Shelving reaches toward the ceiling. Books are organized by genre and then by subject. The original floorboards of the shop show their age. The house dates to pre-1800.

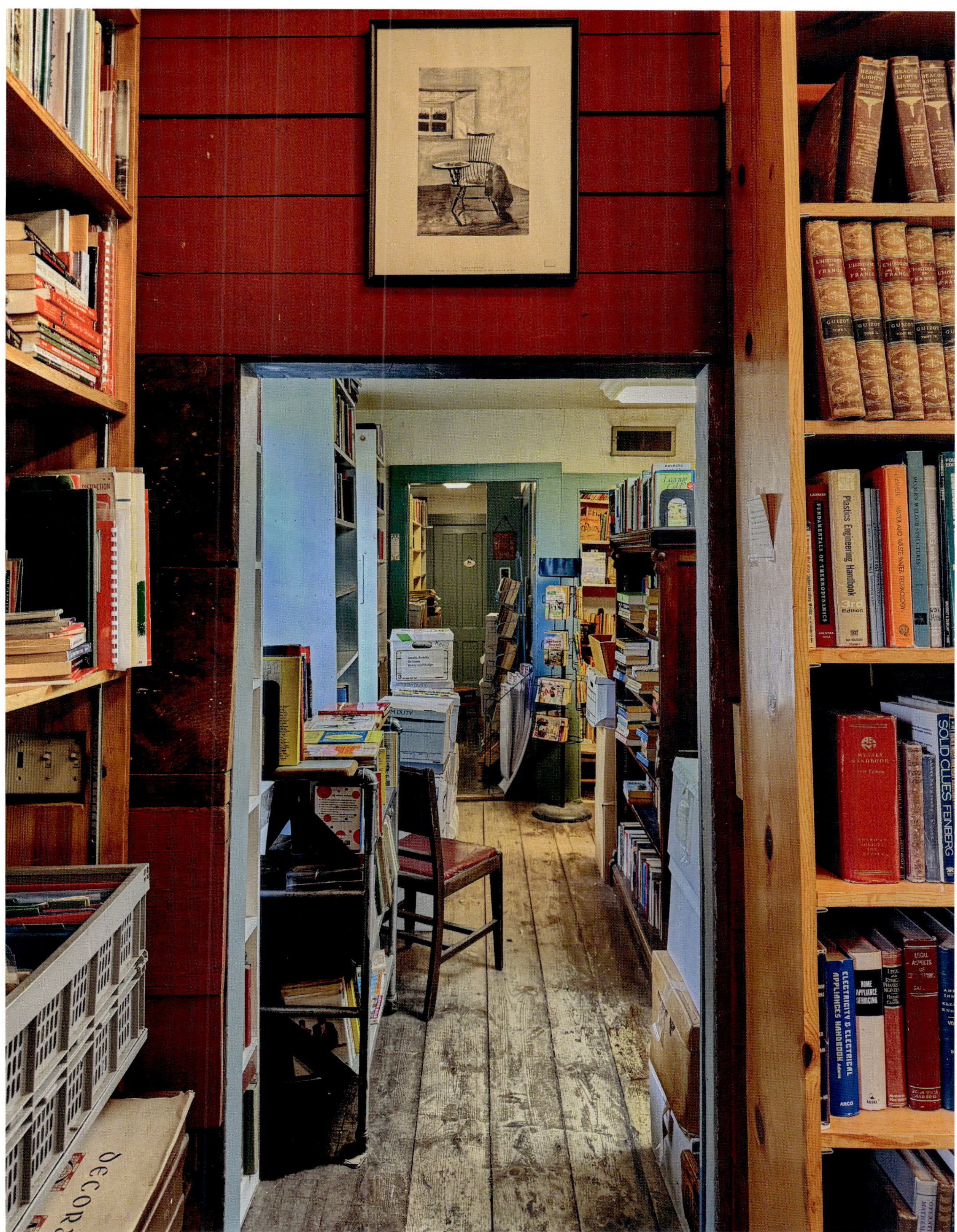
BEACON LIGHTS OF HISTORY
L'HISTOIRE DE FRANCE
GUIZOT
FUNDAMENTALS OF THERMODYNAMICS
Plastics Engineering Handbook
3rd Edition
MODERN WELDED STRUCTURES
WATER AND WASTEWATER TECHNOLOGY
METALS HANDBOOK
SOLID CLUES
FEINBERG
ELECTRICITY & ELECTRICAL APPLIANCES HANDBOOK
HOME APPLIANCE SERVICING
LEGAL ASPECTS OF
ARCO
DECOR

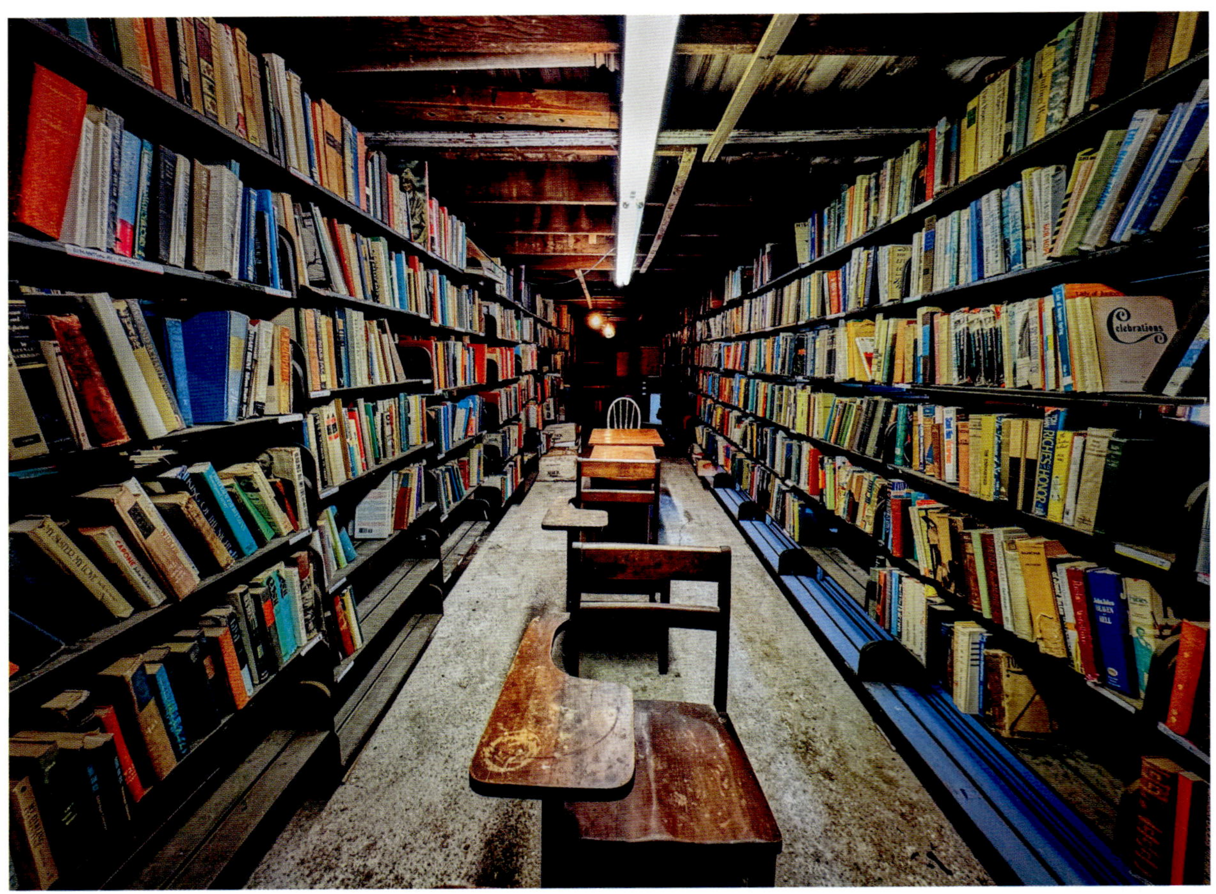
Celebrations

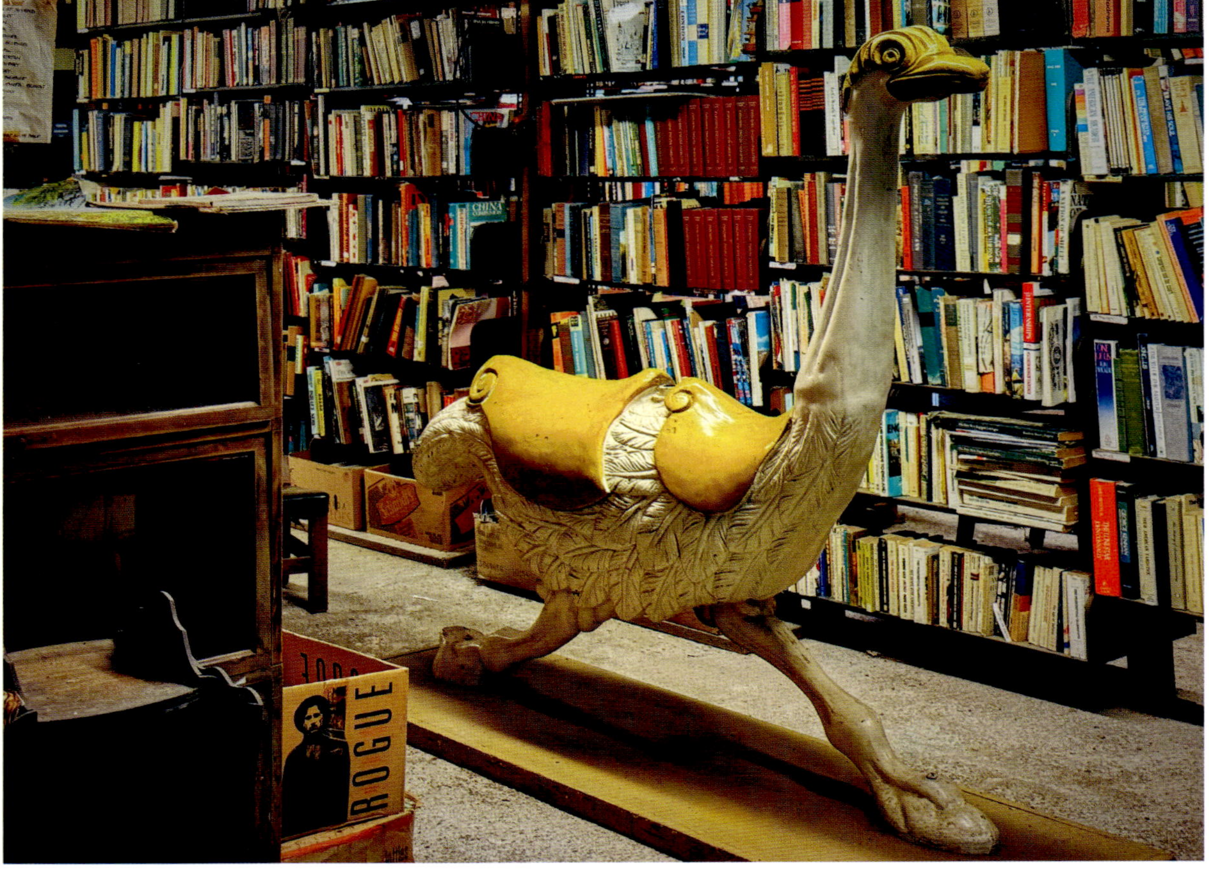
ROGUE

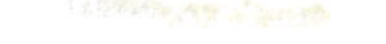

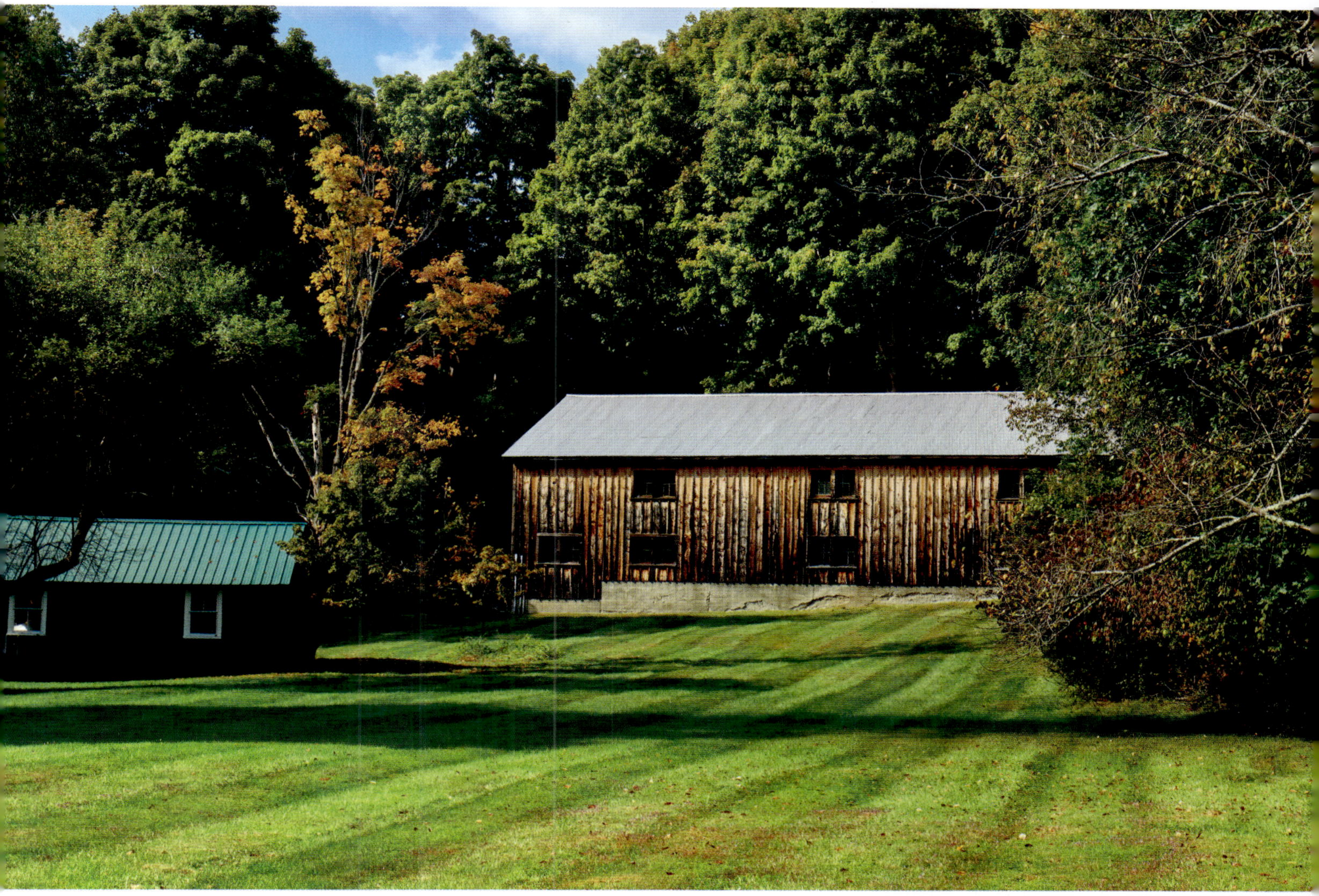

opposite, top
Rows of reasonably priced books line the dusty shelves of the book barn. The variety of Sharon's stock is impressive. School desks offer a place to read or to place a stack of books to take home.

opposite, bottom
A hand-carved ostrich, named Glinda, is a menagerie figure from a carousel. Her yellow saddle may be used as seating in the rows of books inside Librarium's barn.

above
The barn sits on a slight hill behind the house.

Roxbury, New York

Upstate New York is made up of small cities, villages, and hamlets. Albany, the state capital, is one of the few that qualifies as a major city, with a population of more than 102,000 residents within the city limits as of 2024. Many of the smaller villages have grown up around an industry. For example, Hudson, New York, was established in the eighteenth century as a whaling center. Troy at one time was the richest city in the state, based on steel production and its location near the Hudson and Mohawk rivers. Kingston developed around limestone, a natural component of cement, and as a transportation hub.

In some cases, the towns of the Hudson Valley and Catskills had a single patron who made a mark on the place. This tradition continues in many towns and has helped modern-day revivals. Also, cultural institutions and universities have put and kept small towns on the map. Bard College in Annandale-on-Hudson, Vassar College in Poughkeepsie, and Rensselaer Polytech Institute in Troy are just a few examples. Each city, village, and hamlet has a history and trajectory all its own.

Roxbury, New York, located in the Catskills, is a hamlet on the rise. It was the birthplace of Jay Gould, known as one of the "robber barons" of the nineteenth century. His father was a farmer, and Gould left the town as soon as he could. Yet, at the end of his life, he promised to build a church in Roxbury but died before its construction. His children took up the project, finished the building of the church, and dedicated it to their father's memory. The Jay Gould Memorial Reformed Church was finished in 1894. Gould's daughter, Helen Miller Gould Shepard, also developed a connection with the town and made an impact on its history.

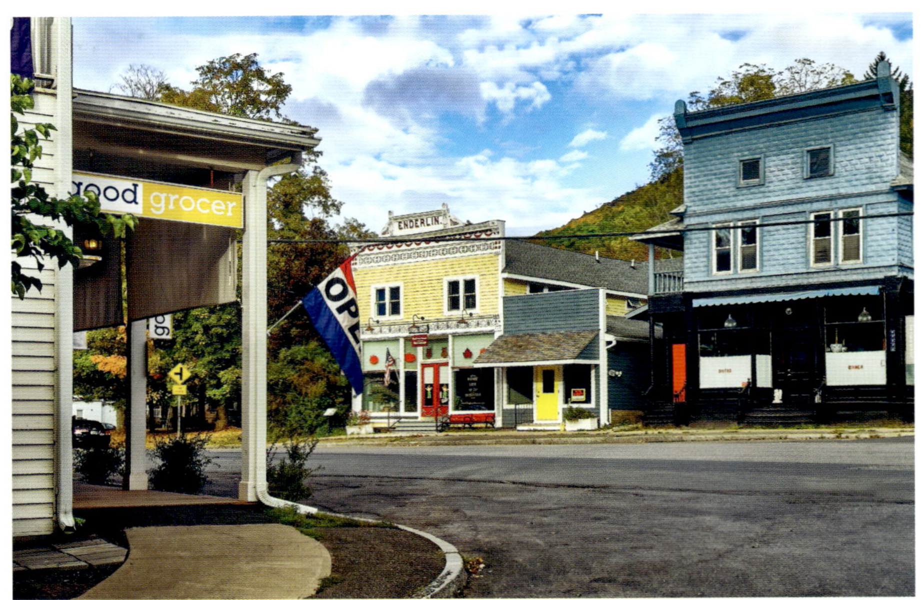

A glimpse of Roxbury's main street on Route 30. The grocery store, Good Grocer, opened in 2023. It took over a space that started out as a corner grocery. It used to be that the main street of these tiny towns had everything a resident needed, from a grocer to a hardware store.

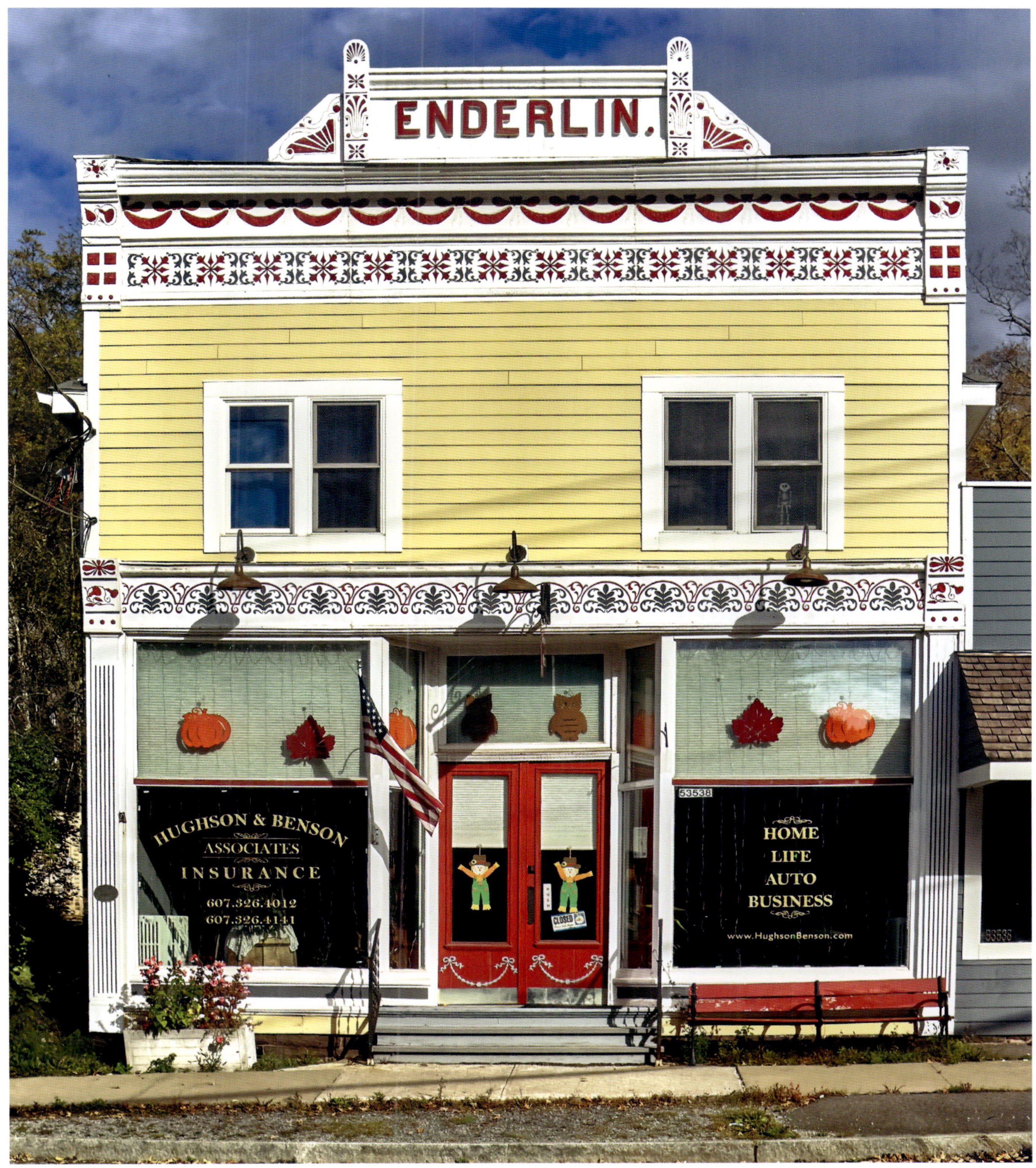

Jay Gould's father purchased a tin shop in the first iteration of this building, which was constructed in 1840. Later, in 1905, Frank Enderlin added a two-story facade to the front of the hardware store. His name is still on the facade. The store is part of the town's historic district.

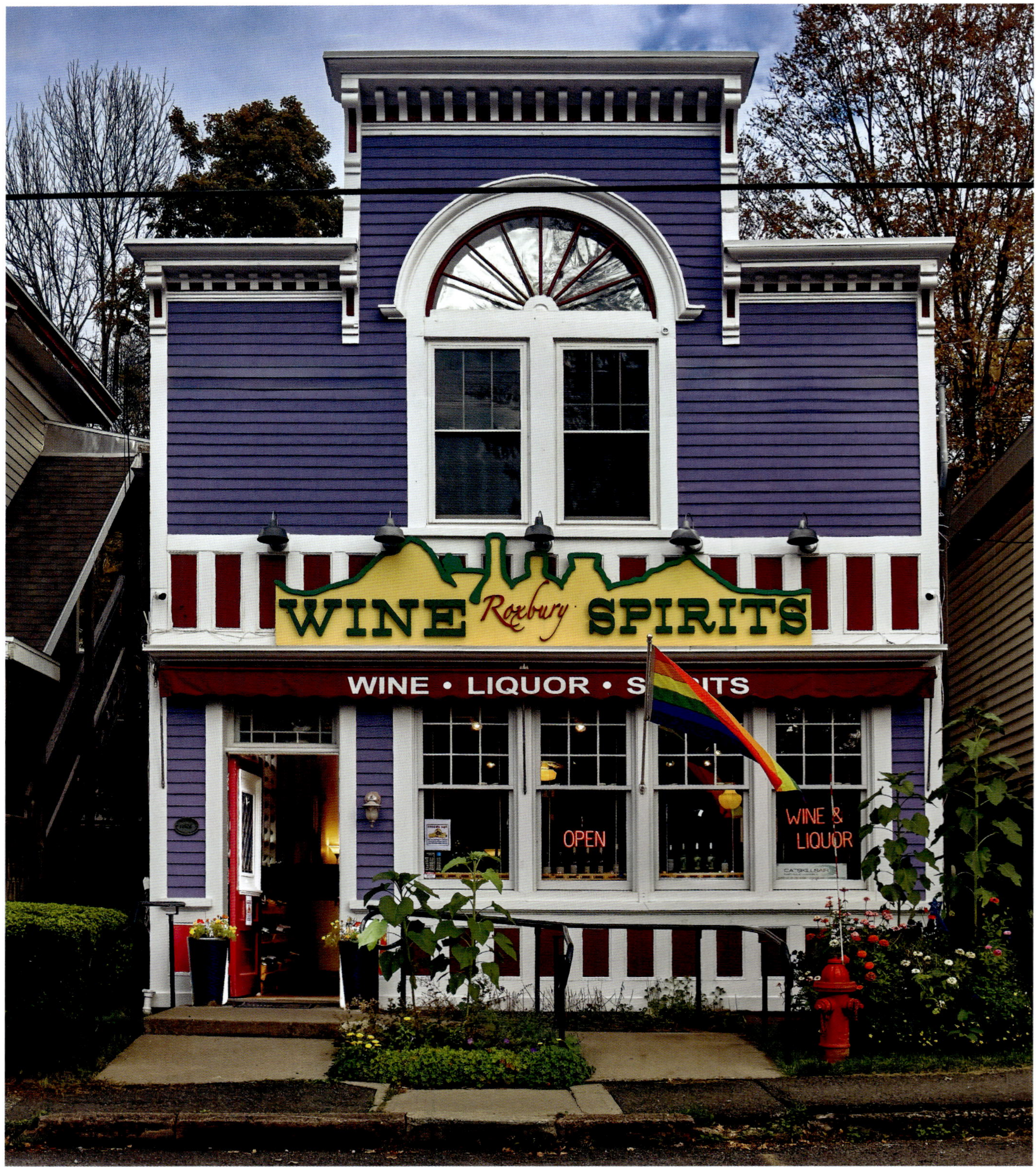

above and opposite
The buildings on Route 30 range in age from the late 1800s to the early 1900s. These days, the businesses on the main street serve a variety of residents' needs, from the practical to the enjoyable. The Roxbury Wine and Spirits store was built in the 1880s. The Fierce Grizzly Bistro once occupied the first floor on the corner building.

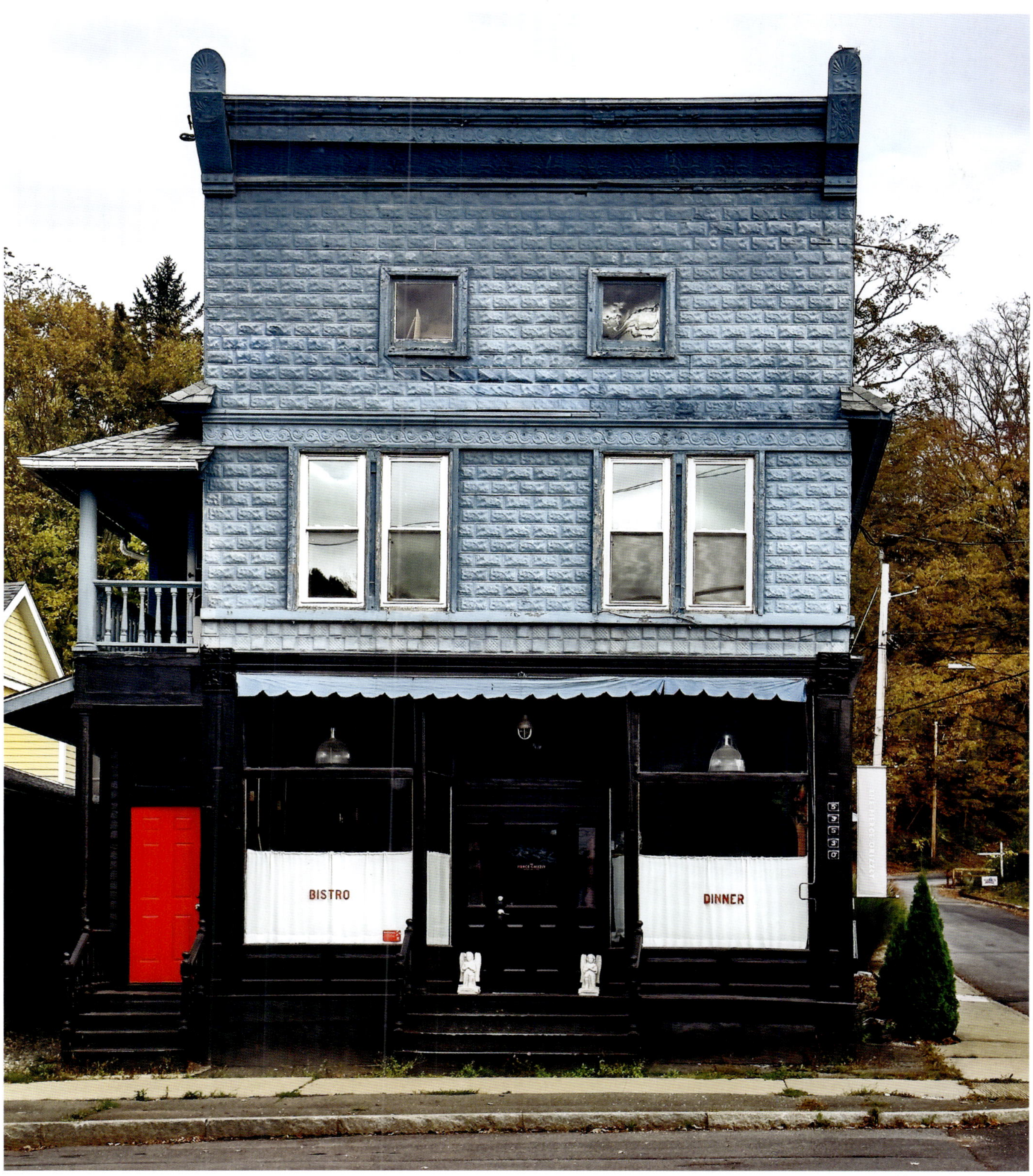
BISTRO
DINNER

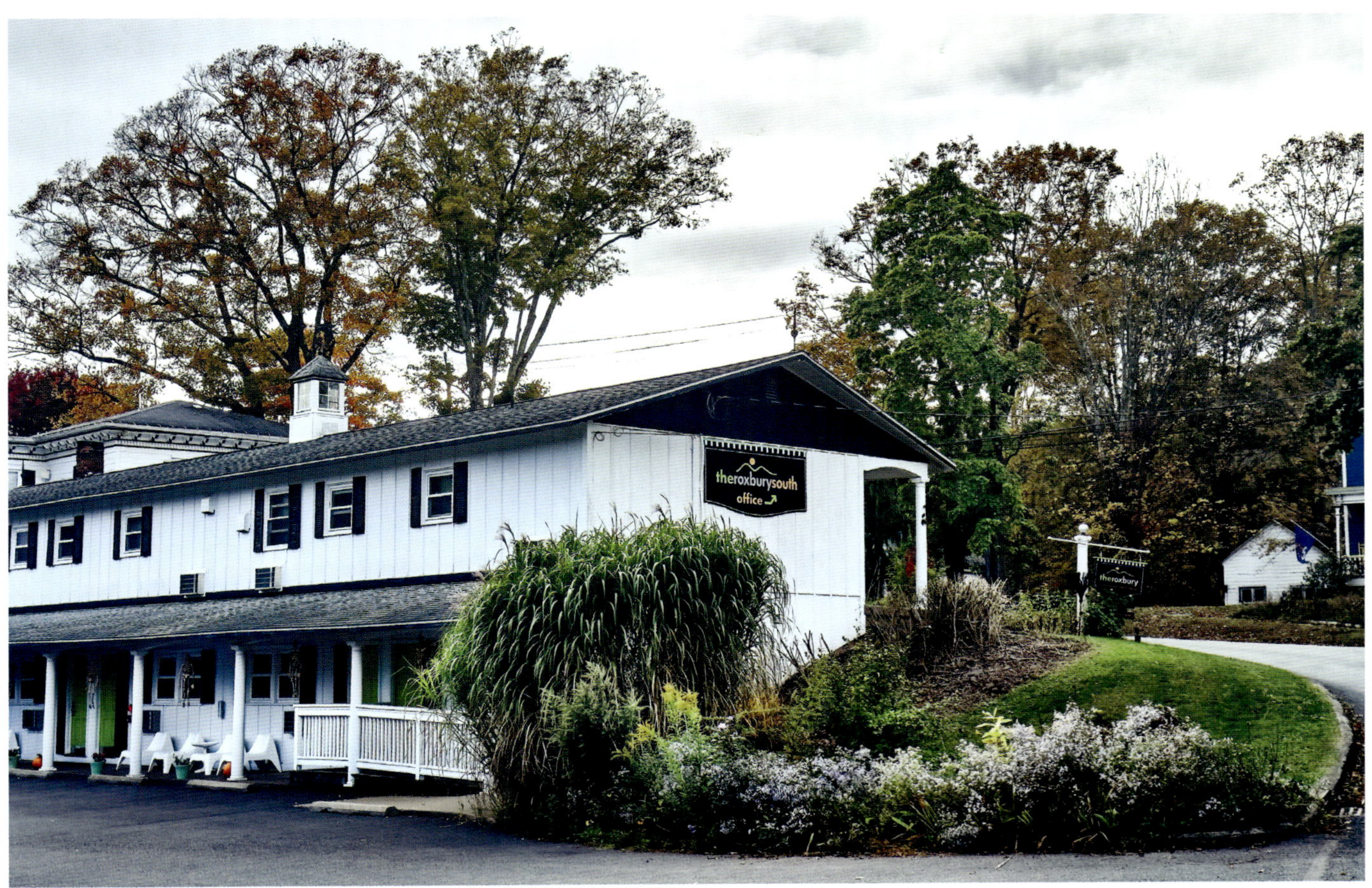

Roxbury experienced a boom-and-bust cycle. In the 1980s, the state transportation department wanted to widen Route 30, the road that goes through the main street of Roxbury, but the citizens rallied and stopped the effort. The downtown redevelopment has turned historic buildings into new businesses. When the Roxbury Motel was bought and redesigned, tourists had a place to stay. With its colorful decor, the motel became a draw and contributed to the revival of the town. In 2024, New York State Downtown Revitalization Initiative awarded Roxbury and nearby Grand Gorge a $10 million development grant for the towns' main streets. Individual business owners will apply for grants to enhance their establishments and grow the town's main street.

above
The Roxbury Motel was built in 1963 and purchased and renovated by Gregory Henderson and Joseph Massa in 2004. The motel expanded across the street in 2006. The owners continue to update and add more rooms and experiences. The motel brought renewed tourism to the town.

opposite, top and bottom
The Roxbury Art Center's current home was once the town's YMCA. The building was erected in 1911. Jay Gould's daughter, Helen Miller Gould Shepard, commissioned the building, which had several uses before the art center. The gallery is a few yards from the main street.

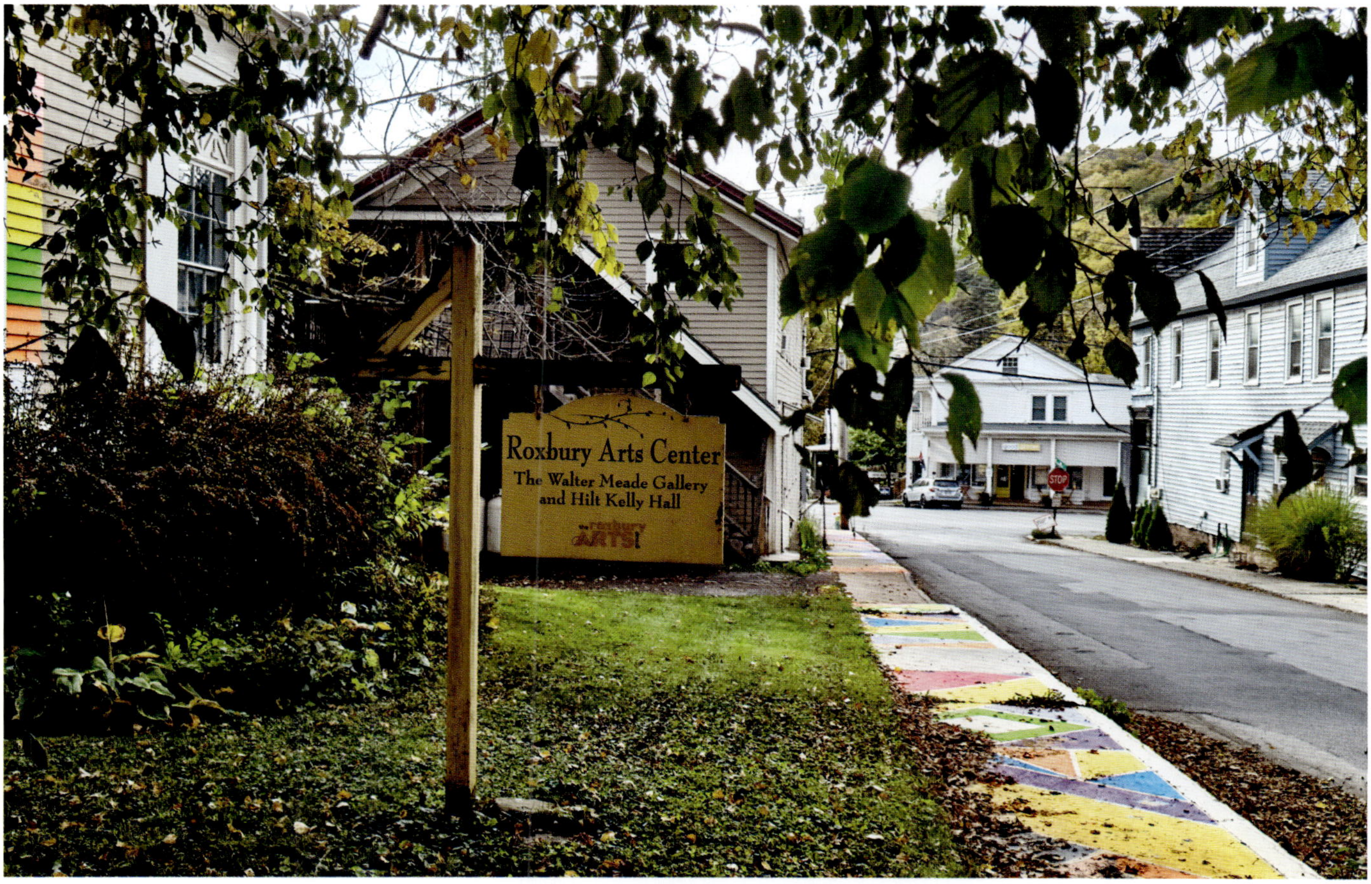

Roxbury Arts Center
The Walter Meade Gallery
and Hilt Kelly Hall

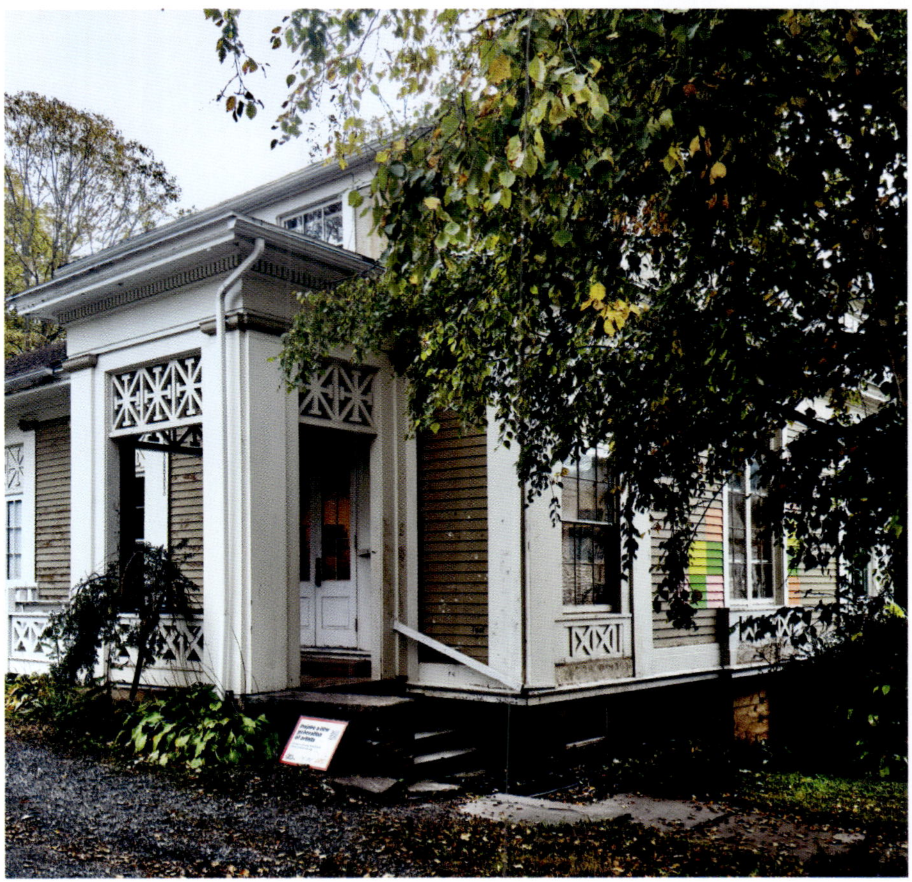

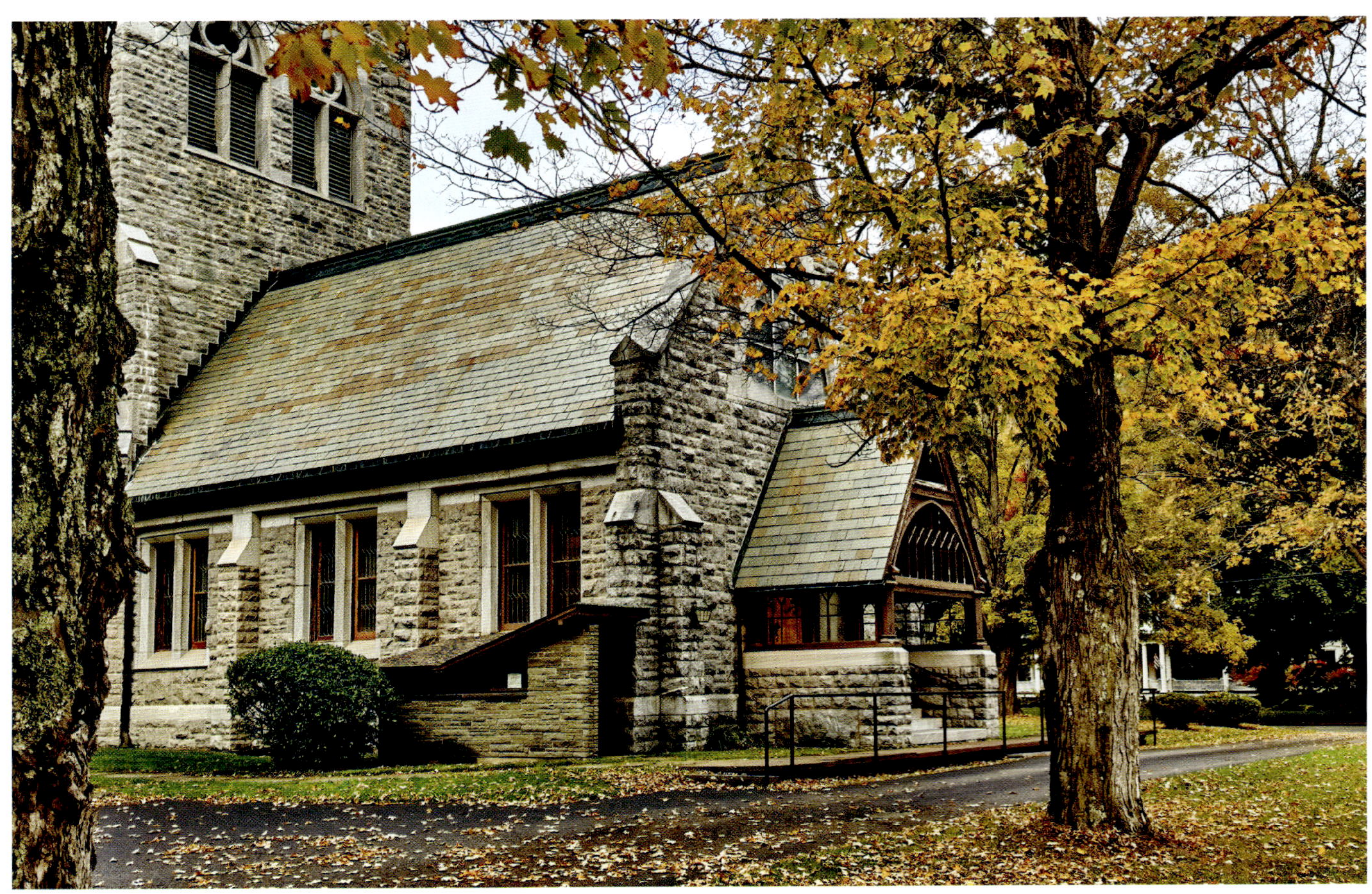

above and opposite
The Jay Gould Memorial Reformed Church was built and dedicated by the financier's children. The building was designed by Henry Janeway Hardenbergh, a renowned architect in New York. Tiffany glass windows were installed in the nave of the church.

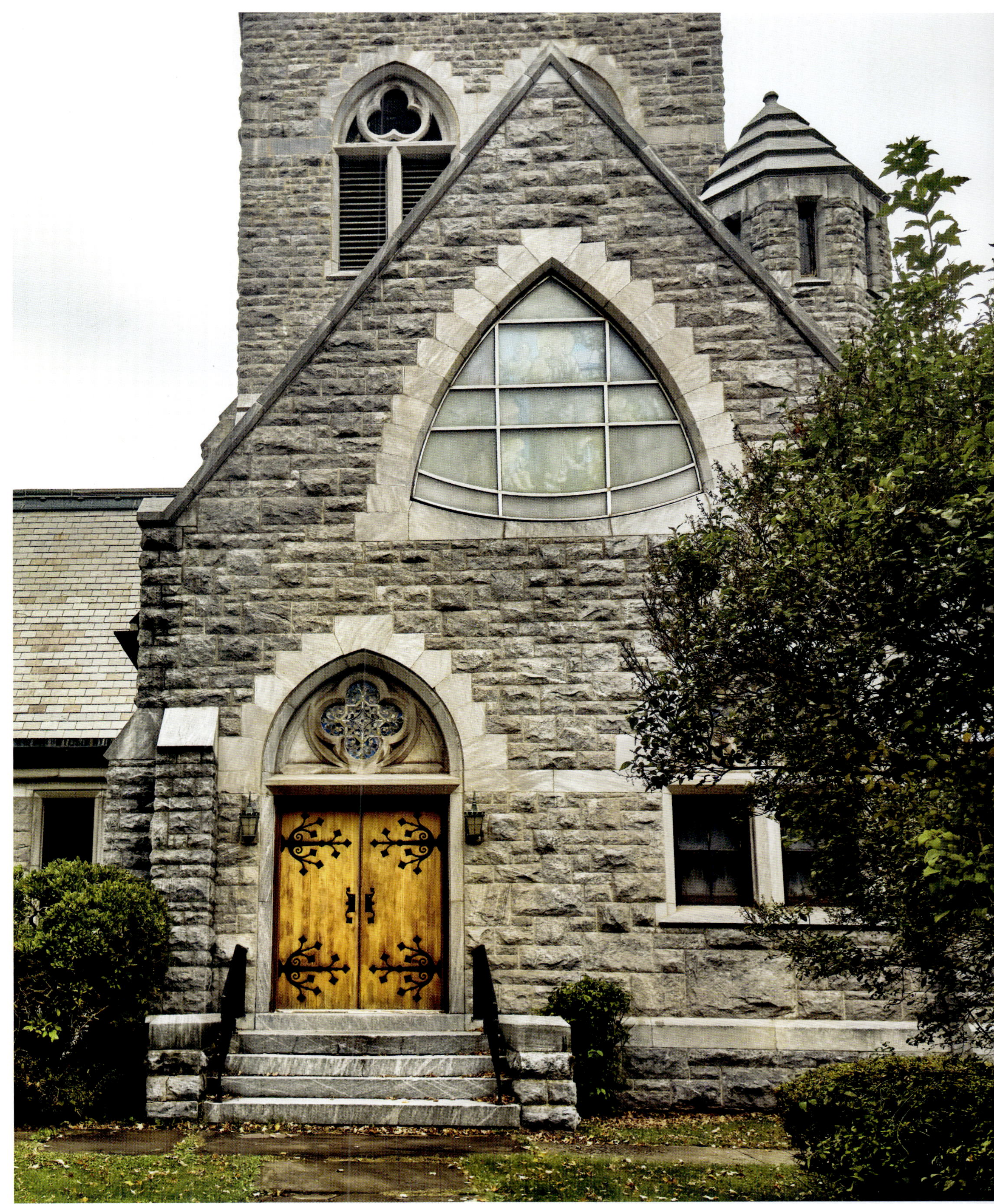

II. Art

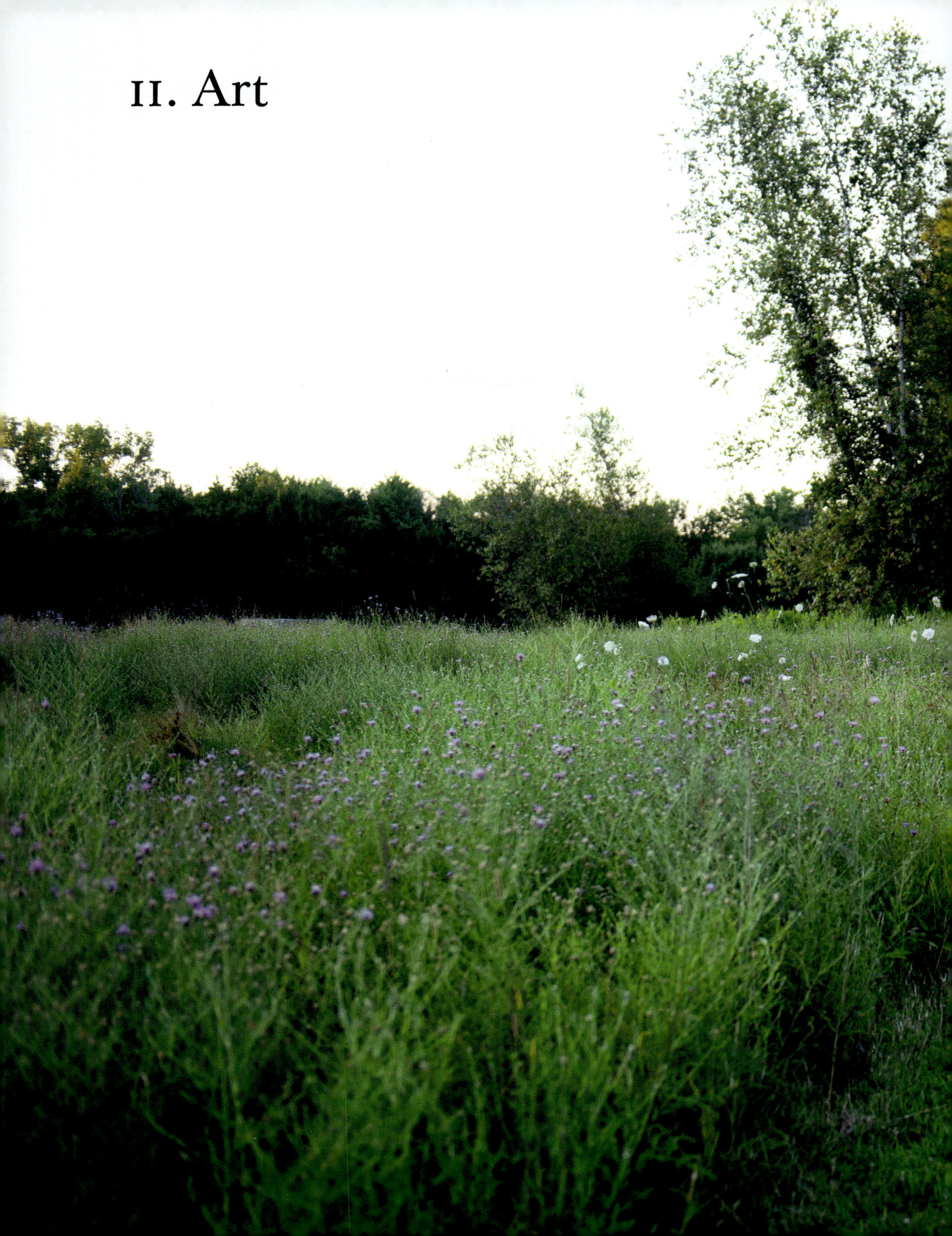

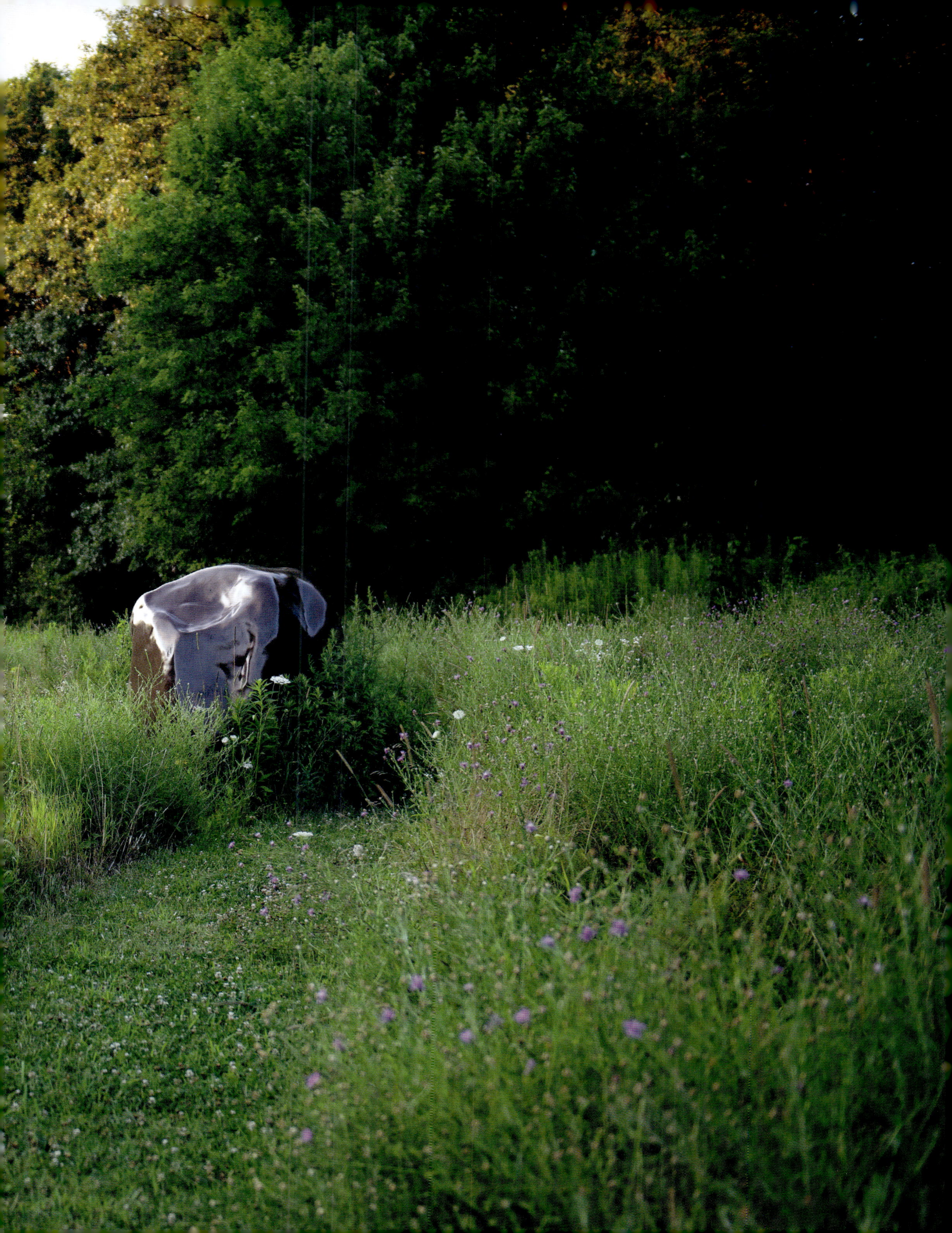

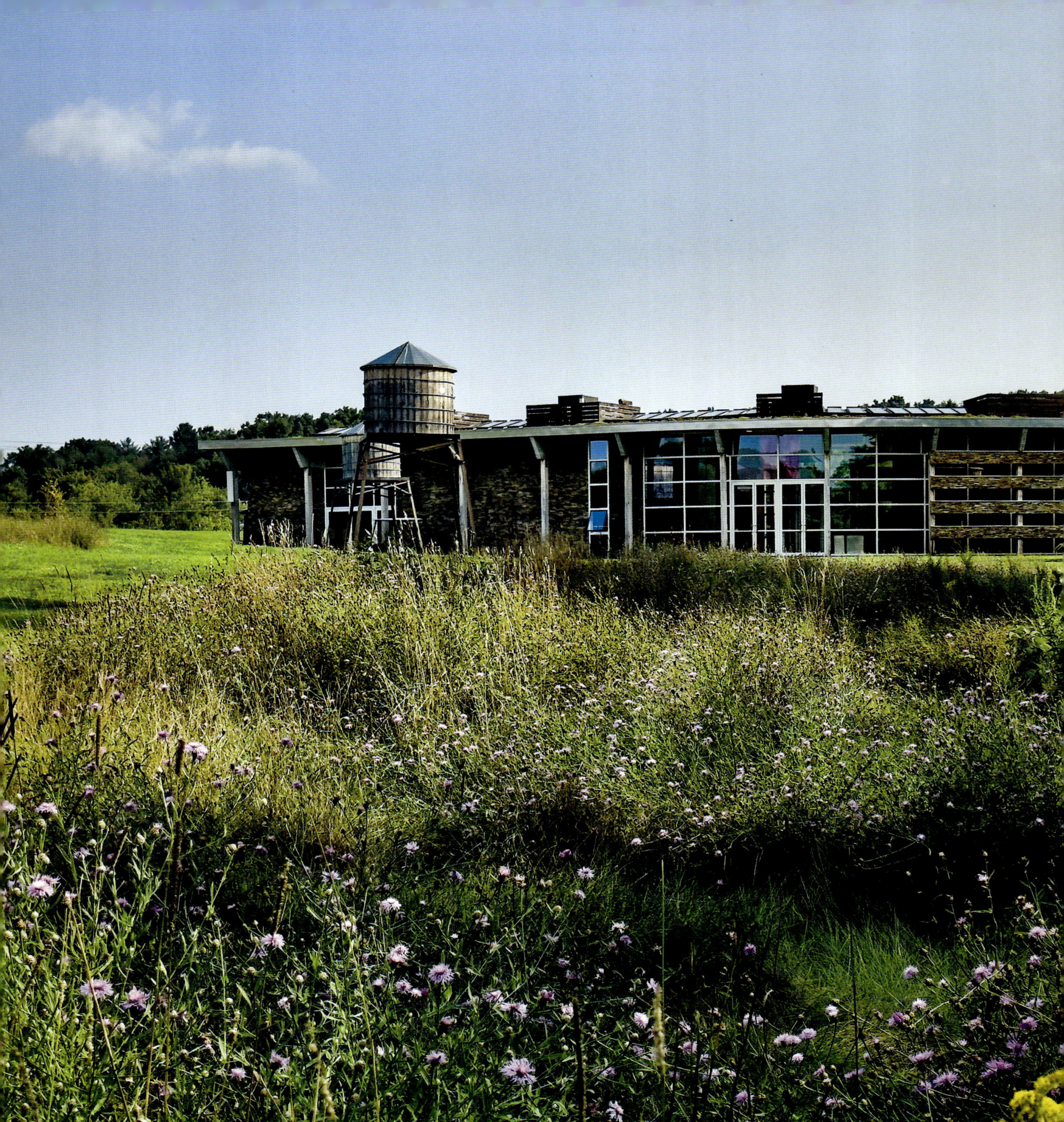

previous
Dan Colen's work *Brown M&M* (2014) is nestled among the native plants of the Sculpture & Architecture Park at Art Omi.

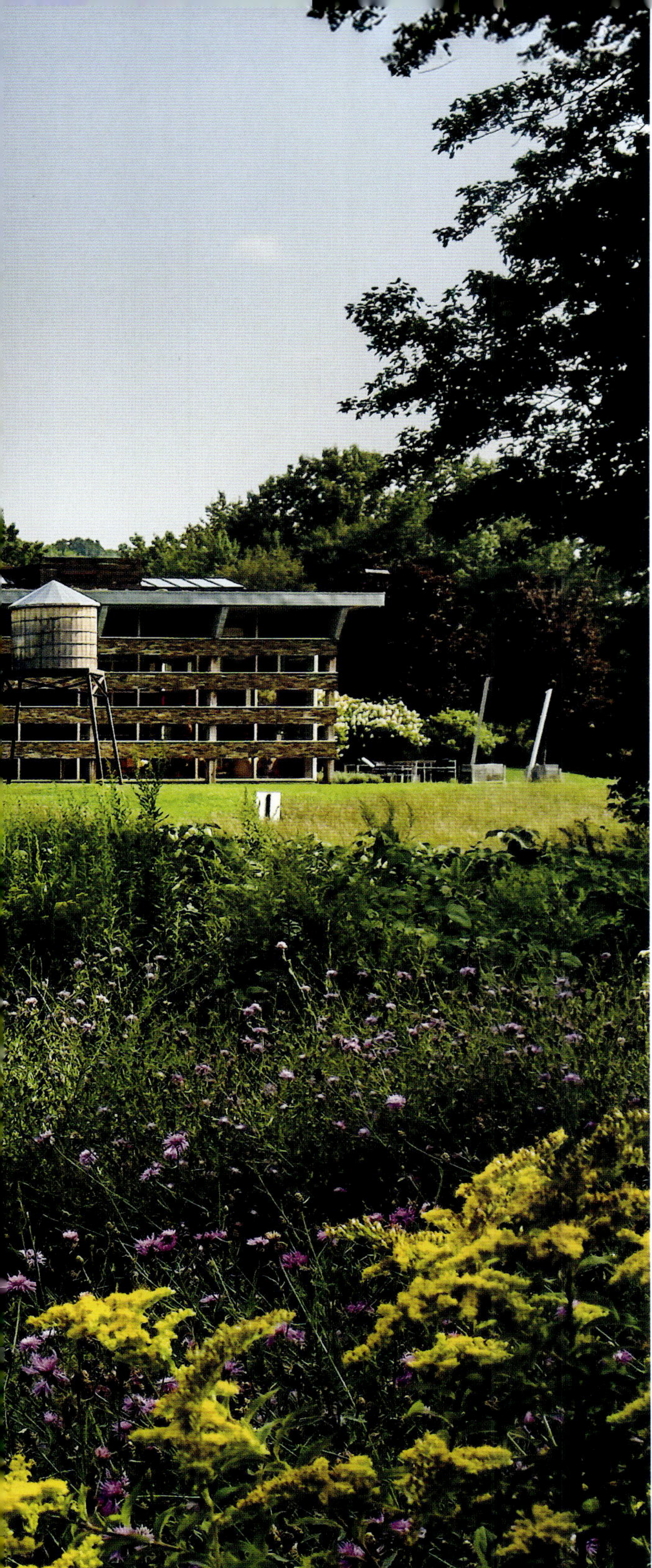

Art Omi

Ghent, New York

Driving along a country road through the hamlet of Omi, part of the town of Ghent, clouds rise above a field. Those blue clouds, made of powder-coated aluminum and steel, are a 2014 work by artist Olaf Breuning. The piece is installed near the entrance of the nonprofit arts center Art Omi's Sculpture & Architecture Park, part of the 120 acres of former farmlands that Art Omi acknowledges were once the unceded lands of the Mohican, now known as the Stockbridge-Munsee Community living and thriving in the state of Wisconsin. The art center was founded in 1992 by multi-hyphenate entrepreneur, real estate investor, literary agent, and passionate arts philanthropist Francis J. Greenburger with the help of friends and artists.

Art Omi's programming includes a residency that over the years has brought and continues to bring artists, architects, dancers, and writers collectively from approximately 120 countries and regions to the site where they spend time making art. Farther down the road from the art park, a barn has been converted into artists' studios. Art Omi is fully integrated into the community. Readings, exhibitions, and performances, some held at the visitor center gallery, bring artists' work to the public. Perhaps its lasting impact is through the children's arts education program that takes place in the summer and on weekends. Children explore the fields of artworks, later making their own pieces in the Newmark Gallery to take home, developing their relationships to art and making. In the winter, the center welcomes cross-country skiers on the property, and dog walkers are present year-round from dawn to dusk. In 2024, Art Omi broke ground on a new project: Art Omi Pavilions are scheduled to open outside Chatham, New York, in 2026.

The Charles B. Benenson Visitor Center, designed by architects Kathleen Triem and Peter Franck of FT Architecture + Interiors, was completed in 2008. The 4,200-square-foot space has a gallery and a café. Iván Navarro's work *This Land Is Your Land* (2014) was installed nearby.

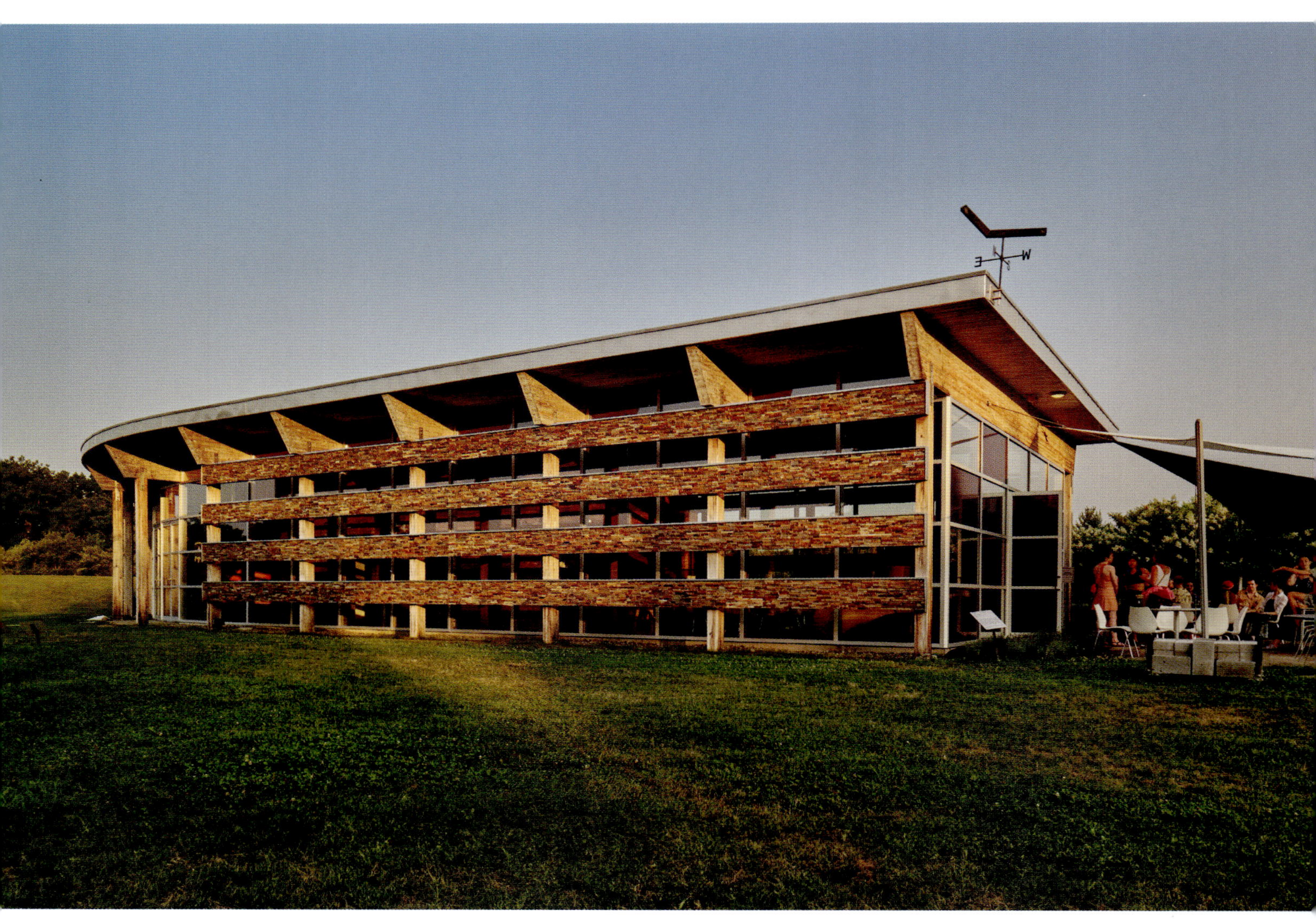

The exterior of the visitor center is wrapped in a band of local slate stones that help mitigate the temperature of the building, reducing the need for additional energy to cool the building. The solar panels cover some of the energy usage of the building.

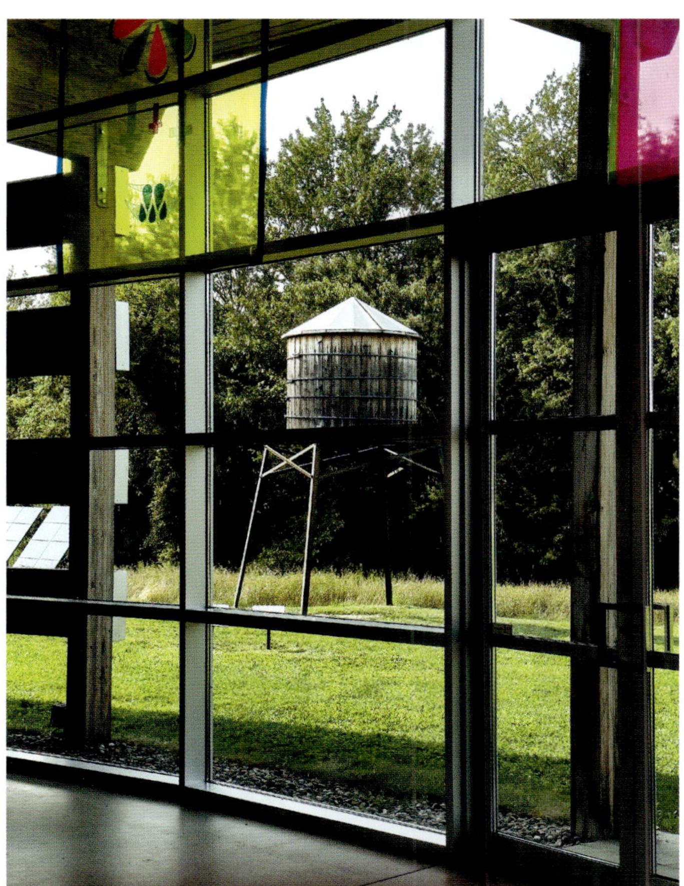

left
A view from the interior of the visitor center to the sculpture fields, where Iván Navarro's water tower–like piece titled *This Land Is Your Land* (2014) is installed. Nathan Young's work from the exhibition *Tune It or Die!* (2024) extended into the center's lobby. Three transparent banners, two of which are visible near the gallery ceiling, are seen here too.

below
Artist Riley Hooker's *Body, Language* (2024) includes the installation of colored films on the glass walls. Riley's installation flows through the café space. The colorful, inflatable sculpture *SIT(UATION)* (2024) and layers of carpeting and pillows are meant to be used as a place of repose.

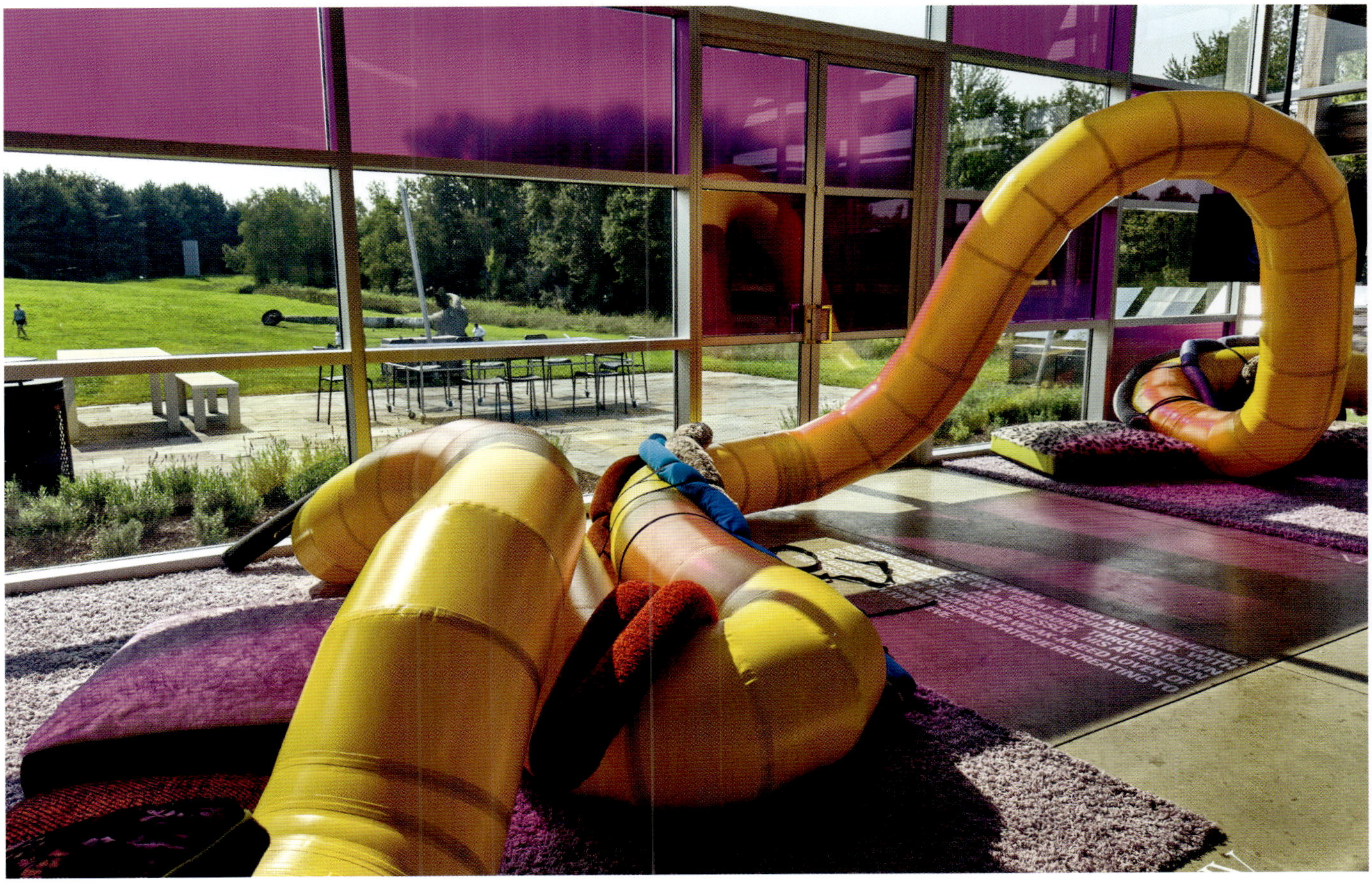

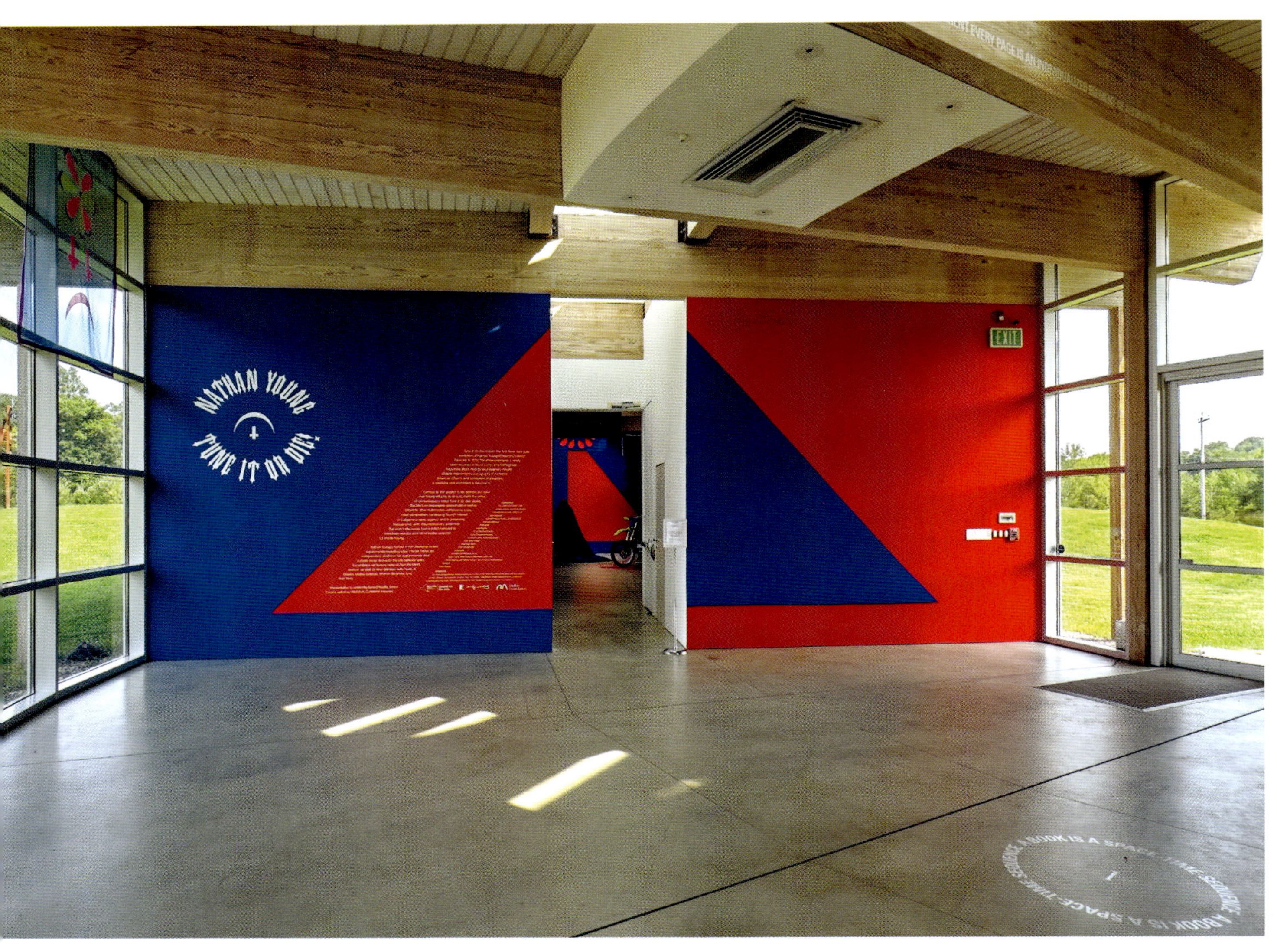

above and opposite
In 2024, Nathan Young's exhibition *Tune It or Die!* was shown in the Newmark Gallery. The entrance features bold graphic design that mirrors the exhibit inside the gallery. Young's multimedia work includes color, flags, sculptural pieces, objects, and sound.

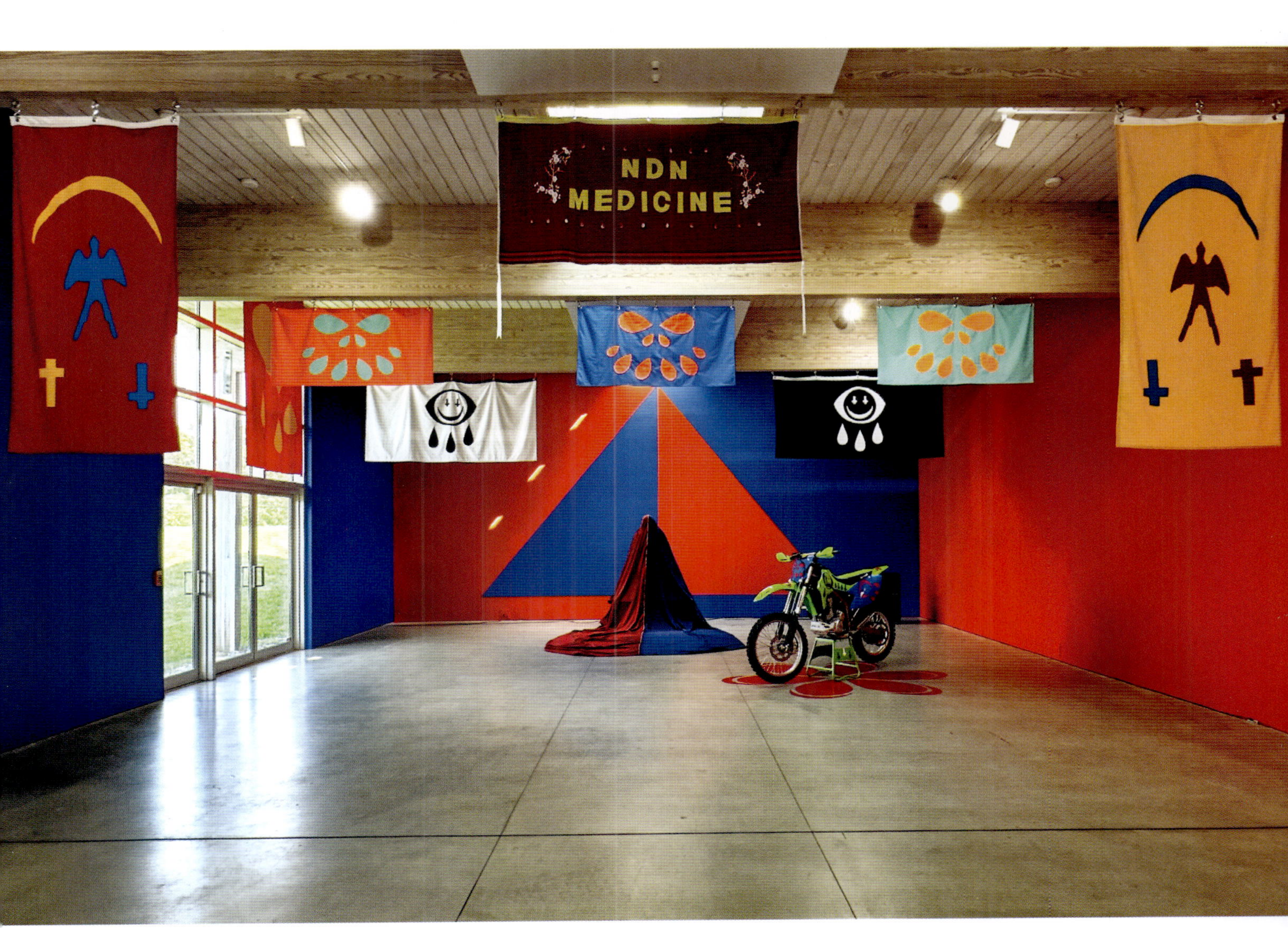
NDN
MEDICINE

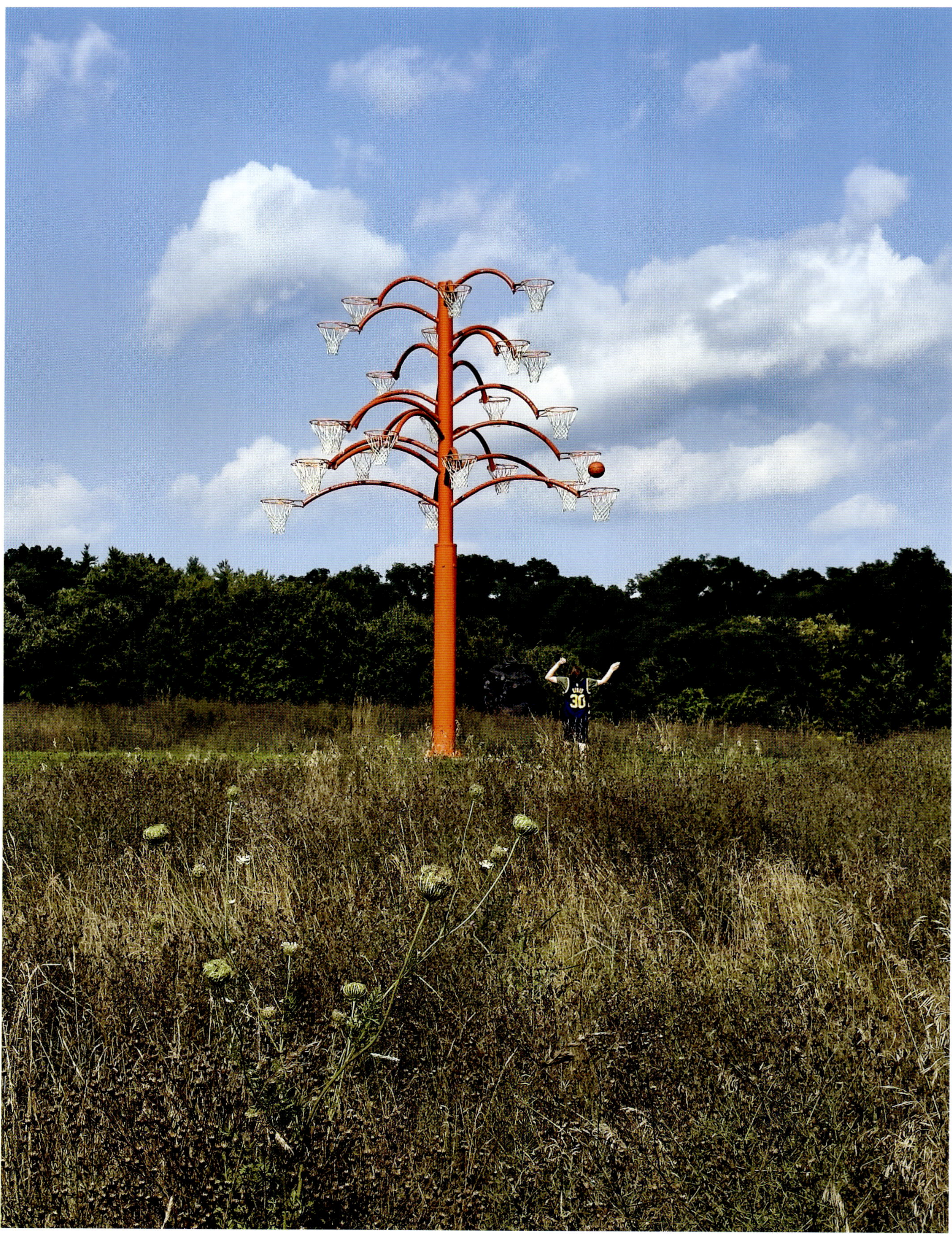

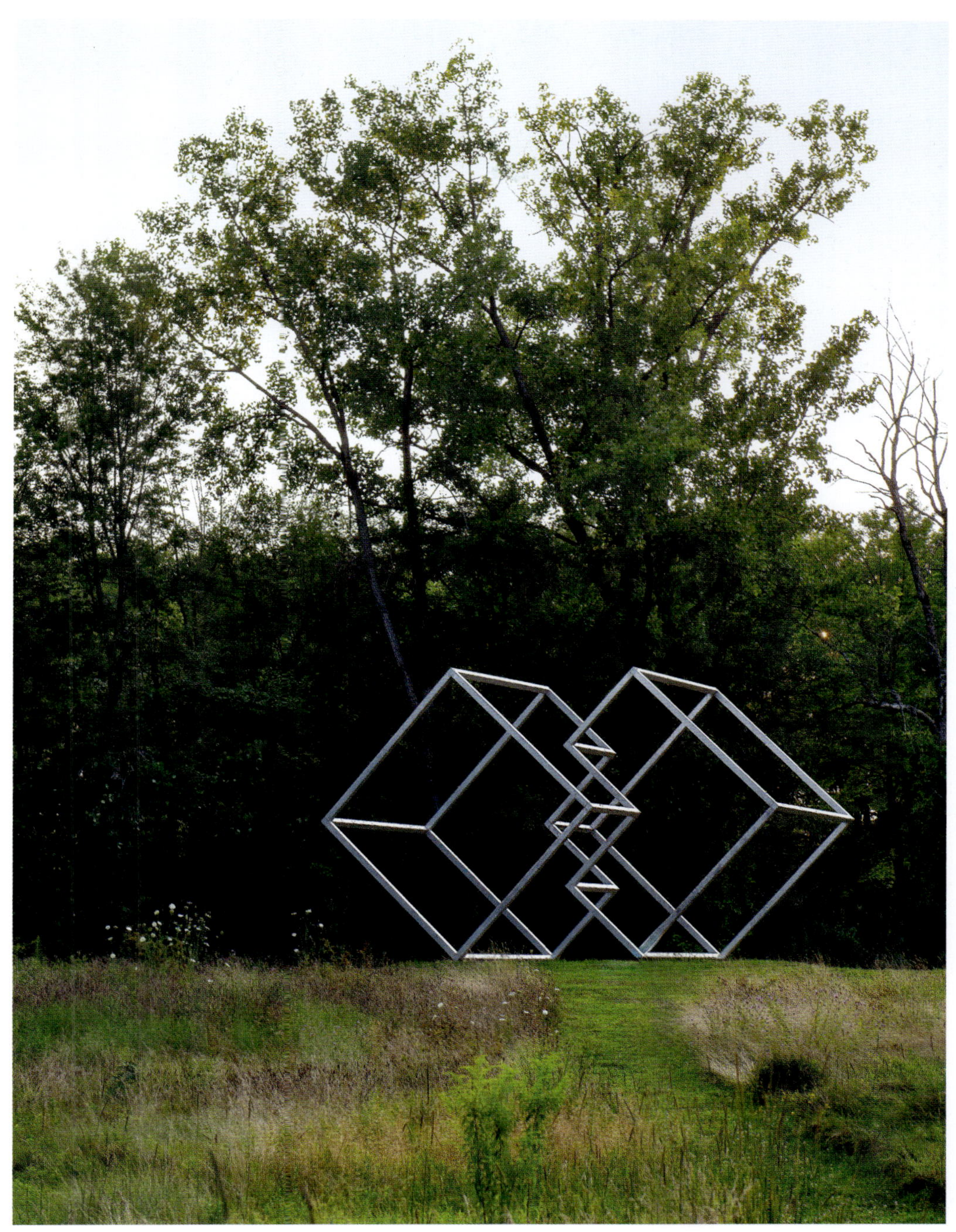

opposite
Alexandre Arrechea's *Orange Functional* (2022) is an interactive structure. Basketballs are provided for visitors to test their hoop skills. The work was commissioned by Art Omi.

above
The environment plays an important role in the perception of Forrest Myers's *Valledor* (1969). The work either is framed by or frames the surroundings. At Art Omi, nature is on display.

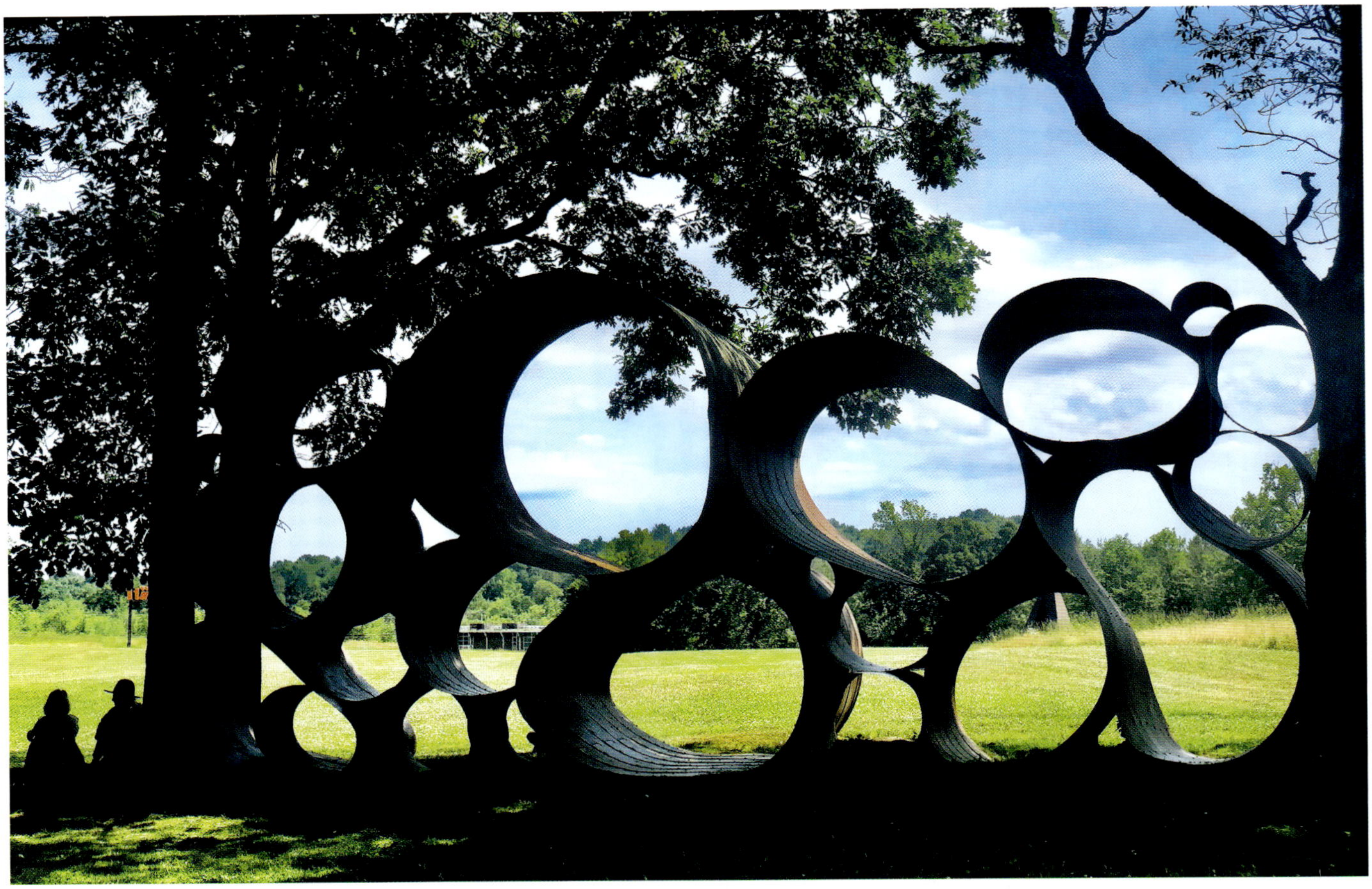

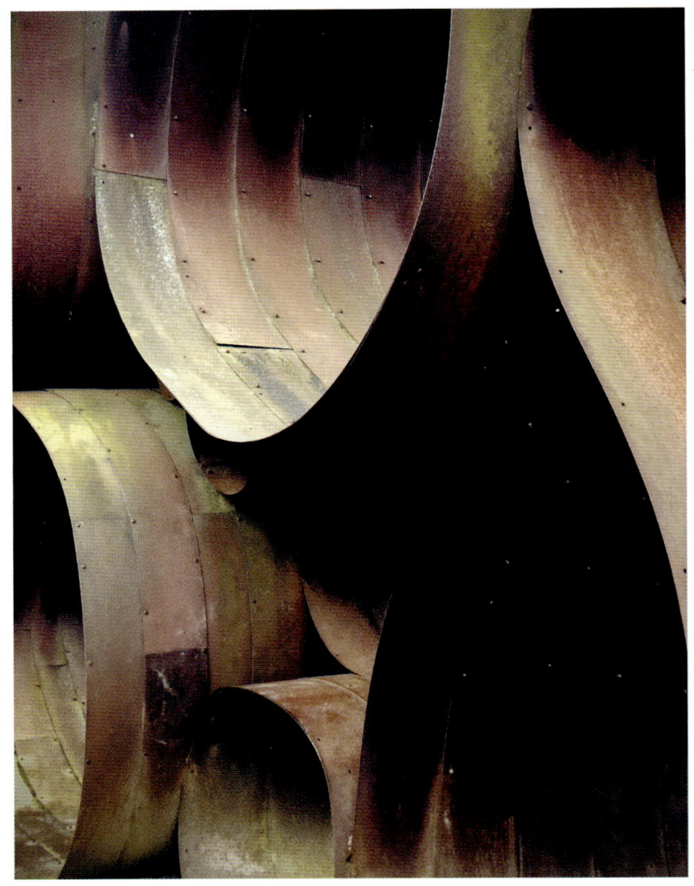

above and right
DeWitt Godfrey's *Picker Sculpture* (2005) was installed between two trees on the site. The Cor-Ten steel hoops change as they weather the environment. The piece was deinstalled in 2020. The Sculpture & Architecture Park displays pieces for extended periods of time before rotating them out to allow other works to be exhibited. This practice makes these fields a renewable source of inspiration, with recently installed and familiar works sharing the same place.

opposite
Alex Schweder and Ward Shelley's *ReActor* (2016) is no longer on display at Art Omi. It was shown on a hilltop of Architecture Field 01 from 2016 to 2023.

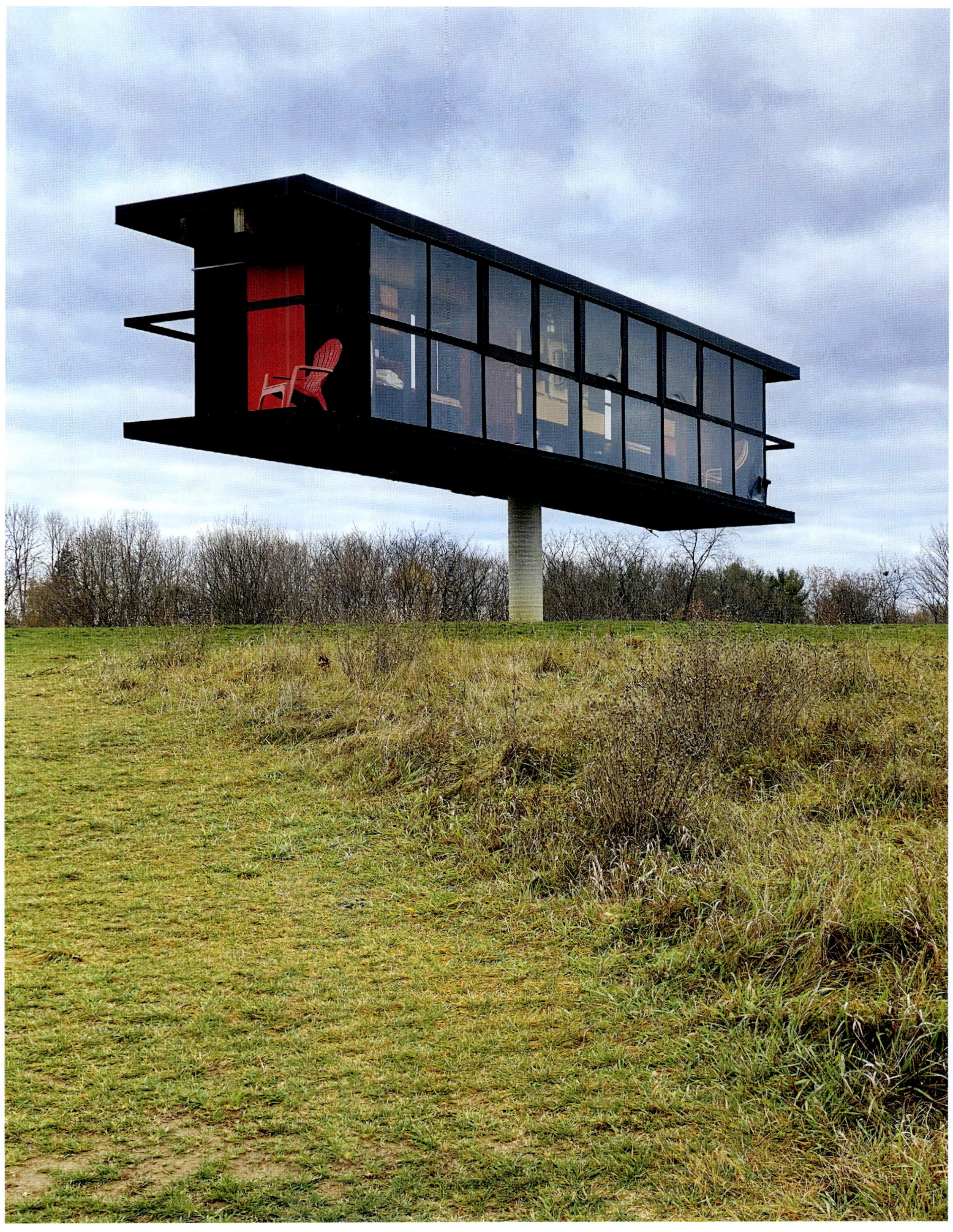

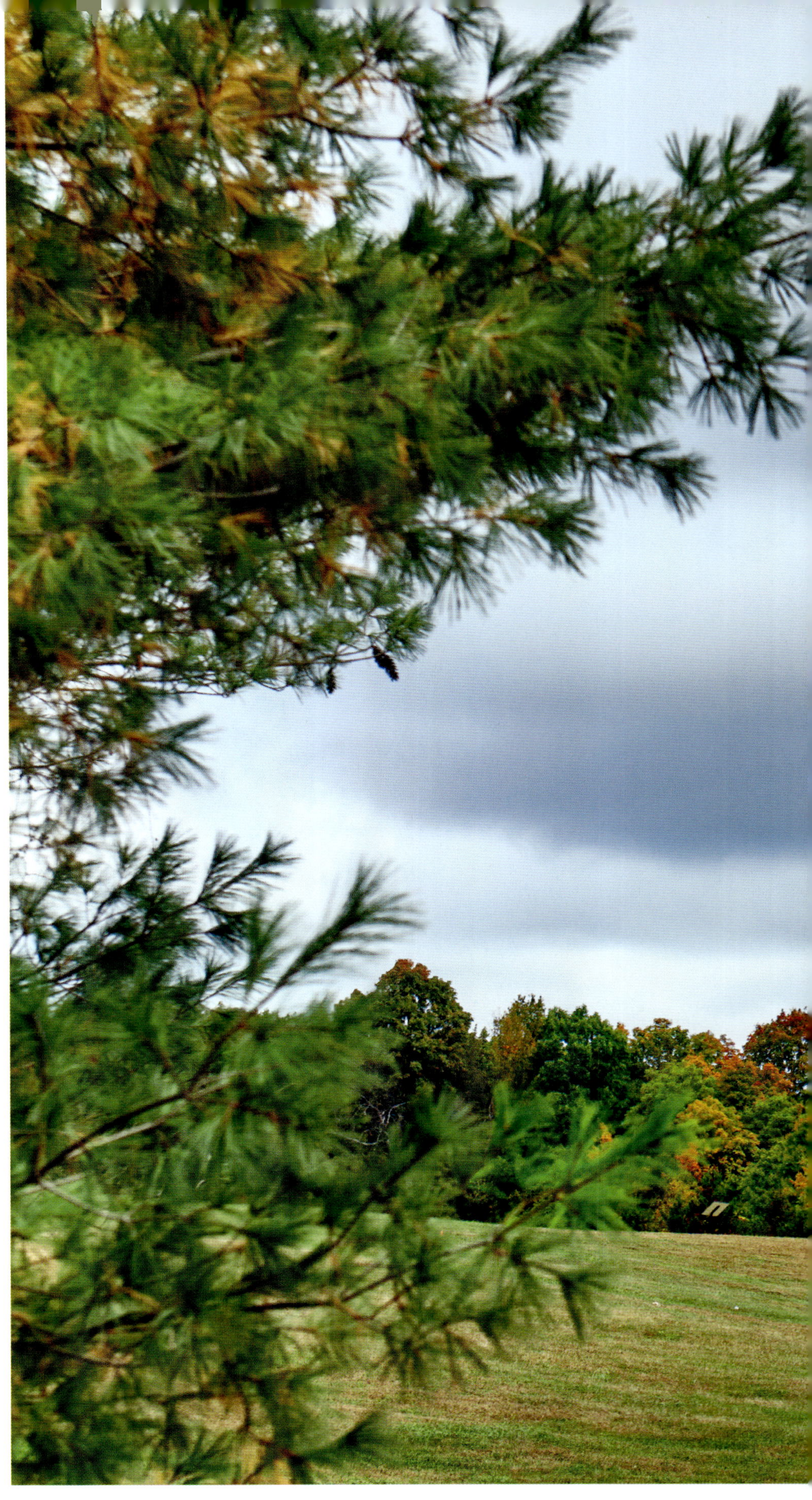

Clouds (2014) by artist Olaf Breuning welcomes visitors to Art Omi.

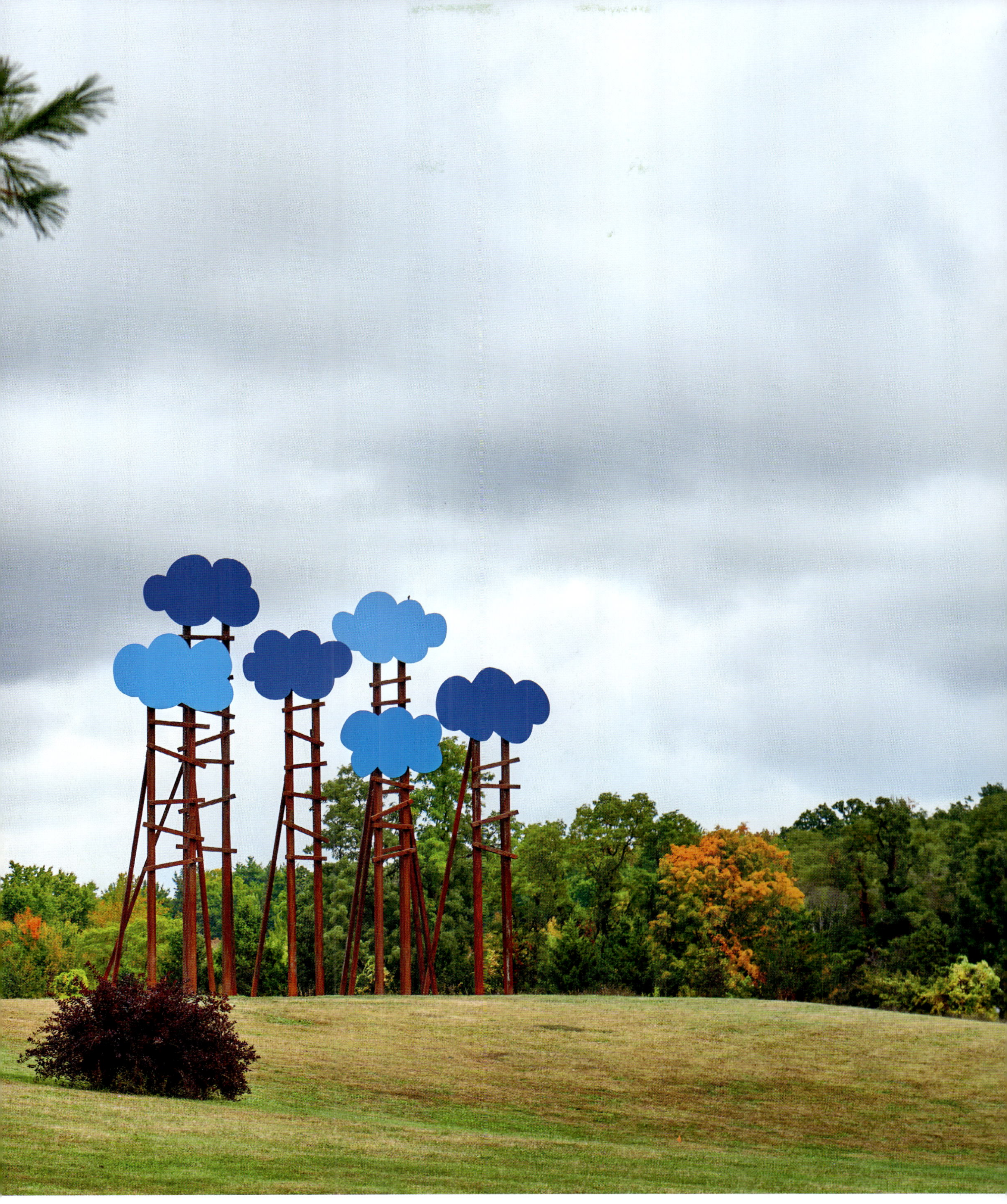

Bill Arning Exhibitions

Kinderhook, New York

Bill Arning's career in the nonprofit New York art world led him to visit hundreds of artists' studios from the mid-1980s on. After leaving New York City to work as curator at the MIT List Center for Visual Arts, he became director of the Contemporary Arts Museum Houston. When his tenure in museums ended, he opened a gallery in Houston. Then, in 2023, he decided to move Bill Arning Exhibitions from Houston to the Hudson Valley. His partner, Aaron Skolnick, suggested the space in Kinderhook, New York, as a potential gallery.

The gallery is an 1812 carriage house and, at one time, was the office of a newspaper and later a car dealership. The intimate size and the location in town—down the street from other galleries, including The School and September Gallery—fit Bill's business model. He travels to art fairs around the country, showing a varied group of artists, many from the surrounding Hudson Valley area. He also exhibits some of the artists he first visited in the 1980s, 1990s, and 2010s in New York City.

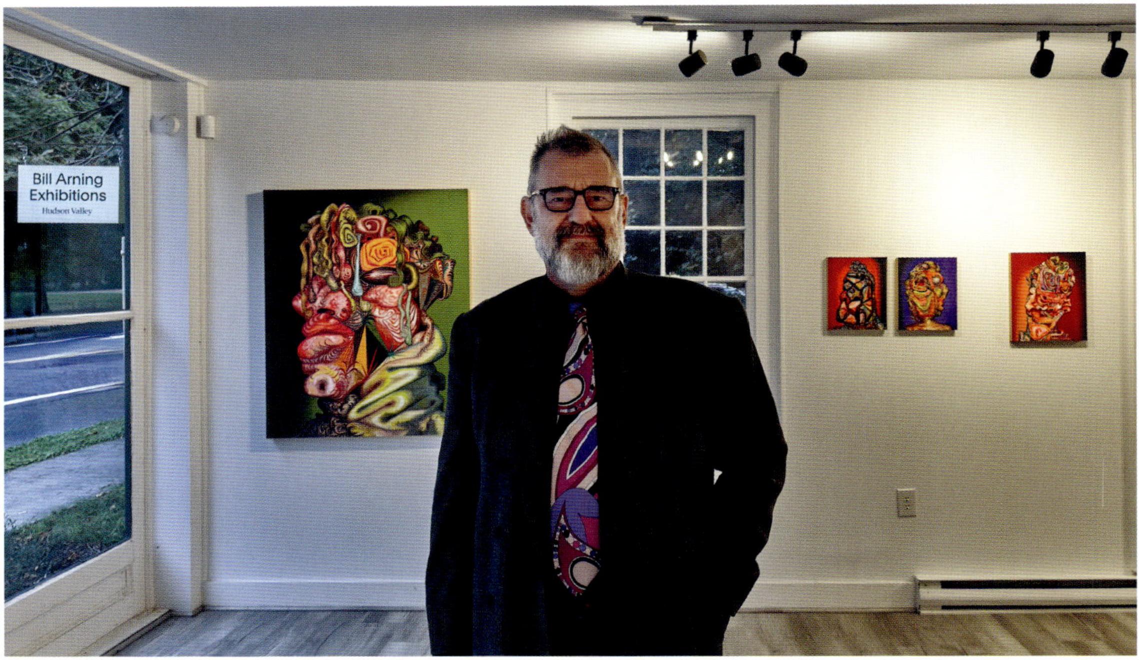

Bill Arning was once the director of the groundbreaking nonprofit White Columns in New York City. Paintings (from left to right) by James Esber, titled *Teenager* (2023), *Fissures* (2021), *Concaveman* (2021), and *Apertures* (2023), were shown in the gallery exhibition "Other Beings" on view from August 16 to October 13, 2024.

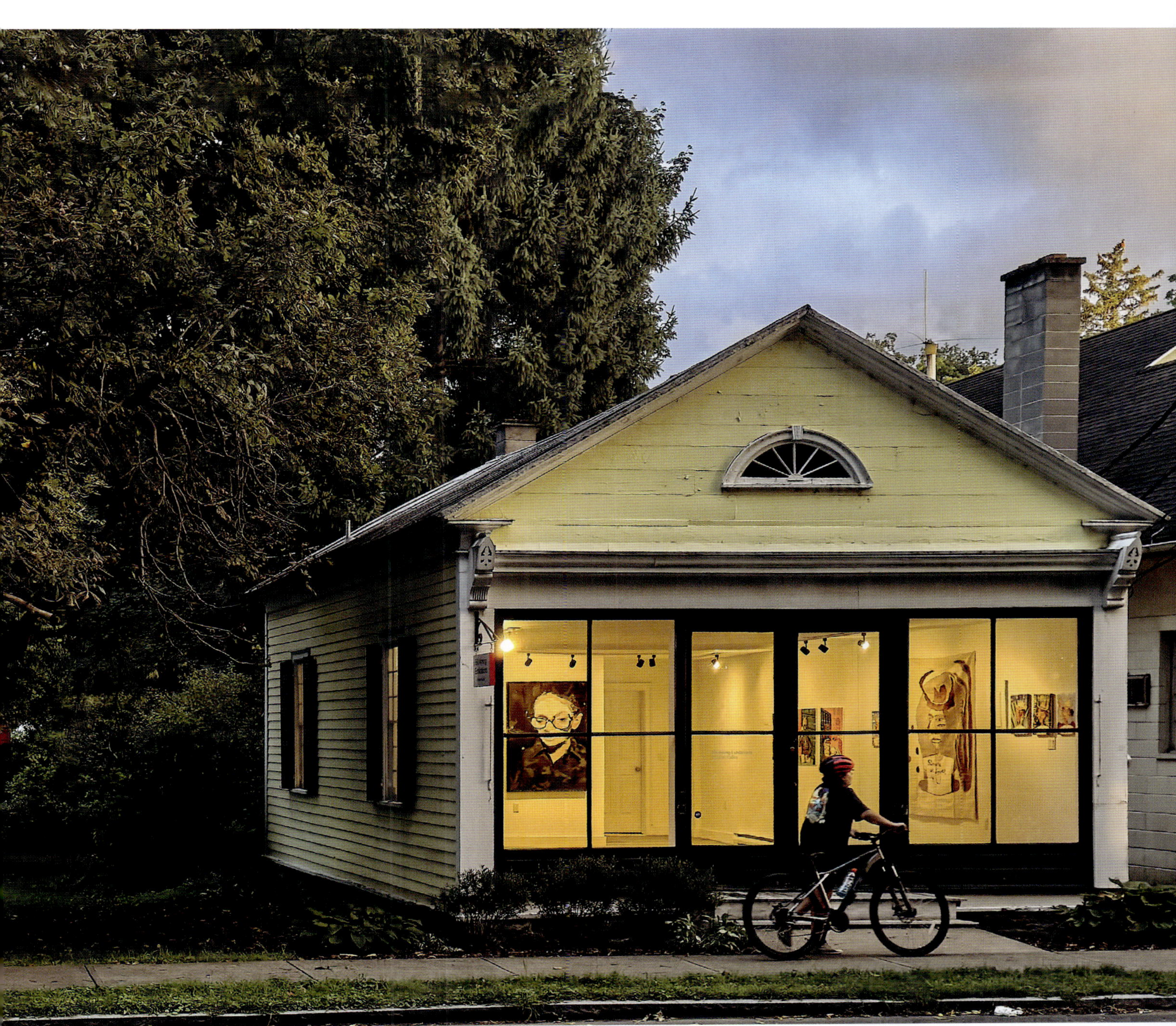

In the evening, Bill leaves the gallery lighting on so those who are out at dusk or later can take a moment to view an exhibition. As the sun sets, the one-room space glows like a beacon.

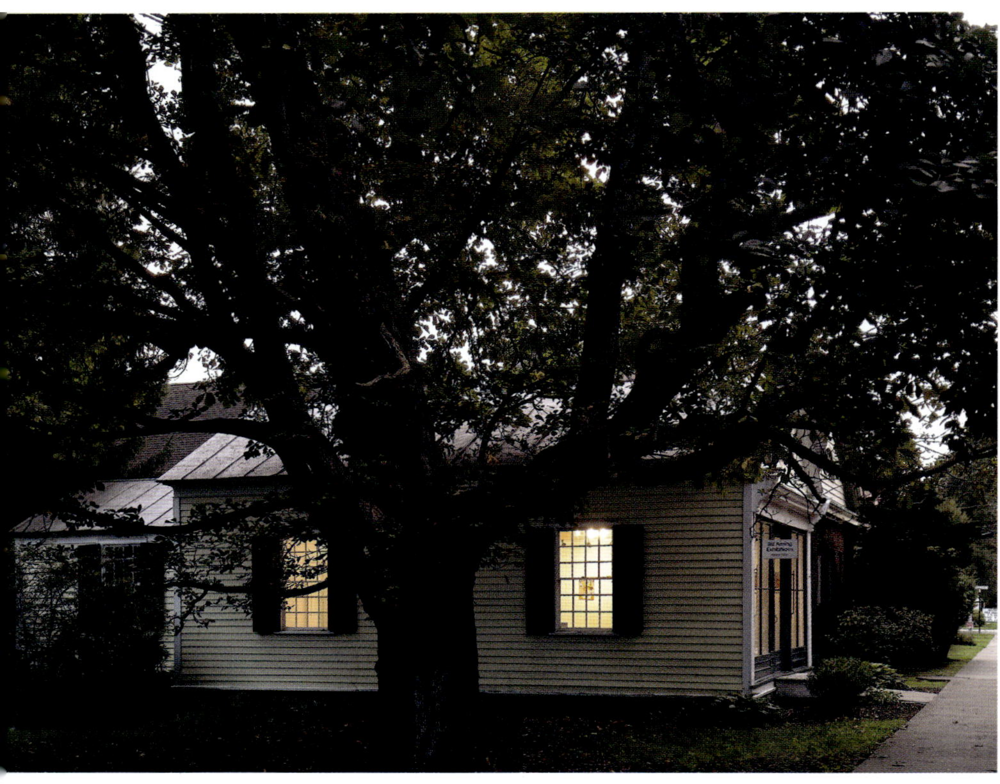

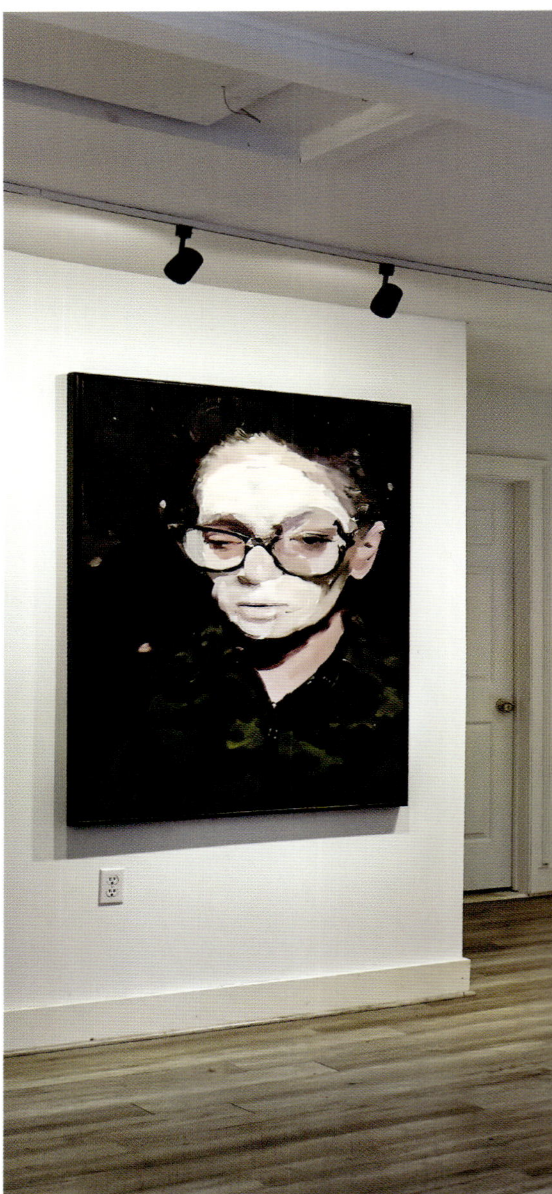

A chestnut tree in the neighbor's yard provides shade in the summer and a connection to nature throughout the year.

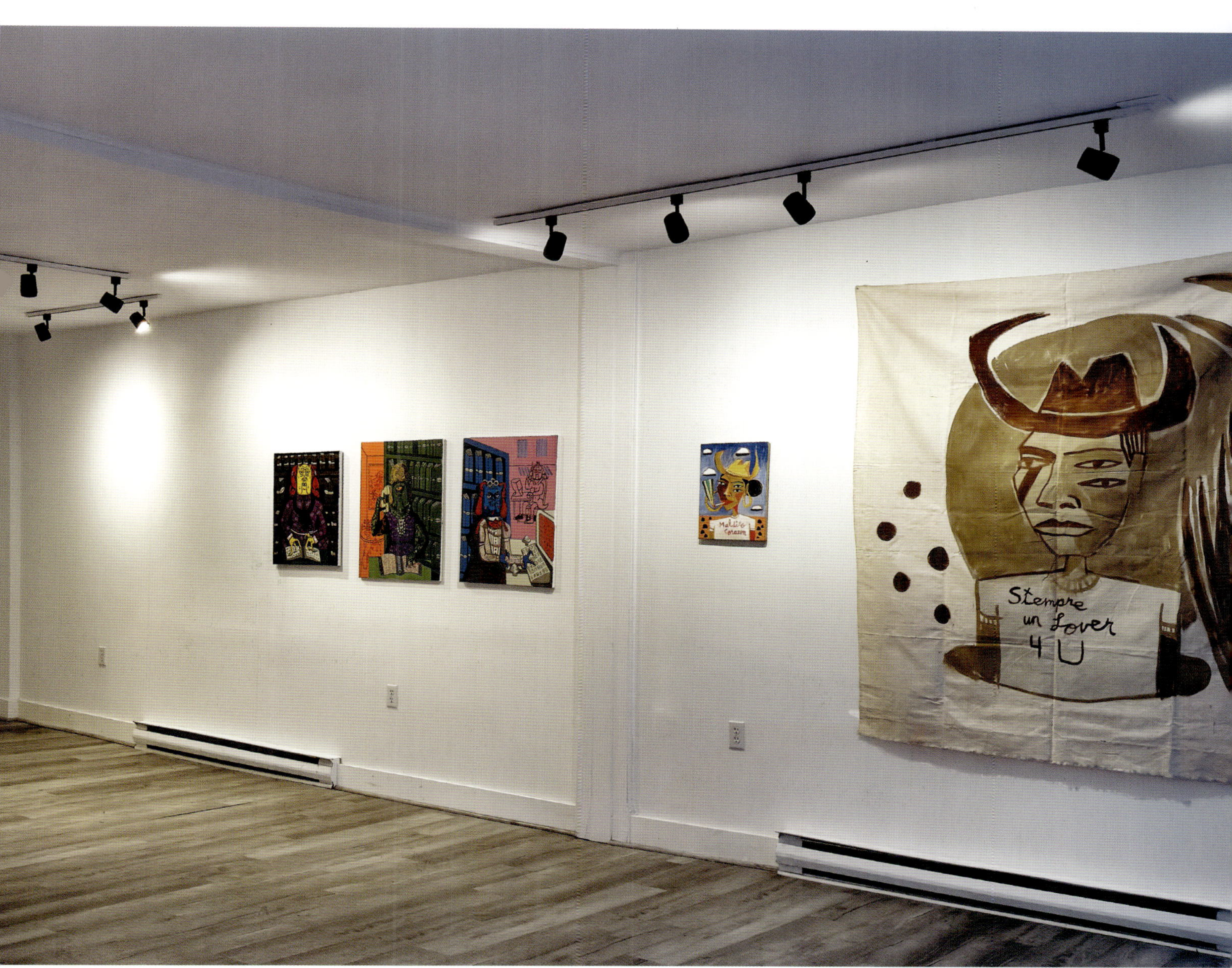

“Other Beings” also included (from left to right) Richard Butler’s *MAGGIEINCAMO* (2020); Hannah Barrett’s *Rare Books* (2023), *One Ring-a-Ding* (2022), and *Vertical Blinds* (2023); and Cruz Ortiz’s *Dos Dios Con You* (2024) and *4U* (2023).

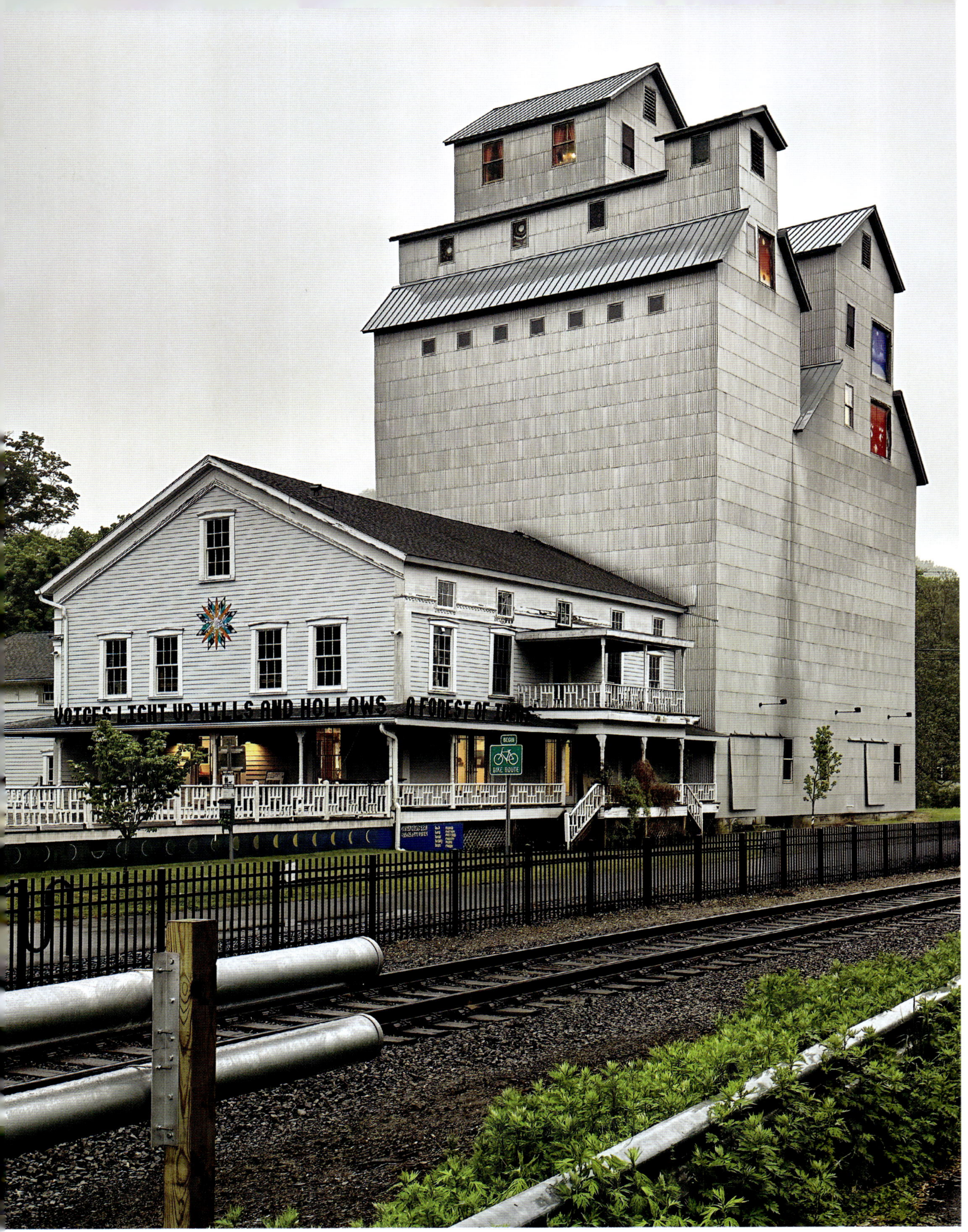
VOICES LIGHT UP HILLS AND HOLLOWS
BEGIN
BIKE ROUTE

The Wassaic Project

Wassaic, New York

Most New Yorkers recognize the name Wassaic as the end stop on the Metro-North commuter train's Harlem Line. But many don't know that the tiny hamlet was once a center of industry. Iron ore produced by the Gridley Iron Works, Borden's condensed milk factory, and grain from local farmers helped the town thrive for years. These days, remnants of those earlier times still exist, and not by accident. It's still possible to drive by the nineteenth-century stone iron ore furnaces and visit the grain silo, known as Maxon Mills, built in the 1950s, that has become the Wassaic Project. Upon first sight, the seven-story building's scale is impressive. Entering the first-floor galleries, the realization of how much work it took to transform the space to use as a non-profit art center sinks in. The massive size of the interior's exposed wood beams is equally surprising.

Efforts to protect Maxon Mills from being demolished began with Sharon Kroger, a university professor who lived nearby. Then the building was purchased by Tony Zunino and Richard Berry, developers who specialized in preservation. They renovated the structure, installing a new staircase and roof. Tony's daughter, artist Bowie Zunino, and her fellow artist friends, Eve Biddle and Elan Bogarin, started a summer festival at the mill in 2005—one that continues to this day. Later, Jeff Barnett-Winsby, Bowie's husband, joined the directors team.

After years of living in Wassaic and experiencing the needs of the community, they saw the potential for the site as an arts and education center. Since then, outreach and programming have grown and expanded. The Wassaic Project added two more buildings to the campus. Now there is a residency program with artists' studios in the old Luther auction barn. There are exhibitions on every floor of the mill and installations around the complex. Performances take place in the Gridley Chapel that was built in 1873 by Noah Gridley, owner of the iron works factory, for his wife, Emeline—a poignant connection to the family, who, in 1857, urged Cornelius Vanderbilt to bring a railroad to the town. Just like the railroad brought people to the town, the Wassaic Project draws not only community members but also artists and art lovers from all over.

opposite
The seven-story grain mill was known as Maxon Mill. Artworks are displayed outside as well as in the galleries. *VOICES LIGHT UP HILLS AND HOLLOWS — A FOREST OF IDEAS* (2020) by Steffi Drewes and Jesse Walton is a text-based piece installed on the edge of the roof.

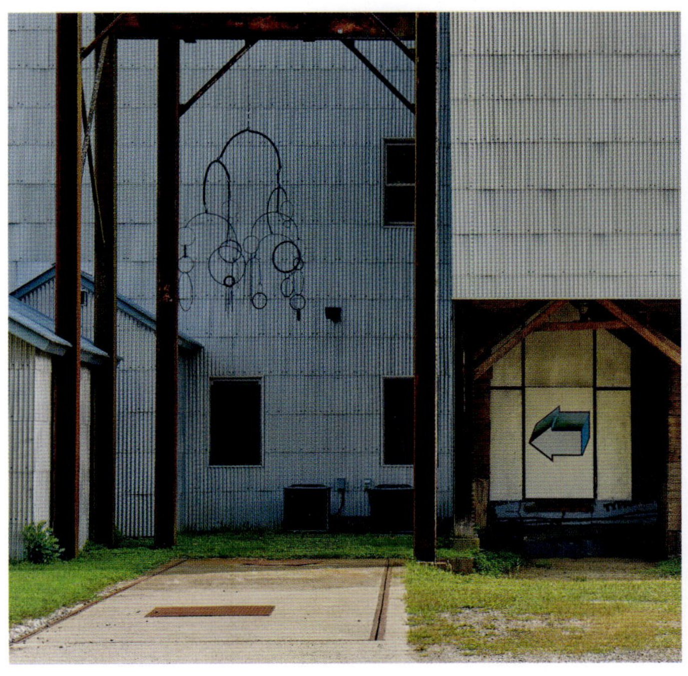

right
Throughout the center's grounds, there is an inventive use of space. Beth Campbell's *THERE'S NO SUCH THING AS A GOOD DECISION* (2022), which hung from a grain loader, and Daniel Carello's *Rubric* (2020), displayed on the back wall of the building, occupy what might have been unusable space.

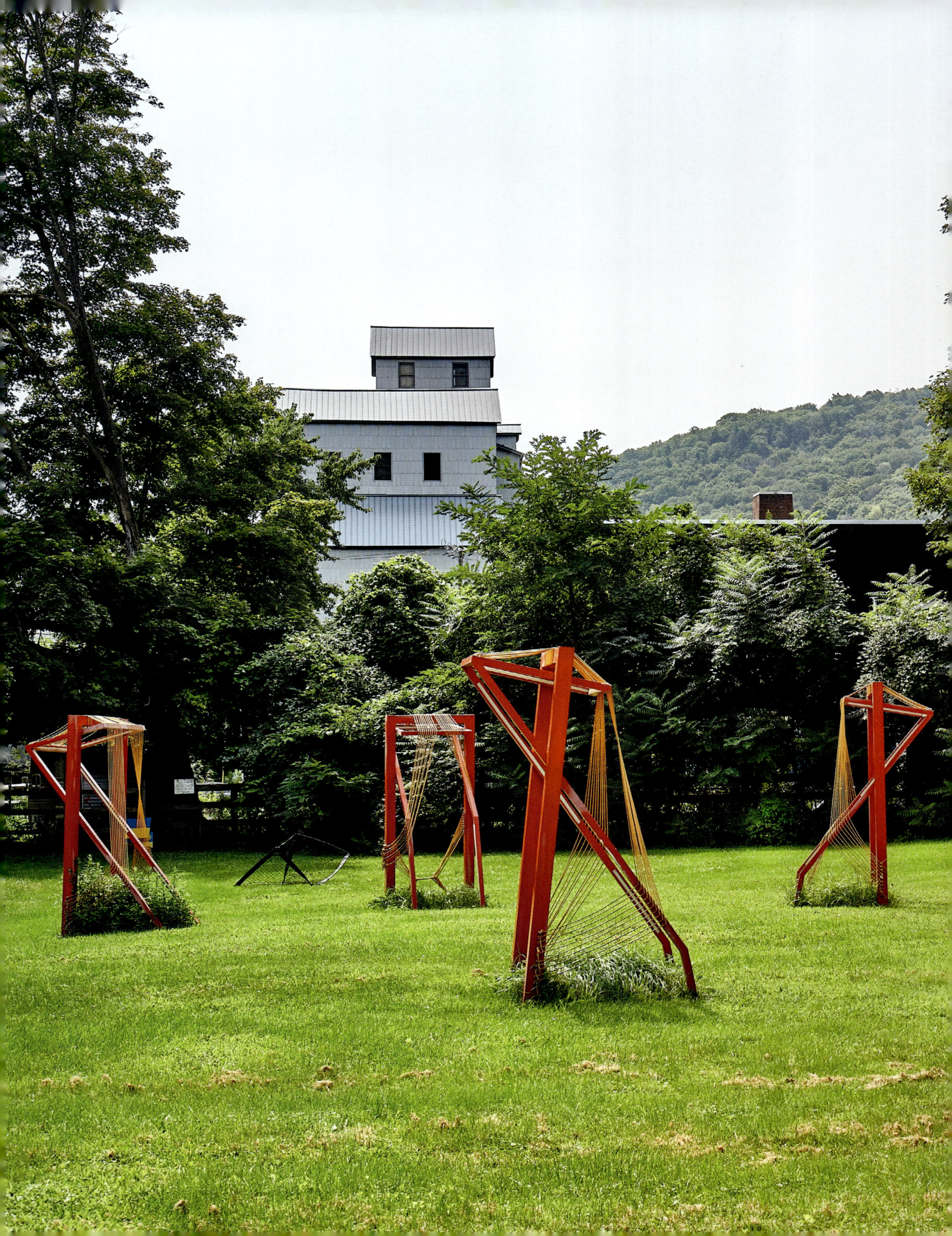

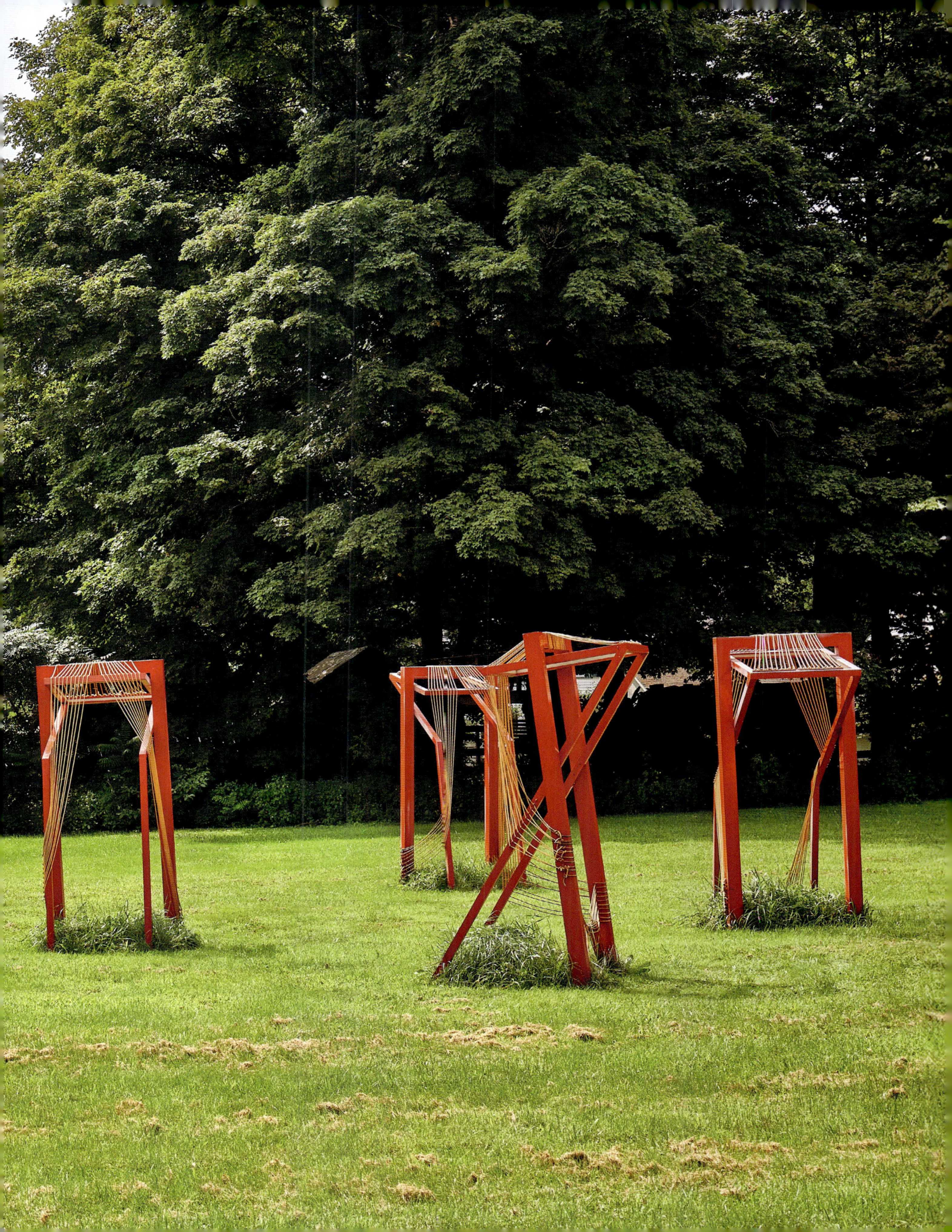

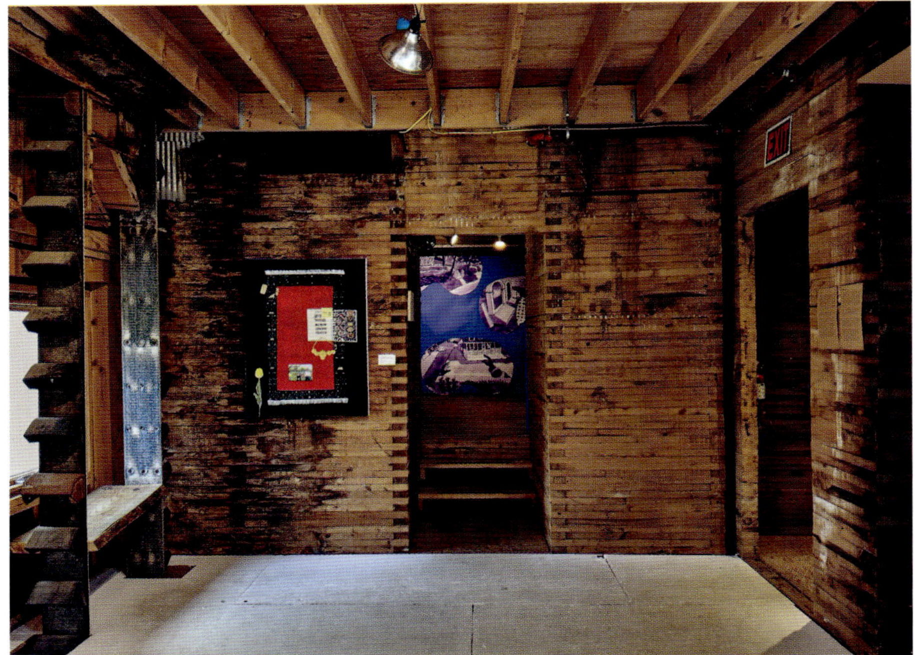

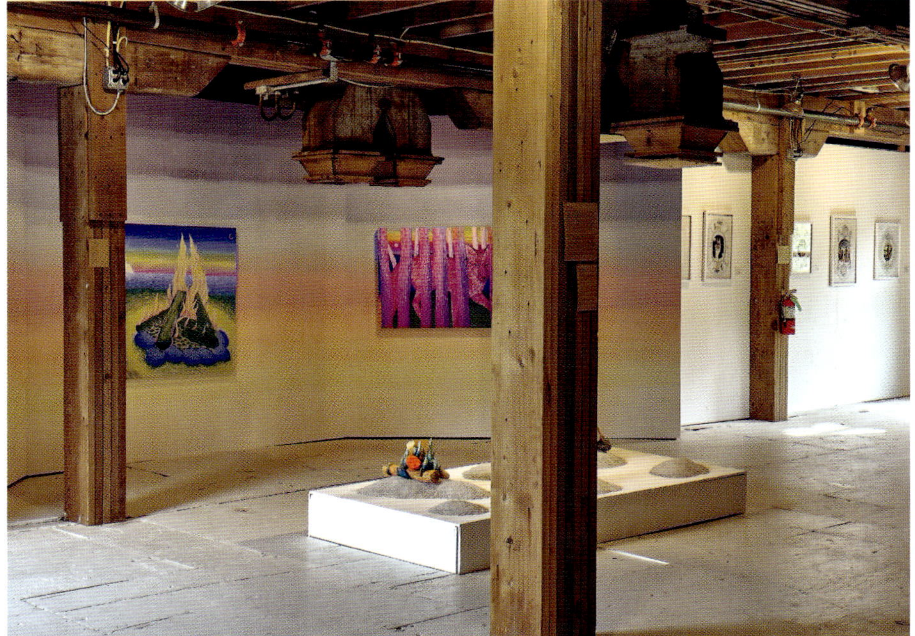

previous
Nina Cooke John's *Point of Action* (n.d.) is sited in the Luther Barn Field.

top
The restored mill offers rich textural surfaces to exhibit artwork. Haley Darya Parsa's acrylic painting, titled *A love letter to Texas tulips that never die (May their place be green)* (2024), is hung against the original lath substructures. The adjacent gallery shows Beth Livensperger's *288 County Road 81* (2024), from her series *Here Is Somewhere Else*, an installation of watercolor and acrylic paintings on paper.

bottom
Grace Hager's oil on canvas paintings, *Radiance* (2023) and *Mirage* (2023), as well as her ceramic sculptures on the raised platform, including one titled *Kindled* (2022), are shown as part of "Tall Shadows in Short Order," the 2024 summer exhibition. While some gallery walls retain the character of the structure, others have been drywalled and painted.

opposite
On the third floor, Maria Stabio's *Shelter* (2021) greets visitors at the entrance to the galleries.

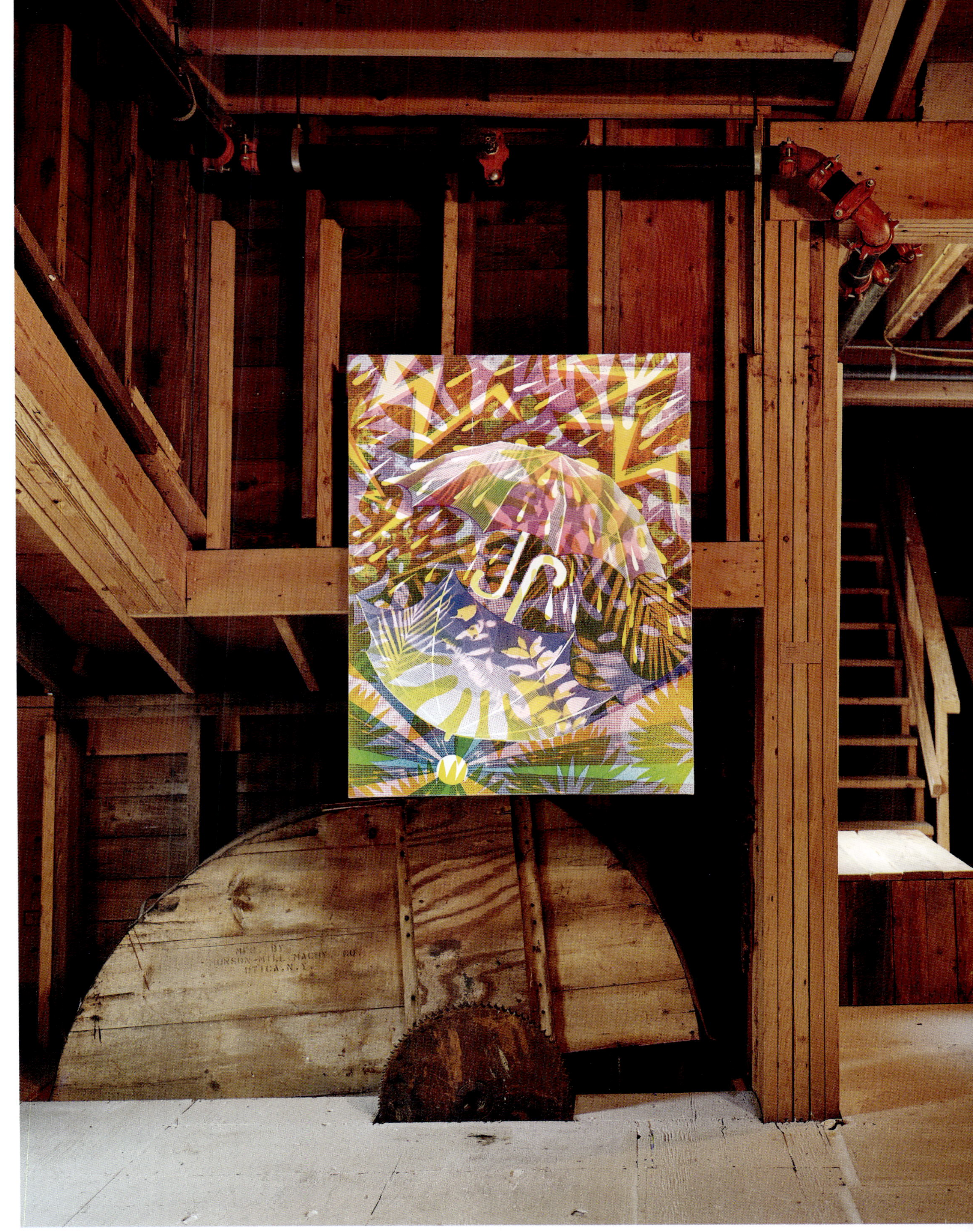
MFG. BY
UTICA, N.Y.

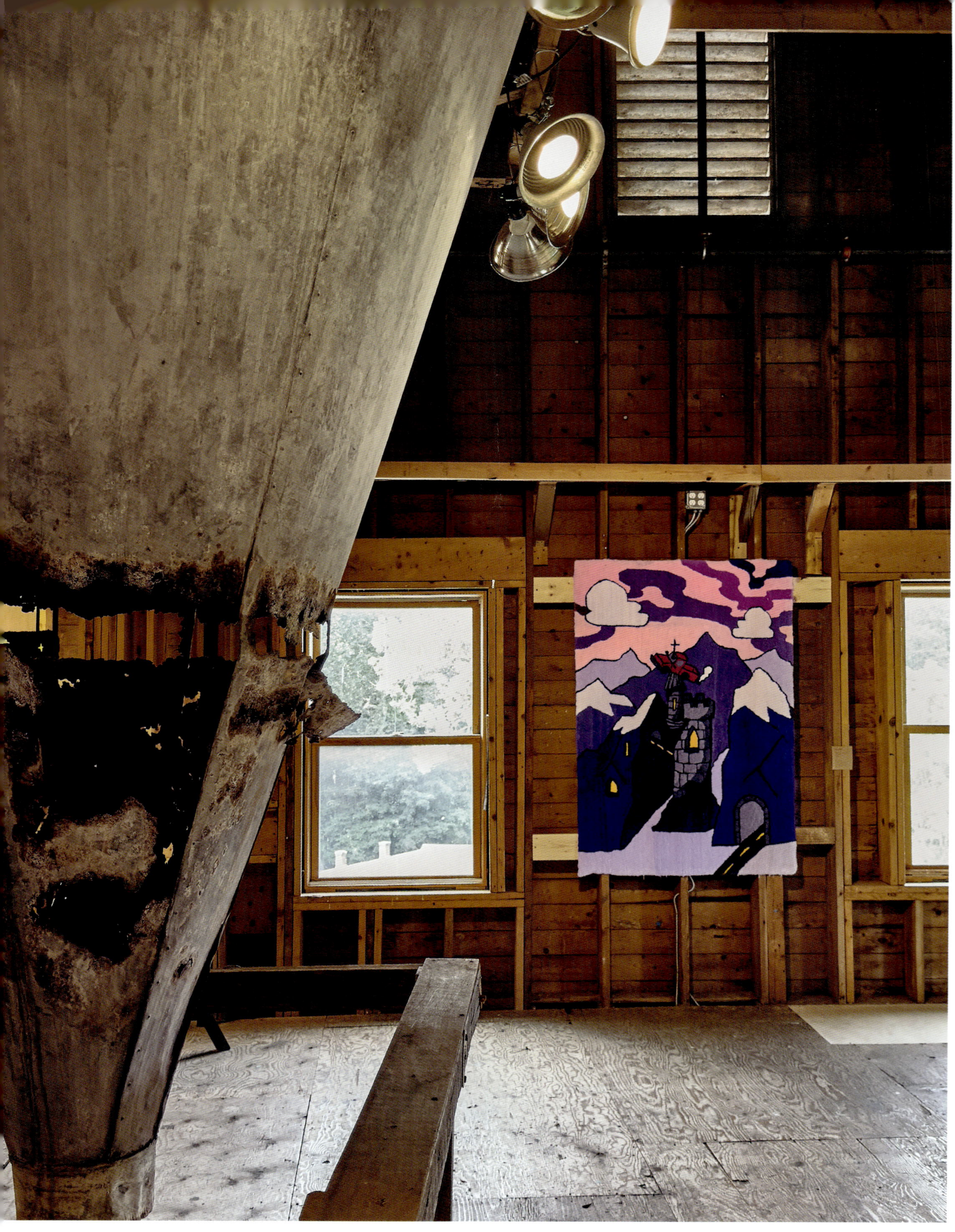

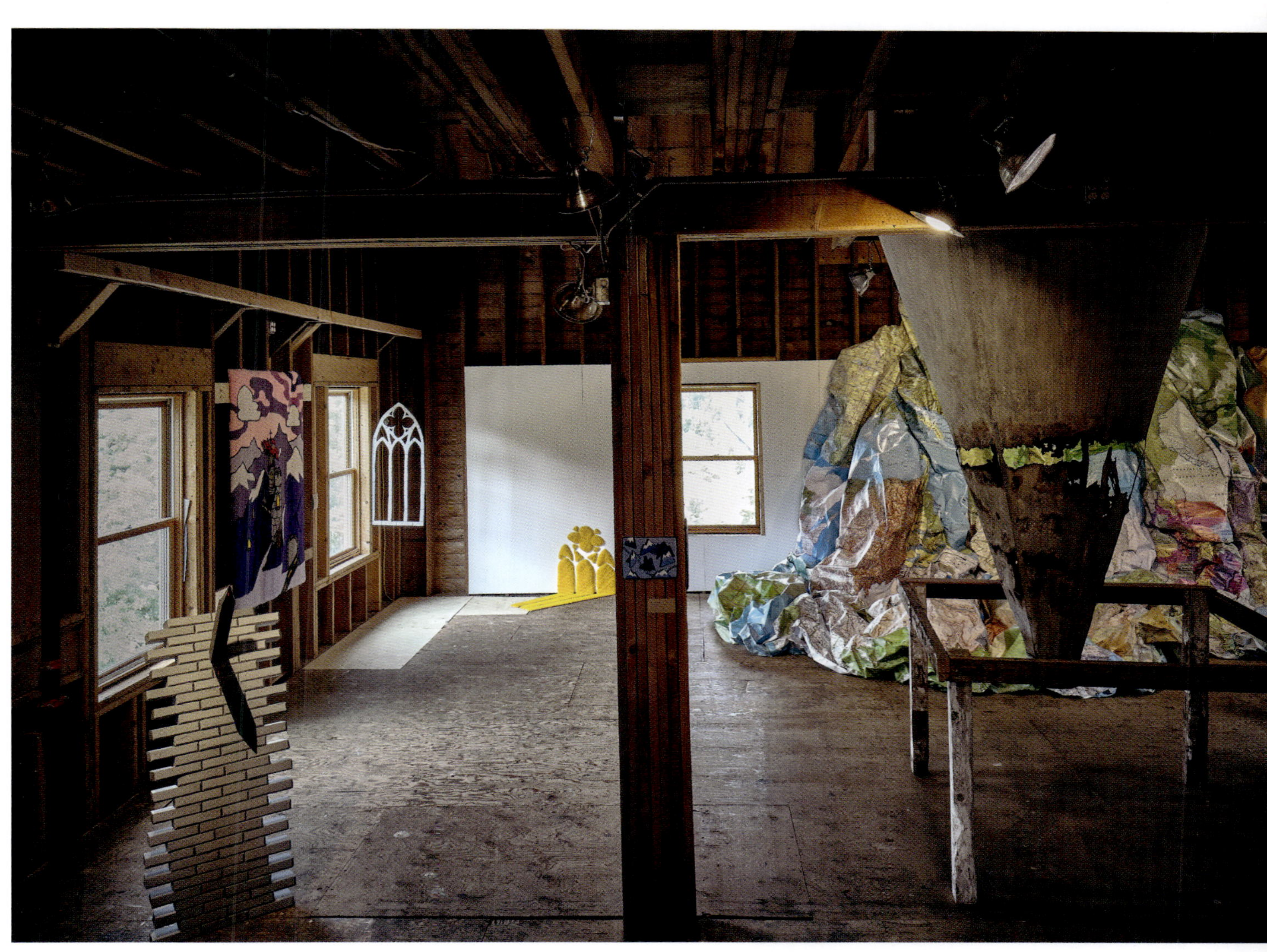

opposite
On the sixth floor, Matthew Gilbert's wall piece, *Orange County Gothic* (2023–2024), made from brightly colored yarns, stands in contrast to the metal hopper bottom cone, a remnant of the old mill that was purposefully left in place.

above
Matthew Gilbert's wall and floor pieces, *November* (2023) and *load-bearing, barely* (2022), made of foam board, share a gallery with Luciana Abait's work from her *Displacement* series.

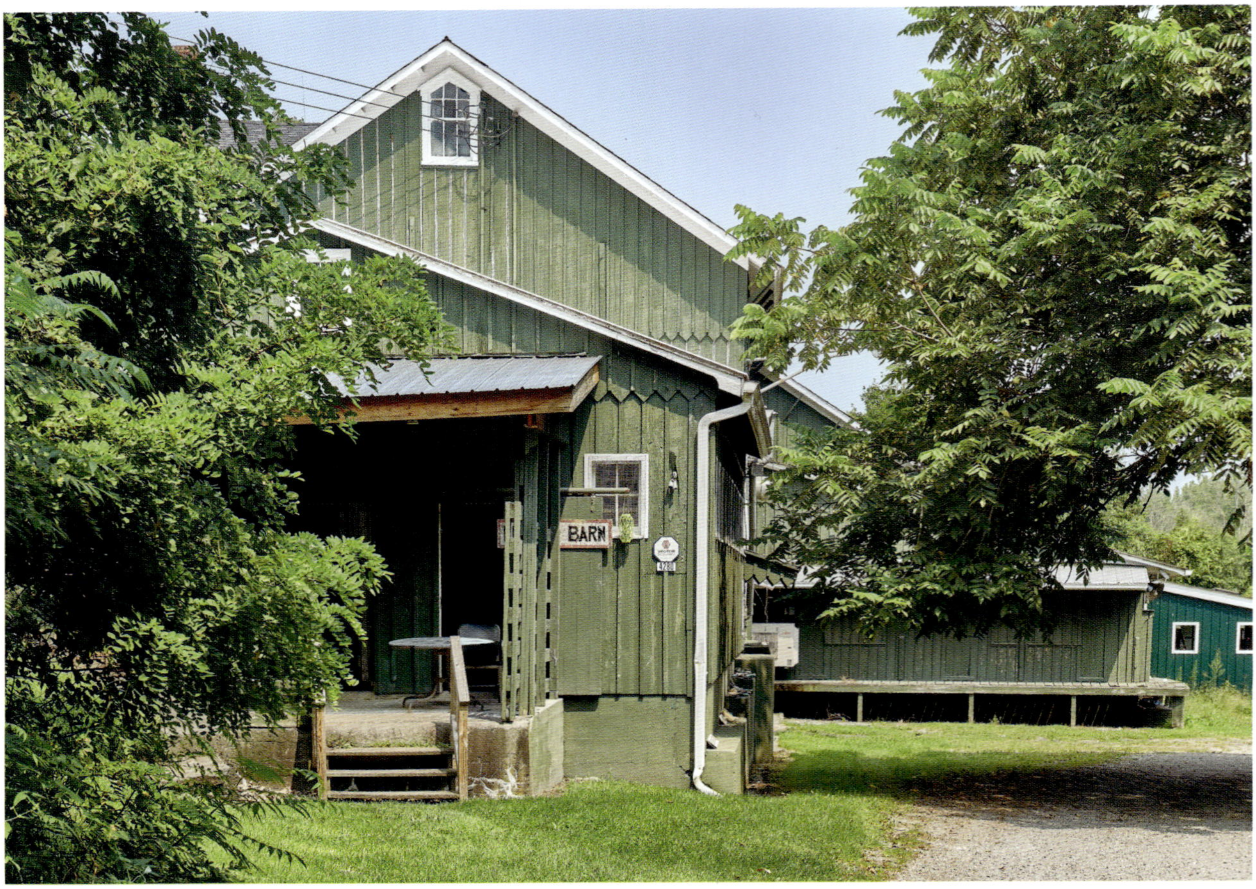

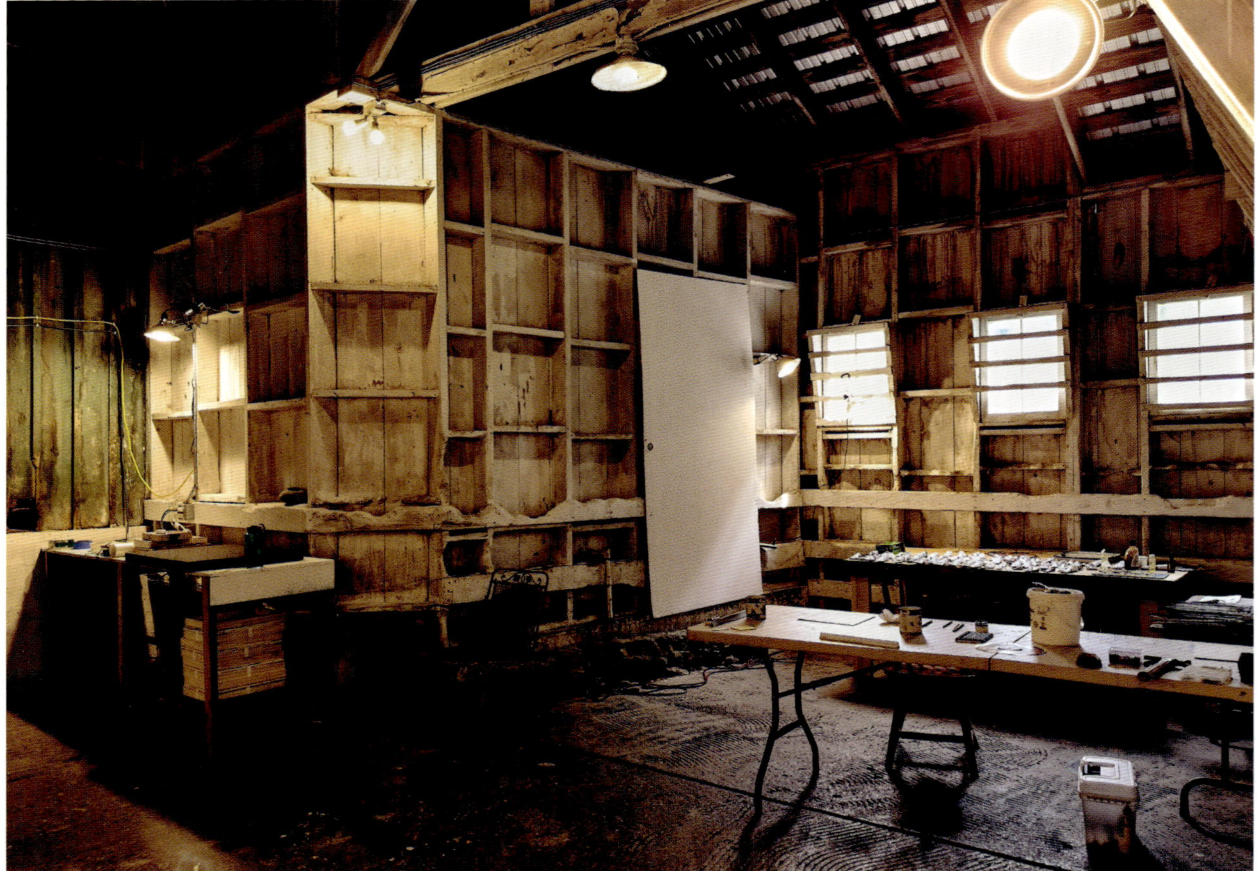

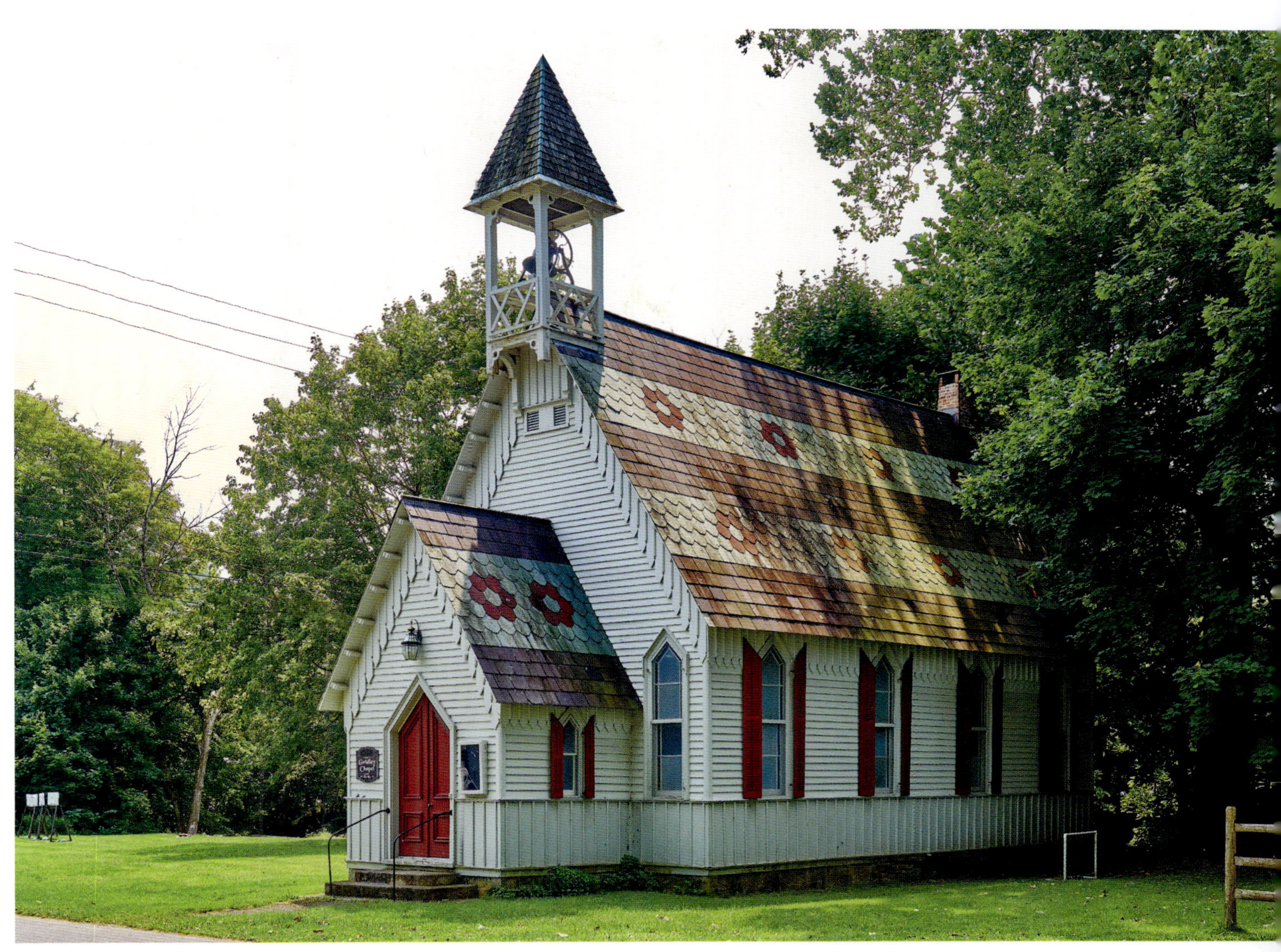

opposite, top
The livestock auction barn, not far from Maxon Mill, is repurposed as artist studios.

opposite, bottom
In the barn's upper level, another studio is set up with the artist's paints and palette and a blank canvas. The barn's rustic architecture has been kept while the use of the building has changed.

above
Performances take place in the American Gothic-style Gridley Chapel.

overleaf
Jesse Walton's *Boredom Is a Luxury* (2024) is placed on the empty lawn next to the Gridley Chapel.

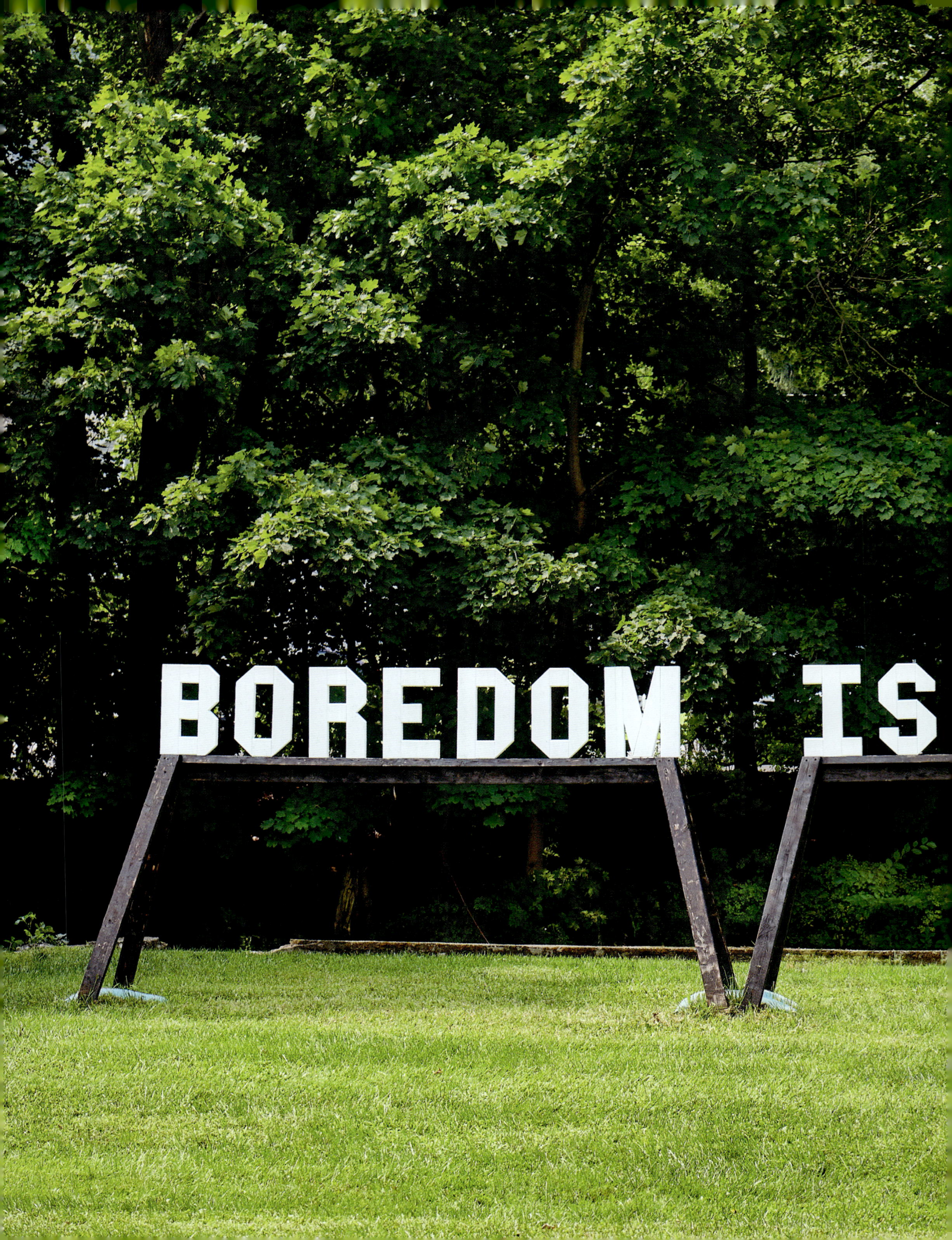
BOREDOM IS

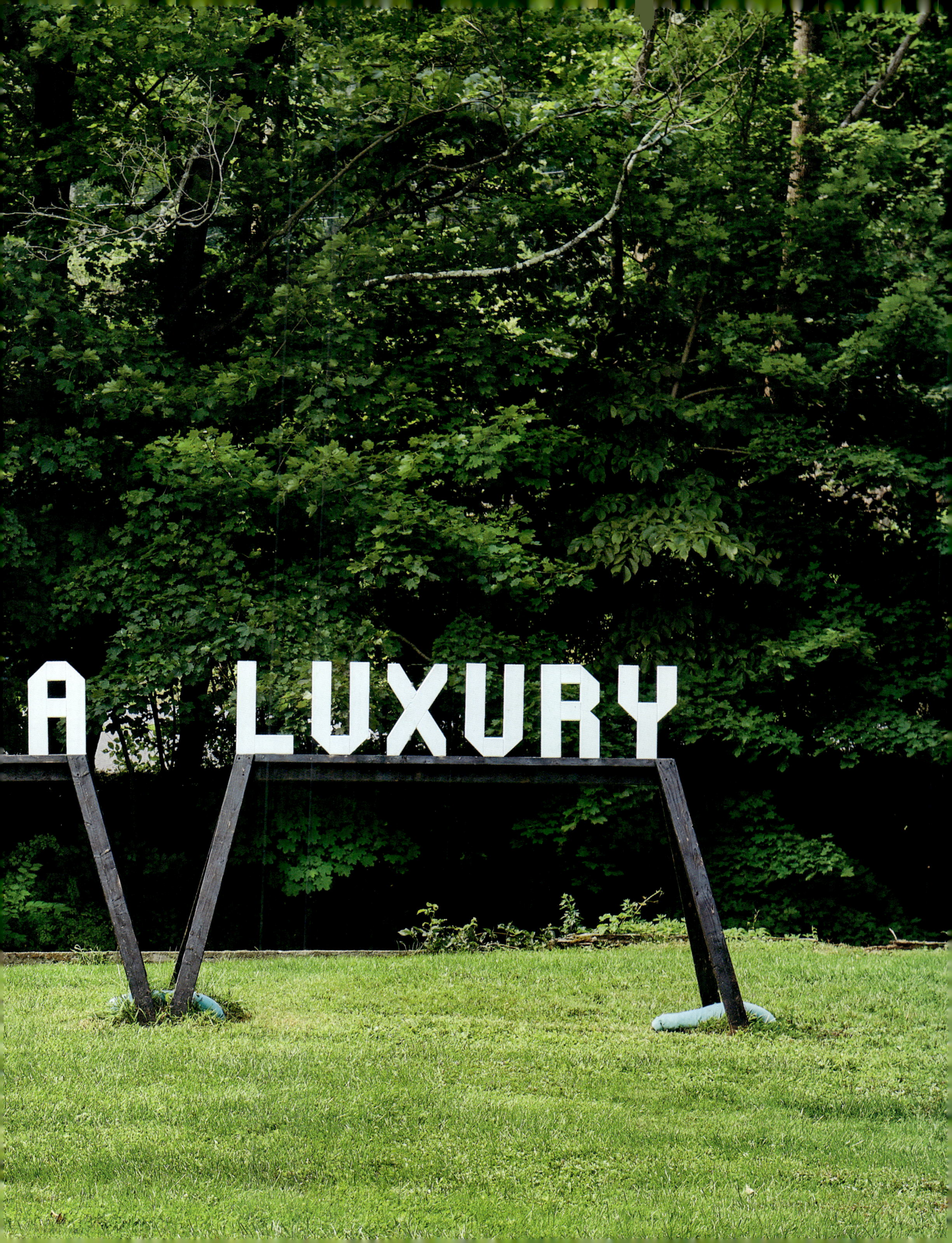
A LUXURY

Caitlin MacBride
Foreland
Catskill, New York

Artist Caitlin MacBride moved from Brooklyn to Hudson in 2020. She took a studio at Foreland, a campus of three buildings that includes a converted Civil War–era mill in Catskill, New York, just over the Rip Van Winkle Bridge, twenty minutes away. In 2021, the artist studios in the building on Main Street, known as the Foreland Front Building, were just being completed, and Caitlin was able to sketch out the parameters of her space. Her studio has two windows that look onto the alley that leads from Water Street to Main Street past a corner public garden. She works on both canvases on the wall and on easels. Her space has room to store and display finished works.

For the last few years, Caitlin's subject matter has incorporated objects that have become part of the iconography of the Shakers, an early American Utopian community that first settled in upstate New York, such as weaving looms, tools, furniture, and Shaker costumes including bonnets. She has also painted images of tools and sample books of dyed fabrics. Her process starts with deep-dive research on each object, making the connection between objects and community, as well as the concepts of value and use. Her work was recently shown in New York City and Detroit, and at the Shaker Museum's pop-up gallery in Kinderhook, New York.

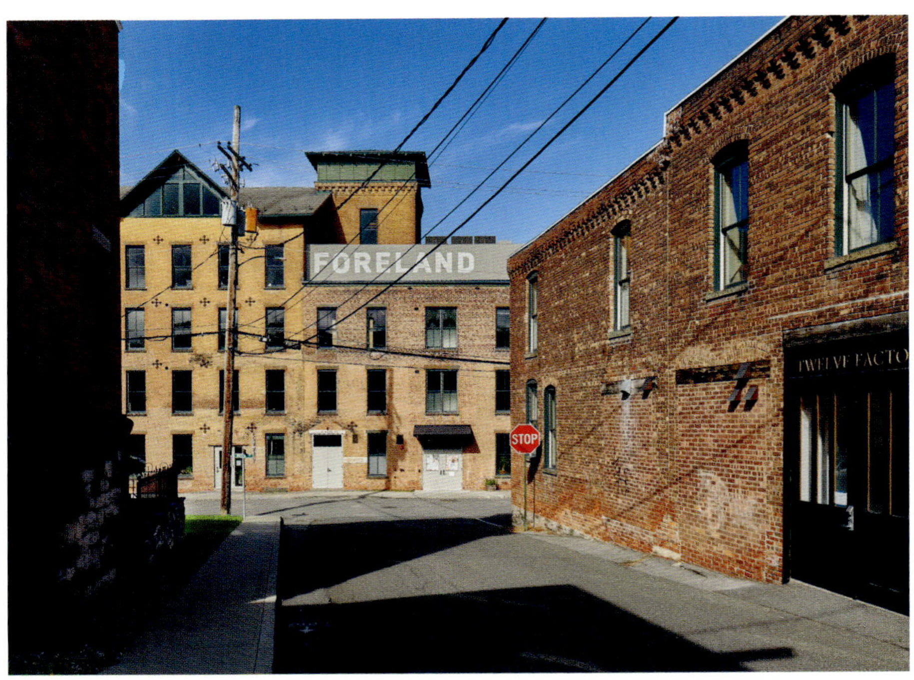

above
Foreland, an art and commercial venue in Catskill, New York, consists of three nineteenth-century buildings. Caitlin's studio is in the Foreland Front Building and overlooks this alley.

opposite, top
The artist in her Catskill studio. The 2022 oil on canvas painting *Select a reverential broom, twill be a labor of surprise (for Eldress Rosetta Stephens)* hangs behind her, as does a smaller work.

opposite, bottom
A corner of Caitlin's studio with works in various stages of completion.

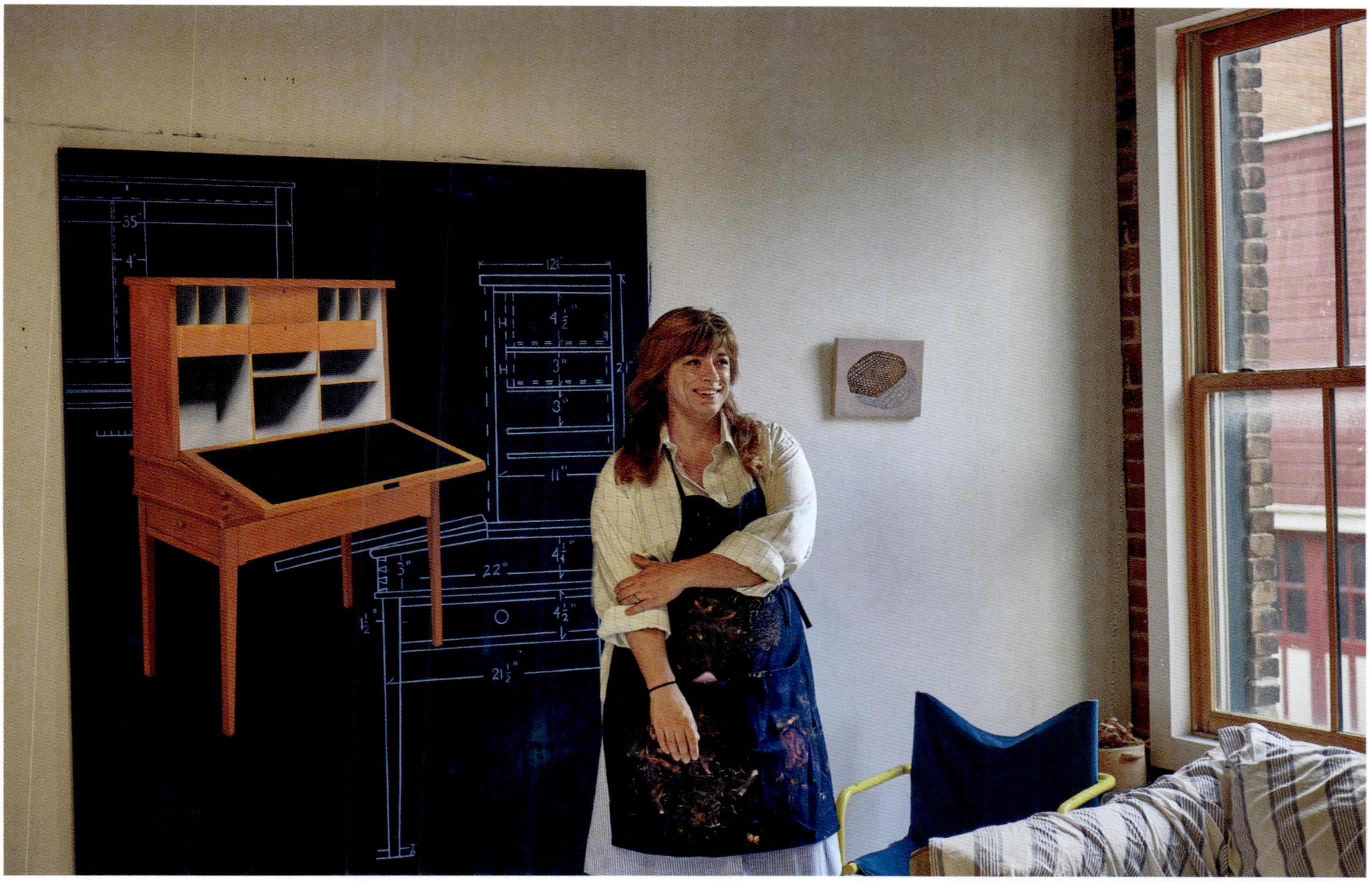

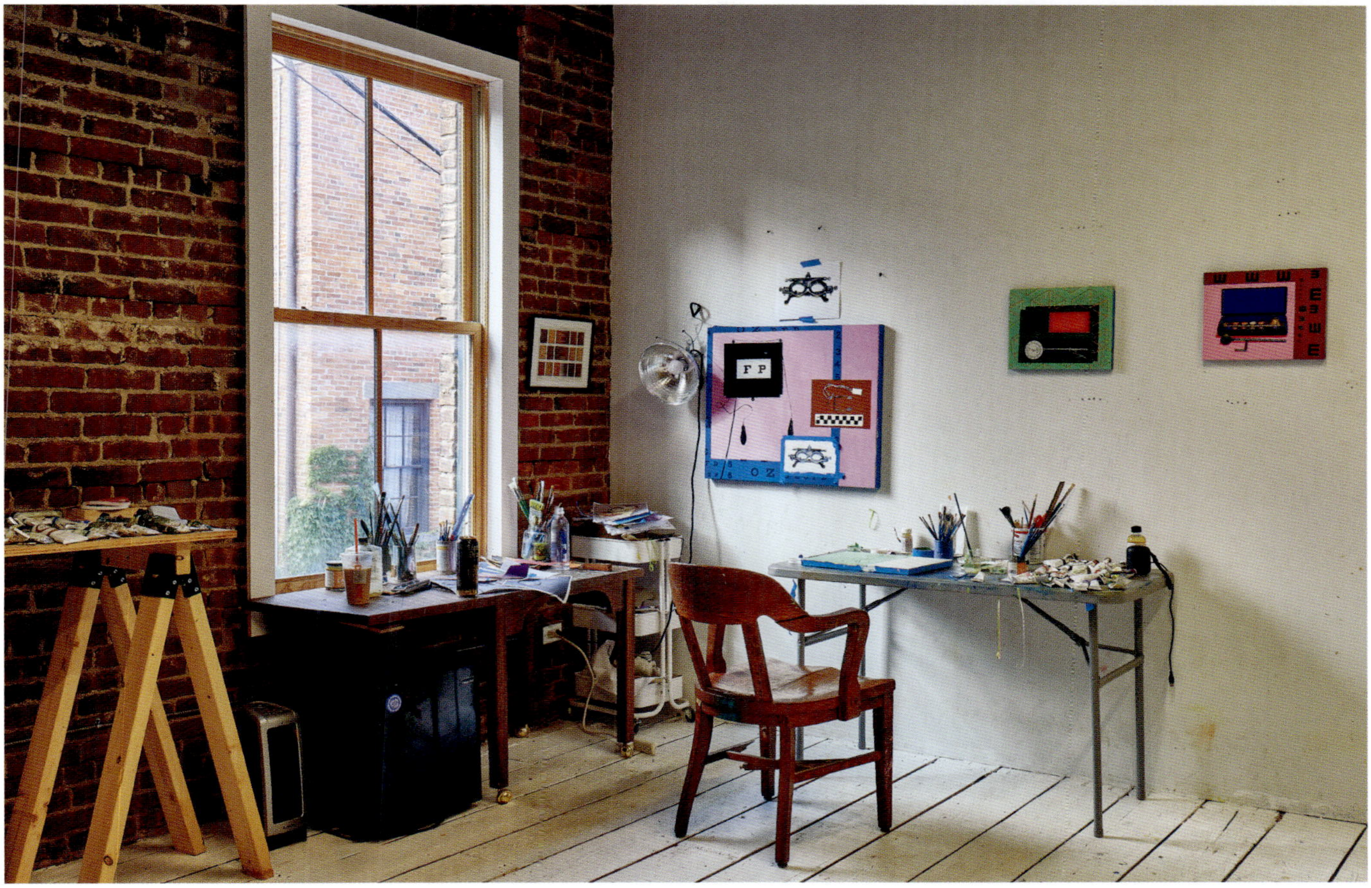

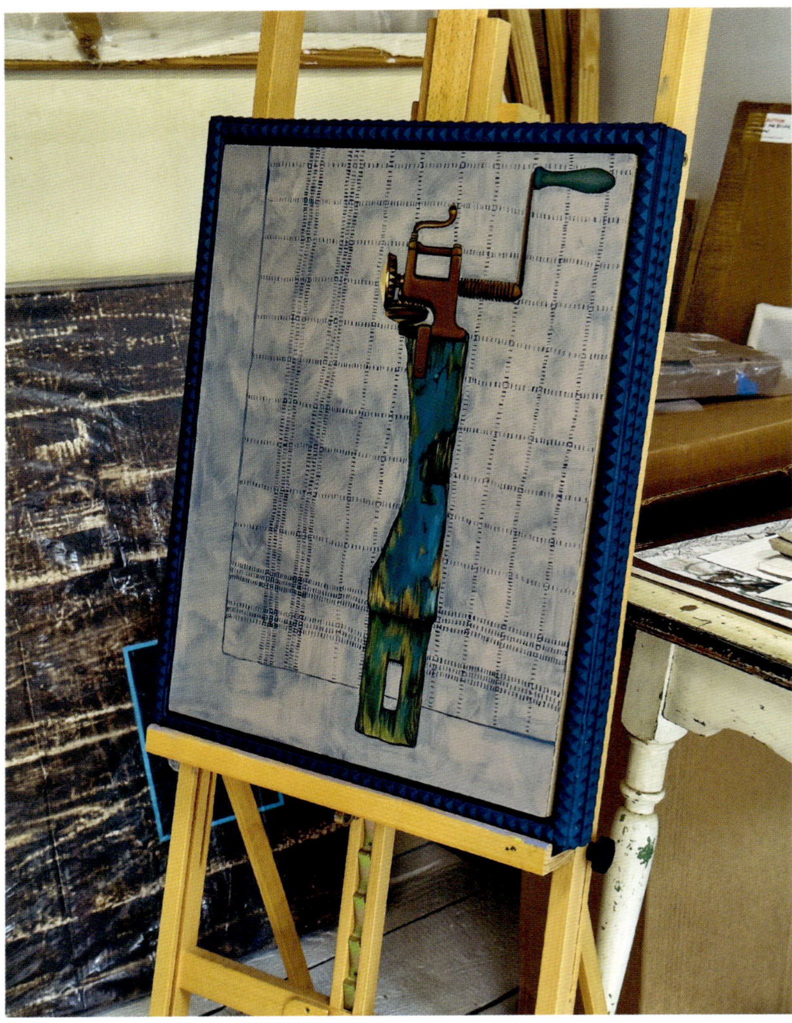

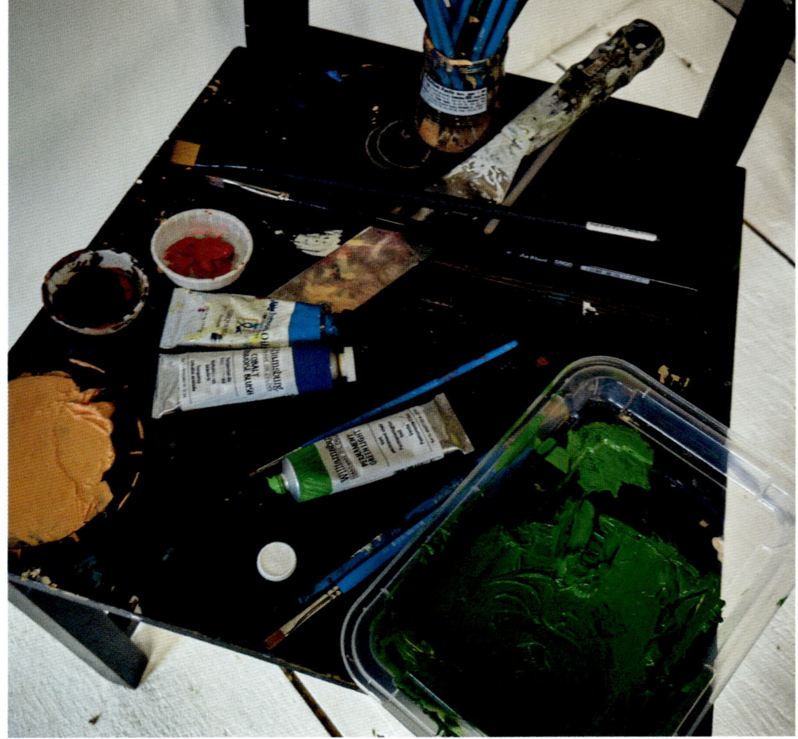

top
Cossaduck Hill (2020), a painting of a metal crimper, is based on an object from the Colonial Williamsburg Collection.

left
A studio chair becomes a temporary worktable holding paint tubes, brushes, and other tools.

opposite
The painting *Mill* (2021) is displayed against the brick wall of the studio.

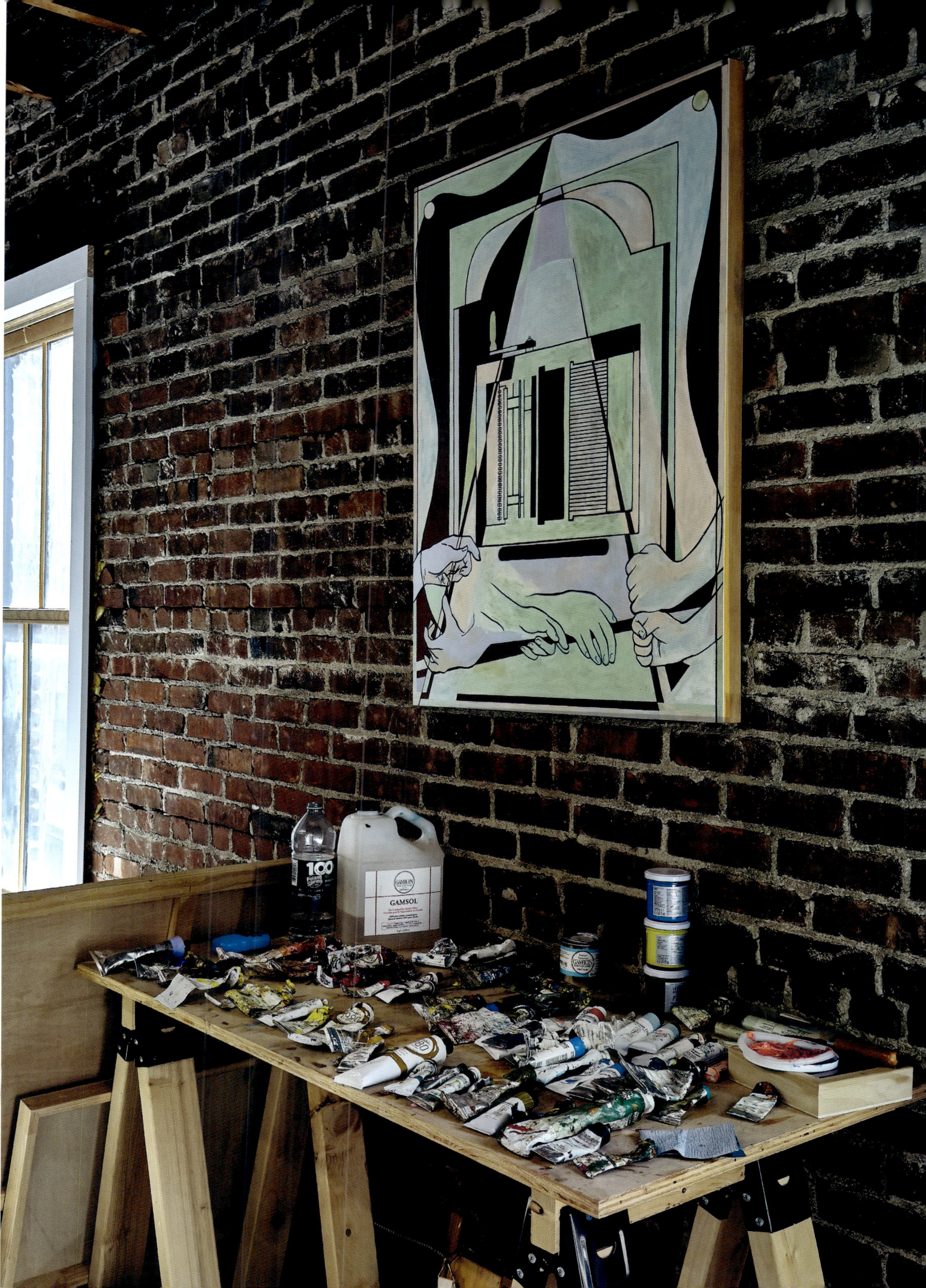

100
GAMSOL

The Campus

Claverack, New York

The Campus is the latest large art space to join the Hudson Valley art scene, opening in June 2024. The project takes advantage of existing architecture, in this case, the 1951 Ockawamick School in Claverack, New York, near Hudson. While the presentation of art in an empty school is not necessarily a new concept (think MOMA PS1 in Queens, New York, or Jack Shainman Gallery's The School in nearby Kinderhook, New York), this interpretation of the school-to-gallery model is fresh. The exhibition spaces are far-from-pristine white boxes. Furnishings and finishes, such as lockers, lab desks, bookshelves, blackboards, and faux wood paneling, remain and are incorporated into the galleries. Indeed, the intent was to "preserve the soul and history" of the place. Modifications are minimal; floating walls are installed as needed in former classrooms. Art is shown in relationship to these remnants of the history of the building. These leftover artifacts of school days and the memories and associations attached to them are now memorialized. The environment is part of the overall experience, whether in harmony with or in juxtaposition to the works on display.

Art dealer Andrew Kreps started the search for storage upstate and found the school. He spoke to another art dealer, James Cohan, and they decided to bring together six "midsize" New York City galleries—Andrew Kreps, James Cohan, Bortolami, Anton Kern, Kaufmann Repetto, and Kurimanzutto—to create not only a place for art storage but also an exhibition space that includes outdoor space for the exhibition of large-scale sculptures and other artwork, something not easily found or accessible in New York City. For the first exhibition, which was up for five months, curator Timo Kappeller selected pieces from more than two hundred artworks from the galleries' collective inventories. In addition, the New Haven, Connecticut-based arts incubator that supports both artists and curators, NXTHVN, founded by Titus Kaphar and Jason Price, was invited to curate and install art made by their artist fellows.

The first opening was a success—more than three thousand people came for the event. The crowds were made up of not only local artists and contemporary art connoisseurs but also those willing to travel to explore new art destinations. Collectors and other gallerists came to see the possibilities and world-class art that upstate has to offer.

opposite, top
The Ockawamick School, built in 1951 in Claverack, New York, was both a public elementary and a high school. It has been adapted to become an exhibition space, owned and organized by six New York City galleries. It opened in June 2024.

opposite, bottom
The triple-door entry lobby of the school is still intact except for the hallway flooring, which was removed to reveal the concrete floors underneath. The school's receptionist office now serves as the gallery's front desk.

overleaf
The gymnasium near the front entry is part of the gallery topography. The bleachers are still intact and opened for use. Yinka Shonibare CBE RA's *Moving Up* (2021) is shown in the middle of the gym. Andrea Bowers's neon *Climate Change is Real (Global Climate Action Summit, San Francisco)* (2018) is shown on the back wall of the stage. Also on view are Lara Schnitger's *Class of '24* (2023) and *Leader of the Pack* (2023).

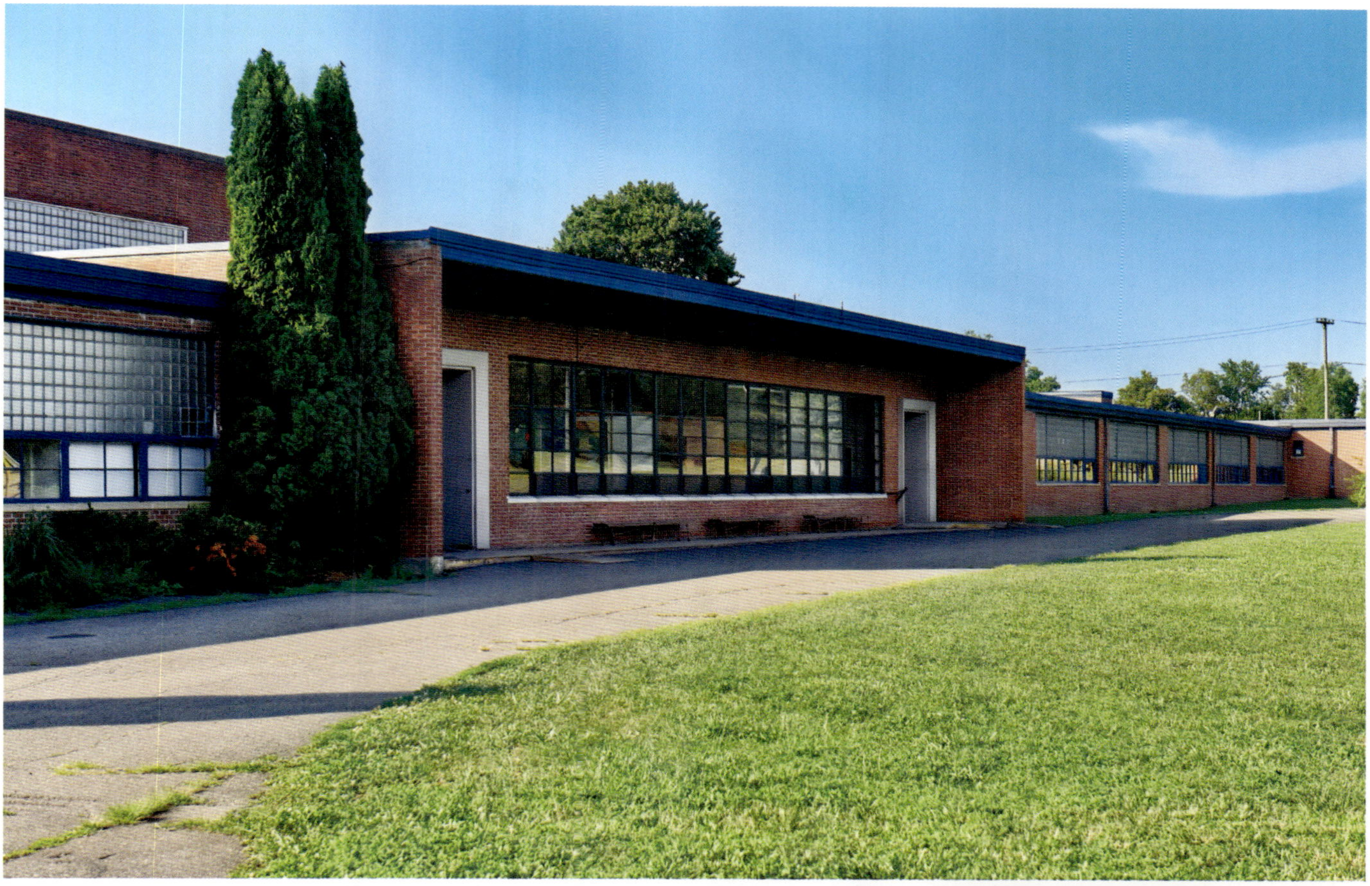

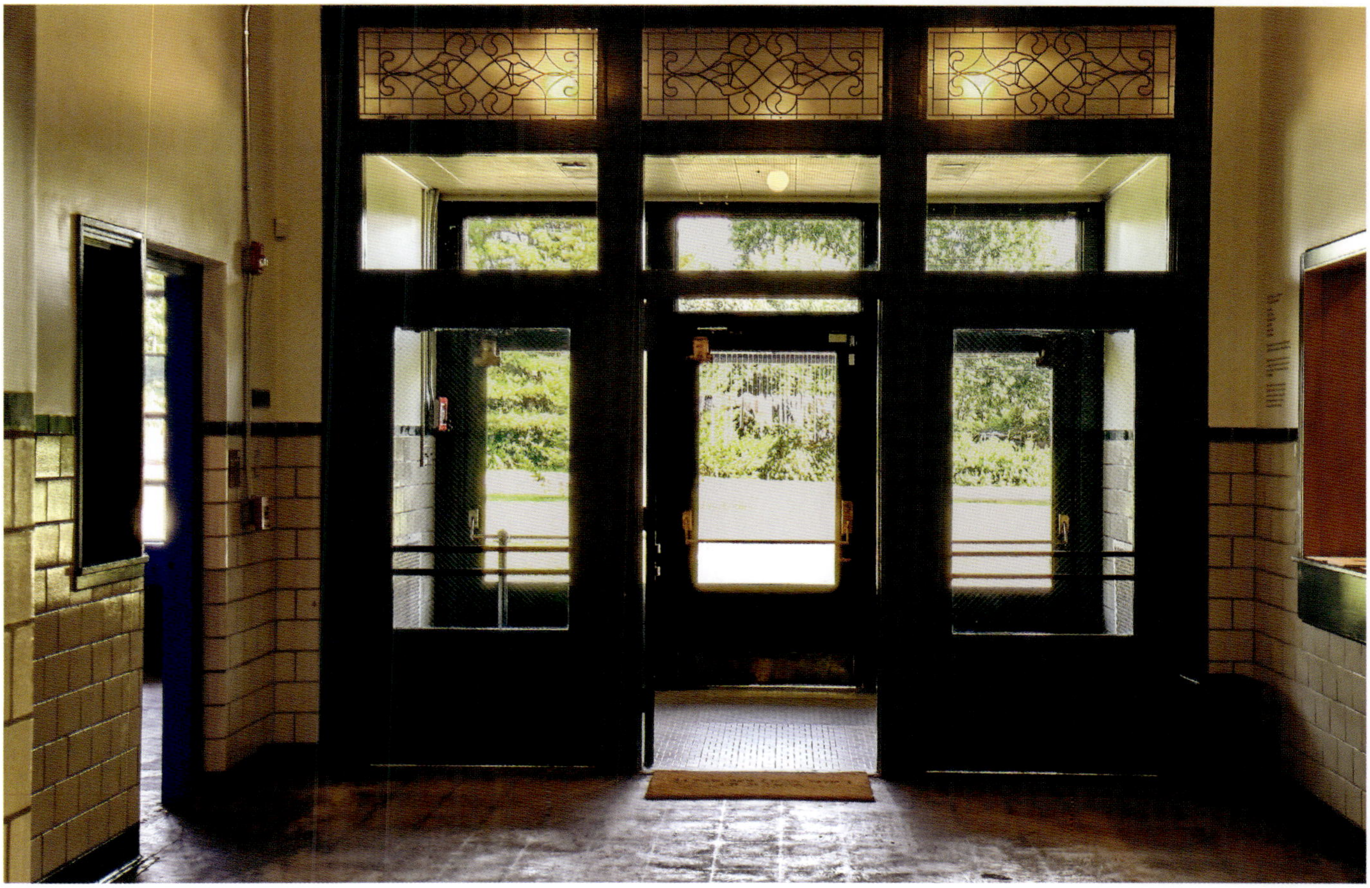

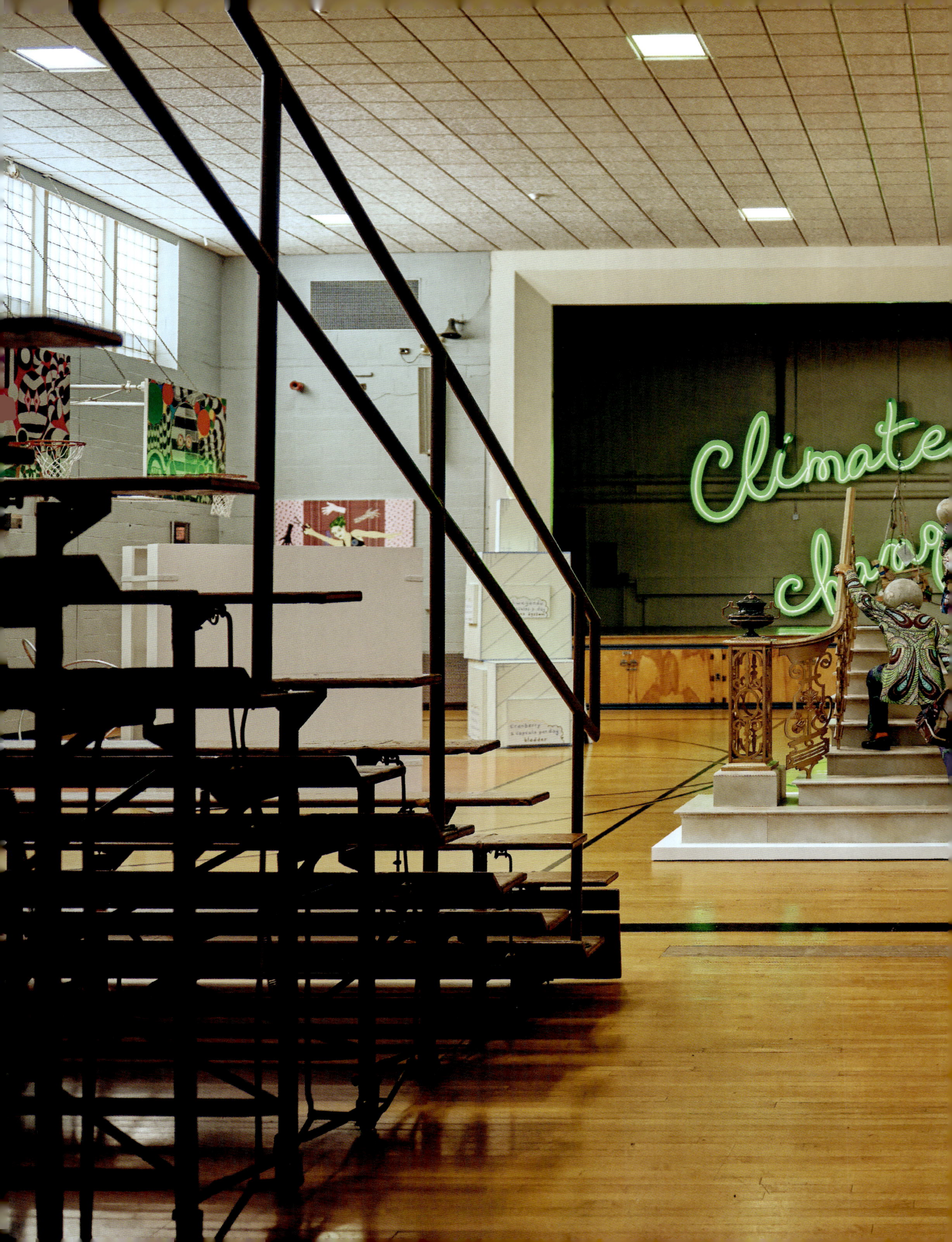
Climate
Cranberry
1 capsule per day
bladder

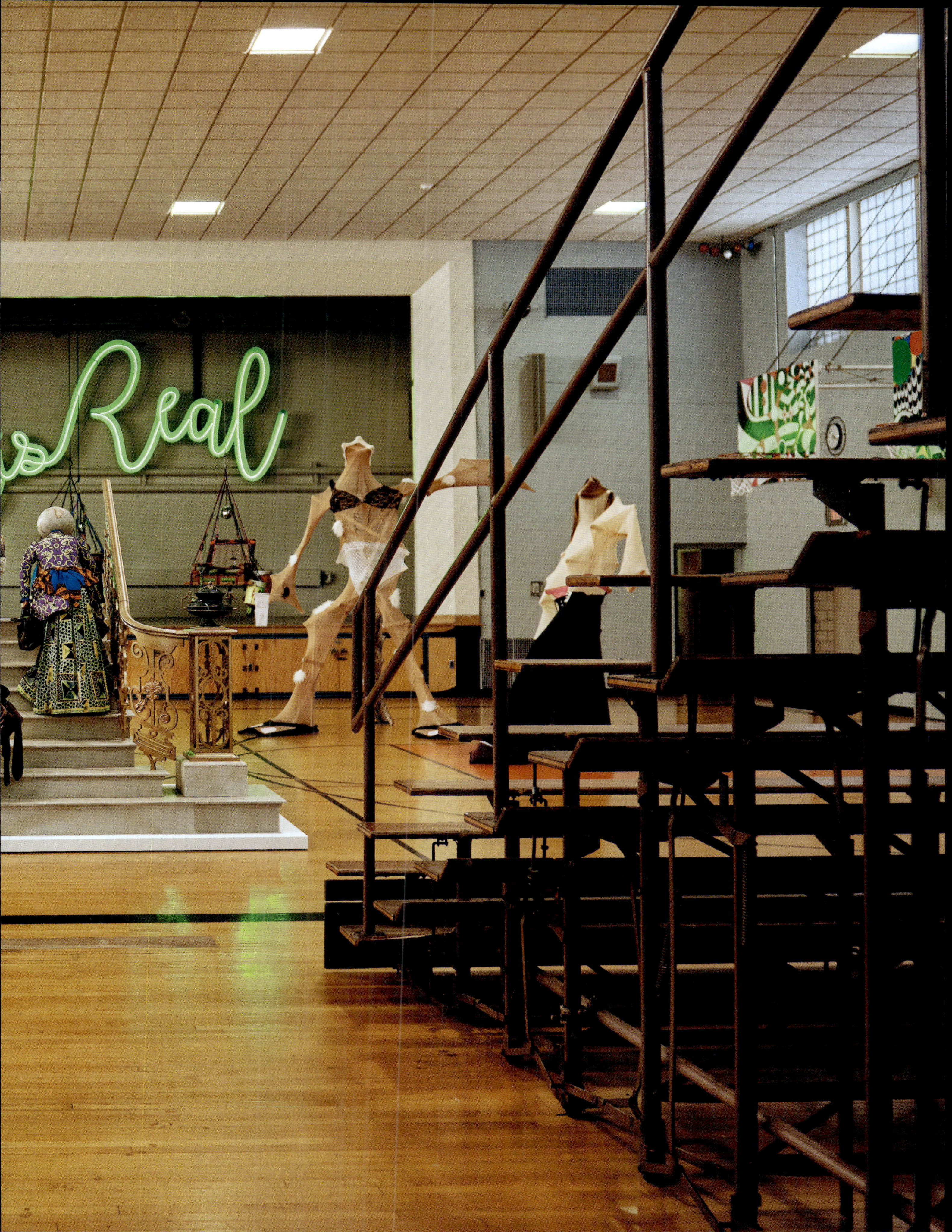
Real

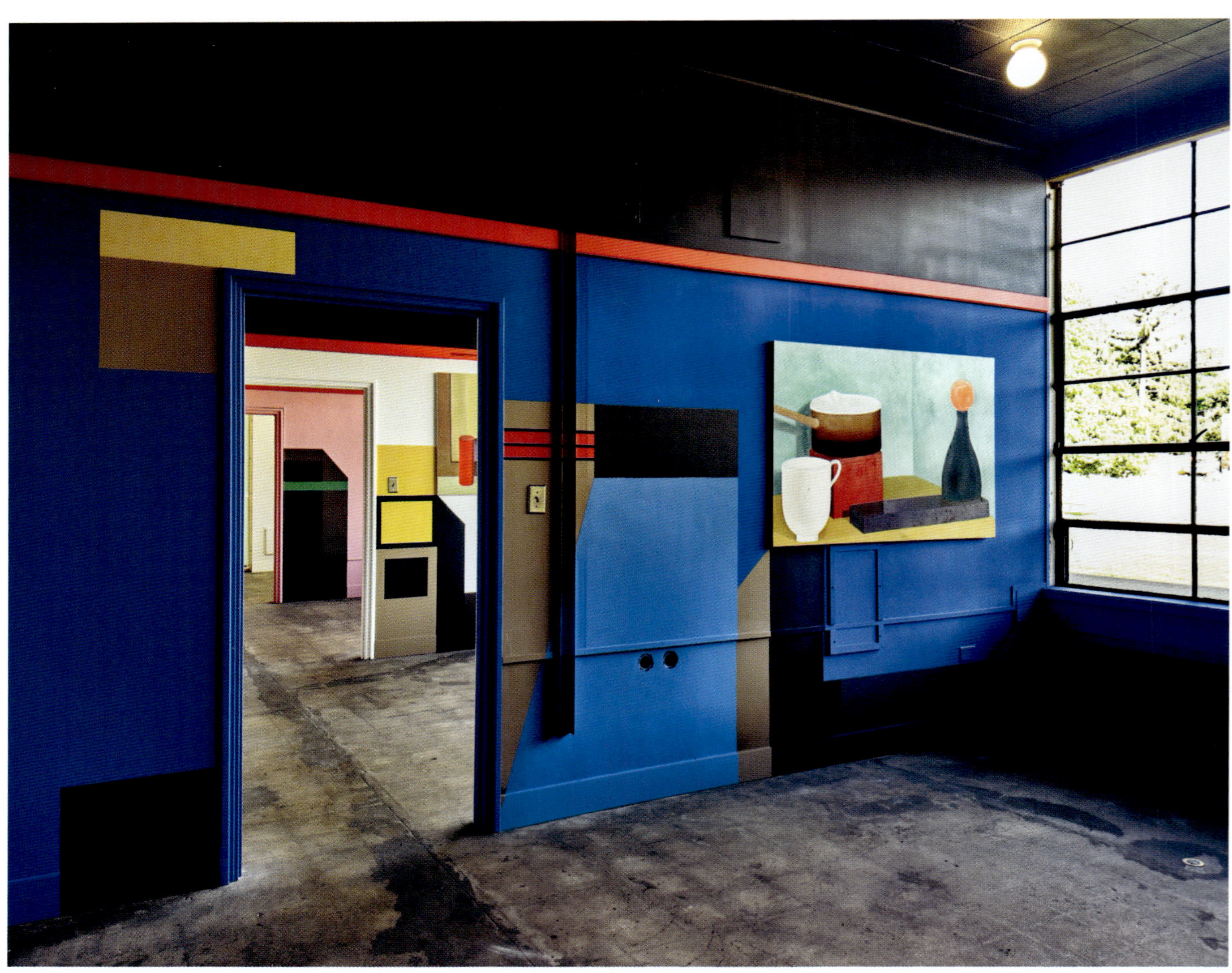

above
Nathalie Du Pasquier's *Untitled* (2007) is exhibited on a wall painting also made by the artist.

opposite, top
Gallery 13: A diptych painting by Jutta Koether titled *HMTQ/DCMG 2* (2015) was displayed back to back.

opposite, bottom
Galleries 20–21: Adrian Armstrong is a Cohort 05 alumni of NXTHVN's studio fellowship. His work, *A Gathering of the Congregation, Austin, TX Chapter* (2024), is a mixed-media piece. The work is displayed on a floating half wall that is a new addition to the site. Jamaal Peterman is also a Cohort 05 alumni; his work, *This Is America* (2023), is shown on a back wall of the former classroom. These rooms were curated by Marquita Flowers and Clare Patrick, both recipients of the NXTHVN's curatorial fellowships.

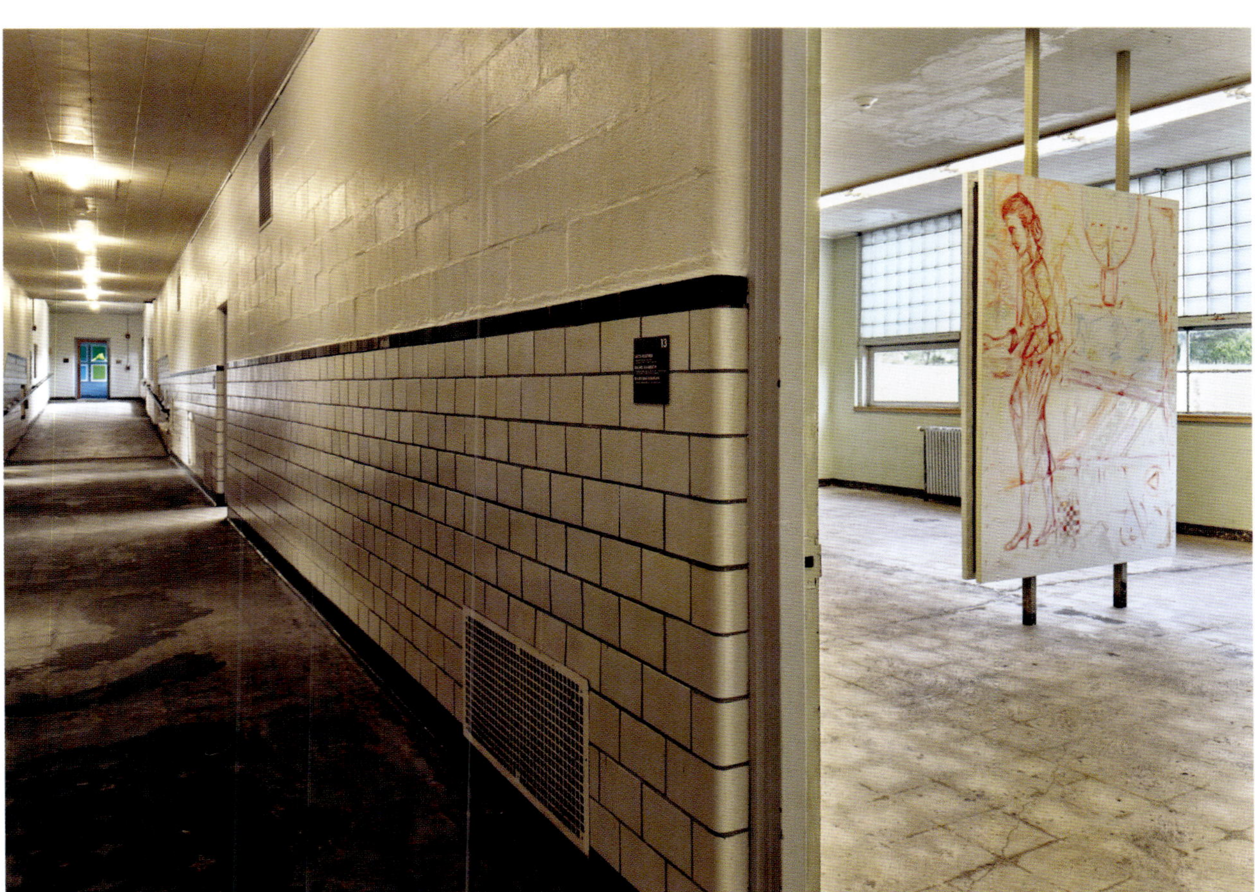

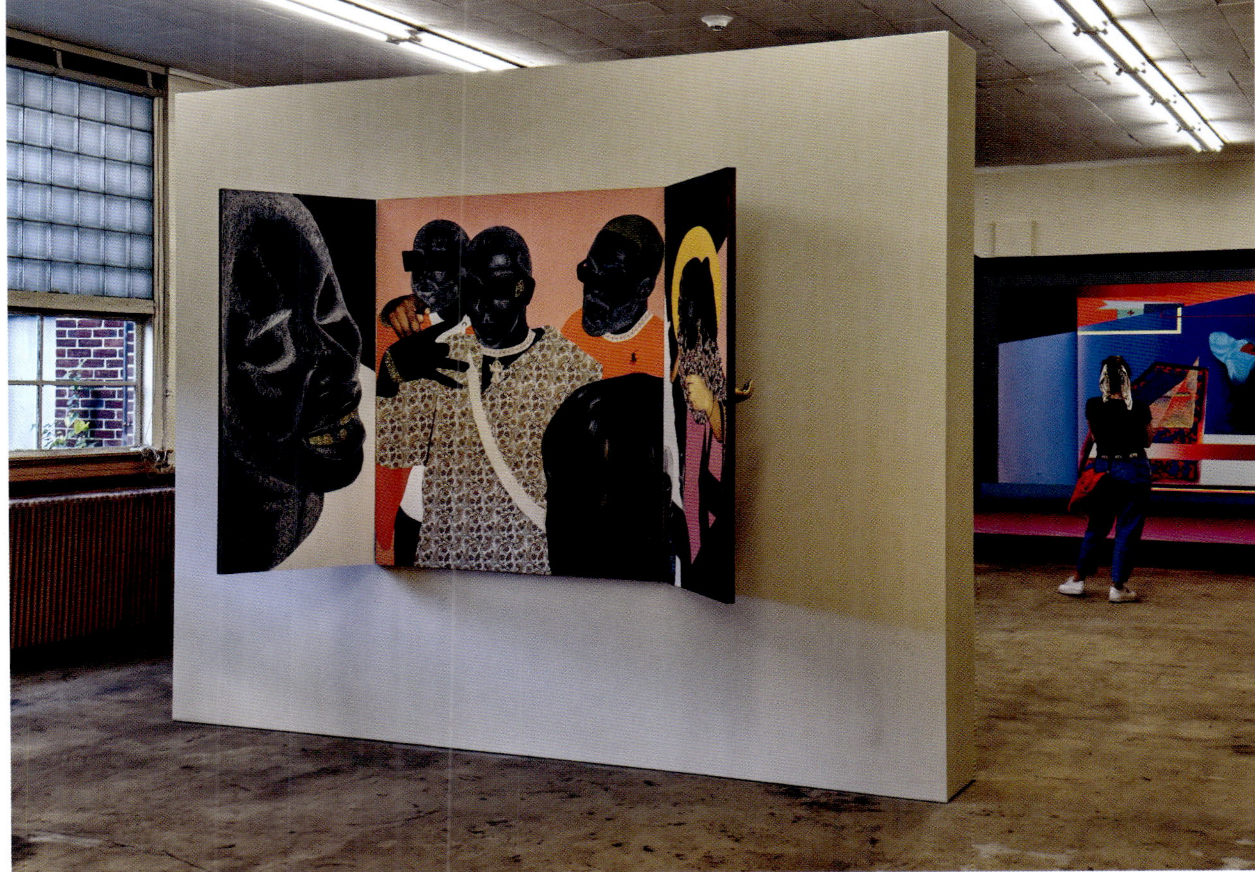

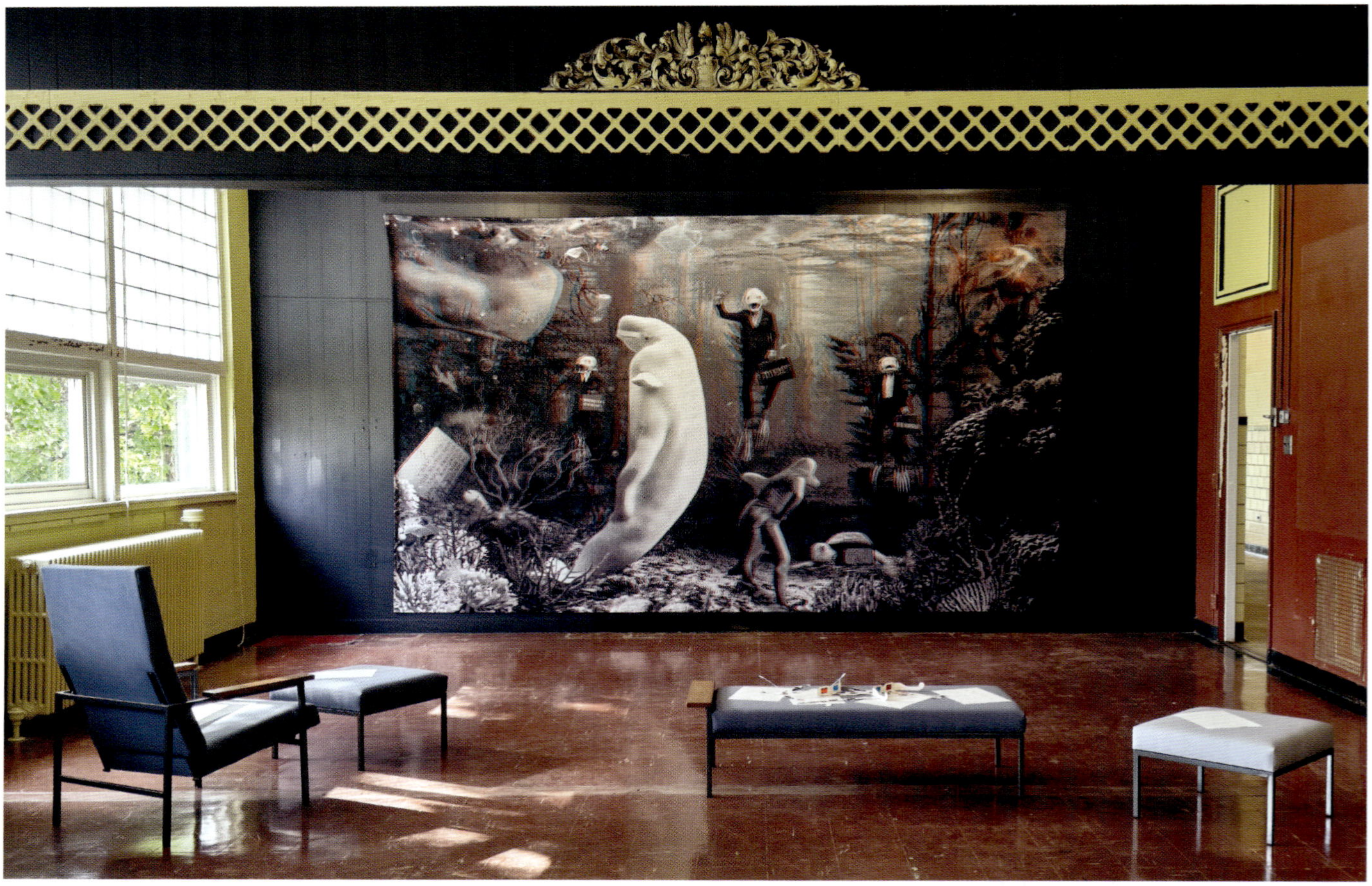

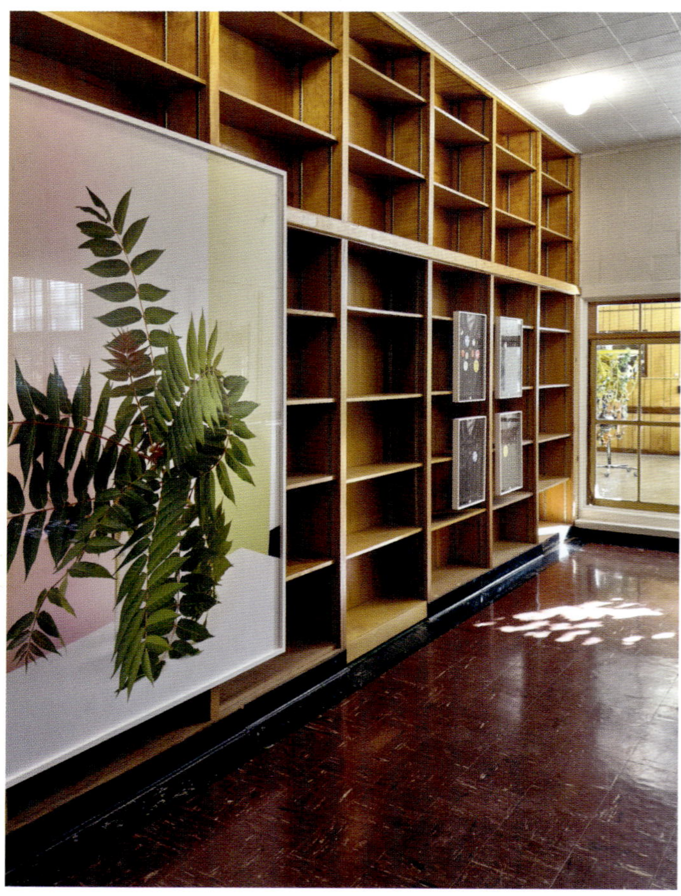

above
Goshka Macuga's work includes the woven 3D tapestry *Who Gave Us a Sponge to Erase the Horizon?* (2022) and four custom-made furnishings, *Declaration of Law of Insects (IMPTBC)* (2012), *I* (2012), *Seat for a Polish MP* (2012), and *Not Everything I See Is Art* (2012).

right
Sumach / Essigbaum (2023), an archival pigment print by Annette Kelm, hangs against empty bookshelves of the former library.

opposite
Sonic Lunar Eclipse Type K—Medium Ultralight #28 (2014), a sculpture by Haegue Yang, hangs between the science lab stations.

overleaf
A courtyard garden between buildings has been used as a site for Erika Verzutti's bronze sculpture *Venus of Cream* (2020).

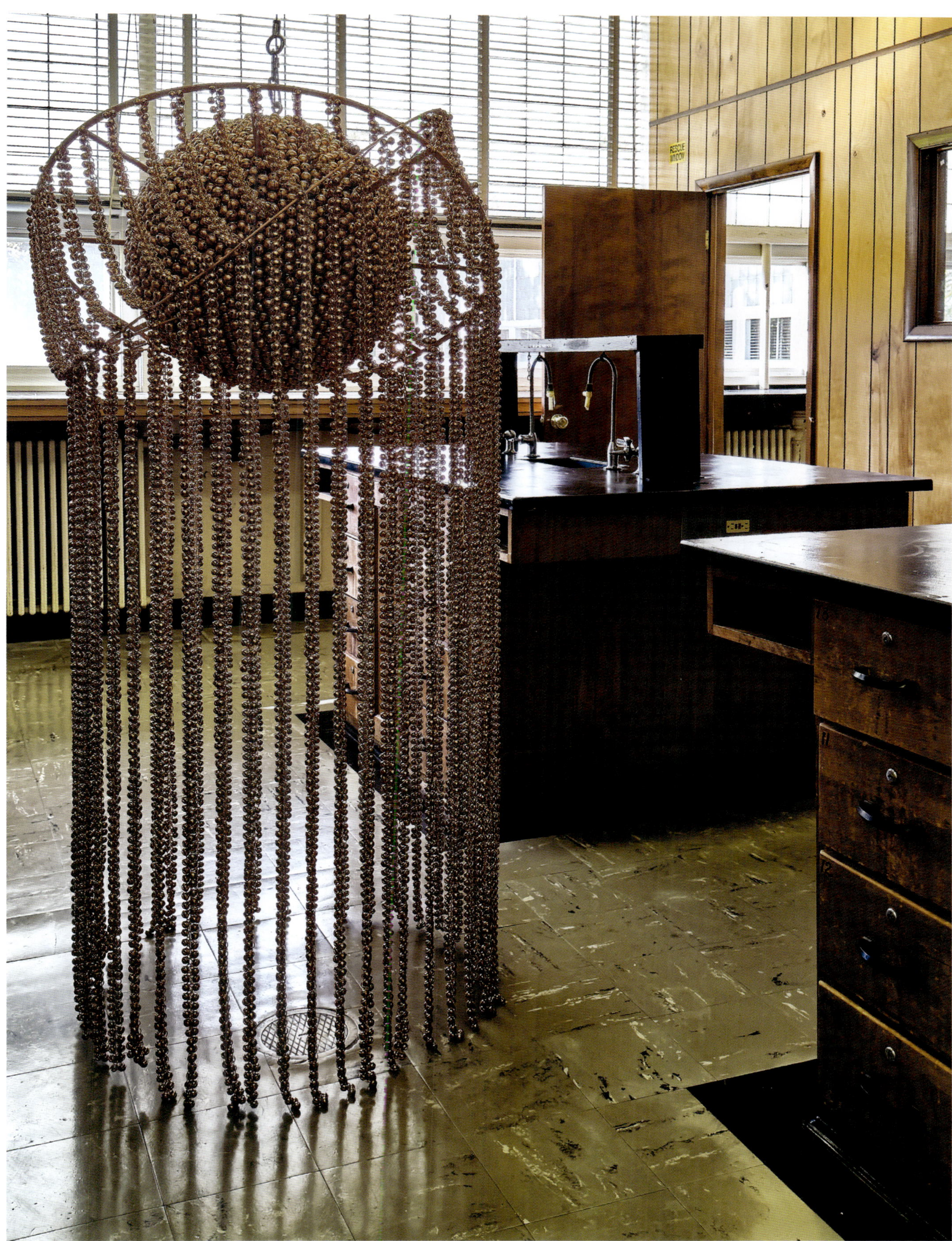
RESCUE

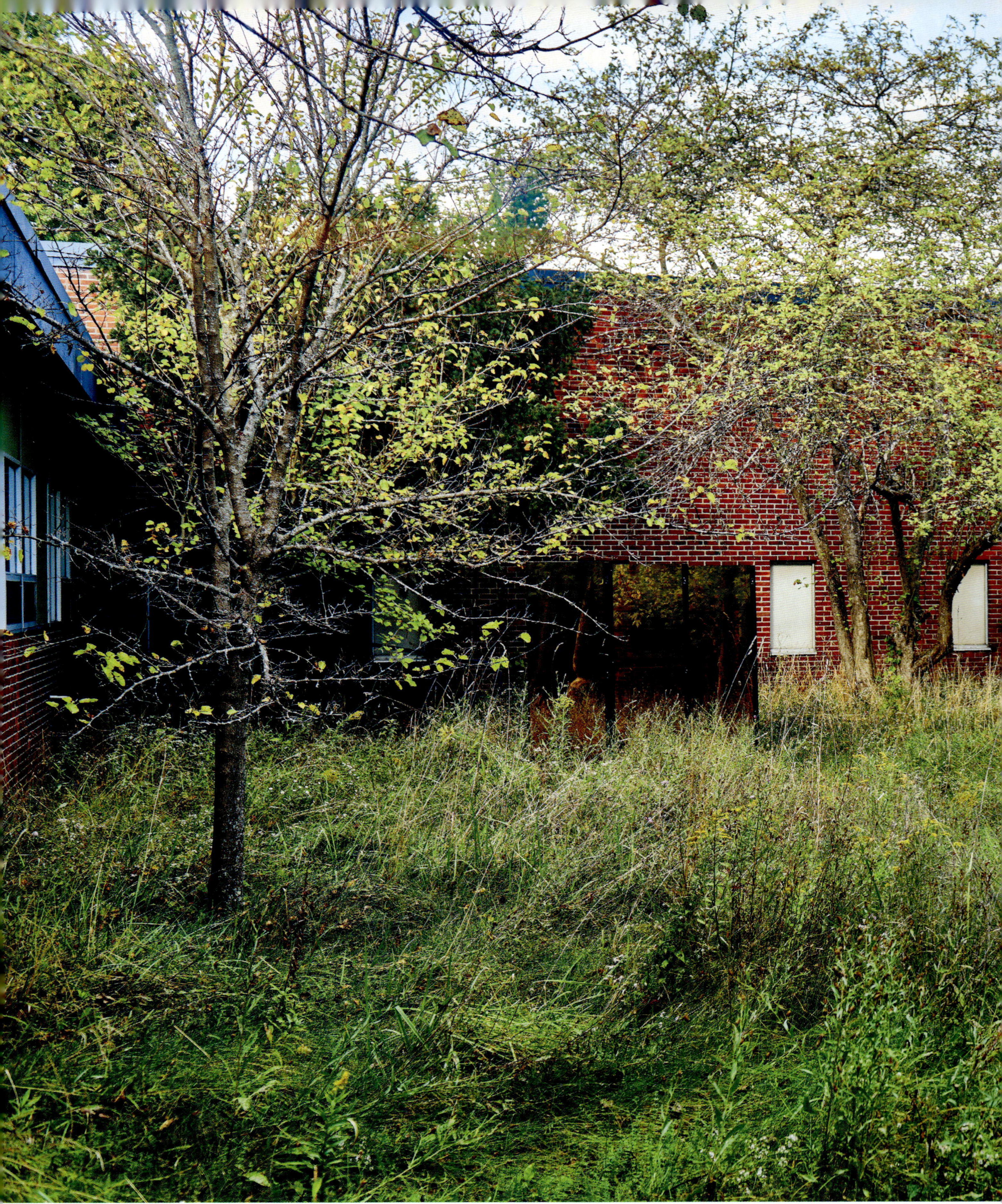

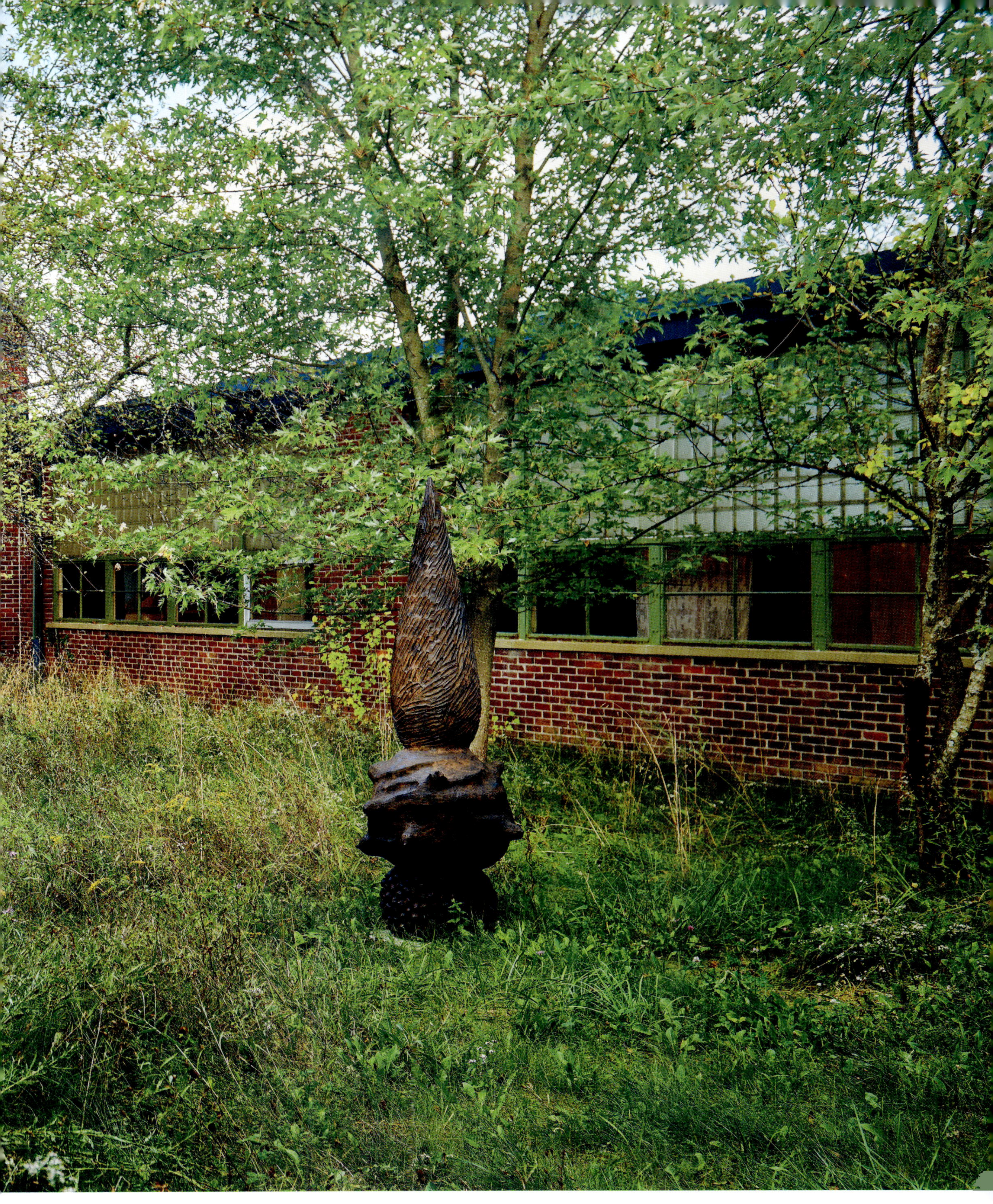

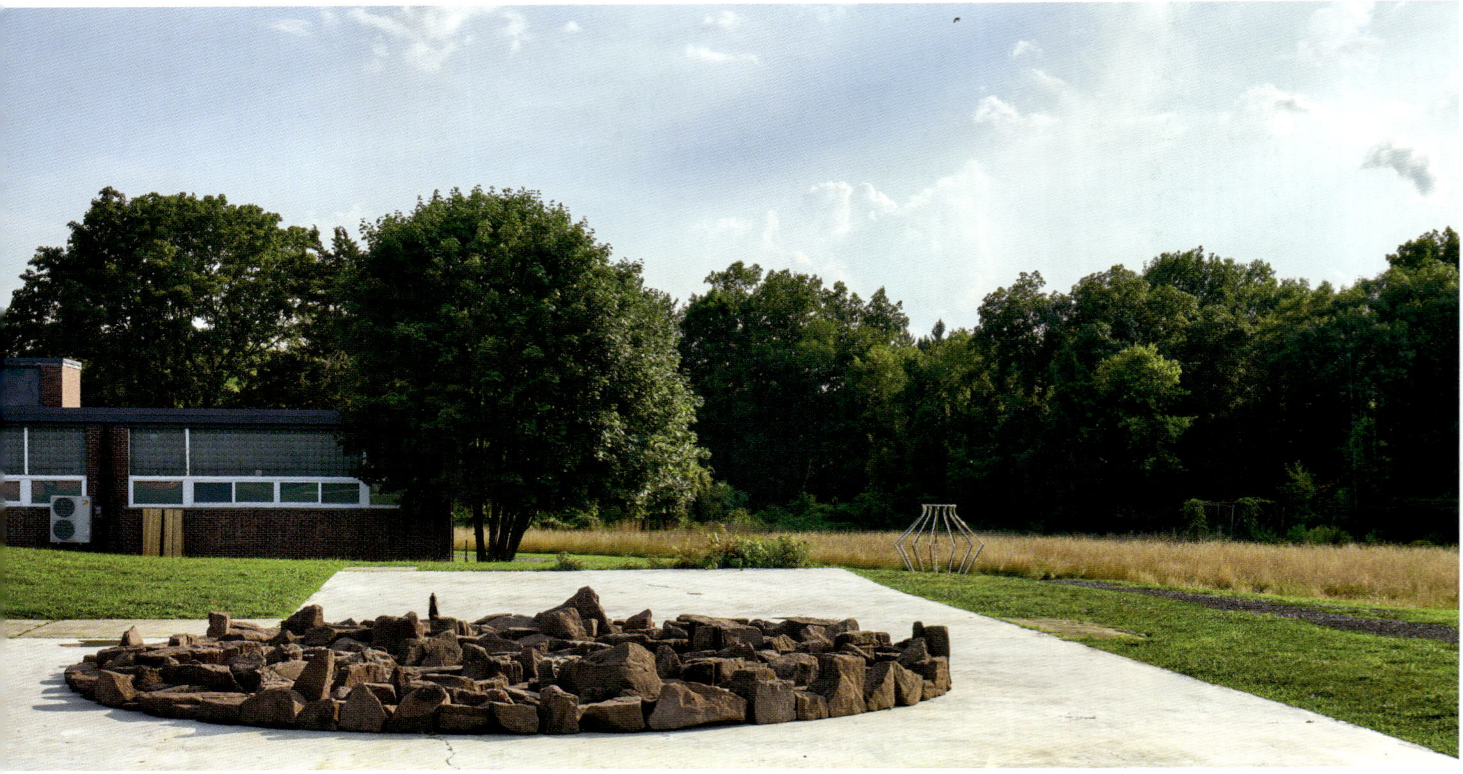

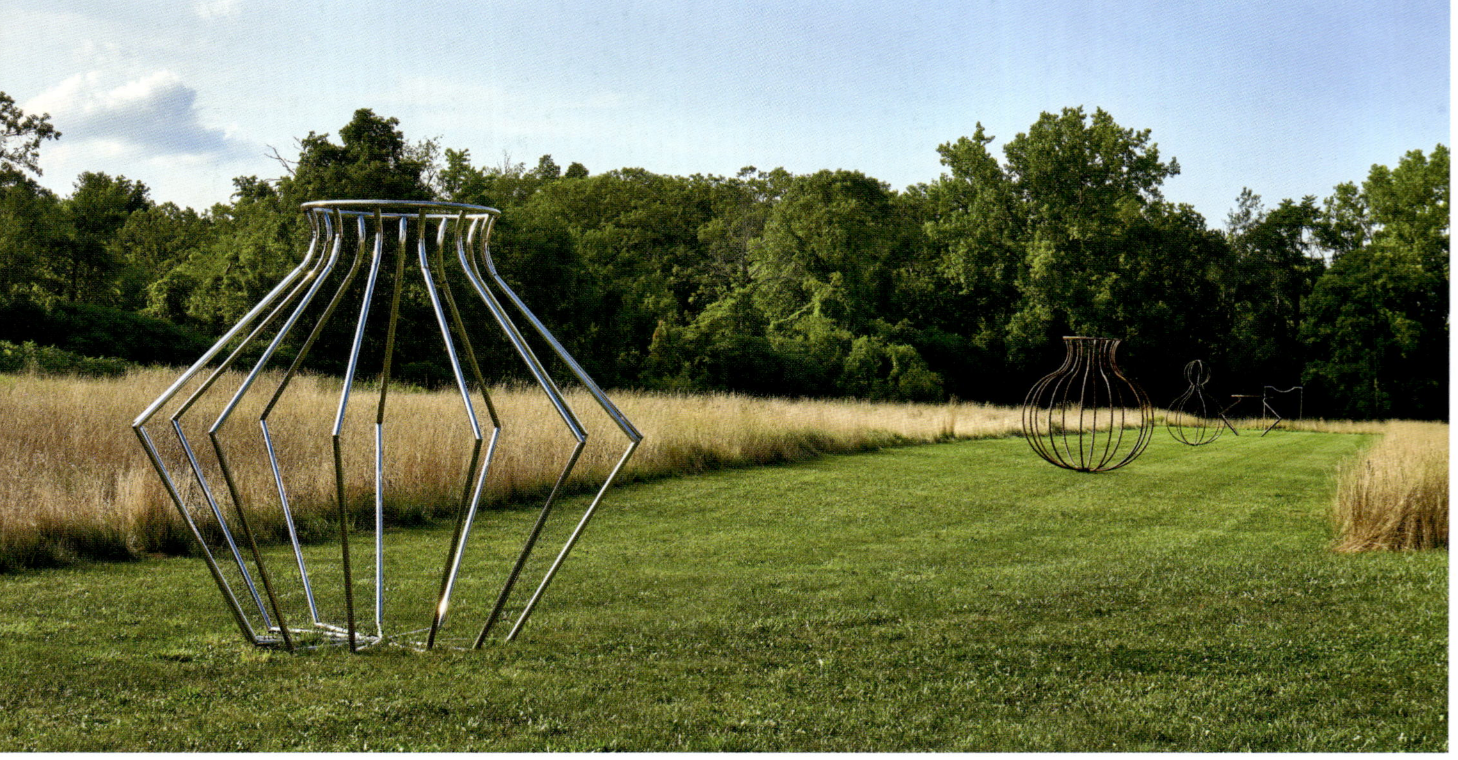

top
Richard Long's *Brownstone Circle* (2000) is one of the artist's major works on view on the Campus's grounds.

bottom
A row of sculptures by Maren Hassinger, titled *Vessel 1* (2022), *Vessel 3* (2022), *Vessel 8* (2022), *Vessel 9* (2022), and *Vessel 10* (2022), are installed across a field behind the school.

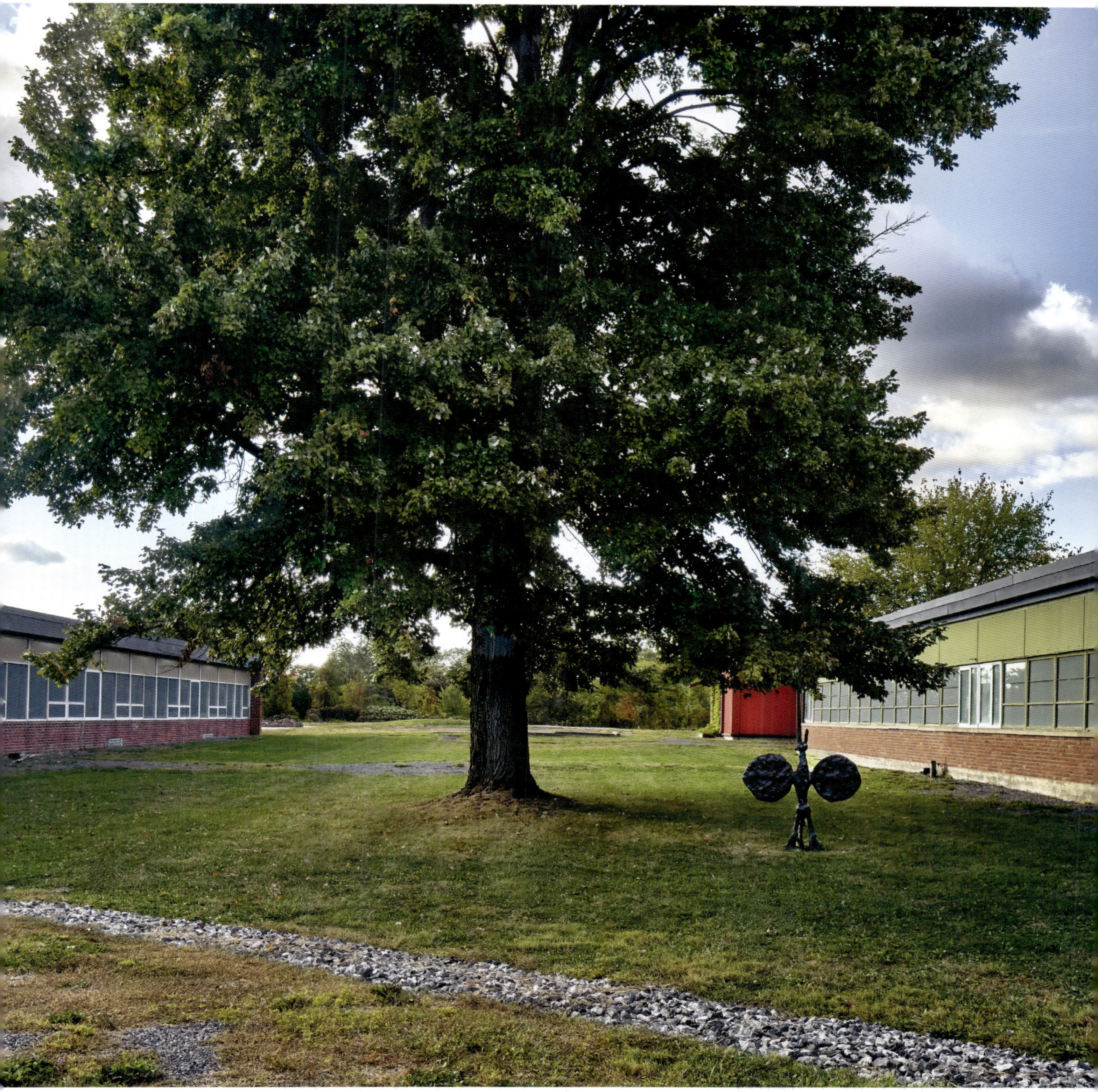

Fledermäuse (2020), a bronze sculpture by Danish artist Tal R, was placed under the large maple tree and is also seen from inside the galleries.

Private Public Gallery

Hudson, New York

Christopher Freeman took three years to transform the former Ohav Sholem Synagogue, built in 1865, into a home and gallery. The building had a commercial past too. It had been Woodman's Hall, a men's boxing and meeting club; a secret dance hall in the 1920s and '30s; and a plumbing and heating company's office. It is located one street over from Warren Street, Hudson's main street.

In 2005, Chris, who is an artist, designer, builder, and now gallerist, was looking for a place to live. He and a friend, Laura Powers, decided to purchase the property together. Eventually, they bought the houses next door too. They created two living spaces in the building: a ground-level loft for Chris and a top-floor apartment for Laura. In 2021, Chris and his partner, Matthew McNamara, fixed up their living space to accommodate their new family. They also added a gallery, where Chris could show other artists' work and create his own paintings. He named it Private Public Gallery, and the inaugural exhibition opened in September 2021.

Private Public Gallery has established an active and varied program, from an installation of Donna Dennis's immersive work to Stephen Maine's colorful abstract paintings. Chris, Matthew, and their daughter, Roxanne, have created an inviting home. Artists from the gallery and Chris and Matthew's paintings fill the walls. Dinners after openings usually take place at their dining room table or in the courtyard. Chris says, "When we opened the doors of the gallery, suddenly there were hundreds of artists in our lives. My life has completely opened up. Our house has become a center where [the] community [of artists] meet one another."

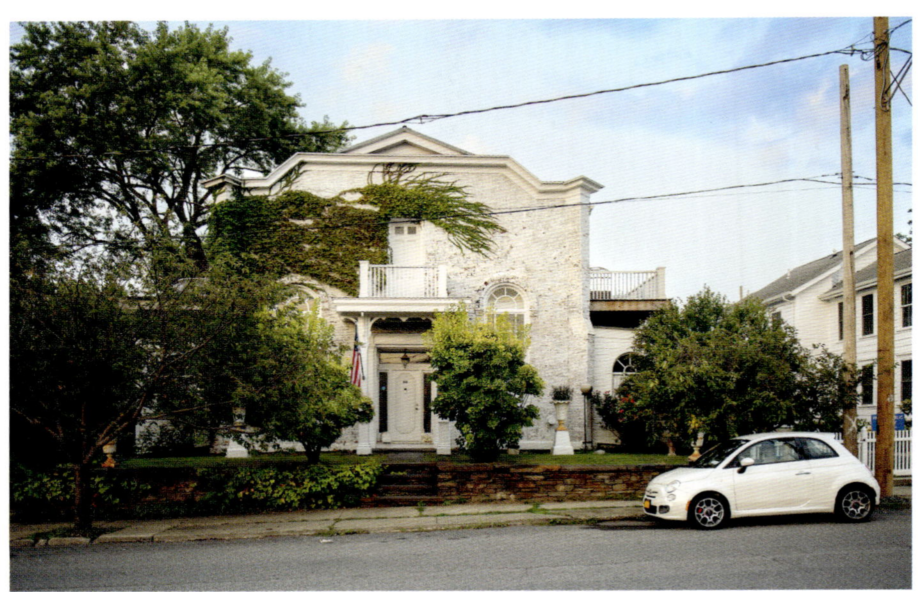

above
The front entryway was updated with columns and a small Juliet balcony above. The front yard was landscaped with steps and a rock wall. The original windows with the brick arch cornices were restored.

opposite
Urns filled with flowers, a white picket fence, and a smoke bush tree add color against the white facade. The garden and landscaping took a couple of years to complete.

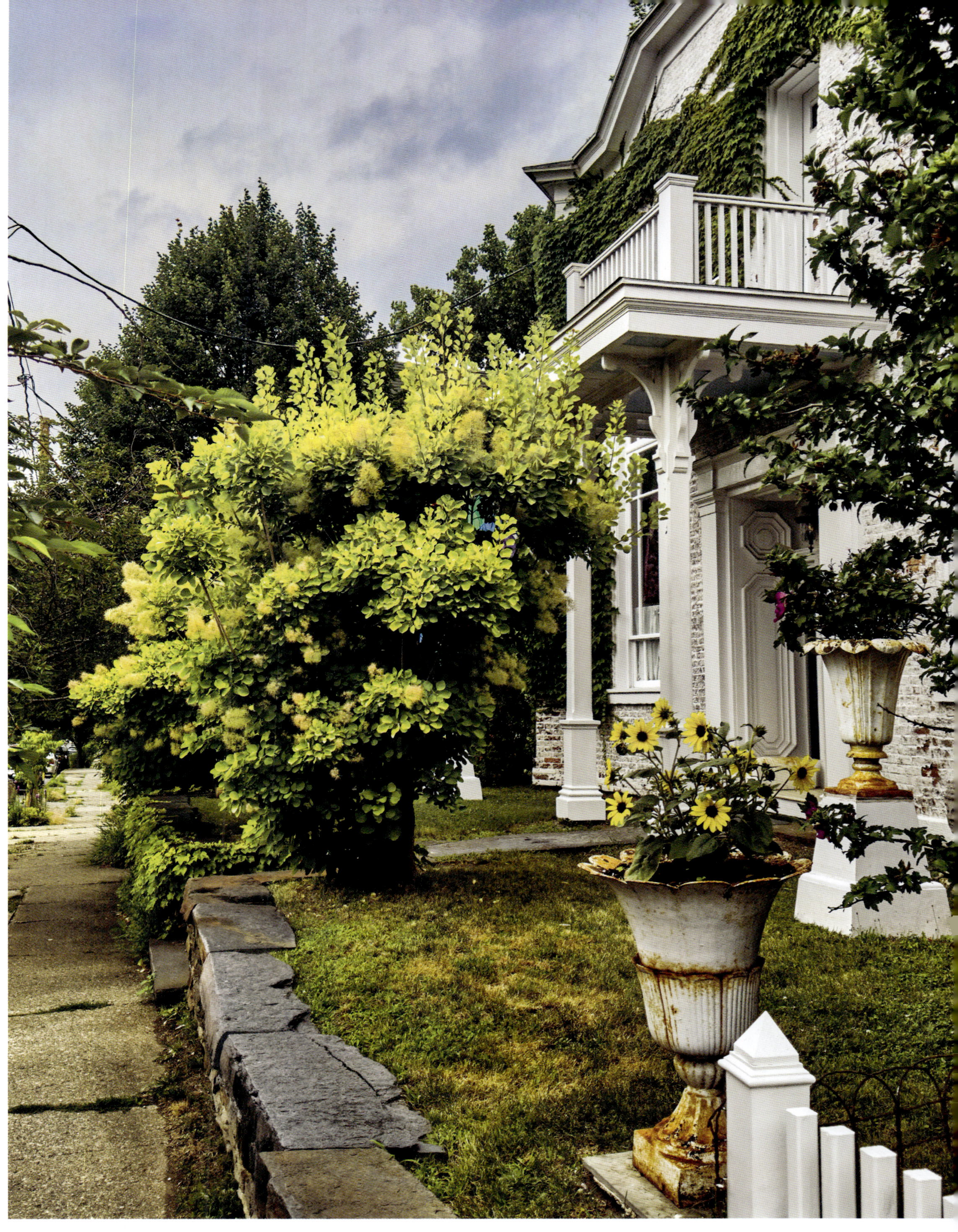

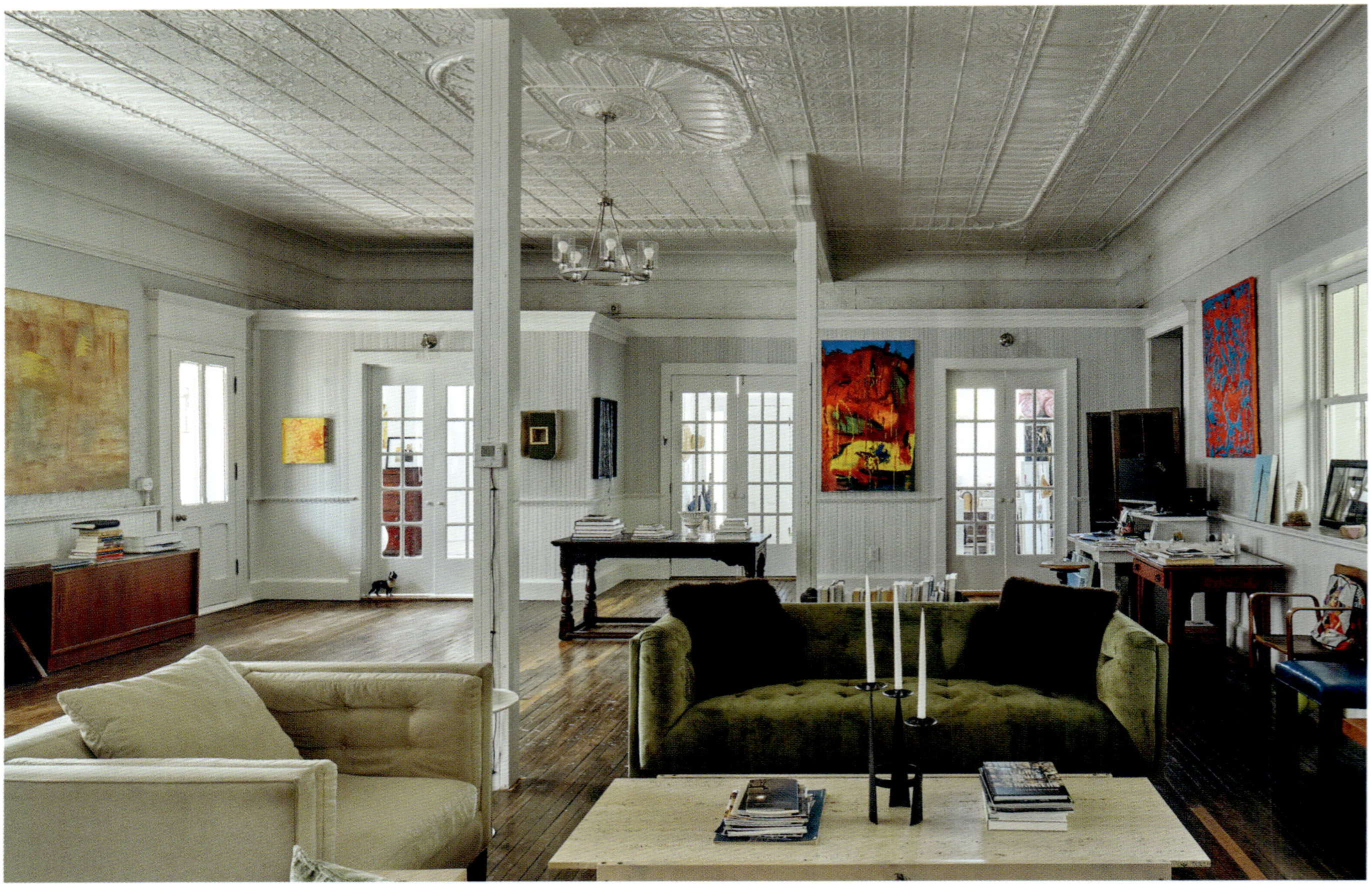

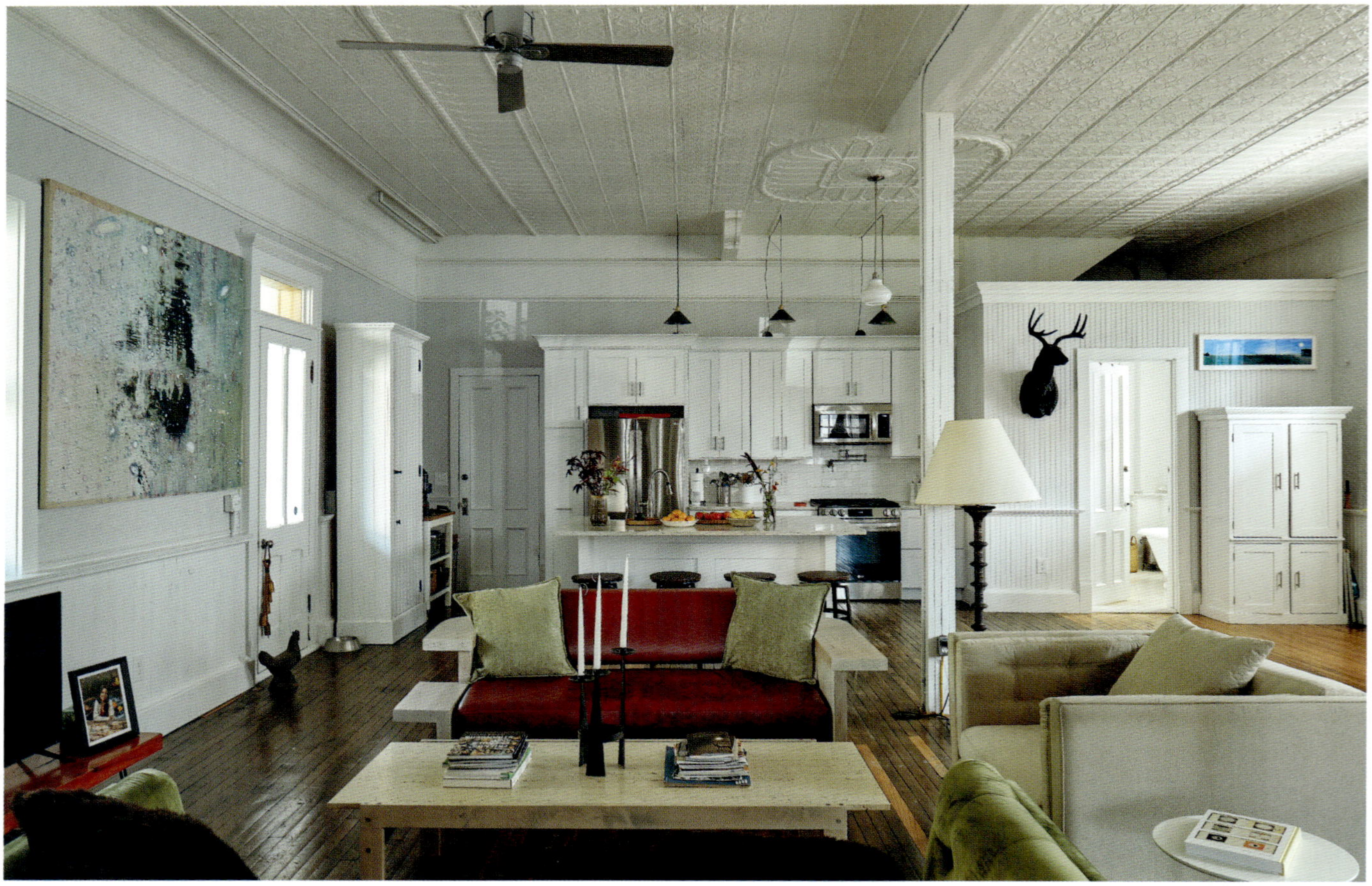

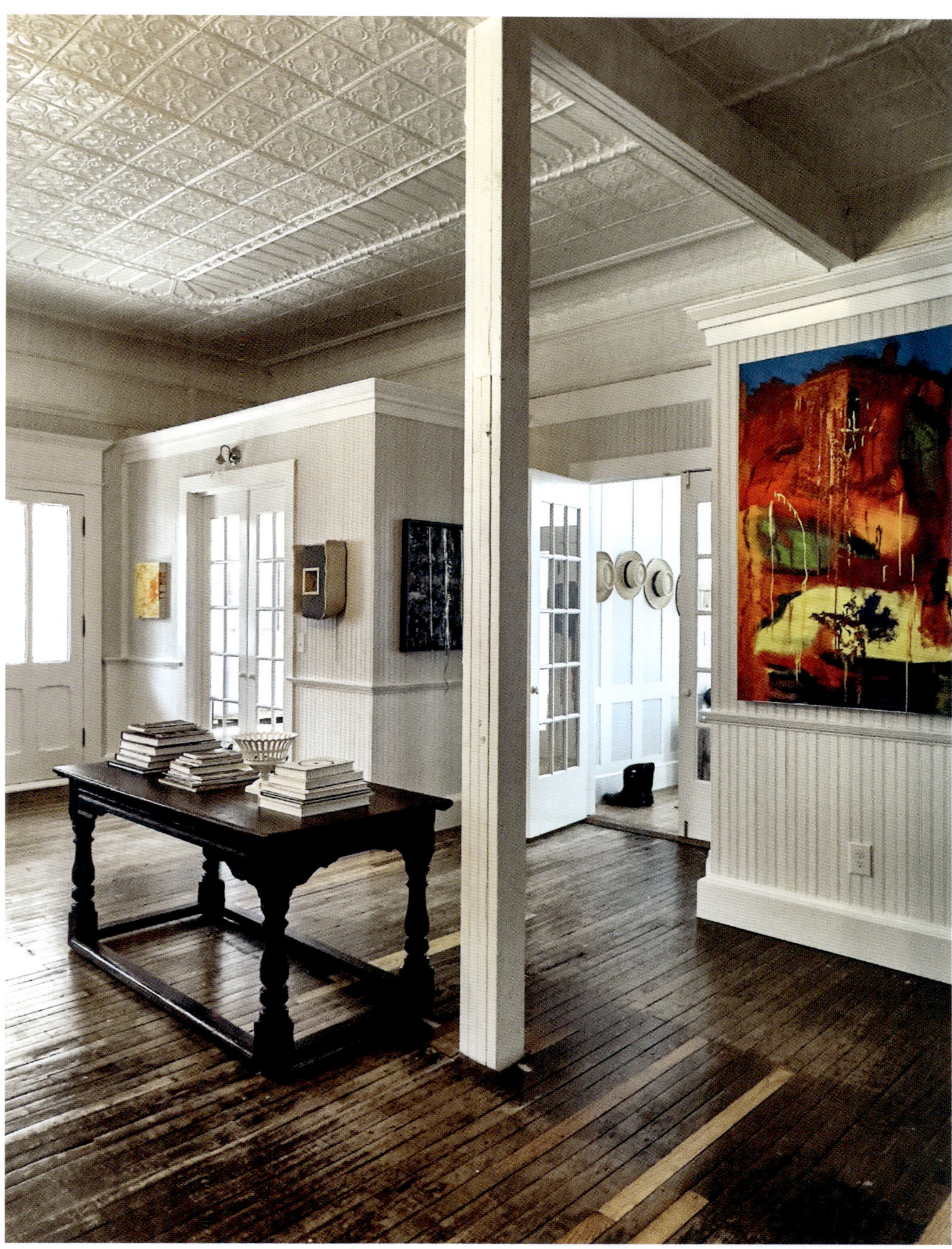

opposite, top
The interior feels like a combination of a classic New York City loft and a gallery. The open plan has no walls between the living, dining, and kitchen areas, only structural columns. Paintings of all sizes hang around the room; from left to right, Deborah Darcy's *The Conversation* (2024), by the door, is across from *Untitled* (1994), one of Chris's works. A small painting titled *Inverted Reverse Painting* (2022) by Howard Schwartzberg hangs opposite Matthew's *Desert Landscape* (2003). *P24-0221* (2024), a painting by Stephen Maine, is also installed in the space.

opposite, bottom
Looking toward the kitchen, seating is in the center of the space. Natural light permeates the room from the windows and doors on both sides. Heide Fasnacht's painting *Echo River (O Pioneers)* (2023–2024) hangs by the door to one of the side terraces. Donna Denis's *Ship and Dock* (2018) was placed above a cabinet.

above
The entrance hallway and bedrooms have French doors, which allow light into the center of the living and dining area. Matthew's *Desert Landscape* (2003) stands out against the white interior. The tin ceiling and hickory floorboards were installed when the building became the Woodman's Hall, a men's boxing club and meeting space.

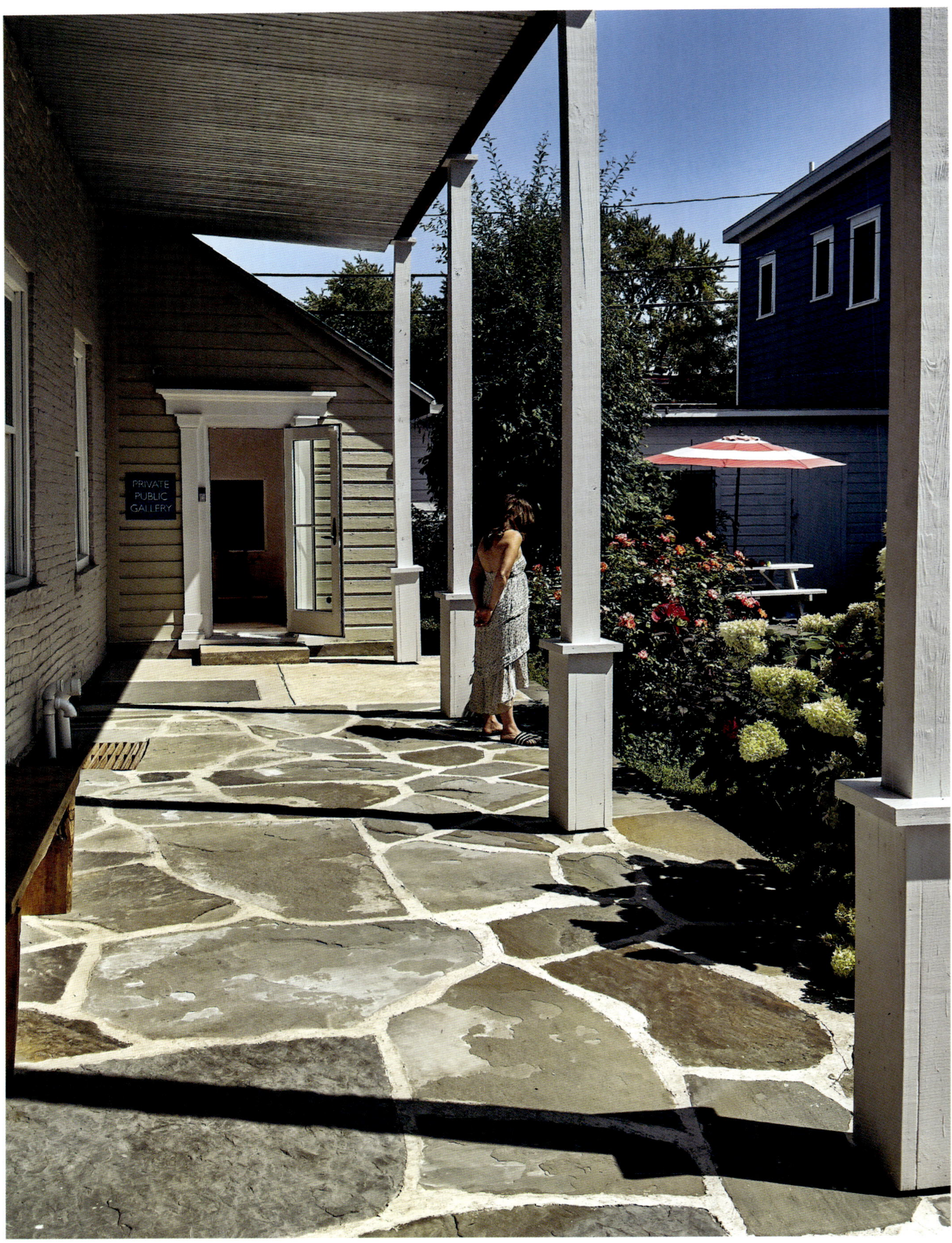
PRIVATE
PUBLIC
GALLERY

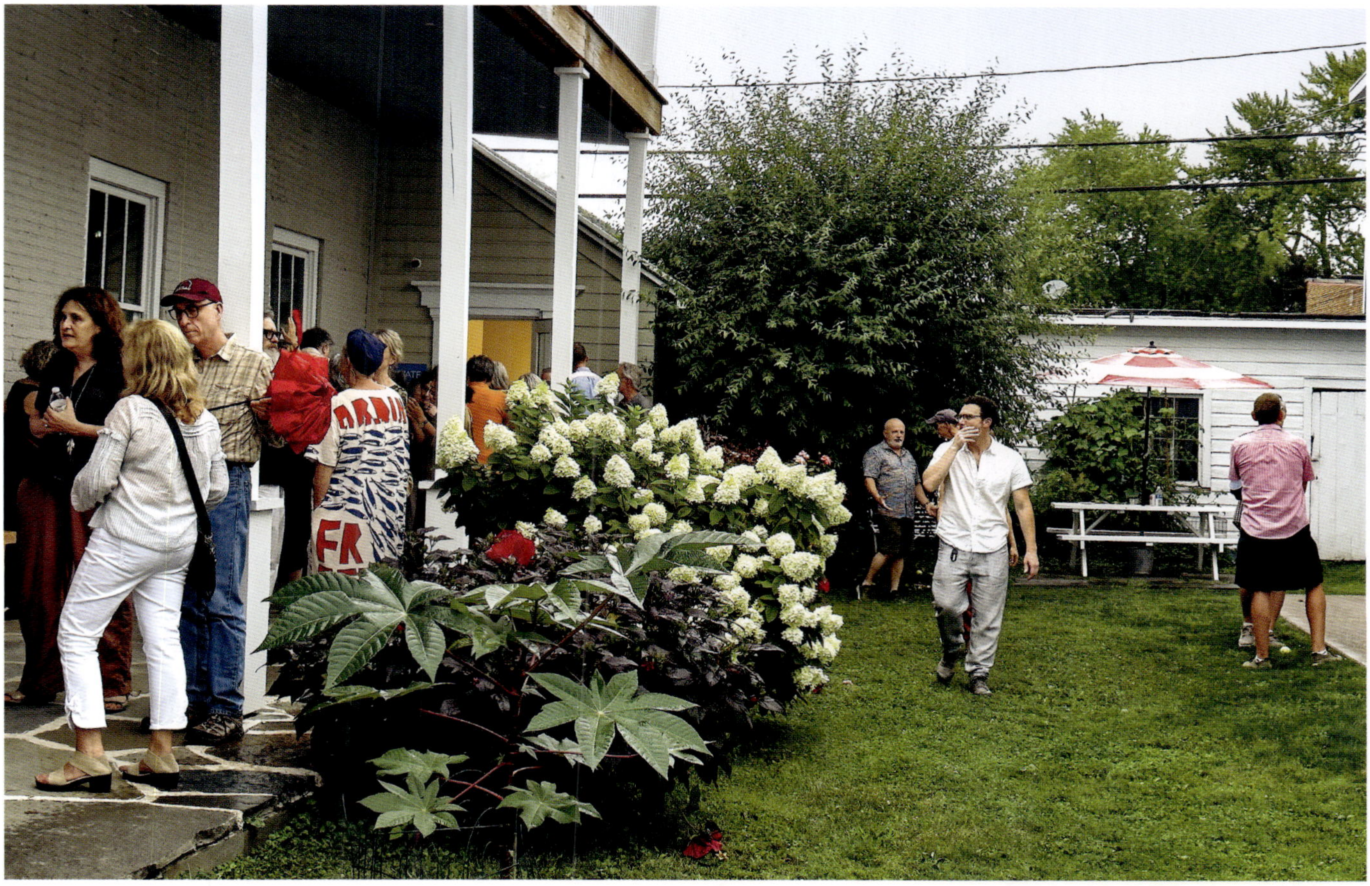

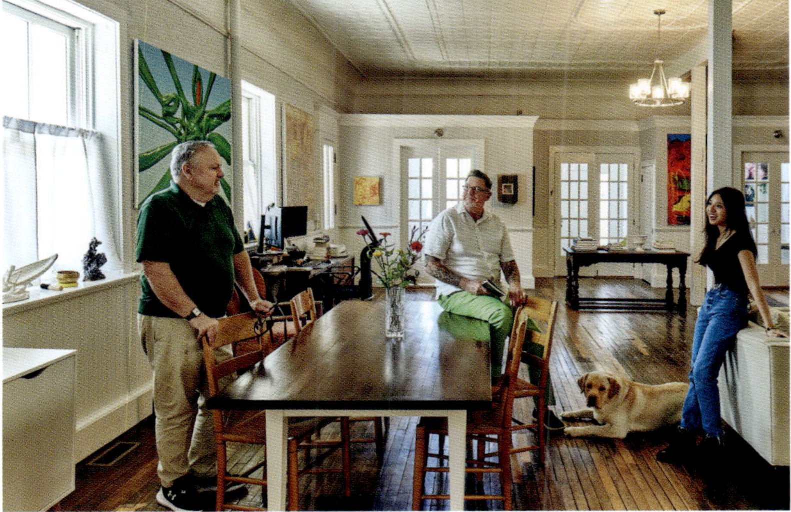

opposite
A stone path leads to the gallery entrance.

top
Gallery-goers congregate after an opening. Chris added the two porticos, one on each side, to the old building, originally a synagogue. At certain times of the day, they provide shade for the path and protection from the sun. Chris created a shared courtyard lawn between his home, the gallery, and the other rental properties.

bottom
Chris, Matthew, Roxanne, and their dog, Teddy, gather around the dining room table. This room also has become a gathering place for artists after the gallery openings. Alexander Ross's painting *Untitled (Green Knot)* (2012) was installed near the table.

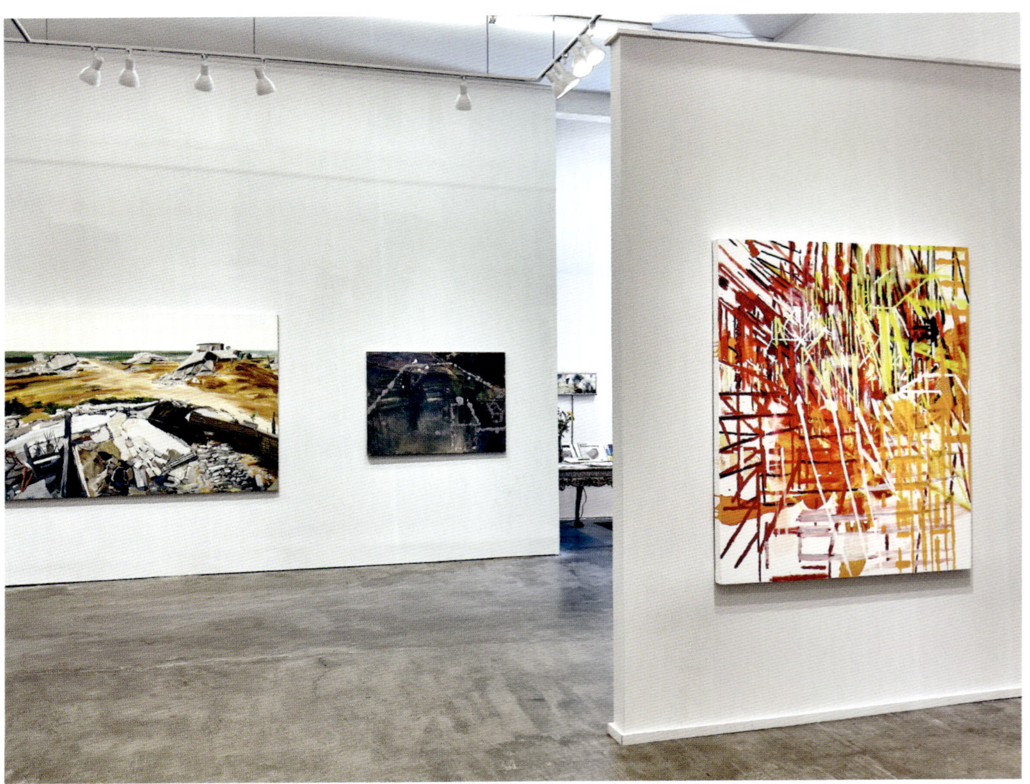

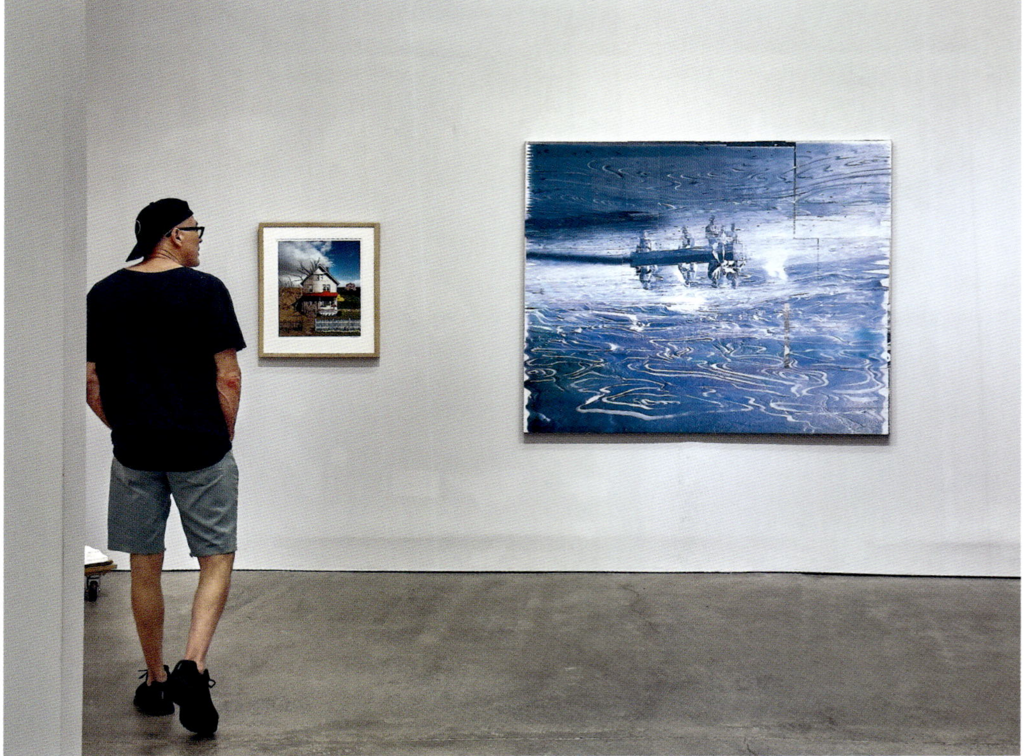

top
Chris designed the gallery to be a flexible space. He changes the interior half walls' configuration as required for an exhibition. Noa Charuvi's *Tel* (2009) and Hanneline Røgeberg's *In the Field I* (2017) are shown on a permanent exterior wall, while Kylie Heidenheimer's *Skye* (2019) is displayed on a temporary half wall.

bottom
From left to right: James Casebere's *Cloudy/Sunny Skies* (2013) is shown next to Heide Fasnacht's mixed-media piece, *Echo River (Slip Stream)* (2023).

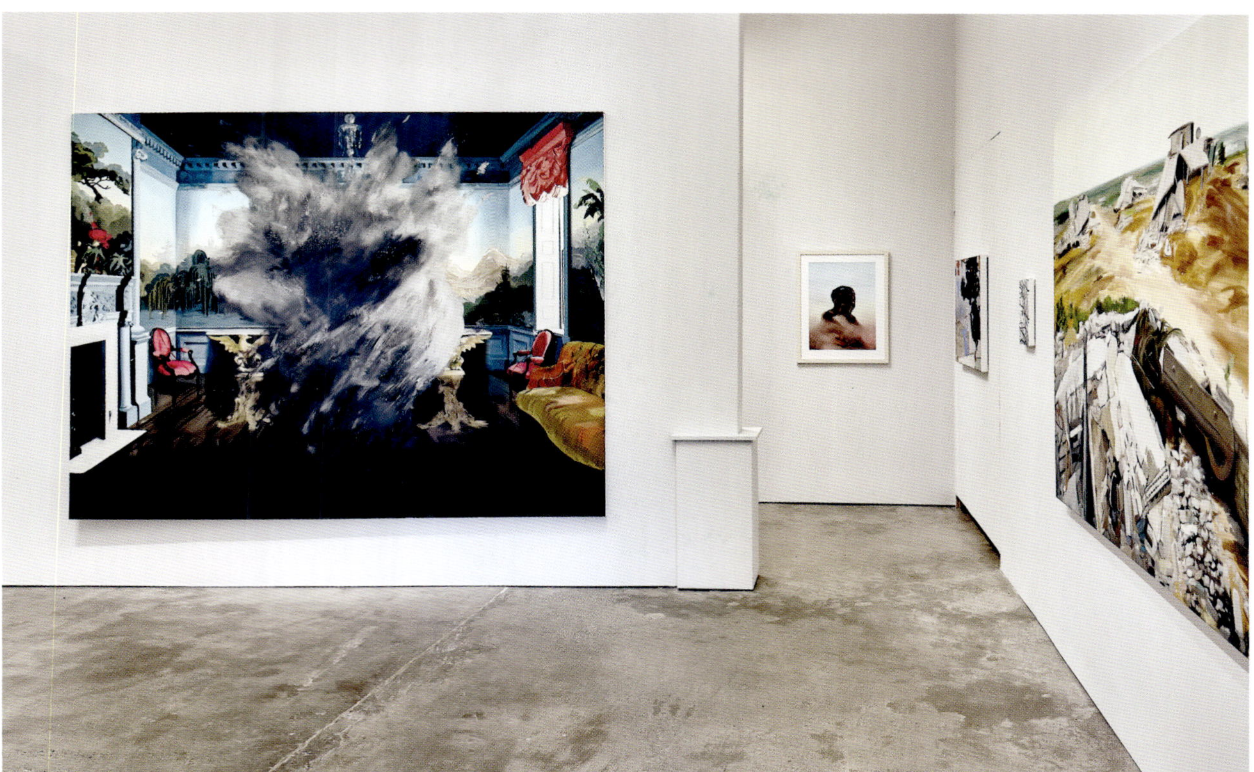

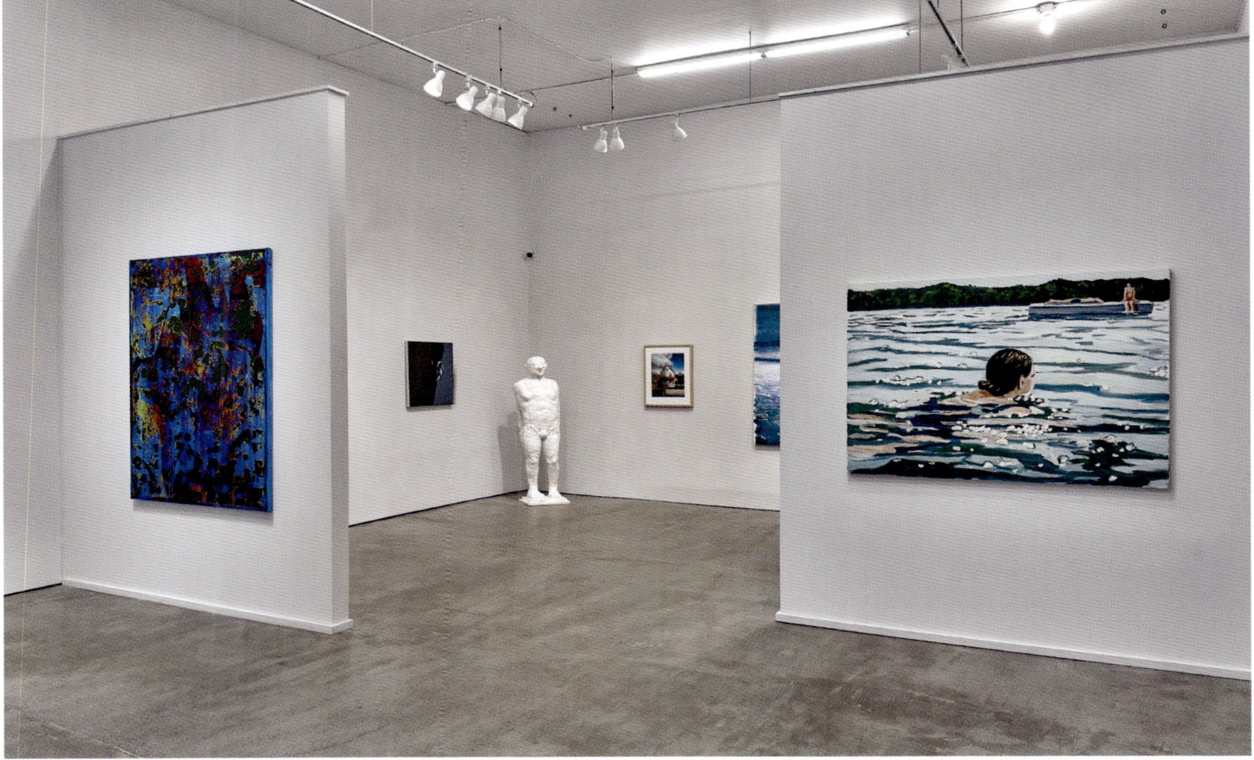

top
In the summer of 2024, Private Public Gallery presented *The Summer Disaster Show 2*. Works included, from left to right, Melora Kuhn's *El Dorado* (2014, 2020), Viktor Witkowski's *Figure (10)* (2019), and Noa Charuvi's *Tel* (2009).

bottom
Bruce Gagnier's sculpture titled *Citizen* (2022) stands in the back corner of the gallery. Two half walls show Stephen Maine's painting *P24-0402* (2024) on the left and Richard Bosman's *Raft* (2002).

Bobbie Oliver and Frank Kitchens

Long Eddy, New York

Some thirty years ago, New York City–based painter Bobbie Oliver and her husband, Frank Kitchens, a former chef and bakery owner, were looking for a weekend retreat upstate. They had certain criteria in mind: a close distance to the city and a large space for a studio for Bobbie. With the help of a local real estate agent, they found a one-hundred-year-old church in Long Eddy that was being offered for sale by the Methodist Church. The building had some damage, including to the steeple, so Bobbie and Frank went about restoring the property. In their restoration of the church, they left as many original details as possible. They never winterized it, choosing to use it as a summer place. Instead, when the Grange, a building next door that had been used as a community center and a hunting lodge, became available, they bought that property, adding insulation and heat. They created a studio for Bobbie on the second floor.

Walking through the front door and along a narrow hallway, the space opens to a large sitting room, formerly the sanctuary of the church. On the first floor are the living and dining rooms, kitchen, a guest bedroom and bathroom, and a corner office. Folding wooden doors separate the living areas from the kitchen. During the renovation, storage cabinets were also added. The moldings on soaring 21-foot-high ceilings were painted in contrasting yellow. Bobbie and Frank added a back door to the area that was once a knave. An outdoor patio is now a few steps away. In the summer, a large dappled willow at the back door attracts dozen of birds, including hummingbirds.

Many people who live in historic or old buildings often have deep feelings of responsibility for the place. They see their role as stewards or guardians of a particular time or history. Bobbie and Frank loved the process of rescuing these two historical buildings. And in the meantime, over the years, they've also built a close relationship to the community of neighbors and friends.

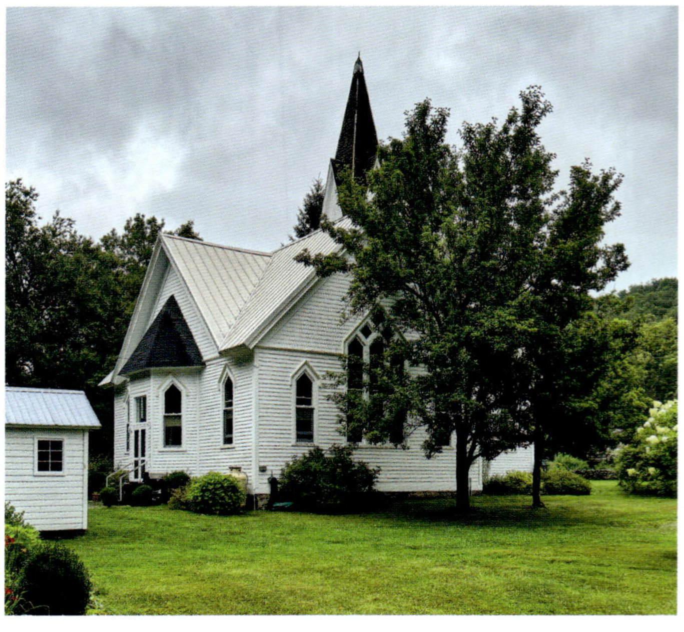

right and opposite
The process of converting the 1893 church into a summer residence started in 1993. The exterior has remained the same in the renovation. Bobbie and Frank spent their first year's budget repairing the damaged steeple. Driving along the country road, no one would guess the church is now a home. The bell in the belfry was removed to the schoolhouse down the road.

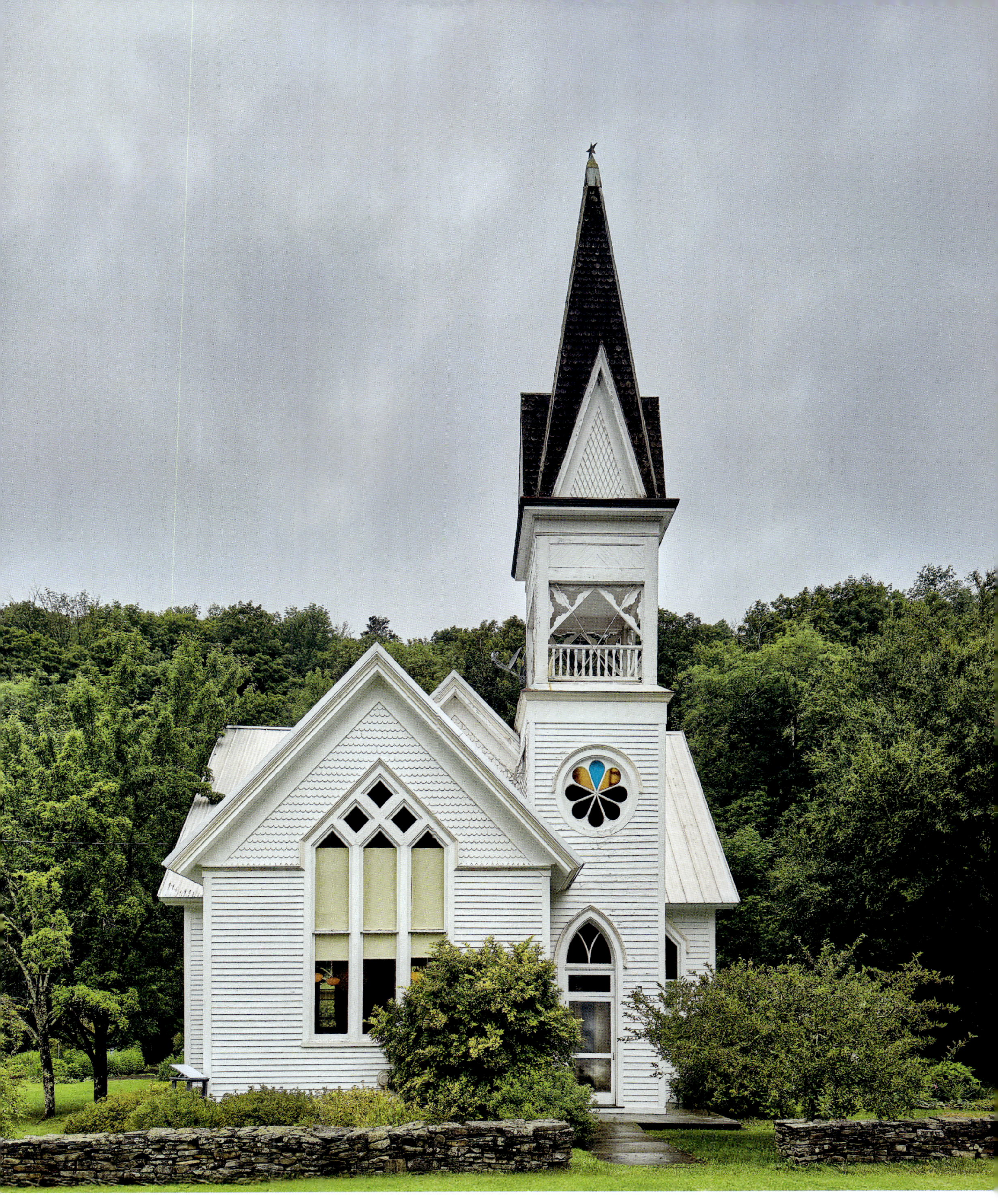

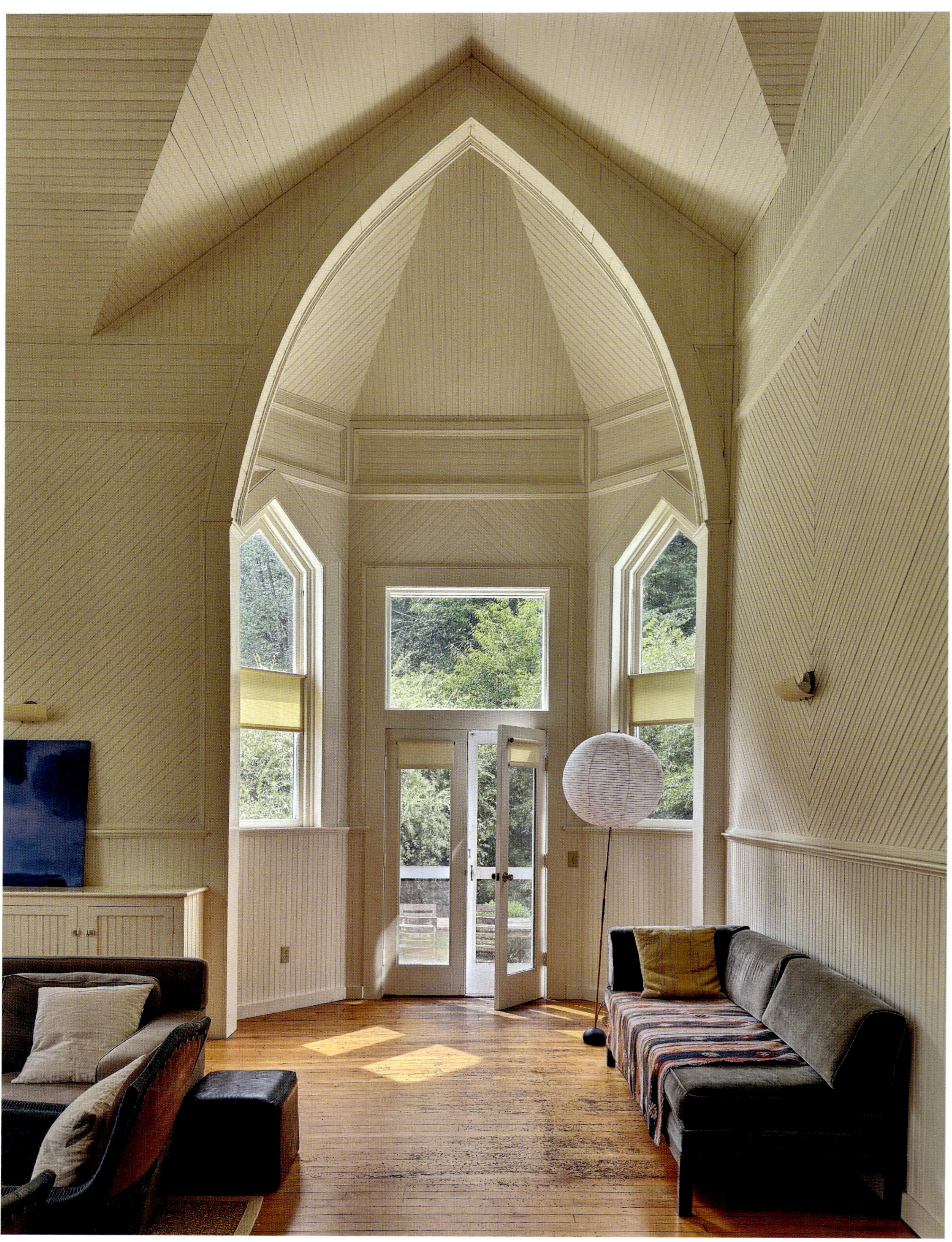

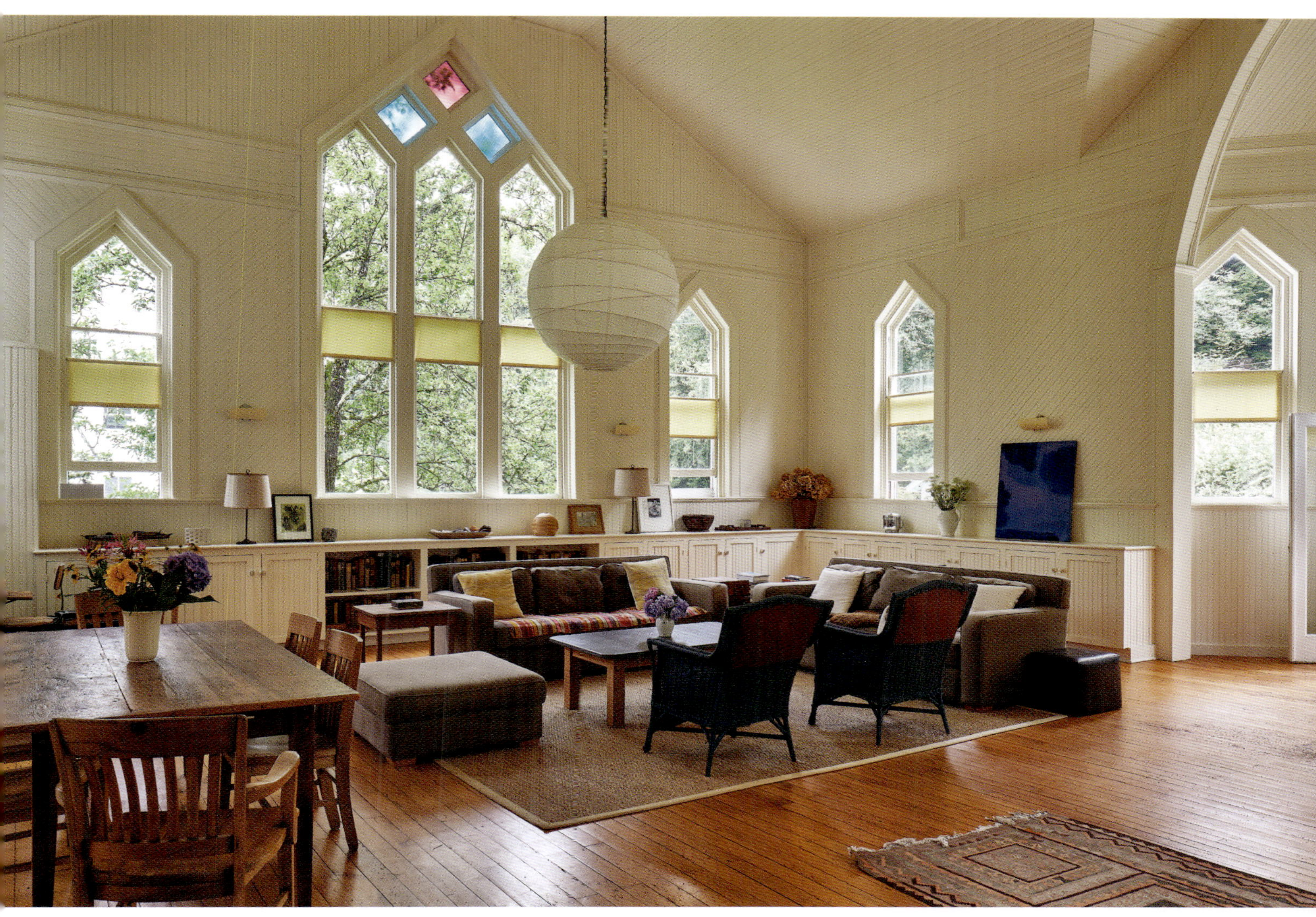

opposite
A back door to the patio was added to give a second egress on the first floor. A window above the door was added to bring in light. The wainscoting, wood paneling, and ceiling were painted white, which allows the architecture to stand out. A Noguchi standing lamp is placed by the sofa near the door. Bobbie worked with the artist/designer when she first moved to New York.

above
The living room is in the former sanctuary. Bobbie and Frank decided to make very few alterations to the interior architecture, especially the soaring vaulted ceiling and window placements. Color panes in the windows were replaced with clear panes, and shades were hung throughout. The wood floors are also original to the church.

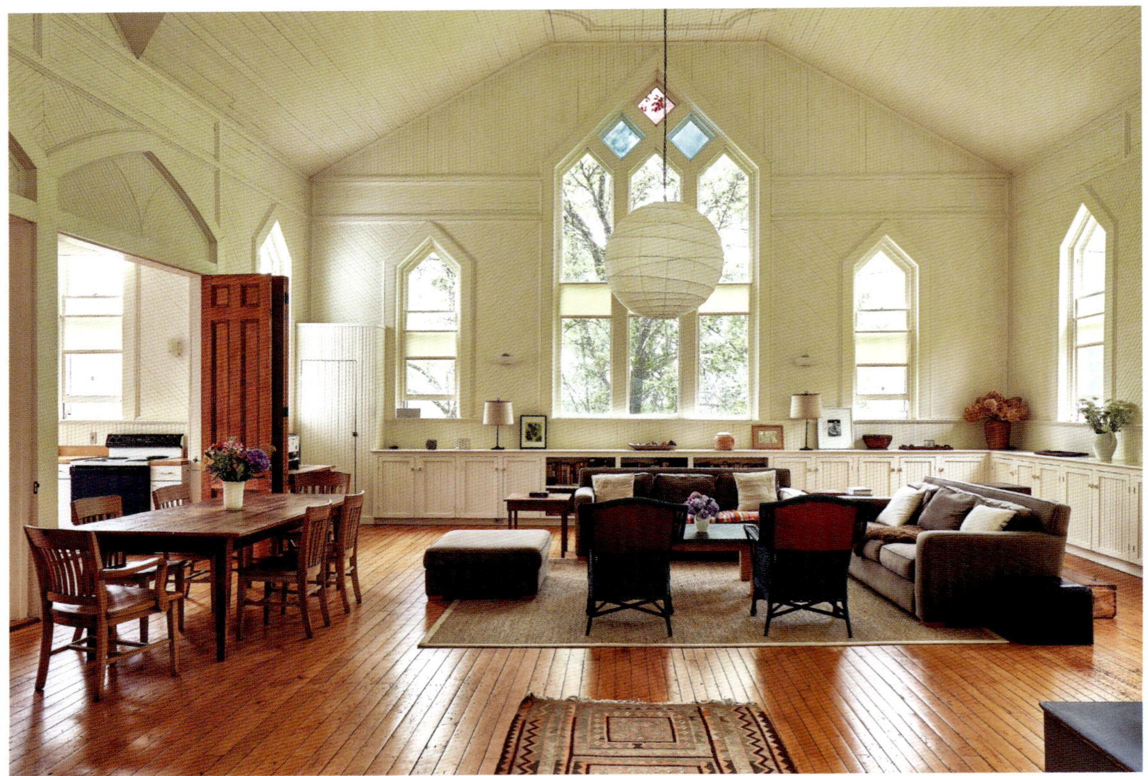

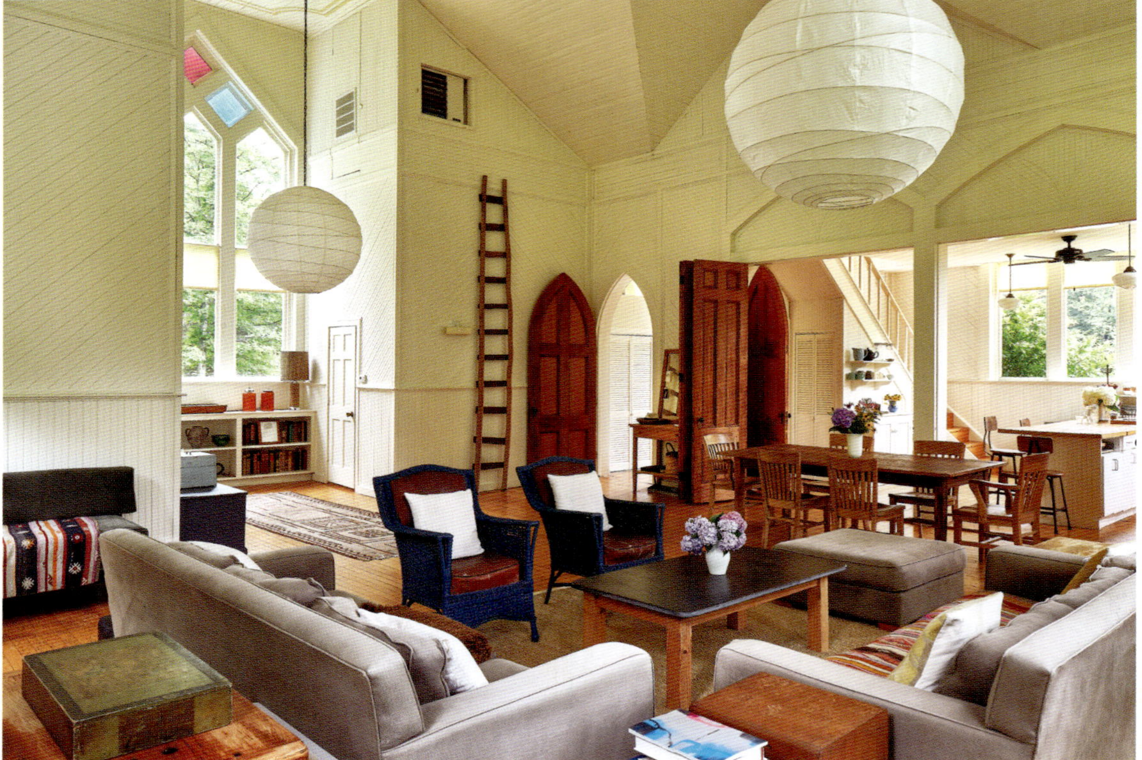

top
The symmetry of the windows and the woodwork over the doorways add to the calm and ordered feeling of the room.

bottom
The open plan of the living and dining area felt very familiar to Bobbie and Frank because they live in a top-floor loft building in New York City.

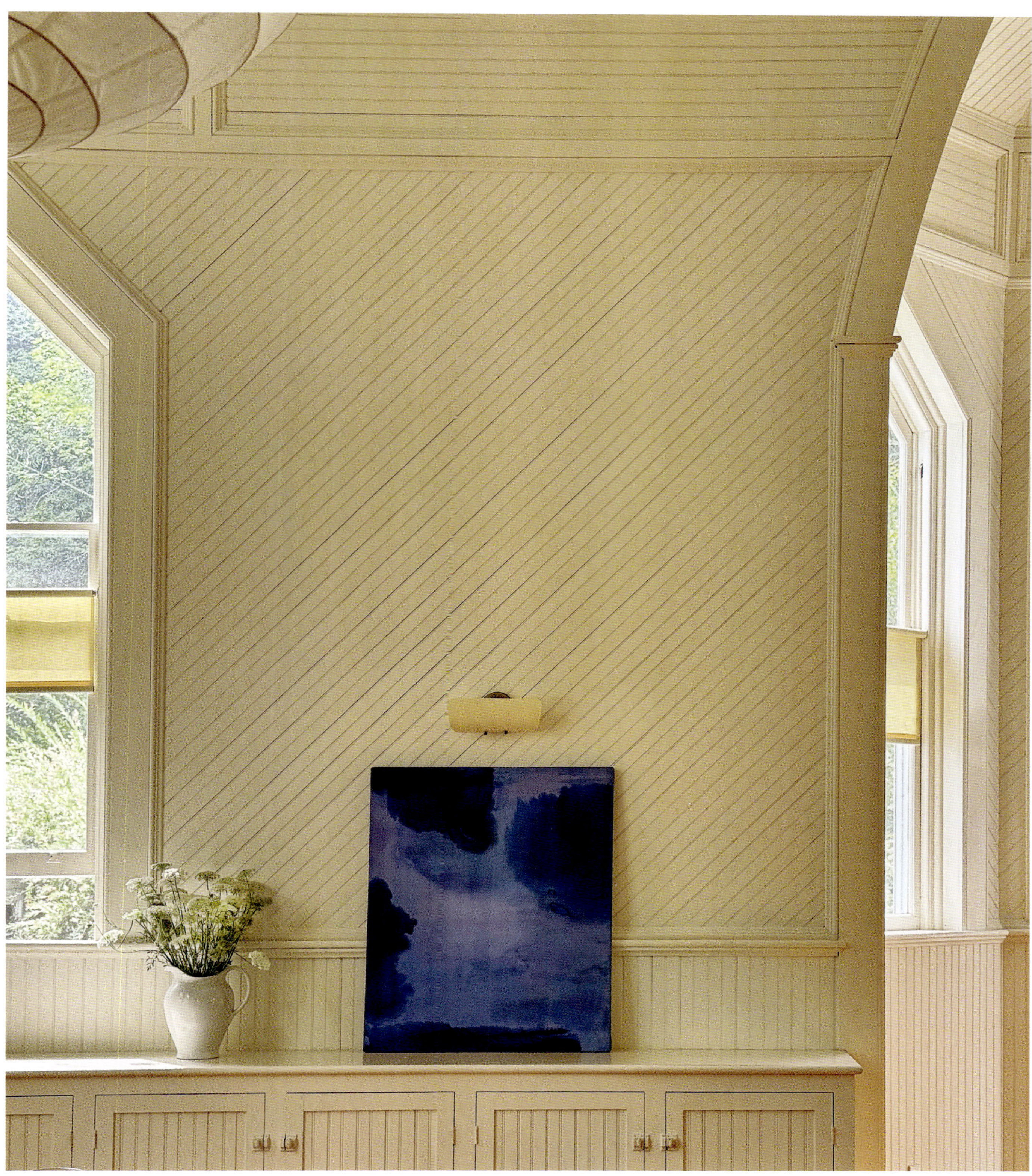

Bobbie put one of her paintings, *Delaware* (2011), on display, leaning against the painted woodwork of the church. The lower cabinets were added to the living room area. They are used to display flowers, collectibles, and artworks.

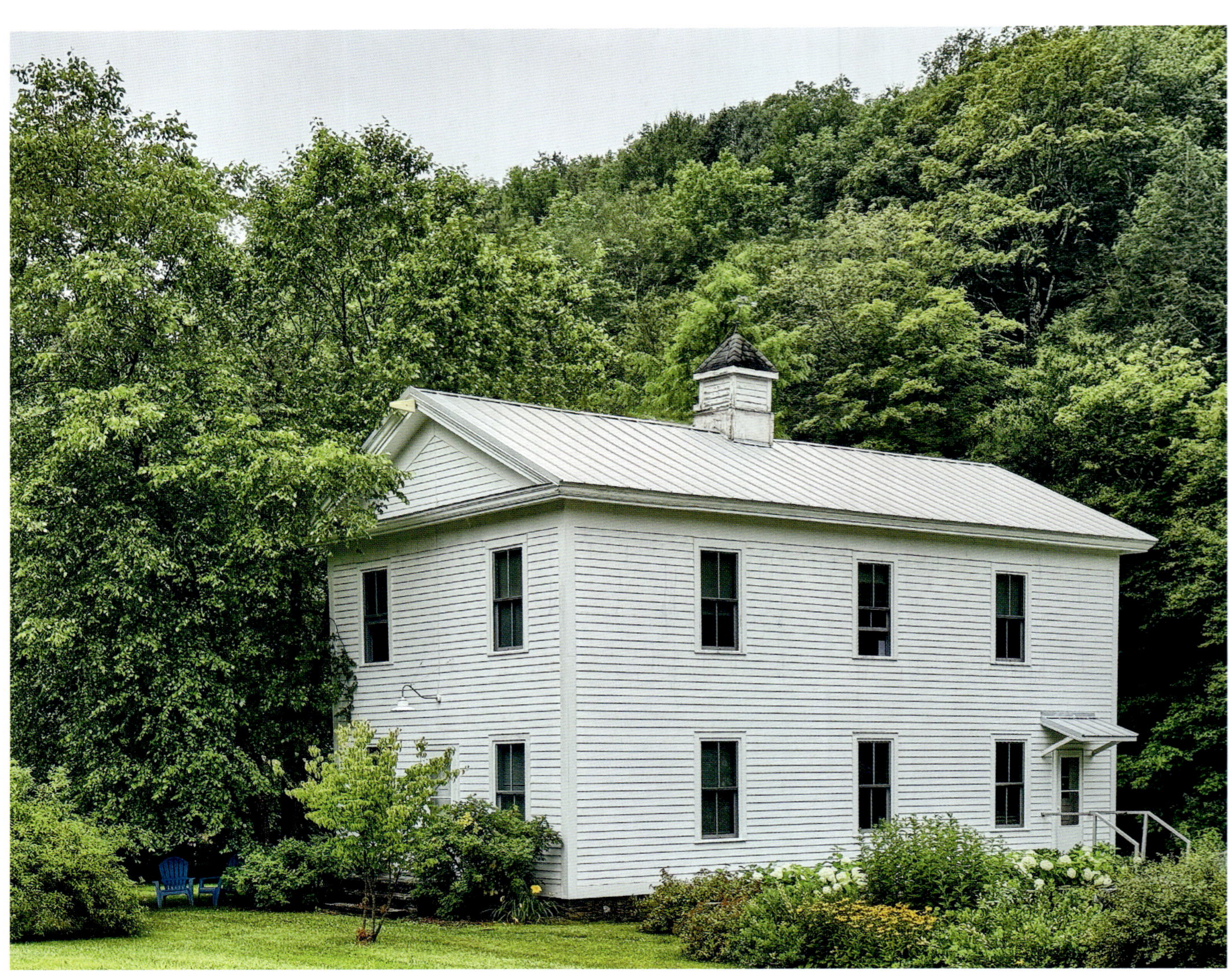

above
The Grange was built in 1886 and bought by the couple five years after they moved into the church next door. Bobbie and Frank did more work on this building than the church, first stabilizing the structure, then upgrading the heating and insulation.

opposite, top
A row of white hydrangeas grows by the stone wall at the side entrance of the Grange.

opposite, bottom
They grow both flowers and vegetables in their backyard.

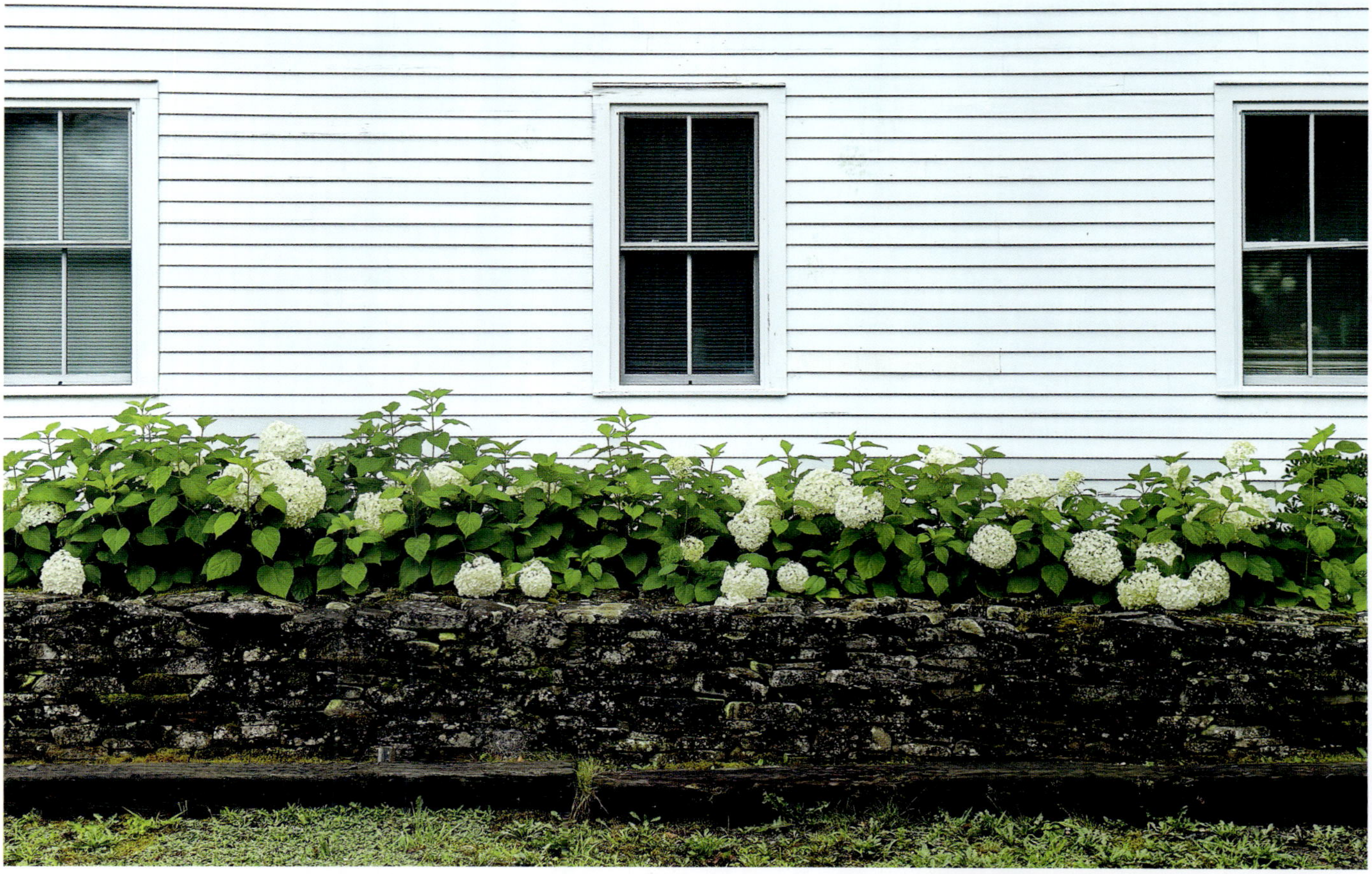

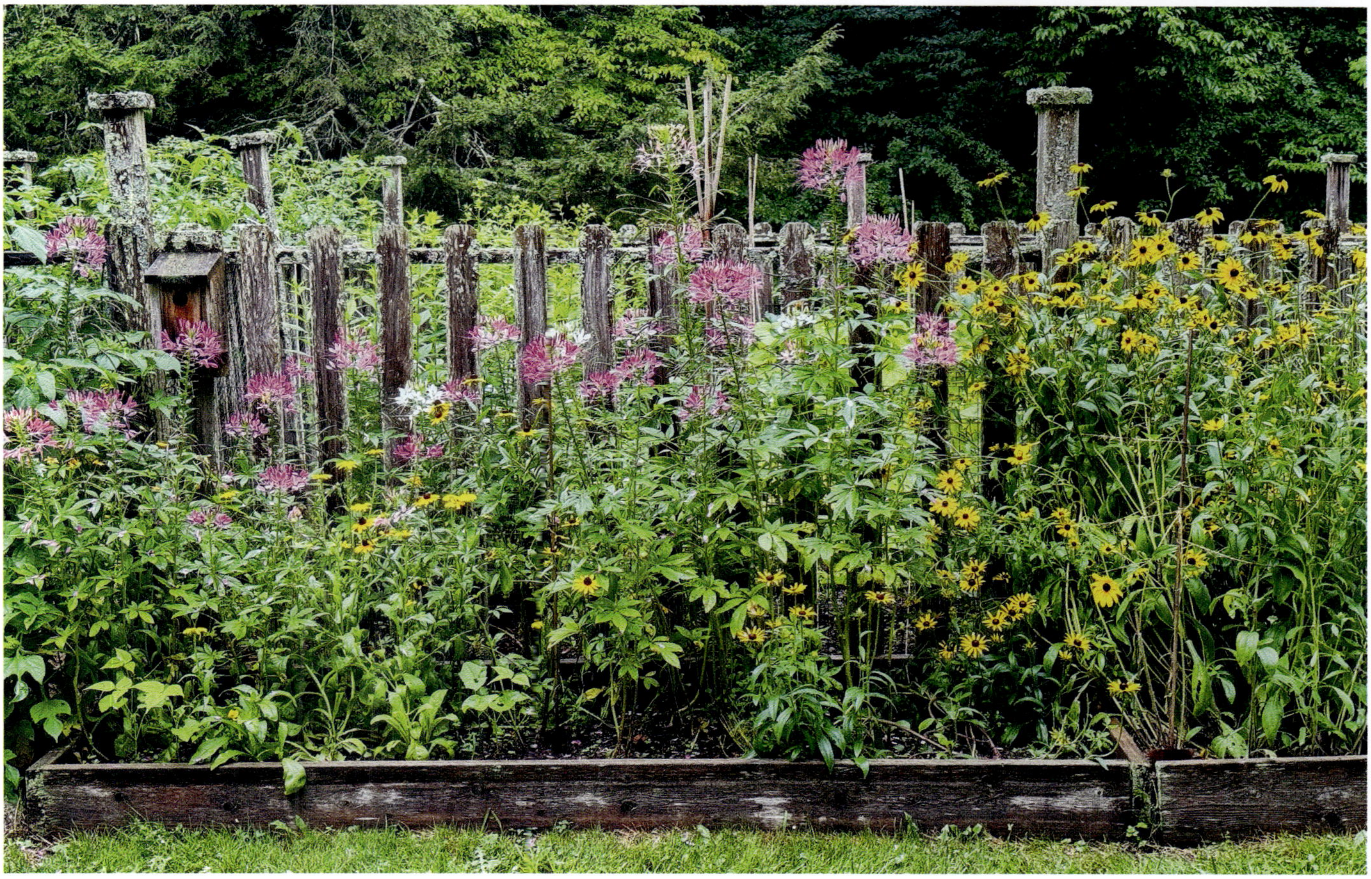

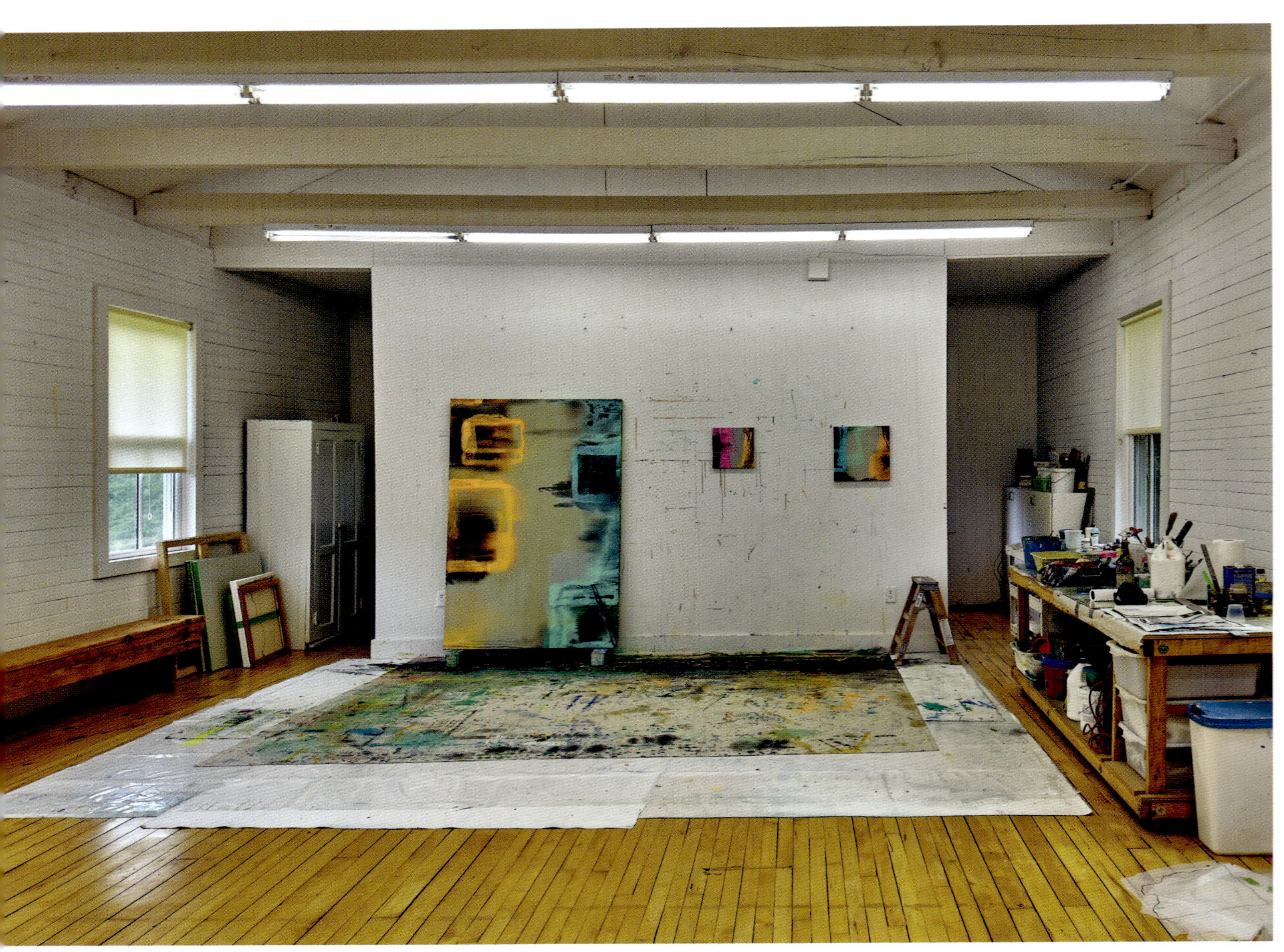

The studio is well organized: a long table placed against an outer wall holds Bobbie's materials and supplies. Daylight tube lights are an even lighting in addition to the natural light from the windows on both sides of the room. Behind a half wall, there are finished paintings. A canvas cloth protects the original wood flooring, as she lays the stretched primed canvas flat on the floor and applies the paint.

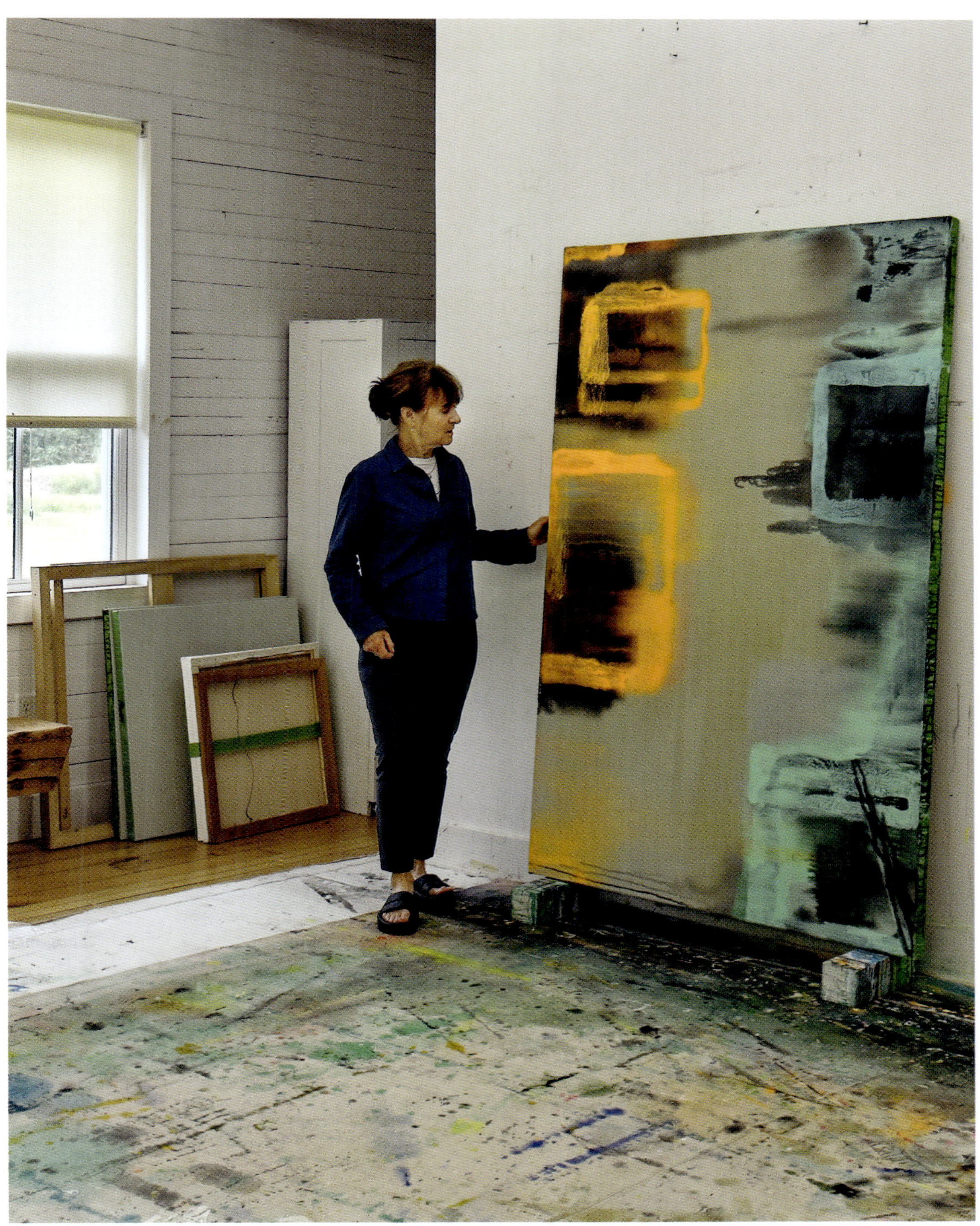

Bobbie stands next to one of her paintings, a work in progress. She has been showing and involved in the New York art world since she moved from London in the late 1960s. Her medium is acrylic water-based paints. The canvases are saturated with color, whether monochromatic or variable. Light seems to glow from within. The fluidity suggests forms, but standing in front of her works, it is easy to lose your bearings.

Rock Valley Schoolhouse

Long Eddy, New York

Just down the road from Bobbie and Frank's house and studio is a schoolhouse that was built in 1885 and was used as a school until the 1940s. Afterward, because of its proximity to the entrance of a local cemetery, the building was used as a gathering place. Later it became a community polling station. In 2006, the school was restored and placed on the New York State and National Registry of Historic Places.

Today the Rock Valley Schoolhouse functions both as a nonprofit museum dedicated to the vernacular buildings of its time that were part of the rural landscape and as a place for cultural activities and performances. At first, poets were invited to read in the one-room classroom, and now musicians are invited to play for the public. One hundred forty years later, the desks are once again filled with those eager to listen.

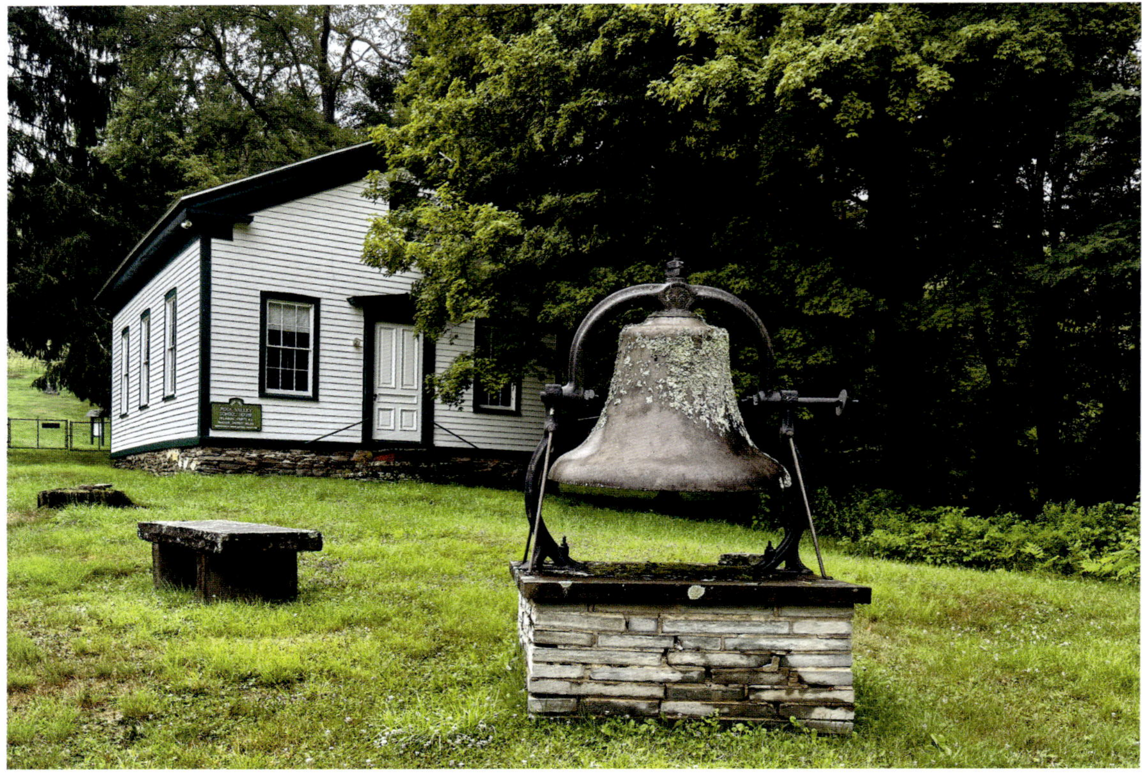

The Rock Valley Schoolhouse is organized by a committee of citizens, including Bobbie Oliver and Frank Kitchens, who want to see the space brought back to life. The bell from their steeple was donated to the school and placed in the front yard. A community graveyard is just behind the schoolhouse.

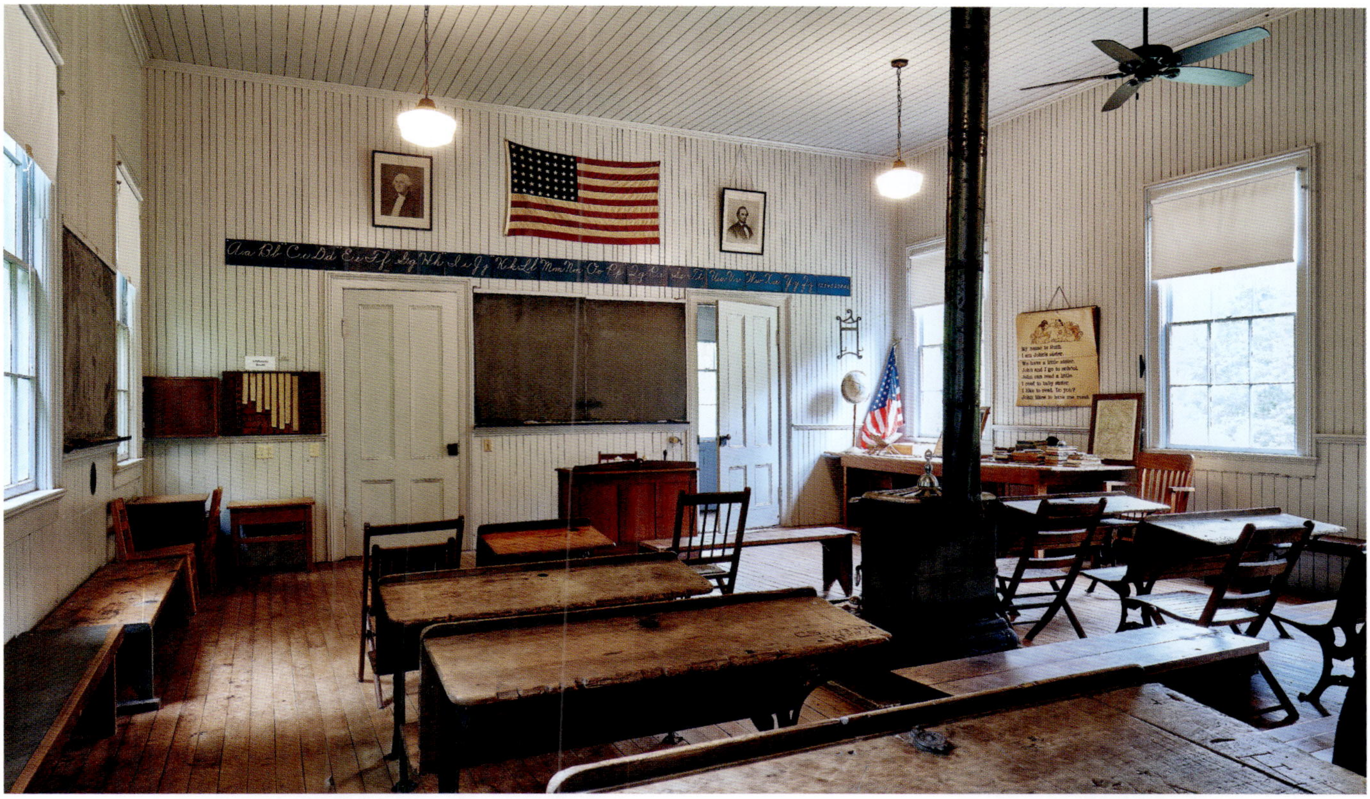

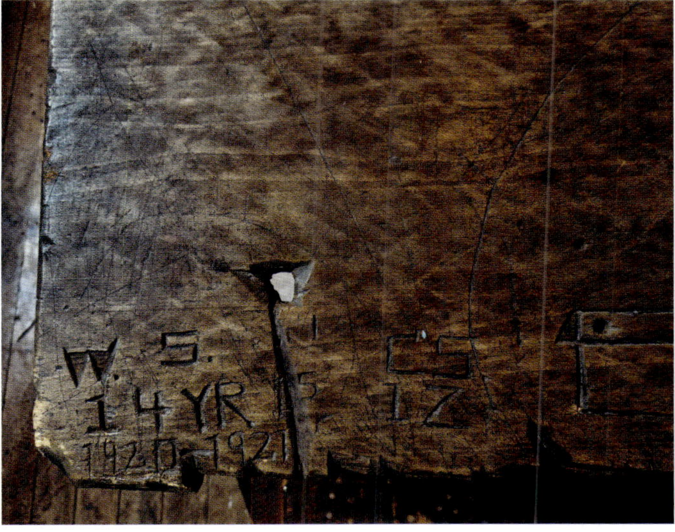

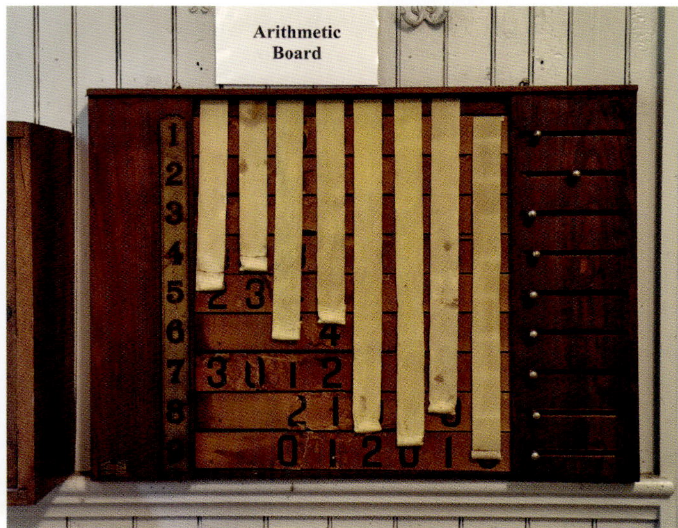

The classroom is filled with wood desks. During concerts, audience members take these seats.

Bull Farm 1856

Rock Tavern, New York

Simone Gogel Eisold, a fashion designer turned interior designer, and her husband, Mark Turner, a decorative painter, were looking for a new home. Walking through the front door, they fell in love with an old stone house not far from Newburgh, New York. The house had been left empty for twenty years, and they soon discovered its history: It was built in 1856 by a successful farmer, John S. Bull, on land formerly owned by the Clintons, one of New York's important political families. Over the years, other families owned the house, but one owner, Randolph Den, a Tokyo gallery owner from Taiwan, kept it as an investment. Simone and Mark spent three hours with the older gentleman. At the end of the tour, he told them that he believed they were the right people to take the house into the future.

Mark had previously restored several old houses. As he and Simone began to renovate the house, slowly and by themselves—a hard and time-consuming job—the couple realized how they wanted to make changes. They thought about what they wanted to do with the place. "It didn't feel right to just be the two of us," Simone said. "We wanted to share the old beautiful home."

The first open house in October 2021 was for friends and family. They put Mark's extensive collection of tribal art on display. Next, they organized a fundraiser to support Ukraine. Forty-six artists participated. That event put their house/art gallery on the map and helped to develop a community quickly.

Newburgh is a manageable distance from New York City. "This area is a new place for people who wanted to decamp from Brooklyn," says Mark. Tallix, an art foundry, is close by, and artists who worked there, including the late Frank Stella, stayed in the area. Simone and Mark curate the exhibitions together. They reach out to both local artists and those they admire in other cities. During Upstate Art weekend, they had more than a thousand visitors.

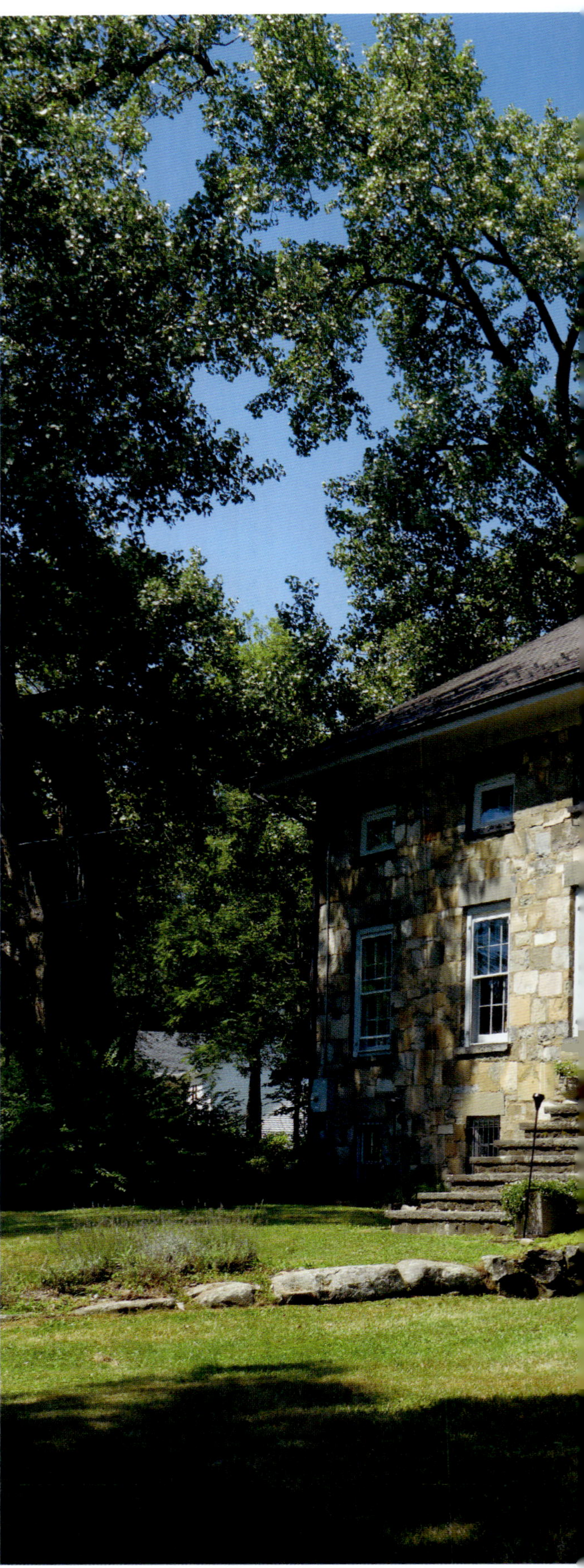

The stone house was built in 1856 by the Bull family, who farmed the land.

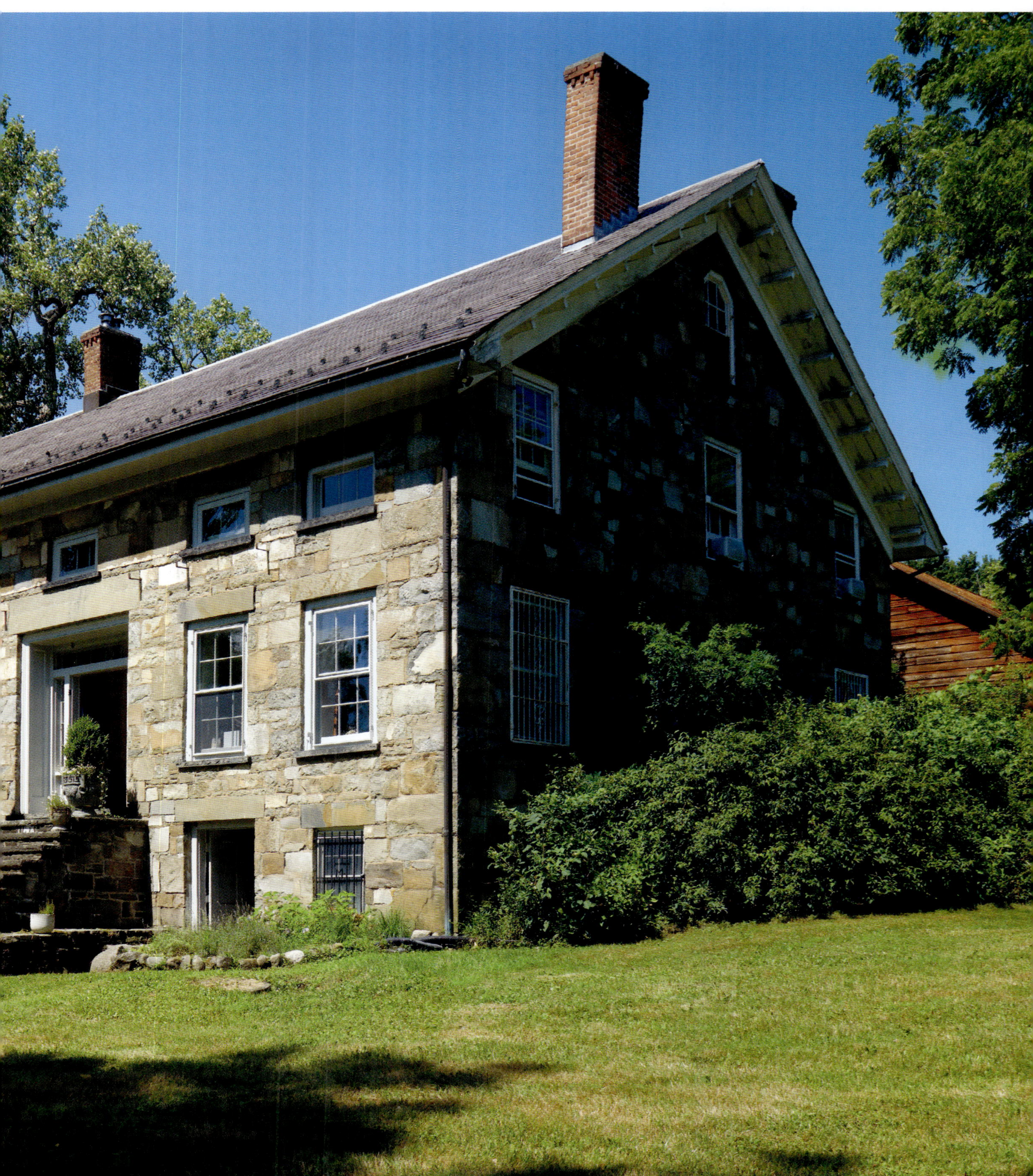

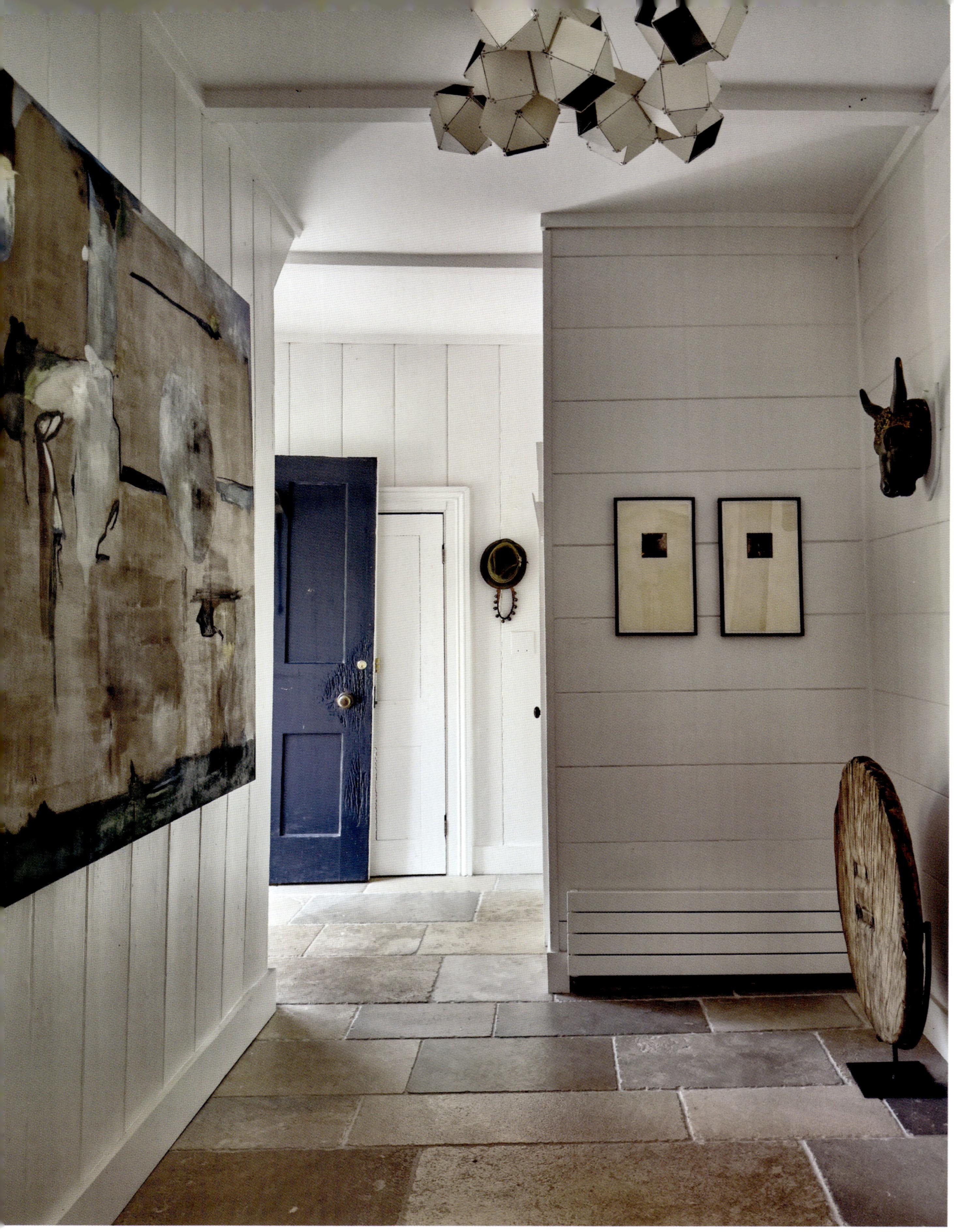

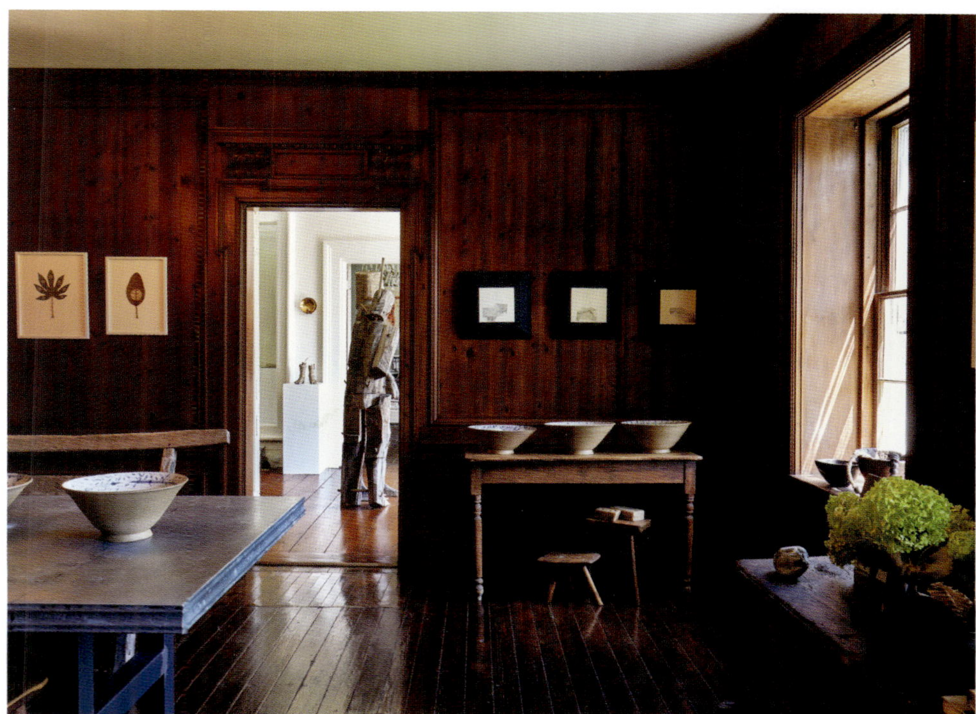

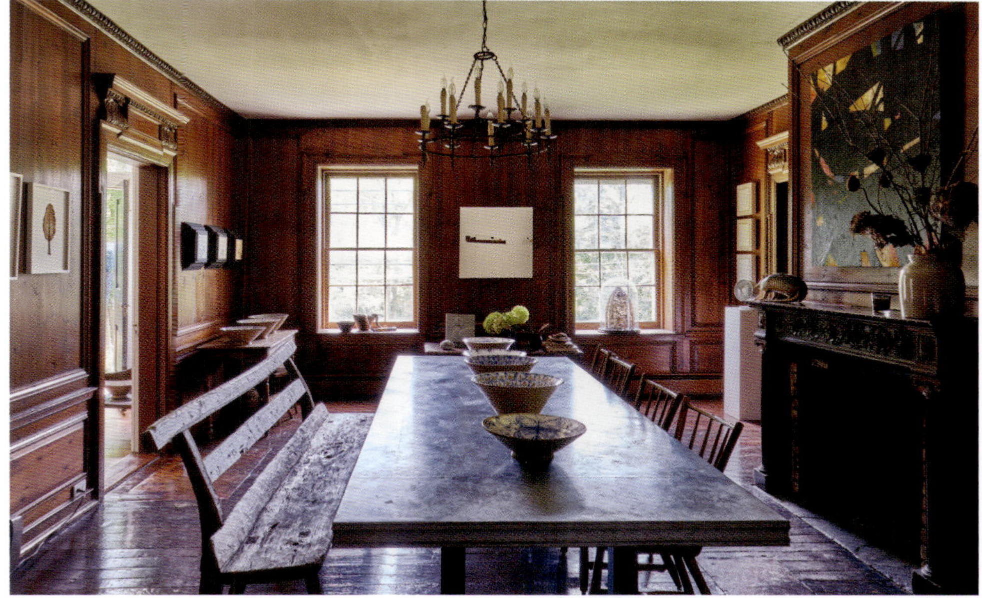

opposite
The side entryway was completely renovated by the couple. The new stone floor continues the materials on the home's exterior. This space was the entrance of the schoolroom on the upper floor for the owner's and the farmworkers' children. The painting in the hallway is by Joshua Elias, titled *After Life Map-One* (2024).

top
Works by Susanna Bauer using leaves as a medium, *Seven* (2022) and *Moon.70* (2024), as well as Leon Johnson's framed works, *Creatures in the Map [FOLD] #1 -3*, are displayed against the dark wood walls of the dining room. Valerie Hammond's and Emil Alzamora's works can be seen in the center hallway.

bottom
Simone placed a long bench along the zinc-covered dining room table. Ken Carbone's painting *Beyond the Periphery* (2024) was hung over the fireplace mantel. Ceramics by Leon Johnson, who lives close by in Newburgh, New York, are displayed on both the main dining table and a side table. An untitled painting by Gonzalo Pita is placed between the two windows of the room, and a small ceramic sculpture of ceremony beads from Ginny Redgate's series is shown on the window ledge.

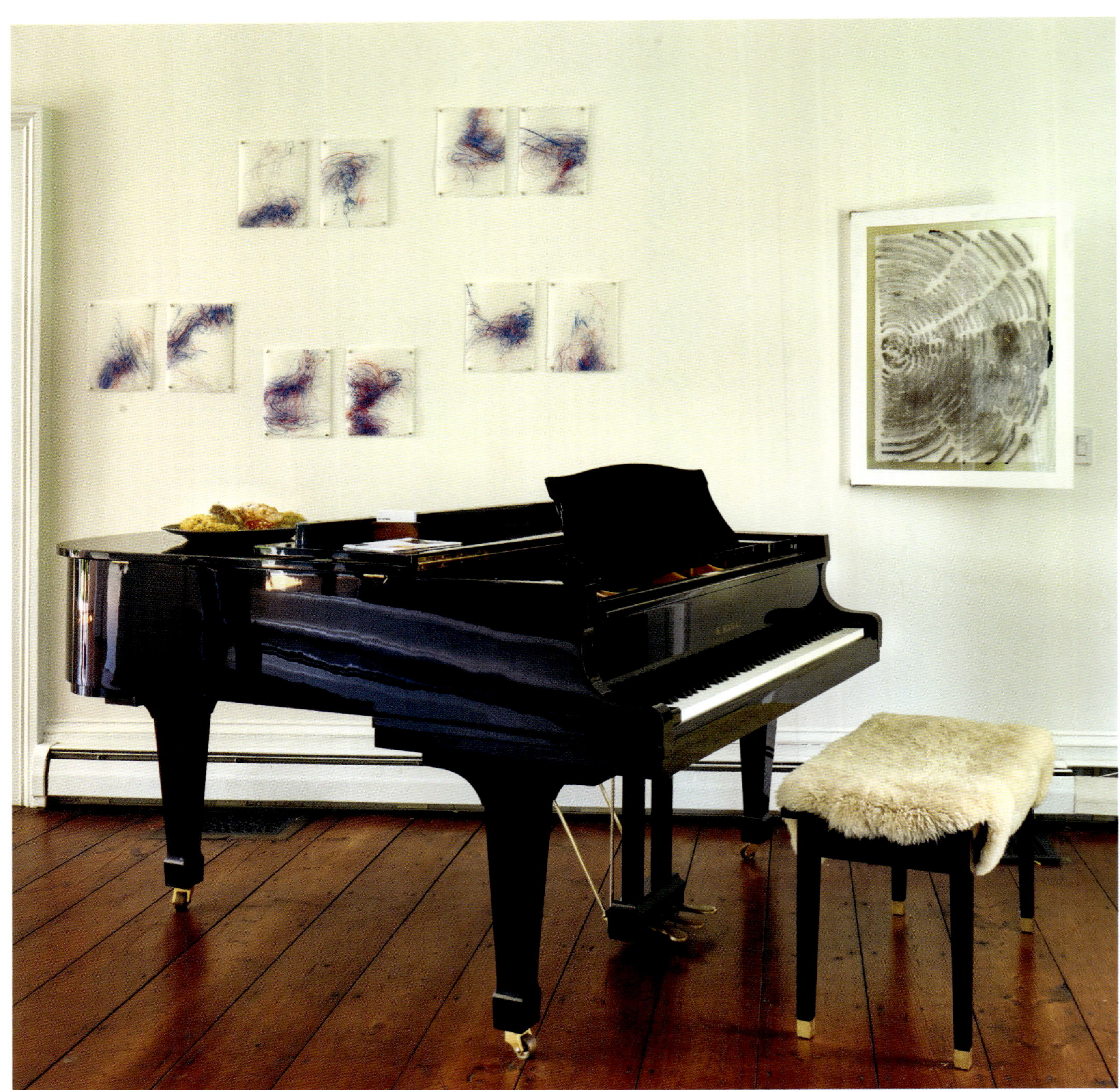

above
Ephemeral drawings in color pencil by Jaanika Peerna, titled *Wind Graphs* (2024), and Audra Wolowiec's work, *waveforms* (2018), are hung in the center hallway over the piano.

opposite
Two figurative sculptures by Emil Alzamora, *The Sound of Trees* (2019) and *Soliloquy* (2014), dominate the center hallway that is transformed into a gallery. Works by other artists including Valerie Hammond, Susan Magnus, Ekaterina Leiva, and Leon Johnson are also displayed on the walls and pedestals. The long mirror was recycled from a hotel in New York City. It was installed by a previous owner.

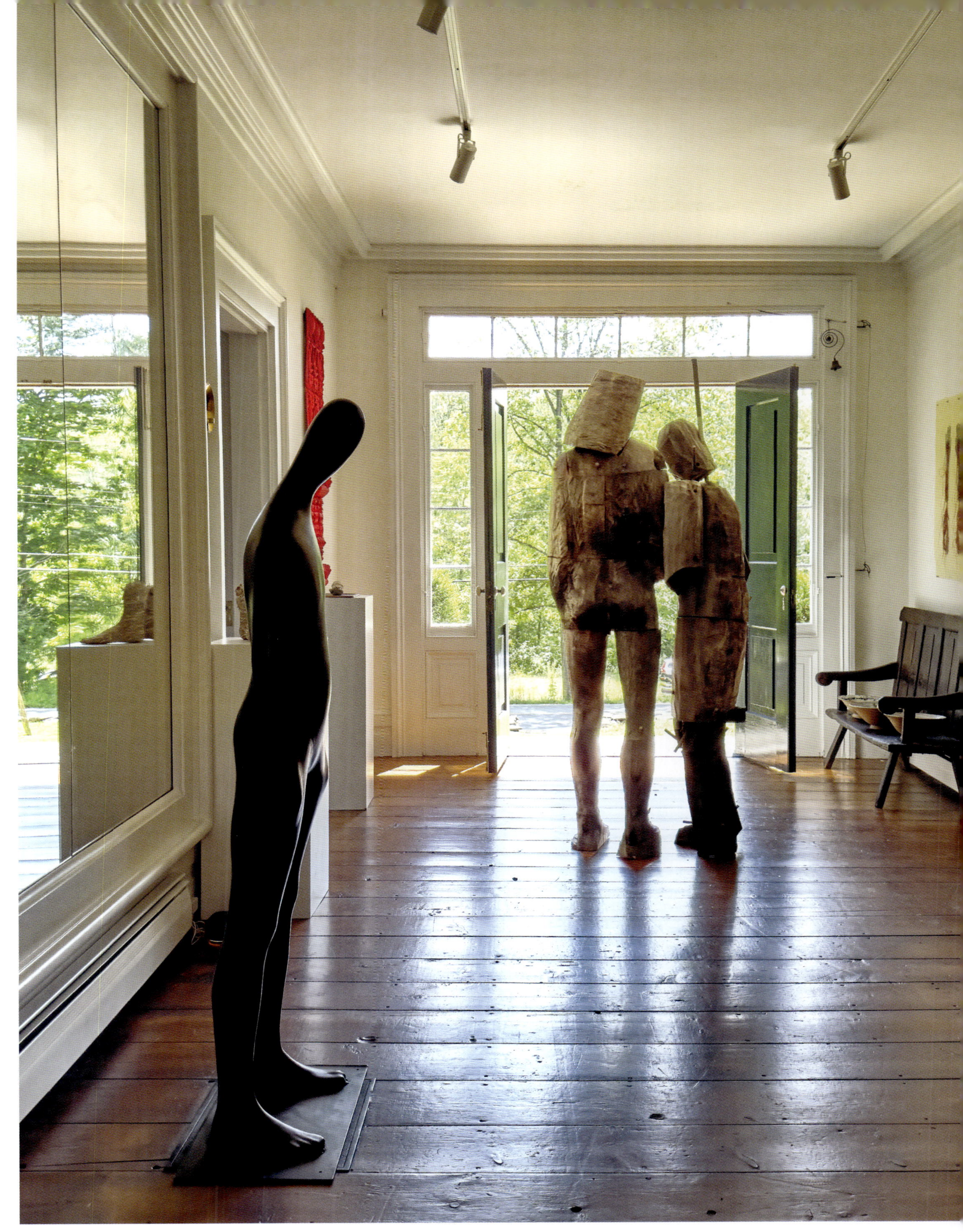

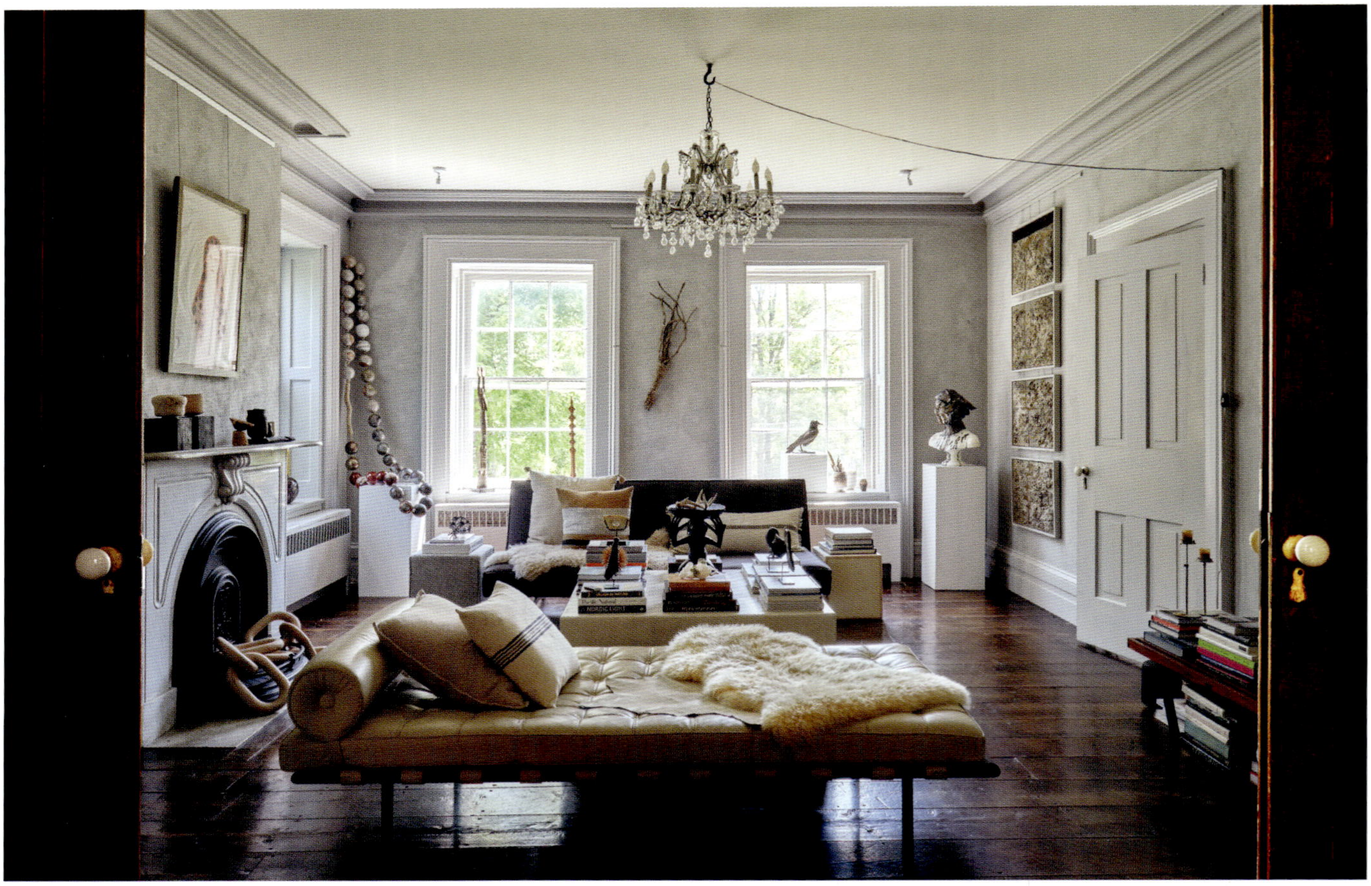

above
Ginny Redgate's *Memory Portrait: Bonticou Crag* (2024), made of glazed ceramic beads in colors that reference natural influences, are hung in a corner of the room. A Valerie Hammond sculpture titled *Arm* (2024), made from wasp nest, paper, and wood, is installed above the sofa. A daybed separates the study from the library in the back. Simone sources furnishing from antique stores, garage sales, and estate sales, and many items are custom pieces created in collaboration with makers, a process she loves.

right
Simone and Mark have an extensive collection of art and design books. Some are arranged on the coffee table with smaller "objets." Emil Alzamora's *Axis Mundi III* (2018) is placed on a pillar in the corner. Four works by Ekaterina Leiva, *Untitled* (2022), hang together on the plaster-finished wall.

opposite
Mark, a decorative painter, created the gray marmorino plaster finish made from lime putty and ground marble in the study. Artworks are mixed with the couple's many collections. Valerie Hammond's ink and watercolor work, titled *Garden* (2023), is hung above the fireplace mantel. Paz Sandoval's carved vessels, made from trees such as local American sycamore and black walnut, are arranged below. Dove Bradshaw's *Without Title* (2013), made with honey locust thorns, plaster, and gesso, is displayed to the left.

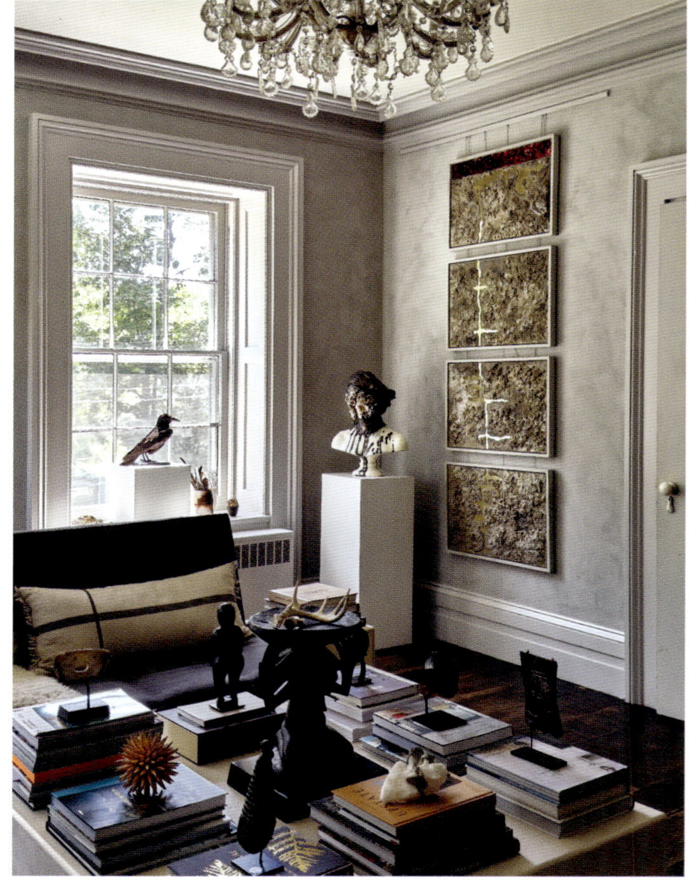

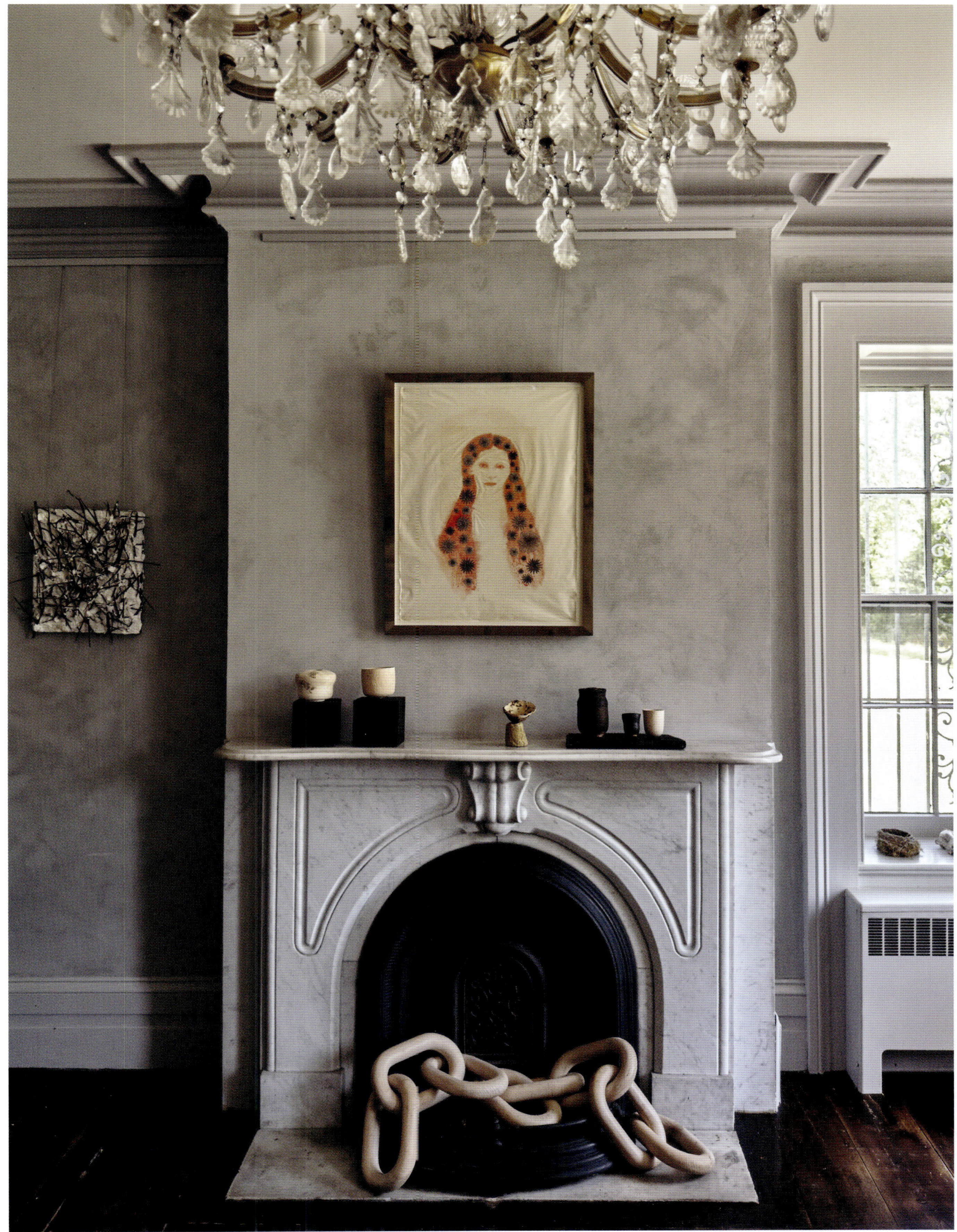

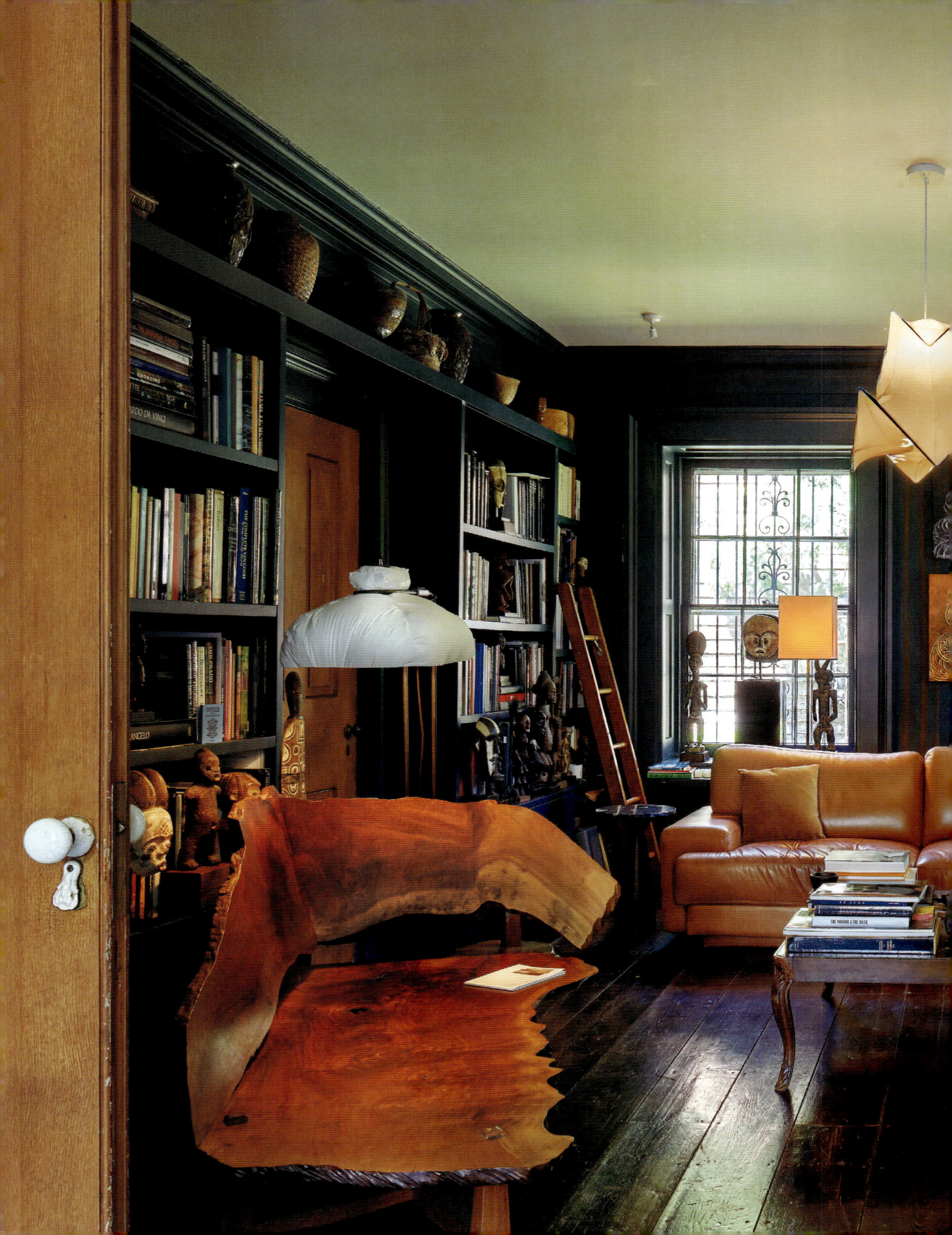

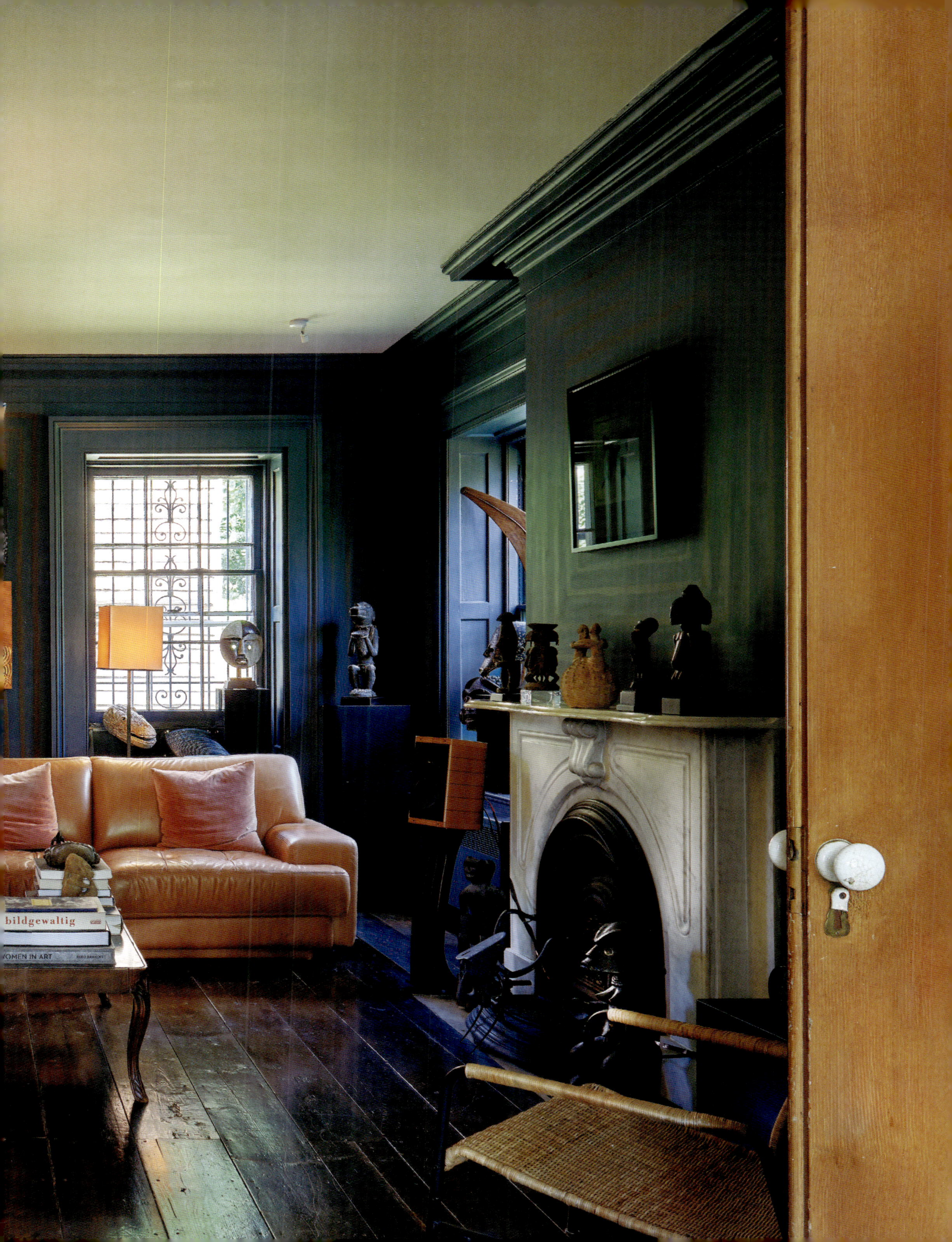
bildgewaltig

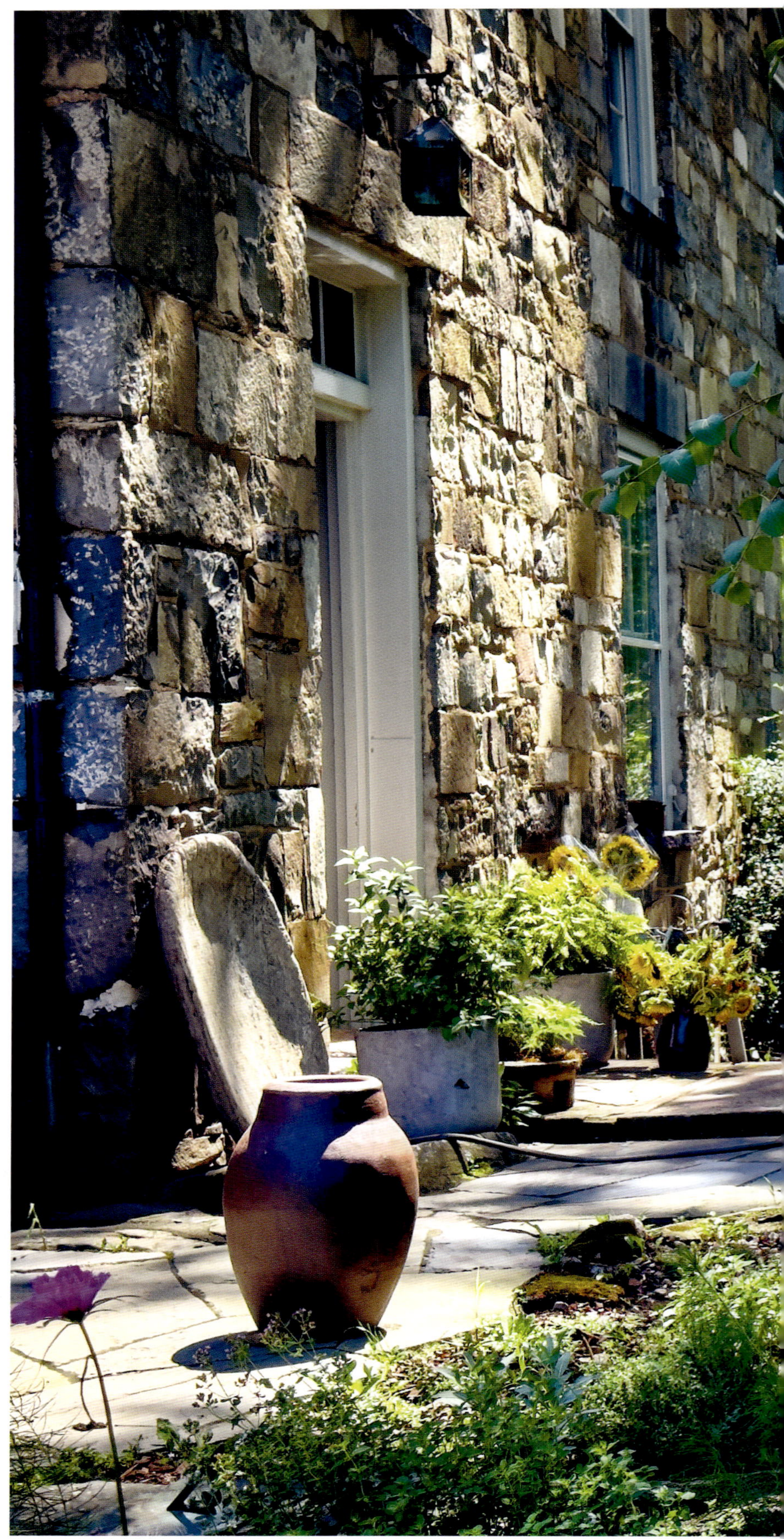

previous
Ian McMahon's sculptural pendant hangs above the darkly painted back sitting room. A second one of his lights, titled *Headbanger* (2023), stands in front of a built-in shelving wall of books, next to Daniel Oates's walnut live-edge chaise. Other artworks in the library include Susan Magnus's piece *Papilio alcibades* (1999) over the fireplace and two works by Emil Alzamora, *The Taste of Copper II* (2024) and *The Deep* (2024), between the windows.

right
The back door of the old stone house has a stone patio that was installed in 2023. The look is very organic, with stones spilling into the grass. Planters are placed by the entrance. An eastern cottonwood tree provides some shade.

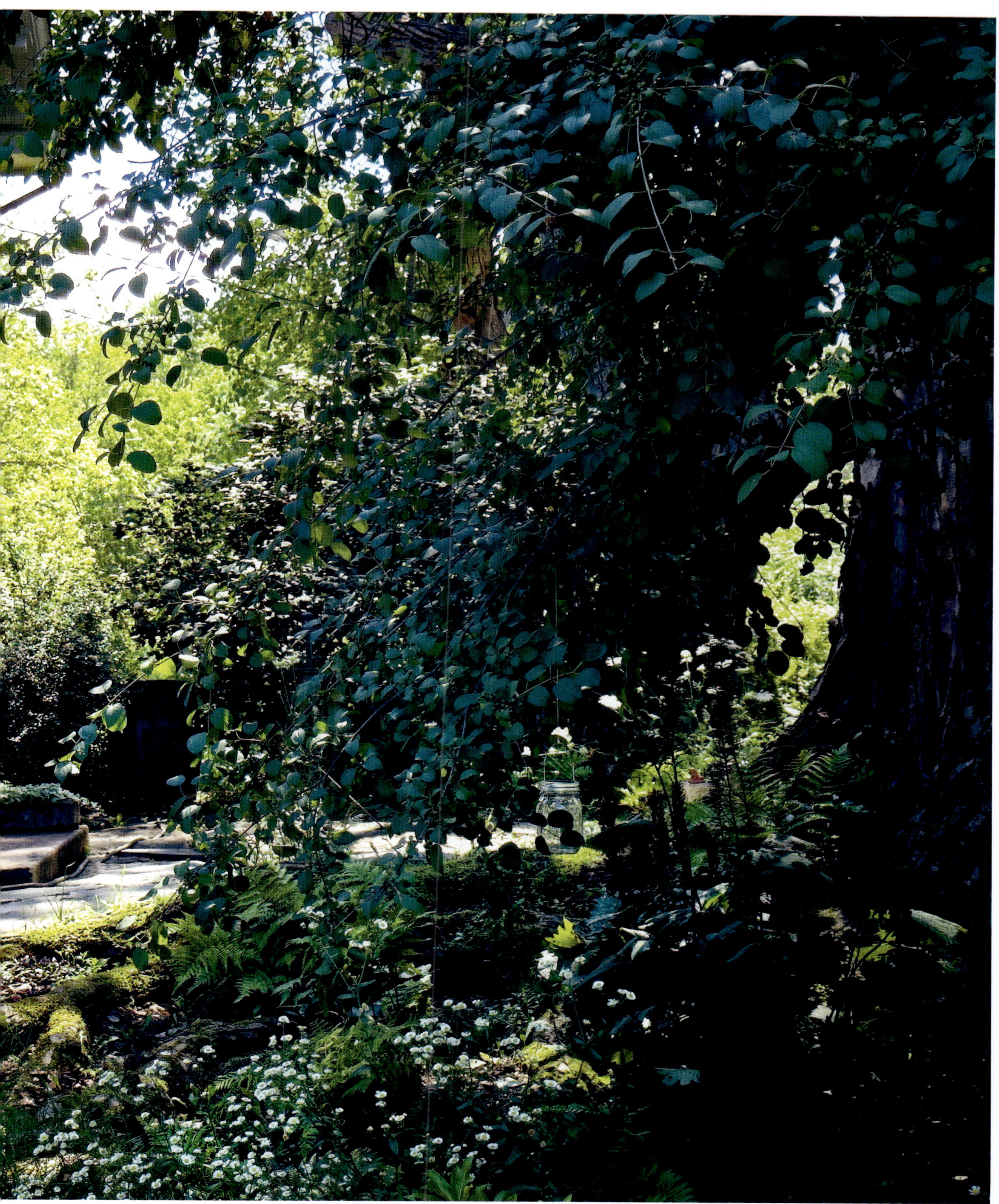

III. Design

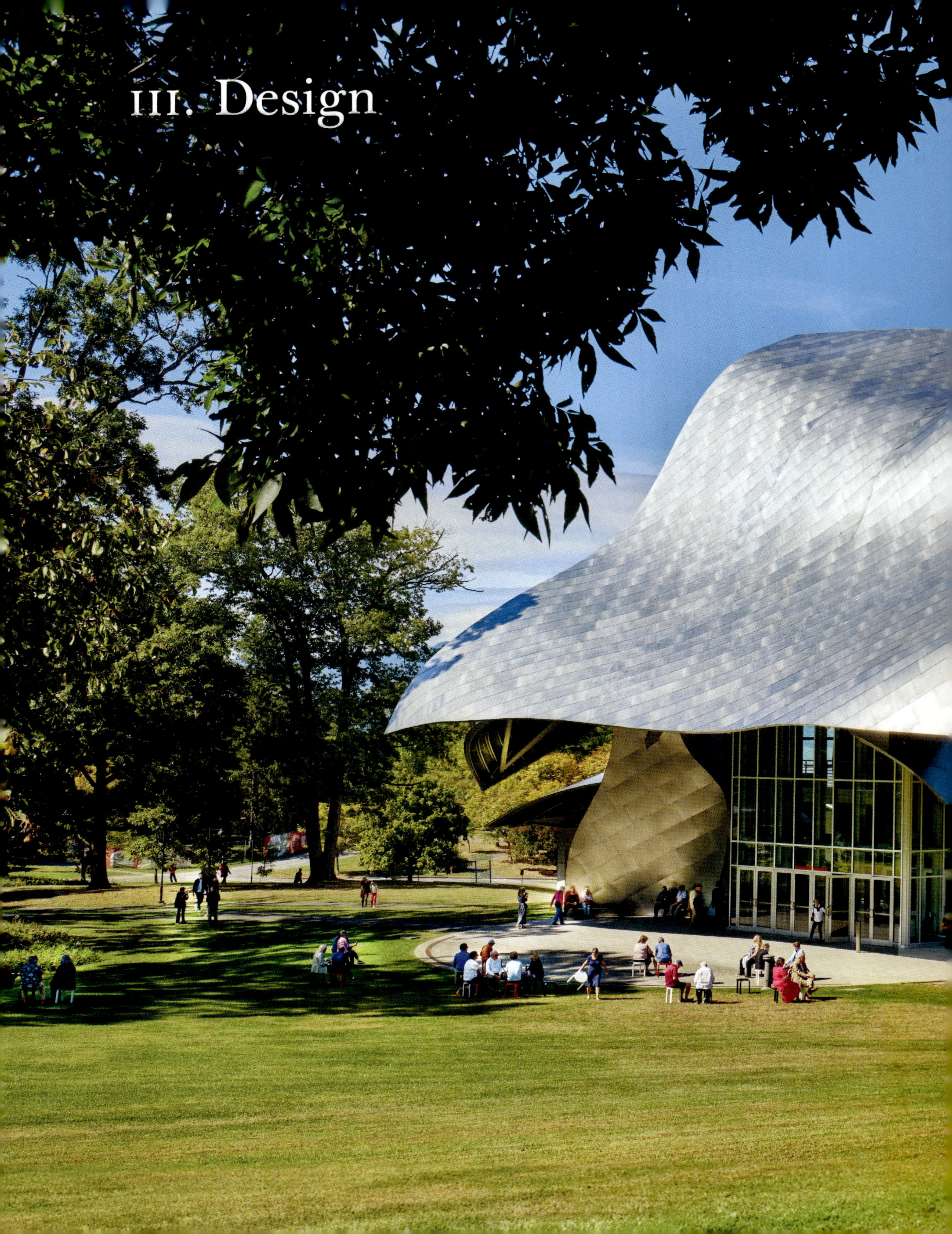

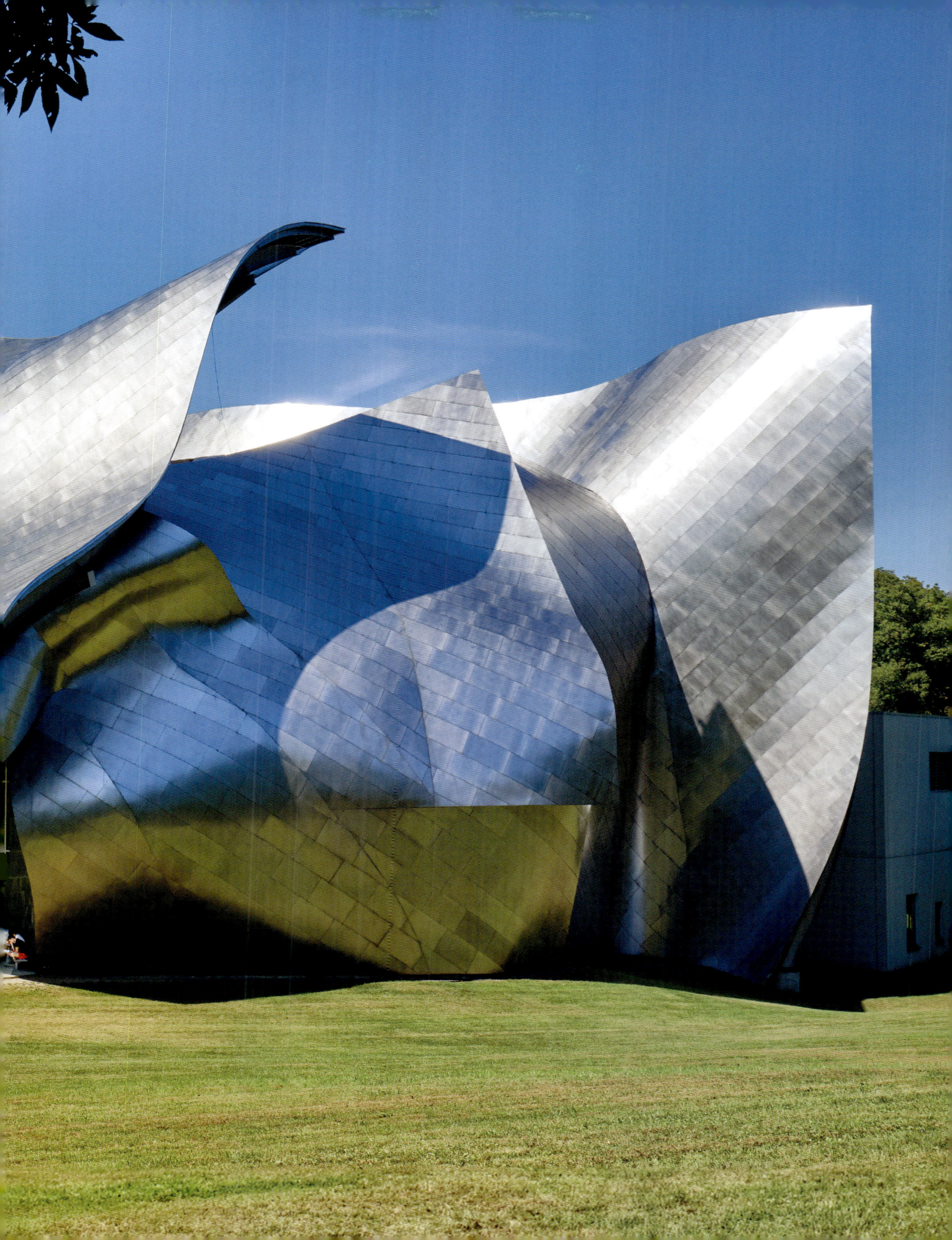

Fisher Center for the Performing Arts at Bard College

Annandale-on-Hudson, New York

Over twenty years ago, the Fisher Center for the Performing Arts opened on the campus of Bard College in Annandale-on-Hudson. The building filled a void on the 600-acre campus. Until that time, the college, which is known for its liberal arts curriculum, including extensive studies in the performing arts, lacked a sizable professional facility. The Fisher Center was designed by architect Frank Gehry and completed in 2003. It consists of two theaters: the Sosnoff Theater seats eight hundred people and the LUMA Theater seats two hundred. The LUMA Theater also has rehearsal spaces and practice rooms. The building sits on a hilltop with western views of the Catskill Mountains.

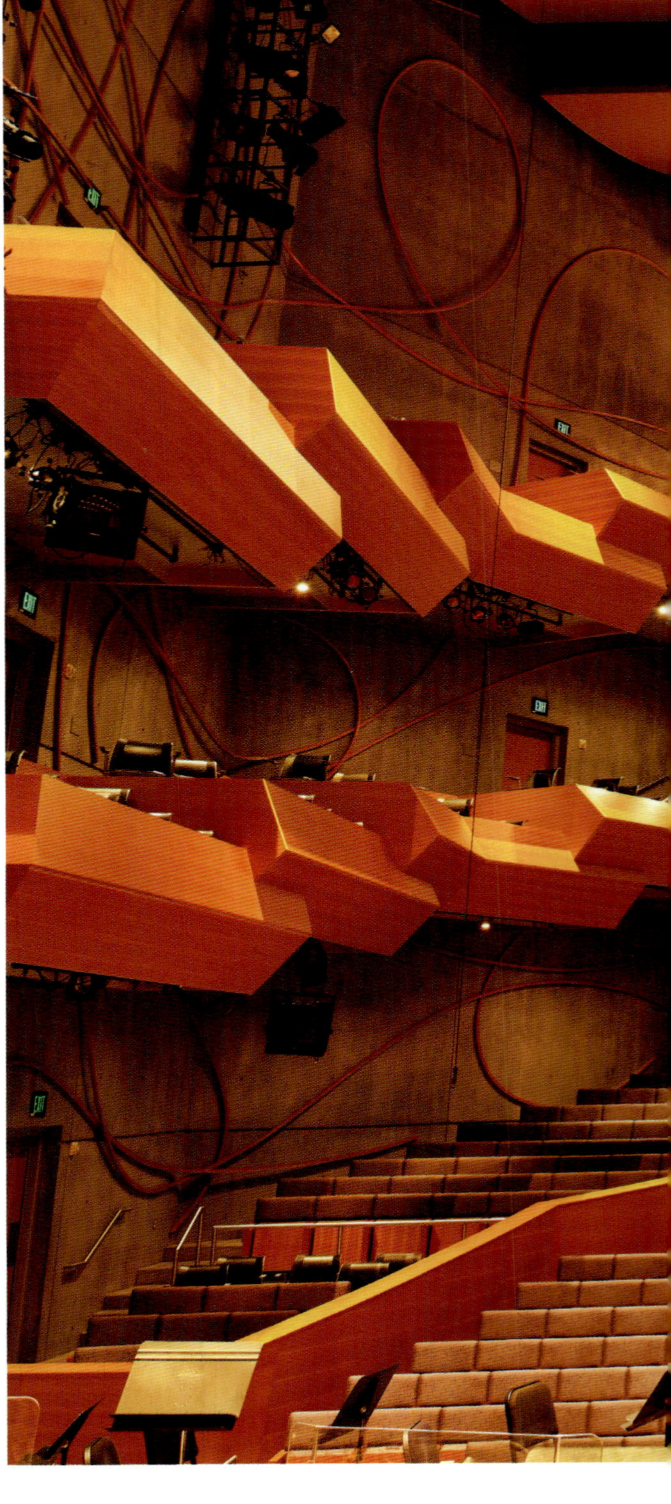

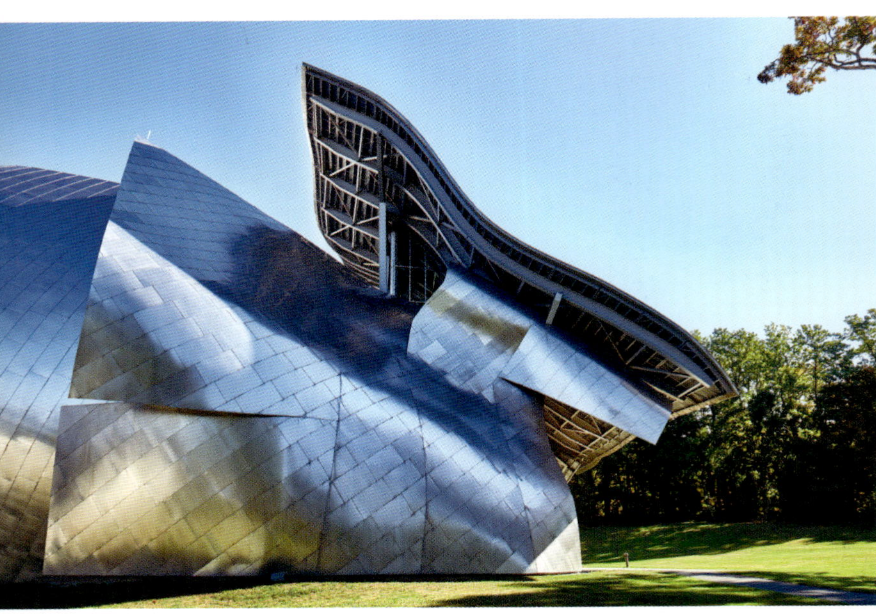

previous
Concertgoers await entry into the Sosnoff Theater of the Fisher Center on Bard College's campus. High-end public architecture is not exclusive to urban areas, as this project by Frank Gehry proves.

above
Viewed from the side, the sculptural nature of the design is even more apparent and dramatic. The Fisher Center at Bard uses geothermal energy and heat pumps, which also consider the environment.

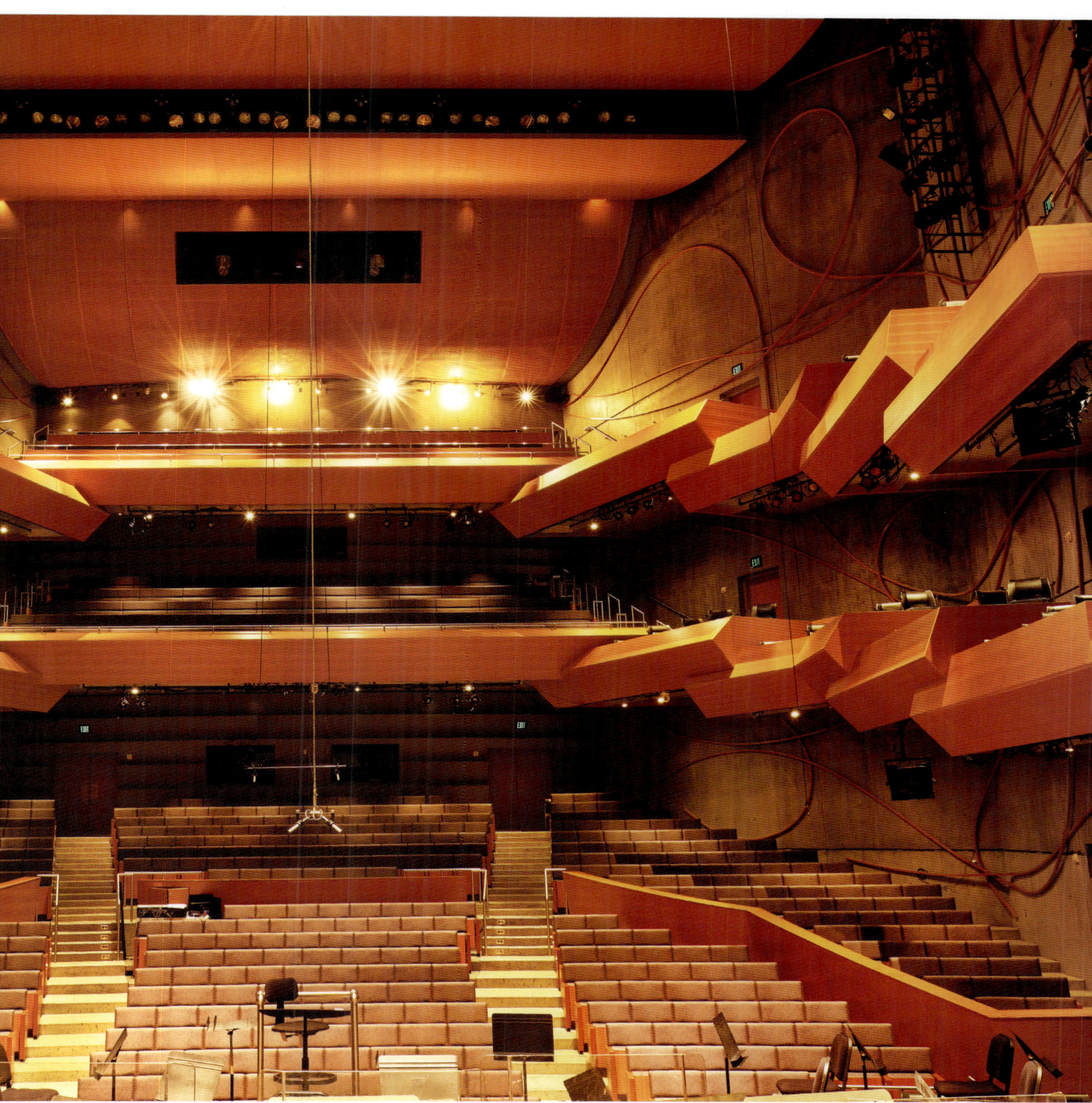

The interior of the Sosnoff Theater is wrapped in a Douglas fir veneer. The wood, ceiling height, and other elements influence the quality of the sound produced in the hall. The front of the theater is designed for maximum flexibility. Backstage are cavernous rooms with rolling doors that allow for stages and equipment to move with fluidity.

Deer Mountain Inn

Tannersville, New York

Tannersville, New York, is in the New York State–protected Catskill Park. The drive to Deer Mountain Inn goes up and up in elevation, past the trailhead to Kaaterskill Falls, the subject of Thomas Cole's famous painting. According to historian Jane Curley, at one time, the trip from New York City to Tannersville took up to ten hours by boat on the Hudson River and then by carriage to the town. After the Civil War, railroad expansion shortened the trip, which made development in the area possible.

The shingled inn with its diamond lattice windows, trimmed in a forest green color, and a bright red door with deer antlers above seems like it's from another time. Indeed, the building was constructed in the late 1880s. Interior designer Iliana Moore and architect Lewis Jacobsen restored the inn for its owners, the Royce family, who bought the place in 2013. There was a lot of work to do, as the building had been used as a church-run children's home from 1965 to the 1990s. However, the first-floor public rooms had survived intact.

Iliana's design and Lewis's work speaks to the historical aspects of the building's past and the surrounding area. The Onteora Club, an artist colony, was established just down the road by Candace Wheeler, considered the "mother" of American decorating. Wheeler's firm, Associated Artists, opened in 1883, a few years before the Deer Mountain Inn's main lodge was built. She did the interior design of many cottages on the grounds of Onteora. Wheeler drew inspiration from the natural world around her. Samuel Clemens, also known as Mark Twain, and his family visited and were among other members

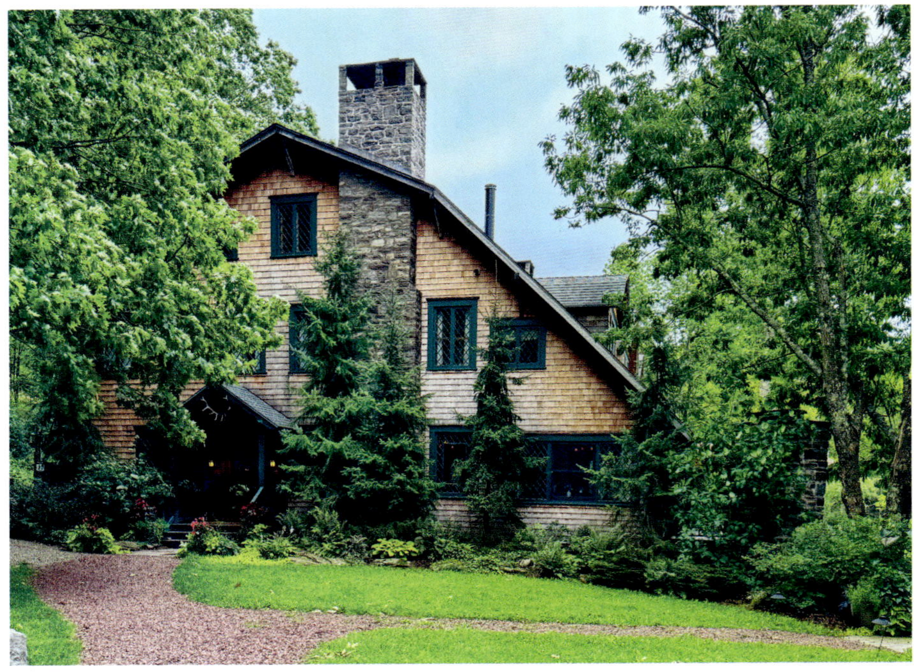

above and opposite
Cedar shakes and a stone chimney define the exterior of the Deer Mountain Inn.

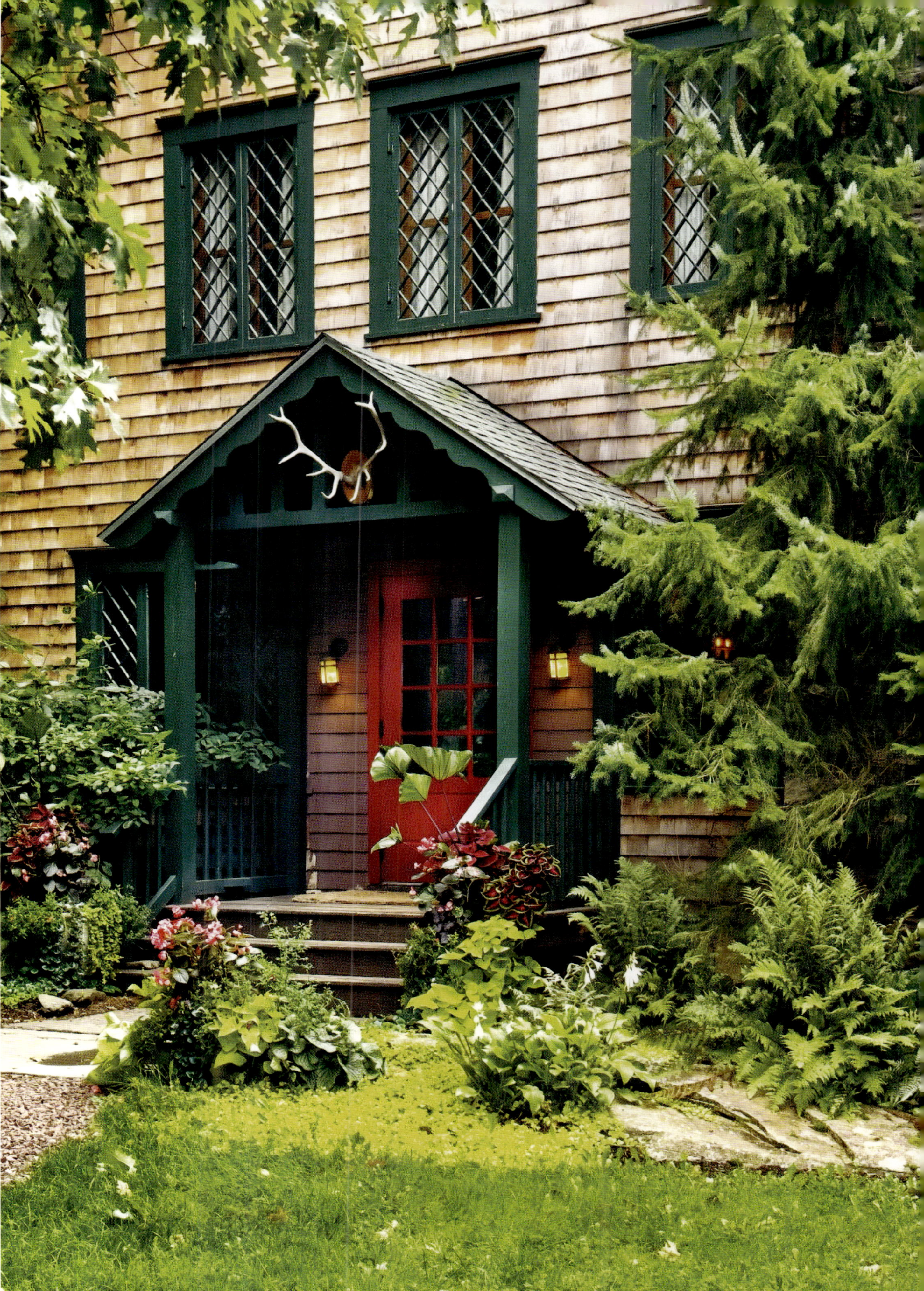

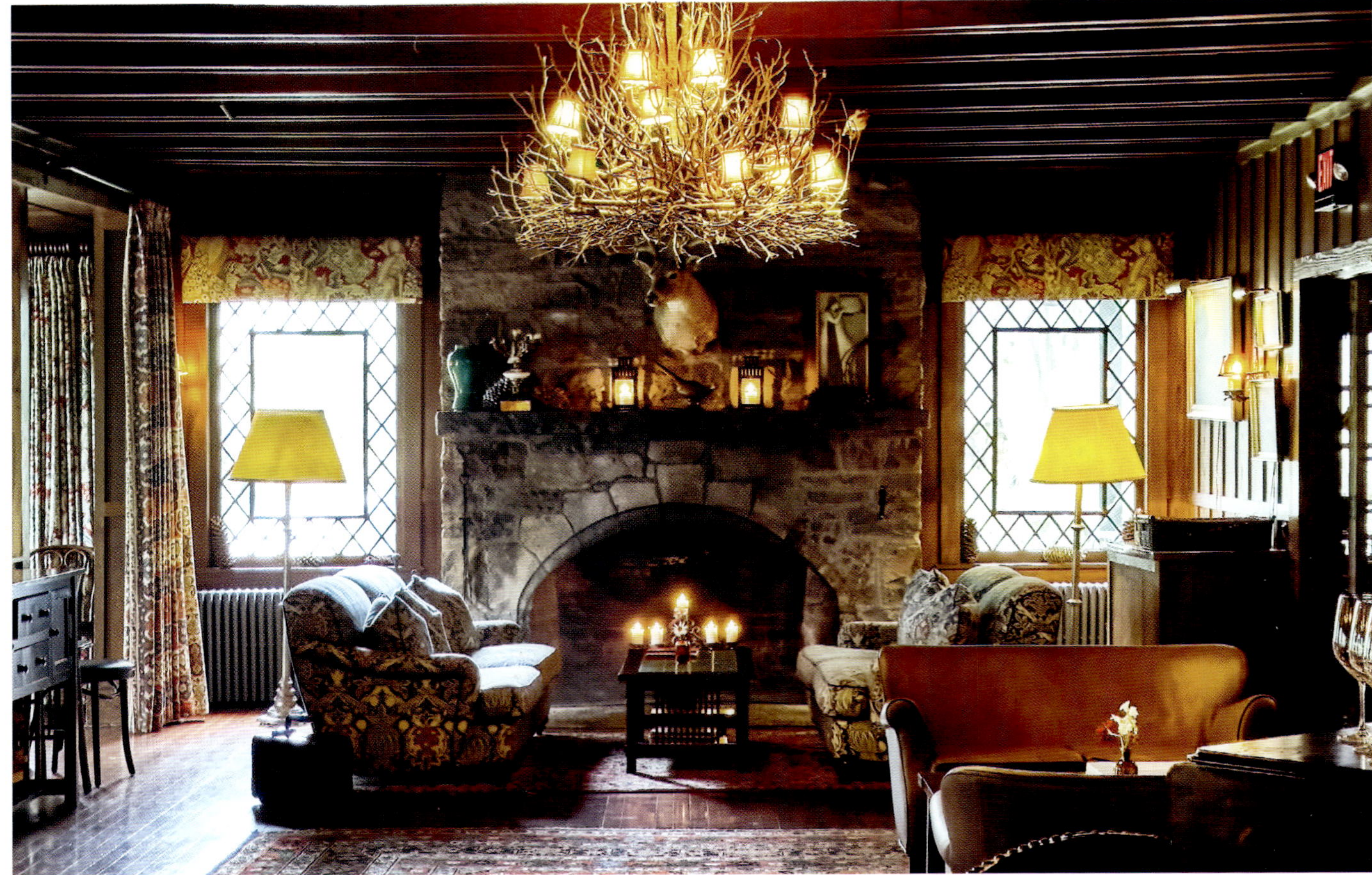

of the literati of the day who were friends of the Wheelers. The updated design that includes all-wood interior wall paneling of Deer Mountain Inn's lodge, Oriental rugs covering the floors, and comfortable furniture in a William Morris floral pattern are in keeping with the Arts and Crafts style that Wheeler was associated with.

The six guest suites and four individual cottages also have a feel of a rustic country aesthetic. Downstairs in the public rooms, bar, and restaurant there is a unified luxurious traditional look. The textures of the drapery and upholstered furnishings exude warmth, even when it is snowing outside. Chef Corwin Kave's menu capitalizes on the abundance of local resources.

Each of the guest suites on the second floor is equally well-appointed. Artworks with traditional Hudson Valley and Catskill Mountain subjects are hung throughout the property and create a welcoming homelike ambience. The second-floor rooms had been chopped up over the years, so everything was taken down to the studs, according to Lewis. The cozy feeling that Iliana creates with her interior designs extends to the four cottages that were recently completed. All have views of the surrounding woodlands. Three of the cottages have two floors, with a bedroom upstairs, a gracious bathroom and kitchen downstairs, and an outdoor deck. For hundreds of years, visitors of all types have sought to escape to the Catskills. Continuing the tradition, the Deer Mountain Inn offers a place of refuge.

above
Two traditional English roll-arm sofas upholstered in a William Morris pattern face each other in front of the fireplace. Drapery around the doors and windows help prevent drafts. Even in the summer the temperatures are cooler at the Deer Mountain Inn's elevation.

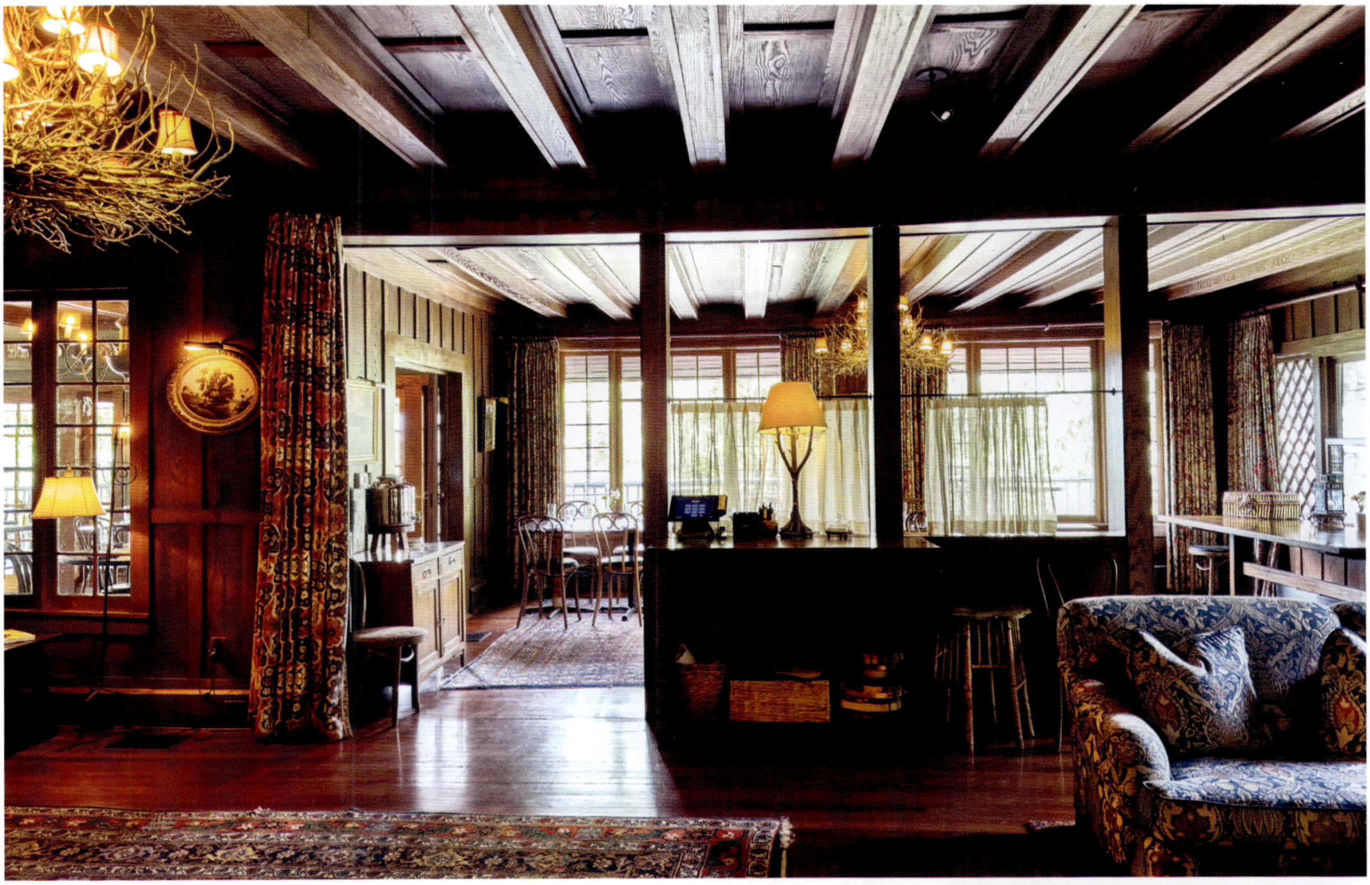

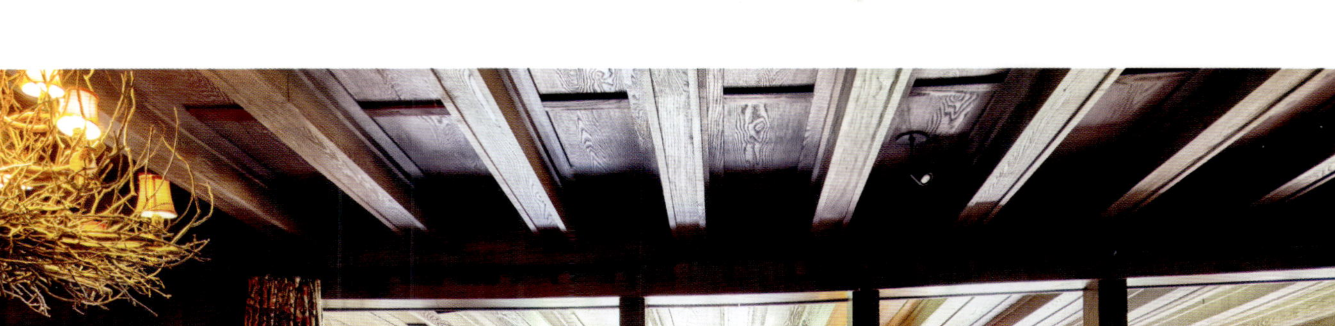

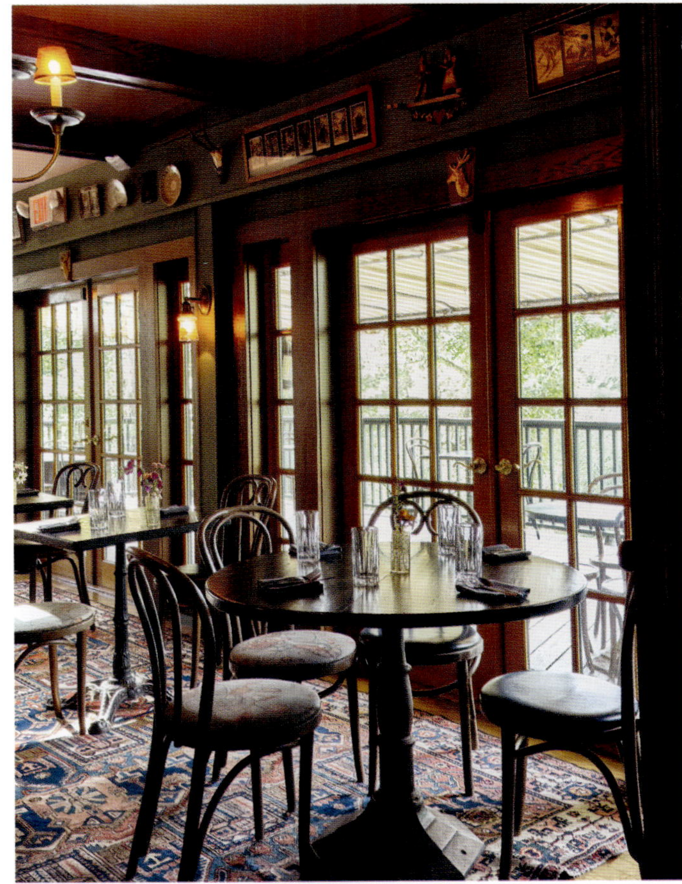

top
The restaurant has two rooms and a bar. A half wall with pillars and café curtains separates the front room from the seating around the fire.

right
Bentwood café chairs and tables are placed by the French doors to the deck.

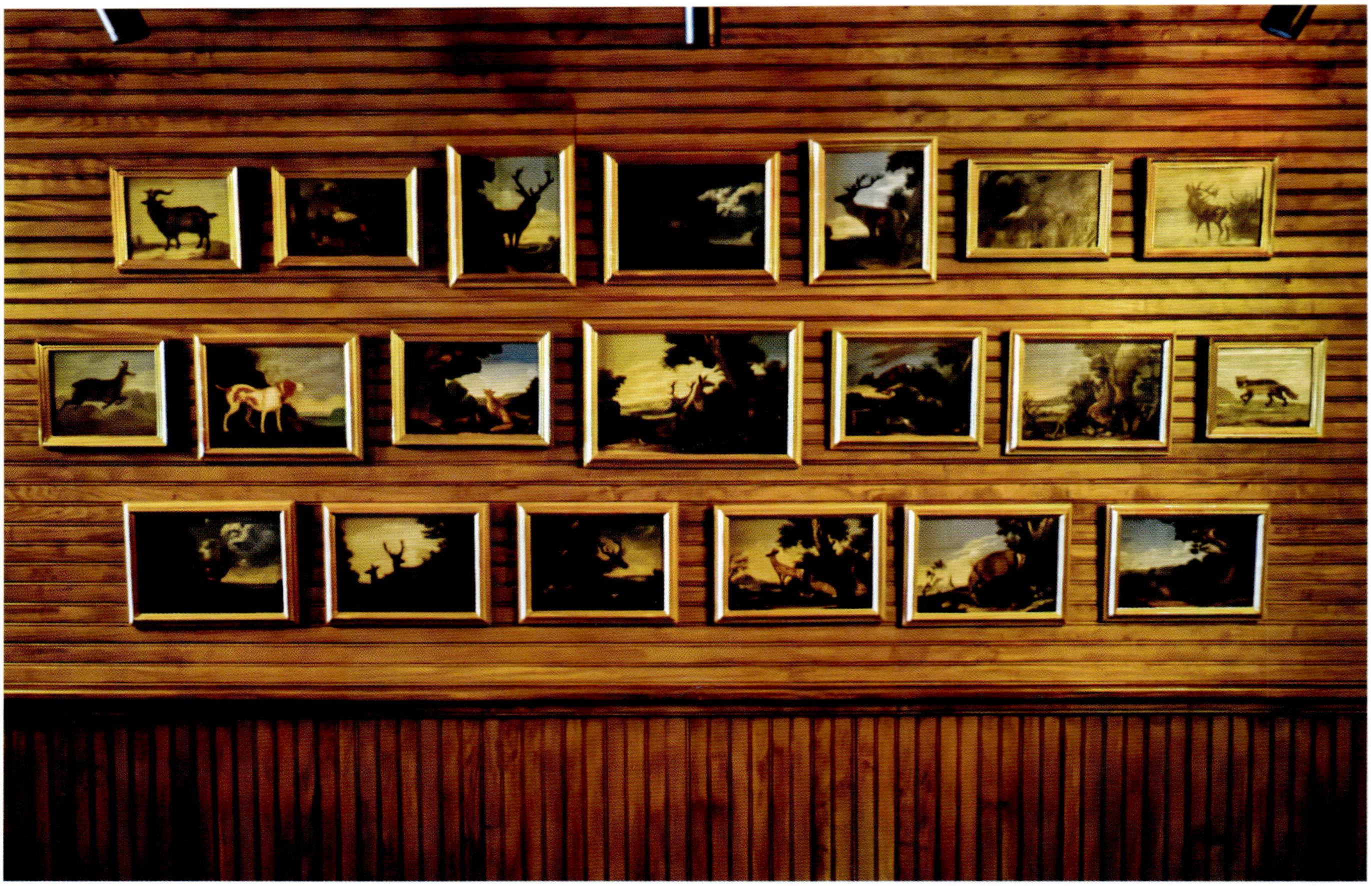

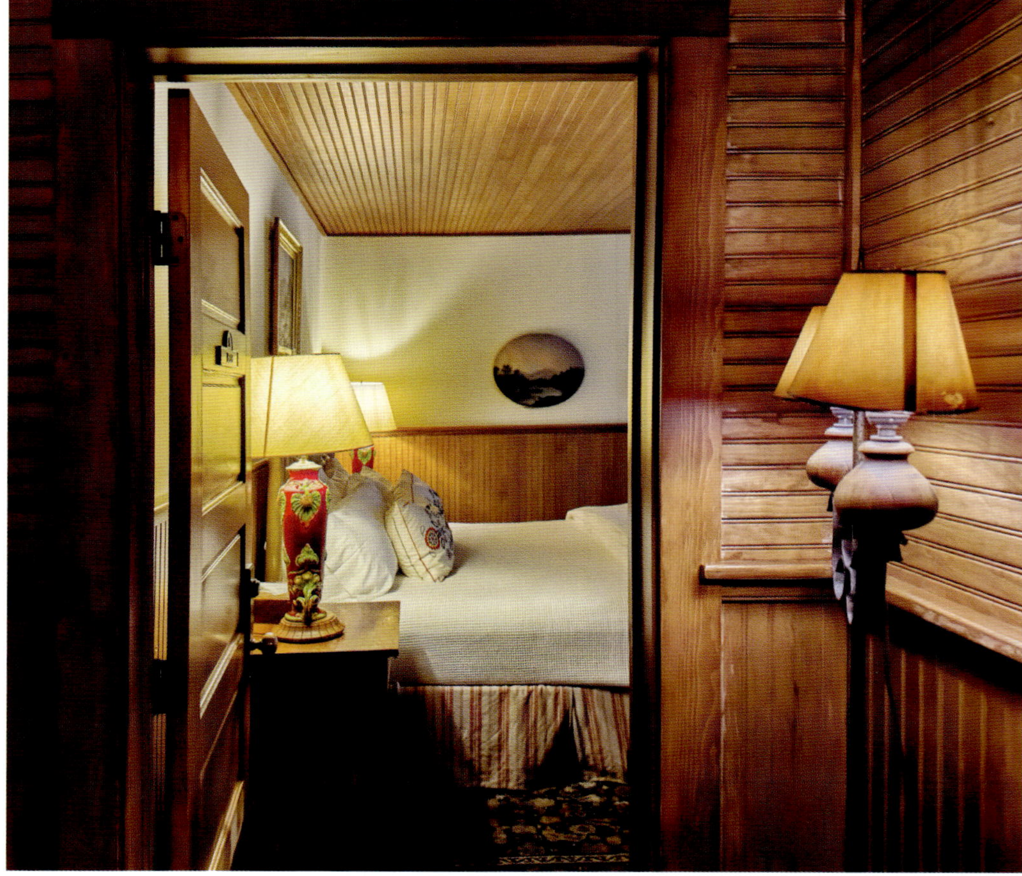

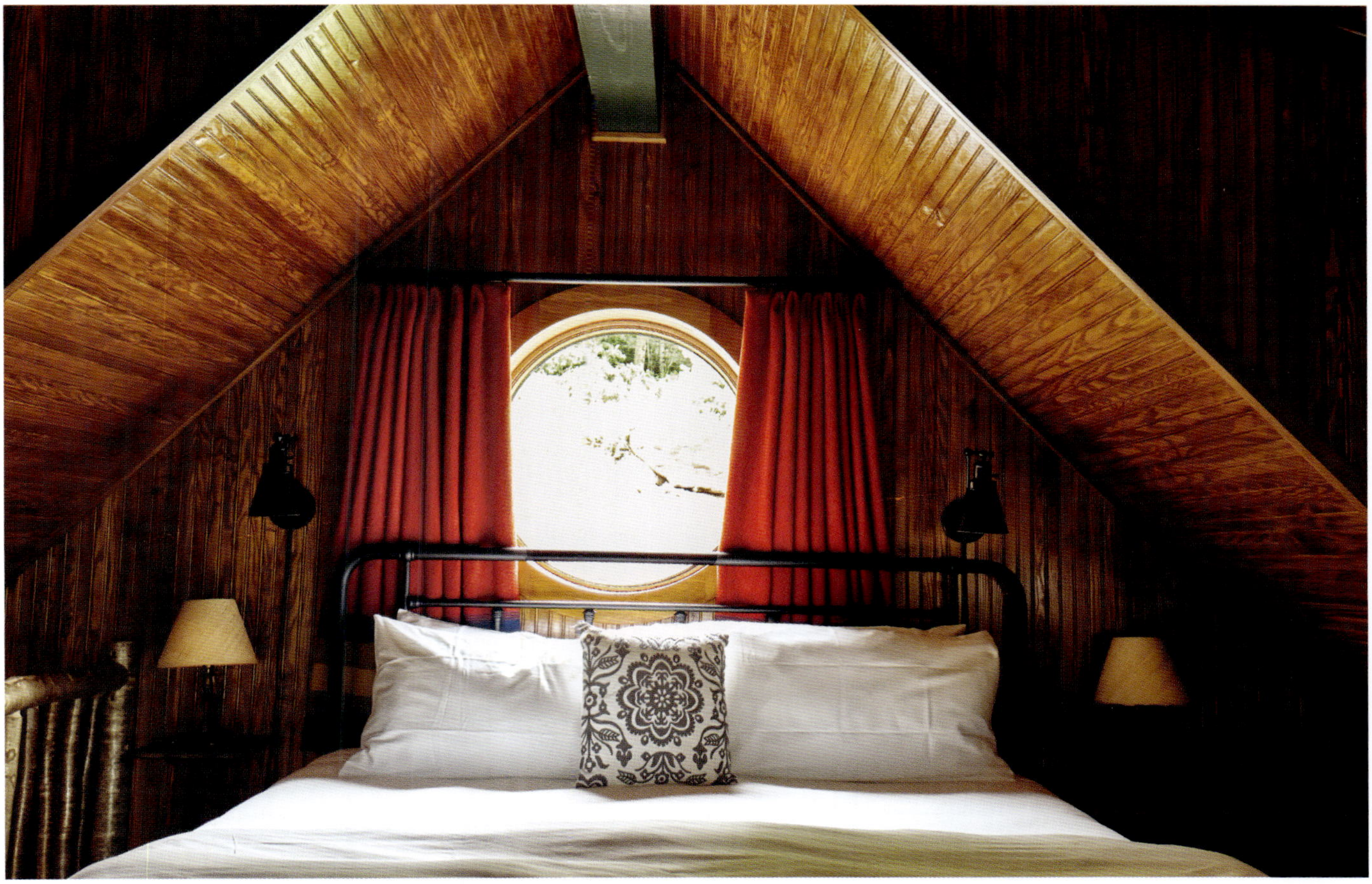

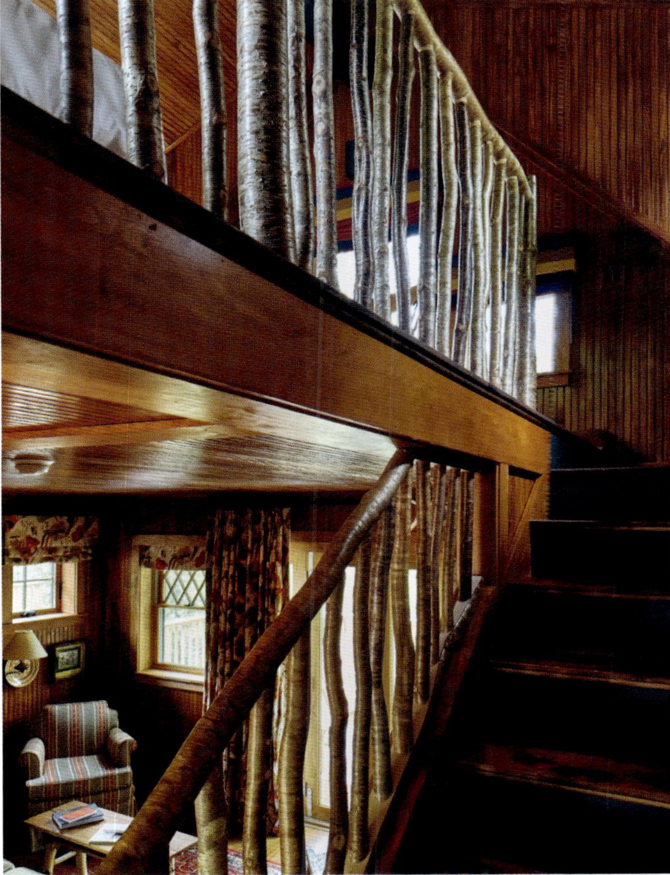

opposite, top
Upstairs in the main hotel, antique artworks decorate the wood-paneled corridor.

opposite, bottom
The Reid and Twain suites share a common entrance. Although each room is designed with the same decorative scheme, one-of-a-kind design details such as antique lighting make them unique.

above
The slanted interior roofline of the cottage's upstairs bedroom harks back to a time when beds were in the eaves of country houses. In the Deer Mountain cottages, the decor is romantic.

left
Each cottage has an element of the rustic mountain decor that Candace Wheeler used in the cottages on her family property. The birch wood balustrade is a style of the area and has been used in mountain cabins for a long time.

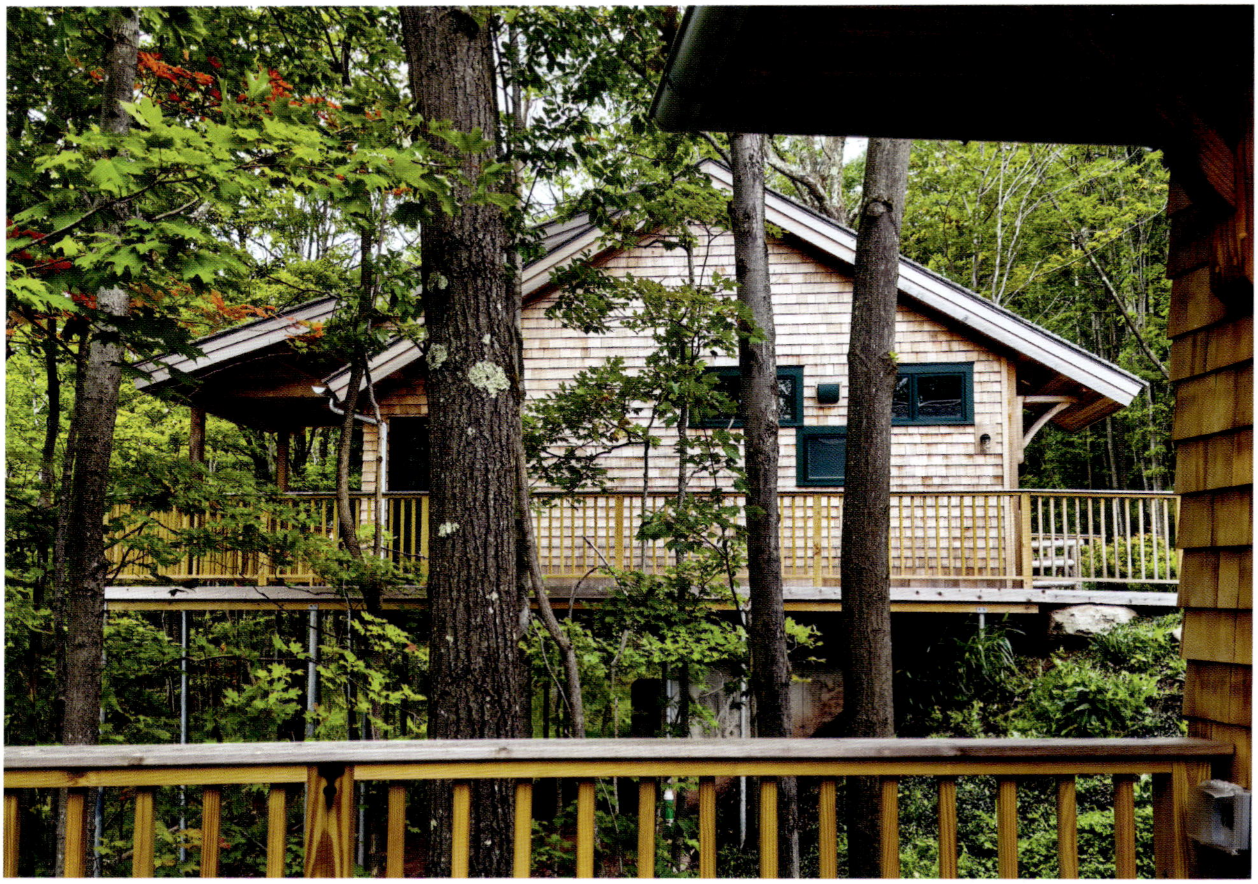

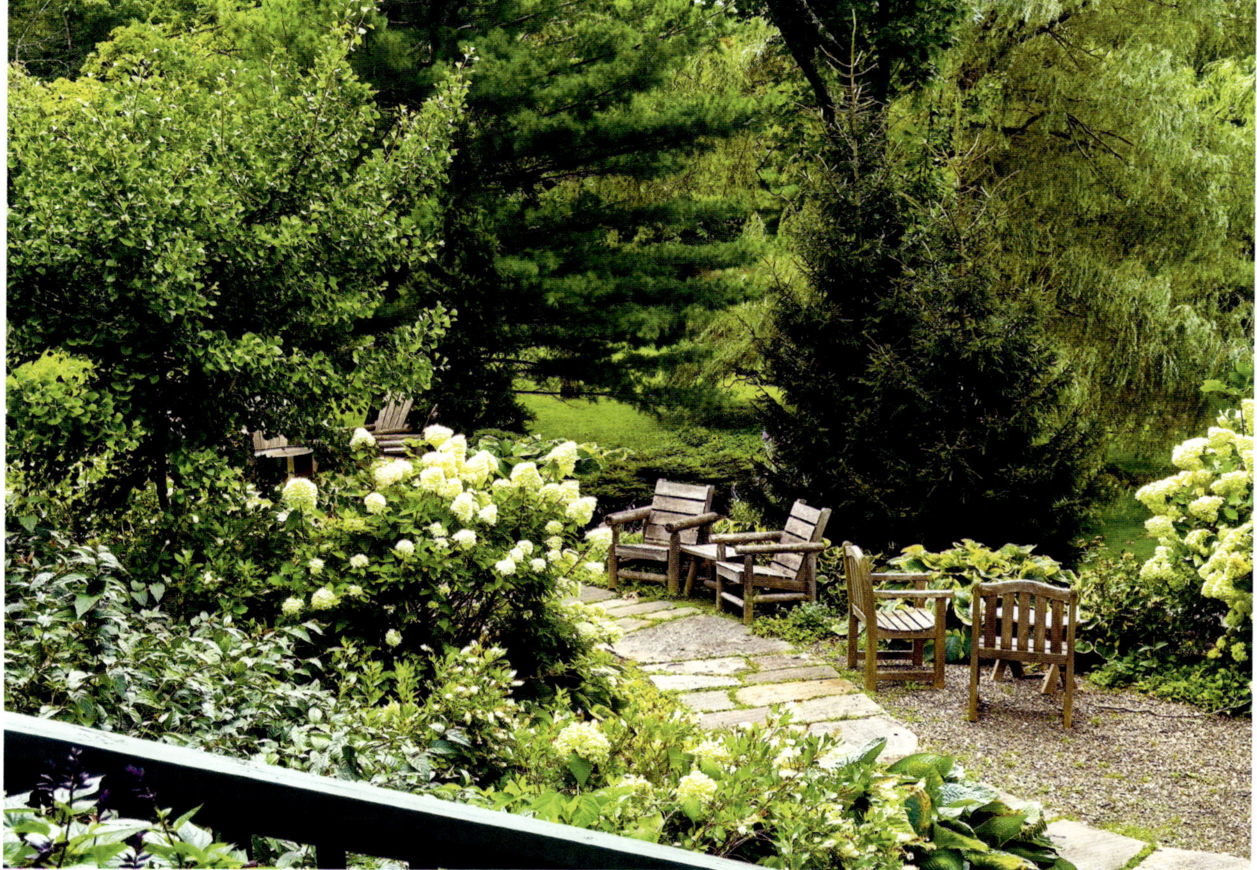

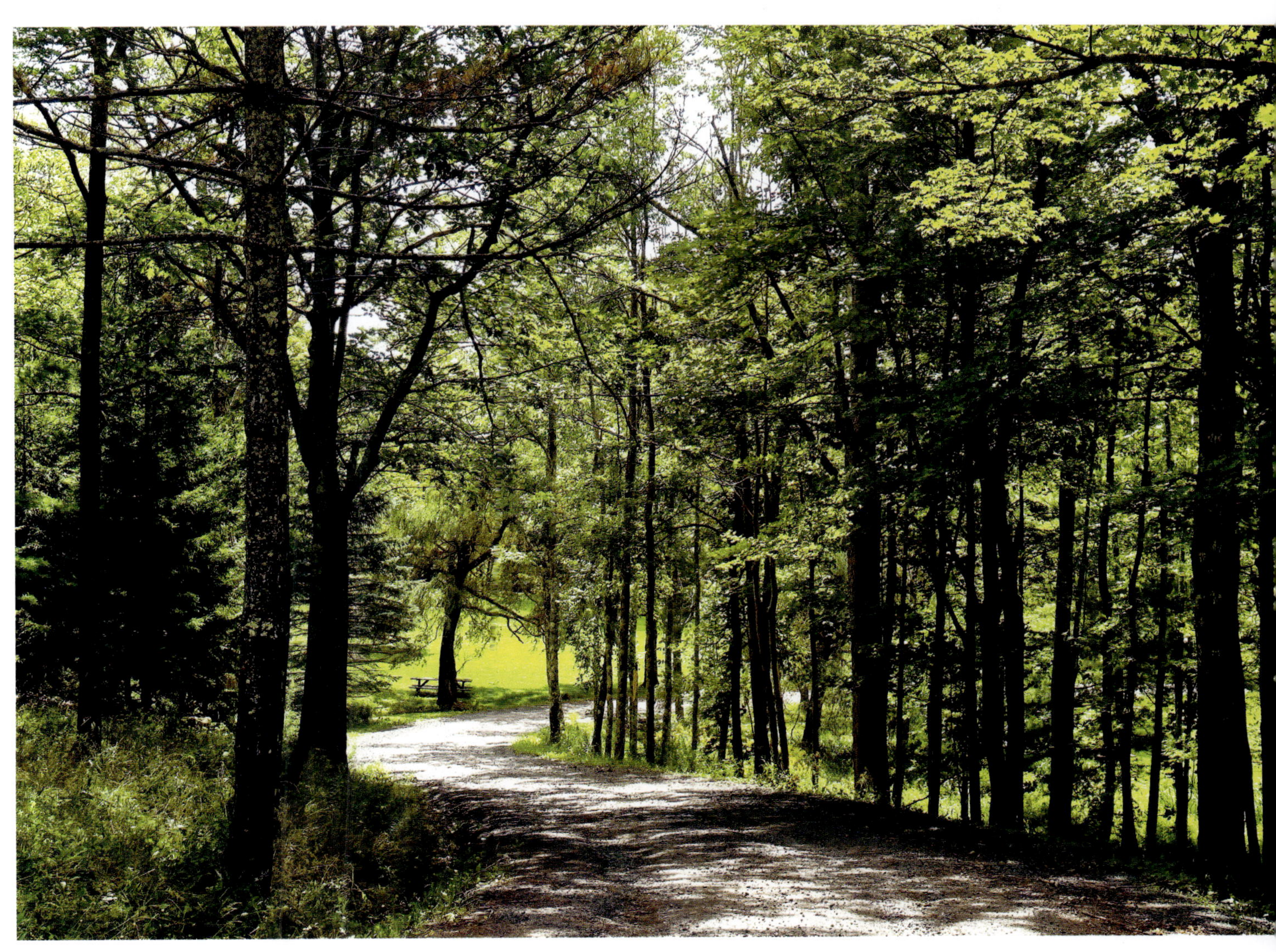

opposite, top
There are four individual cottages not far from the main inn. They all face the forest and are built apart from one another.

opposite, bottom
There are several outdoor terraces, in addition to the porch on the front of the building.

above
The Deer Mountain Inn property is set on 160 acres. A winding road leads to the inn's entrance.

Jim Zivic

Jefferson, New York

This 1863 Greek revival house was a retreat for artist and designer Jim Zivic. Purchased in 1998, it was at first a summer home, a place away from the city, where he built a career making work that focused on materials with industrial associations, such as coal and steel. Jim worked in the fields, sculpting tables from anthracite, a hard coal. In 2004, he made the commitment to live full time upstate in Schoharie County.

The old house is still a work in progress. Jim stands in his kitchen, looking out a window at the pasture. He reminisces about what it took to turn that once almost empty room into a proper kitchen. Each room has a story like that. He runs his hand along the old wallpaper, telling why he chose to keep it—as a "historical document of the house," a "visual memory" of what was. Jim is fascinated with the process of making things, whether interiors, chairs, rugs, a hammock that the design world loves, or stone steps for his front porch. While he may live in a house that is deeply connected to the past, his work is connected to the present. Each interior has an injection of contemporary life in its design, through Jim's furniture and sensibilities.

The reclaimed chicken coop has become his base of operations and home to a new drawing studio. On a U.S. Army drafting table, in the drawings on display, and in the things he collects, there are clues to Jim's thinking. In the design studio, a separate area of the coop, it's not just Jim working alone. He works with assistants who assemble parts of the furniture, sew the rugs, and help him move and load the pieces

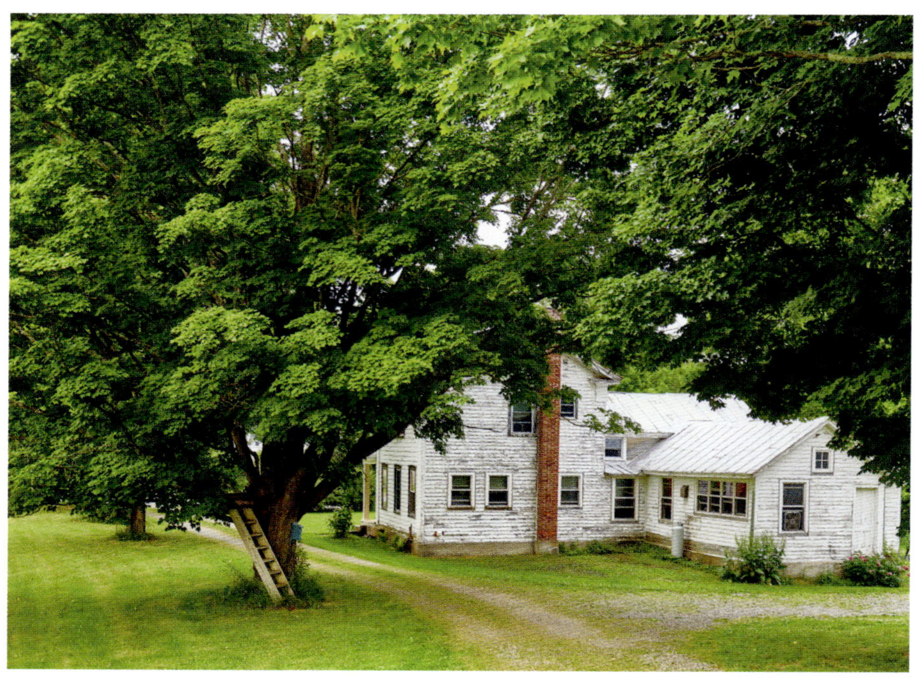

above
The kitchen extension was added to the original house in early times and was renovated in 2003.

opposite, top
Jim Zivic bought the 1863 Greek Revival house in 1998.

opposite, bottom
Jim has been refining the facade of the house. He replaced the columns on the front and made his own versions of Adirondack chairs. He is also painting the house.

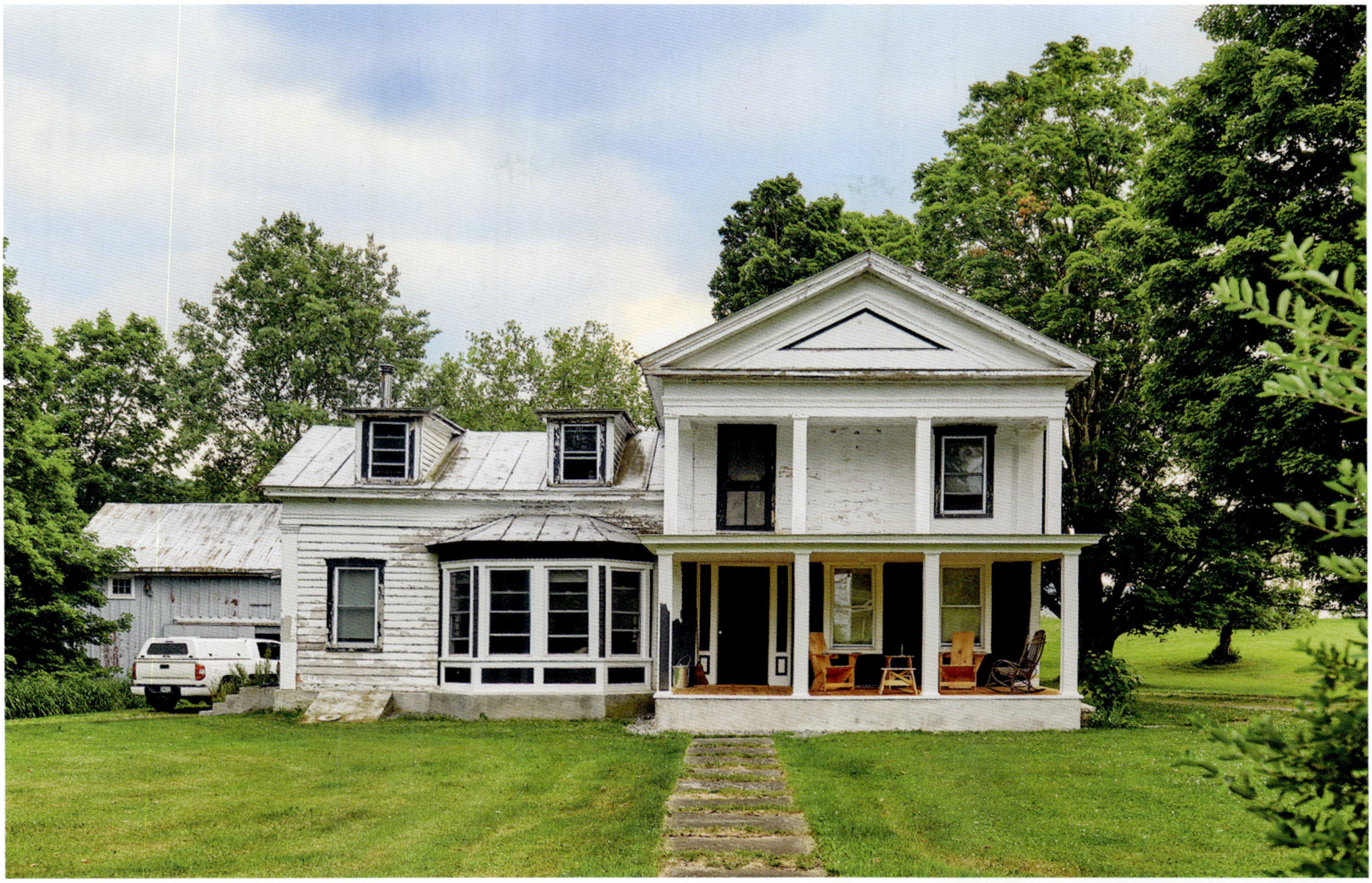

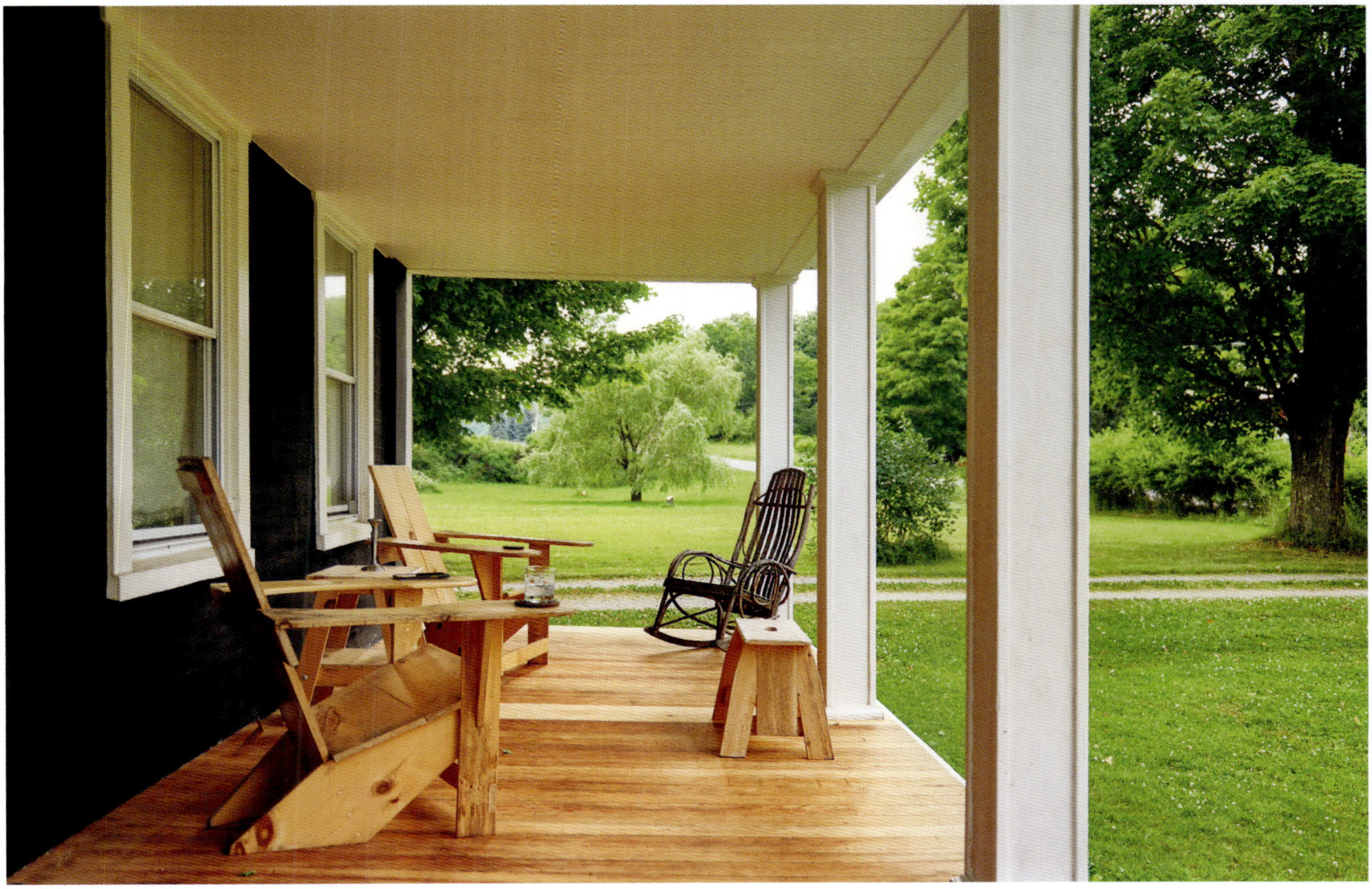

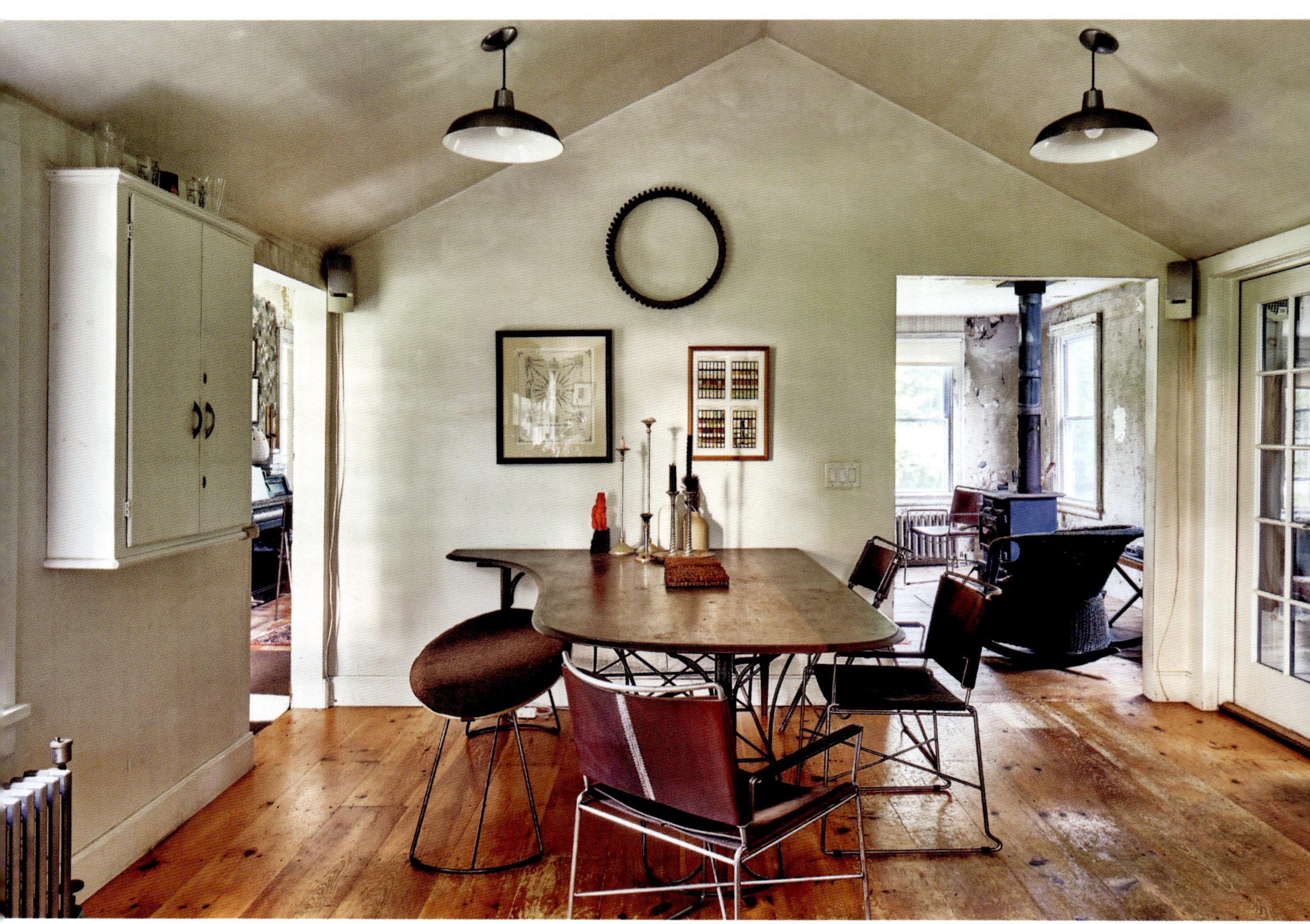

onto trucks that take his designs first to this gallery in New York City and then on to destinations around the world. Jim outsources the production of the chair's forged steel bases to a local company, keeping the work within the community of which he is a part. Jim shares the stories of his neighbors and the town, showing his devotion to the people and place. He continues to pass on that passion to his daughter, Marlo, who returns home during the summers to hang out and help paint the front porch.

above
The kitchen table was made with a baby grand piano lid, wrapped in leather. The chairs, bench, and table all have steel bases.

opposite, top
The living room is a combination of old decorations and new furnishings. Jim kept sections of the old wallpaper he uncovered. He designed the Pullman dining chair by the woodstove. An early map of the United States hangs above the velvet-covered JZD sofa. The coffee table was made from singed oak from a local tree. It is inscribed with lyrics of a song by Melora Creager in poured tin. Jim uses Texas sheepskins as material in his designs, a decorative and practical element that adds warmth to the house.

opposite, bottom
Jim placed a Weed daybed of his own design (named for the material of the wedge headboard made by Joe Holtzman), with its aluminum base, in the bay window of the front parlor.

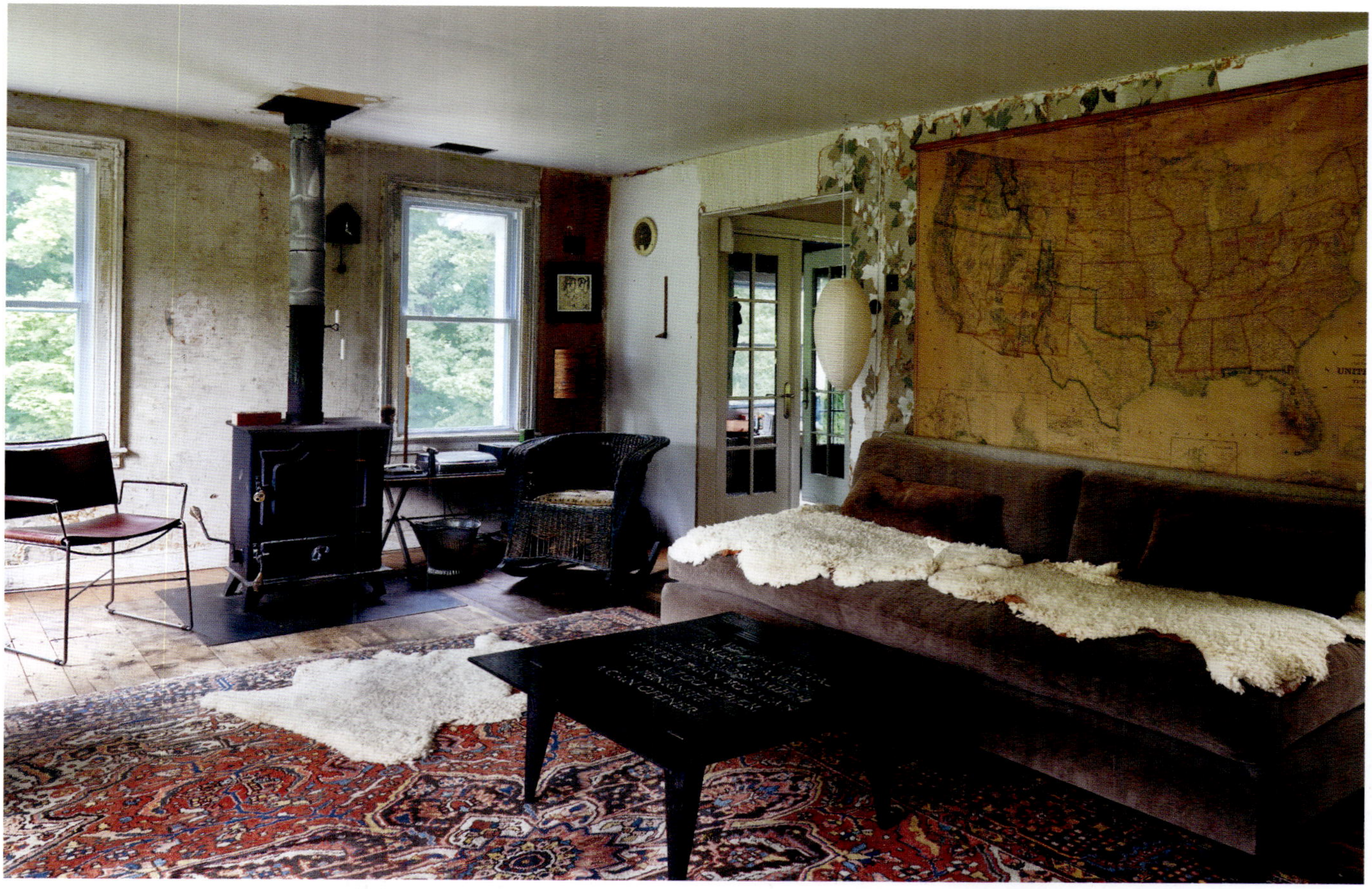

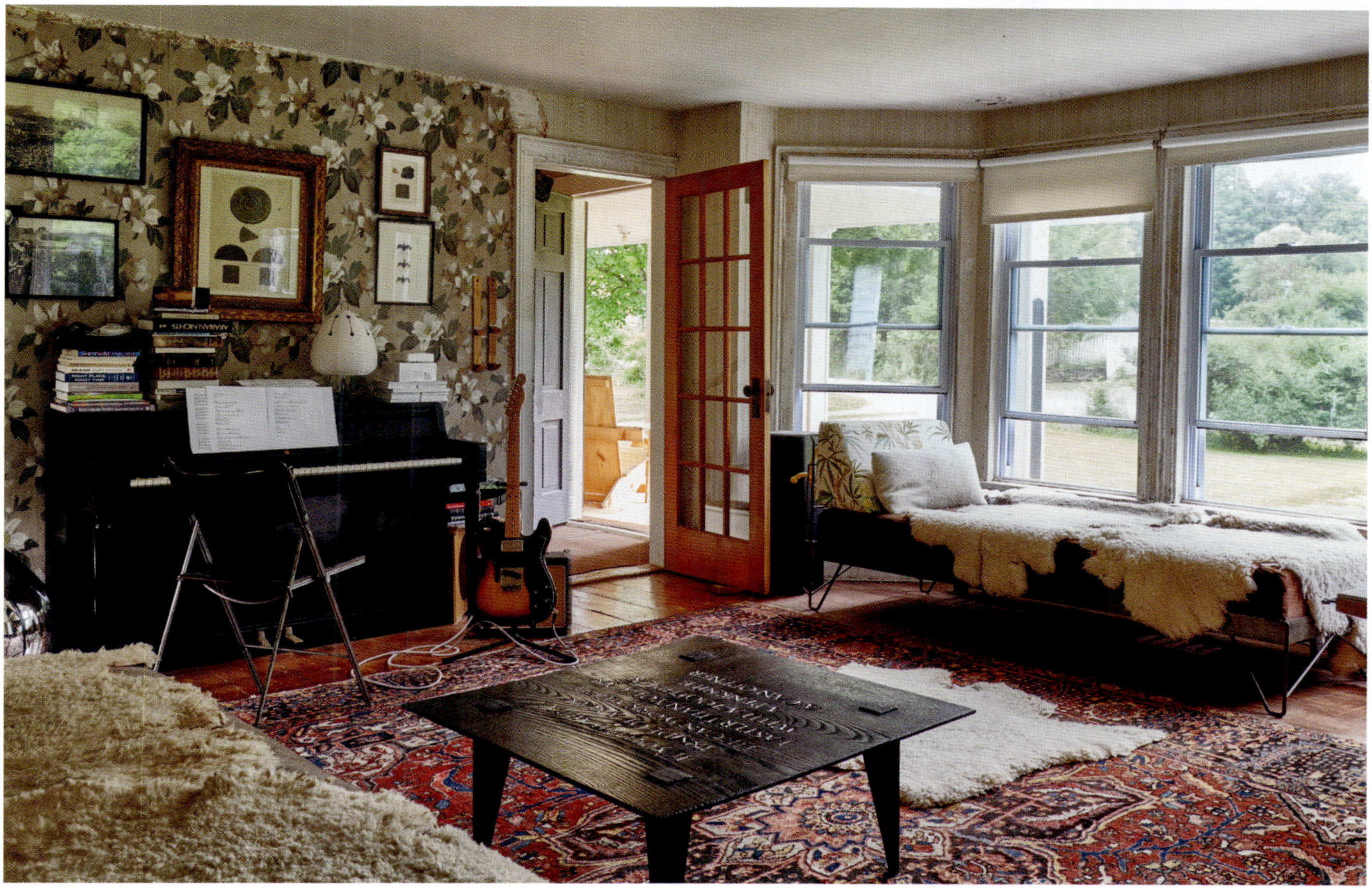

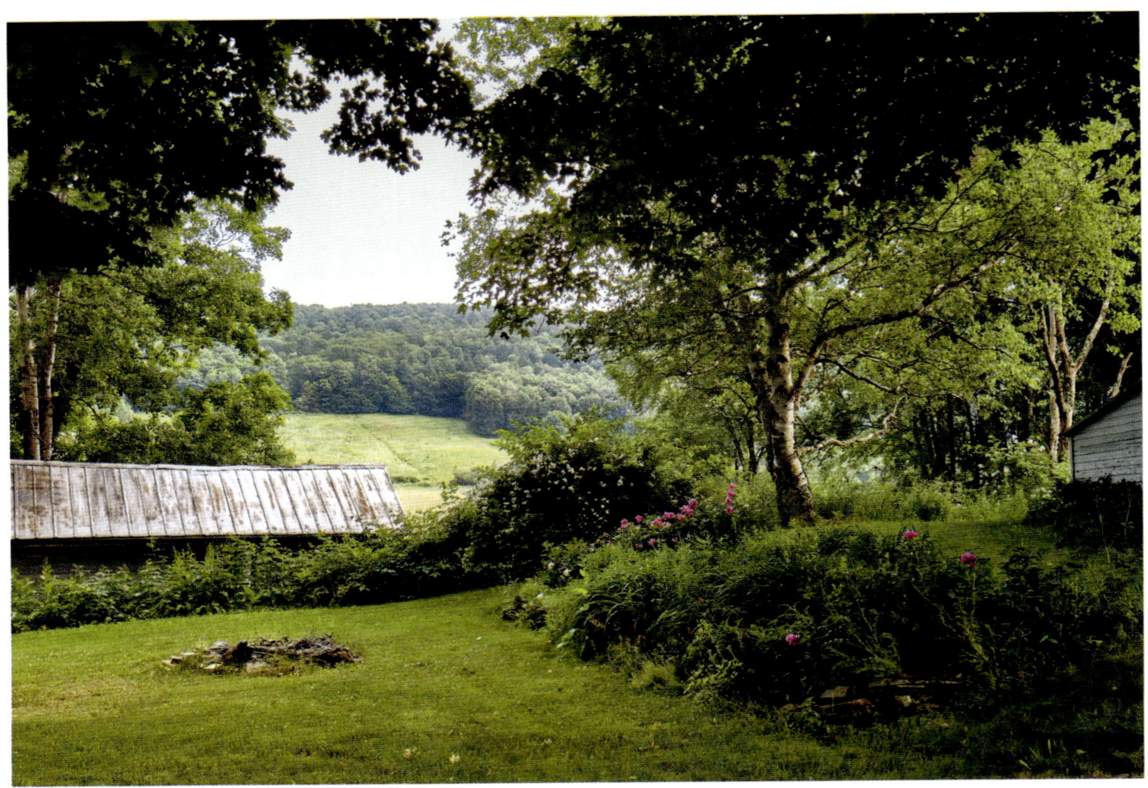

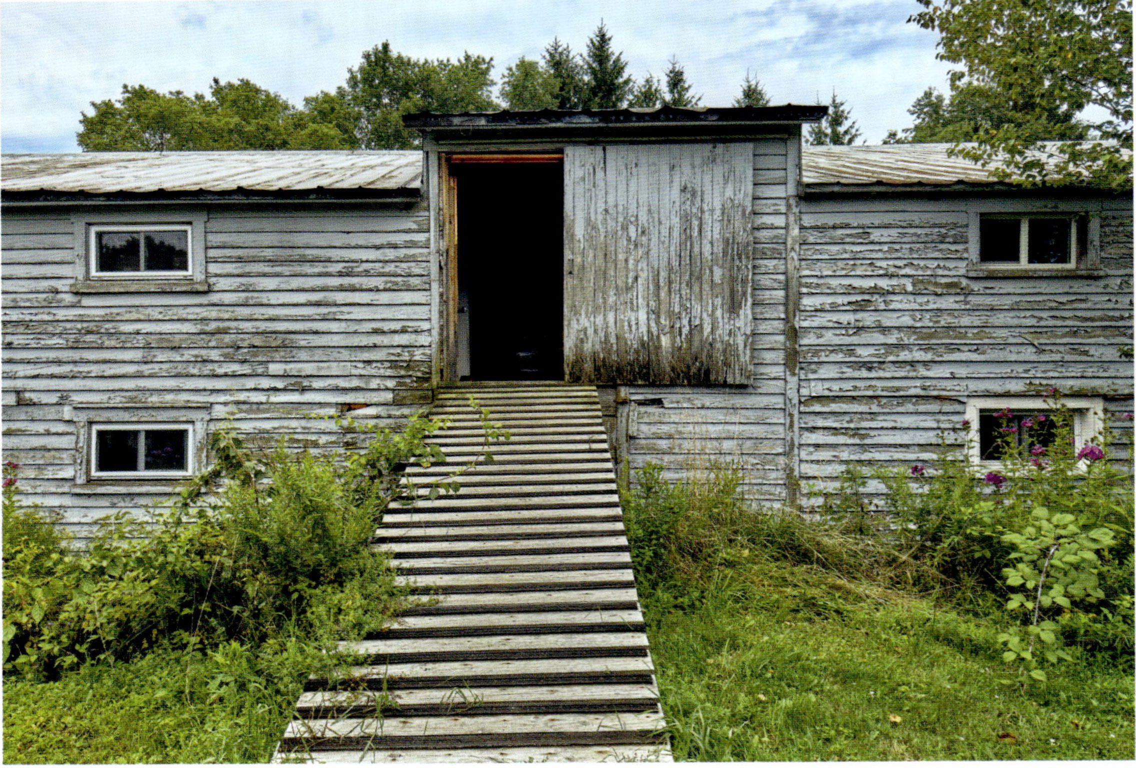

top
A view across the pastures of Jim's and his neighbor's property.

bottom
The old chicken coop on the farm contains an art studio, a furniture manufacturing site, and a music studio. A wood ramp leads inside.

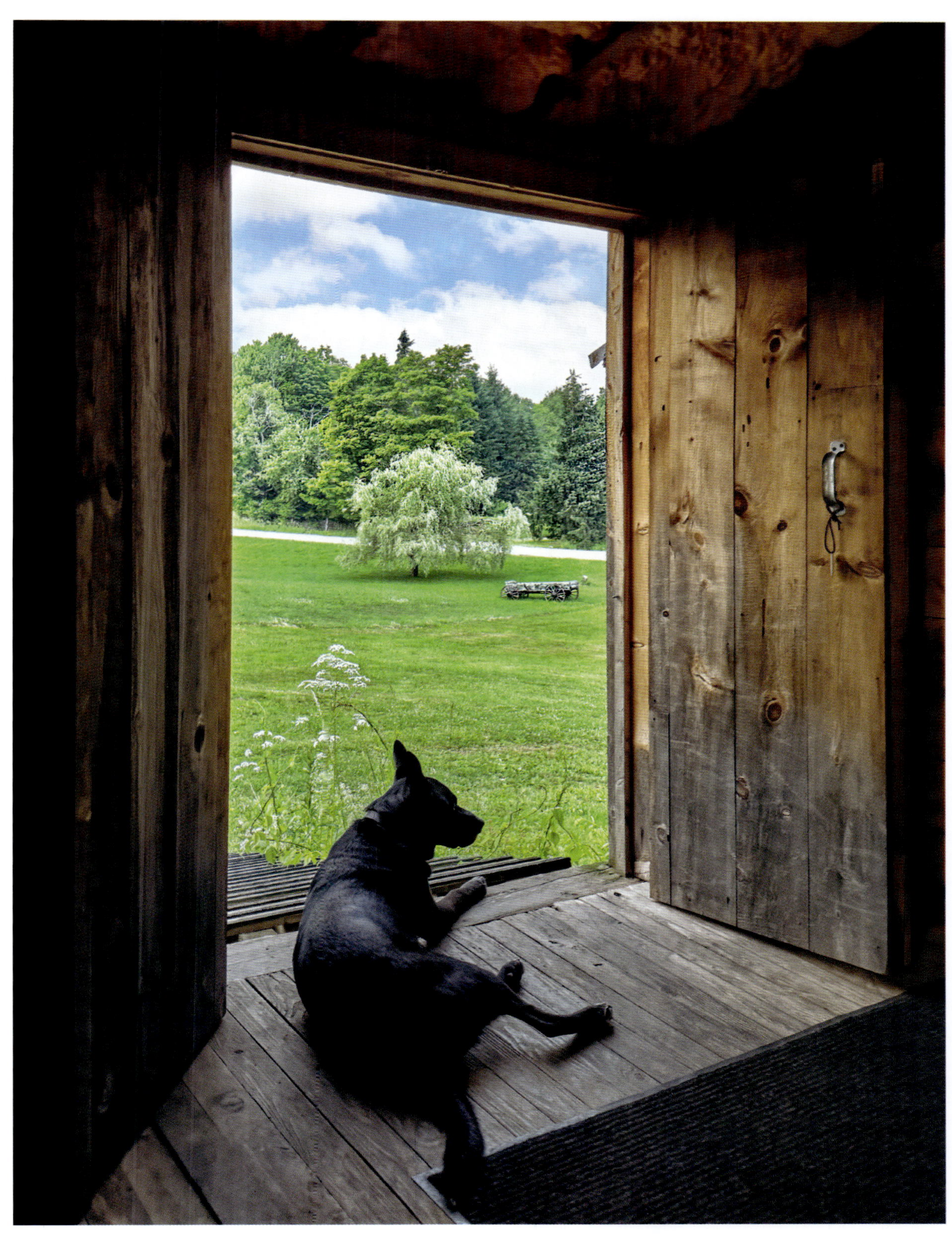

above
Jim's dog, Peter, relaxes in the doorway of the coop.

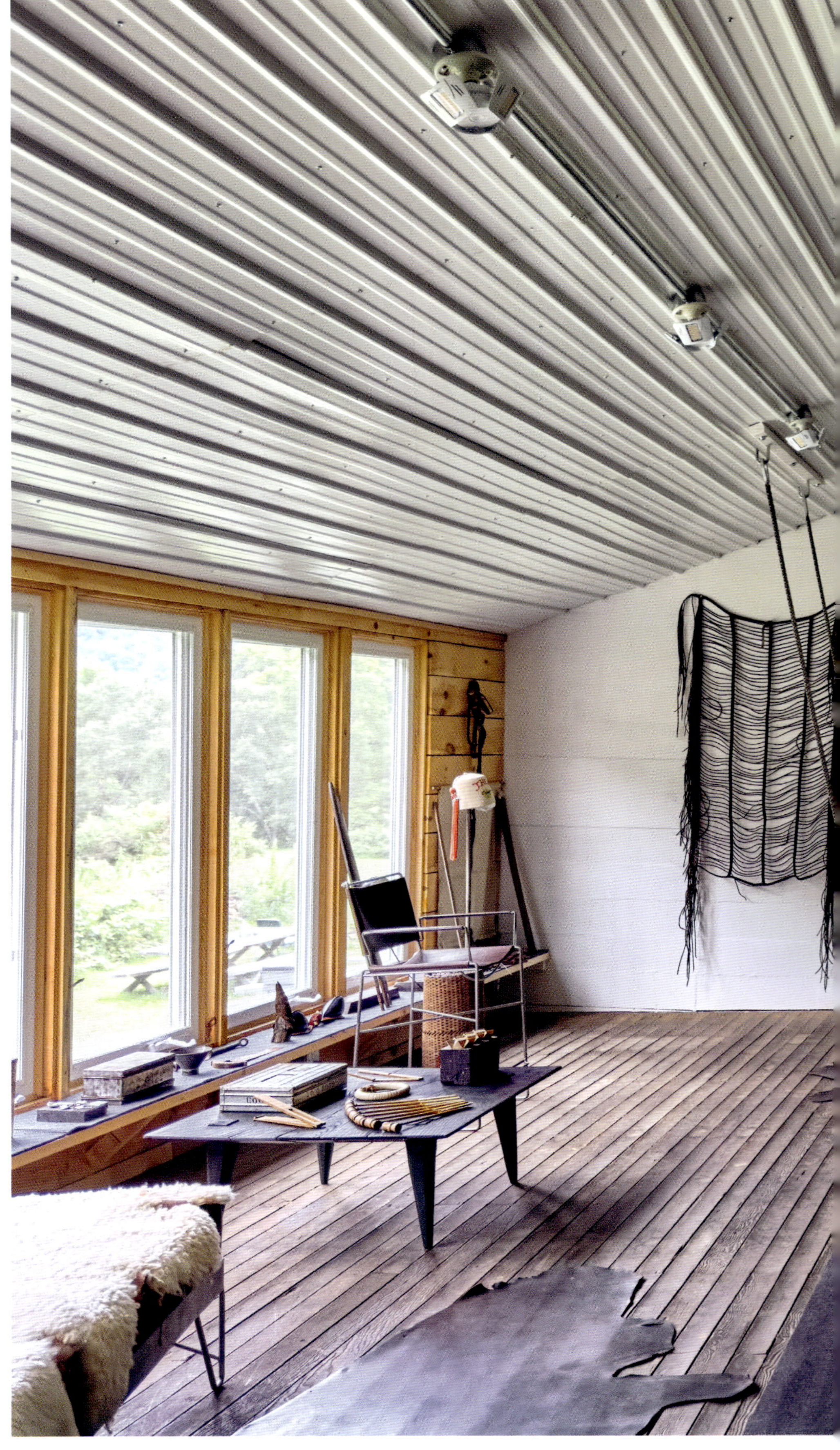

One of Jim's most recent projects was renovating one section of the coop as a studio. He installed one of his most well-known designs—a hammock—at one end. Jim has been making versions of the hammock for over twenty years, but interest escalated once Gwyneth Paltrow featured her custom-made hammock in an article in *Architectural Digest* in 2022. Two leather horse fly blankets hang at one end of the room. The studio has a wall of windows. Jim displays collections of things that inspire him on the window ledge.

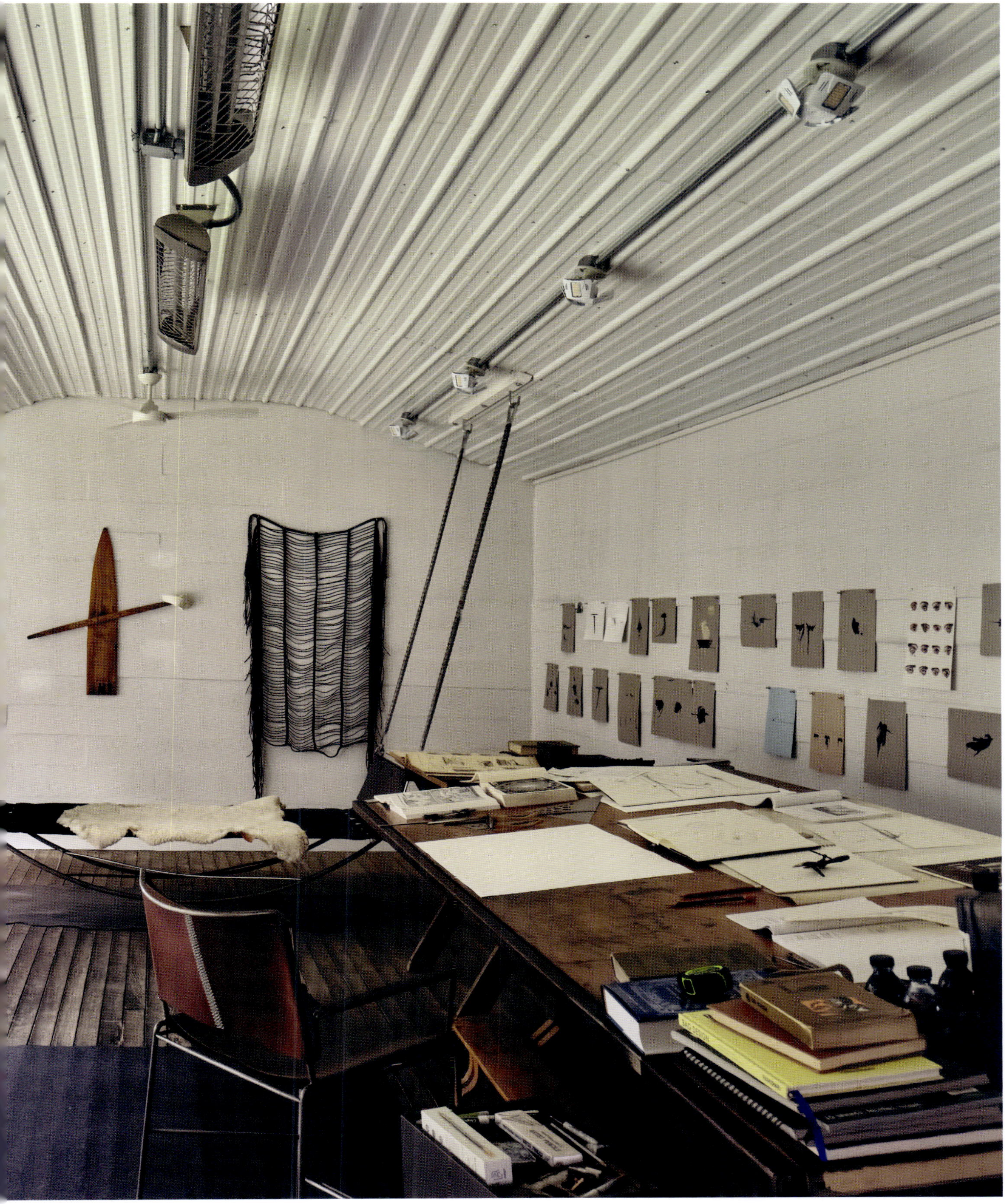

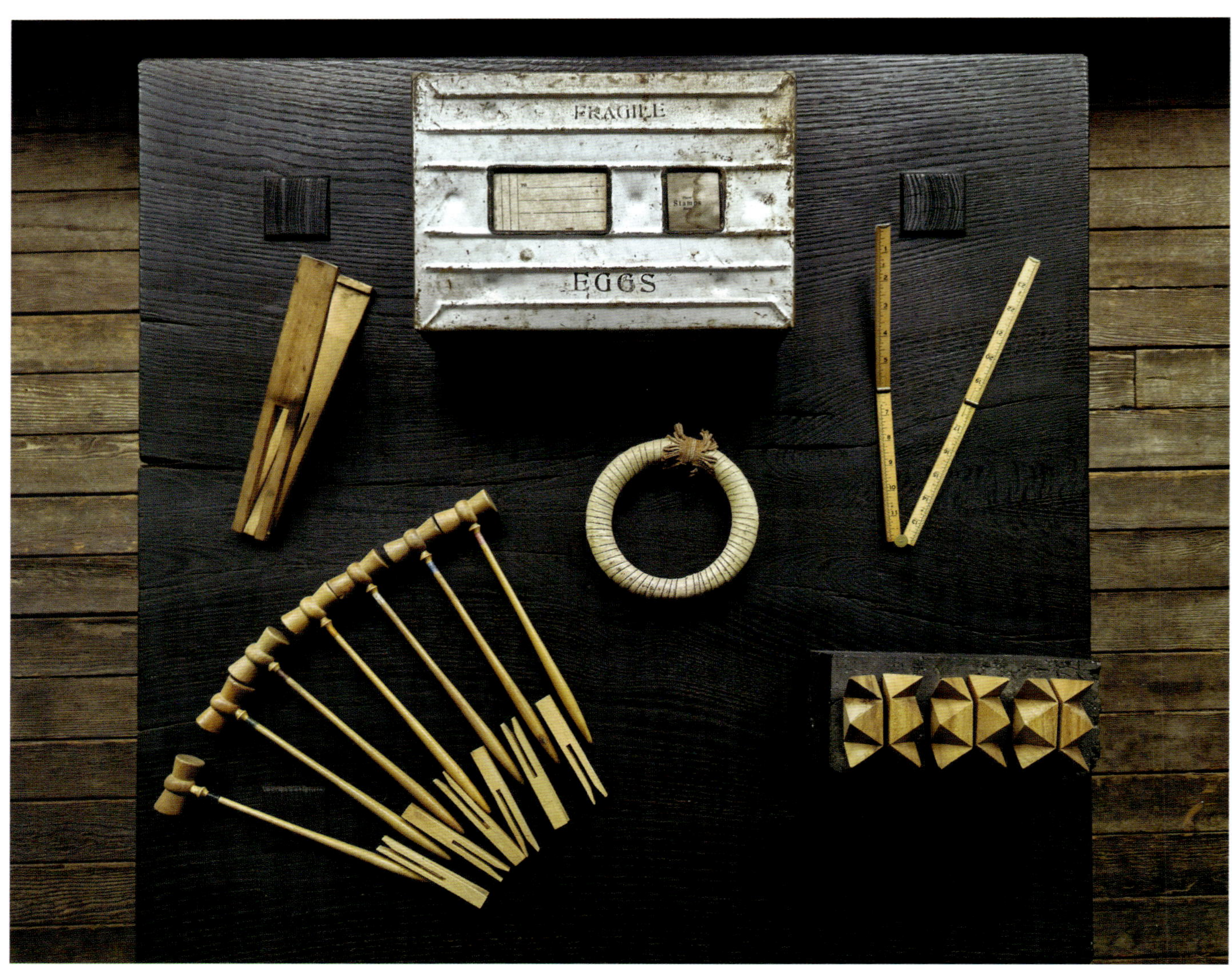

above
Some of Jim's artfully displayed objects: a metal egg carton (with a return address for reuse), part of a wooden measuring tape, local homemade wooden clothespins, wood mallets from a game, a brick of coal with a mind-bender puzzle placed on top, a ring from a saddle, and wooden toast tongs.

opposite, top and bottom
Jim's sketches are made on and hang above a U.S. Army drafting table, a gift that he held on to for years. The table has finally found a home in the studio. It holds a collection of books and diagrams, as well as drawing and measuring tools.

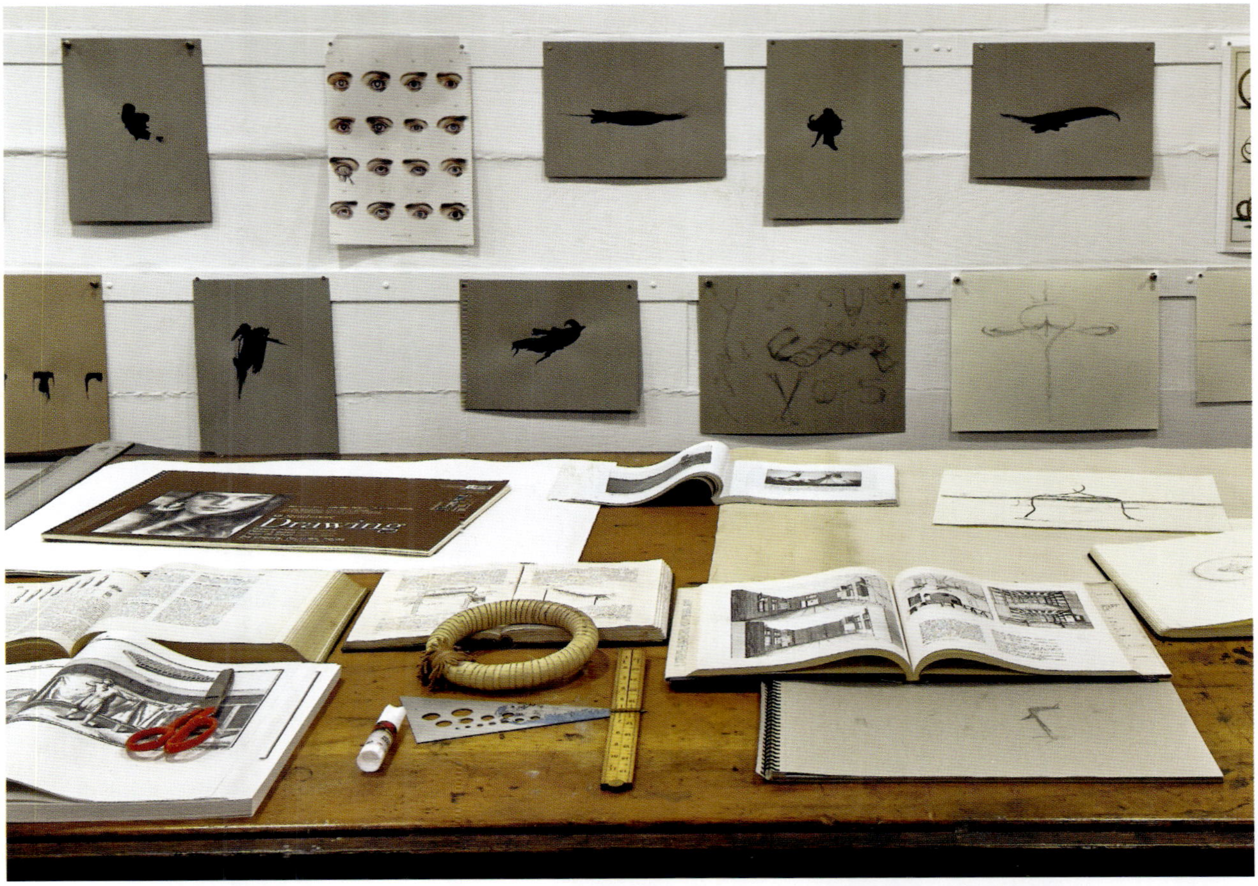

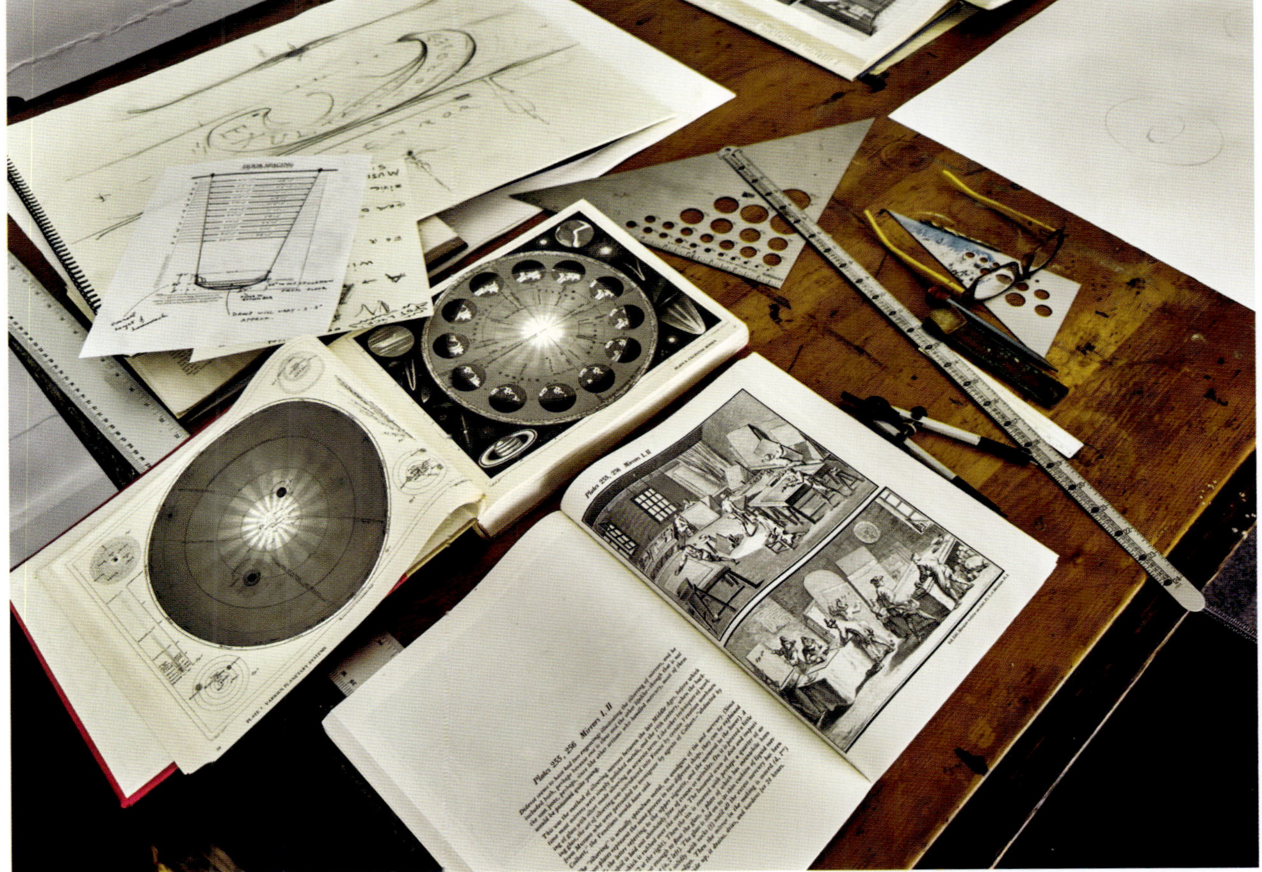

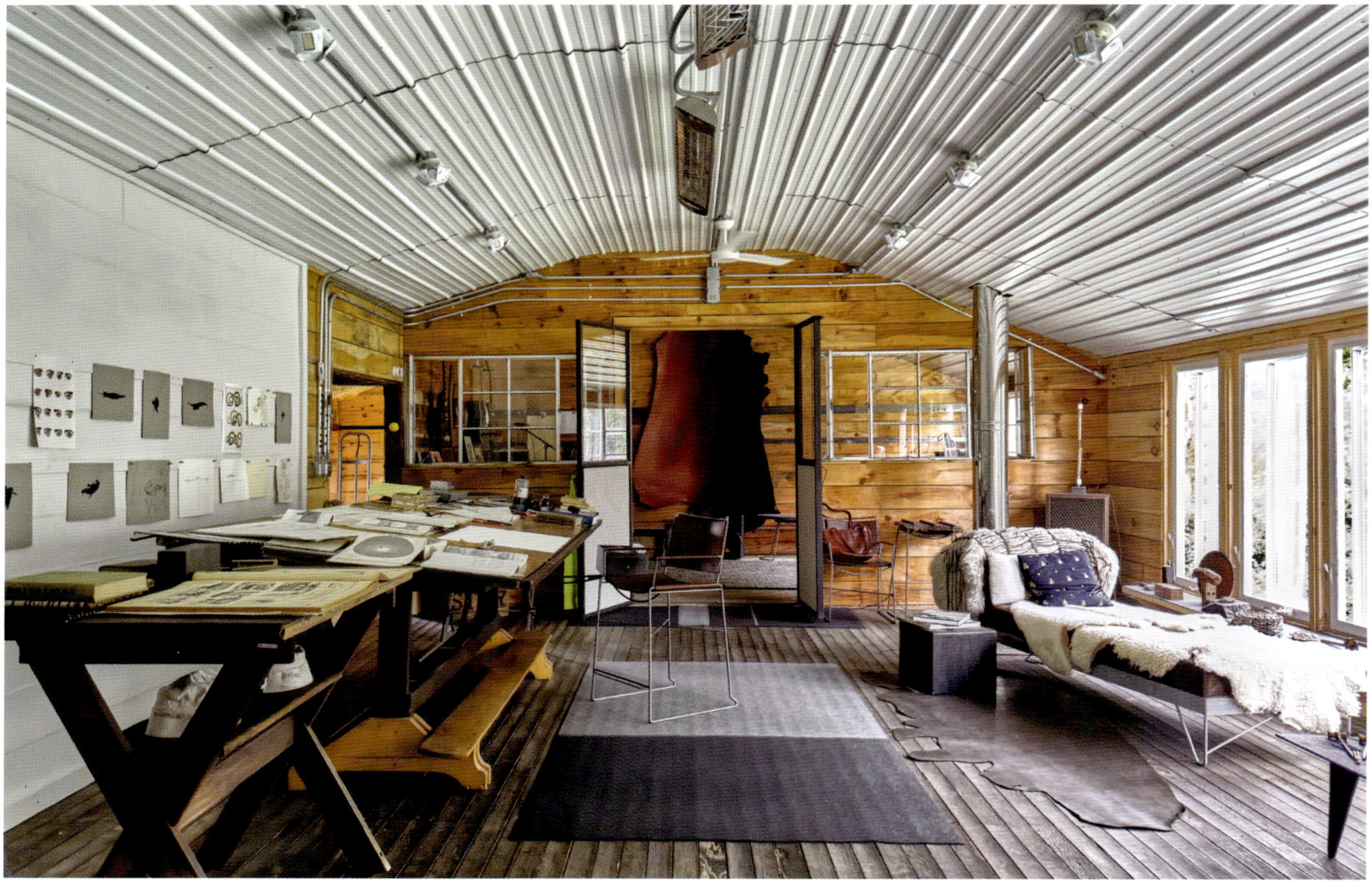

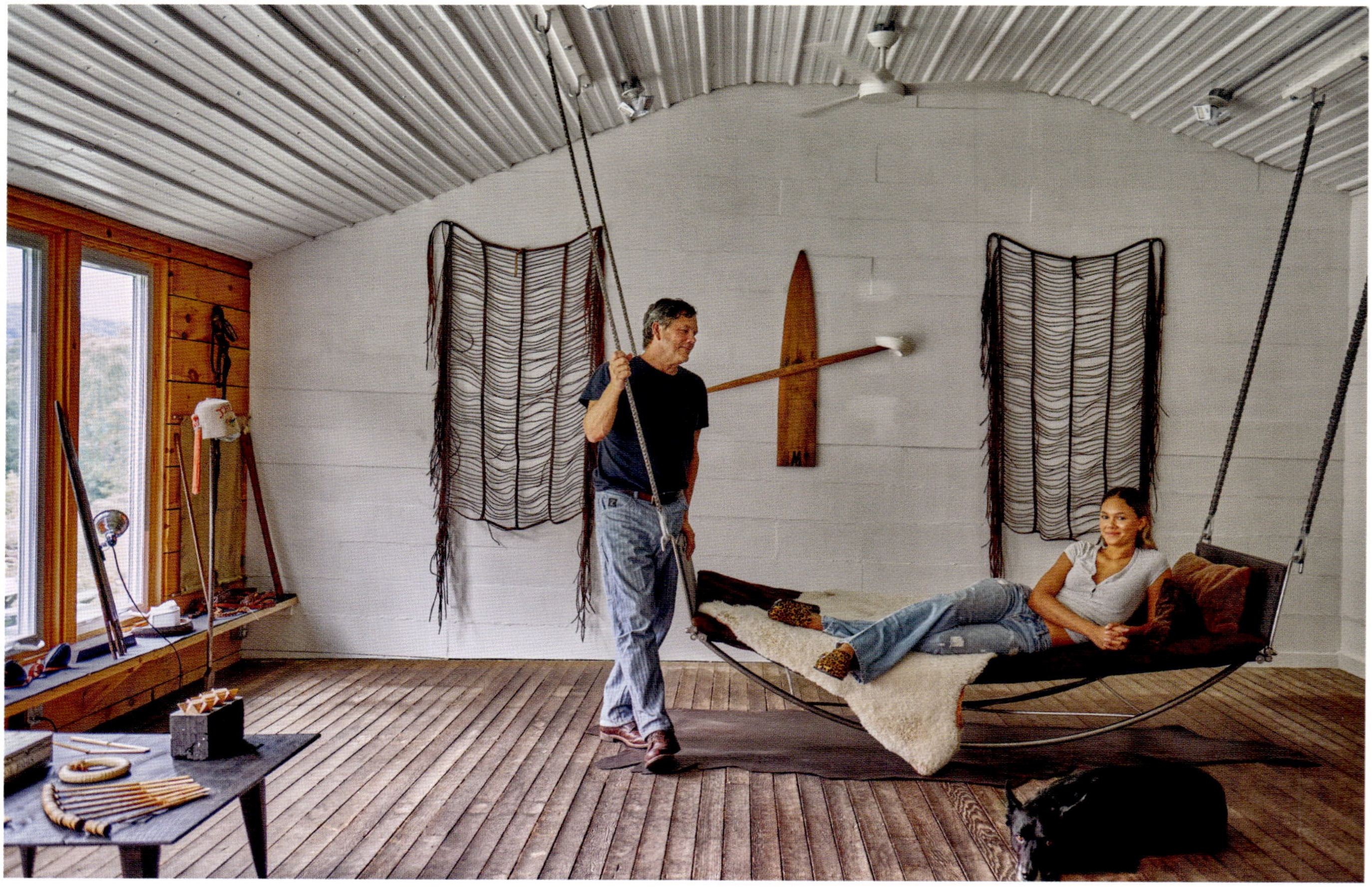

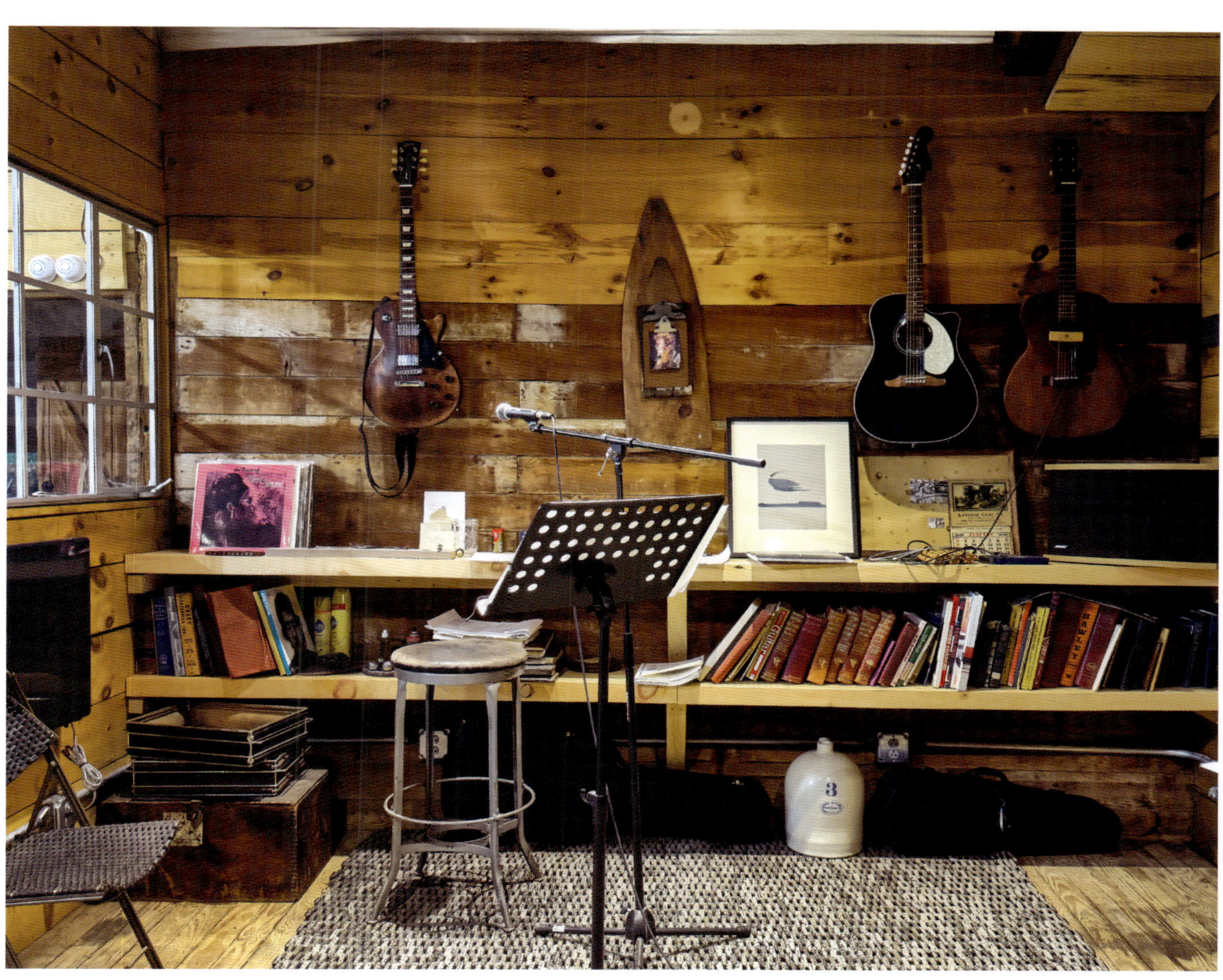

opposite, top
Another view of the studio looking toward the music room. The ceiling of the studio was made with metal roofing material that is normally used on barns or houses. Interior windows and a door separate the two spaces but allow light to flow into both areas. The two-tone felt rug was designed by Jim. He has also used leather as a floor covering. Leather hides hang in the music studio.

opposite, bottom
Jim and his daughter Marlo, hanging out in the drawing studio.

above
In the music studio, shelving was made for his record collection. Guitars hang against a wall made of rough-cut pine from a local sawmill down the road. Jim designed the chair and rug using an industrial leather link material.

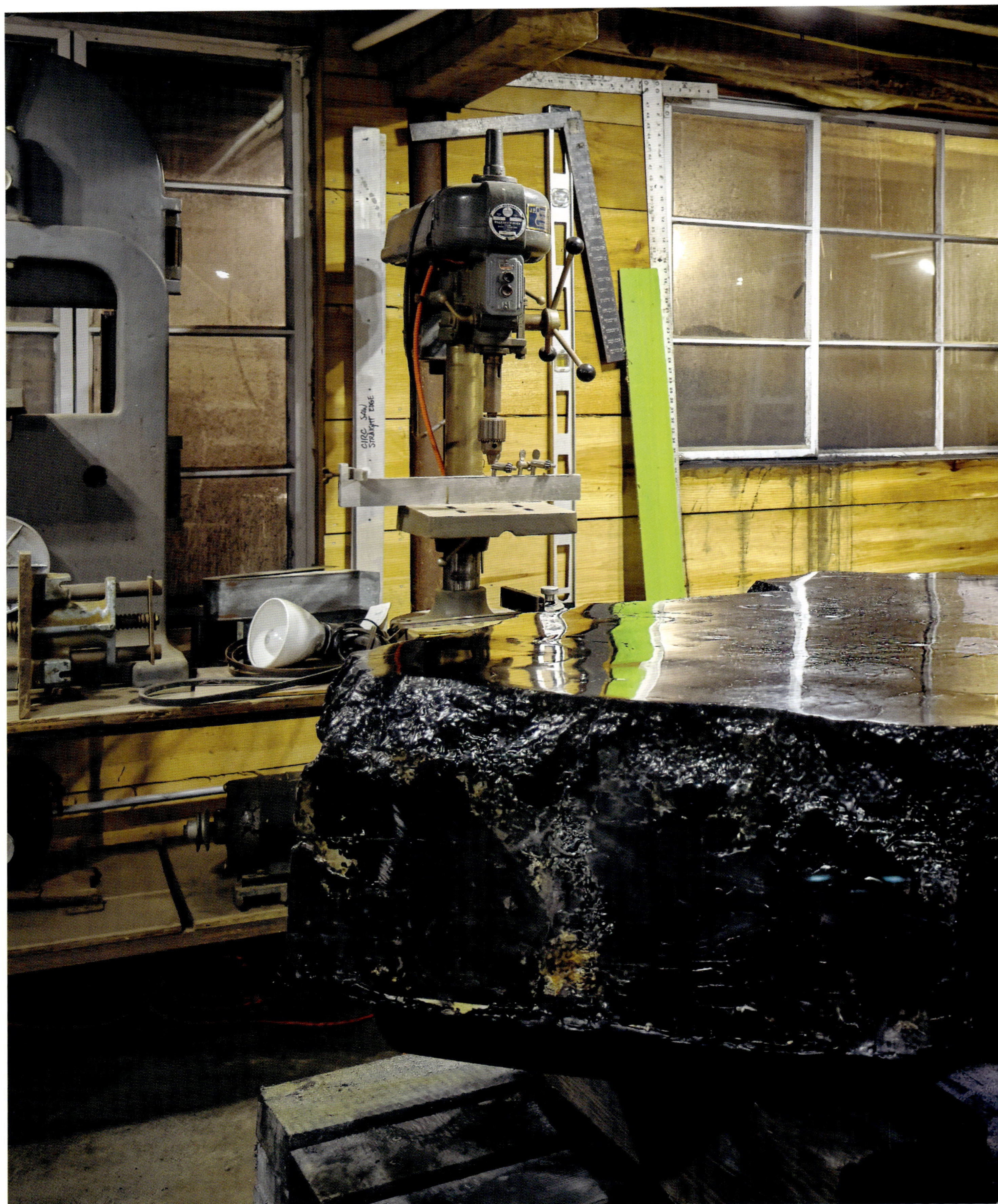
CIRC SAW
STRAIGHT EDGE

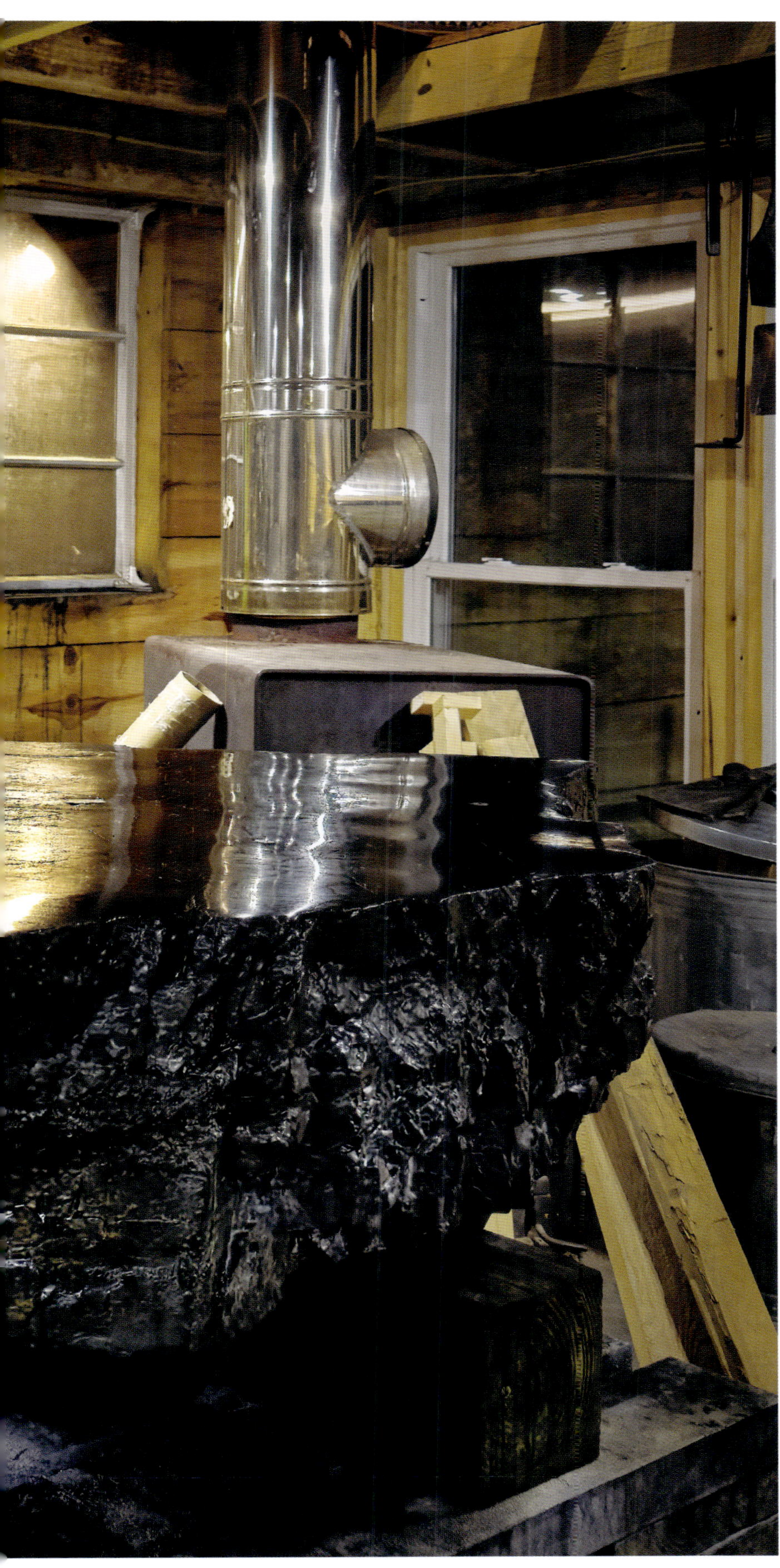

On the lower level of the chicken coop, Jim works on and stores his furniture made with coal. Those pieces are sculpted into shape, then honed and polished, reaching an almost mirrorlike surface.

Chase Booth and Gray Davis

Craryville, New York

Chase Booth and Gray Davis love "lake life." Both grew up near the water—Chase on the Pecos River and Gray's family having a boat and spending summers on a lake in Tennessee. Their Chris-Craft speedboat is docked on Copake Lake in Columbia County. They also have a canoe for trips around Zecky's Pond in front of their latest house in Craryville, a hamlet within the town of Copake. Their social life revolves around the water. In fact, it was a friend who introduced them to upstate New York. Gray is a principal of Meyer Davis, an international design firm, and Chase, his husband, came up from New York City to visit in 1994; they have had a place here since 1996.

This house is their fifth house in the area. They built and sold two of their previous homes—both were on Copake Lake. The last house had an Adirondack style and the house before that was decidedly modern, but this house is different. "I love living in an old house," says Chase. The house was built in 1792. He adds, "We let the old parts remain old and we kept the new parts new." One recent extension was turned into a mudroom and a dining room with sliding doors to a deck with views of the water. They also transformed the newish screen porch into a living room that has both a woodburning stove and almost all glass floor-to-ceiling windows and doors.

Chase and Gray reimagined how to use the existing spaces. For example, the primary bedroom suite is now downstairs in the former first-floor front parlor. Guests have the entire upstairs, which consists of three bedrooms. One small upstairs room became a large bathroom. There is a symmetry to the kitchen that Gray picks up on in his interior interventions. The custom-made kitchen island is parallel to the galley kitchen and proportionate to the small room. The furnishings are a blend of new and vintage finds from antique stores in Hudson, New York, about thirty minutes away. Light reflects off the painted-white wood floors. Above all, water views and nature are front and center, adding to the tranquility of their home.

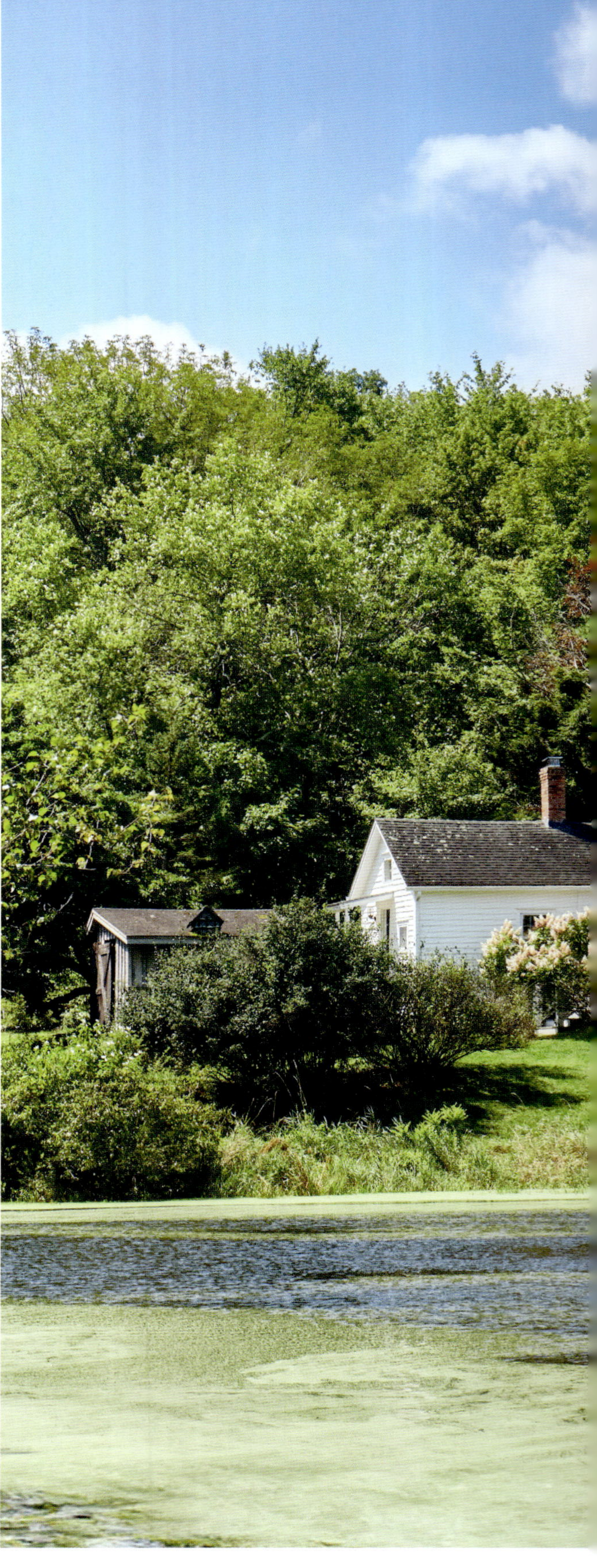

Chase and Gray's upstate home sits beside a small pond in Columbia County.

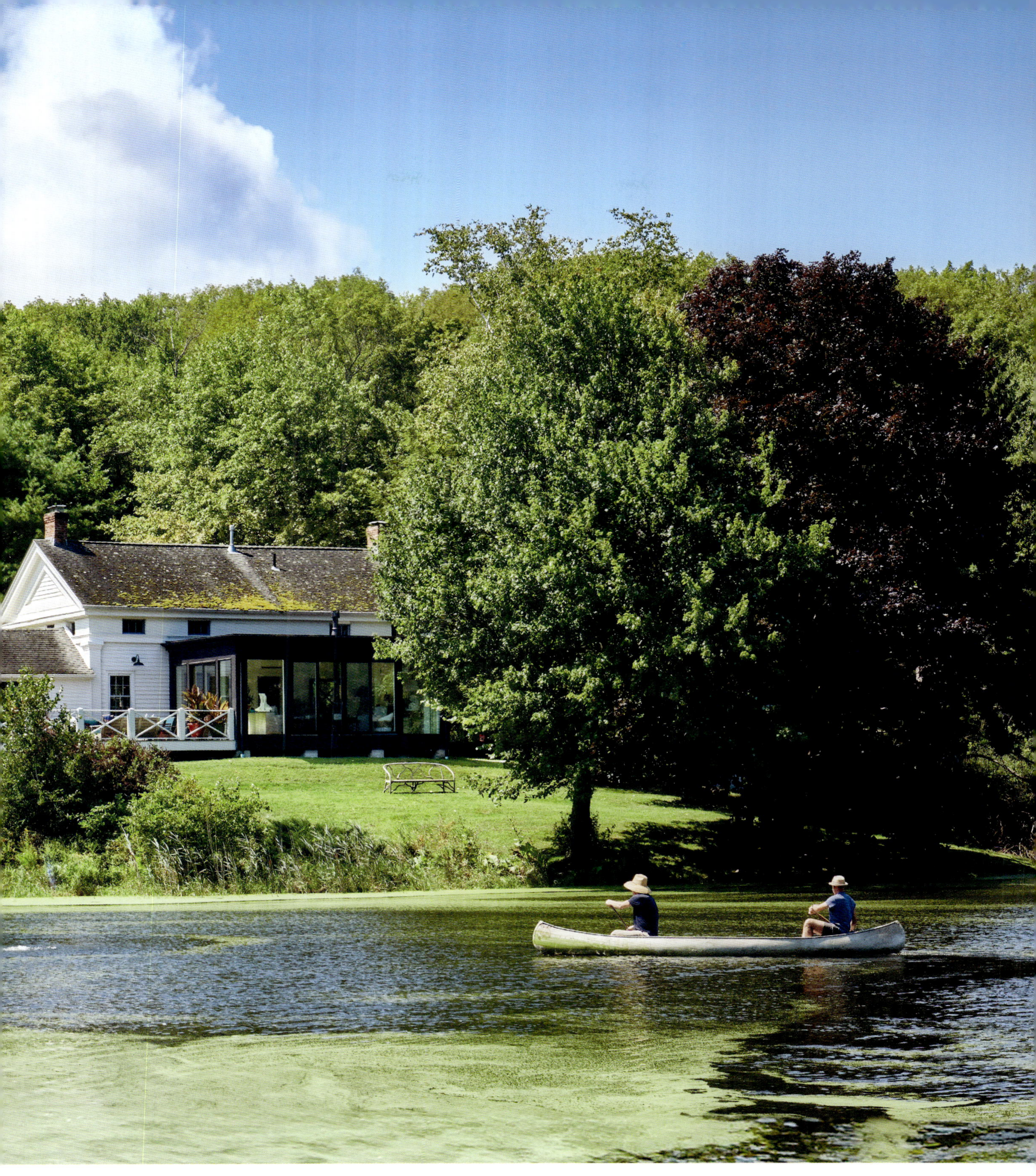

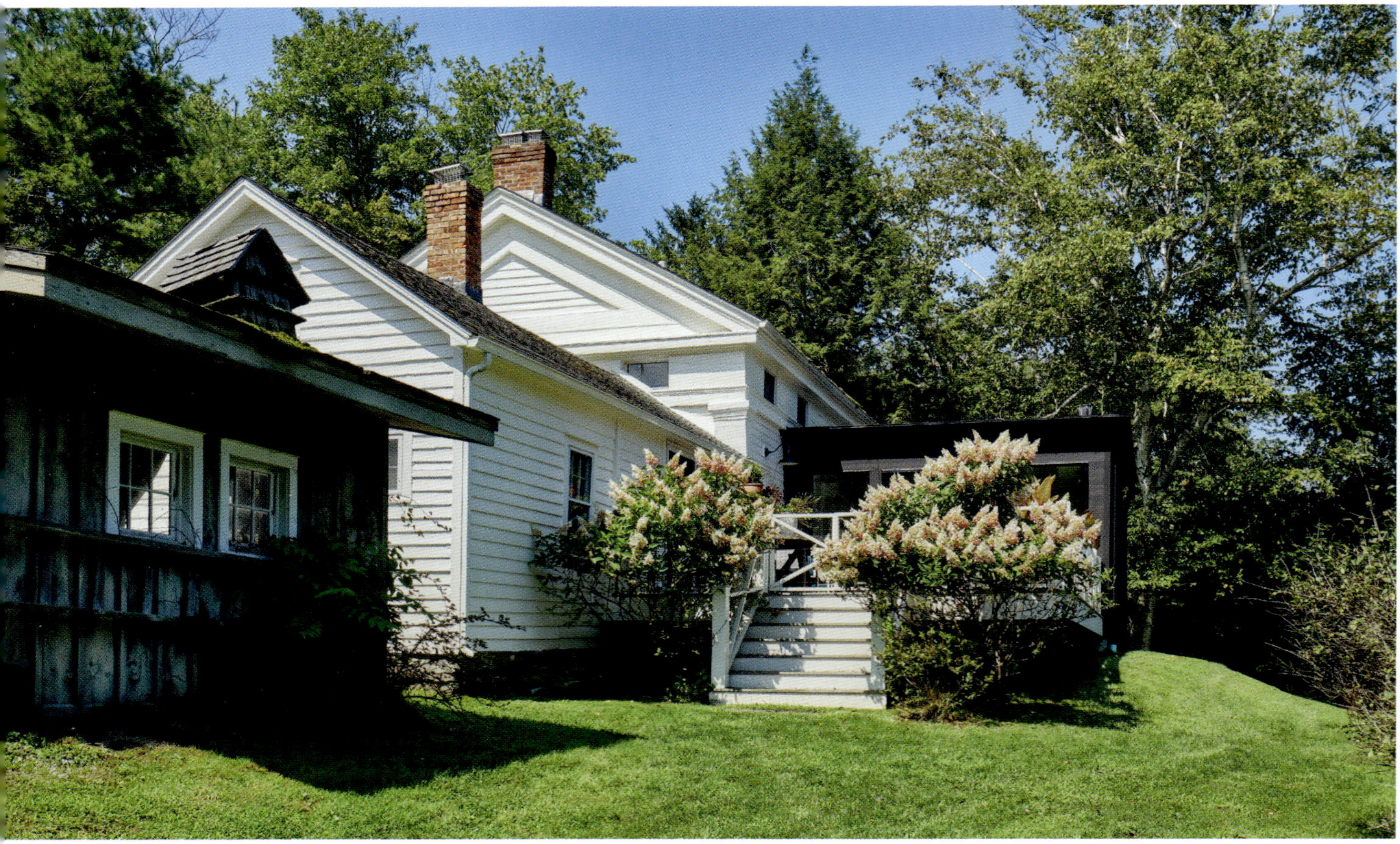

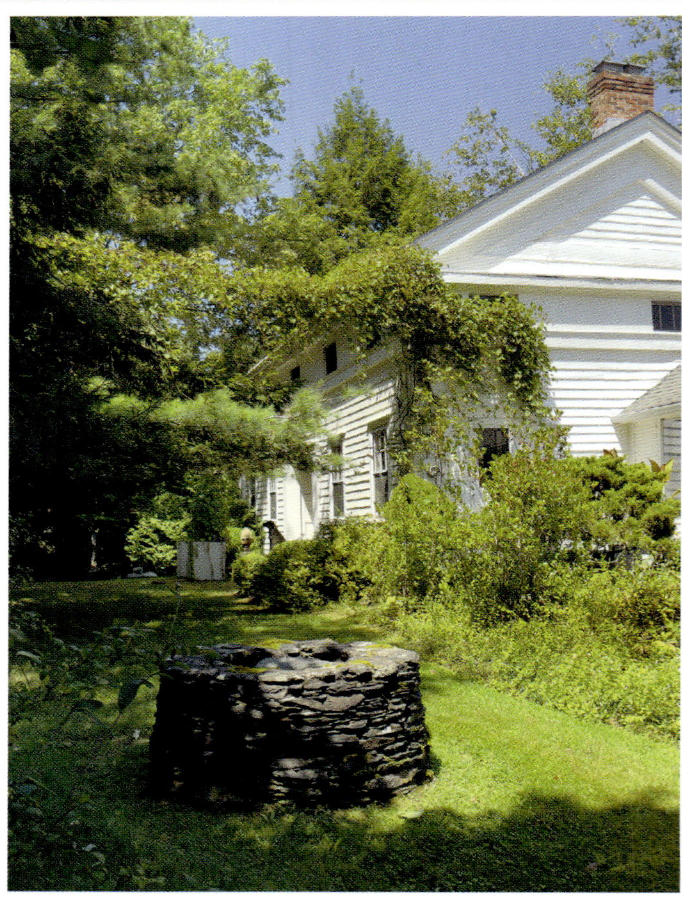

above
Two extensions were added: one, with a black exterior, is now the living room and the other, with a white exterior, the dining room. A deck connects the two rooms. All have water views.

right
The main house is an eighteenth-century Federalist style.

opposite, top and bottom
The house is surrounded by nature. The couple's collection of jade and other potted plants is placed outside in the summer and brought inside during the winter.

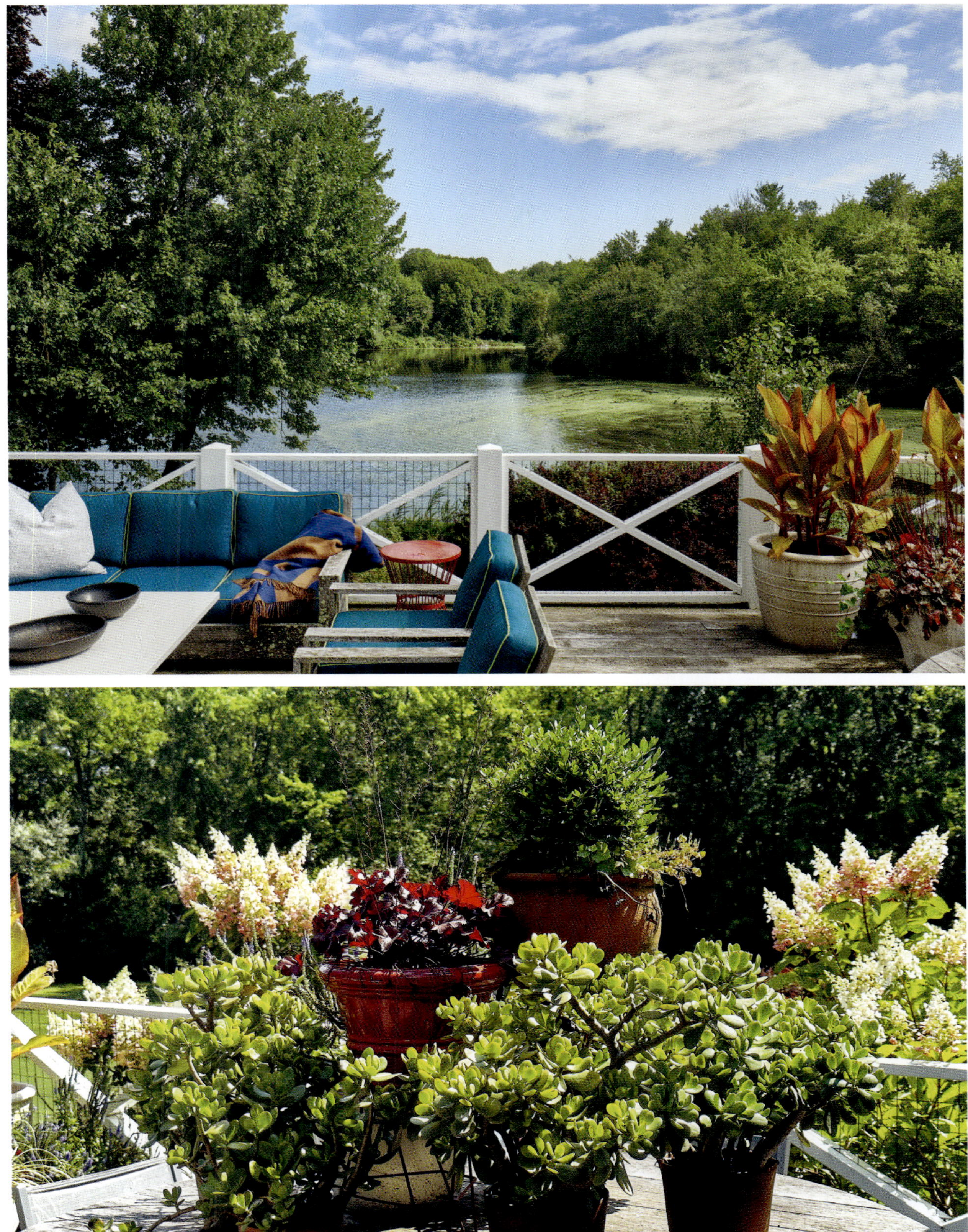

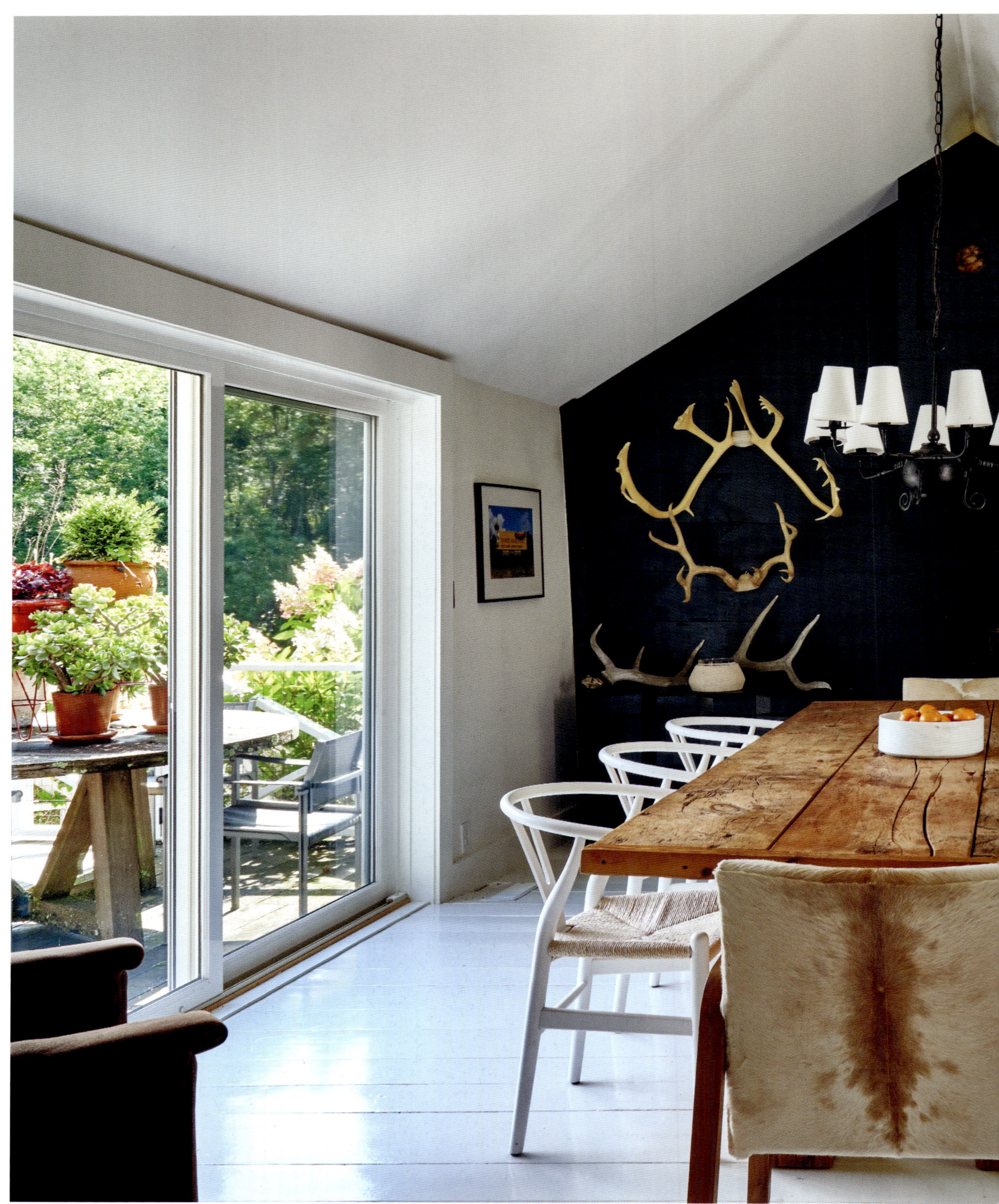

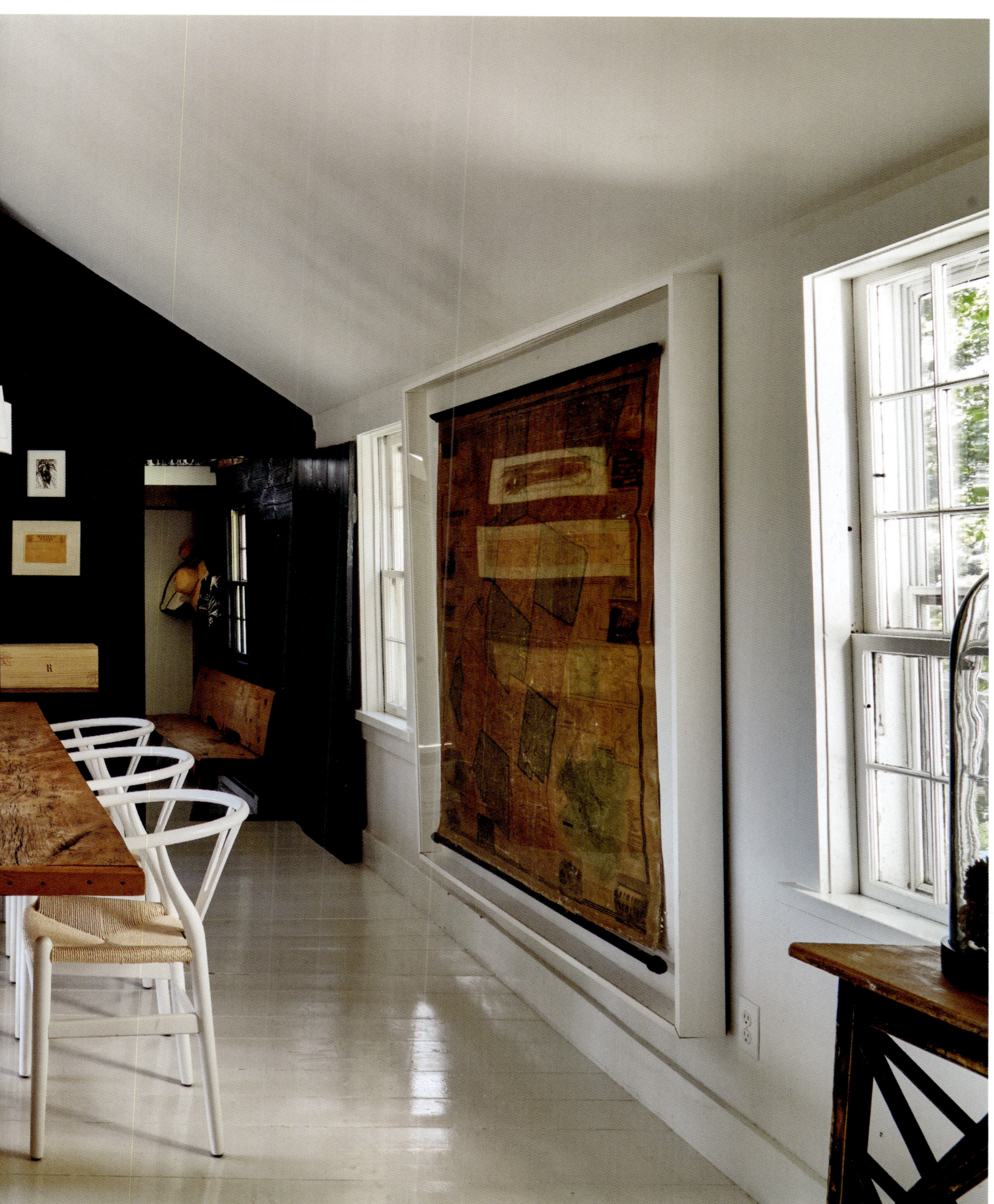

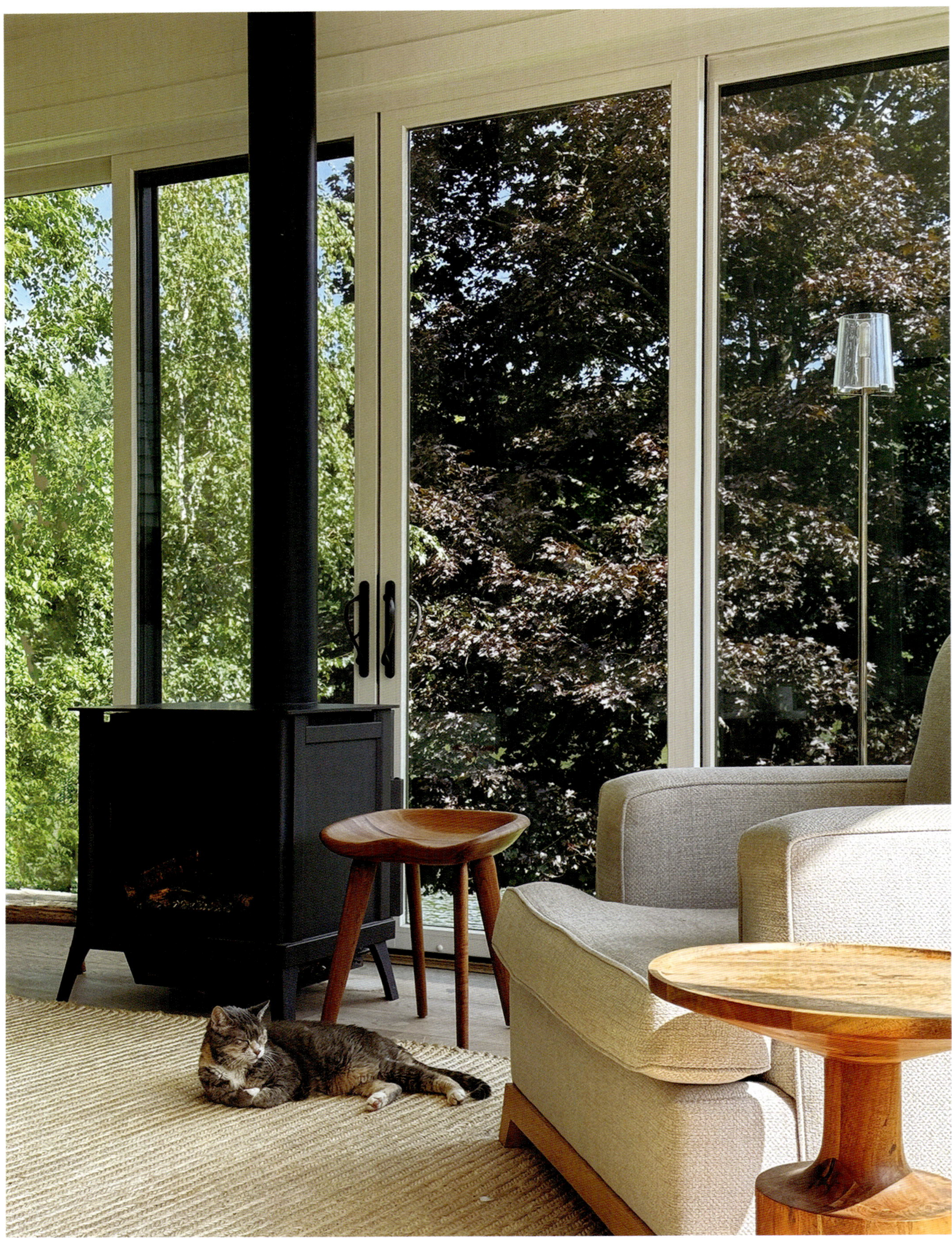

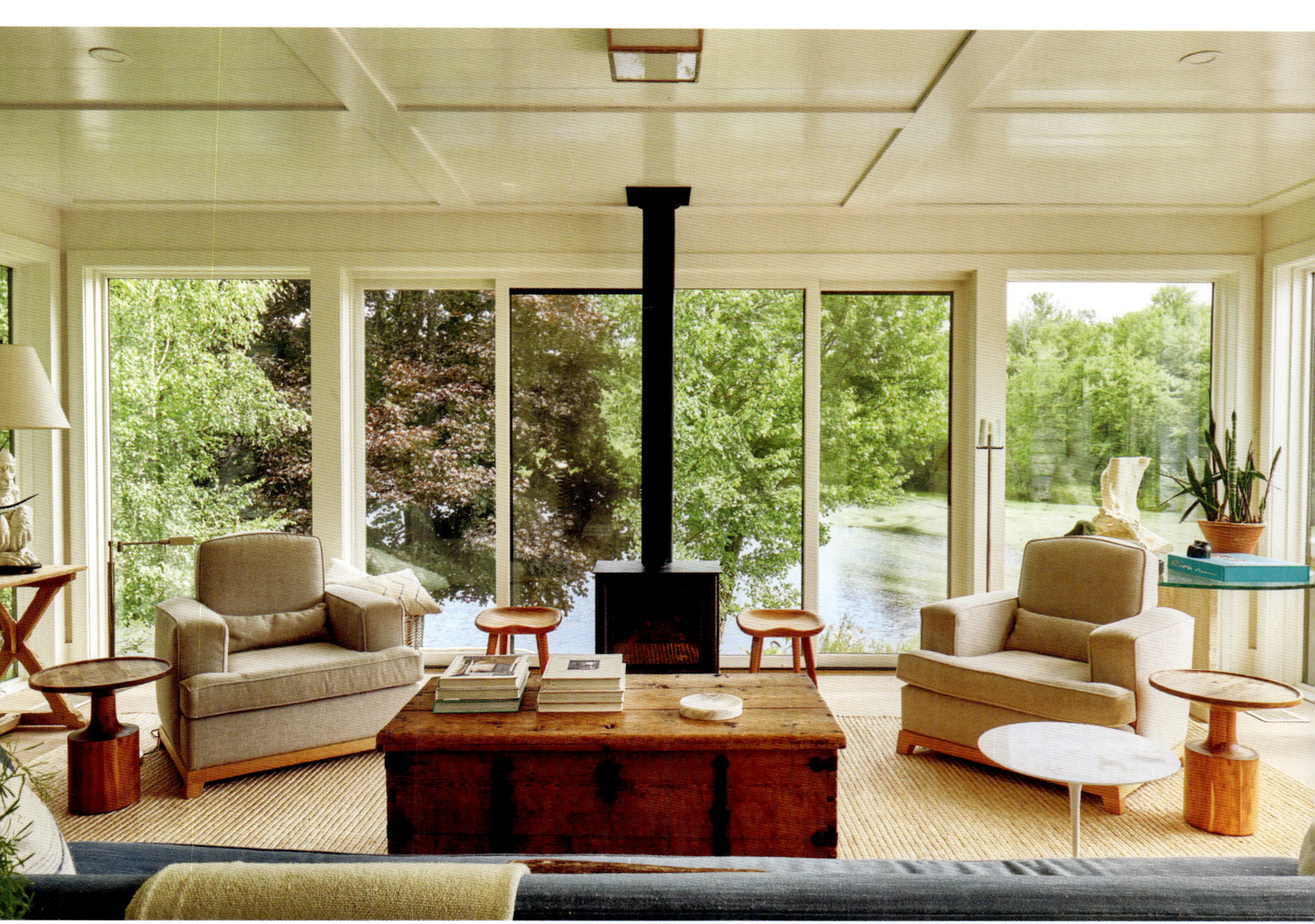

previous
The first extension was adapted to be the dining room. It is located just off the kitchen, part of the original house. One wall of the room is painted black, making it a focal point. The white floors unify the room with the kitchen. An old map of Columbia County takes up one wall.

opposite
In the summer, their cat, Momma Girl, basks in the warmth coming in through the wall of windows. In the winter, she sits by the fire.

above
Gray and Chase turned the screen porch into a weatherized modern living room with a woodburning fireplace. Upholstered furniture pieces and wooden stools and tables complement each other. The long blue sofa was designed by Meyer Davis, the international design firm where Gray is a principal.

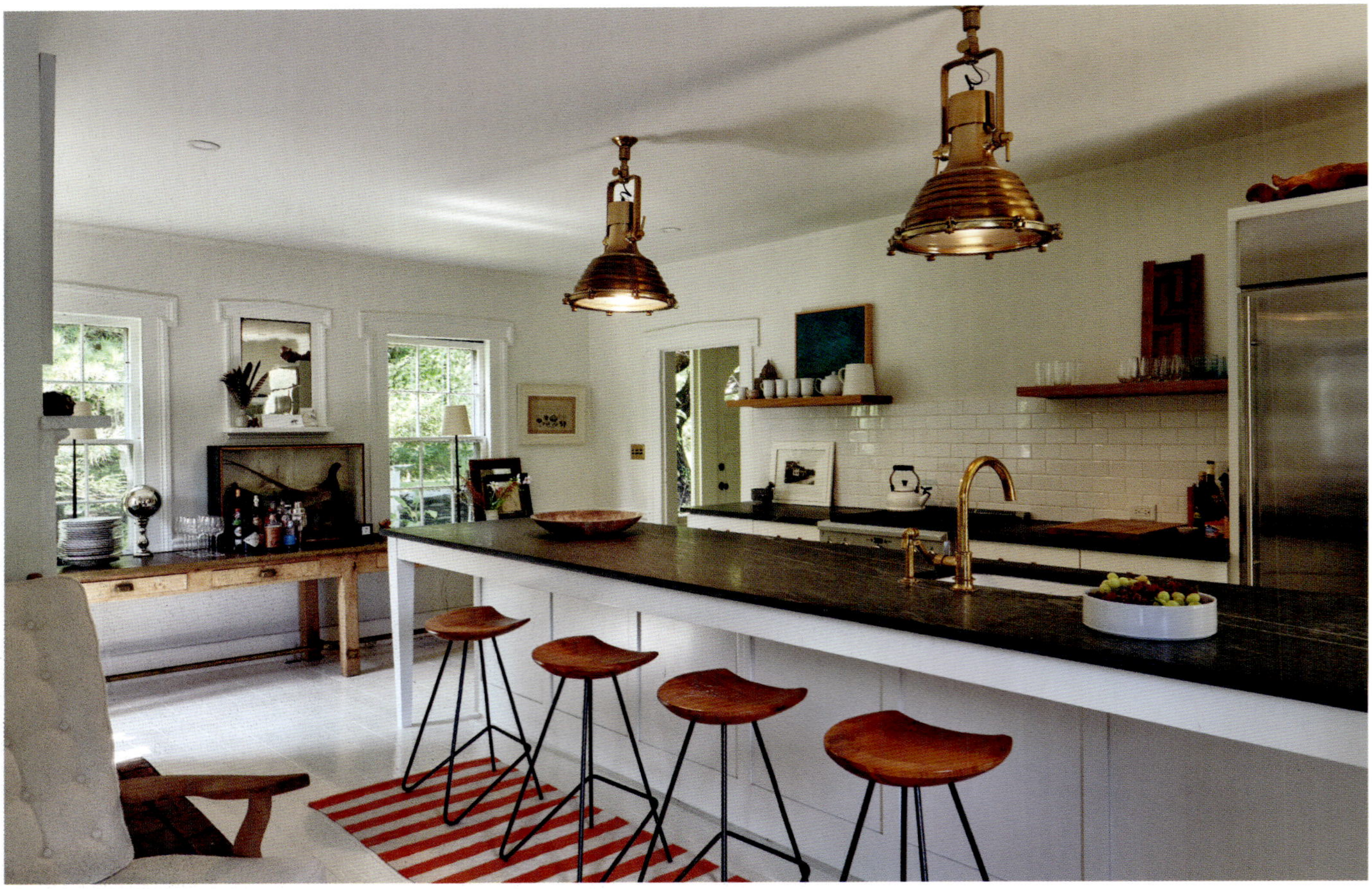

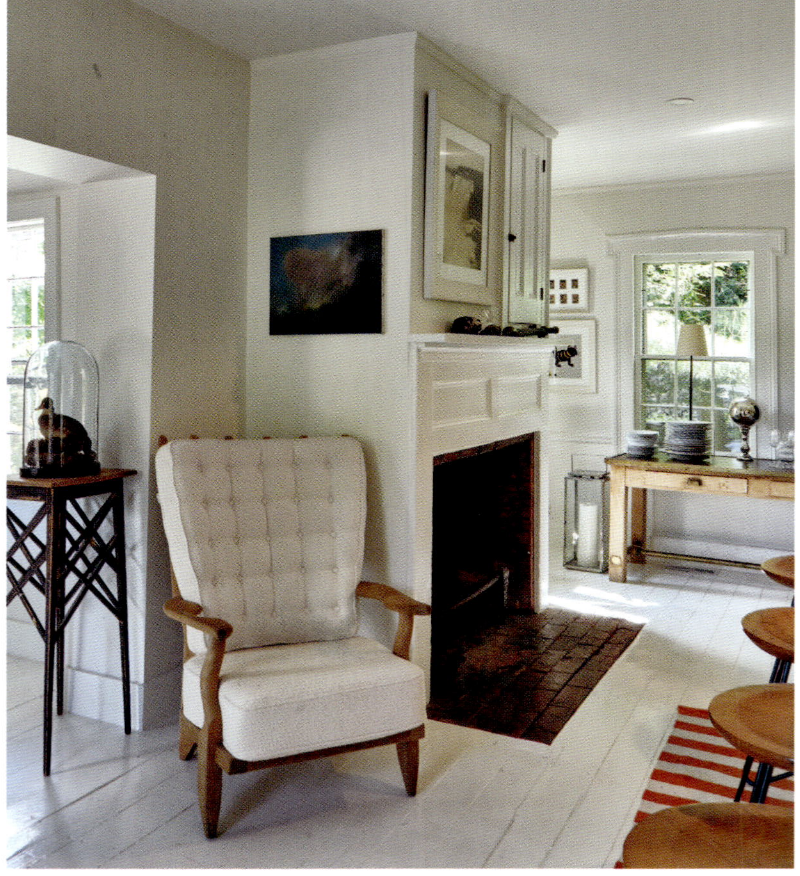

above
Four wood-and-iron stools are pulled up to the kitchen island, which is a workspace, breakfast table, and bar when guests come to visit. The overhead lighting is from Restoration Hardware.

right
Rooms in old houses, especially those built in the 1700s, were not big. When Gray and Chase updated the kitchen, they created a modern kitchen that fit the house and connected to the dining room that was part of an extension. This corner of the kitchen shows the fireplace, the opening to the dining room, and some of the kitchen furniture, including a Danish modern chair.

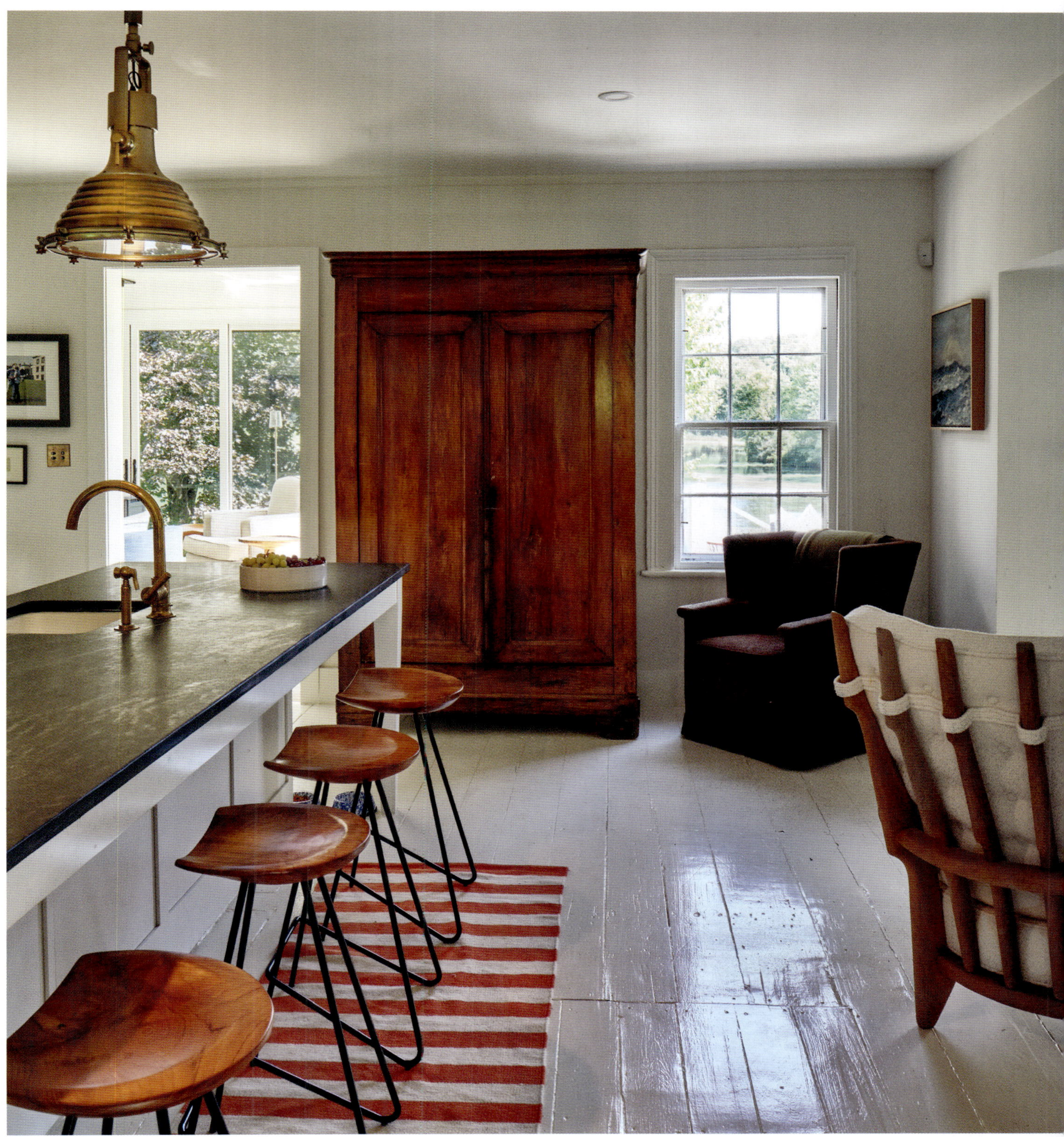

Exposed kitchen shelving and storage were kept to a minimum. Instead, Gray and Chase placed an antique armoire between a window and the door to the sitting room, both of which bring lots of light to the space.

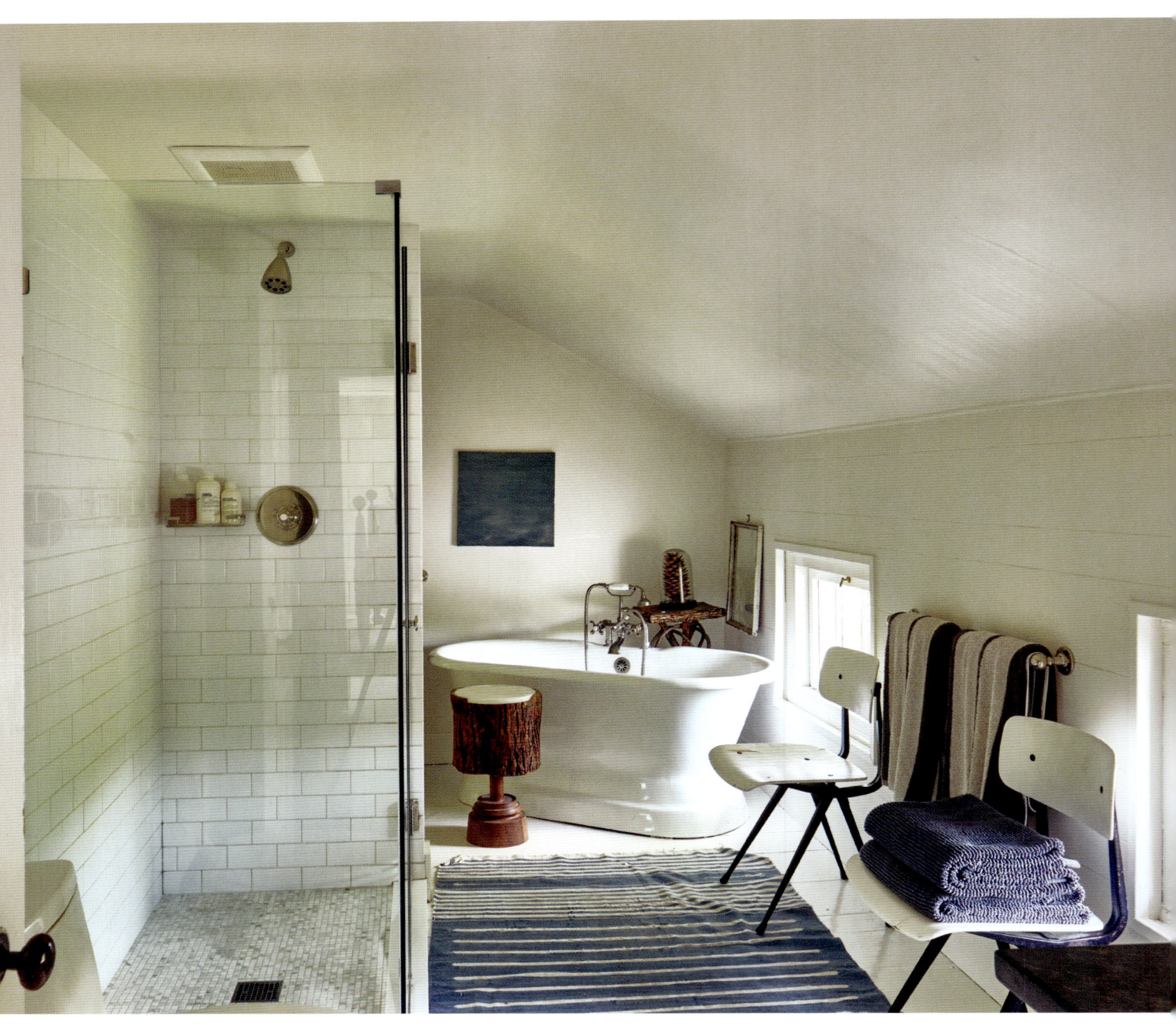

Glass walls and white tiles around the shower increase the space of the full bathroom on the upper level of the house.

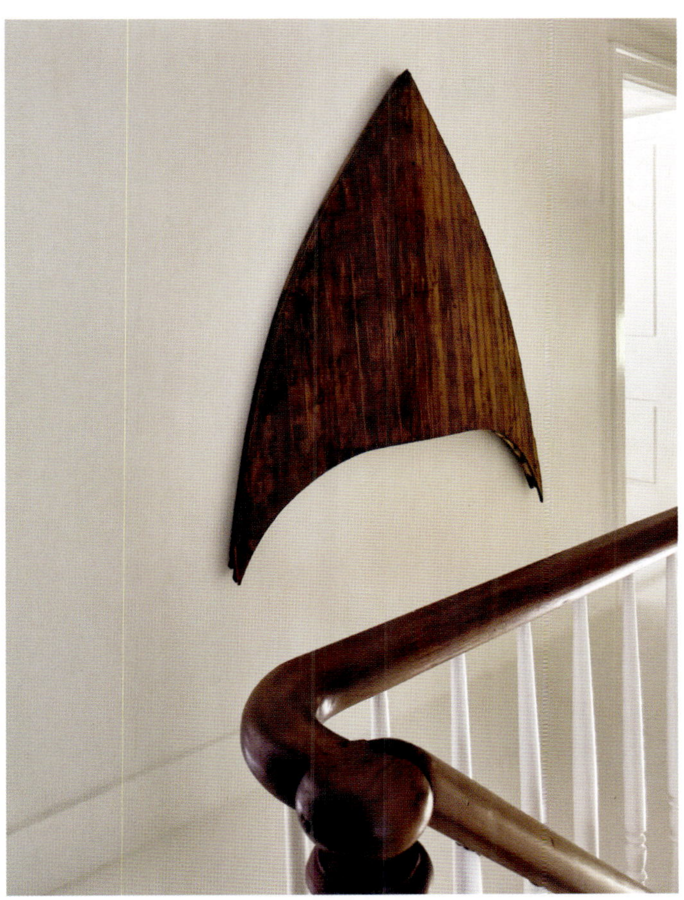

left
A wooden boat bow serves as a sculptural artwork on the upstairs landing.

below
Gray's grandfather's cannonball bed came from Tennessee to be used as a guest bed. It fits perfectly under the slanted roof.

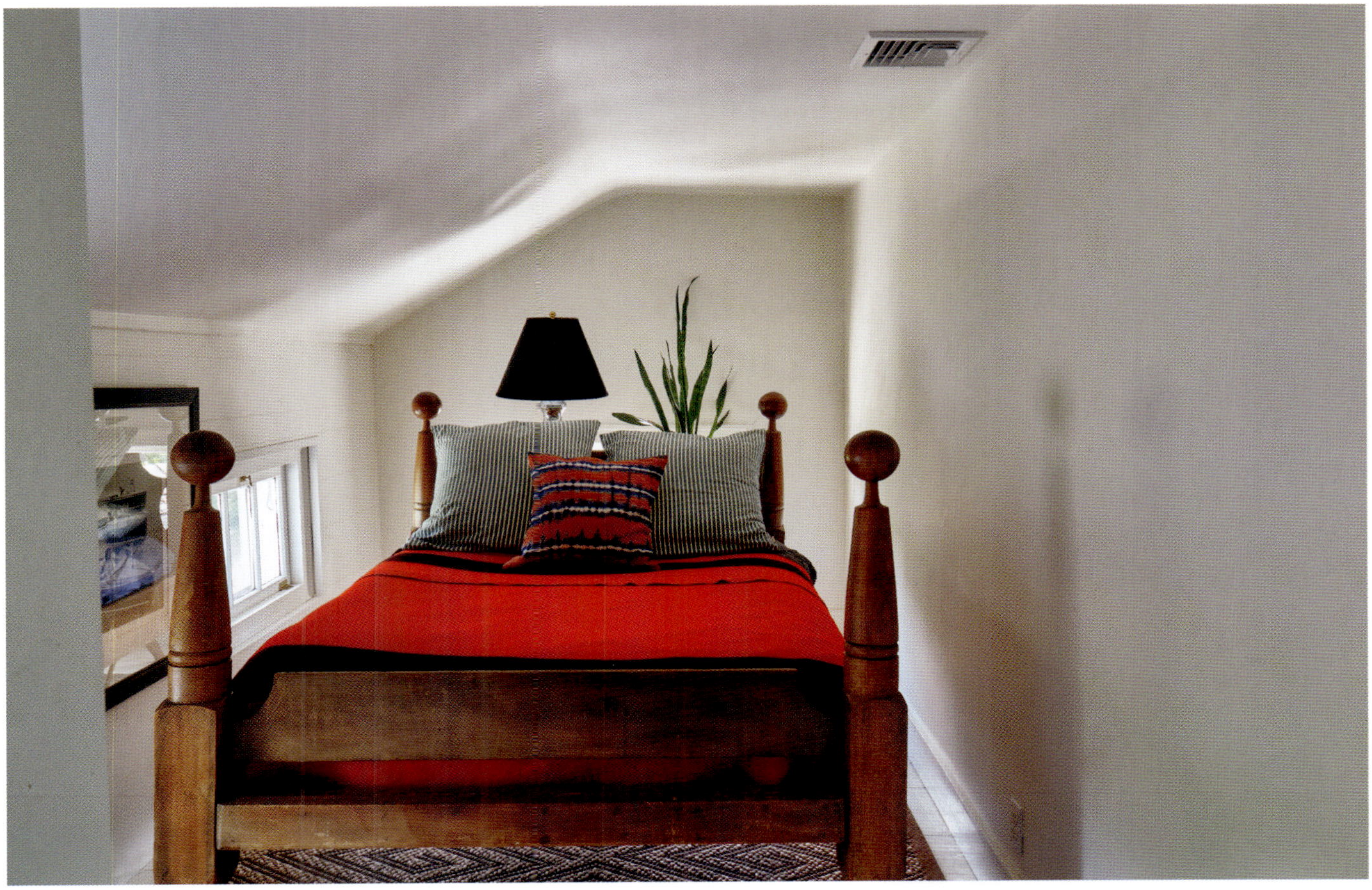

Paolo Volpati-Kedra and Giovanna Battaglia Engelbert

Hillsdale, New York

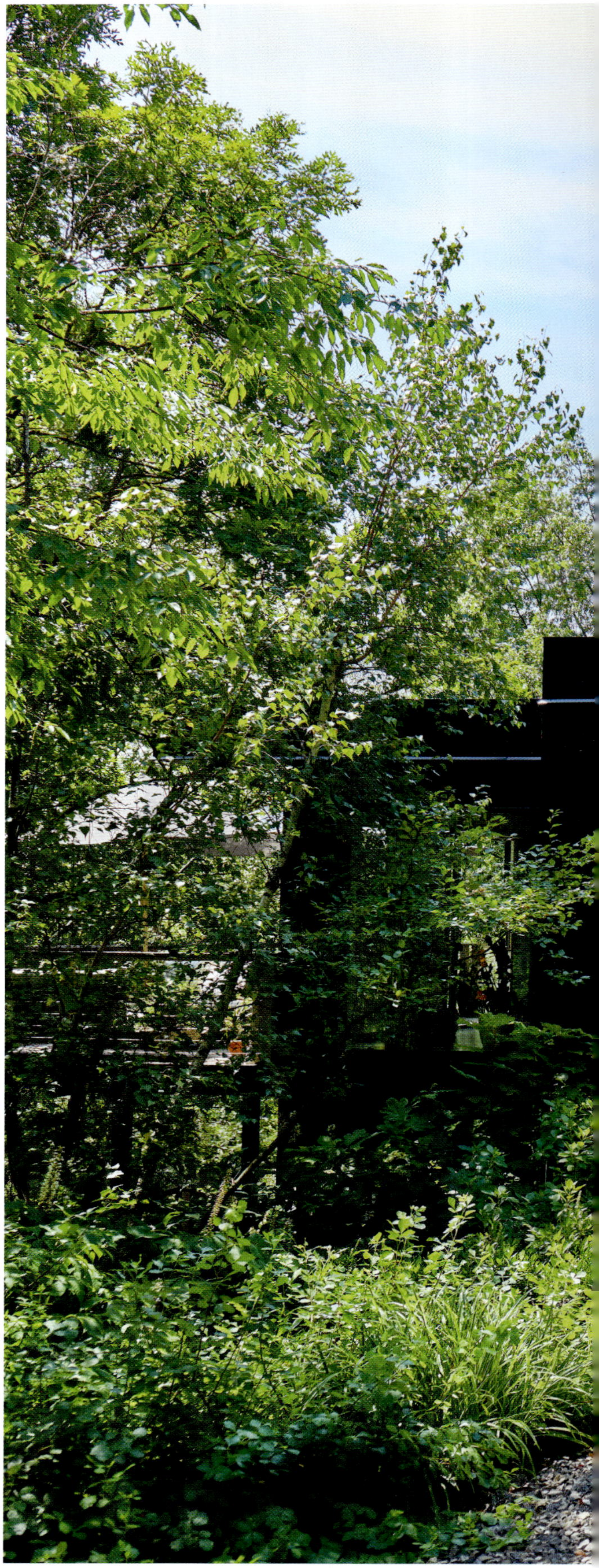

Paolo Volpati-Kedra and Giovanna Battaglia Engelbert met in Milan, Italy. For many years they had a long-distance relationship while he lived in Boston, where he had an established food business, and she had a professional career in fashion in Milan. Then Giovanna's job transferred her to New York City, and they began looking for a place to rendezvous between Boston and New York. Their friends Chase Booth and Gray Davis, as well as other friends, had places upstate. Gray owned a property near Lake Copake. One night at dinner, Gray said, "You are buying the land, and this is your house." He sketched the plan on a cocktail napkin.

The couple joined a community of friends who love "lake living," which Paolo describes as casual and relaxing. "Here, it's about winding down," he says. "Our meeting point is the water." While their house doesn't overlook the lake, they are a short golf-cart ride away. Paolo continues, "The lake has fish, turtles, and other wildlife. It's alive. It's beautiful. It is fed by rain. It brings all of us together." In the summer they spend time on their boat. In the winter, they ice-skate on the frozen lake.

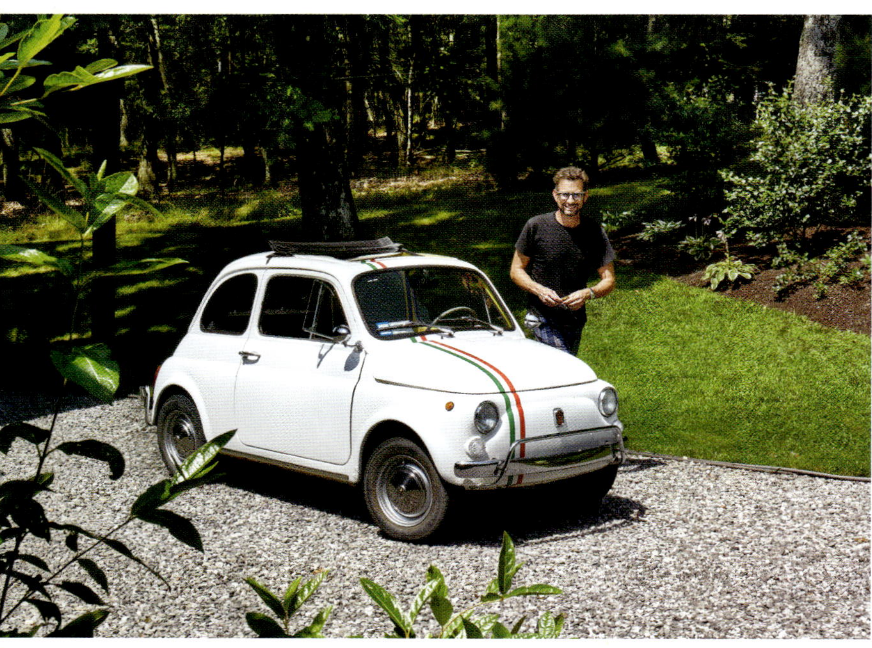

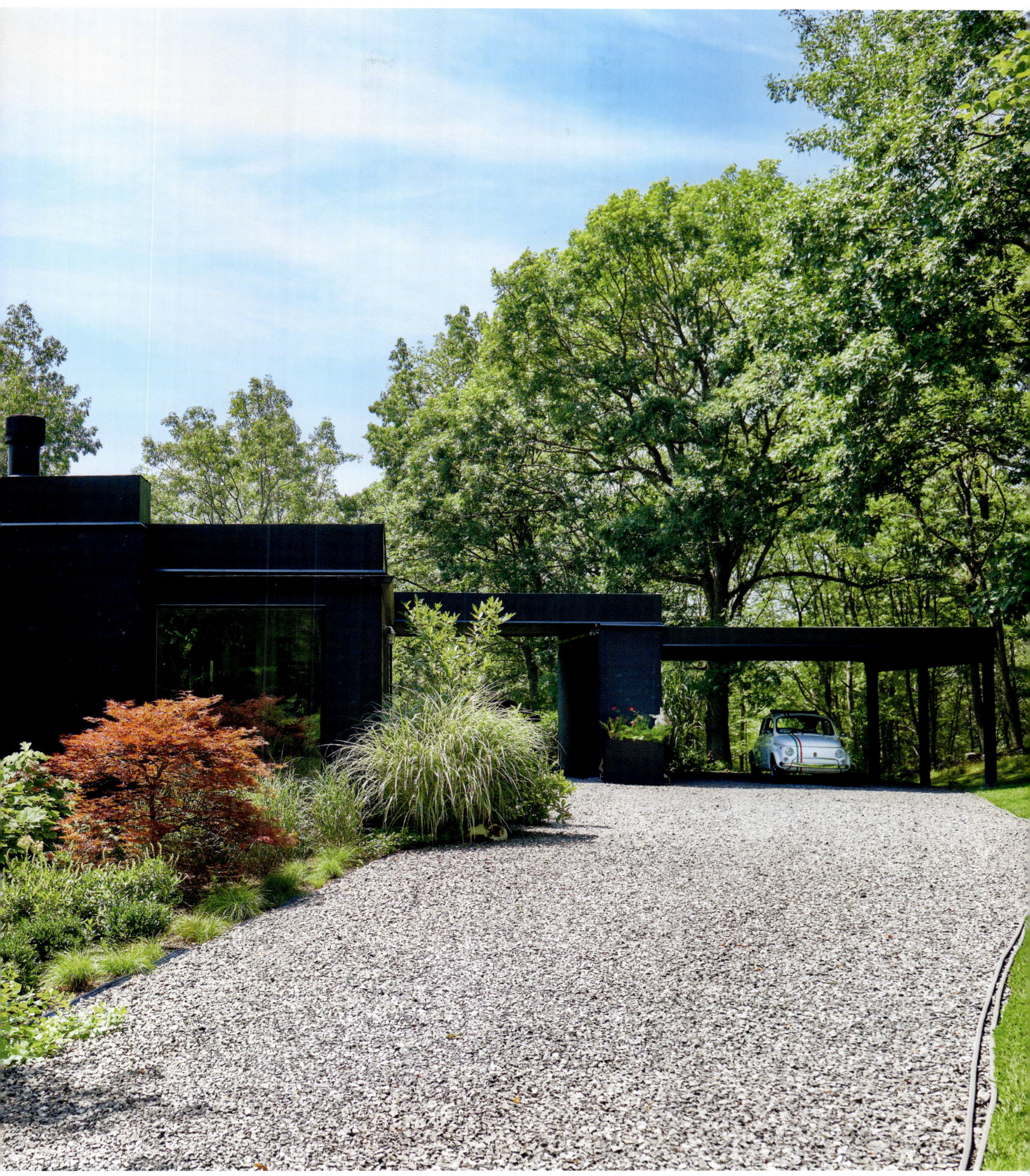

In 2019, just before COVID hit, Paolo sold his company and moved to their Hudson Valley house full time. When the pandemic shutdowns happened, Paolo and Giovanna lived under the same roof for the first time in seventeen years of being together. When the restrictions were lifted, they resumed their split lifestyle. The growth in full-time population was measurable during winter nights when once-dark houses lit up.

The house was built in five and a half months in 2015. It has three guest bedrooms for visiting family from Italy. Choosing the detail finishes, furnishings, and art of the living space together was a pleasure, shared Paolo. They've made it their own. It's a simple house, but there's a lot of room. The lower level was expanded during COVID, adding the office and the gym.

Paolo says the house has the impression of being a tree house. The deck extends into the forest, where oak, birch, spruce, and white pine trees grow. The couple cut down only ten trees in the construction process. They enhanced the garden with native species that thrive here. Paolo and Giovanna spend time observing the changes of light on the artworks and watching the succession of seasons from the deck.

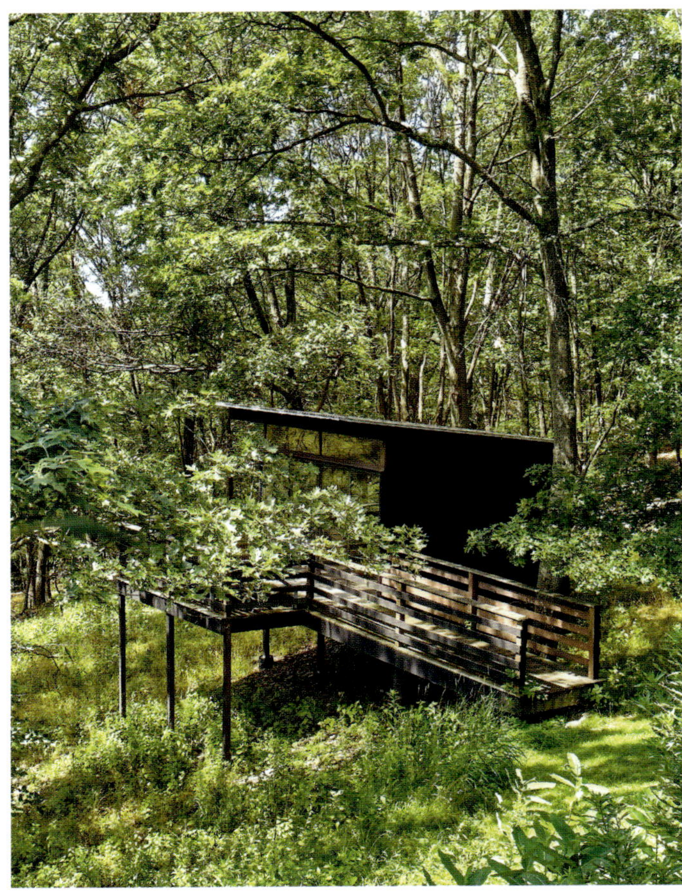

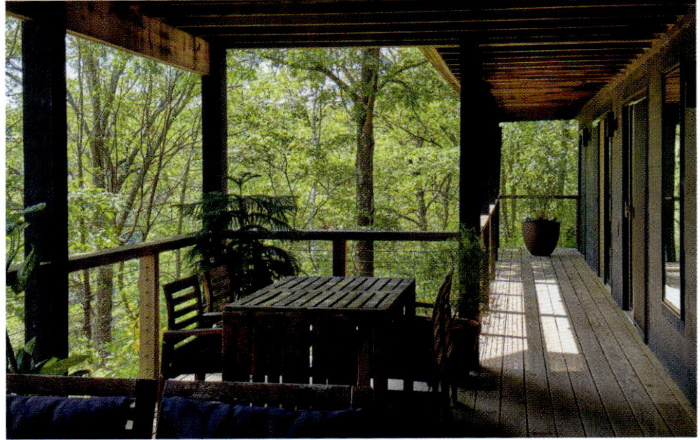

previous, left
The vintage Cinquecento, or Fiat 500, a gift from his father, brings back special memories of Paolo's Italian heritage.

previous
The black house is both perched on the hill and built into the hill.

top
A smaller studio was the first building on the property. It came as a prefab kit and was assembled on-site.

bottom
The downstairs deck is an immersive experience, close to climbing a tree and sitting on a limb.

opposite, top
The couple is surrounded by nature both inside and outside. The fixed picture windows on either side of the fireplace have views of the native plantings and trees of the site.

opposite, bottom
Artworks, books, and modern furnishings, including a suite of upholstered chairs and a couch, complete the look of the room while adding personality and warmth to the space. The artwork, titled *The Vain Man* (2006), by Paul Harbutt has a large presence in the room.

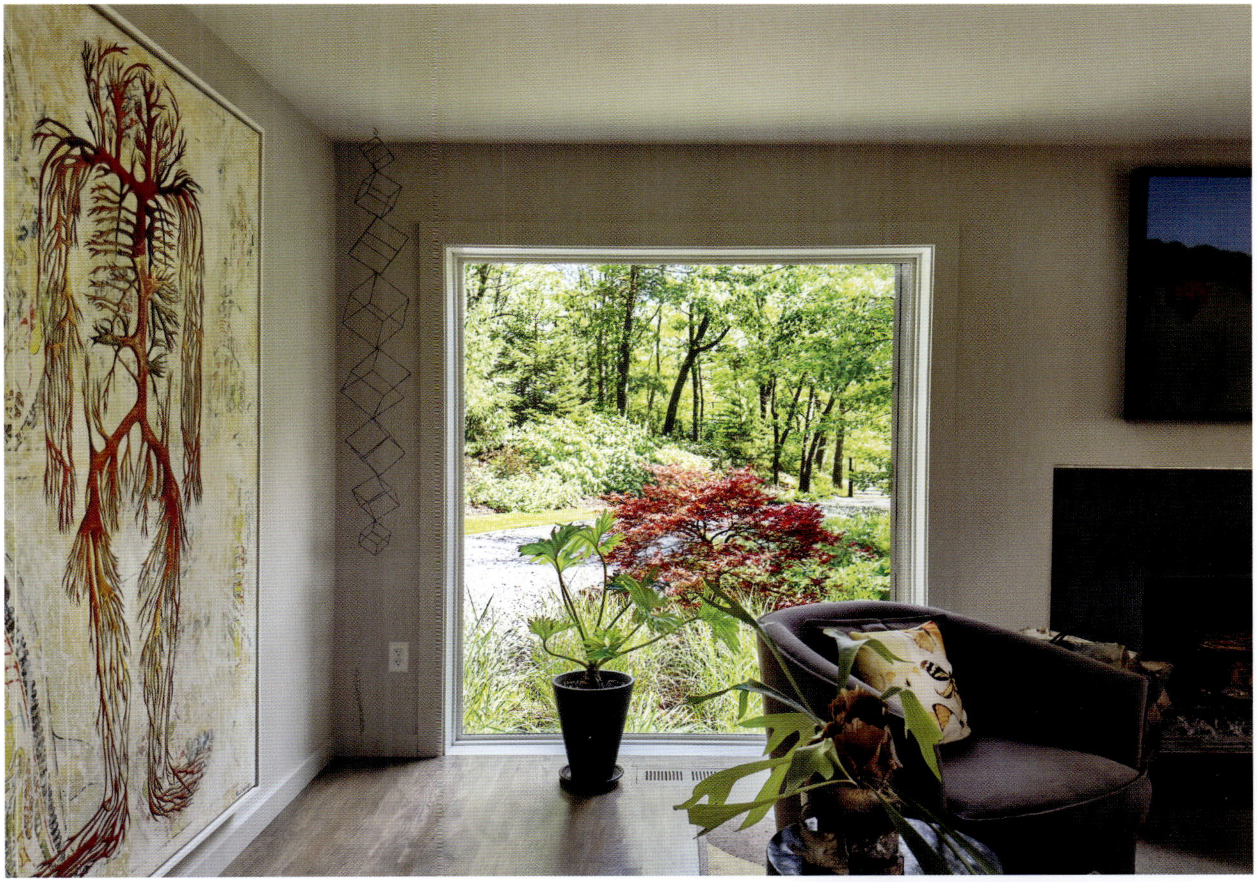

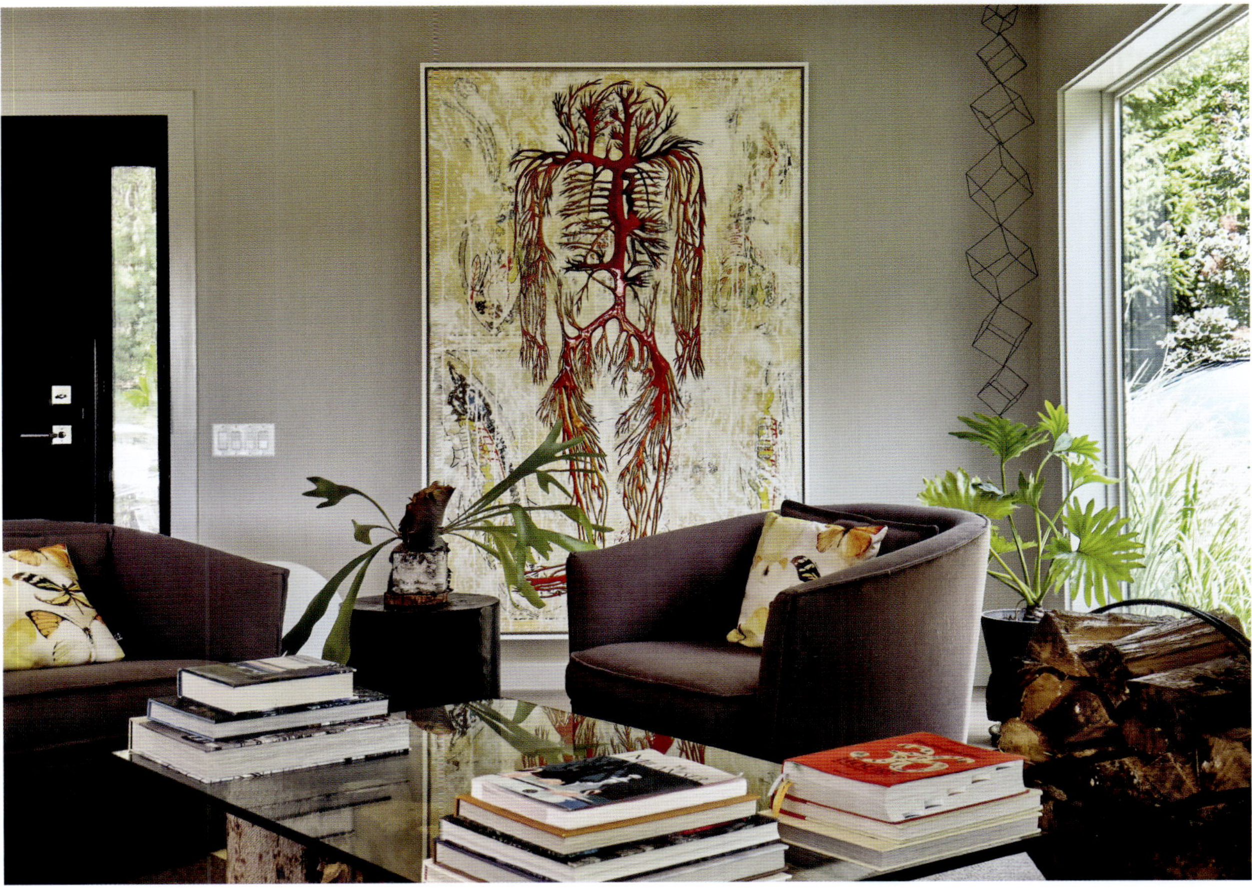

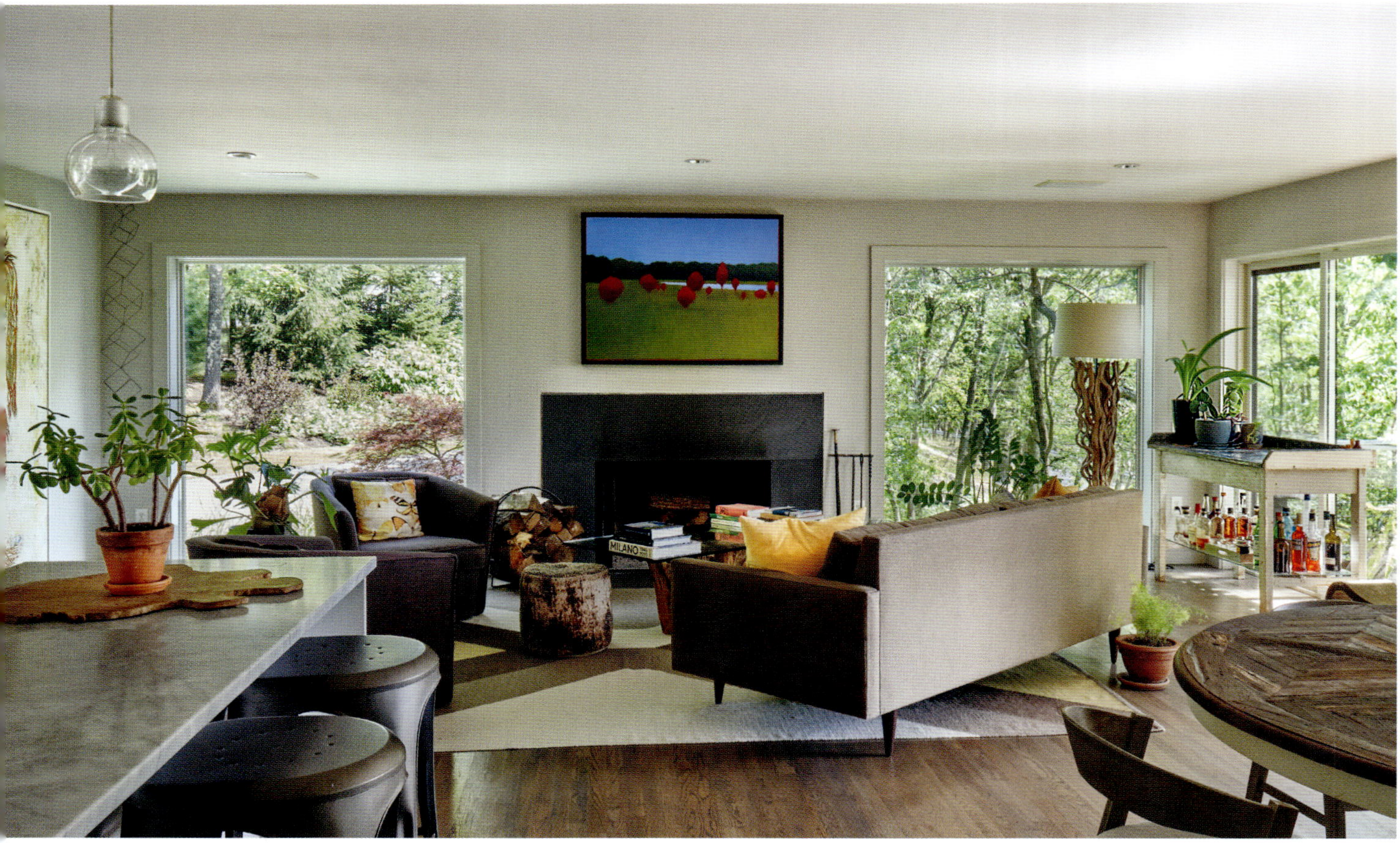

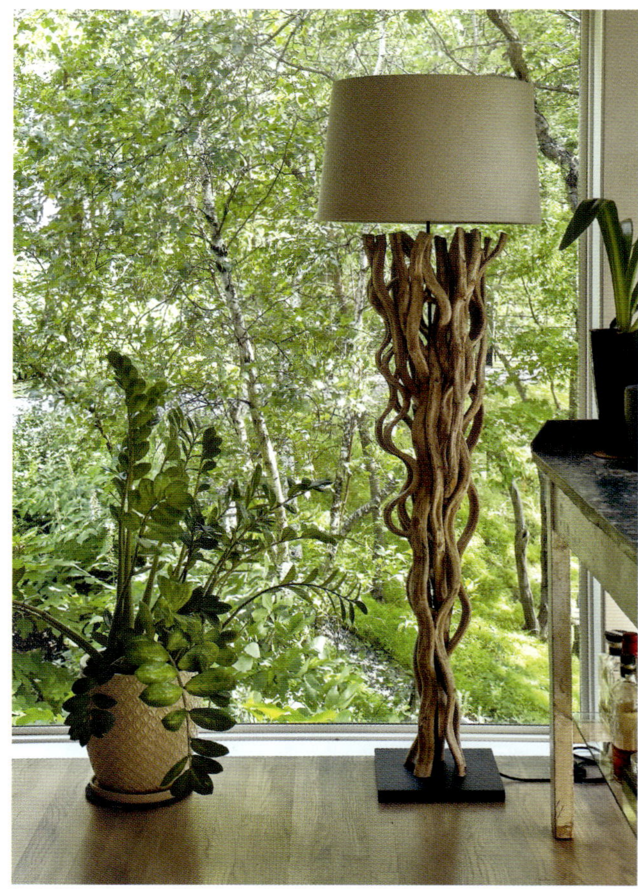

above
Paolo and Giovanna's open-plan design includes living, kitchen, and dining areas. A landscape painting titled *Life Around the Pond* (2021), by Tracy Helgeson, hangs above the fireplace.

right
A standing lamp with a driftwood base and container plants bring nature to the interior.

opposite, top
The view of the kitchen through the dining area.

opposite, bottom
A long, dynamic painting by Bryan Meador, titled *Tulips* (2014), is hung above the round dining table; the staircase to downstairs gives the illusion of a bigger space.

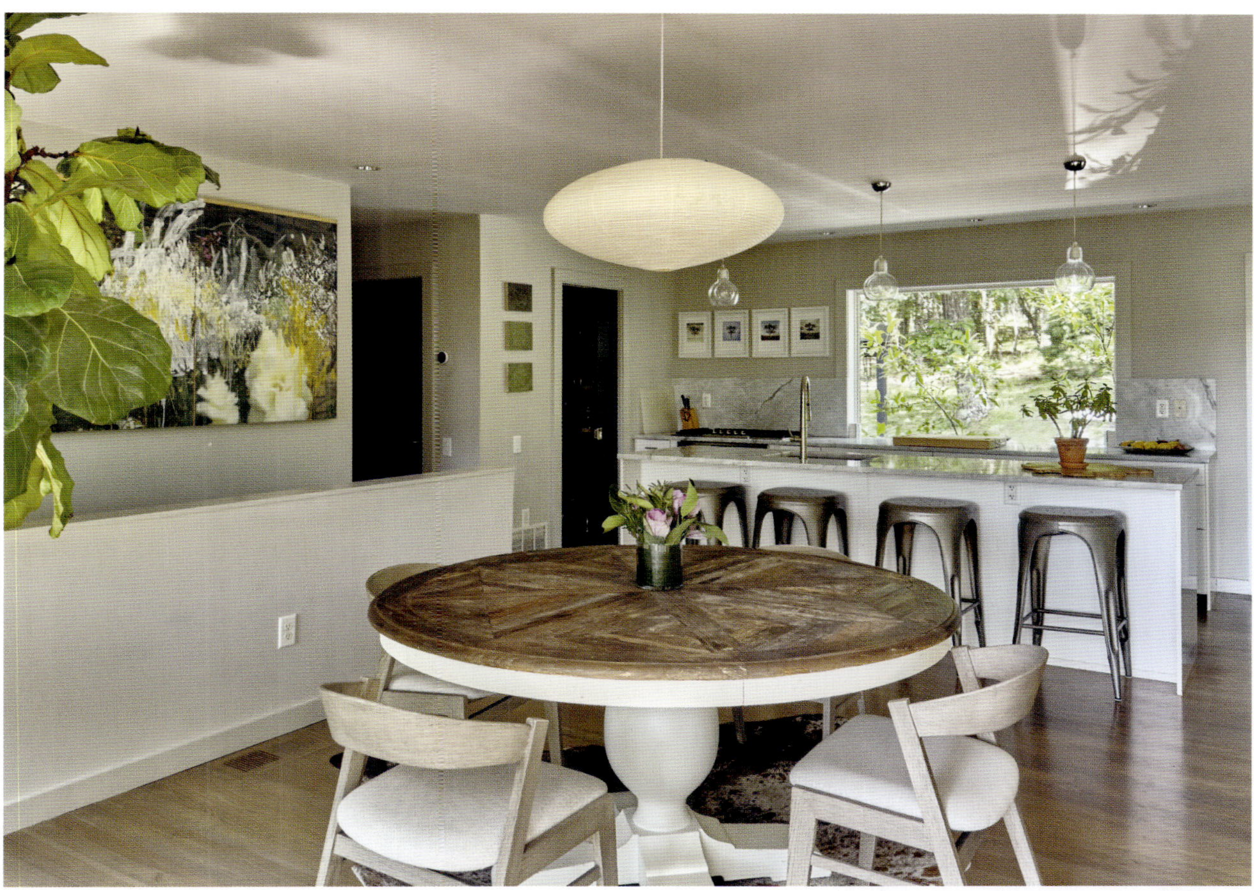

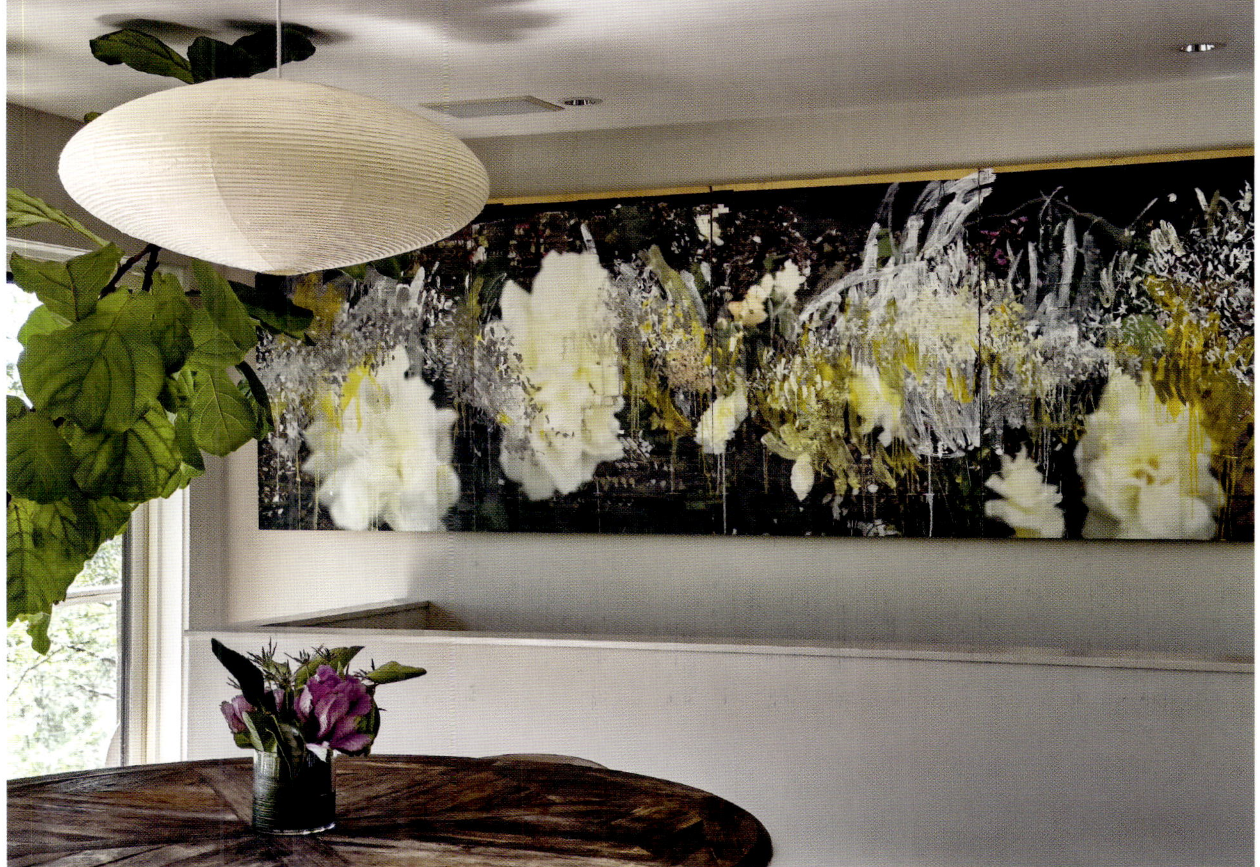

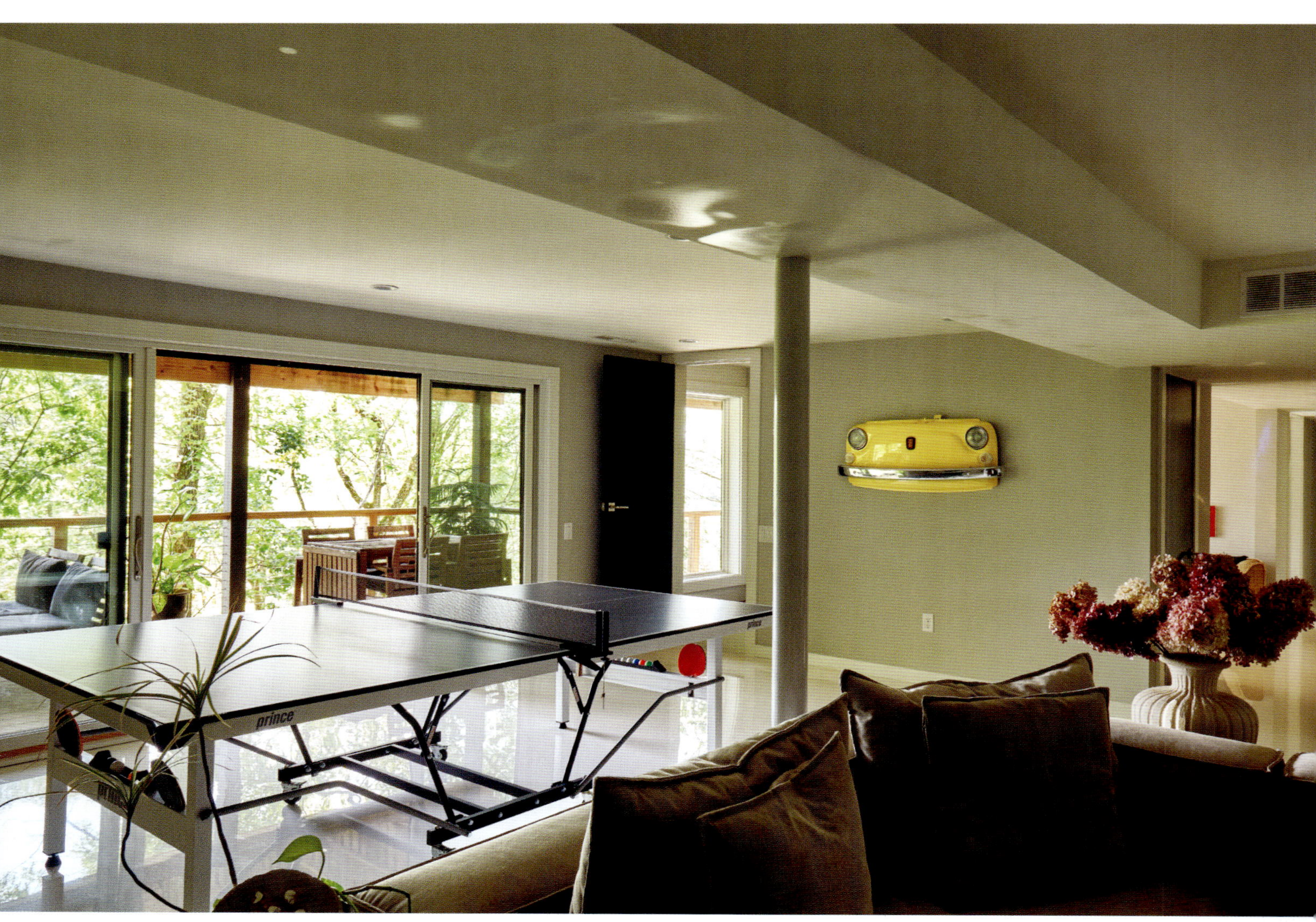

above
Giovanna and Paolo built out the downstairs part of their house, also adding a deck during COVID. The renovated space includes an office and a gym, both of which were important when everyone was sheltering at home and trying to work remotely.

opposite, top and bottom
The upper deck has views of the hills of the Taconic Mountains. The deck runs the length of the house from the living room to the primary bedroom.

overleaf
On Lake Copake, Gray Davis is at the helm of his speedboat. Giovanna dives off the back as Paolo and his nephews watch from a distance. All part of "lake living" in upstate New York.

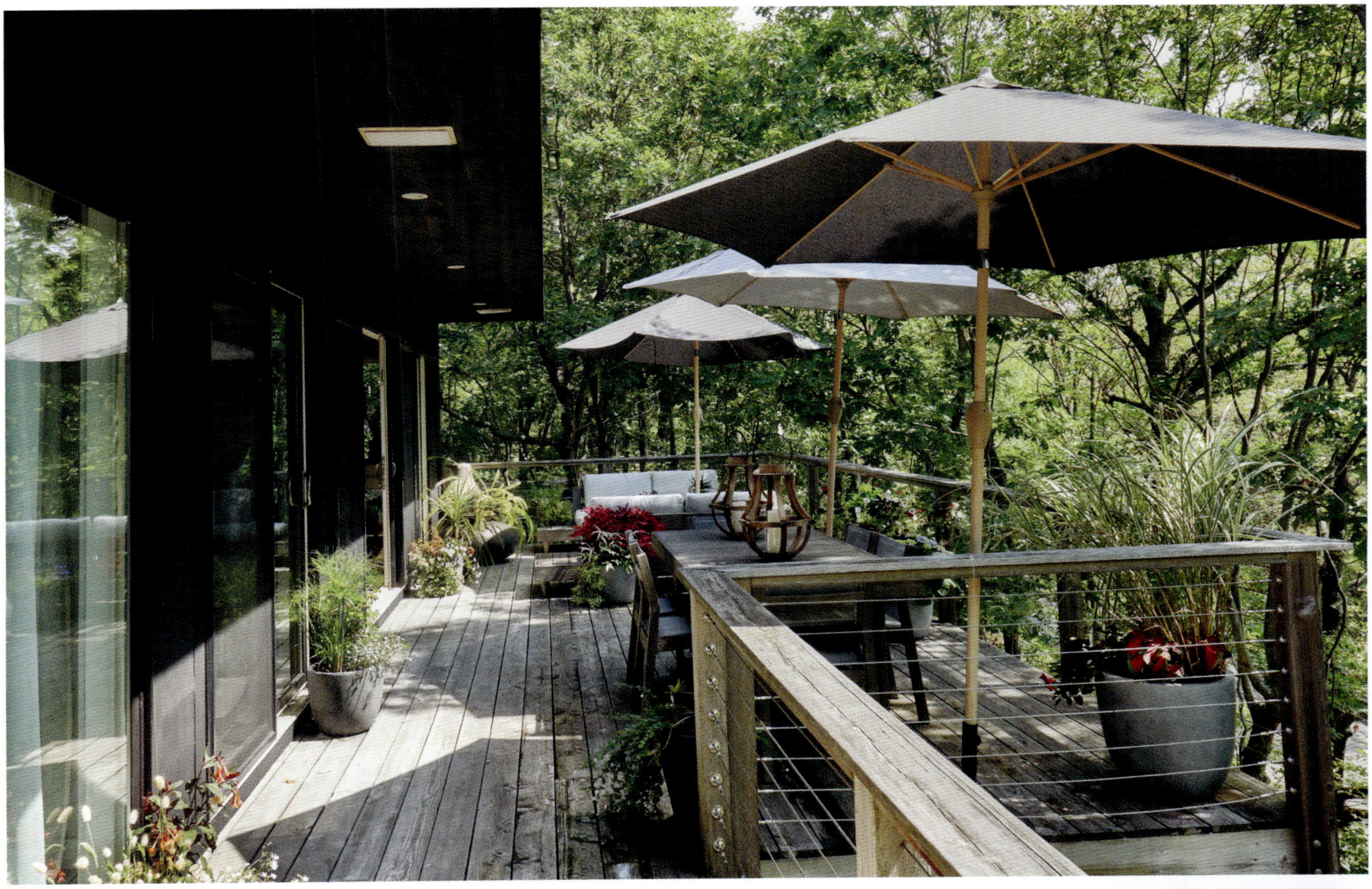

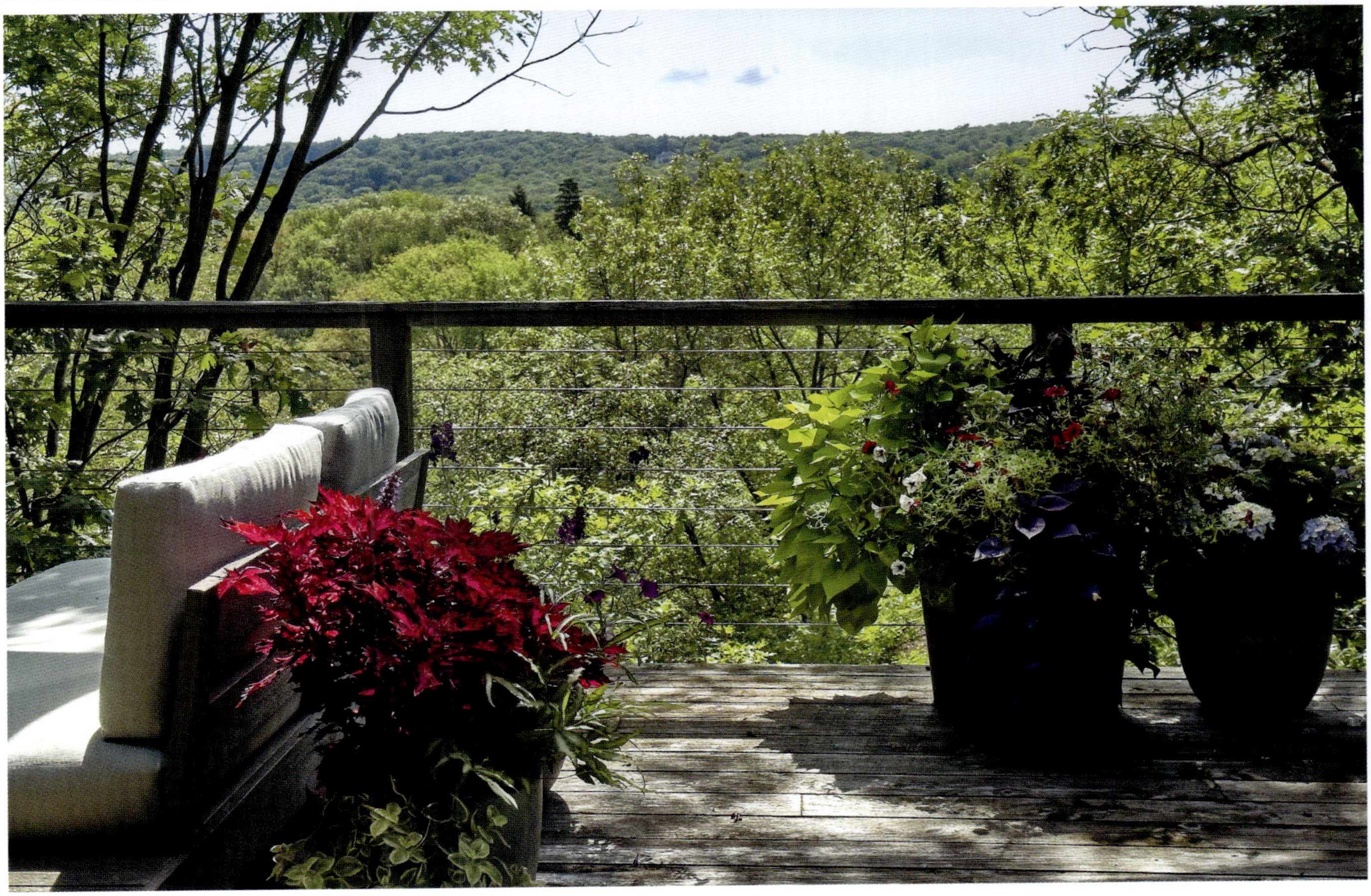

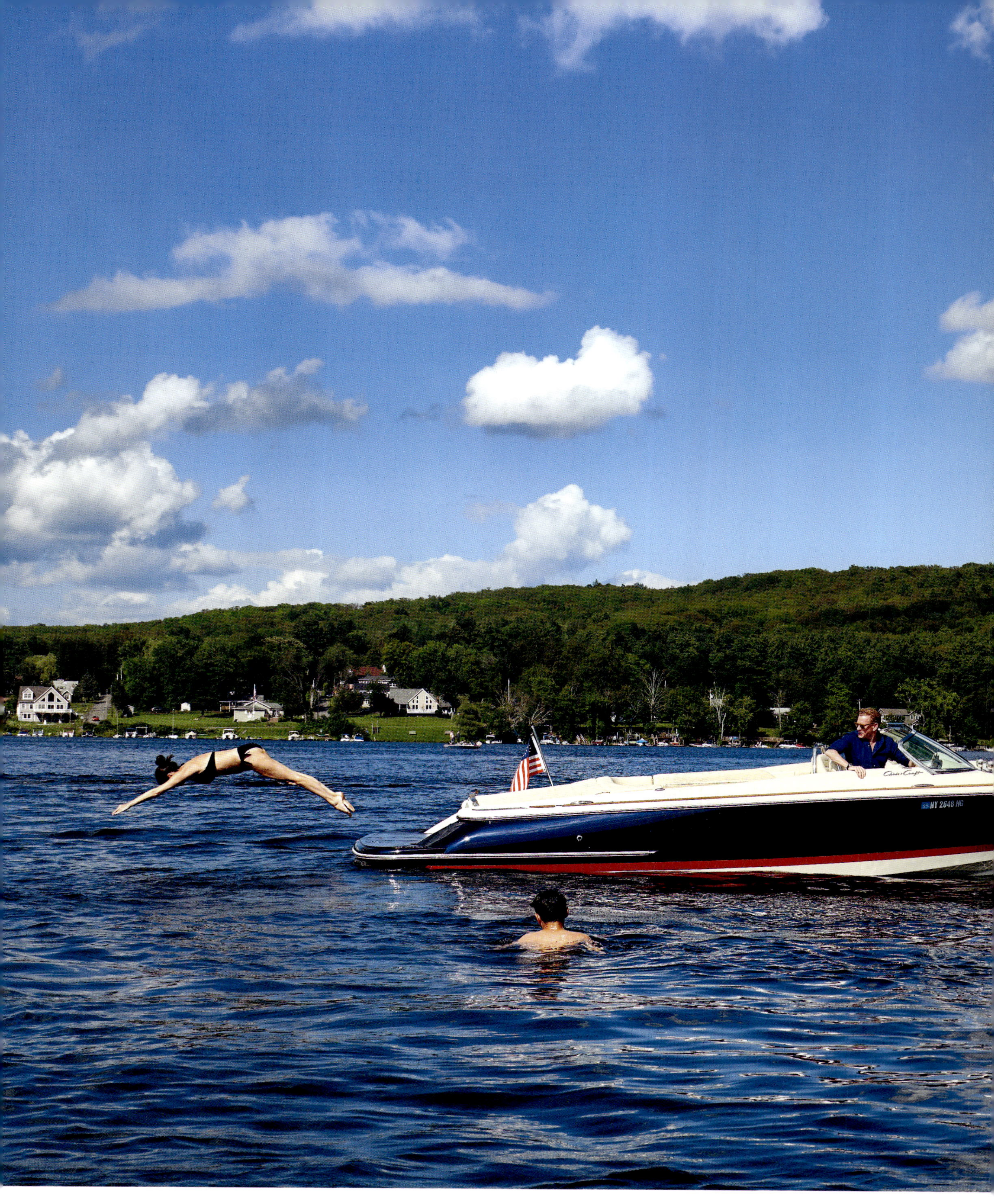
NY 2648 HG

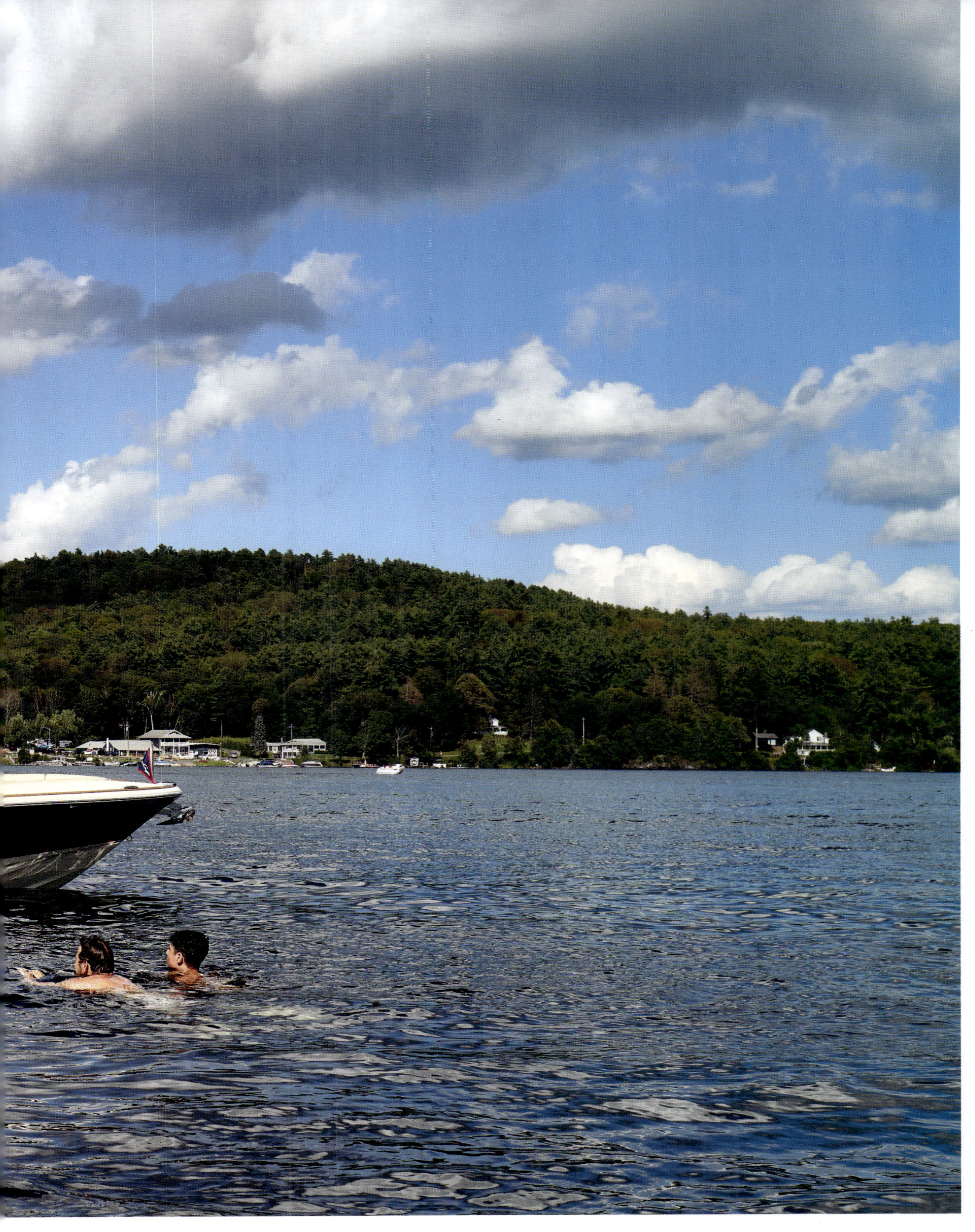

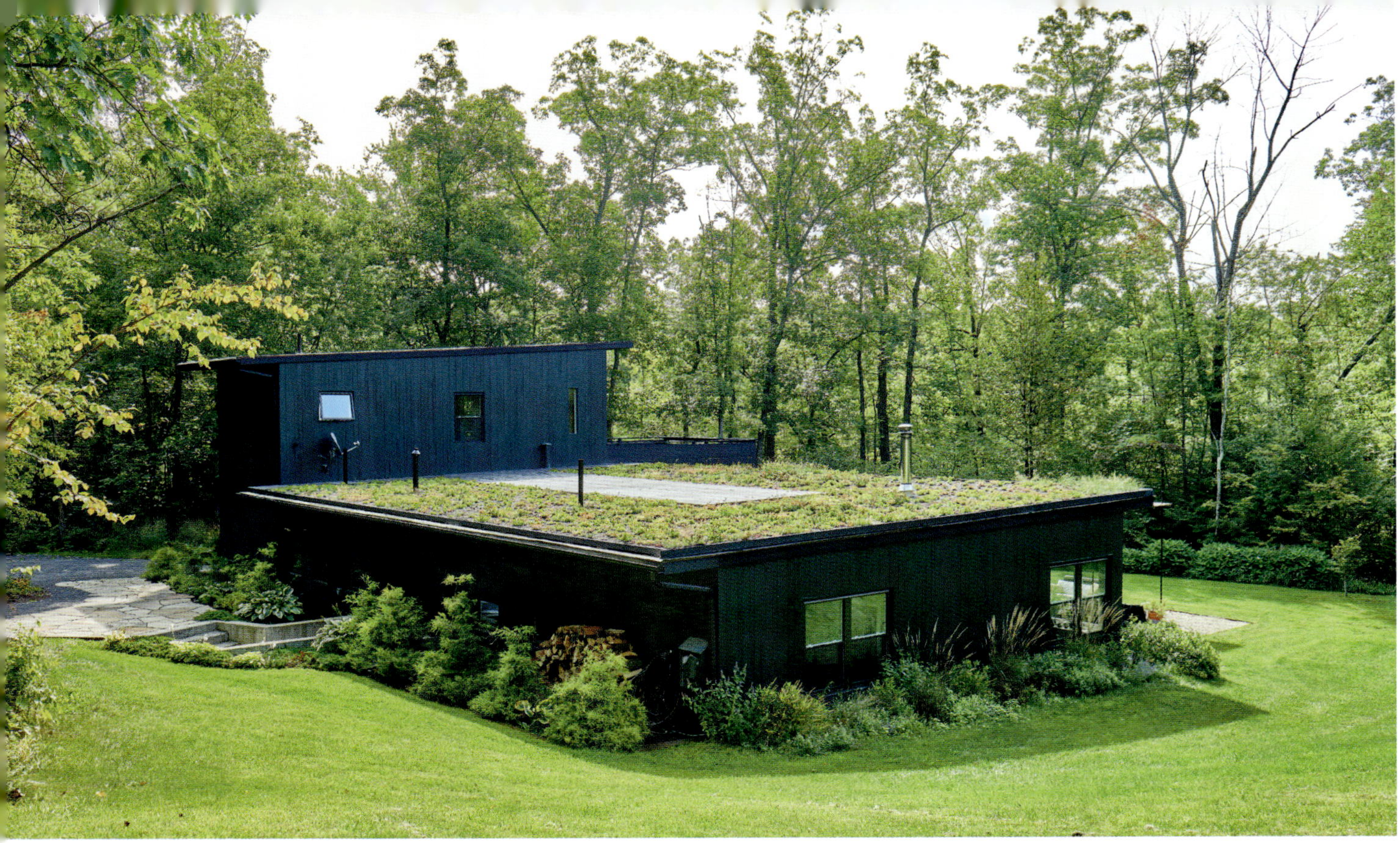

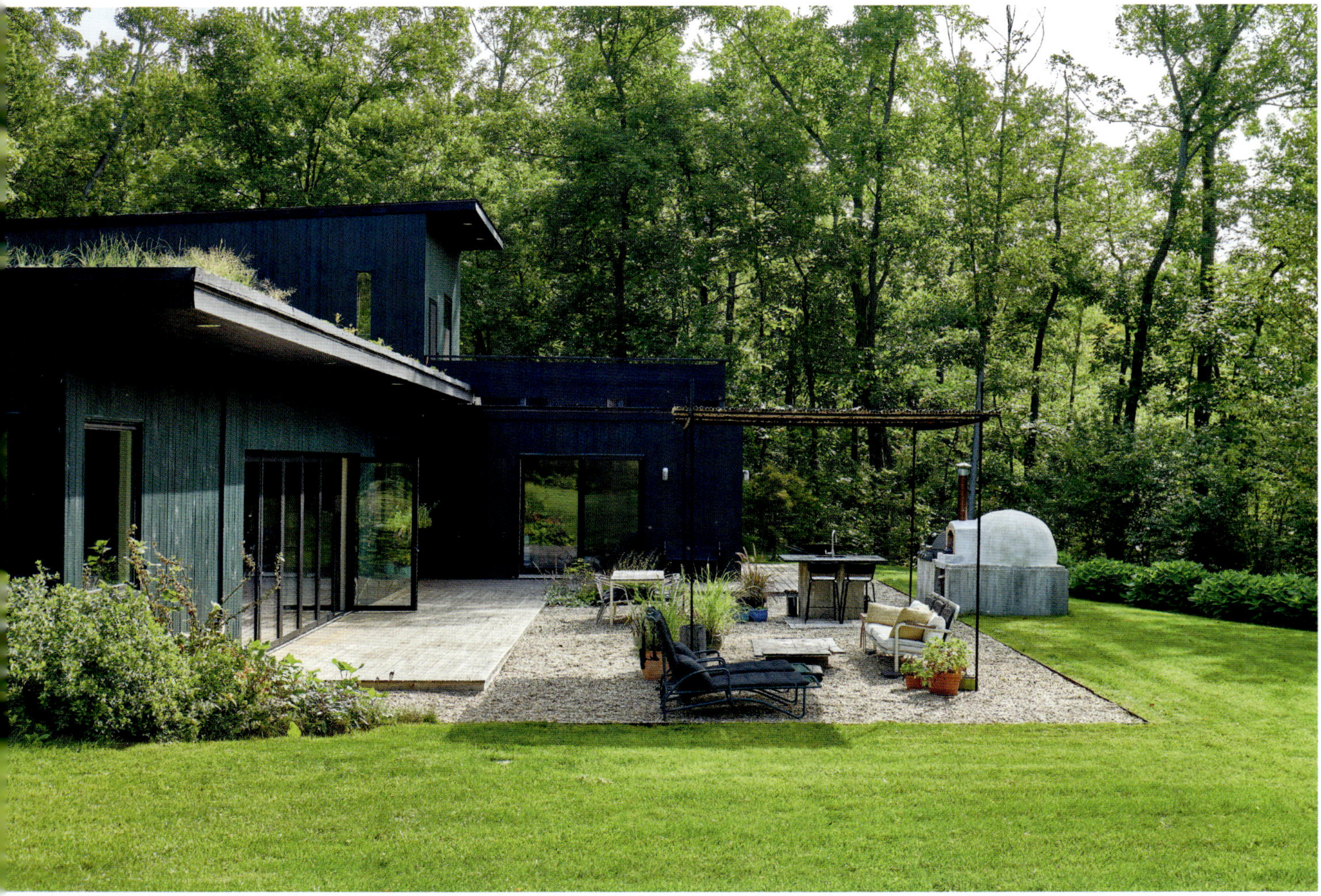

Per Blomquist and Angie Keefer

Ghent, New York

A house in a forest is all about living outside. This connection to nature is what Angie Keefer and Per Blomquist created in Ghent, New York. Per was born in Sweden and Angie in Alabama, but they came together in upstate New York via time in New York City. Per is in the construction and design business. He works on his own projects, renovating old houses and designing and developing new properties. Angie, an artist and writer, trained as a designer and architect. This house is a collaboration of their styles and sensitivity to nature.

Up a long road, in a quiet area with a few neighbors here and there, the house is sited in a cleared section of a forest, facing south to take advantage of the morning light. The main section is all on one floor. The living room has folding doors that open out, extending the living and dining areas to the outside surroundings. Angie and Per organized the outside spaces parallel to the inside spaces: the outside dining table is across from the inside table; the seating area is across from the indoor living area; the kitchen areas are close to each other too. A Scandinavian barrel sauna and an outdoor shower are steps away. The only exception is a two-story extension, where, at night, the couple climbs a staircase to the primary bedroom suite and deck that overlooks the green roof, garden, and forest.

Everything feels close at hand. There is a natural flow between the built environment and the outdoors. With so much going on in clients' homes or with their other design projects, Per and Angie's idea was to simplify their own home and create a place to enjoy.

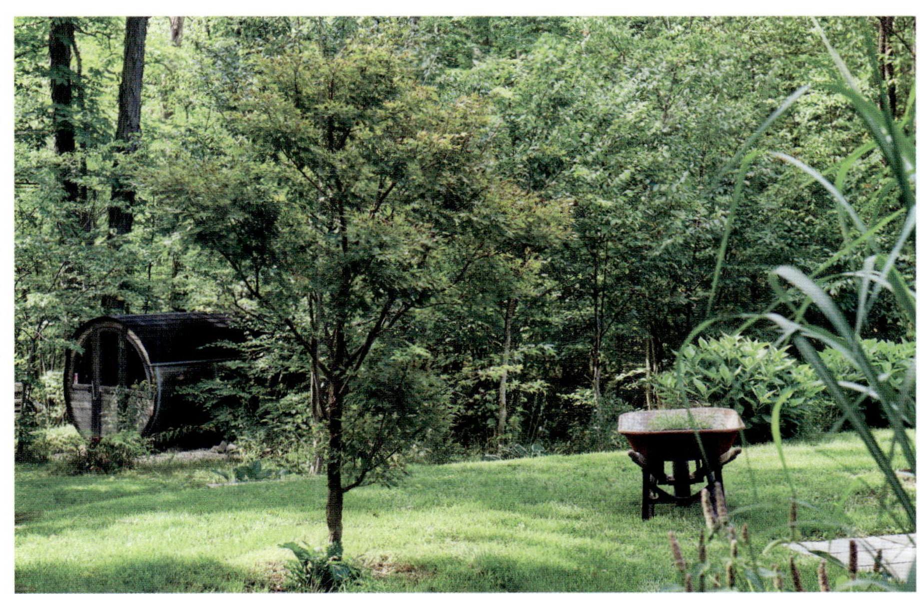

opposite, top
The green roof helps keep the house cool and extends the life of the UV membrane underneath. It also adds a natural element to the design.

opposite, bottom
A view of the house and garden shows the proximity of one to the other.

above
The Scandinavian barrel sauna is close to the house.

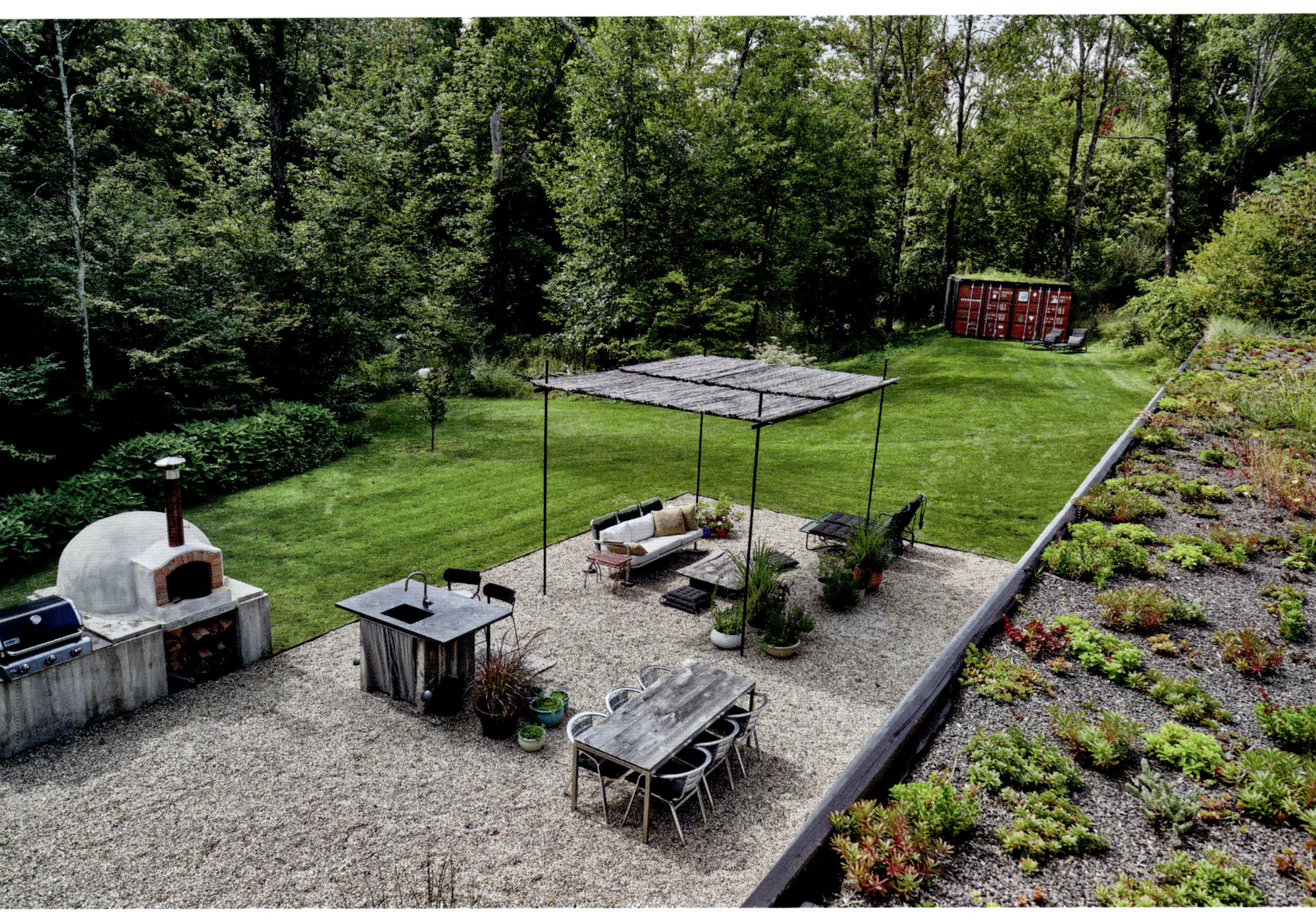

above
The outdoor living space is surrounded by woodlands. In a corner of the garden, a shipping container is used for storage.

opposite, top
Per and Angie sitting under the pergola at their house in Ghent.

opposite, bottom
The outdoor kitchen includes a woodburning pizza oven, a barbecue, a sink, a bar, and a dining table. It is organized for entertaining.

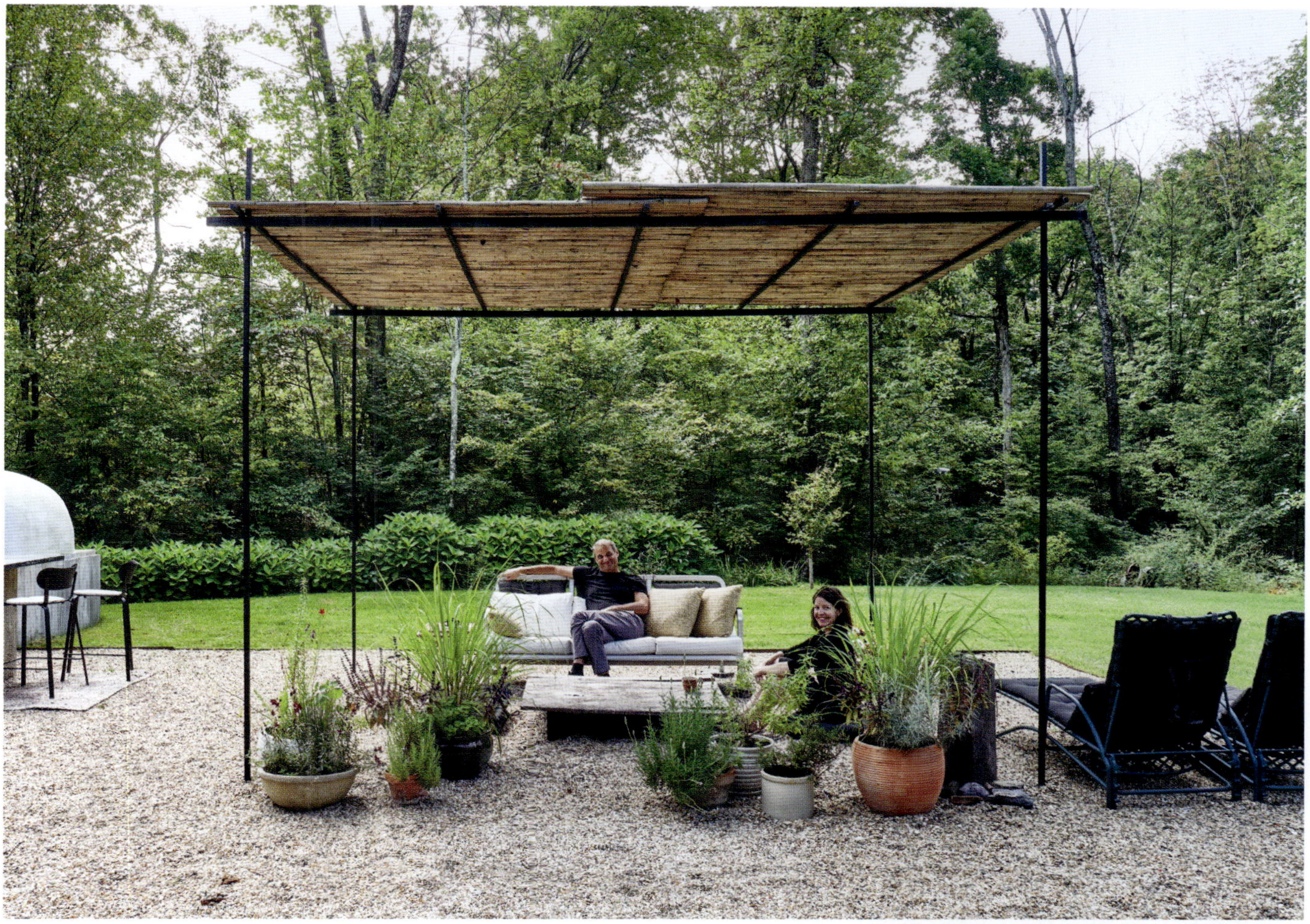

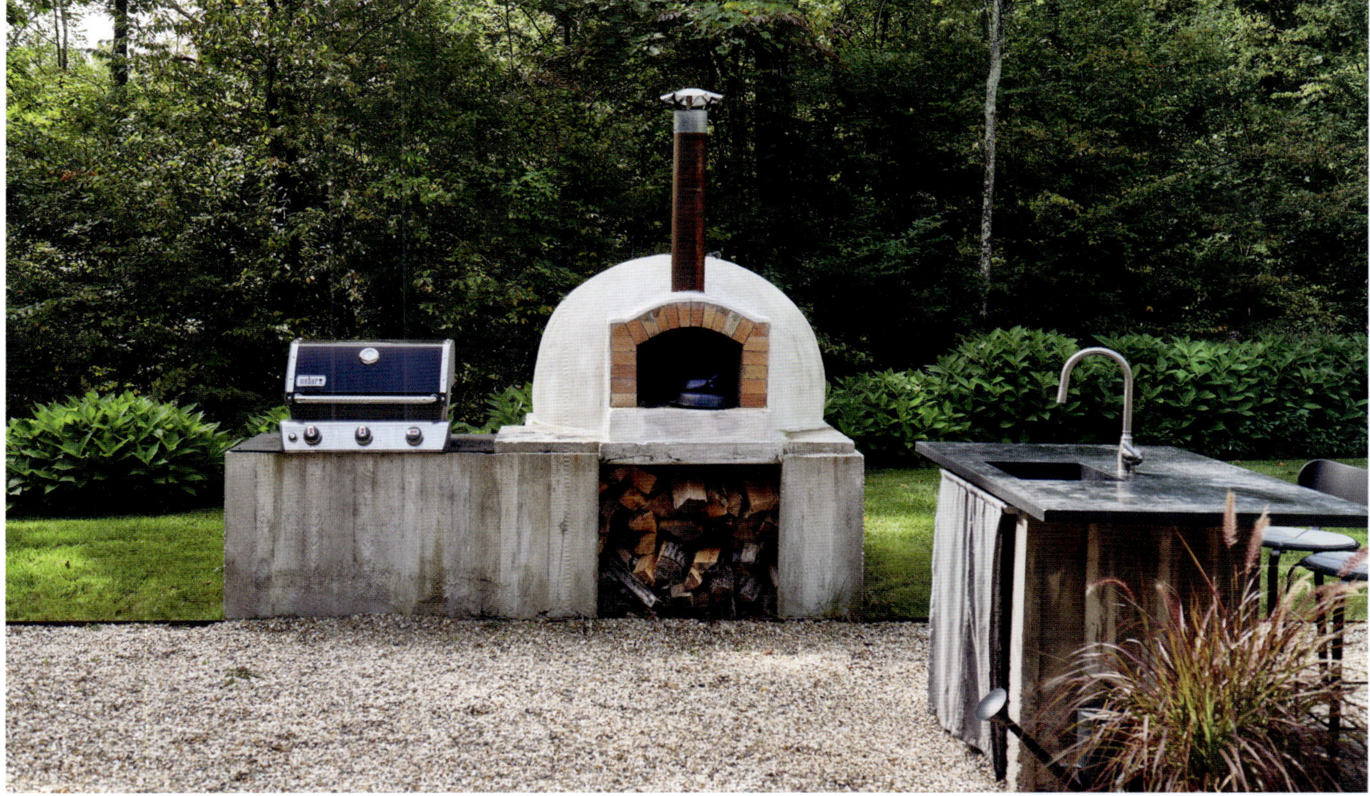

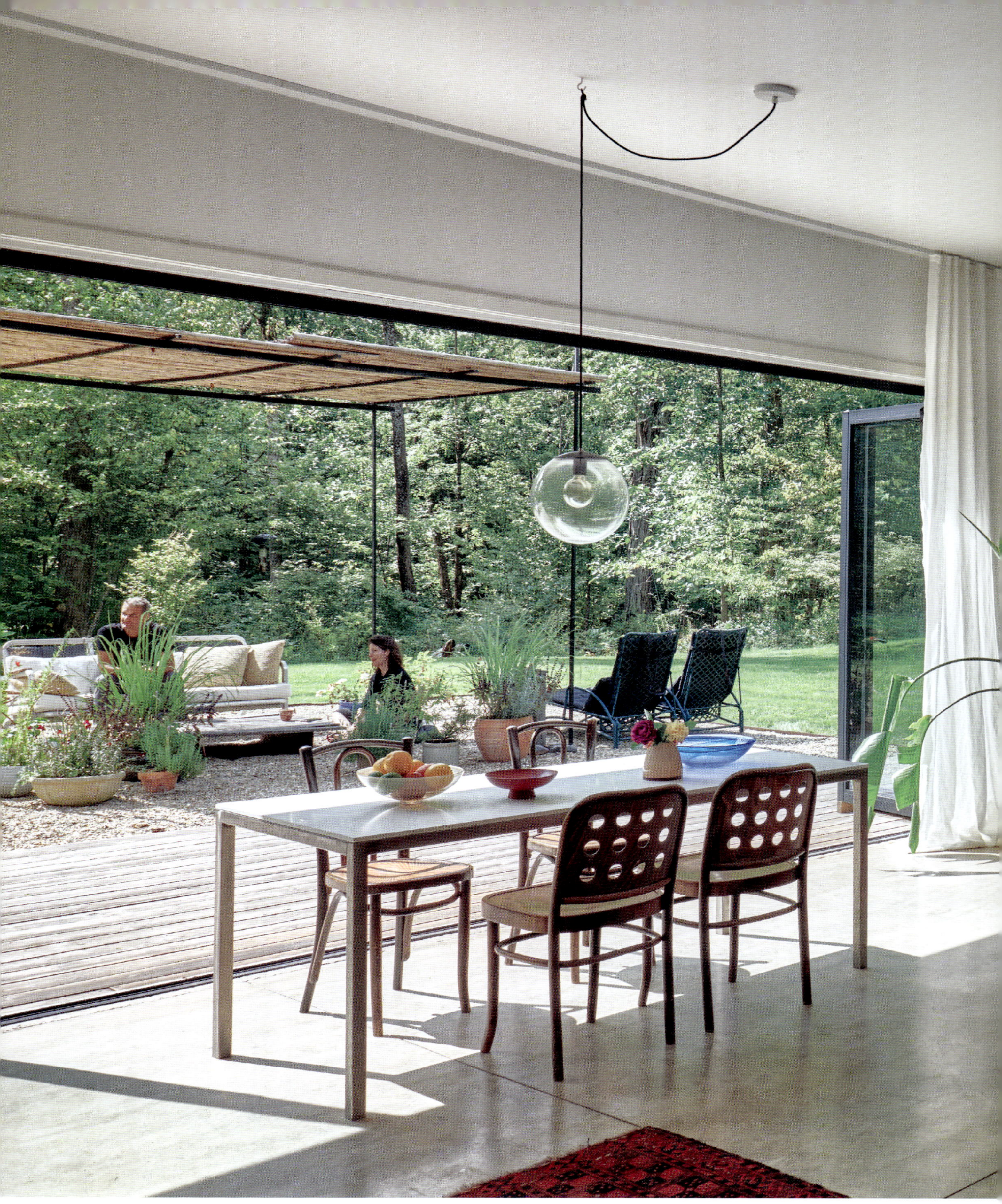

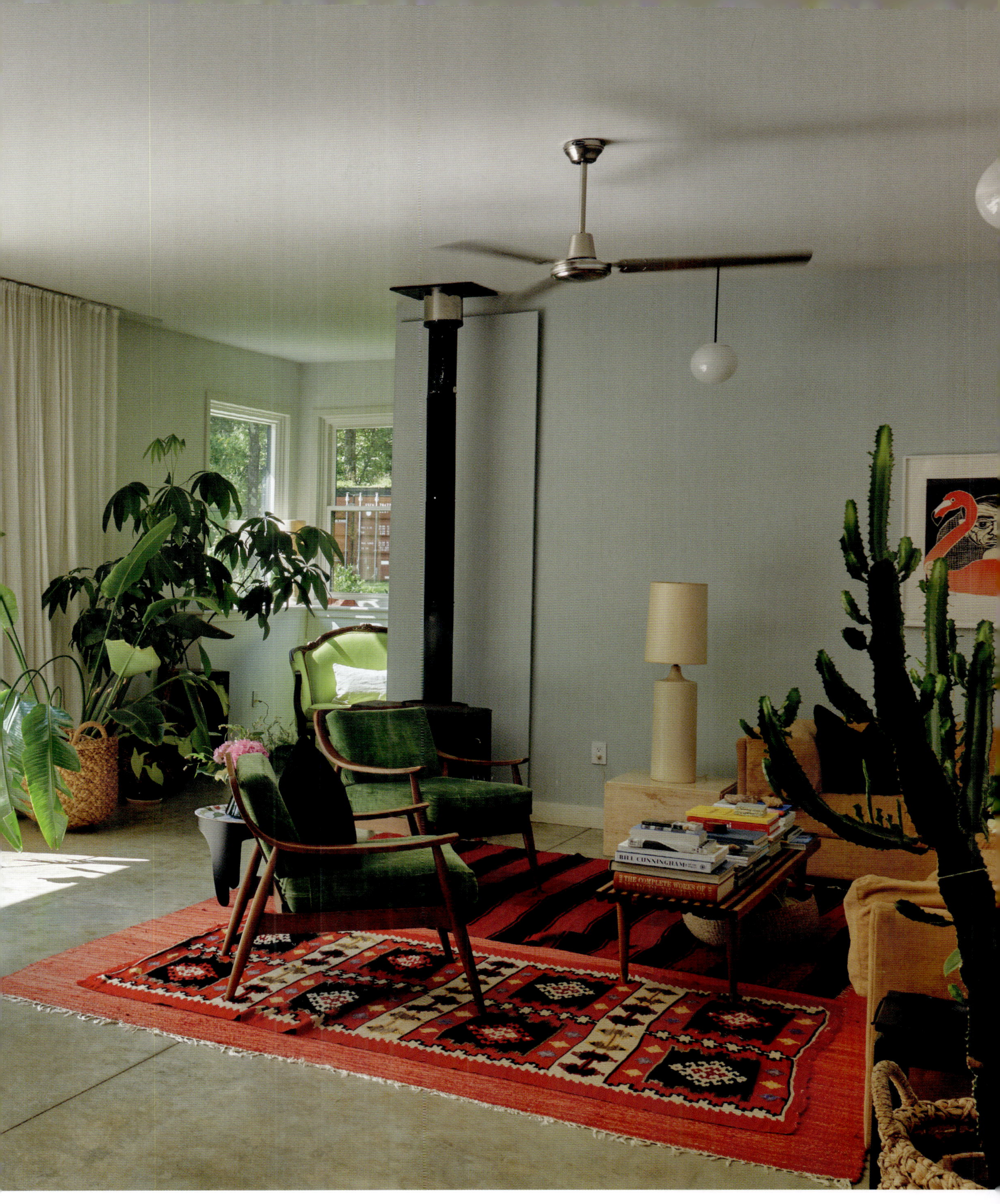

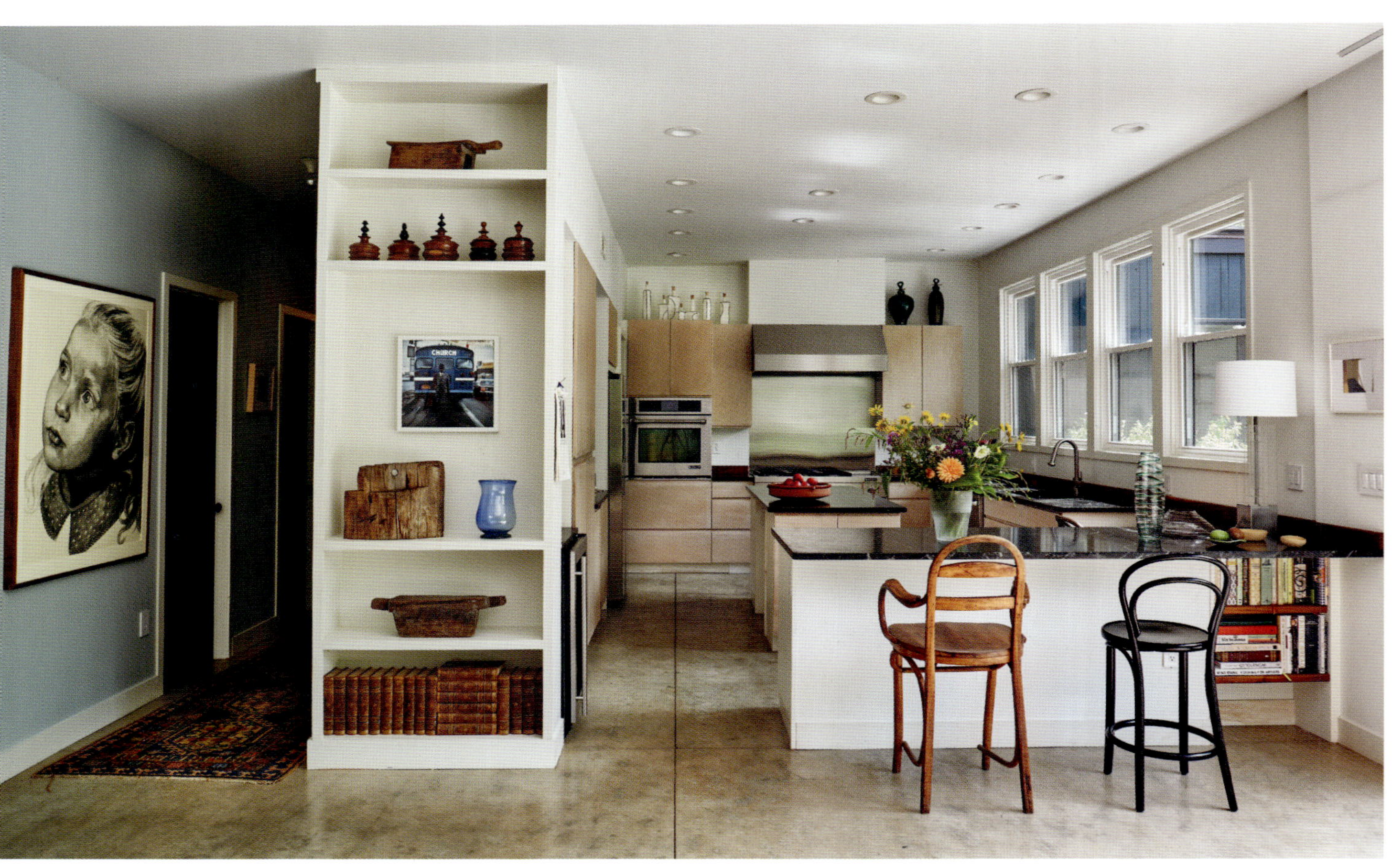

previous
The open-plan living and dining room has a woodburning stove. The modern furnishings and artworks give the rooms their personalities. The polished concrete floors have radiant heating.

above
A wall of built-in cabinets streamlines the kitchen design. A 2007 drawing in graphite, titled *Paulette, Beguiling Orphan,* by artist Anna Craycroft, is at the entrance of the hallway.

opposite, top
The primary bedroom has a door to a deck that overlooks the forest.

opposite, bottom
Angie uses online auctions to source many of the furnishings. An antique red sofa was a discovery. Her penchant for bright colors is found in the decoration of the downstairs media room and in the choice of artworks by local self-taught artist Earl Swanigan, three of which hang above the seating.

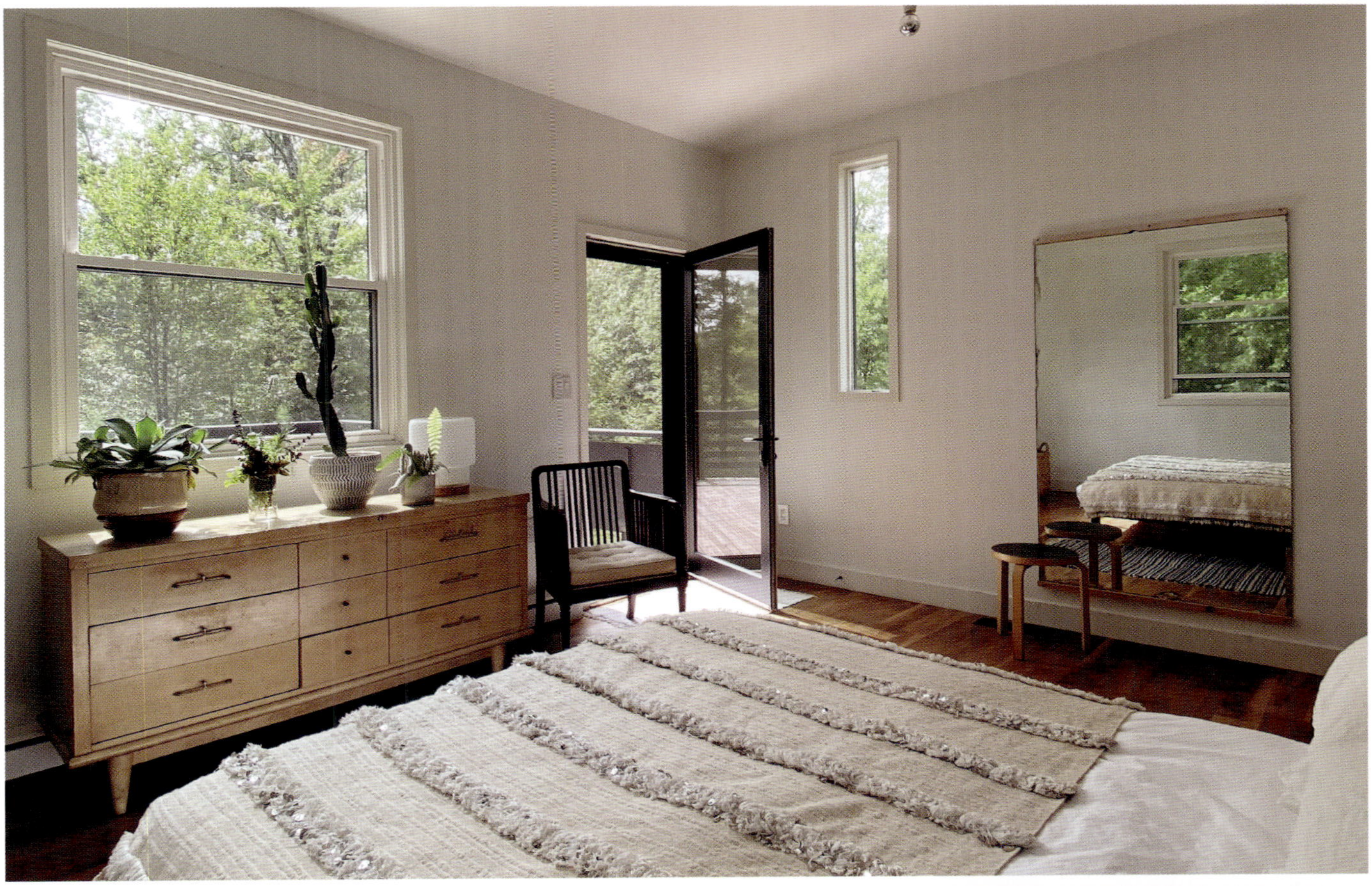

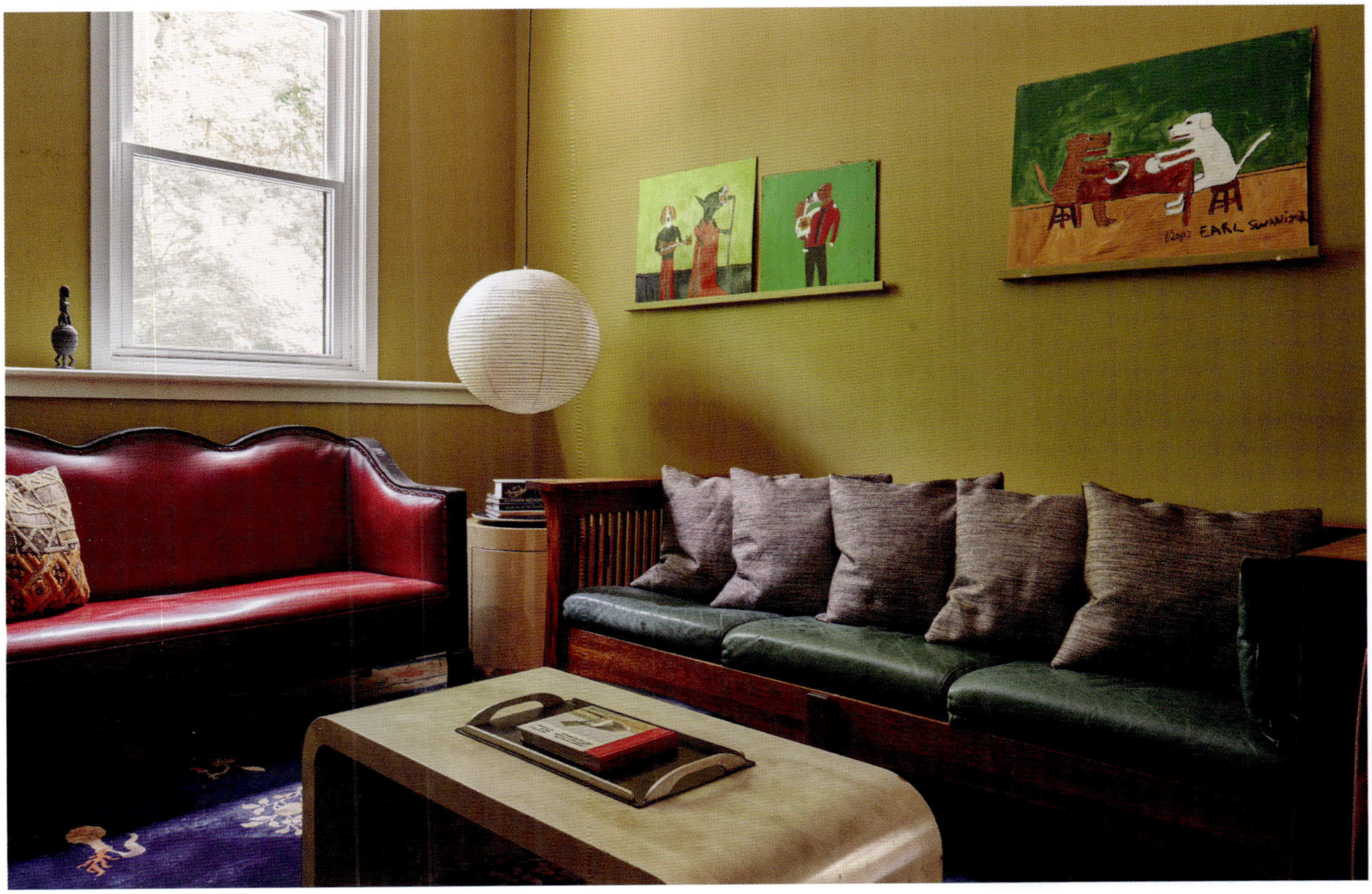

'T' Space / The Steven Myron Holl Foundation Archive and Archive Gallery

Rhinebeck, New York

A handmade sign off a country road in Duchess County indicates the four-space unpaved parking lot of 'T' Space, architect Steven Holl's art center for art, music, and performance, which opened in 2010. It is a one room–two level gallery. Exterior cedar 2 × 2 boards run horizontal to the verticality of the forest. It is a subtle difference that draws a distinction between the natural world and the intended one of the gallery. Action is required to enter or exit; ascending or descending a ramp or a staircase, push or pull open a wall to get in or out. Skylights and windows let light and views of nature into the space. Artworks are installed in relation to these dynamics. The gallery is one of four buildings on the property including Steven's family home—a 1950s stone house that was added to in 2001, two guest houses, and his drawing studio overlooking a lake. Perhaps it is this small structure that makes the most impact.

Farther down the road on a larger piece of land, known as the 'T' Space Reserve, is the Archive and Archive Gallery. It is also the Hudson Valley office of Steven's architecture practice. The expansive building includes an architectural archive of models, furniture, project files, and watercolors, many of which are on display. The Archive Gallery is tucked in an upper level. The Archive Building fits respectfully in its surroundings, not just visually but environmentally with the green roof, the geothermal heating, and the rain-water catch basin near the entrance that adds to the biodiversity of the site.

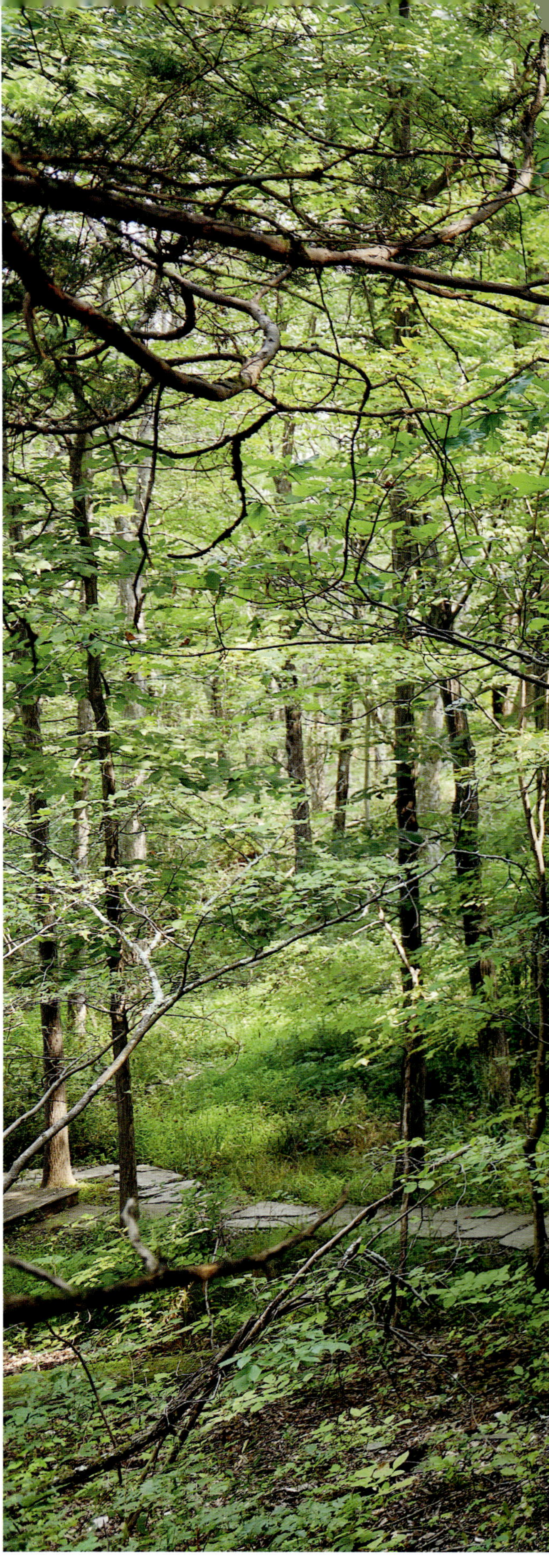

The entrance of 'T' Space. The gallery, set in a thicket of trees, opened in 2010.

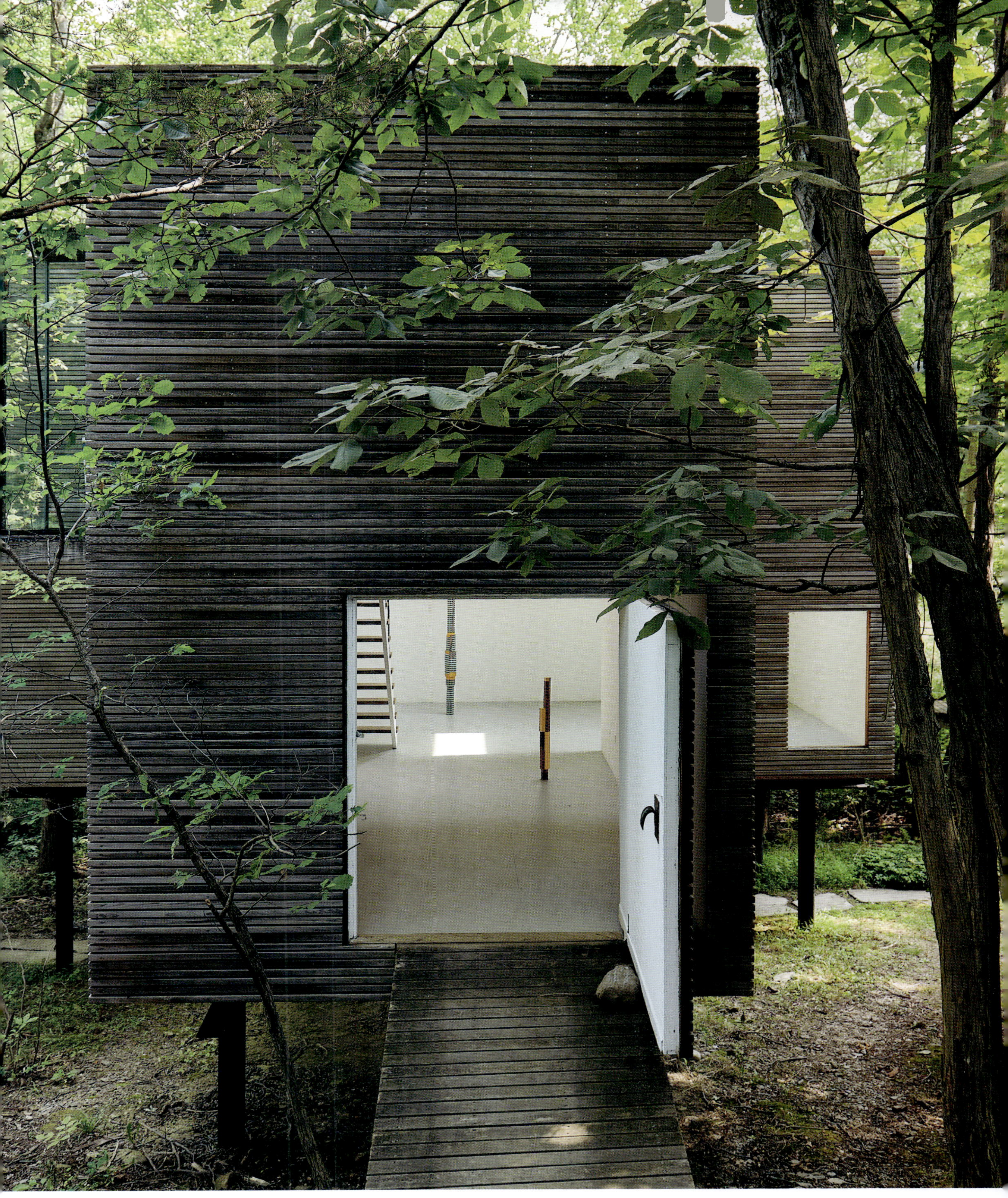

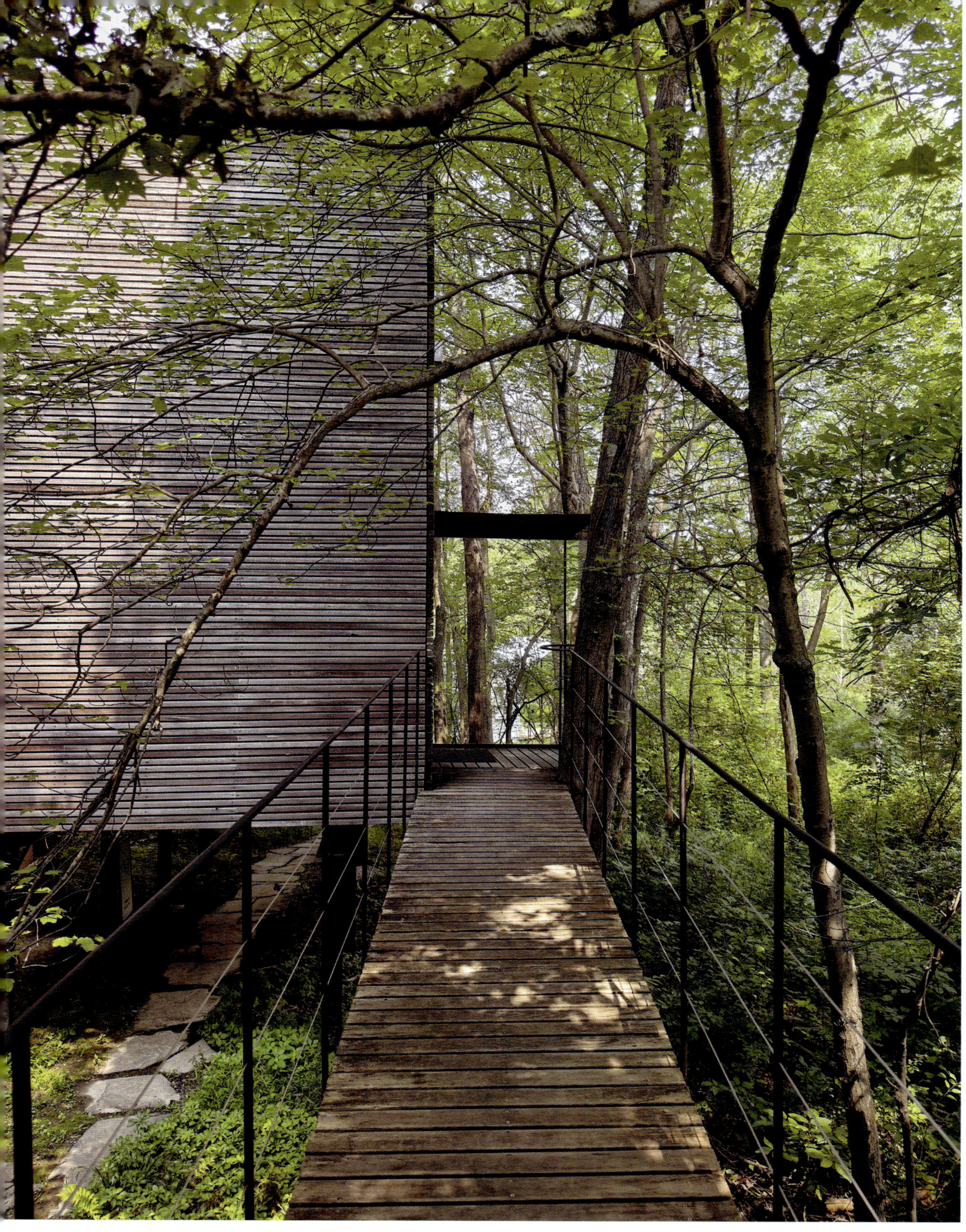

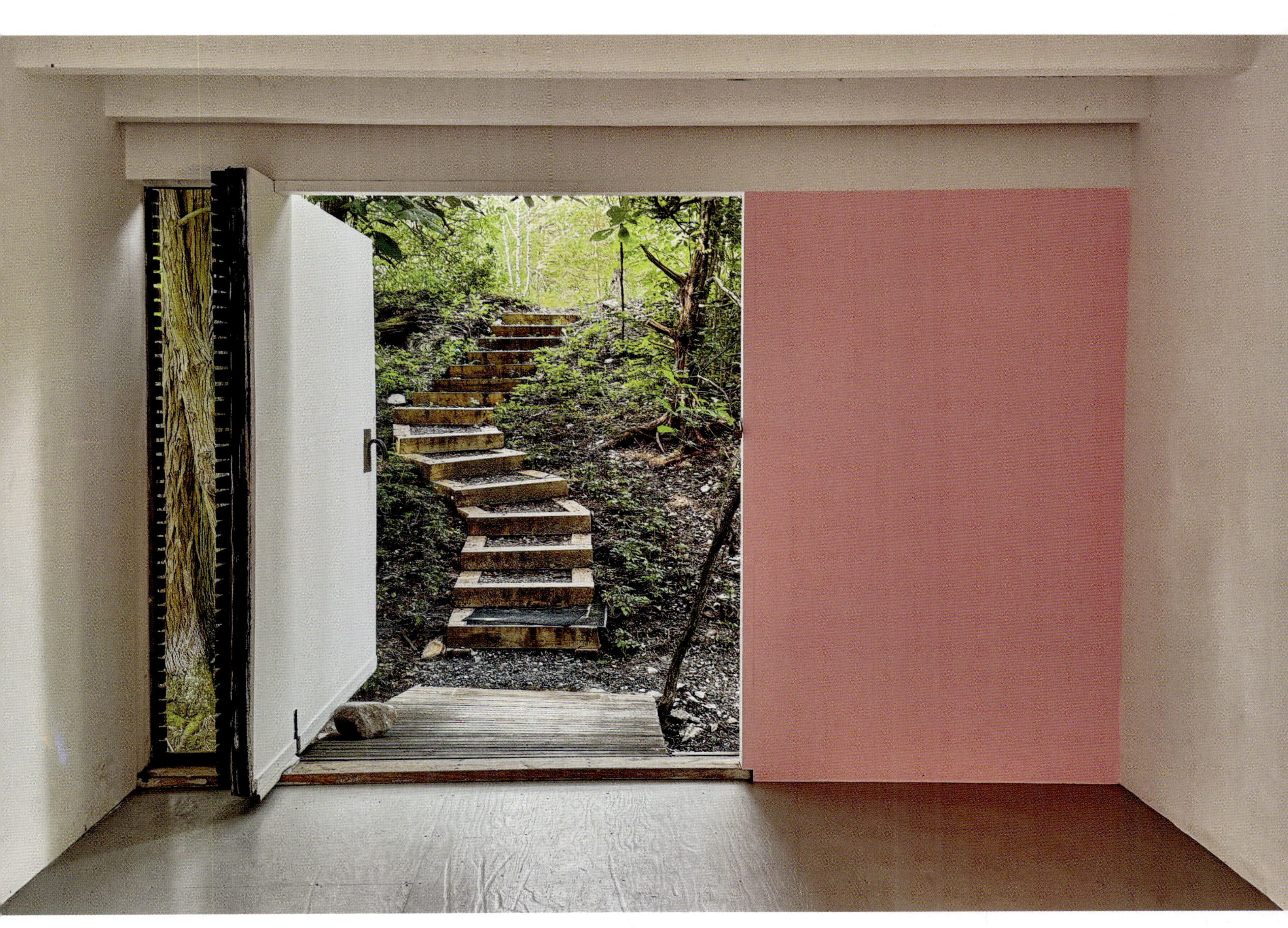

above
From the gallery, the staircase leads to the parking area. Pushing the square front door feels like opening a wall. Peter Halley's painting installation of planes of color were on exhibition in the summer of 2024. The gallery has plywood walls and floors.

opposite
On one side of the building, a ramp leads to the interior gallery space.

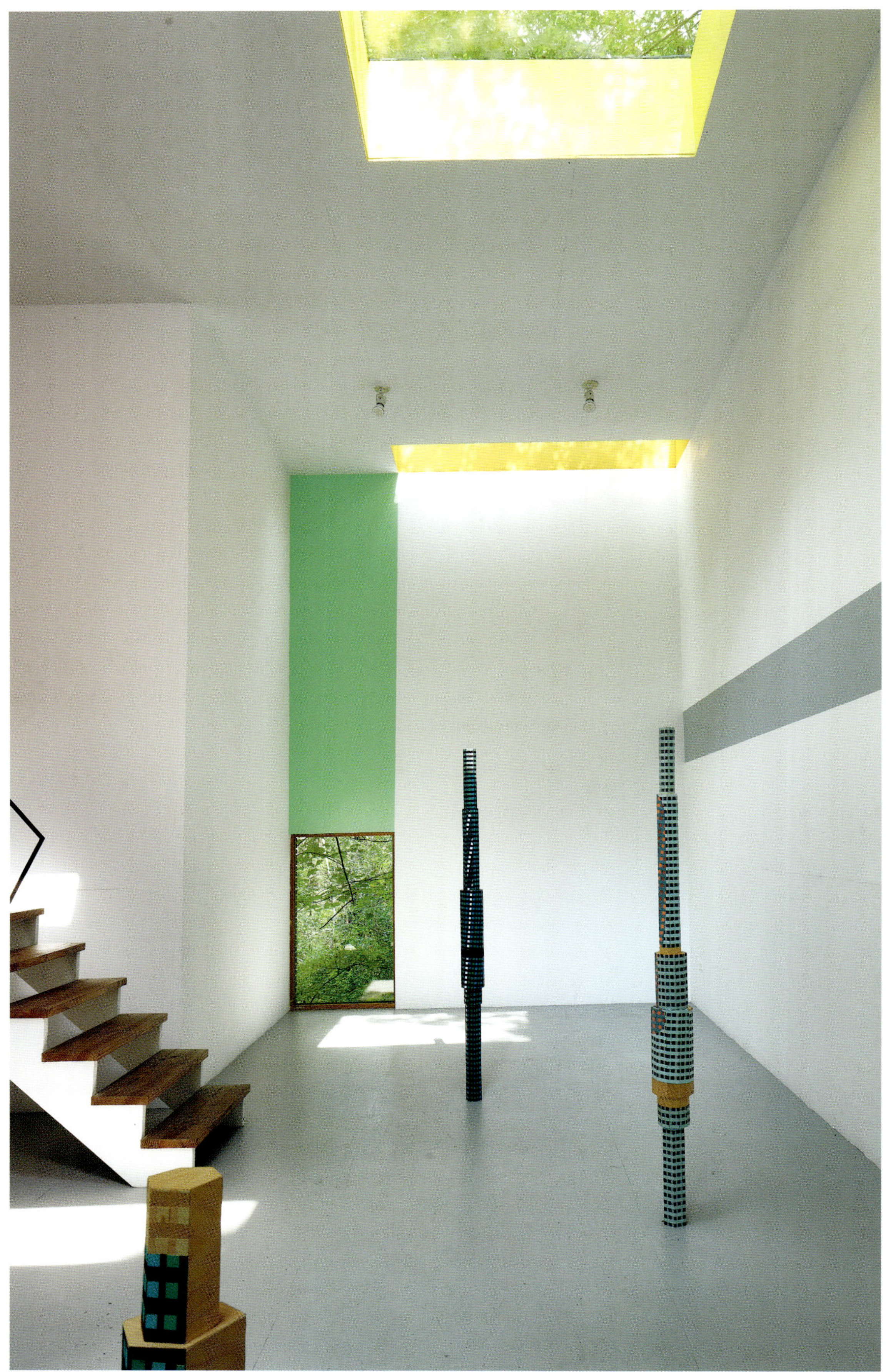

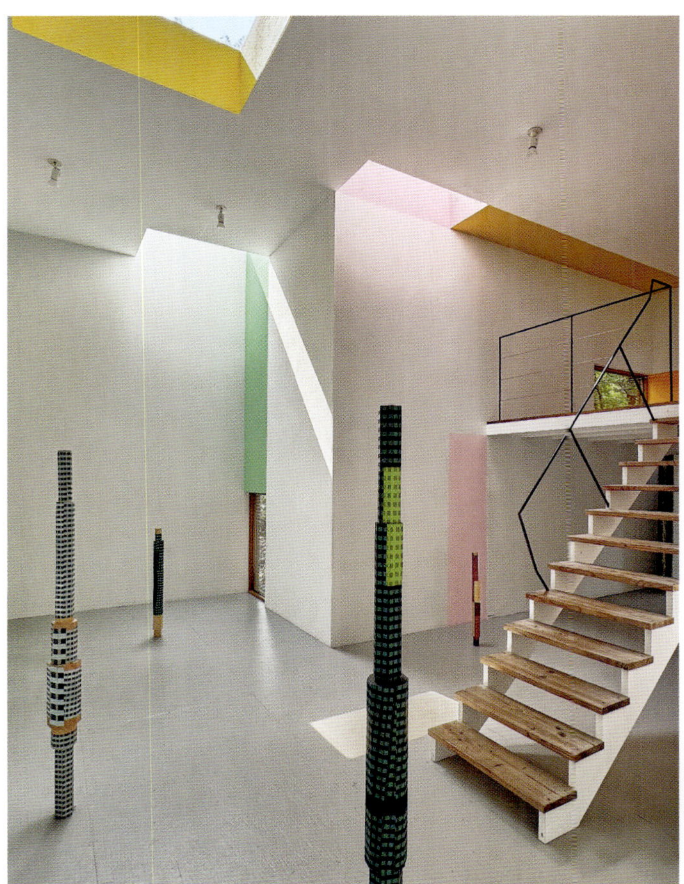

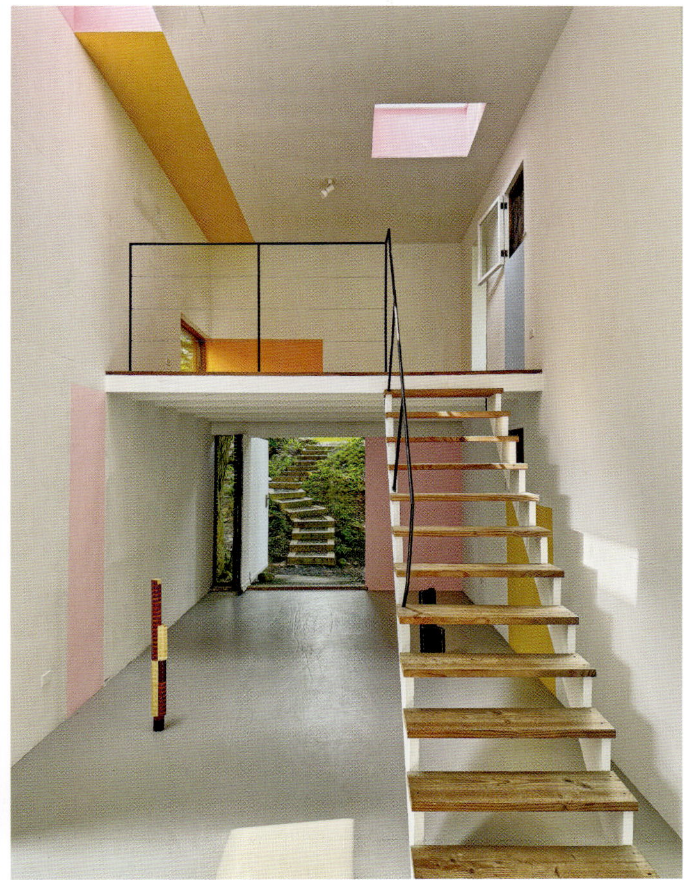

opposite
A simple staircase leads to the second level of the gallery.

above, left
Steph Gonzalez-Turner and Peter Halley's exhibition was titled *Painting/Sculpture*. Steph's vertical works were shown in relationship to Peter's wall paintings. Peter was invited to exhibit at 'T' Space, and he invited Steph to join him.

above, right
Doors, windows, and skylights are the natural light sources for the gallery.

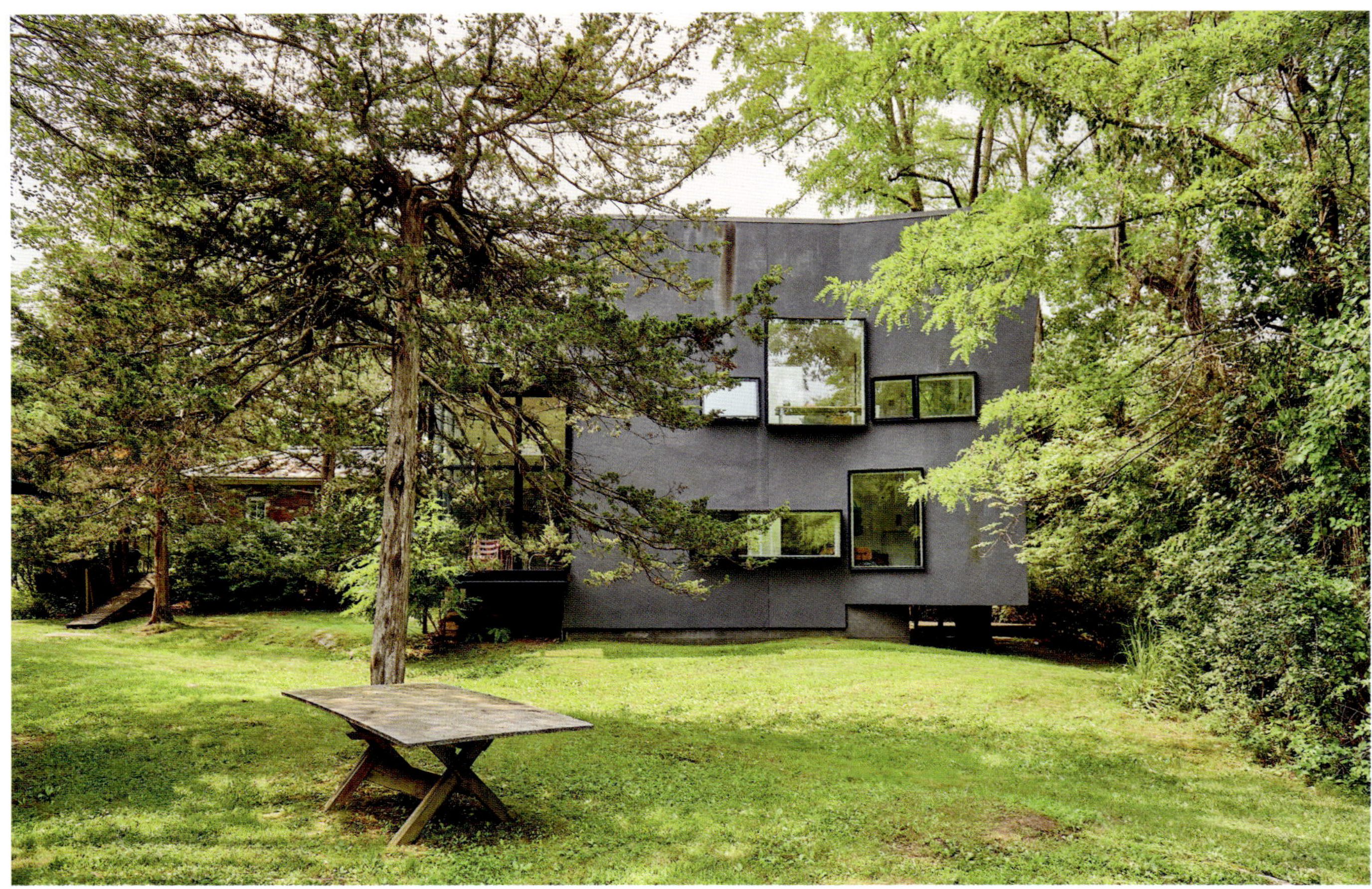

above
Seen from the backyard, the addition to Steven's home, known as Little Tesseract, was completed in 2001. The home has been his rural retreat for forty-two years.

opposite, top
The architect's drawing studio, Round Lake Hut, was built overlooking a small lake, shared by other homeowners.

opposite, bottom
Along the walking path of the property are sculptures by other artists, including Mike Metz's piece *wrench/sled* (1985/2015).

overleaf
Across the Round Hill road, on the twenty-eight-acre 'T' Reserve, is another building, an extension of a 1940s cabin. Known as the Archive, it houses Steven's architectural archive as well as his Hudson Valley office, foundation, and another art space, the Archive Gallery. Among the features of the building are a green roof and a fountain with a rainwater catch basin at the entrance. It runs off a single geothermal well, and the floors have radiant heating. As with all the buildings at the 'T' Reserve, they are sited within the surrounding forest.

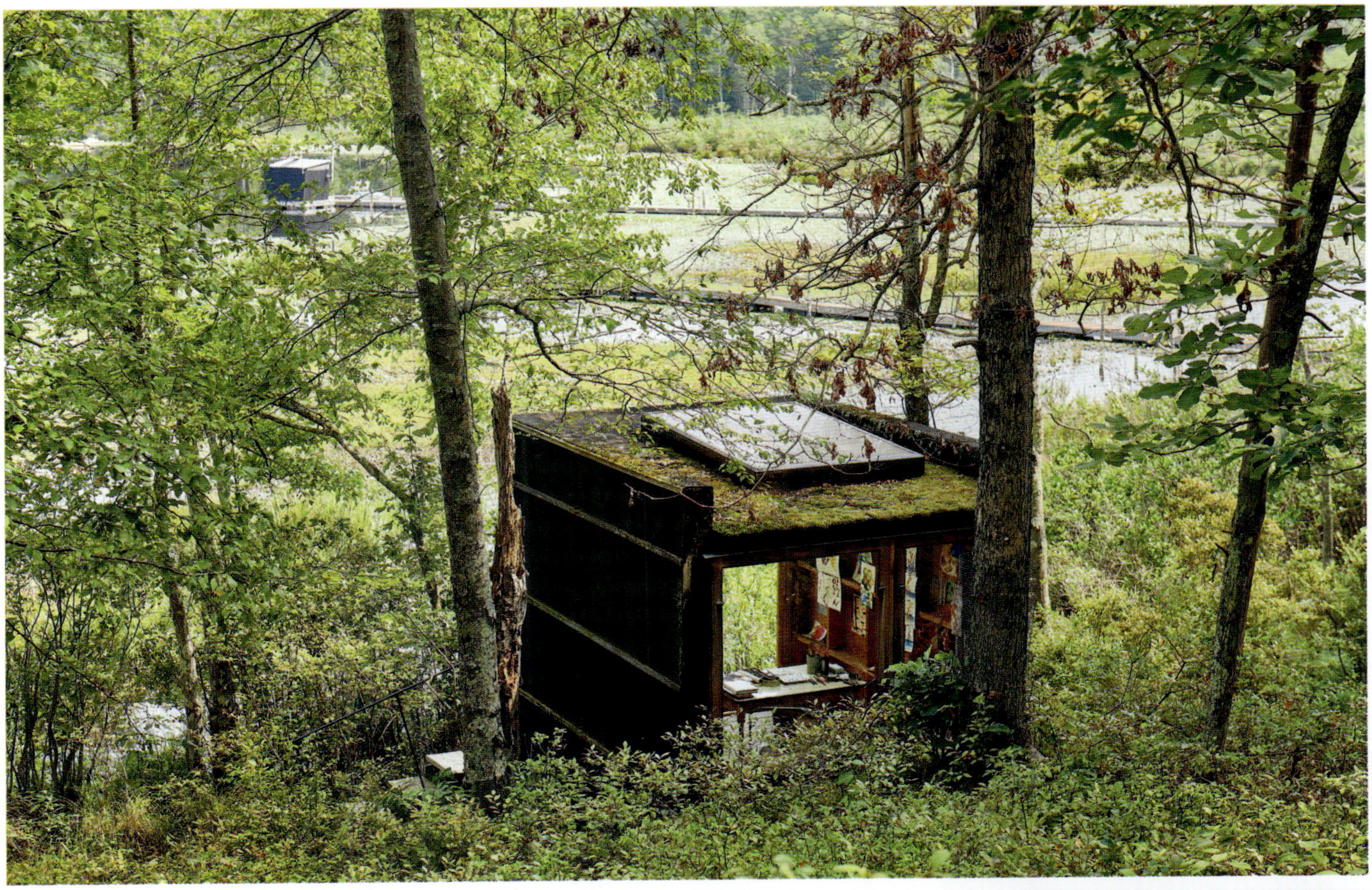

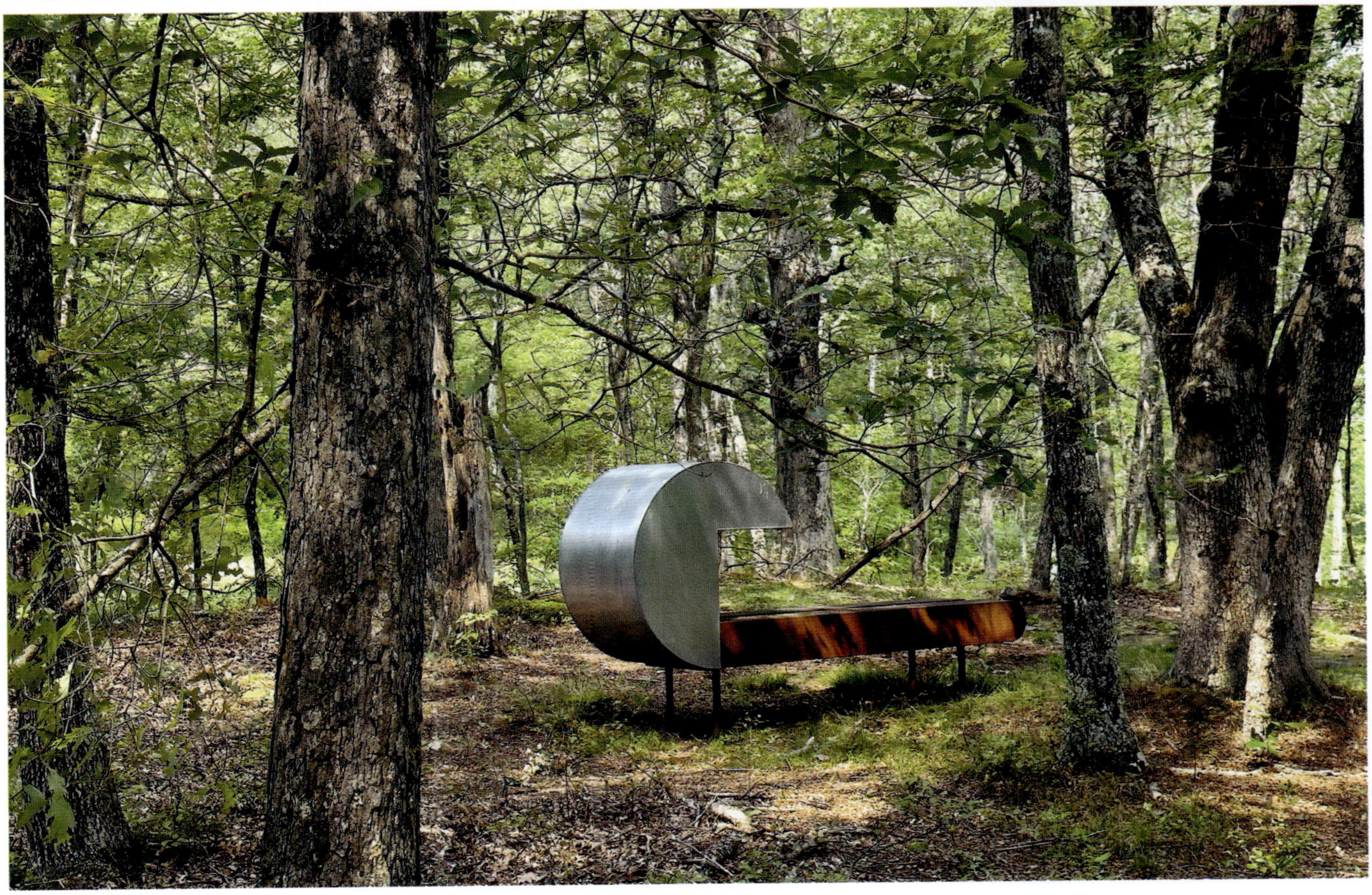

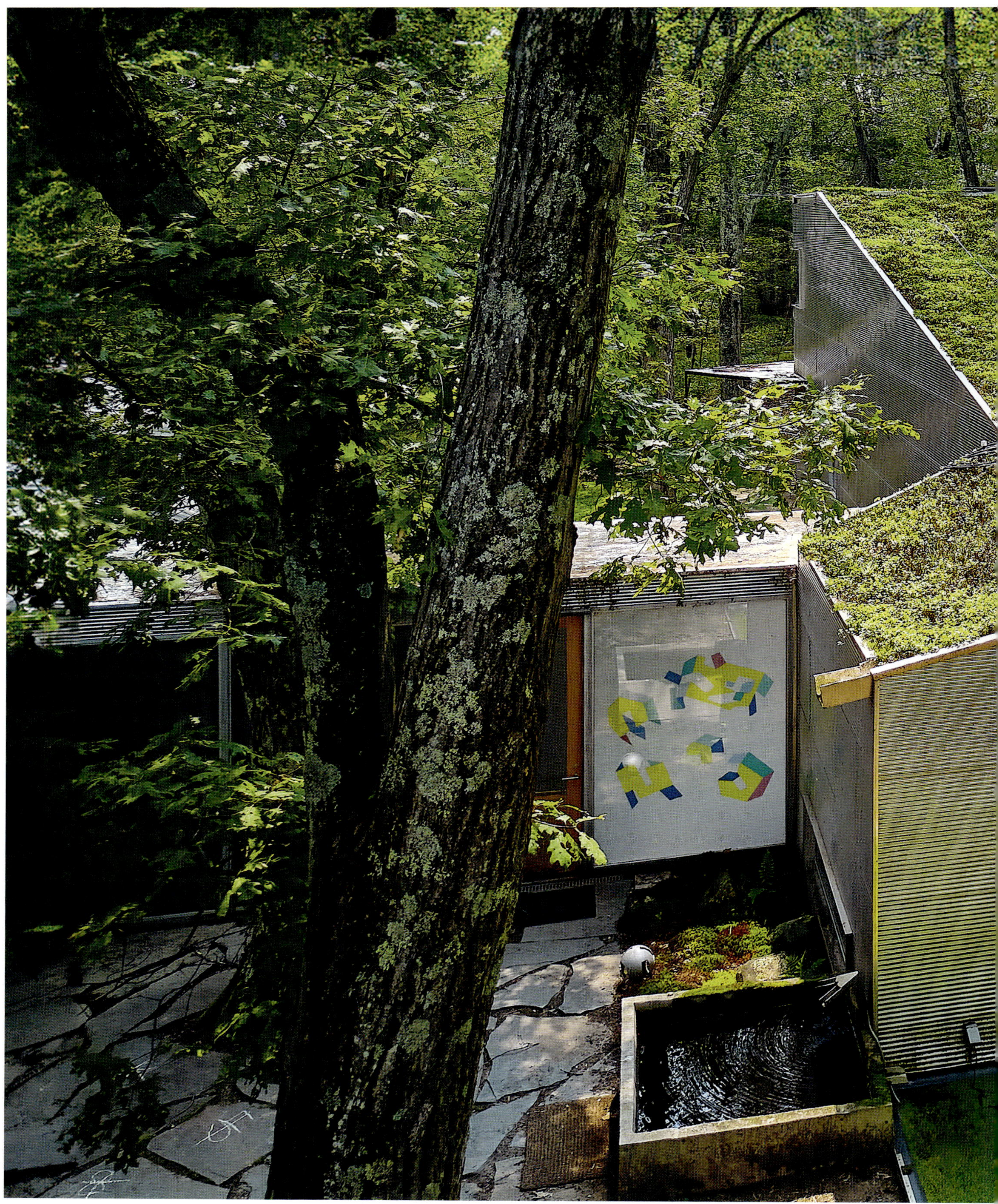

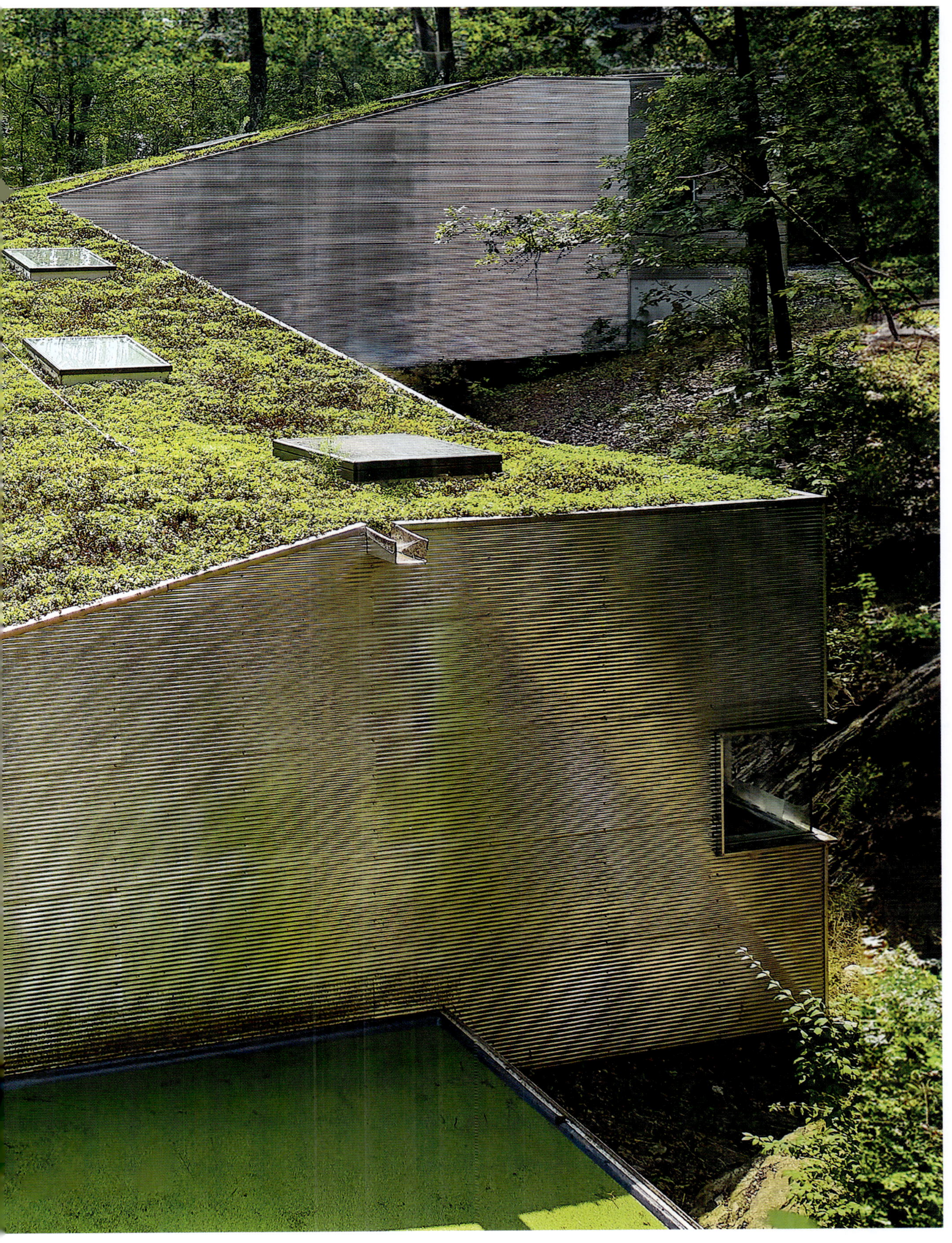

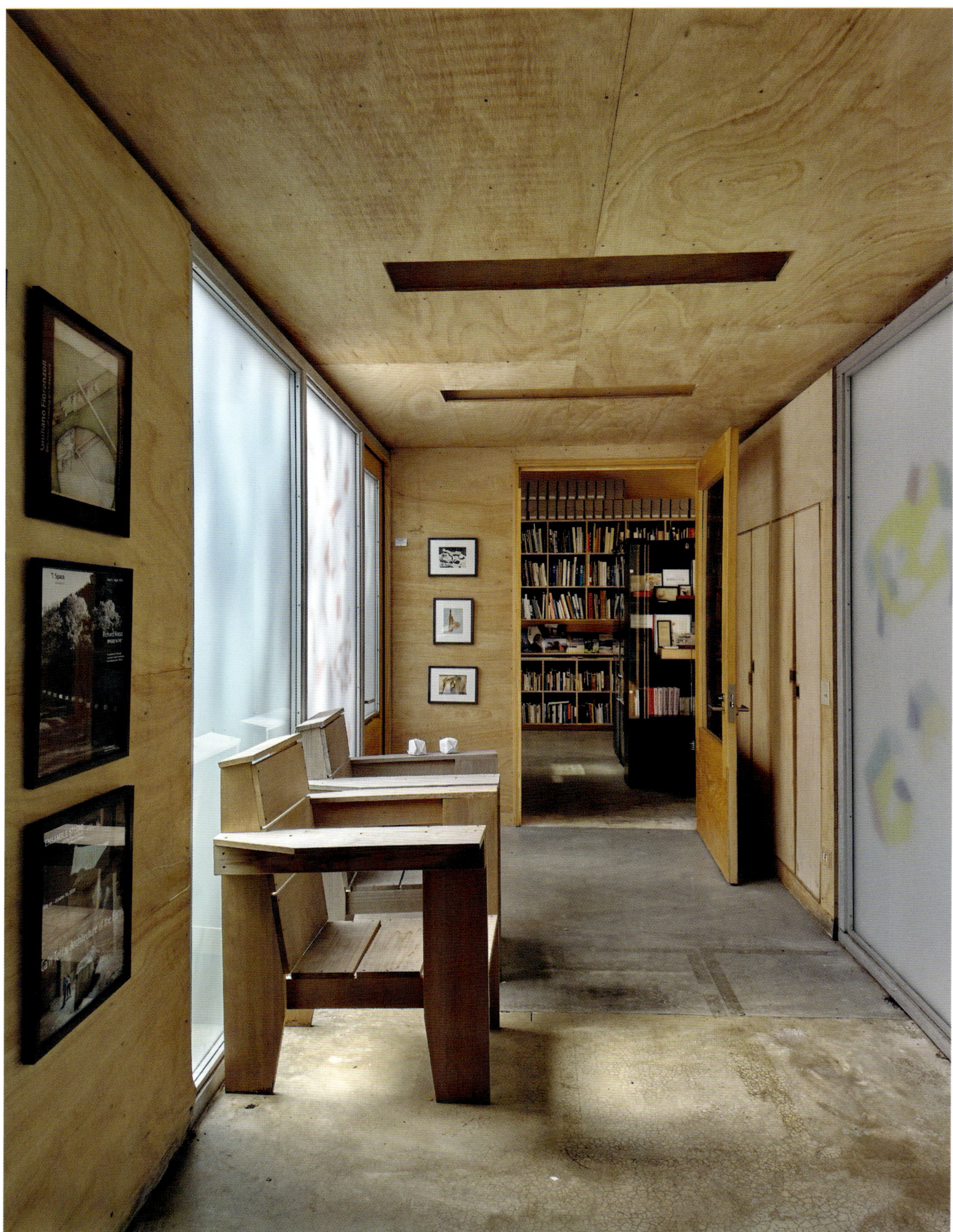
Giuliano Fiorenzoli
T Space
Richard Nonas
ENSAMBLE STUDIO

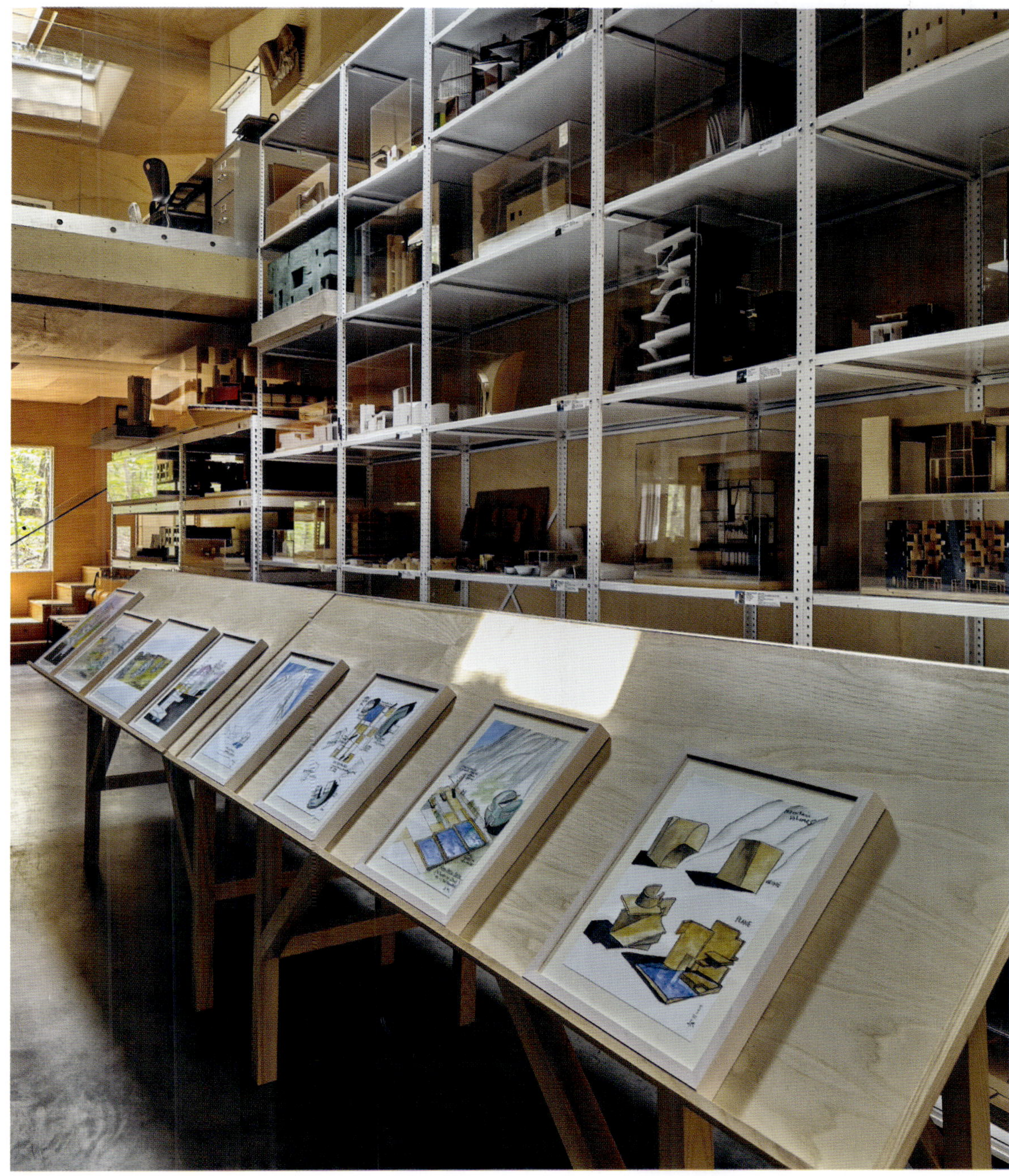

opposite
The entry corridor of the Archive building connects the existing structure, a 1940s cabin, with the extension, a new building. The wooden Manchester chairs were designed by Steven Holl. The walls are made with plywood; the floors are concrete. Silhouettes of project plans are embedded in the windows that are made of an insulating glass by Okalux.

above
The extensive collection of over 1,200 architectural models, numerous watercolors, photographs, books, and drawings are stored and displayed in the Archive, either on shelving or in display cases.

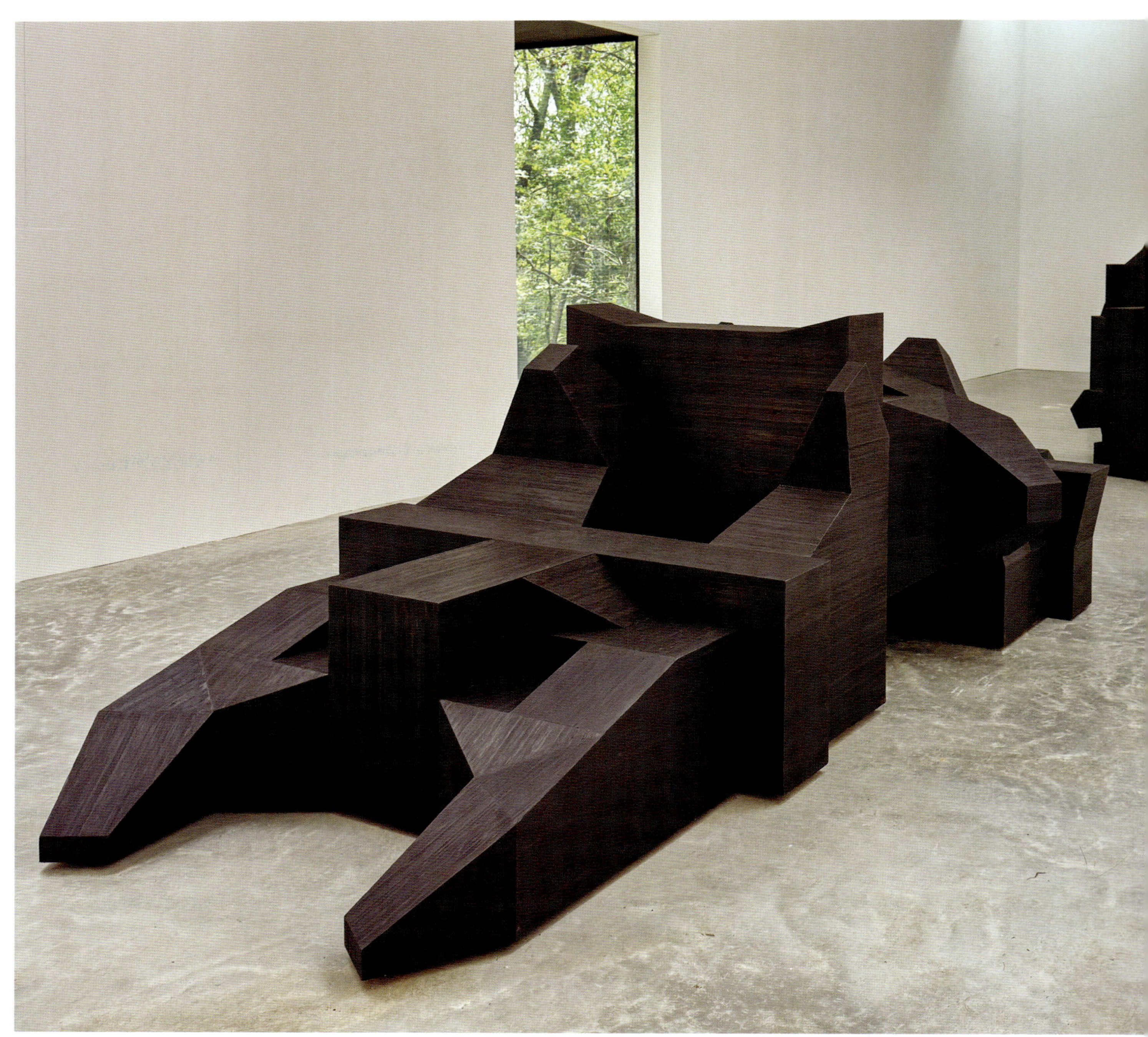

above
The Archive Gallery was completed in October 2023 and adds more exhibition space to the reserve. Exhibitions are four months long, which allows viewers the opportunity to make multiple visits to the location. In 2024, artist James Casebere exhibited his new work, *Shou Sugi Ban*.

opposite
A window-encased platform juts out from the gallery into the trees.

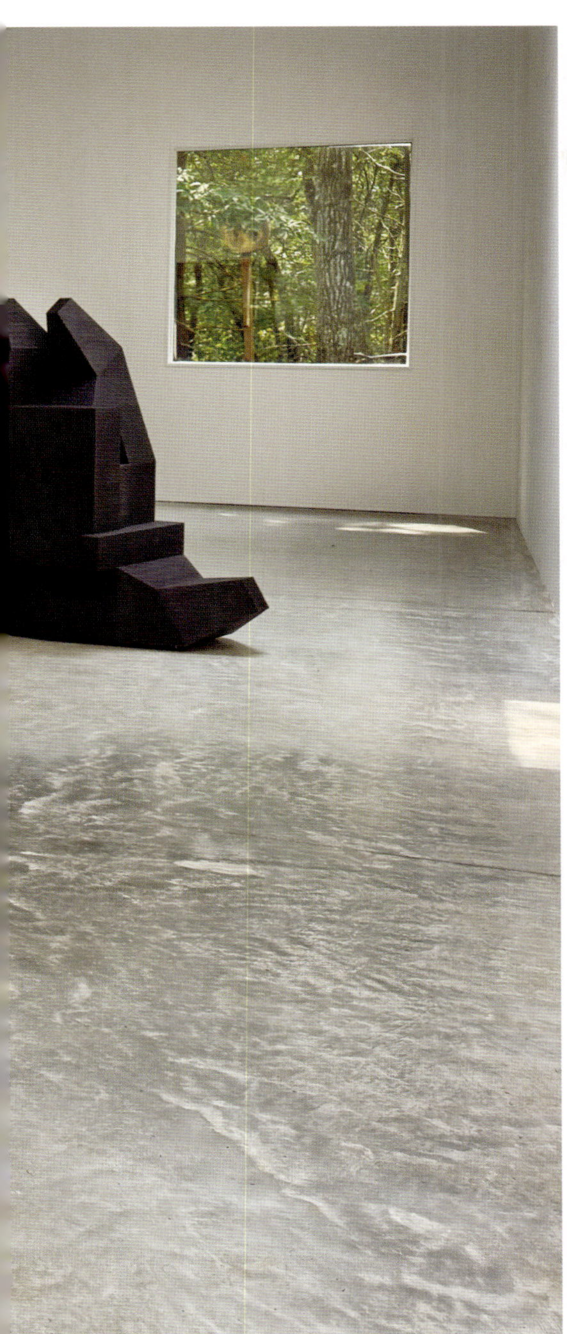

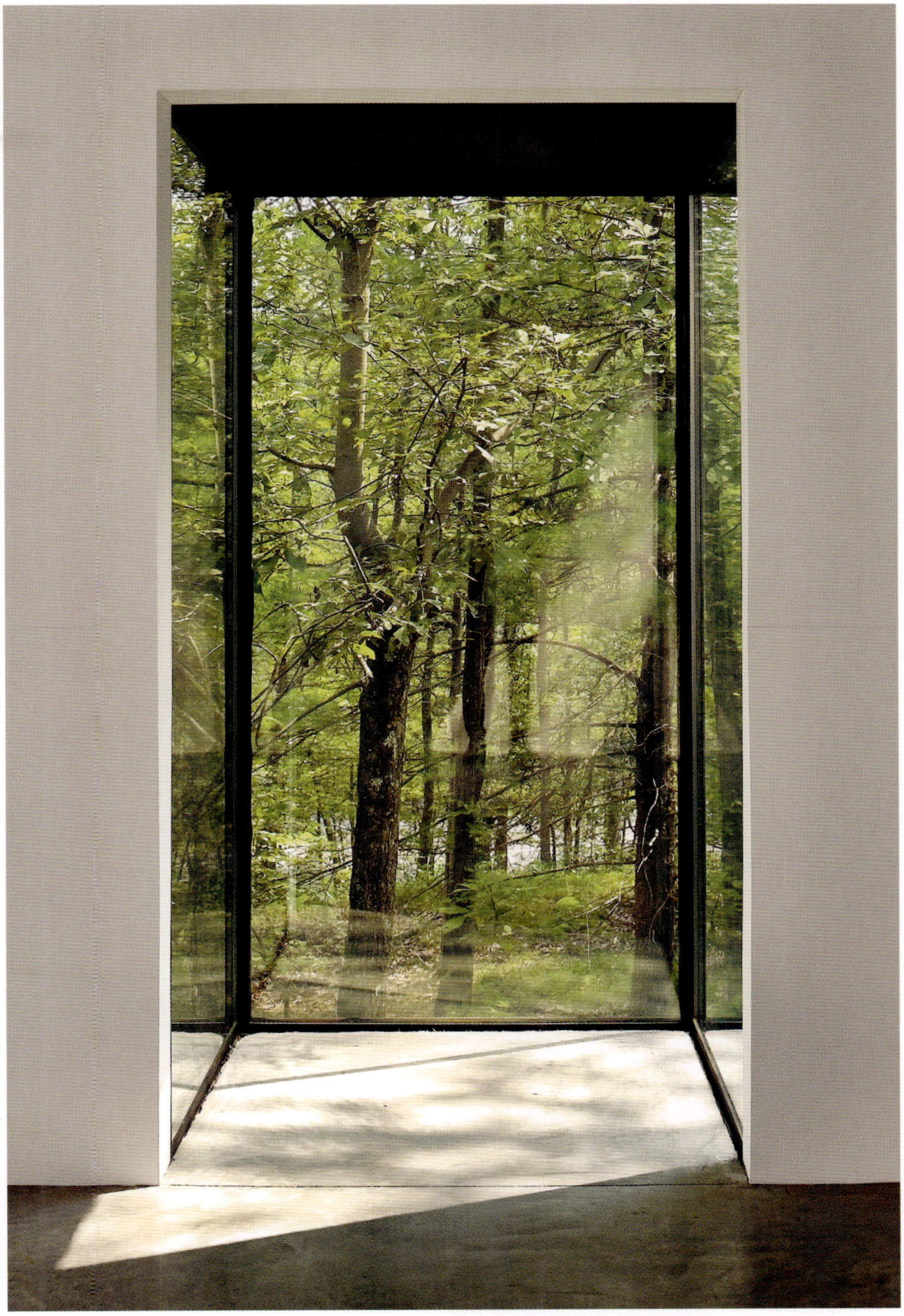

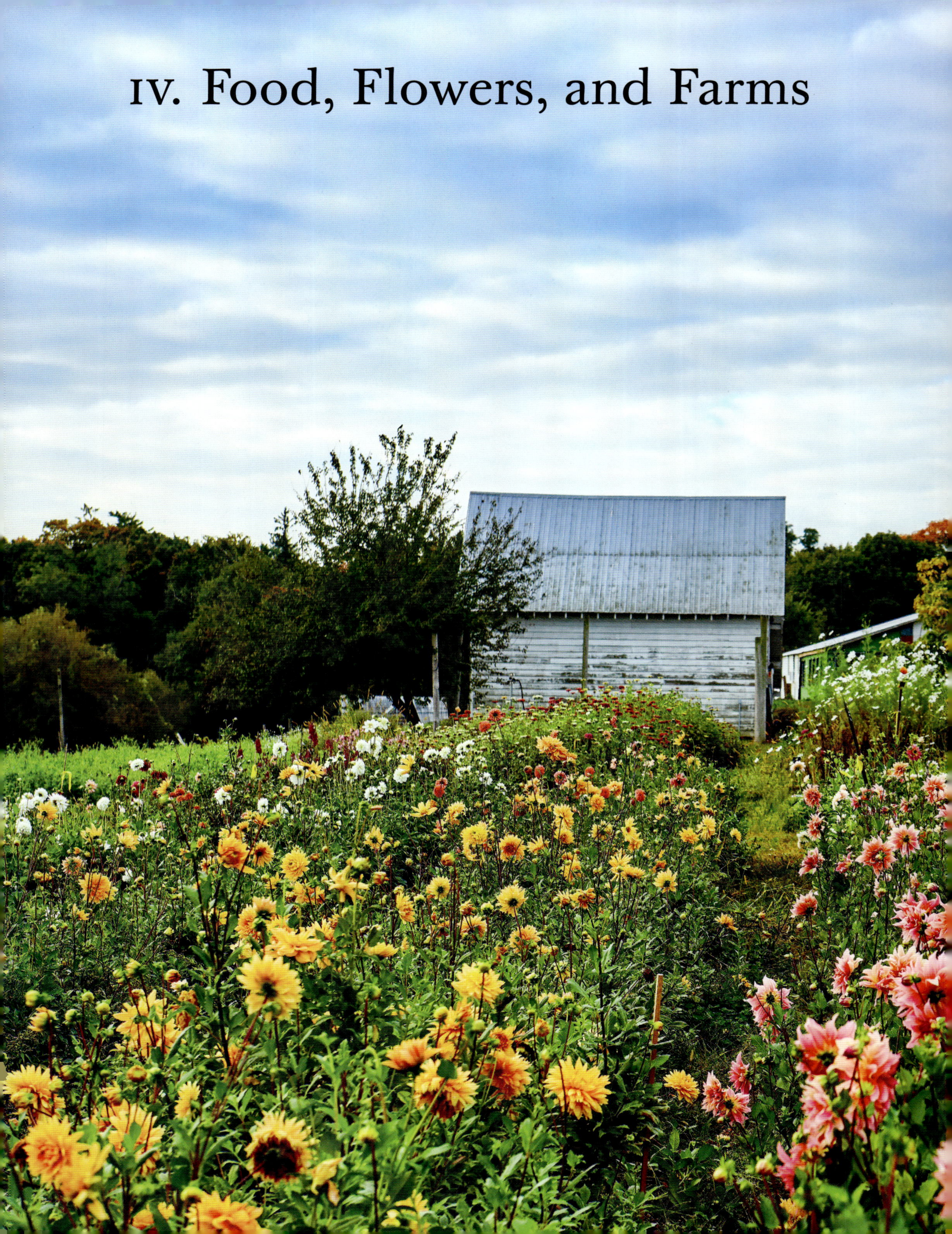

IV. Food, Flowers, and Farms

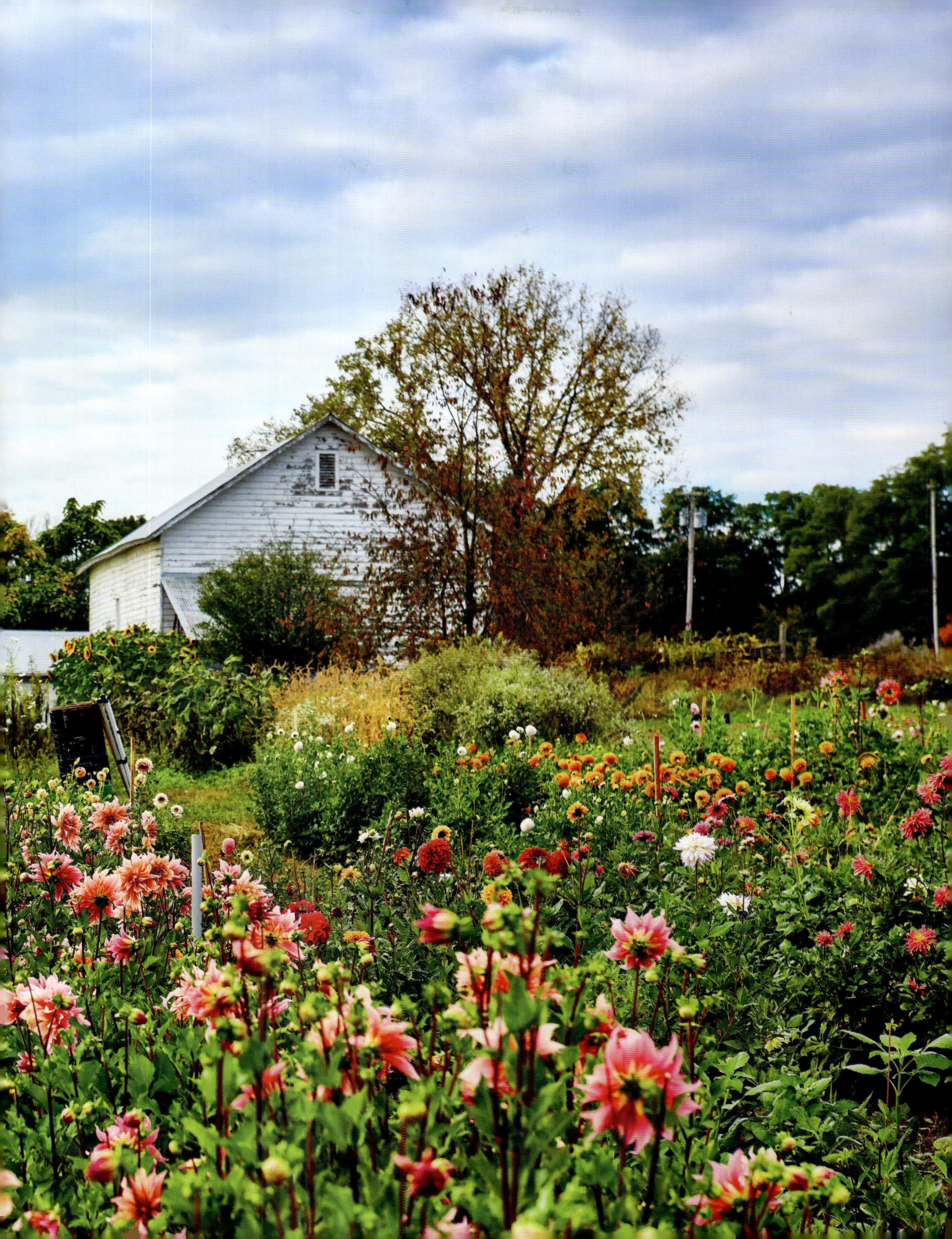

Copake Hillsdale Farmers Market

Hillsdale, New York

In 2002, a Hillsdale, New York, farm was slated for development. A tract of two hundred homes was planned for both sides of Route 22. But the New York State Office of Parks, Recreation, and Historic Preservation stepped in and bought the three-hundred-acre property. The land was transformed into Roeliff Jansen Park, which is managed by the town.

The Hillsdale Farmers Market was started in 2005 by Caroline Stewart and Timi Bates. Seven years later, Roberta Roll started the Copake Farmers Market in 2012. Together, they decided to combine their efforts to form the Copake Hillsdale Farmers Market in 2014. The result is a permanent home at the Harvest Barn, in the Roeliff Jansen Park. Thirty vendors offering a combination of prepared food products, fresh foods, and handmade goods are set up in the covered barn and outside in the barnyard under tents. The market is open on Saturdays from May to November, which is later than most local farmers markets. The covered barn provides shelter in the cool fall months. In the summer, picnic tables are placed outside so that people can enjoy their purchases before taking a hike on the adjacent walking trails of the park. Climbing to the crest of a gentle hill on the path provides views of the Hudson Valley, Massachusetts, and the farm down below.

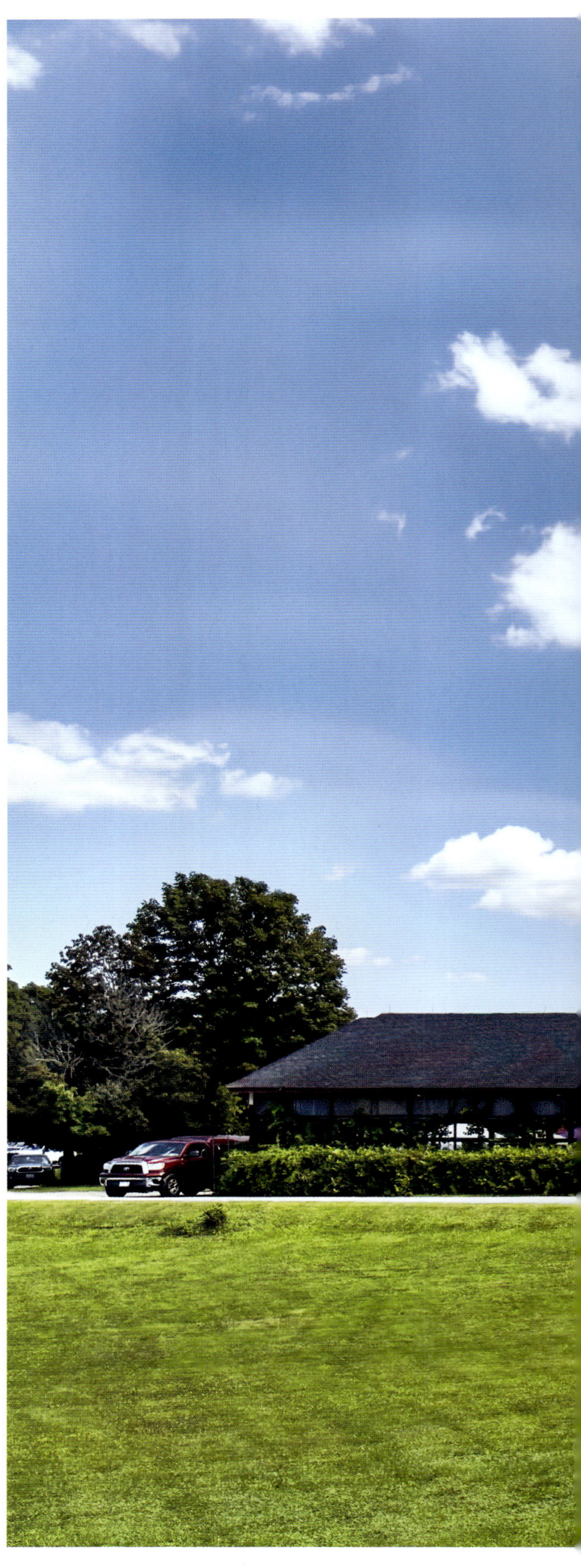

previous
Damsel Gardens is a flower farm in Stuyvesant, New York.

right
The Harvest Barn in Hillsdale, New York, is home to the Copake Hillsdale Farmers Market.

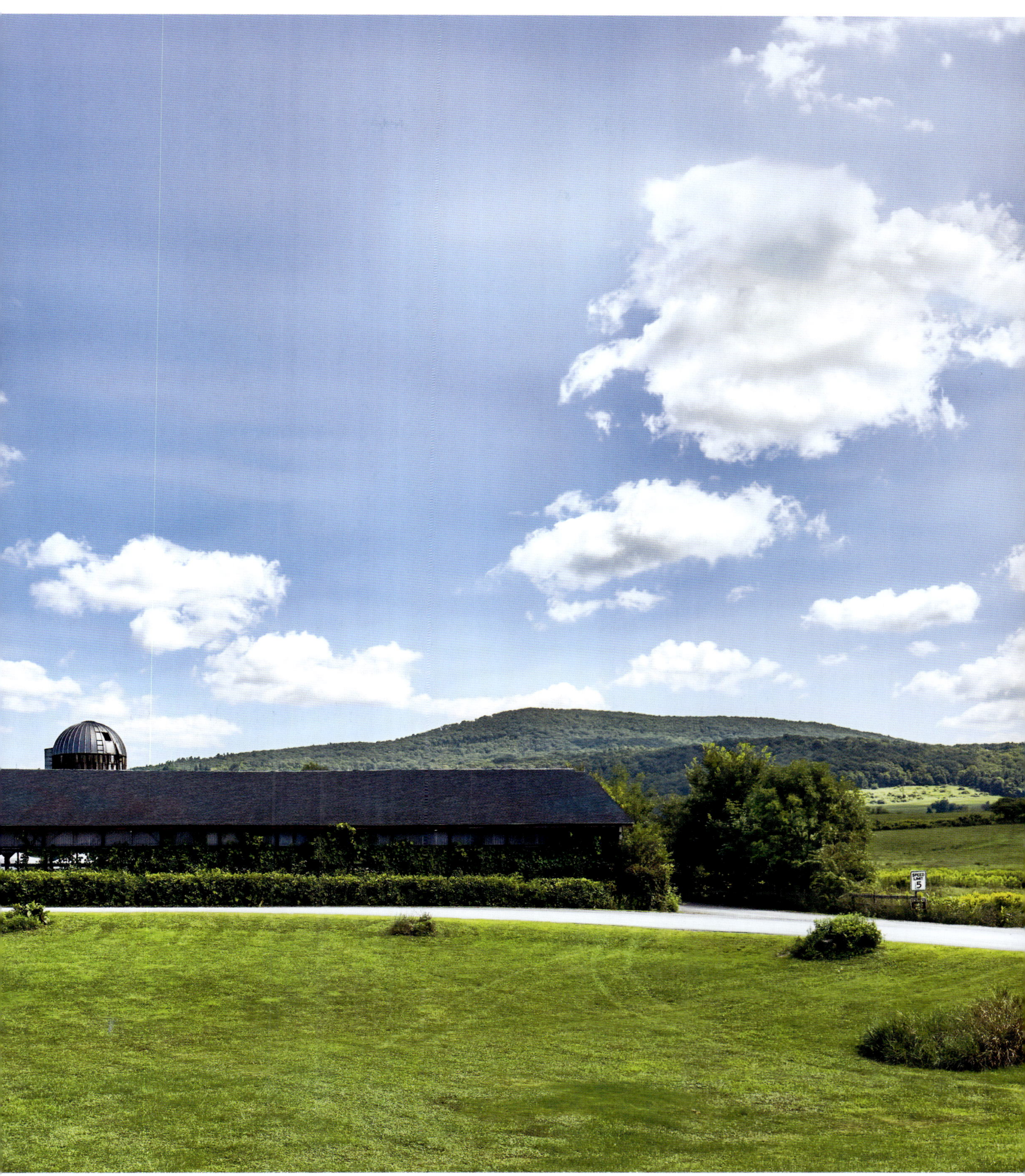
SPEED
LIMIT
5

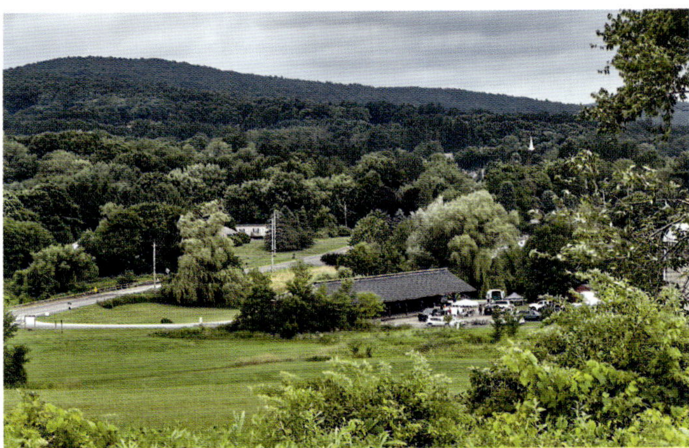

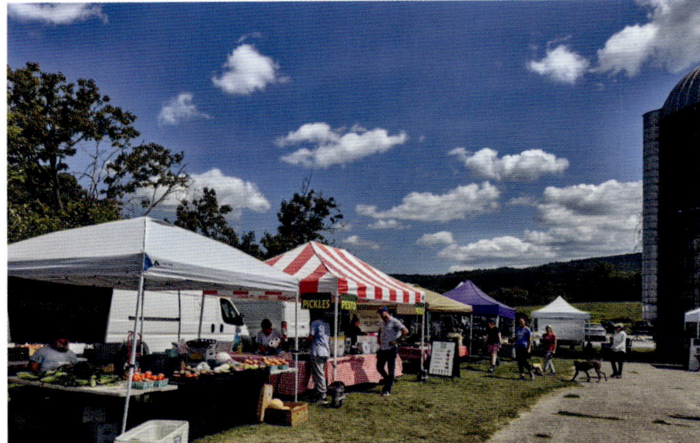

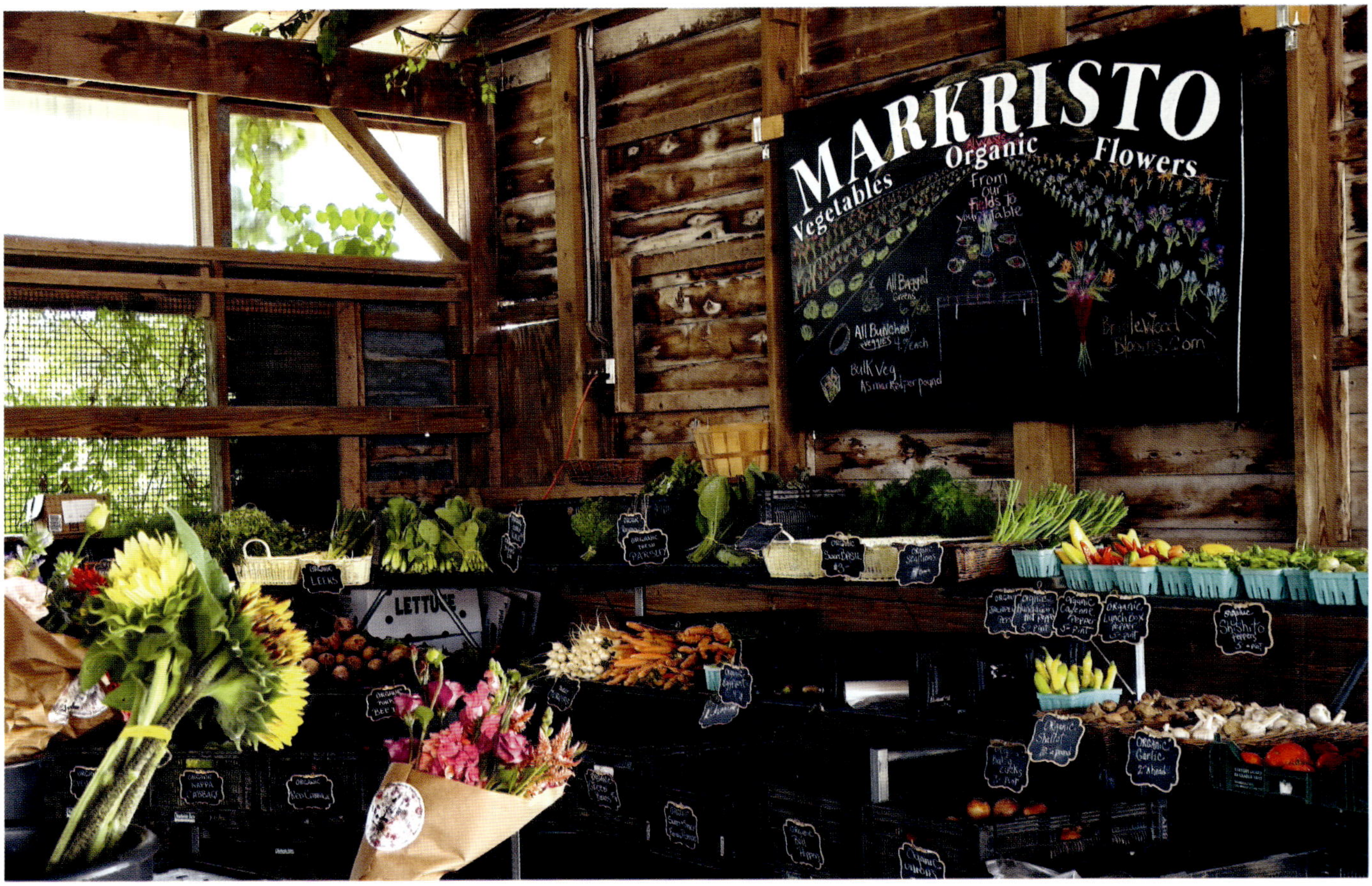

top, left
A view of the Harvest Barn and Route 22 from the top of the Roeliff Jansen Park.

top, right
A row of multicolored tents of farmers and other sellers of local, fresh products are lined up near the farm's silo. Dogs on leash are allowed at the market.

bottom
For farmers displaying their foods, the barn is the perfect rustic setting.

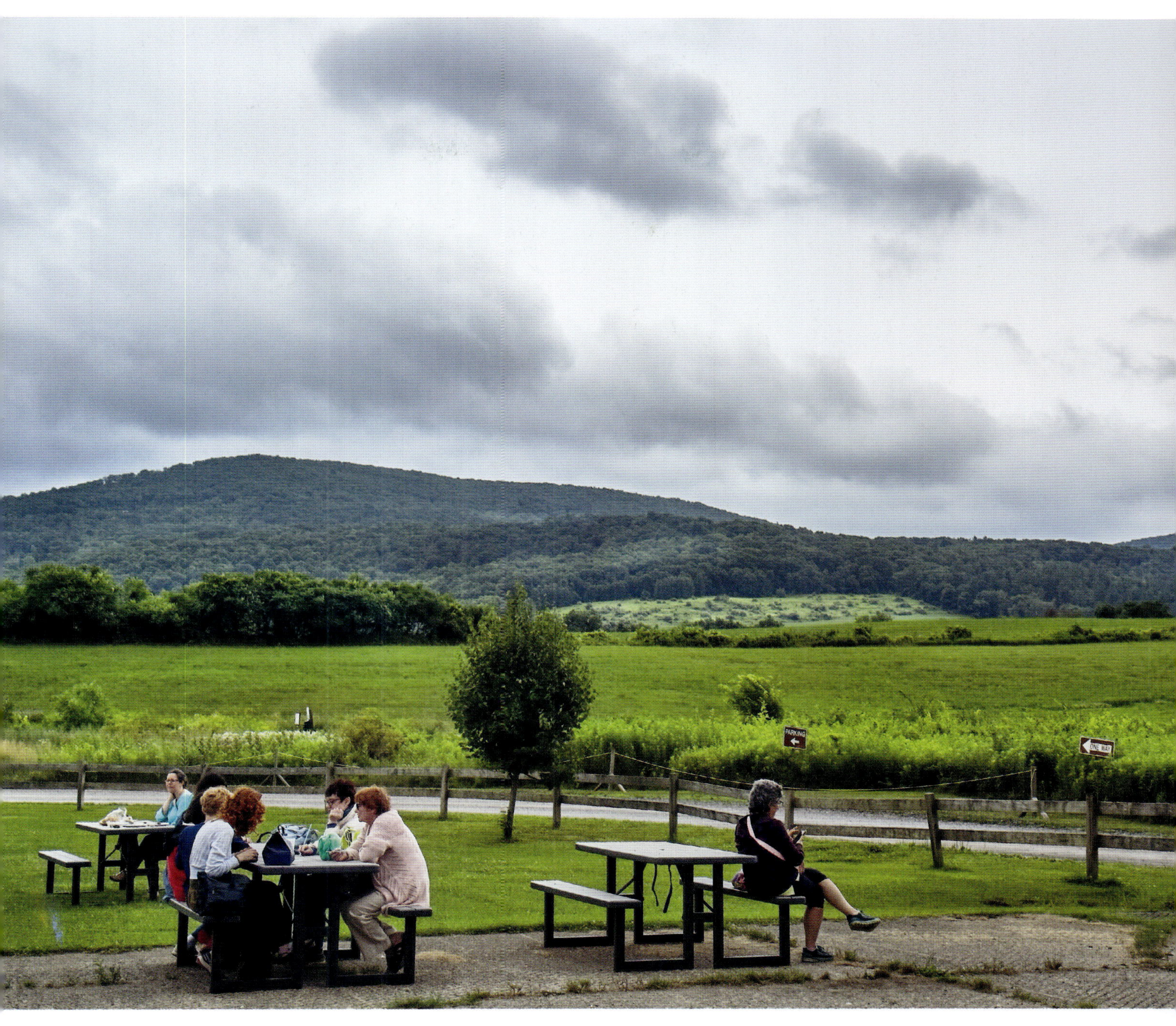

Shoppers gather for lunch made from purchases at the farmers market. The hills of Massachusetts and the expansive park are in the background.

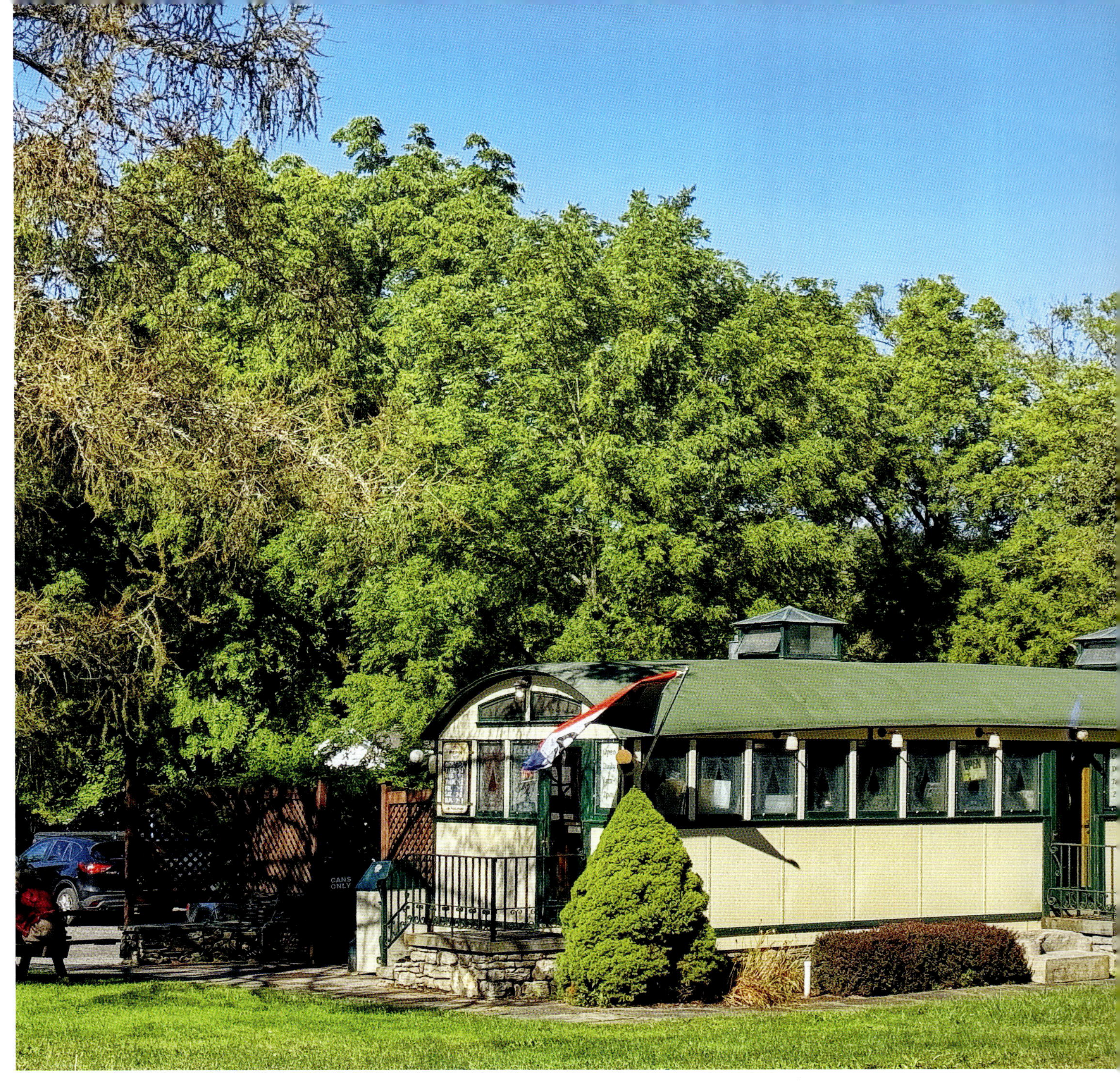

above
The interior of the 1925 diner was totally restored by owner Dan Rundell. The new proprietor, Austen McComb, has run the business since 2021.

right
Dan's Diner was made as a diner. The Jerry O'Mahony company made the first permanent stand-alone diners in the United States in the 1920s. They shipped these diners all over the country.

far right
Dan restored the diner himself, including details such as the tile floor and wood-topped barstools.

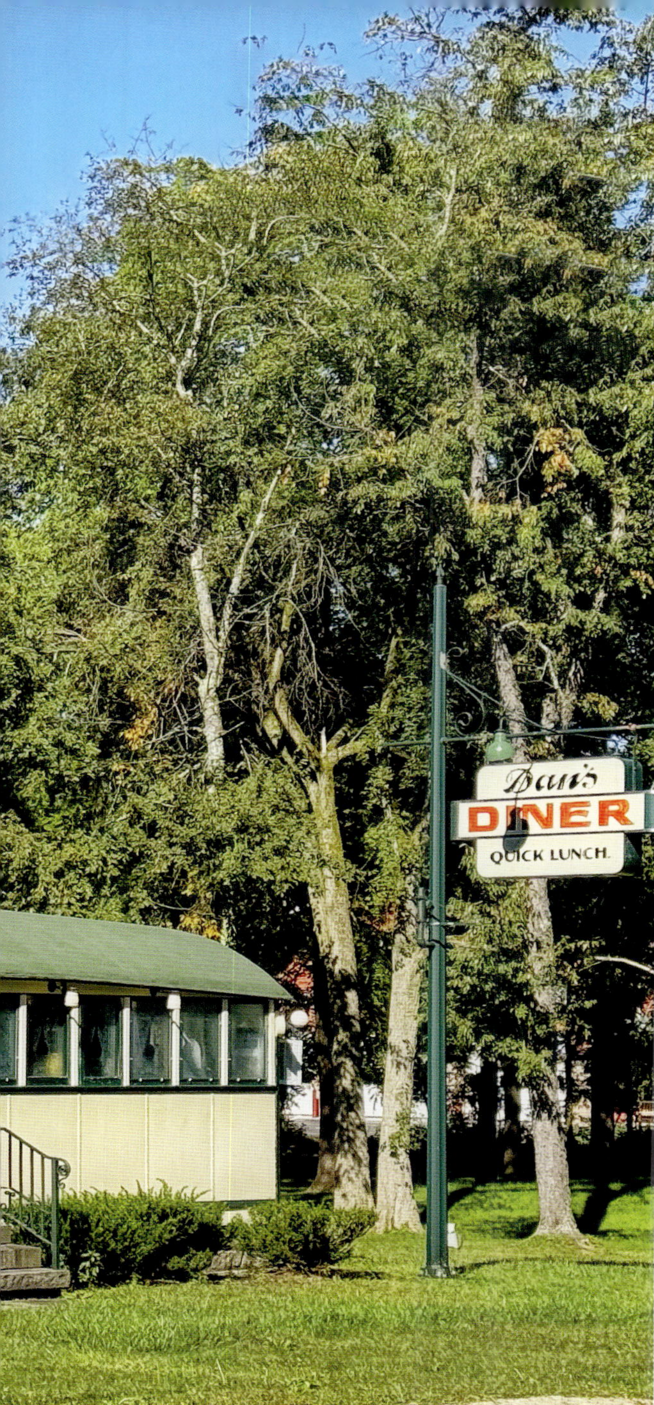

Dan's Diner

Spencertown, New York

Austin McComb believes in diner culture. So much so that when his distant cousin, Dan Rundell, decided he was putting away his apron and looking to lease the diner he had bought and restored, Austin stepped in. He didn't want to see the diner turned into a fancy place. With a background in fast food, Austin knew his way around the grill. He decided that he wasn't going to waver from the traditional diner menu. Breakfast would be on the bill of fare all day. The "Hot Mess," made of eggs, peppers, potatoes, and cheese scrambled together and served with toast, carried over from Dan's original menu. Lunch is served in red plastic baskets with freshly made lemonade in Welch's Looney Tunes jelly jar glasses from the 1970s.

Dan bought the 1925 Jerry O'Mahony diner in 1993. He moved it from Connecticut to his barn, where he restored it. Then Dan moved the like-new diner to its current location along Highway 203 in Spencertown not far from Chatham, New York. It took twelve years to restore the structure, which was built to look like a railroad car. The restoration meant replacing the wood ceiling, repairing the tile floors, repairing and installing the wood-topped metal stools, and replacing the kitchen equipment, grill, fryers, and refrigeration units. Dan opened the diner in 2007. Nowadays, the diner has a steady stream of clients, both regulars and visitors nostalgic for a taste of Americana.

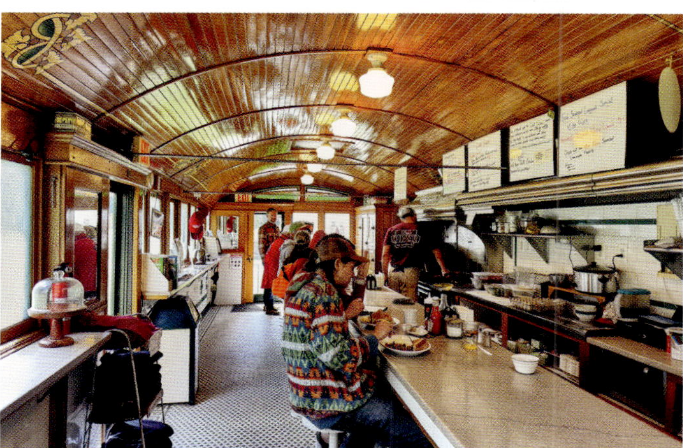

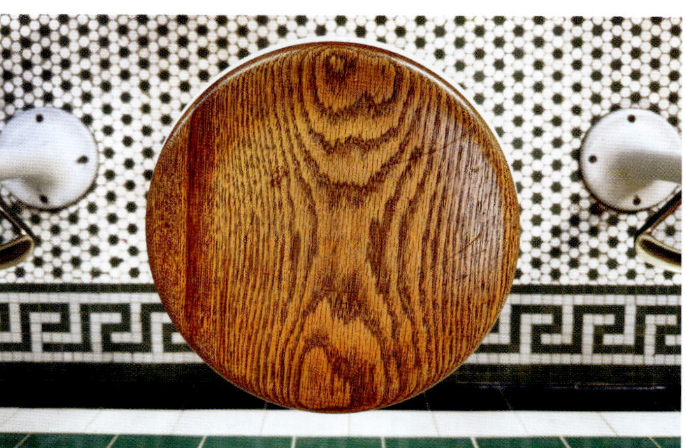

The Chatham Berry Farm and Greenhouse Cidery

Chatham, New York

On Thursday to Saturday nights, the parking lot of the Greenhouse Cidery seems full, but there is always one more spot that becomes available. The cidery is the latest addition to the Chatham Berry Farm, a family business that began in 1982. Two years later, Joseph Gilbert, who is known as Joe, sold his first harvest of strawberries. During those early days, Joe was doing most of the work himself, planning and planting the fields, and he was working at another farm in Connecticut. He would start his day working on the berry farm, then head to his other job. When he started, farms were sinking fast. From Chatham to Albany there were twenty-five farm stands that are no longer in operation. He was a kid from New Jersey and felt the community resistance to his start-up, but that all changed.

The farm is twenty-five acres, and Joe uses eighteen acres to grow small fruit. His blueberry plants have been set in the same place for the forty-two years he has run the farm. He rotates the strawberry field with cover crops. Even currants transplanted from his grandfather's garden overlooking the George Washington Bridge are grown here. Now, he plants different varieties of raspberries on almost five acres and harvests them into October. He used to go to greenmarkets, but he decided to just focus on what he could sell in his shop.

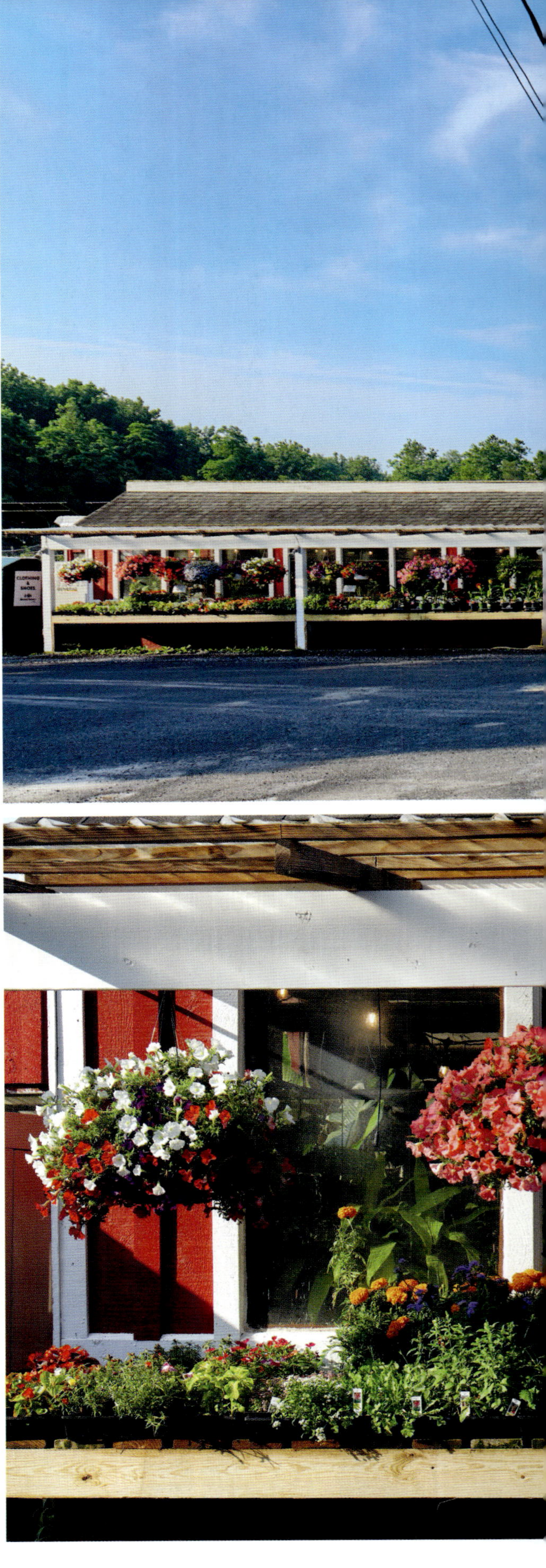

top
The farm store of the Chatham Berry Farm opened in 1982. Flowers and plants and seasonal items such as pumpkins in the fall and wreaths at Christmas are displayed on shelving at the front of the store.

right
Hanging baskets of begonias and geraniums are a summer favorite.

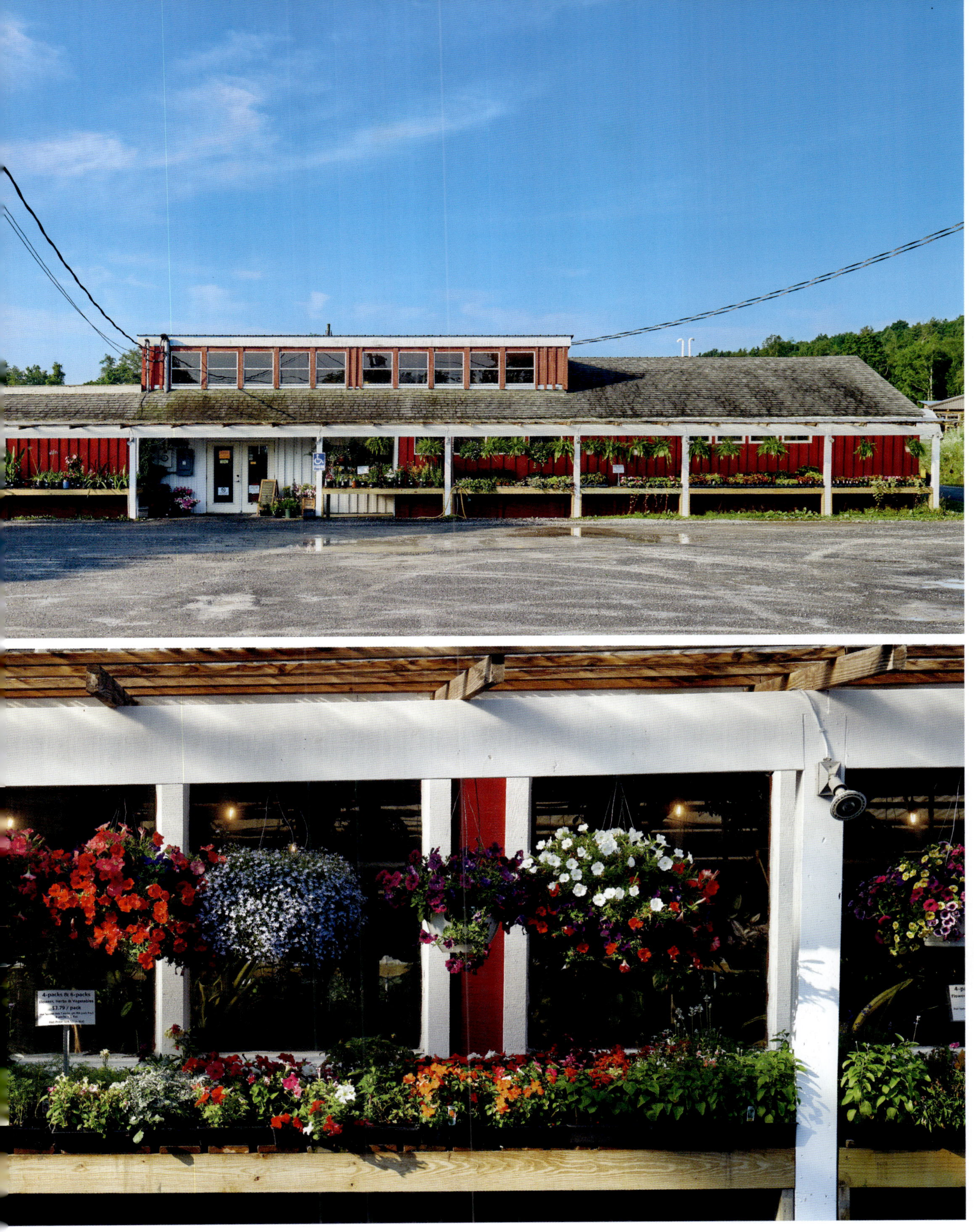
4-packs & 6-packs
Flowers, Herbs & Vegetables
$2.79 / pack

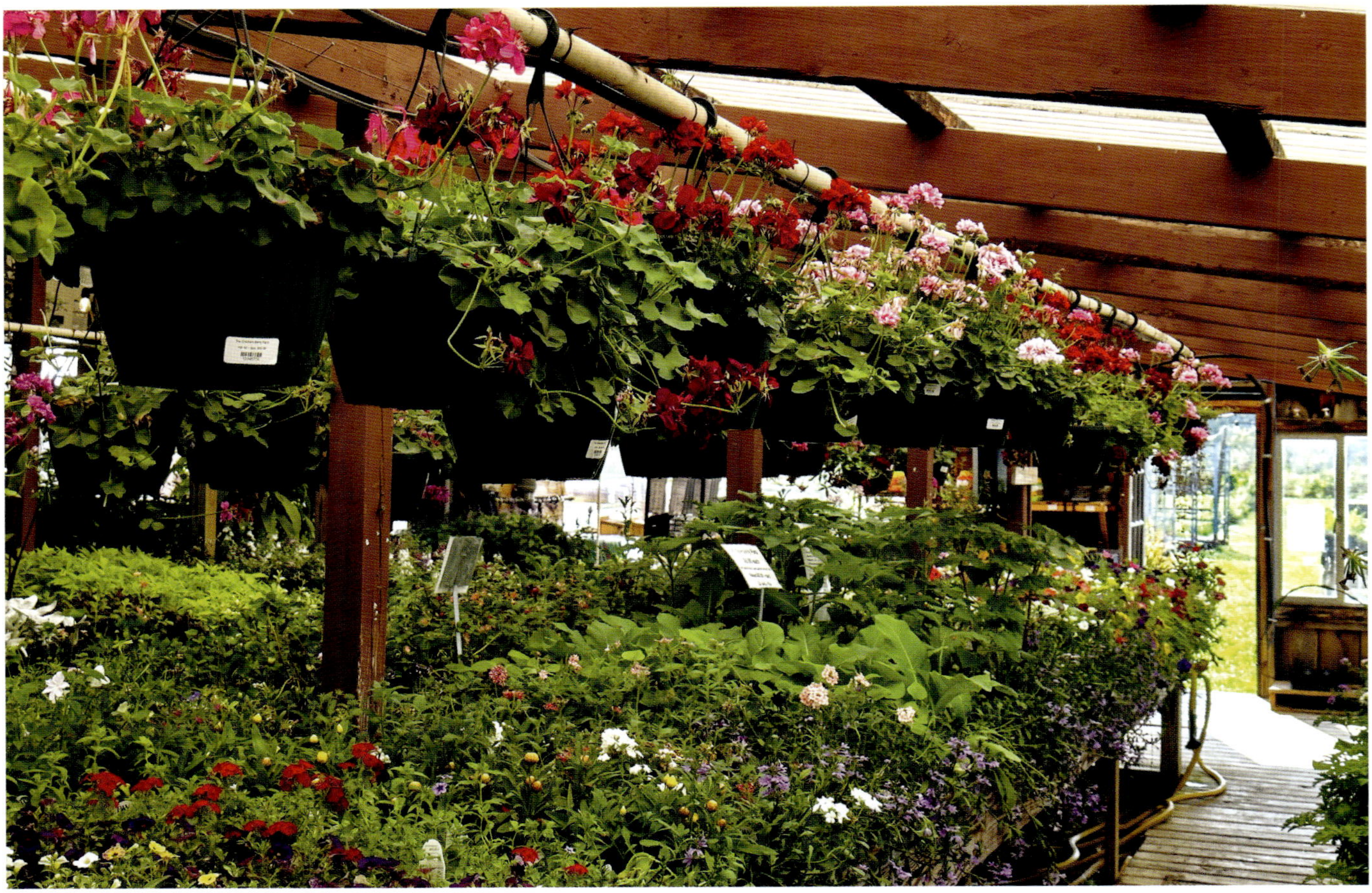

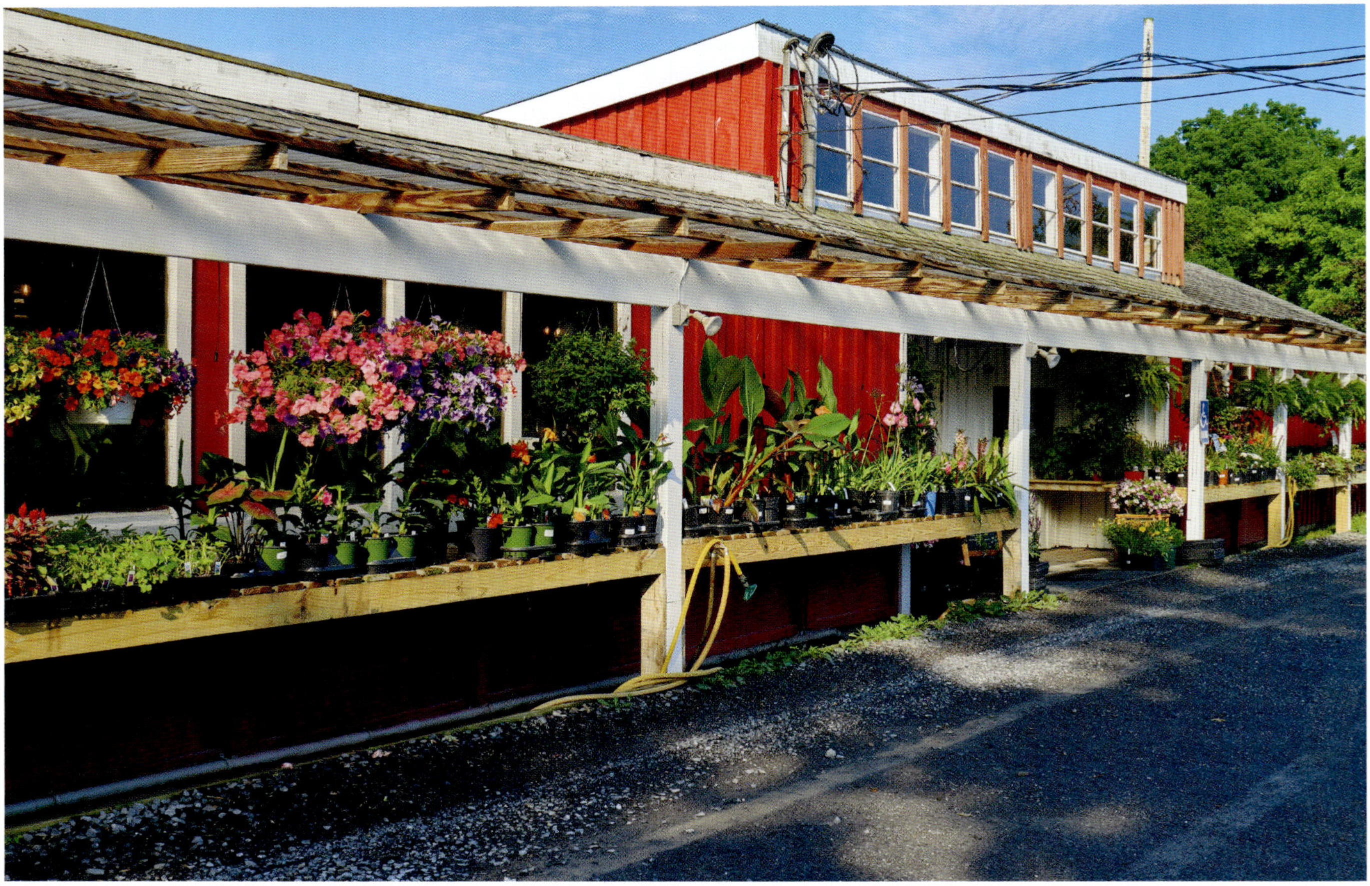

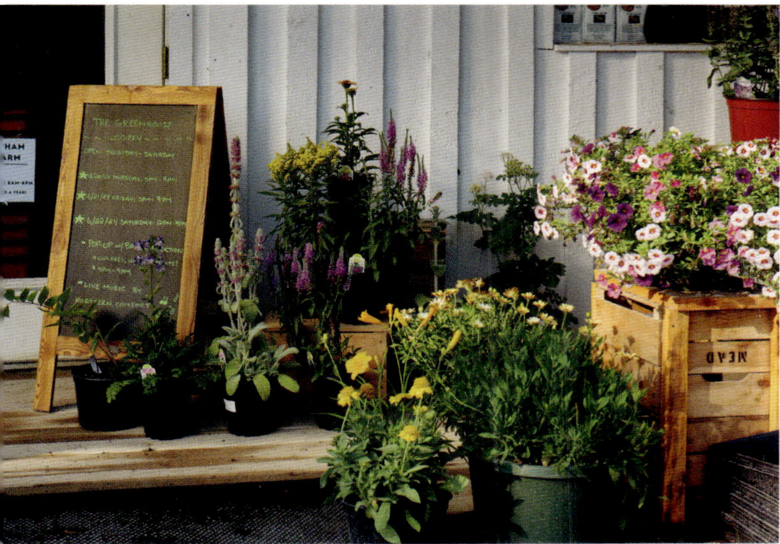

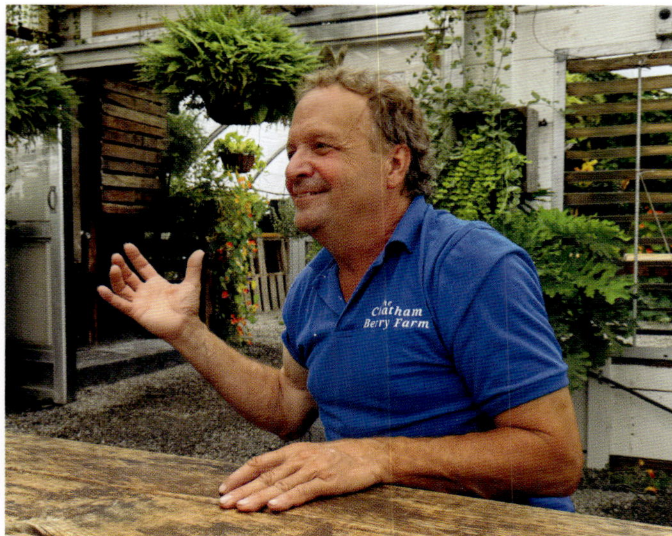

The Chatham Berry Farm is a multigeneration, multi-project farm. All three of his children, Jonathan, Michael, and Lilly, are involved in the business. It was Jon's idea to start the cidery, using pressed apples from nearby Samascott Orchards. He also wanted to add a state-of-the-art hydroponic greenhouse that produces lettuces such as arugula year-round. The farm also grows 140 different kinds of herbs. What produce Joe doesn't grow he buys from nearby farms such as Miller's Crossing near Hudson to sell in the farm stand, along with prepared foods and their own vegetables and fruit.

Joe is always looking to try a more efficient method of farming and land use. Some plans worked out and others didn't. In forty-two years, there has been a lot of trial and error. In 2011, he installed solar panels that now provide half of the farm's electrical needs. Any vegetables that can be used go into seasonal soups sold in the store. And of course, they compost to deal with waste. The farm is pesticide- and GMO-free. They have twenty beehives and sell their own honey. When it is sold out, there's no more until next year.

The Greenhouse Cidery is a popular gathering place. Joe says, "I am just lucky that I like what I do, and that I can make a go at it. Having my own business, I never missed a sports or school event. A lot of people can't do that." His ambition is "just to grow good food..."

opposite, top
The heated indoor greenhouse is part of the farm store.

opposite, bottom
The store has a natural light source, with skylights and windows into the greenhouse.

above, left
Specials are listed on the chalkboard sandwich board at the entrance. The farm grows and sells vegetable and herb plants for home gardens.

above, right
Joseph Gilbert, owner of the Chatham Berry Farm.

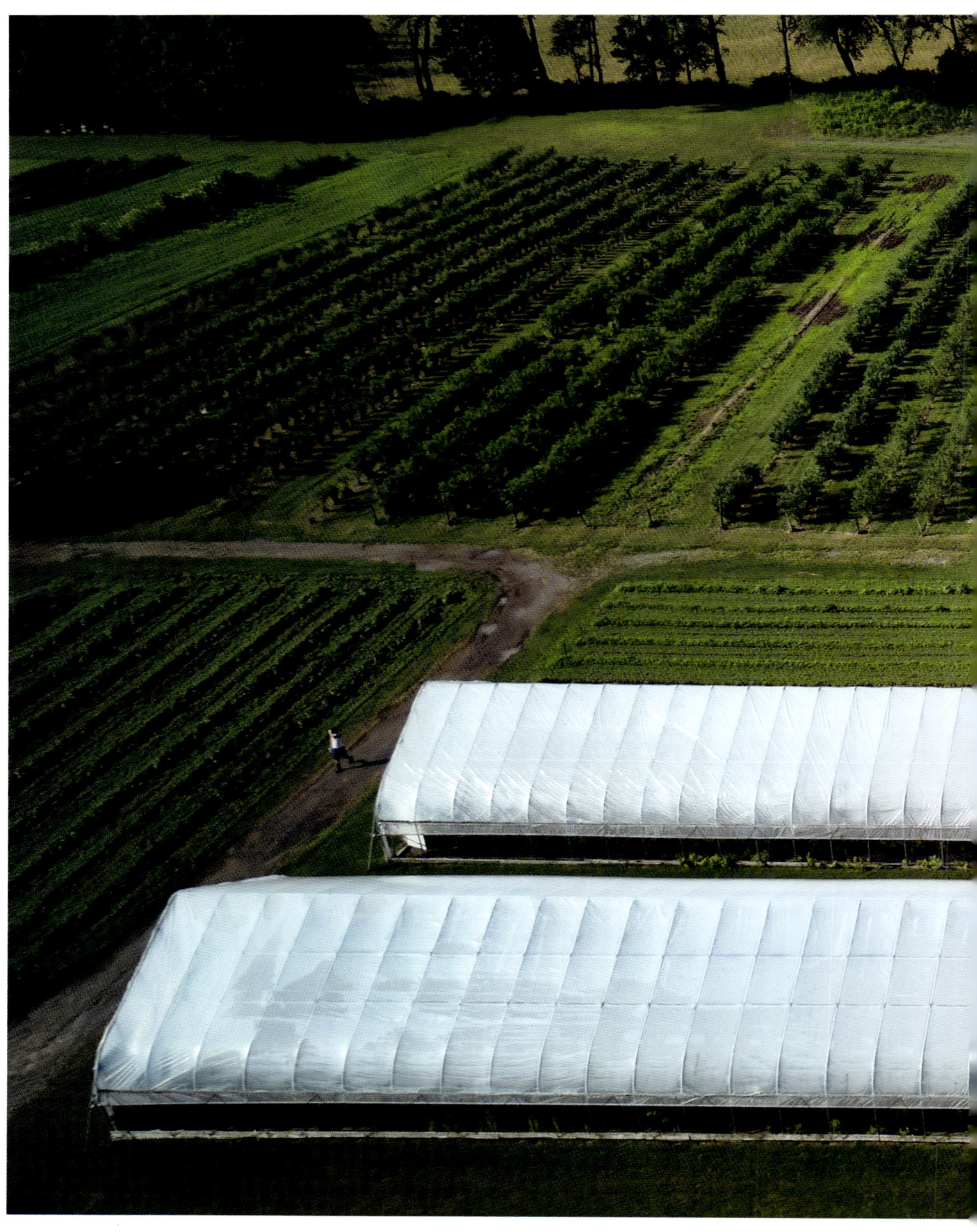

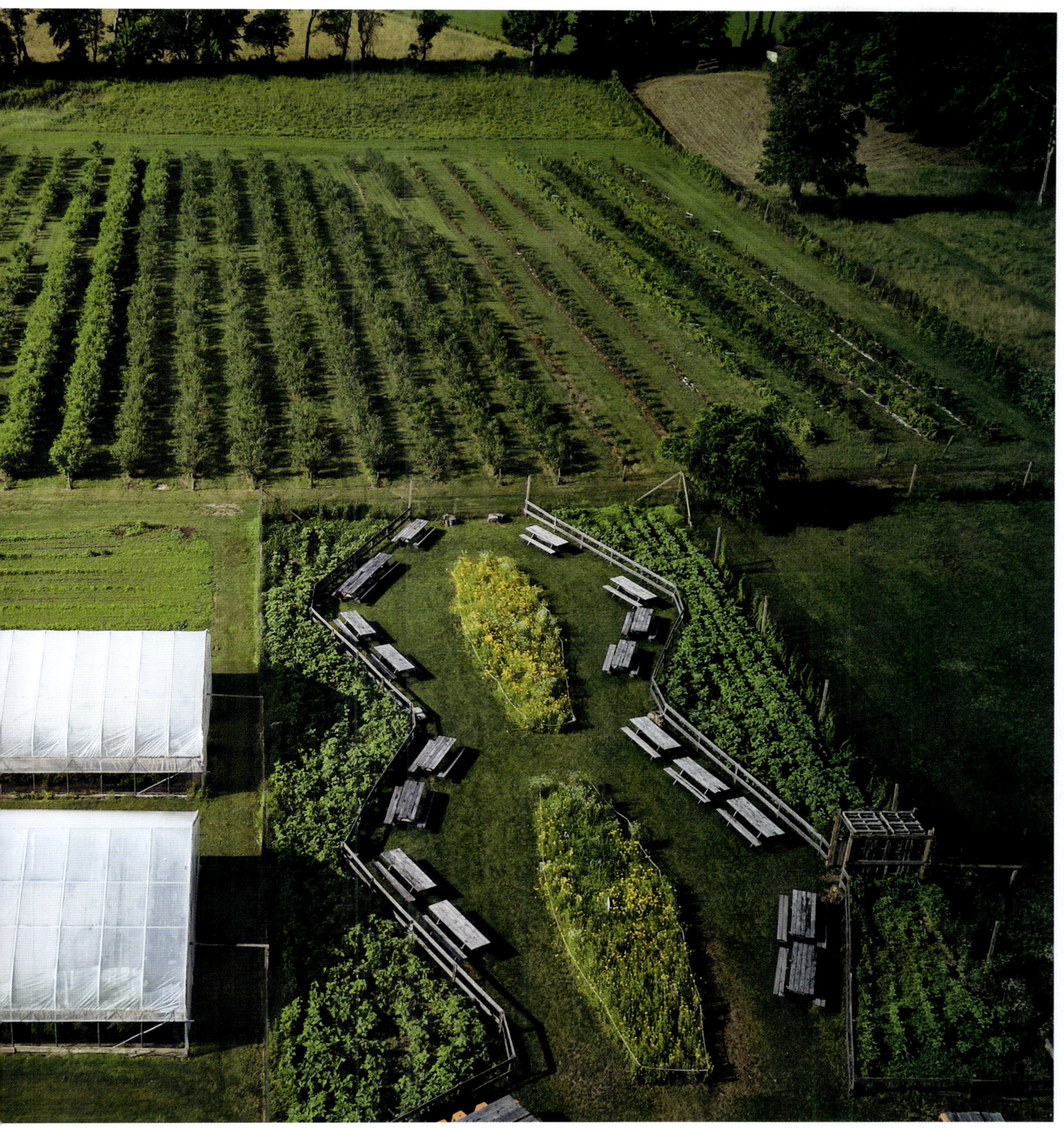

Greenhouses, fields of berry plants, and the outdoor dining area of the new Greenhouse Cidery make up the Chatham Berry Farm's property.

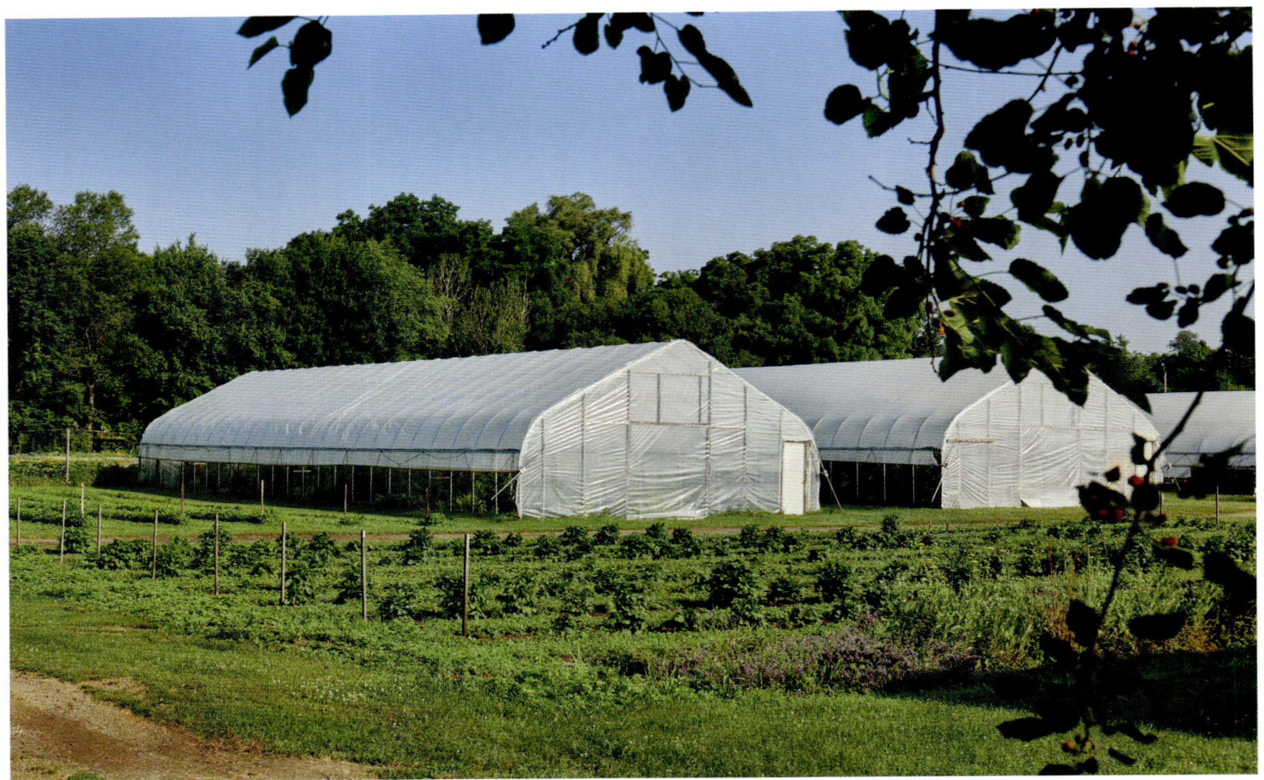

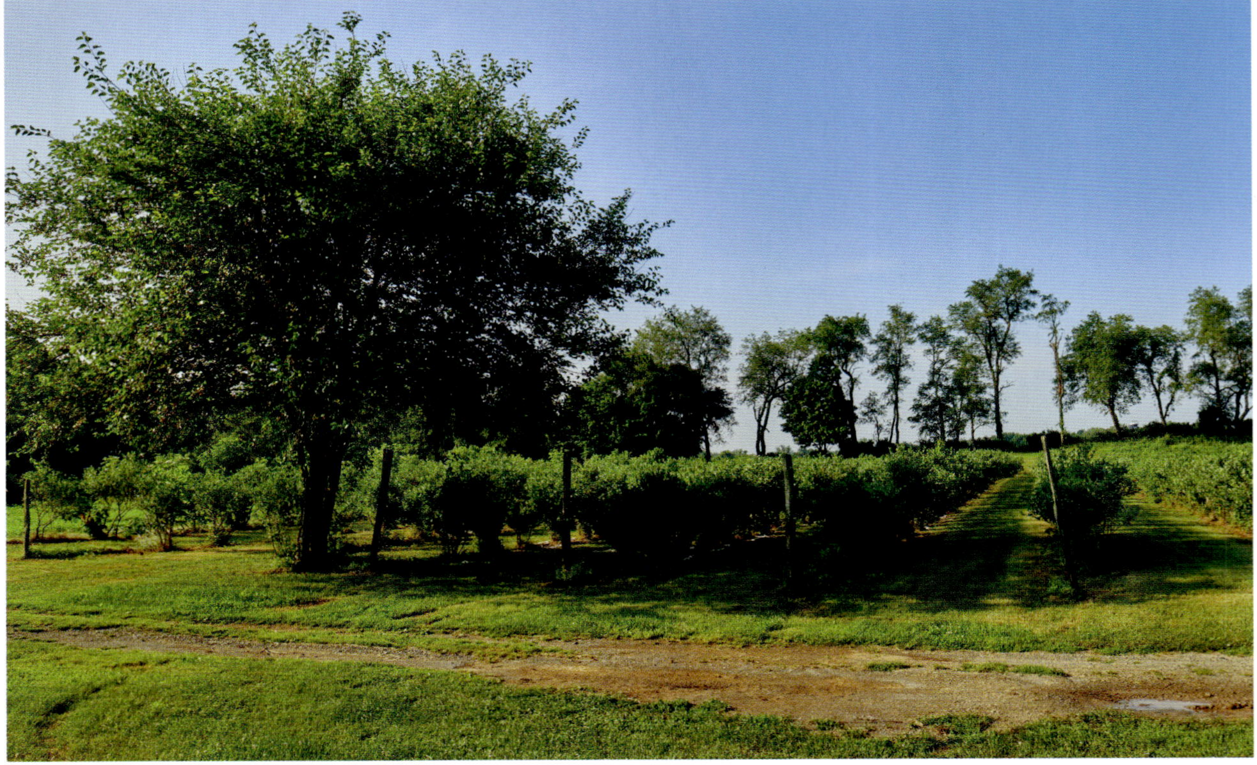

top
Joe has six greenhouses on the farm.
One uses a hydroponic system to grow lettuces.

bottom
The farm focuses on growing fruit, including blueberries, raspberries, and strawberries.

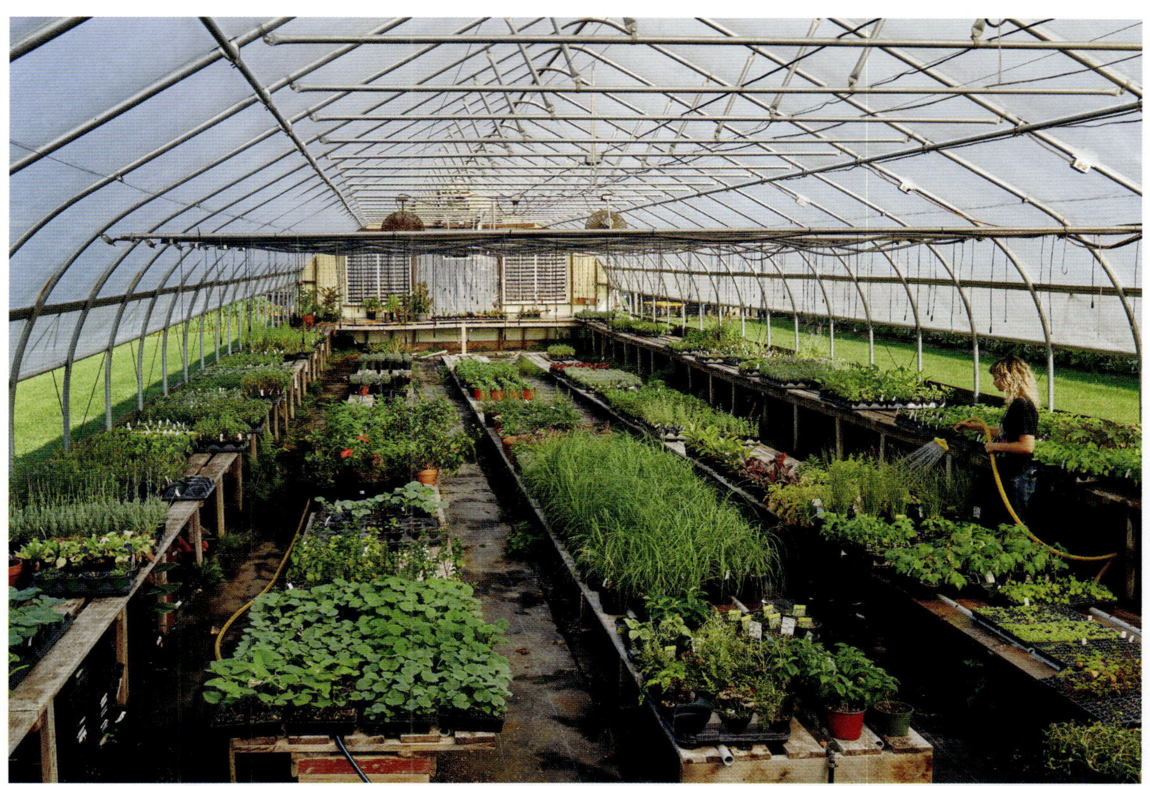

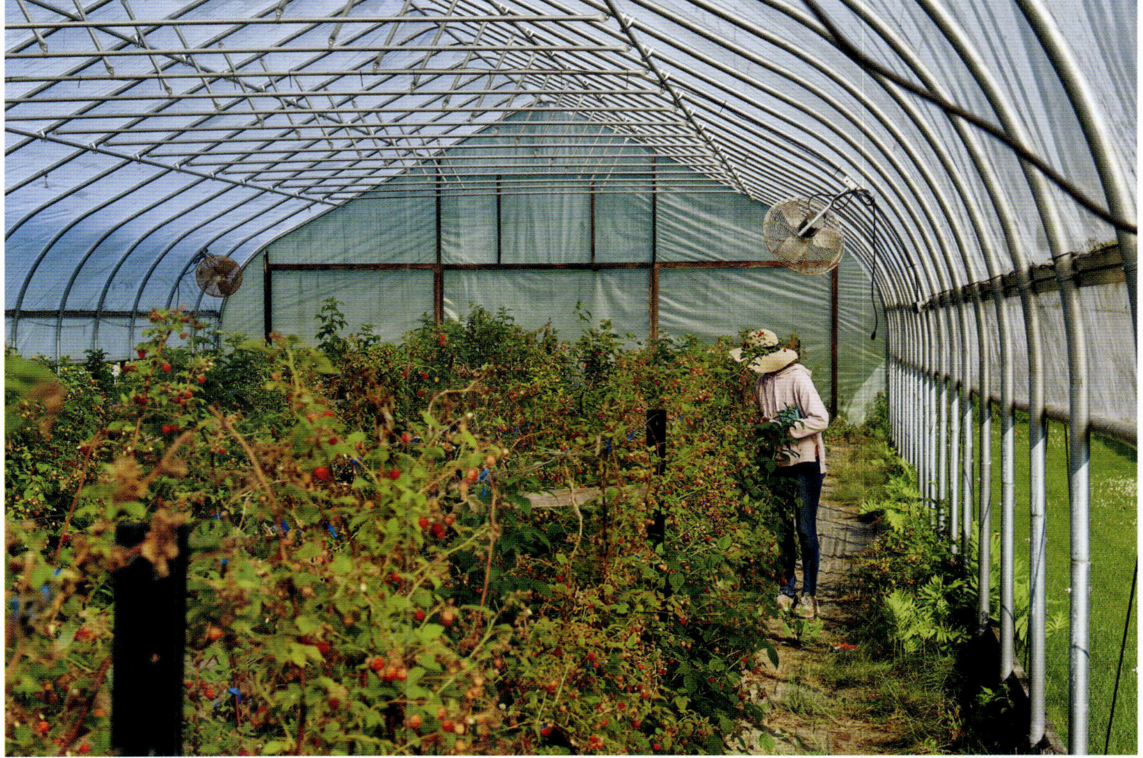

top
Joe experimented with creating a greenhouse below ground level to extend the farm's growing season. Unfortunately, a 6,000-gallon tank of water installed to warm the ground didn't work.

bottom
Raspberries are grown inside one of the greenhouses.

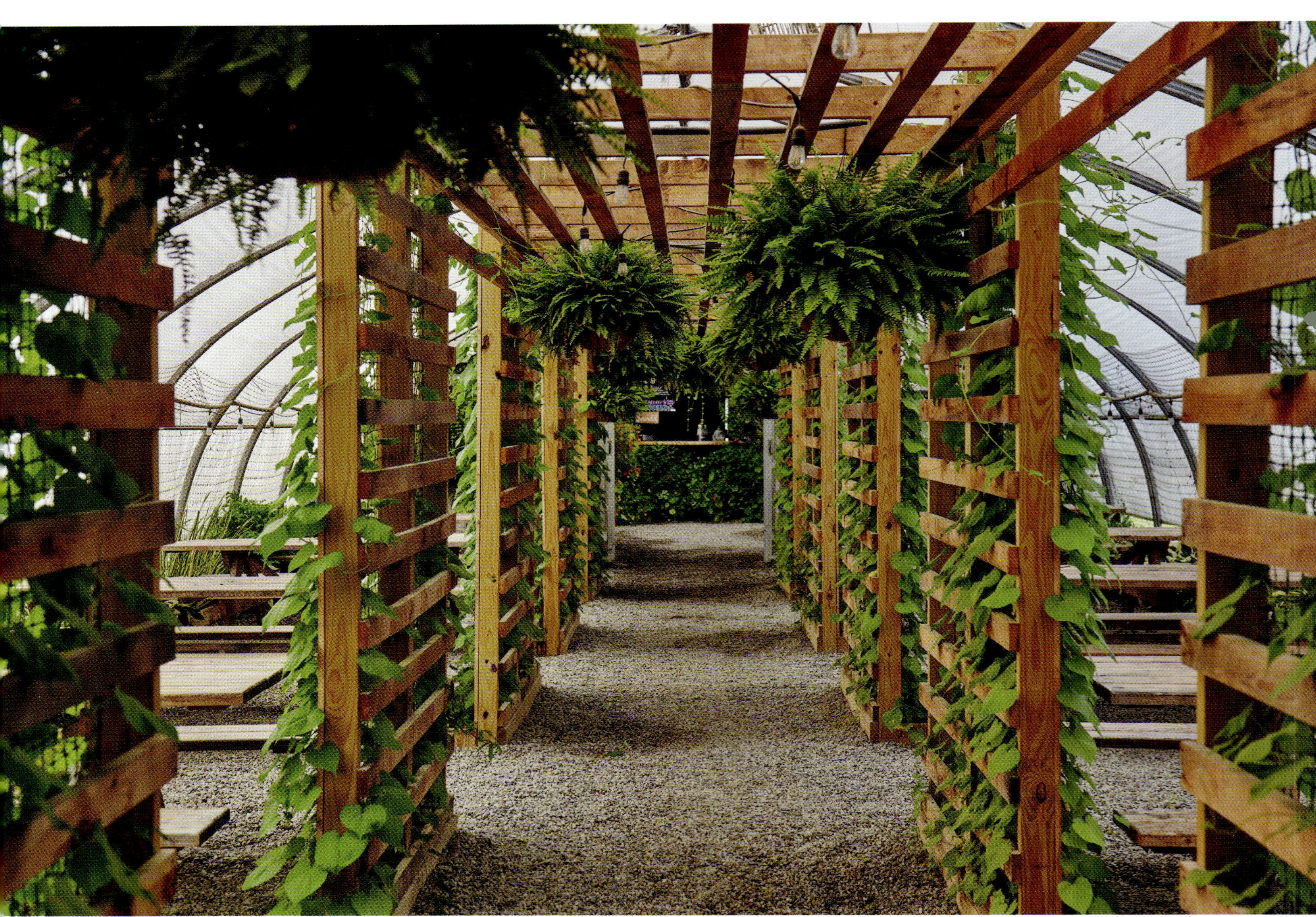

above
The Yummy Kitchen started as a food truck during the early days of the cidery. Now it has become more of a permanent fixture inside one of the greenhouses. Picnic tables are provided for seating. Every spring when the cidery opens for a new season, the greenery in the wooden structures is replaced with new plants.

opposite, top
Ferns and other plants hang and are planted at the walk-up window of the restaurant.

opposite, bottom
The menu is Asian-inspired and constantly updated. Nasturtium grows around the chalkboard.

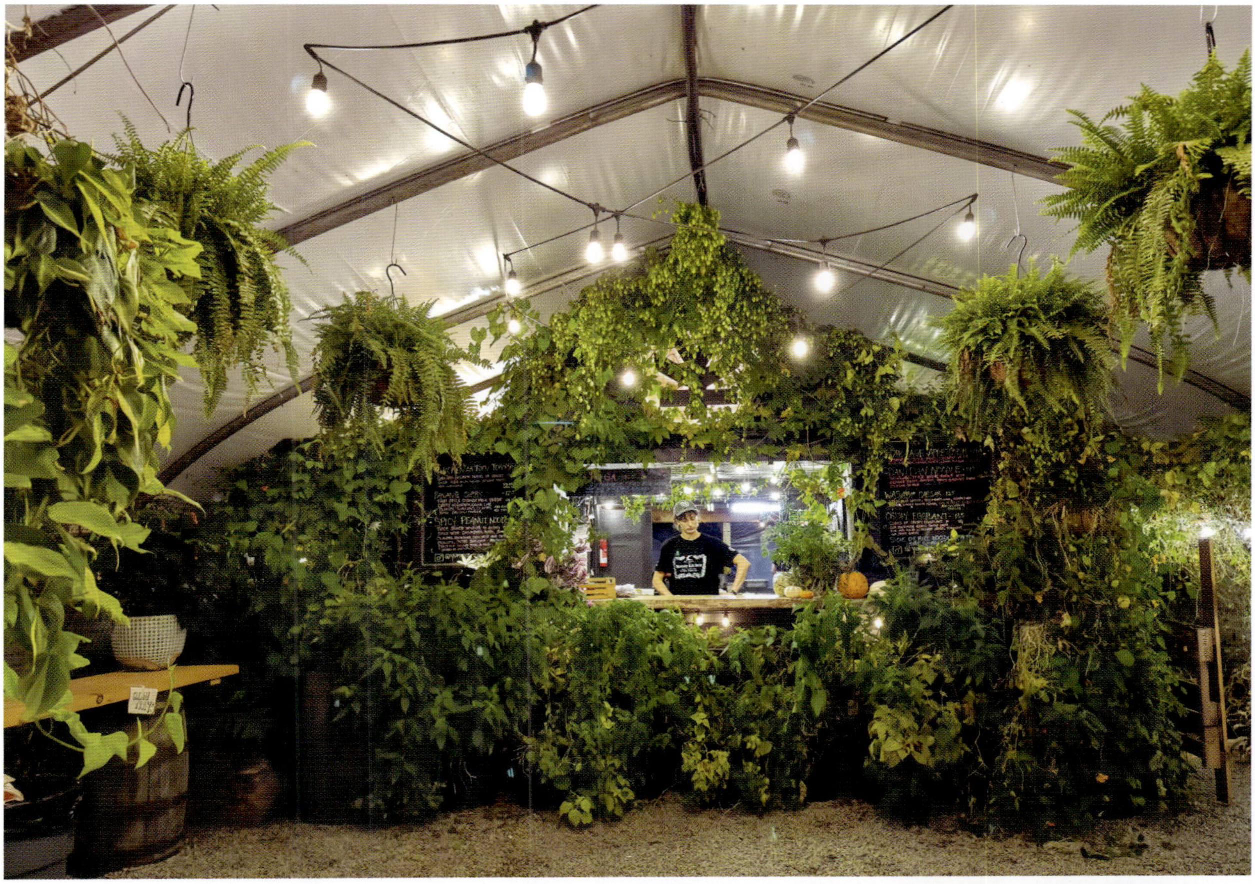

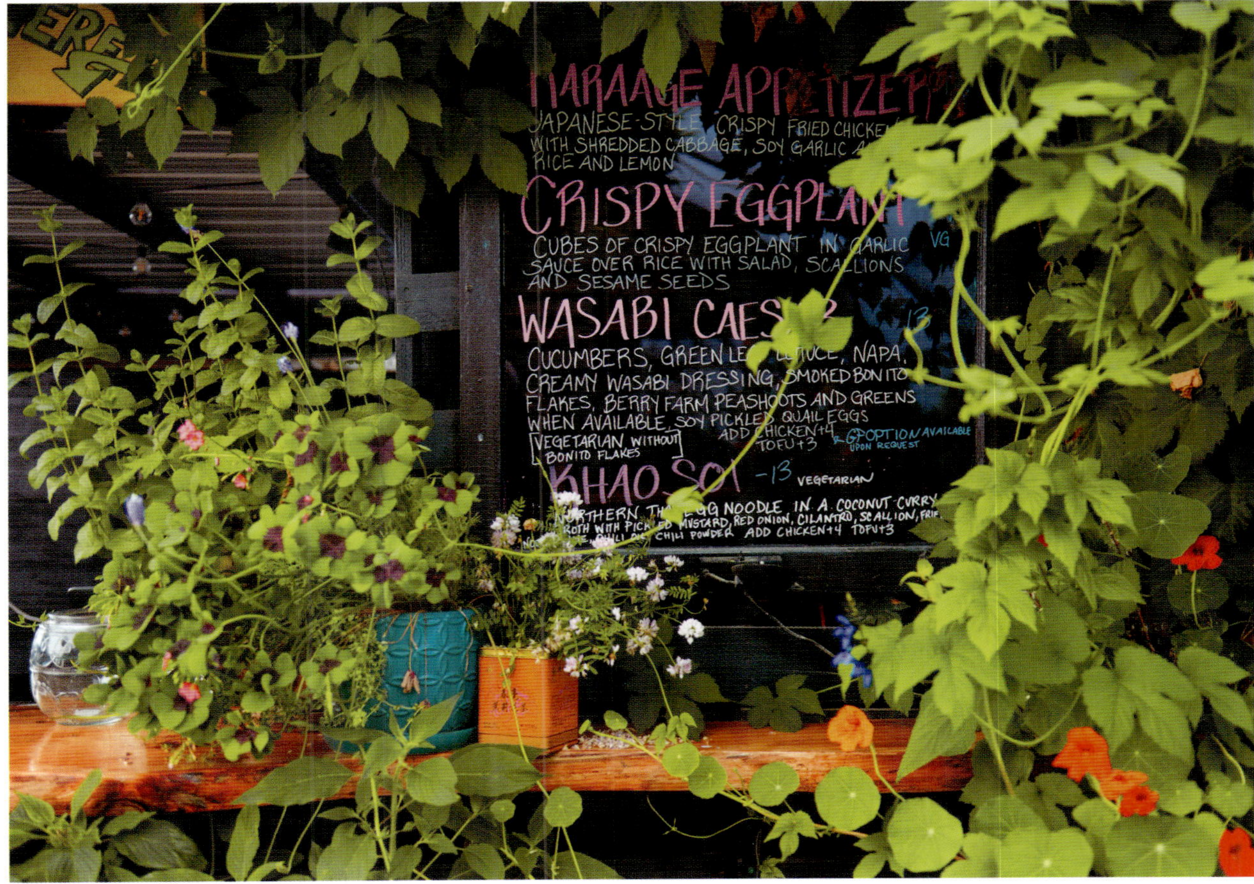
JAPANESE-STYLE CRISPY FRIED CHICKE
WITH SHREDDED CABBAGE, SOY GARLIC
RICE AND LEMON
CRISPY EGGPLAN
CUBES OF CRISPY EGGPLANT IN GARLIC
VG
SAUCE OVER RICE WITH SALAD, SCALLIONS
AND SESAME SEEDS
WASABI CAES
13
CUCUMBERS, GREEN LE
NAPA,
CREAMY WASABI DRESSING, SMOKED BONITO
FLAKES, BERRY FARM PEASHOOTS AND GREENS
WHEN AVAILABLE, SOY PICKLED QUAIL EGGS
ADD CHICKEN+4
TOFU+3
GF OPTION AVAILABLE
UPON REQUEST
VEGETARIAN WITHOUT BONITO FLAKES
KHAO SOI
-13
VEGETARIAN
EGG NOODLE IN A COCONUT CURRY
MUSTARD, RED ONION, CILANTRO, SCALLION,
CHILI POWDER ADD CHICKEN+4 TOFU+3

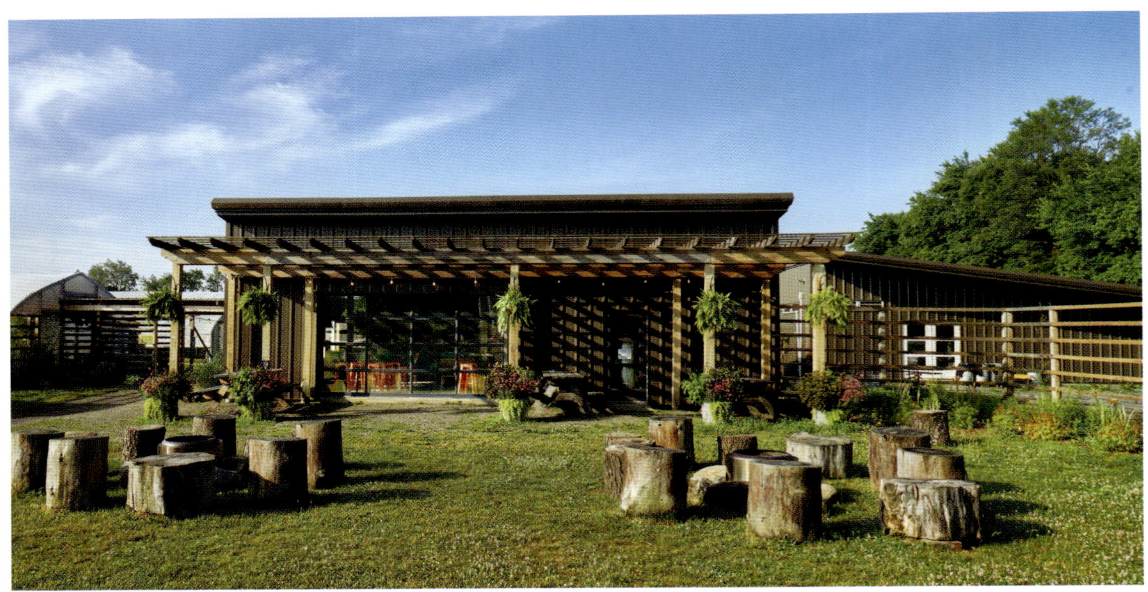

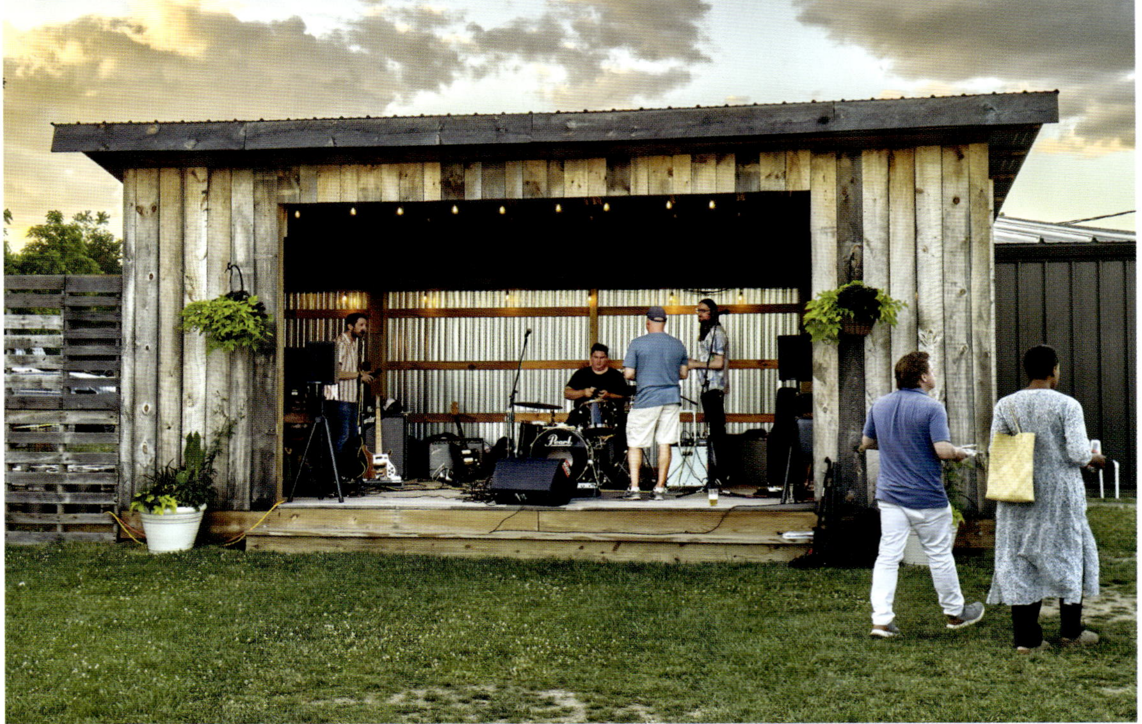

top
Joe gives credit to his sons for coming up with the idea for creating the Greenhouse Cidery next door to the farm stand. Since most of the seating is outdoors, the cidery is open only from April to November. A new bar was built to serve the hard cider they make as well as other drinks. They buy apples from Samascott Orchards in nearby Kinderhook. Customers place an order at the bar after ordering food at the Yummy Kitchen. Logs are used as seating and are placed around the firepits.

bottom
A bandstand for live music performances was added to the cidery. All the new buildings fit the rural style of the farm.

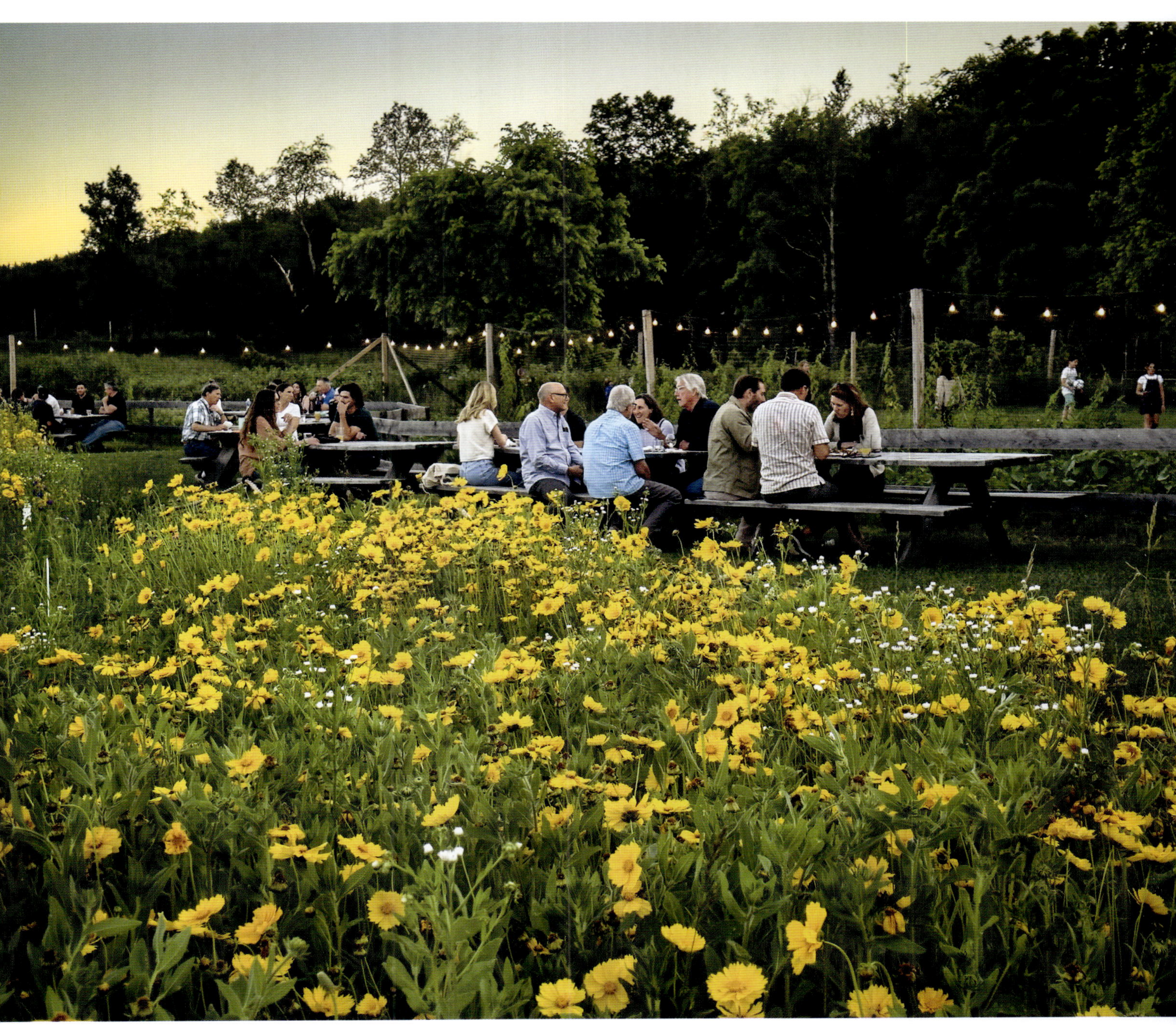

Joe created a garden where customers of the Greenhouse Cidery can gather. In the center, he planted a field of flowers. On the outer edges behind the picnic tables sunflowers grow.

Troy Waterfront Farmers Market

Troy, New York

The Troy Waterfront Farmers Market is one of the busiest markets in the upstate region. It is a city market for farmers and vendors from the surrounding Capital District to bring their produce and wares to the National Historic District neighborhood. In the summer, Monument Square's 1891 fifty-foot granite Soldiers and Sailors Monument is the center of activity. From there, the market spreads out to take over streets such as Second Street, both Upper and Lower River Street, and Broadway. As a year-round market, it moves inside the Troy Atrium in November. The market began along River Street in 2004 and celebrated its twentieth anniversary in 2024. Vendors must apply to be accepted, which keeps the offerings varied and high quality. On Saturdays, the market brings fifteen thousand visitors and locals to Troy, which has been experiencing a revitalization through state grants and an influx of new residents in the past few years.

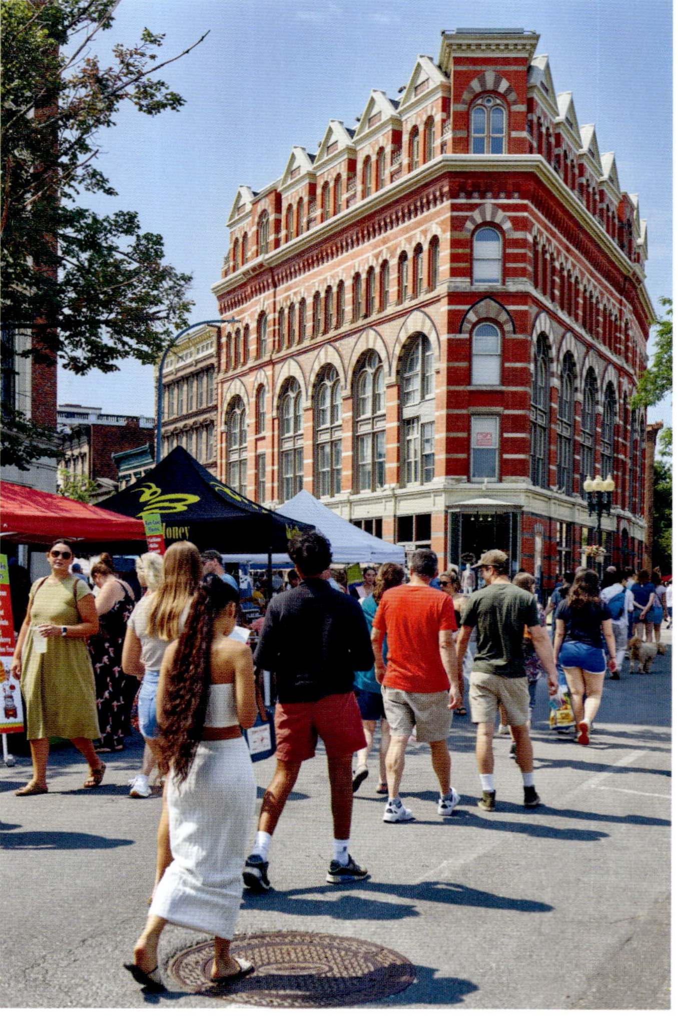

The Rice Building on River Street, built in 1871, stands in the background as marketgoers check out the vendors at the summer market.

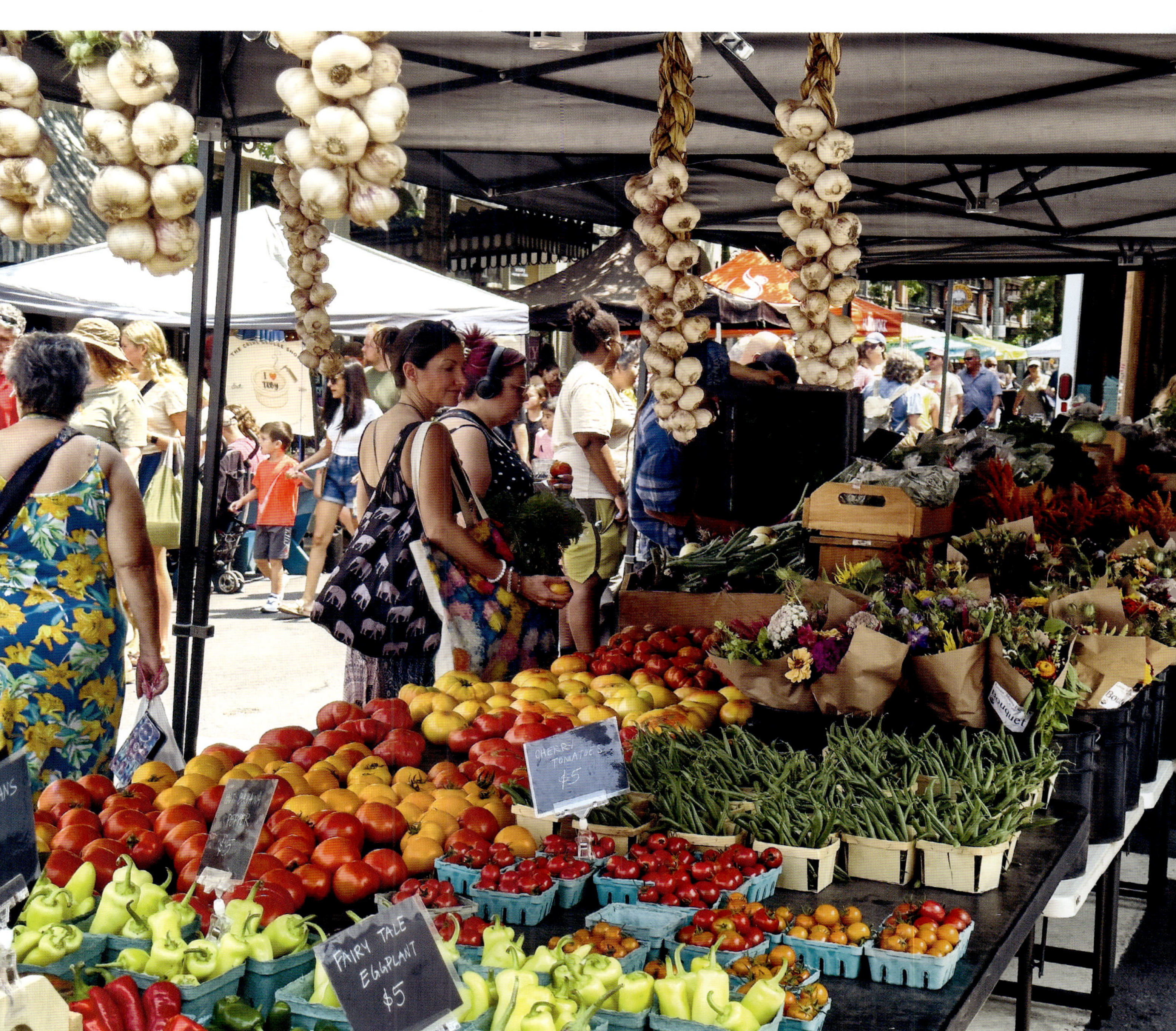

South of France? No, Troy, New York. Over a hundred merchants take part in the summer markets. The scene is a real mix: street food tents are next to tables filled with fresh produce that are next to displays of wellness products.

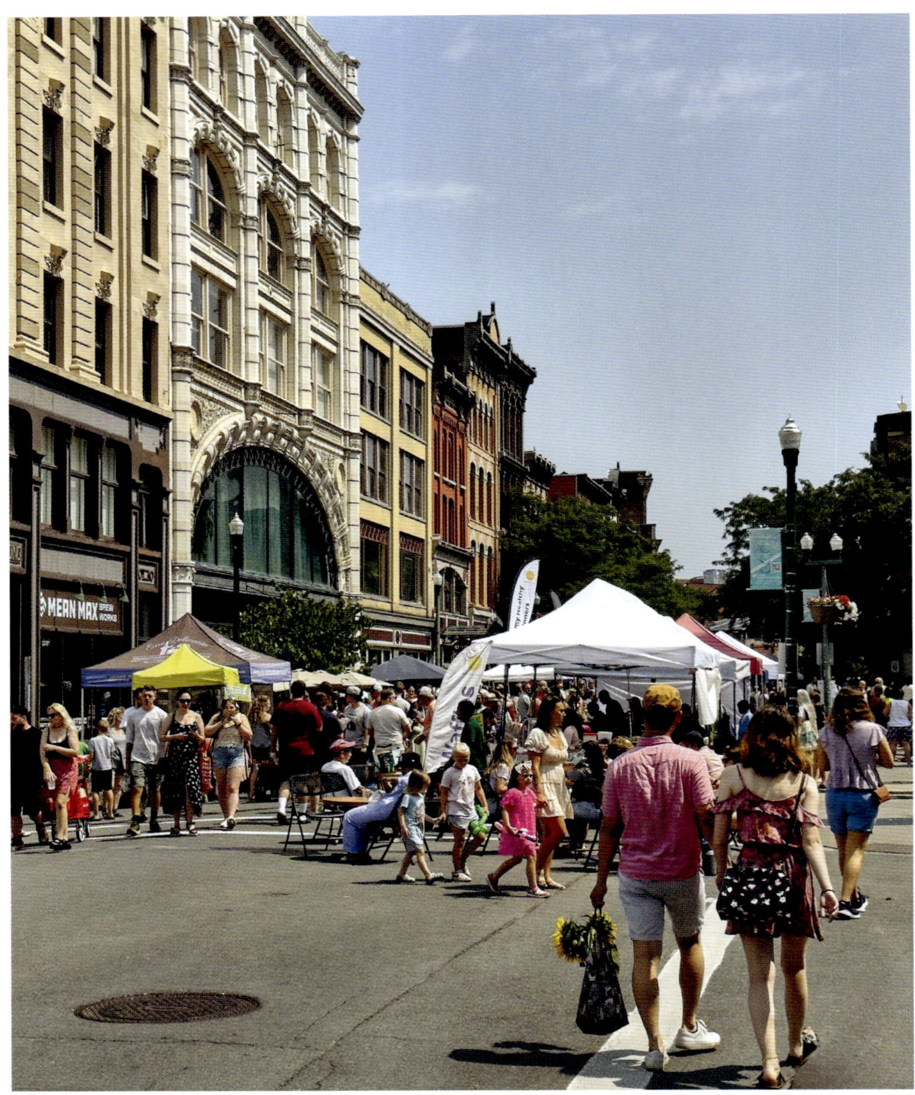

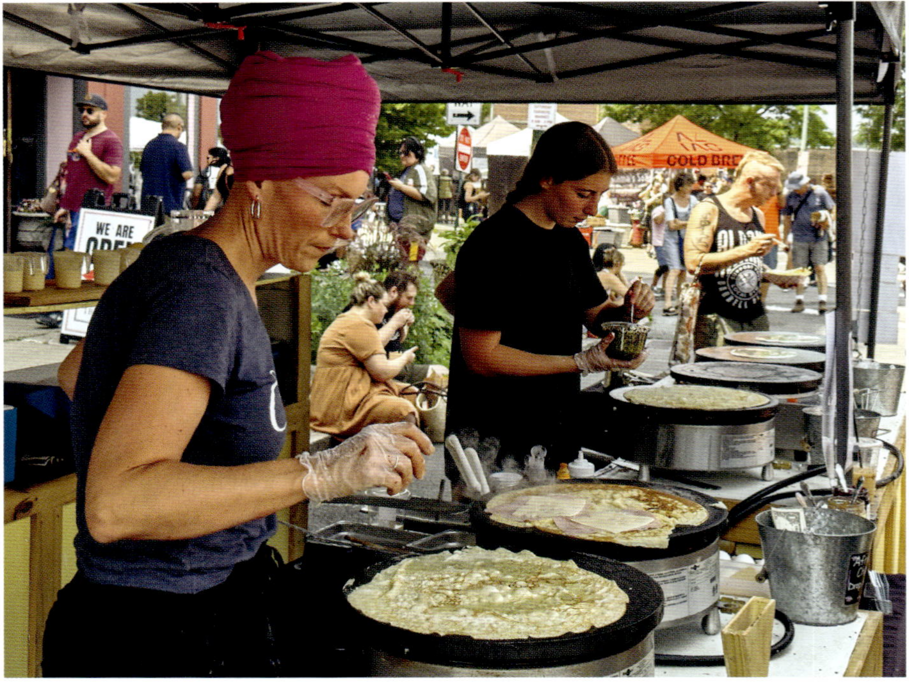

top
The Arts Center of the Capital Region faces River Street, part of the National Historic District, along with other nineteenth-century buildings that have been restored over the years.

right
Holy Crêpe is based in Schenectady but sets up a stall with its cast-iron crêpe plates to serve the French dish to market visitors on Saturdays.

opposite
Street food vendors place their tents around the nineteenth-century memorial to soldiers of the Revolutionary War, the War of 1812, and the Civil War.

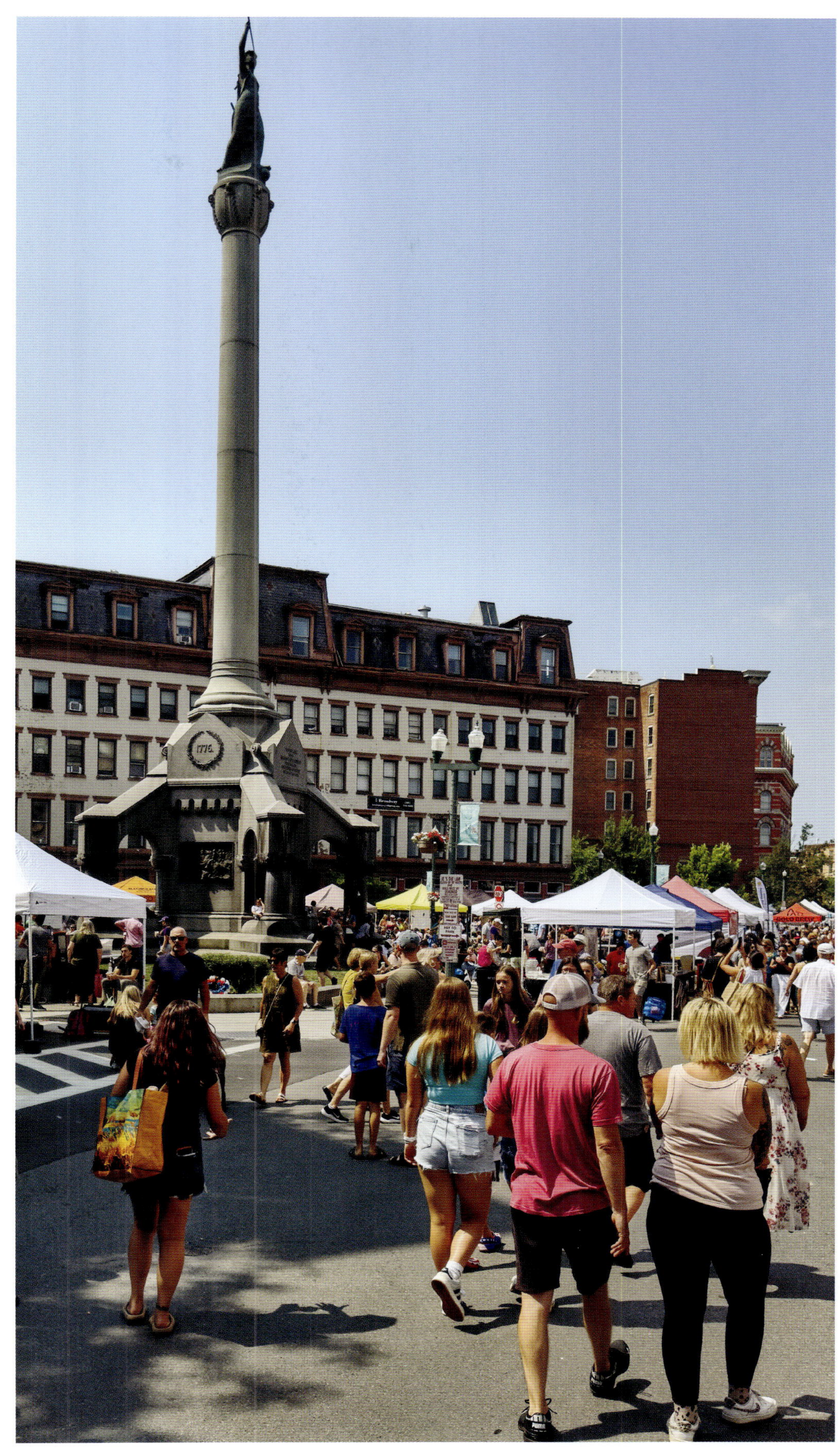

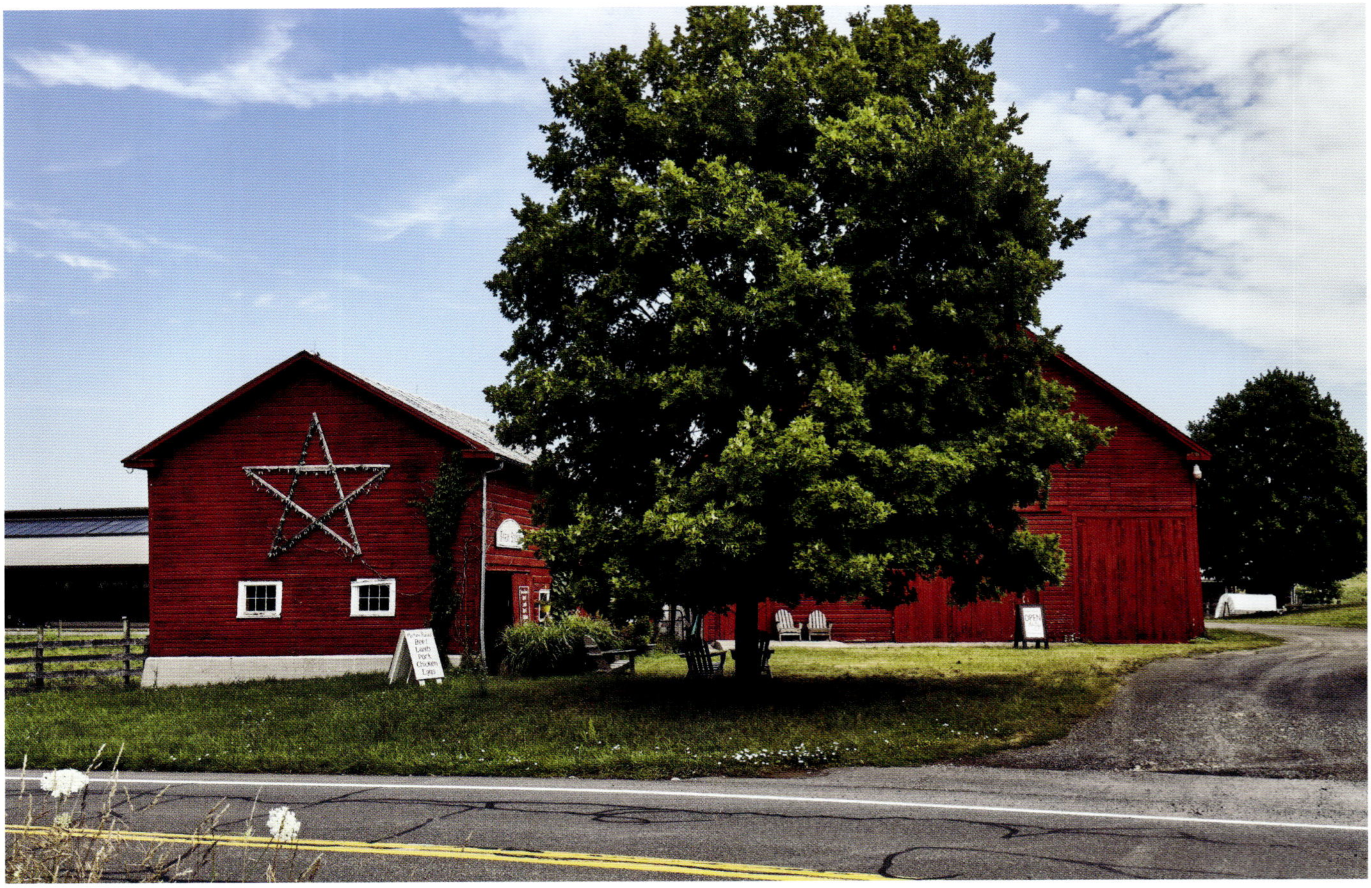

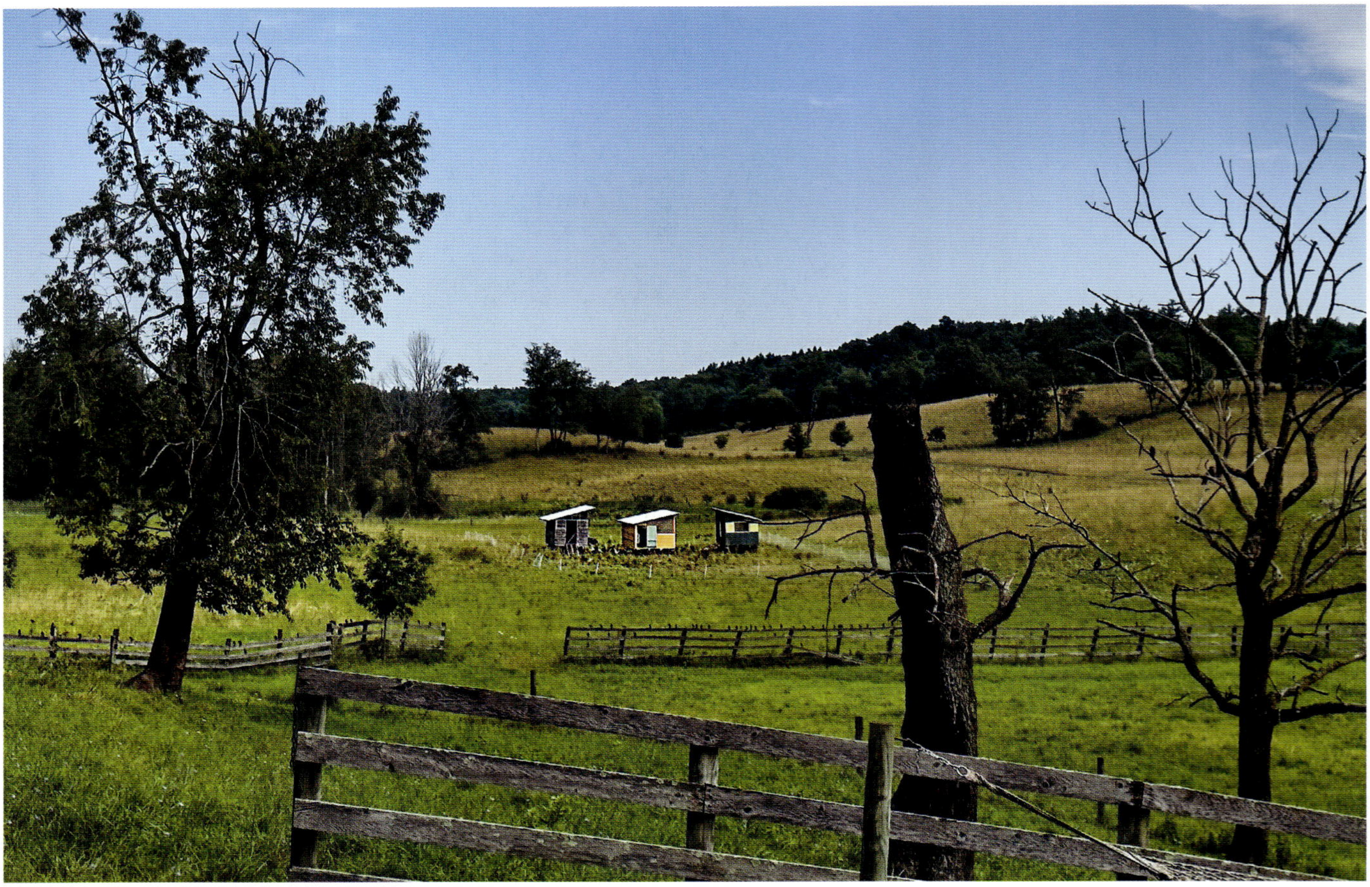

Kinderhook Farm

Kinderhook, New York

Kinderhook Farm is a sprawling 1,200-acre farm that raises pigs, sheep, cows, and chickens. It's a favorite destination on the Columbia County farm tour that happens every September. Visitors on the tour can walk the property, check out the animals and where they live, climb on a tractor, explore the barns, and learn about the daily operations of a working farm. Afterward, most people stop by the farm store, which sells meat, eggs, and other products of the farm to take home.

The farm's history represents the story behind many farms in the area. The Kinderhook Farm was an early Dutch farm, and at one time it was a dairy farm. Eventually, as farms had to change their business models, the farm was sold. In a unique arrangement, Steve and Renee Clearman bought the farm, and their friends, Lee and Georgia Ranney, run the farm with them. In 2004, they decided to make the switch away from the dairy toward meat. They process the animals on the farm, making it a community event. Their meat cows, Black Angus and Red Devon, are grass-fed and pasture-raised. They use guardian dogs trained to protect the animals from predators. The farm has an AWA (Animal Welfare Approved) certificate for its cows, sheep, and chickens. The accreditation certifies that the animals on the farm are treated with the highest animal welfare standards.

In 2011, the farm decided to convert one of the barns on the property to a "farm stay" location. The barn is decorated with rustic and antique furnishings but also has modern conveniences, such as an indoor kitchen and plumbing. Guests can choose to experience feeding the animals, sleeping in the barn, rising with the sun, sitting around the fire at night, and cooking breakfast with food purchased from the farm store. In other words, a taste of rural life.

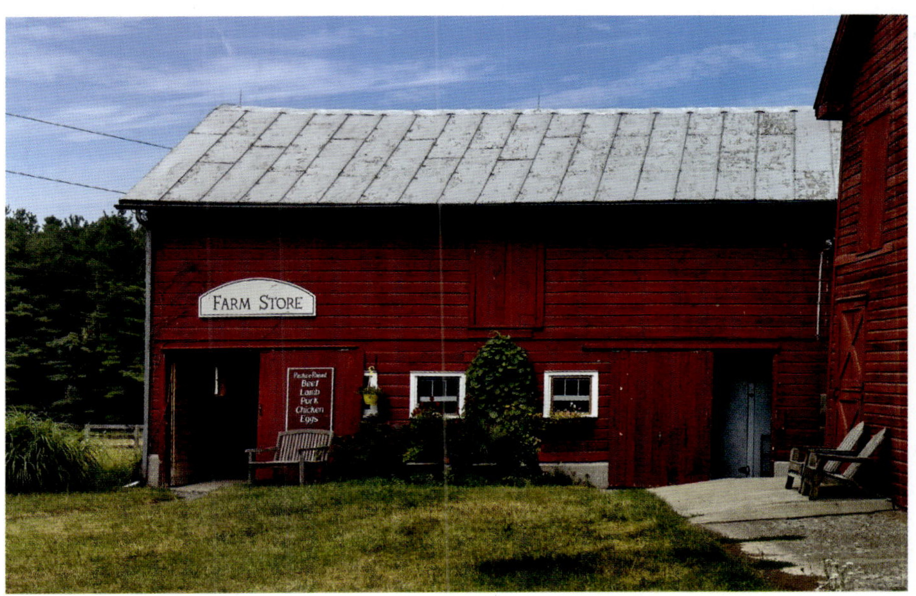

above and opposite, top
On the road to the village of Kinderhook, the two barns welcome visitors to the farm. One has been remodeled as the farm's store. It opened in 2008.

opposite, bottom
Three chicken coops are placed in the open pasture where the chickens run around and feed.

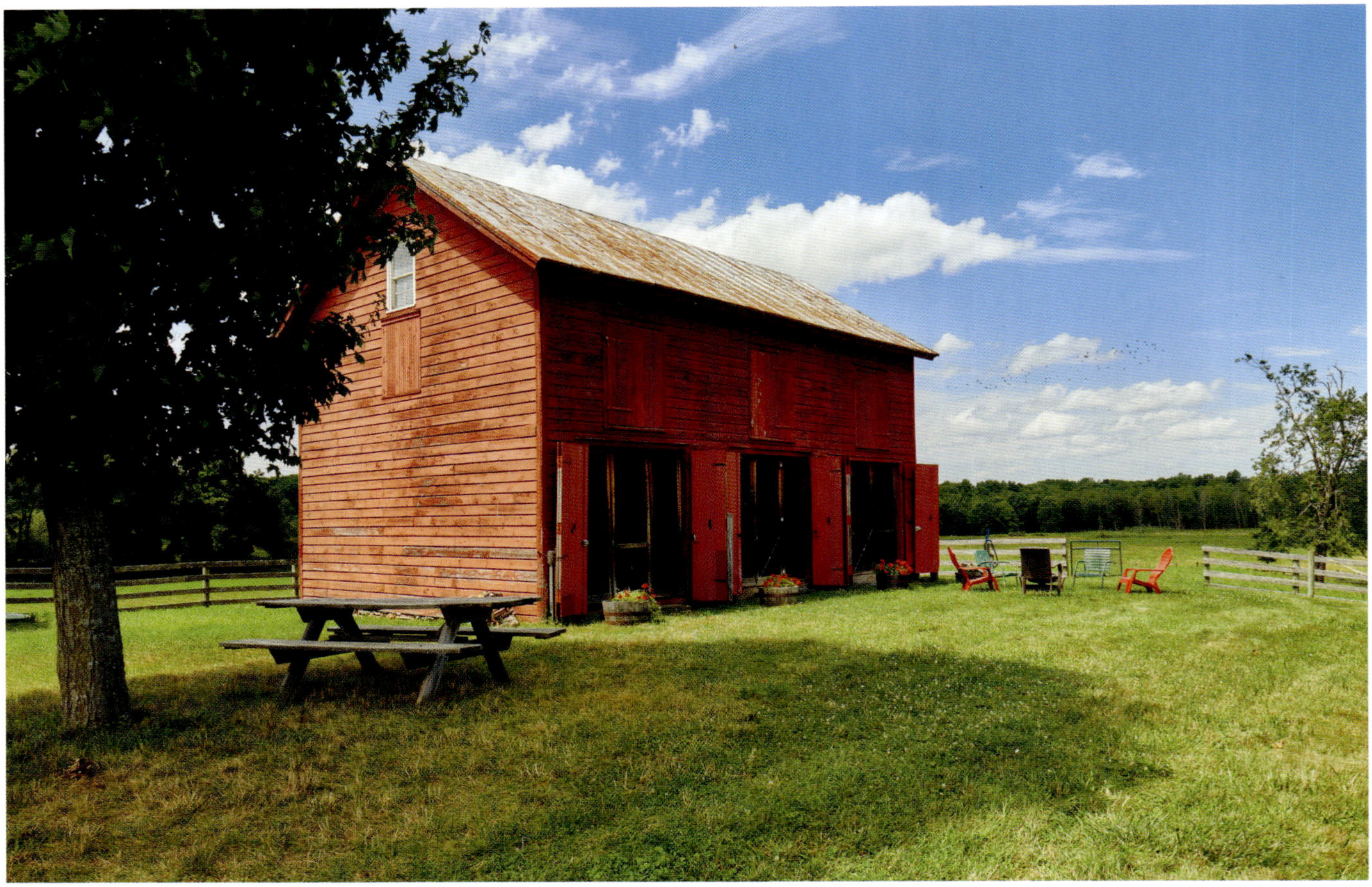

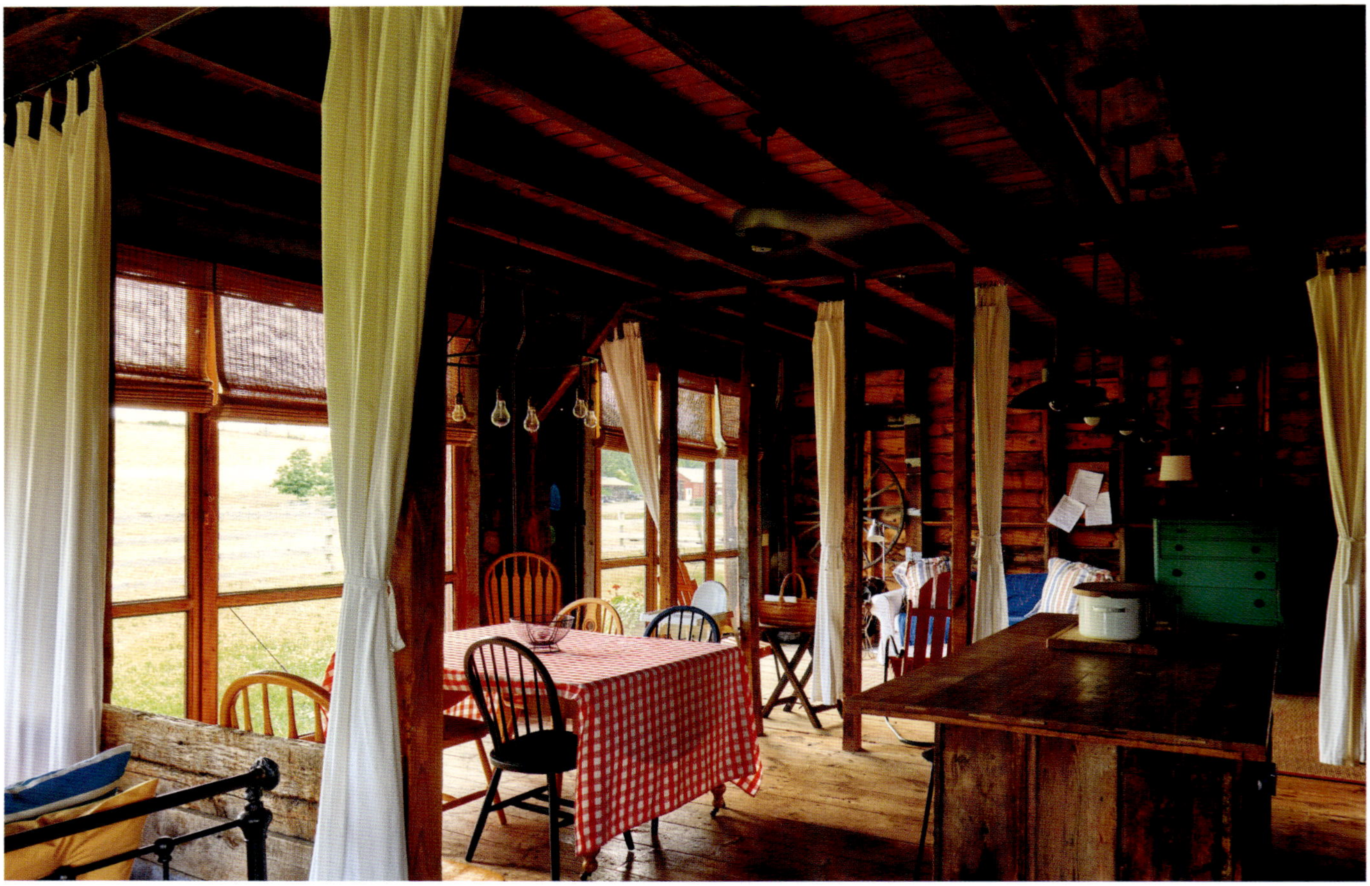

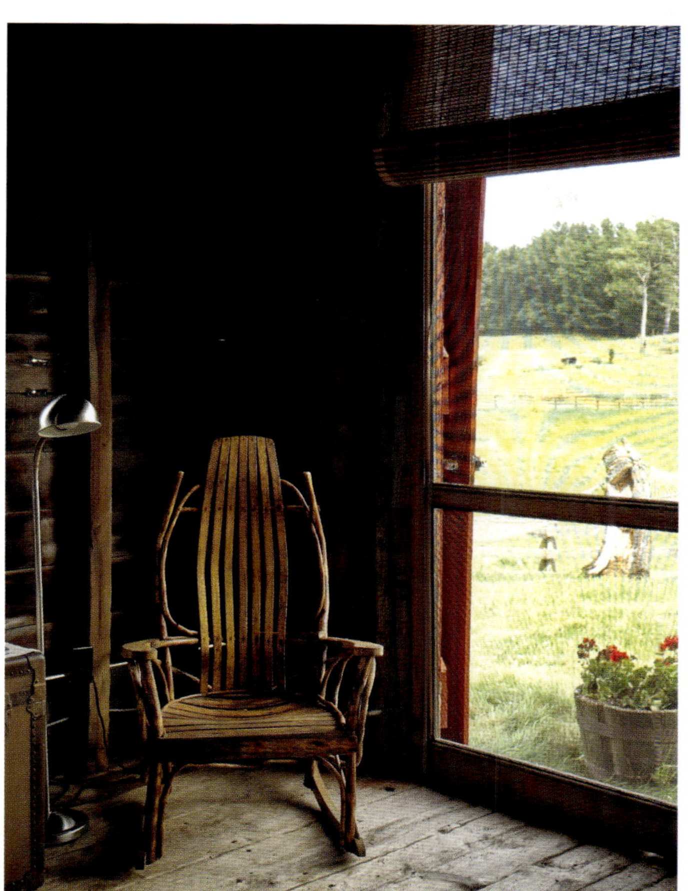

opposite, top
The barn that was converted to the farm stay. The whole barn is rented through Airbnb. A firepit and Adirondack chairs are provided out front.

opposite, bottom
The barn has an open floor plan with the kitchen area between two bedrooms. The exposed wood of the barn's construction enhances the rustic feeling of the interiors. Light seeps through the cracks between the beams. Wood floors creak underfoot. White curtains can be used to divide the space. The front of the barn has screen doors that open to the farm.

left
An antique rocker placed by the screen door overlooks a bucolic view.

below
Two iron beds with floral linens add to the romance of sleeping almost outside.

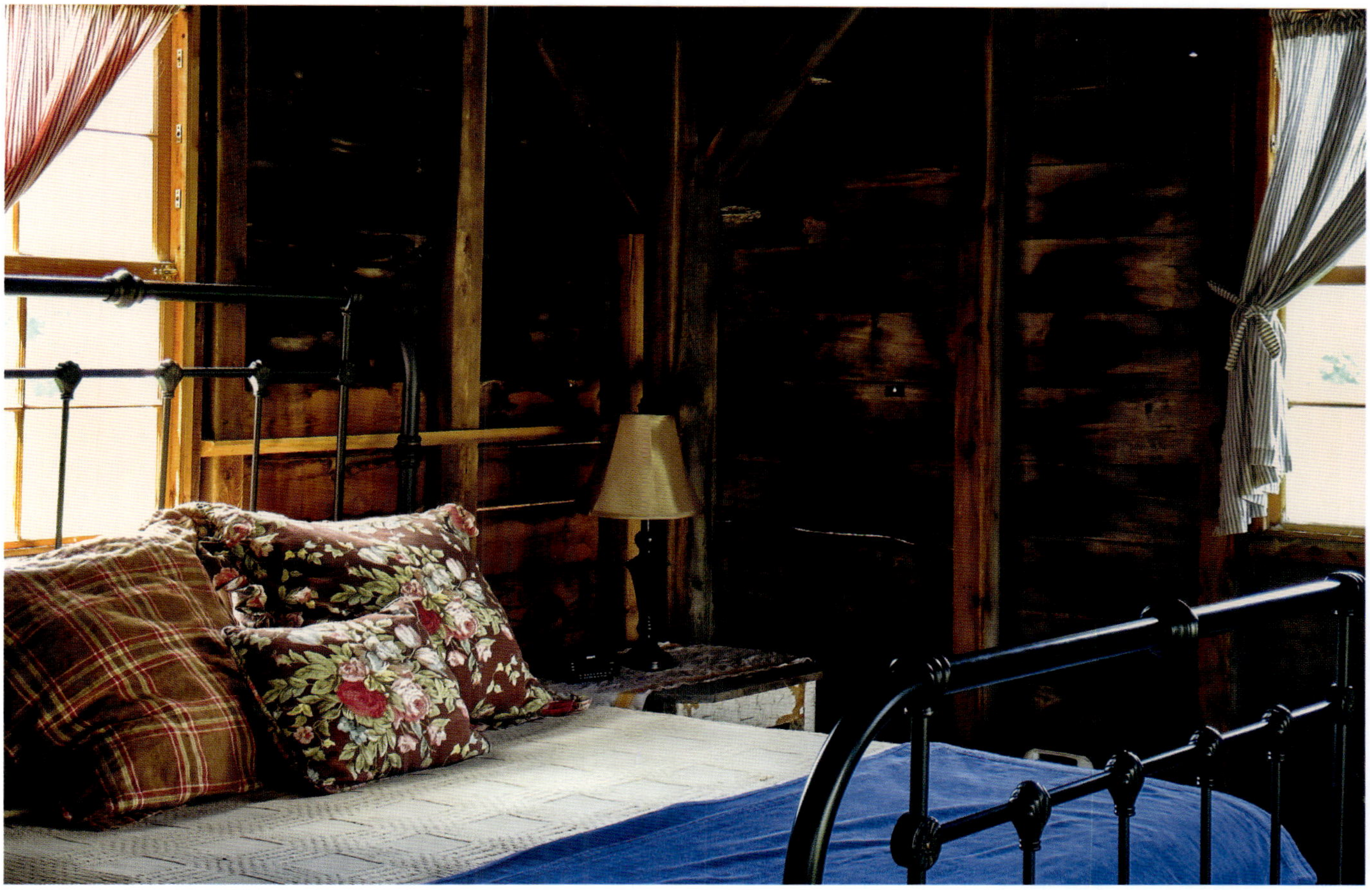

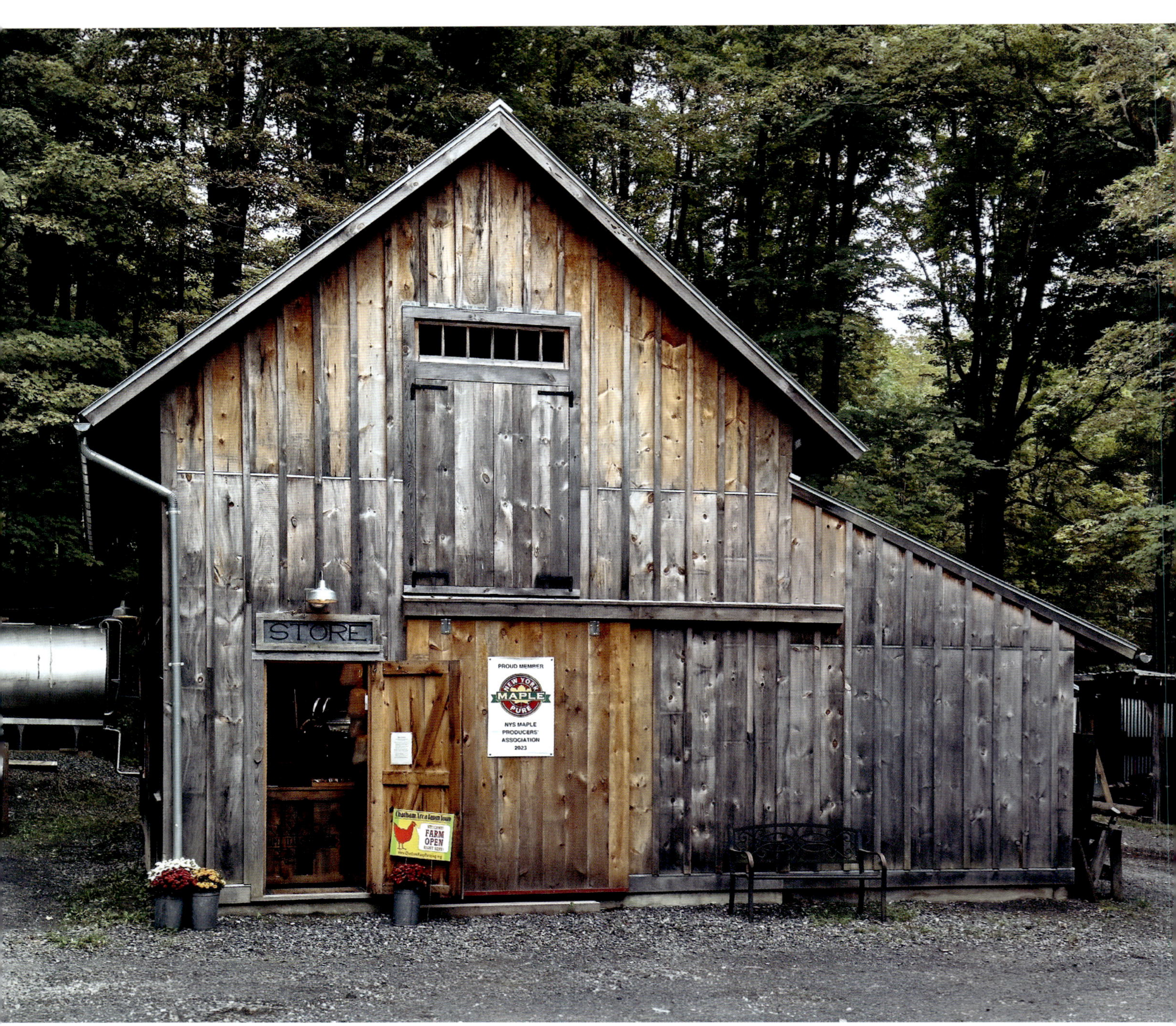

The hand-built sugar shack is nestled in a stand of maple trees. Veronica and Ben also prepared the site for their business, clearing trees and making a road.

Maple Leaf Sugaring

Ghent, New York

Veronica Madey always thought that somehow maple sugaring would be a part of her future with her husband, Ben. When he was about eight years old, Ben and three friends started tapping maple trees in their town of Hillsdale, New York. They had 250 taps and a small evaporator (the machine used to distill the sap). So, she wasn't surprised when the idea to start a maple sugaring business went into full production in 2014.

They started by building the sugar shack. Ben built the timber-framed building himself, felling the trees from their land in Ghent, New York. Veronica carved the pegs that hold the place together. They started tapping the maple trees on their property with 1,500 taps (which is the way to measure the scale of the business), and now their company has over 8,500 taps. Neighbors and friends have asked for their properties and trees to be included in the tapping process.

The company has grown exponentially, and the couple is in full distribution mode with their maple syrup products. Veronica delivers the products; Ben oversees quality control and "cooking." In addition to the sales at the sugar shack, fairs, and festivals, they sell to restaurants and groceries. Ben and Veronica also open the shack to farm tours. They educate visitors on the sugaring process, connecting a product made from nature to the people who love it.

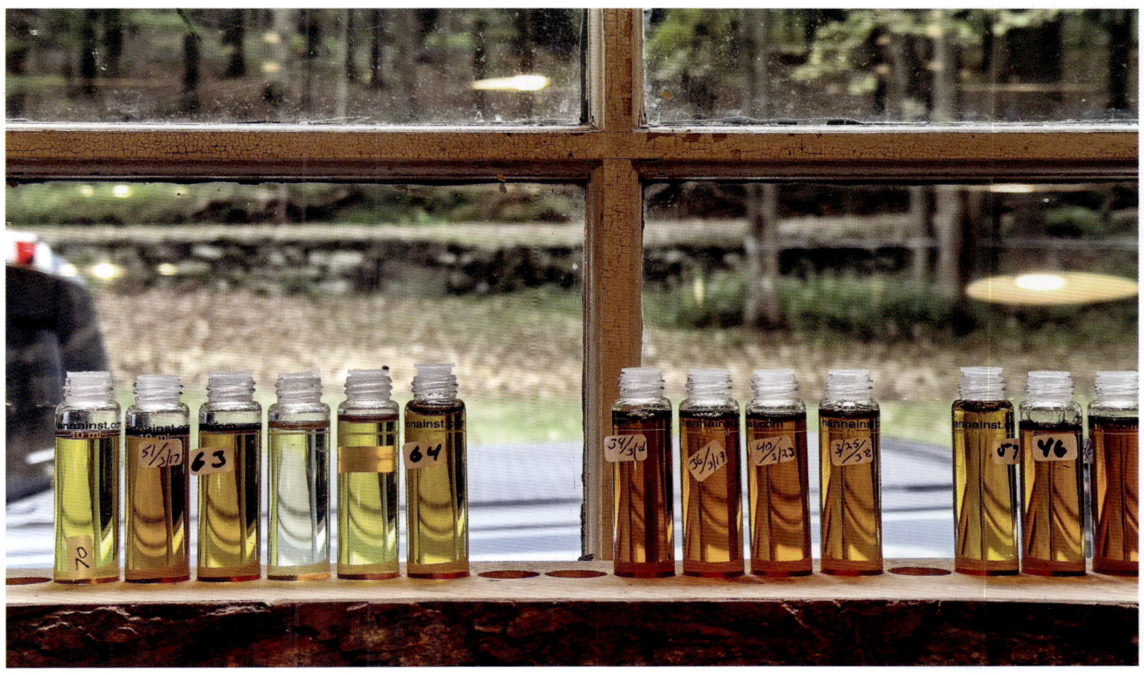

Shades of syrup in glass bottles sit on the window ledge of the sugar house. Maple sugar "season" now starts in February. It's a busy time at the sugar shack as the sap starts flowing in.

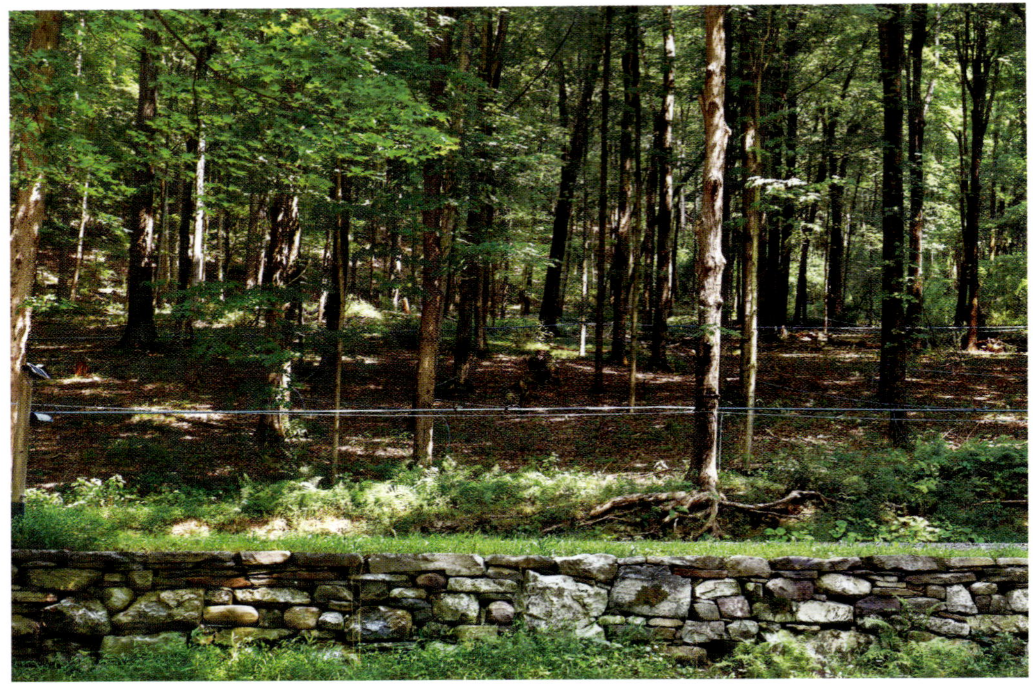

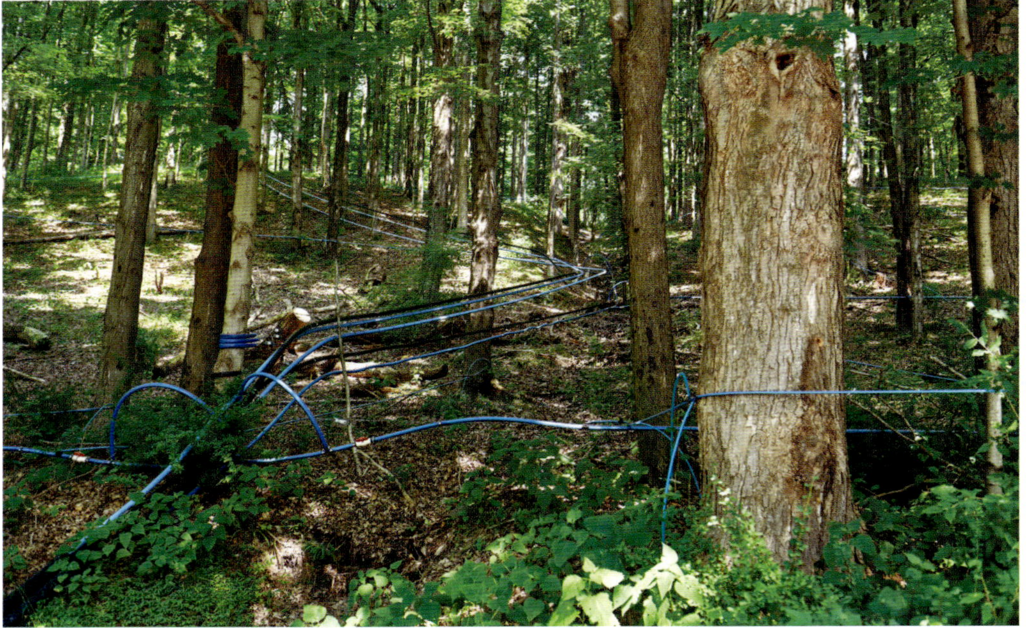

top and bottom
Modern maple sugar production requires a system of tube lines that run between trees. The system creates a vacuum that draws the sap from the trees. Ben explained that one of their biggest challenges in maple syrup production is squirrels. Walking through the forest, it is possible to hear the holes that squirrels have chewed seeping sap. Squirrels are territorial and don't necessarily like the bright blue lines sharing their space.

opposite
Ben standing next to the evaporator that boils the sugar. He's testing the density of the distilled syrup for sugar content. Ideal sugar content is between 66.1 percent and 68.5 percent; 67 percent, before it is filtered, is the best.

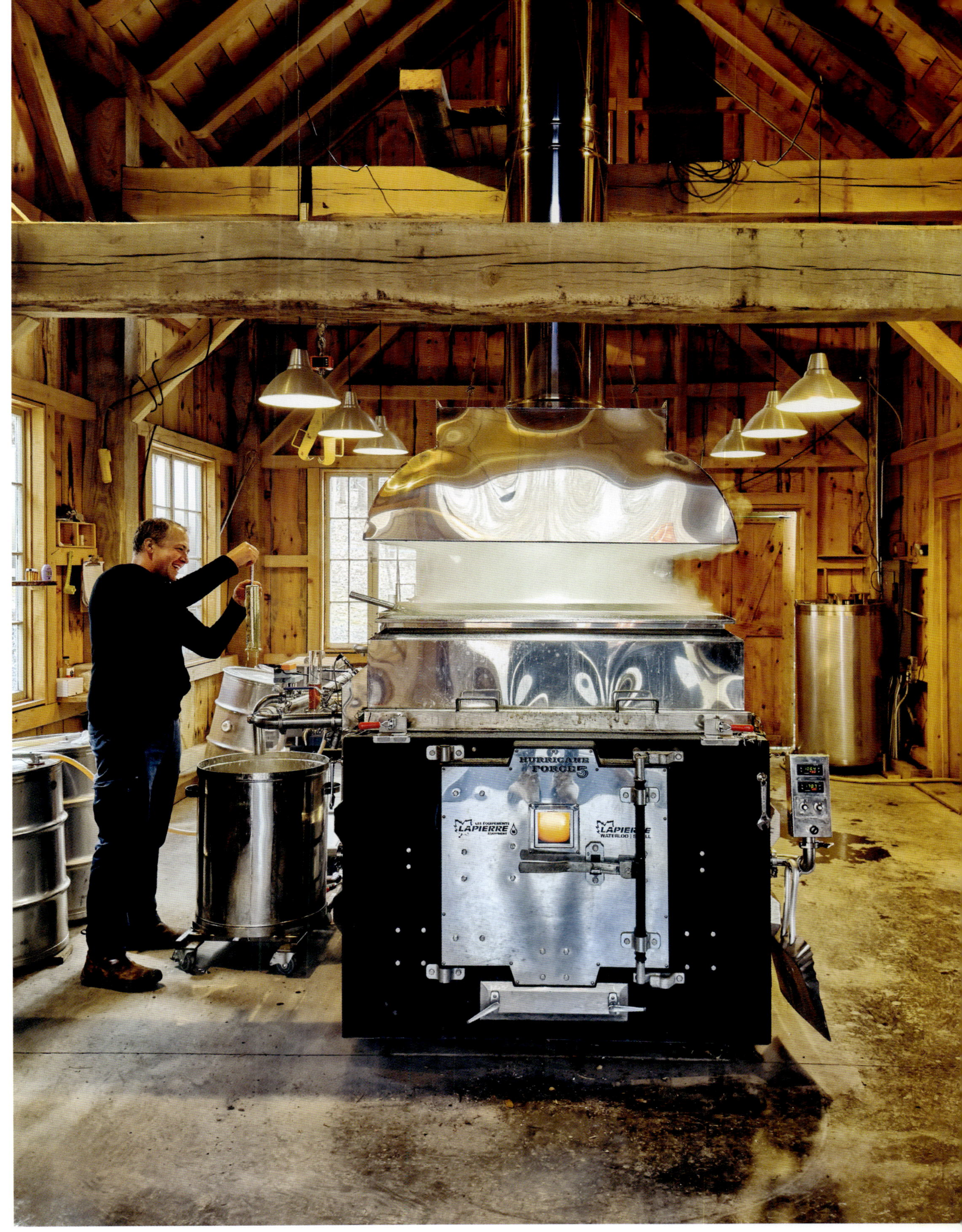
HURRICANE FORCE 5
LAPIERRE

Hudson-Chatham Winery

Ghent, New York

The Hudson Valley has a long history of viticulture. Native Americans grew grapes on their lands, and European settlers brought vines with them. One of the first and longest continually operating vineyards is in the Hudson Valley. For Justen Nickell and Steven Rosario, partners in life and work, it wasn't an ambition to own a vineyard in the Hudson Valley even though Justen's family had a history of homebrewing and fermentation. They both studied at the Culinary Institute of America in Hyde Park and at the time were happily working in Boston in the food industry. On a weekend trip to Hudson, looking for a house in the country as a vacation home, they learned that the Hudson-Chatham Winery had gone up for sale. The timing wasn't great—it was 2020, the start of the COVID pandemic—but they did not let a worldwide health crisis deter them. The farming work that needed to be done was outside. In the process of cleaning up the property, they ended up taking out many of the existing vines. The couple planted hybrid vines such as Marquette, Frontenac, and Itasca, to name a few that could tolerate the cold Northeastern winters. As two thousand new "pieds" (the French expression for grape plants that also means "feet") went in, Steven and Justen were off to a new start, expanding the vineyard to eight acres. Located on the side of a hill between Hudson and Chatham, the vineyard property includes a new tasting room, outside seating in the warmer months, and their home. Five years later they are bottling their 2024 vintage and looking forward to 2025, when the vines they planted will bear fruit.

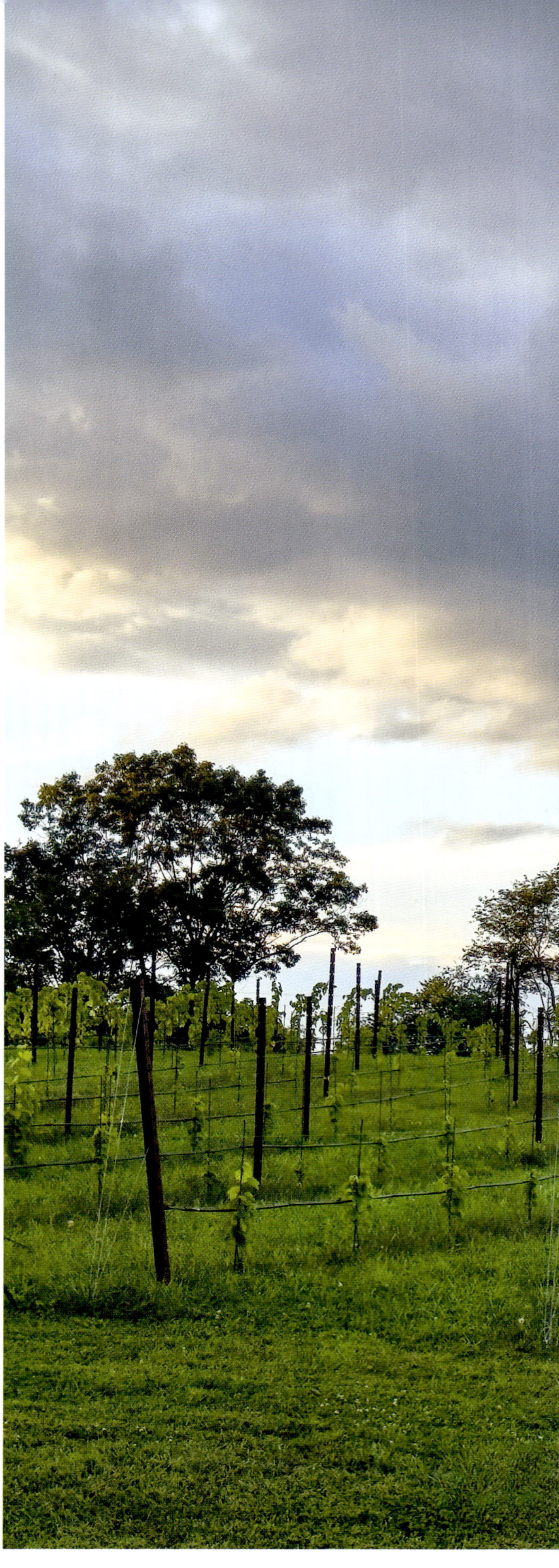

The Hudson-Chatham Winery's new vineyard was planted in 2020. They wrapped up their 2024 vintage in October 2024.

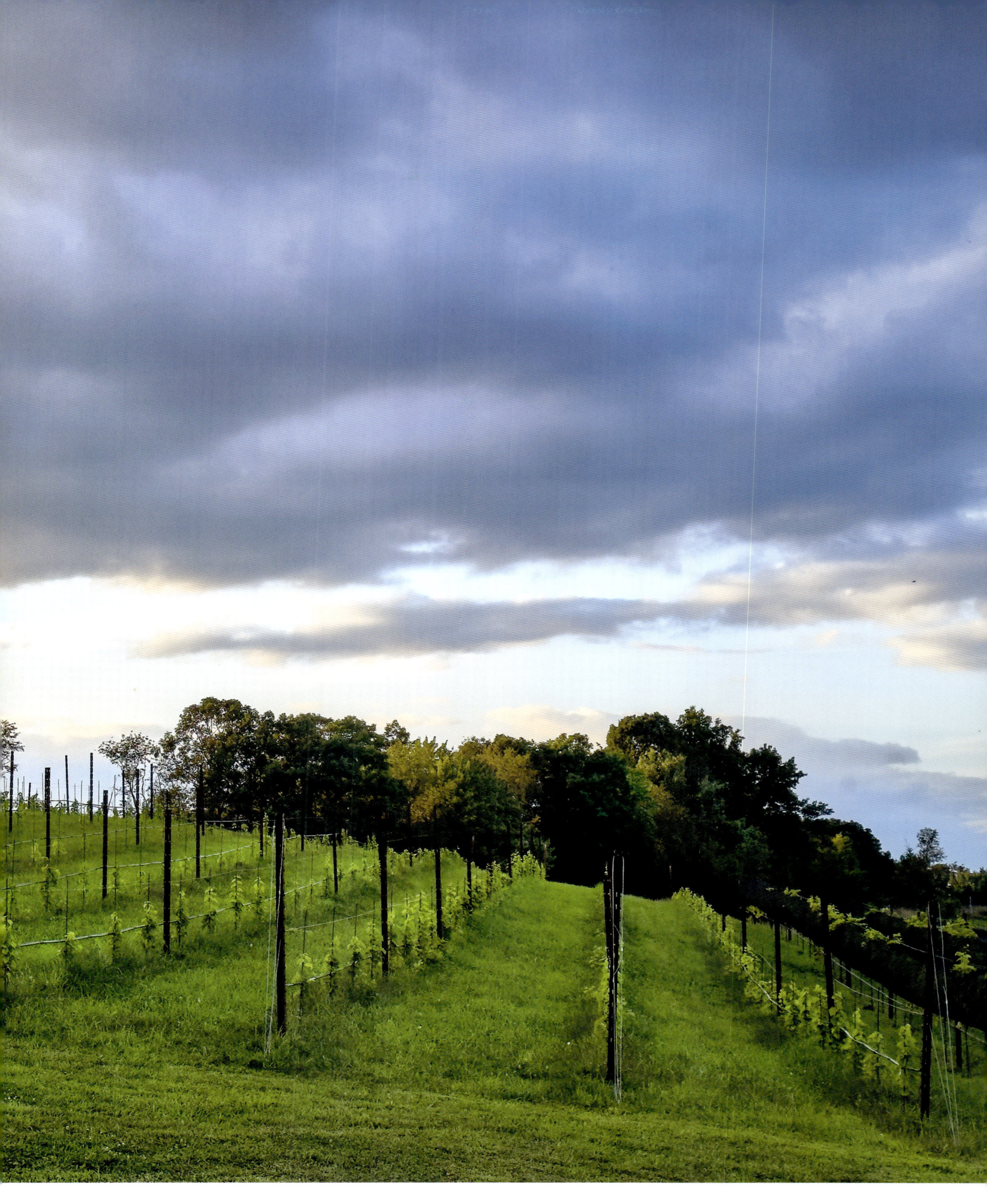

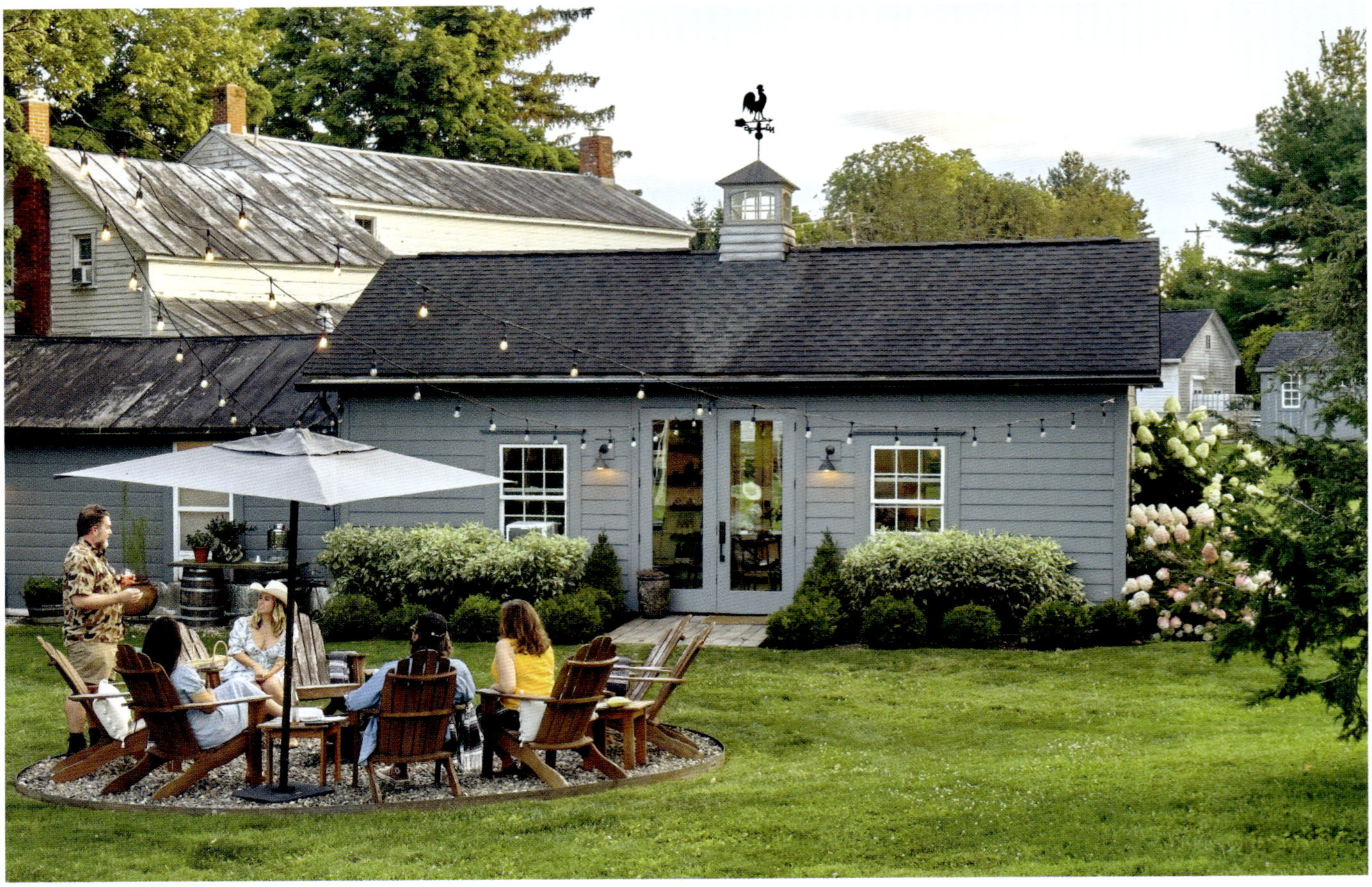

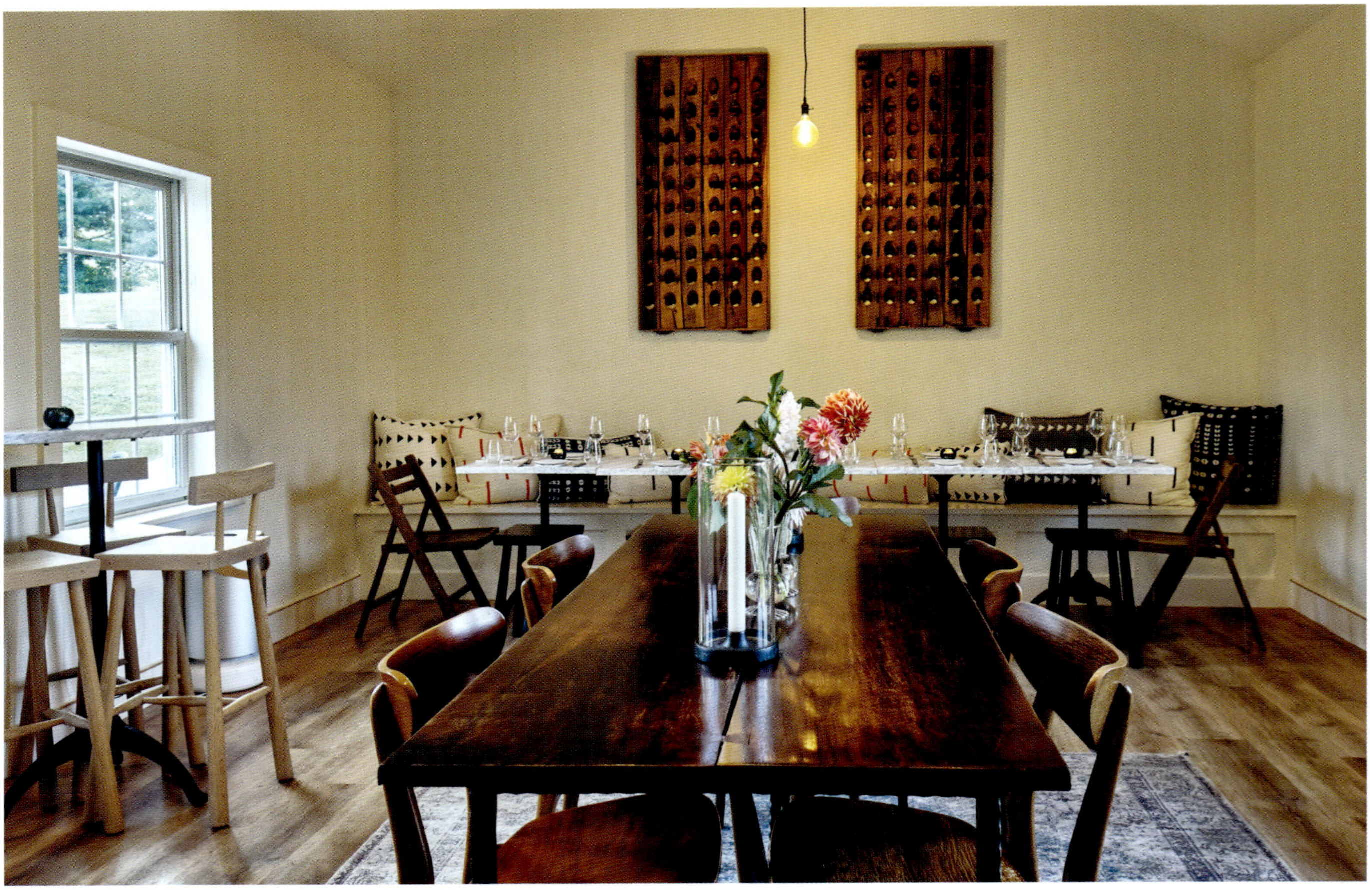

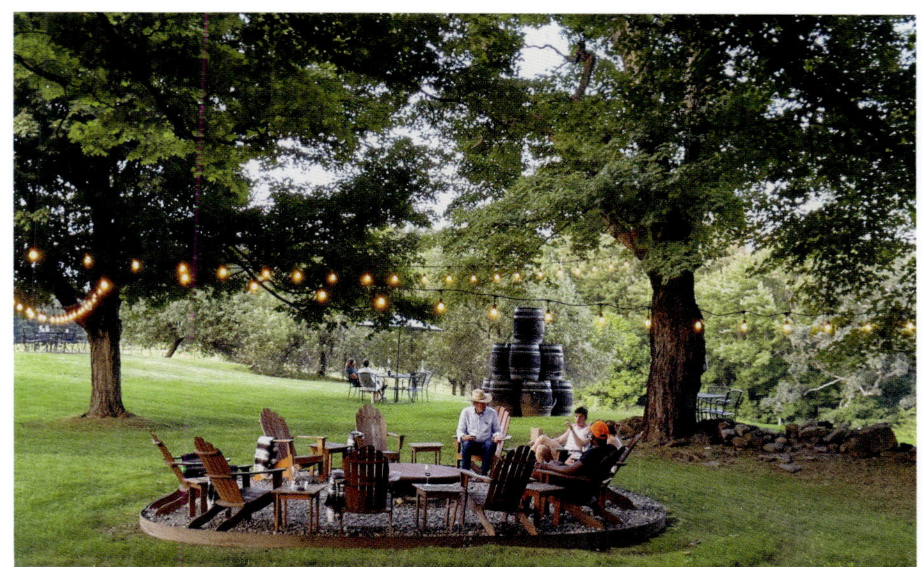

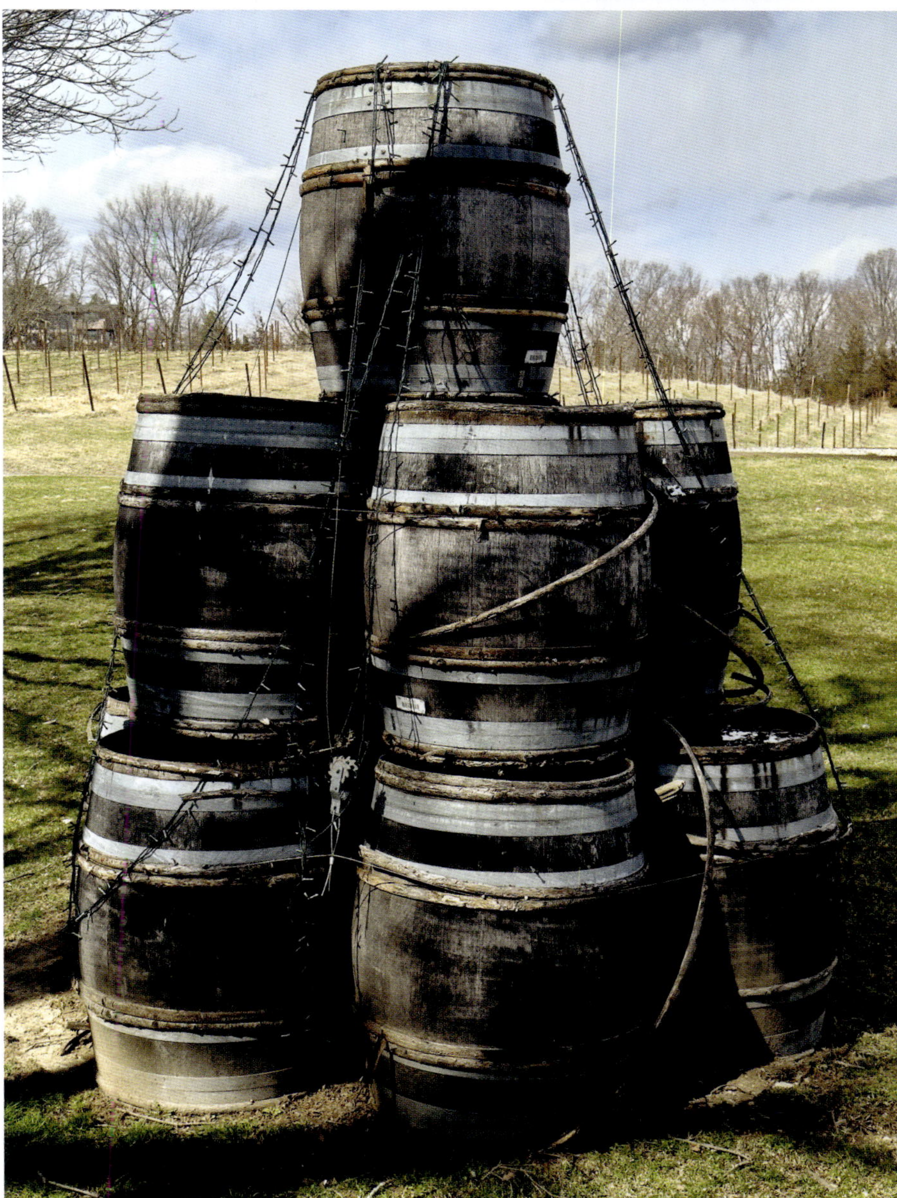

opposite, top
The tasting room was built in 2020 when Justen and Steven took over the vineyard. The outside seating is built around bonfires in the cooler months.

opposite, bottom
The interior of the tasting room is set for a guided tasting event. One of the owners will lead guests through a flight of wines.

top
Guests relax on the winery grounds.

right
Wine barrels are used as a decorative element in the outdoor seating area.

Champêtre

Pine Plains, New York

Chef Michel Jean is going from table to table chatting with guests. Patricia Jean, his wife and business partner, floats through the dining room from the front of house back to the kitchen of the one-room restaurant. Provence, their wildly successful restaurant on MacDougal Street in SoHo, was open from 1986 to 2006. Patricia and Michel sold it after the 9/11 terrorist attack changed downtown and moved full time to their country home upstate. At the time, as avid equestrians, they both wanted to be close to nature.

Now, nineteenth-century antique landscape paintings of the Hudson River Valley, which Patricia has collected over the years, are displayed on every inch of wall space at Champêtre, the couple's latest venture. They opened in 2021. The white-wall space feels like a gallery, and that is the intention. These paintings were also hung in the stairwell at Stissing House, just down the block in Pine Plains, where Michel was chef for fifteen years. But gathering all the works together makes a strong statement about the importance of place. Even the restaurant's name, which in French means "countryside," suggests the here and now.

Early in his career, Michel was part of the New York City French restaurant circuit. He noticed what was missing from the restaurant scene at the time—a casual, bistro-style French place. Provence, with its outdoor back garden, filled in that gap, which is why it became so important to the neighborhood. It was classic French Mediterranean food without the hoopla. Champêtre also fills a gap in the upstate restaurant scene. It is not over-the-top fancy (although some people make it their special occasion spot), but Michel's cooking is precise and inventive. He has a vision and, like the landscape paintings hanging on the wall, the genre may be the same but the distinction is in the details.

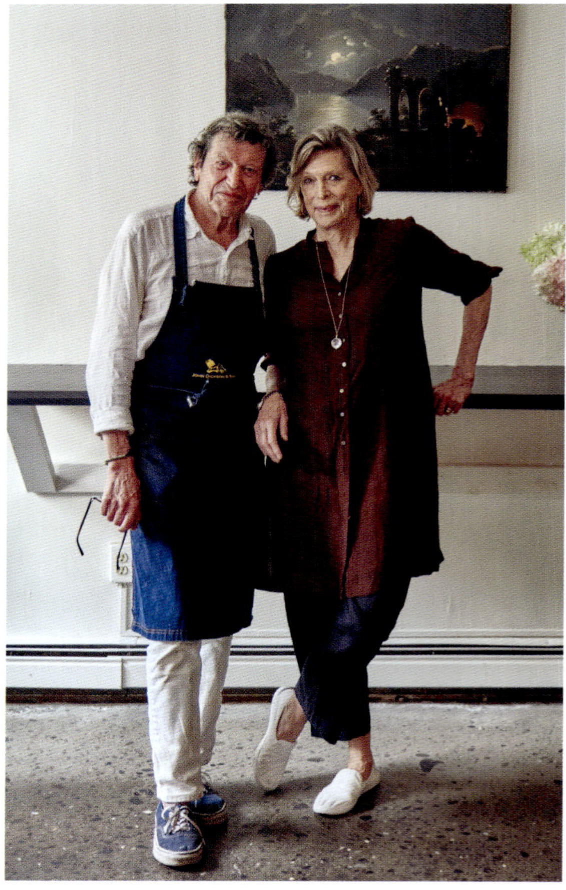

right
Patricia and Michel Jean stand at the entrance of their latest restaurant, in Pine Plains, New York.

opposite, top
Champêtre's terrace has four tables and is a popular spot in the summer.

opposite, bottom
Before service begins, the gallery-style decor is in full view. When filled, the restaurant still has an intimate feel—it is as if you've been invited over for dinner.

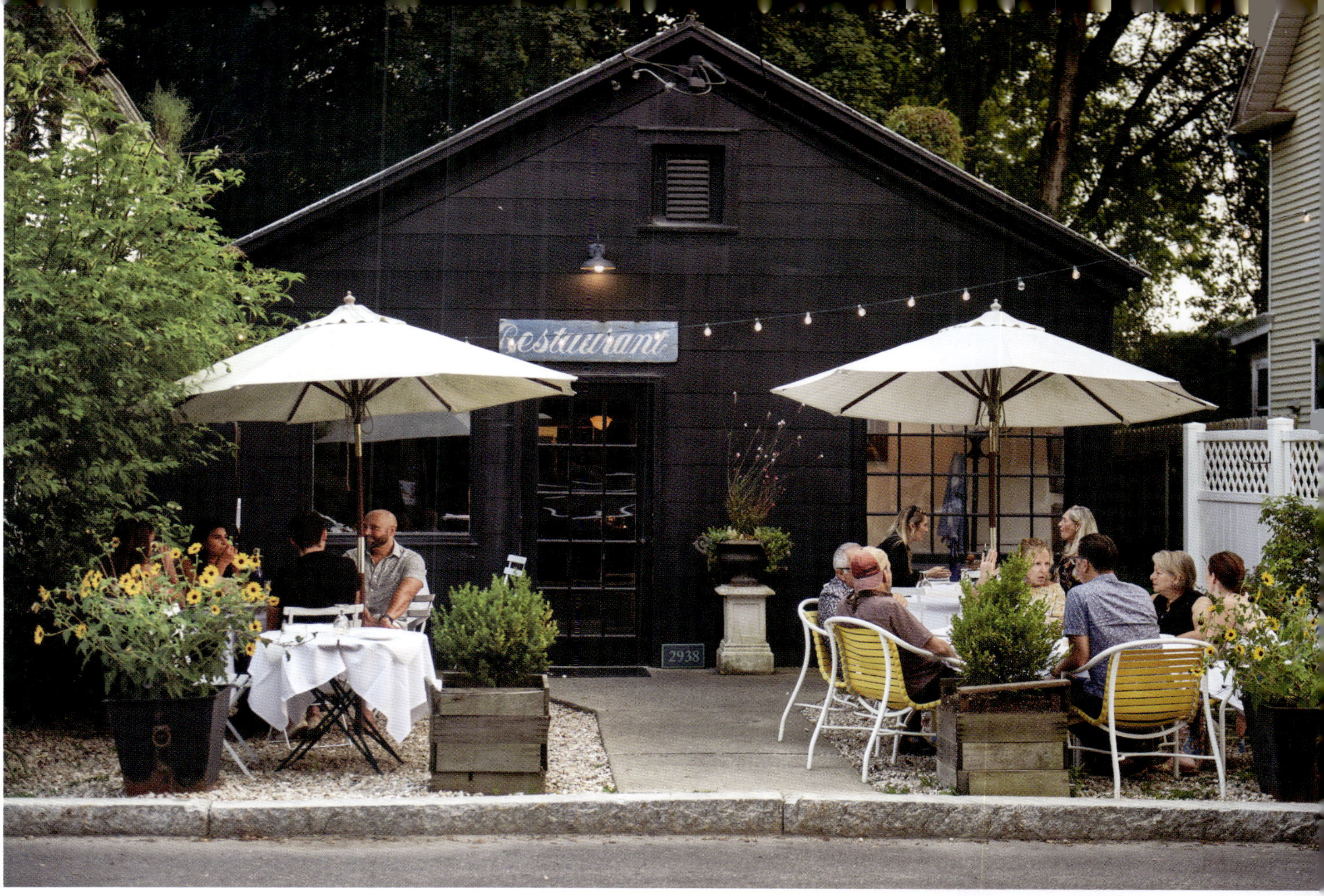

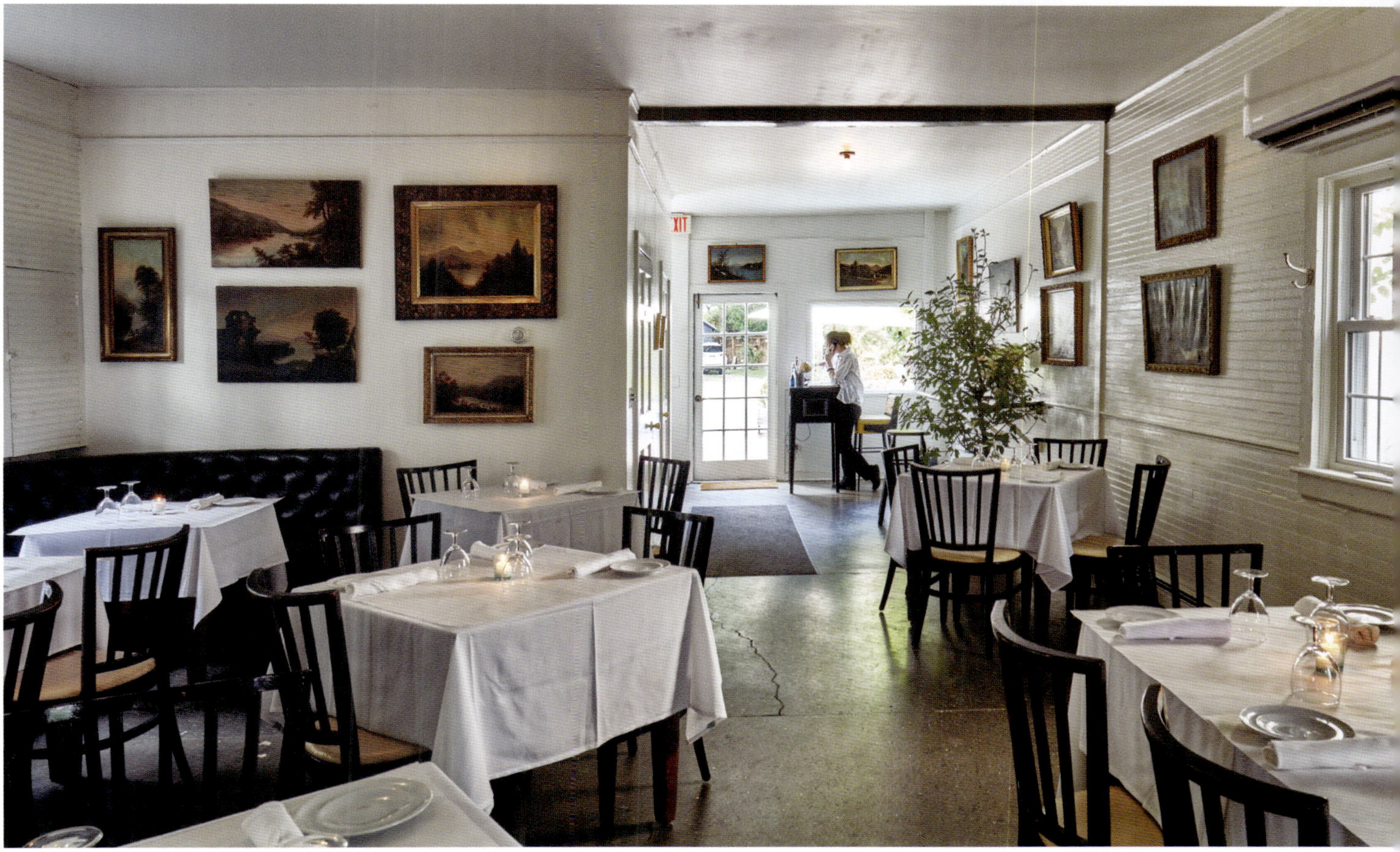

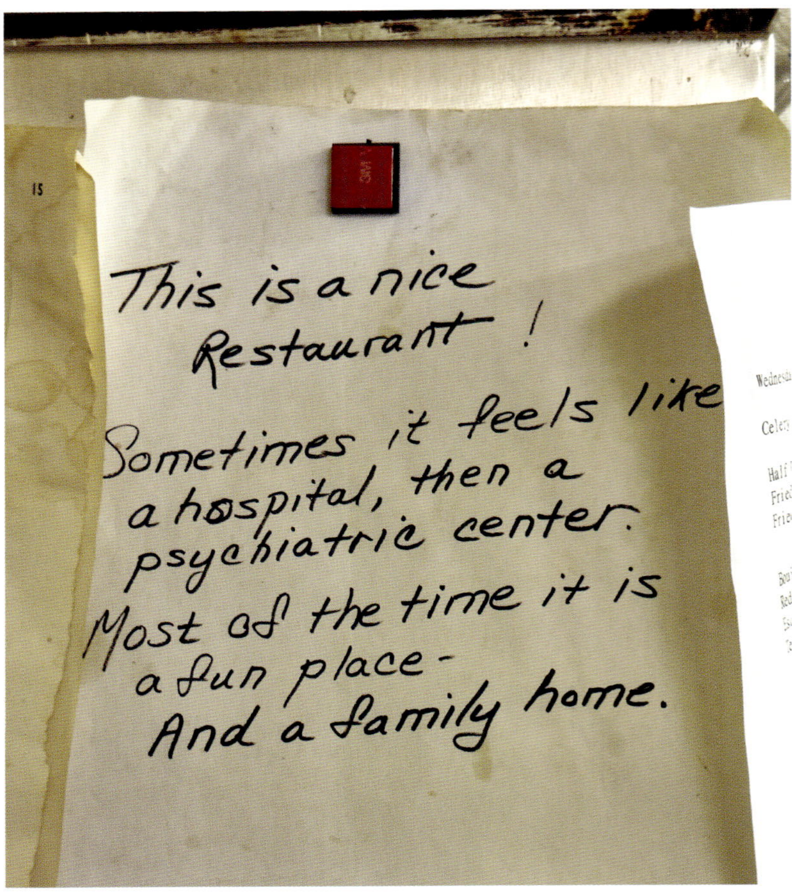

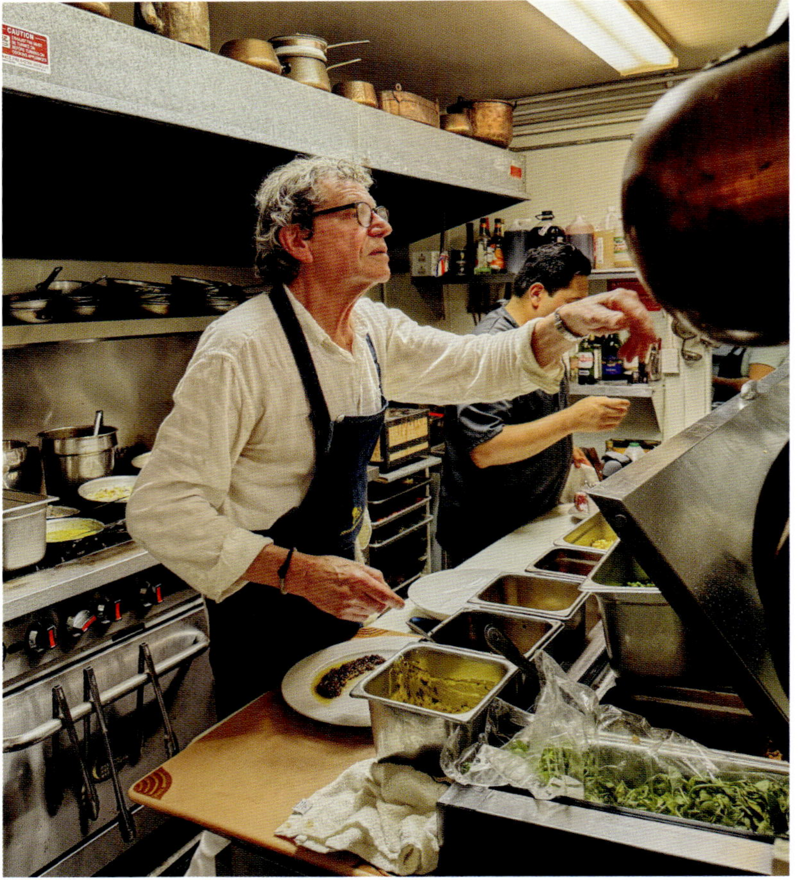

top
Notes in the kitchen include this reminder.

left
Chef Michel Jean is very organized in the narrow kitchen. He works with his sous-chef on the dinner preparations.

opposite, top and bottom
The entrance to the kitchen is behind the bar. The restaurant is compact and efficient in its use of space, including banquettes placed against the walls.

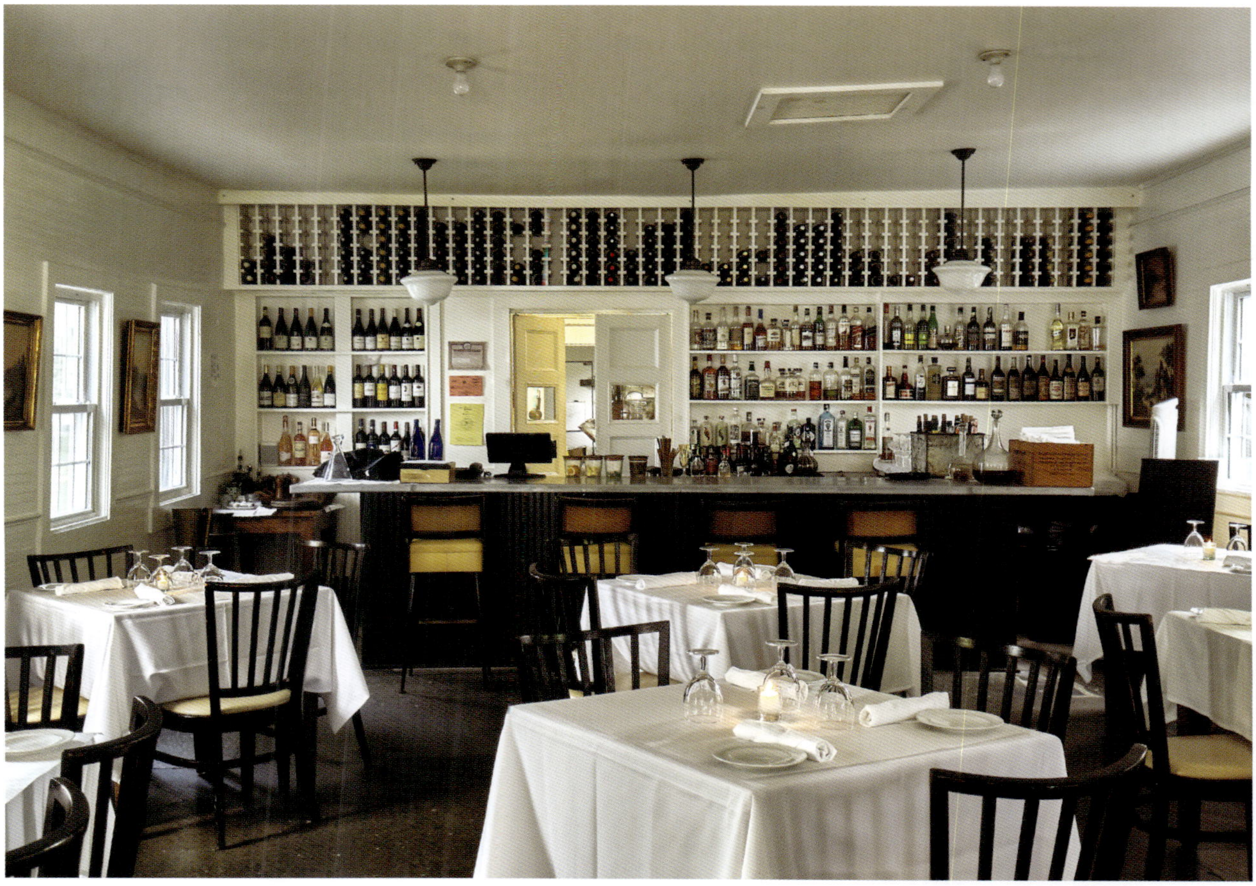

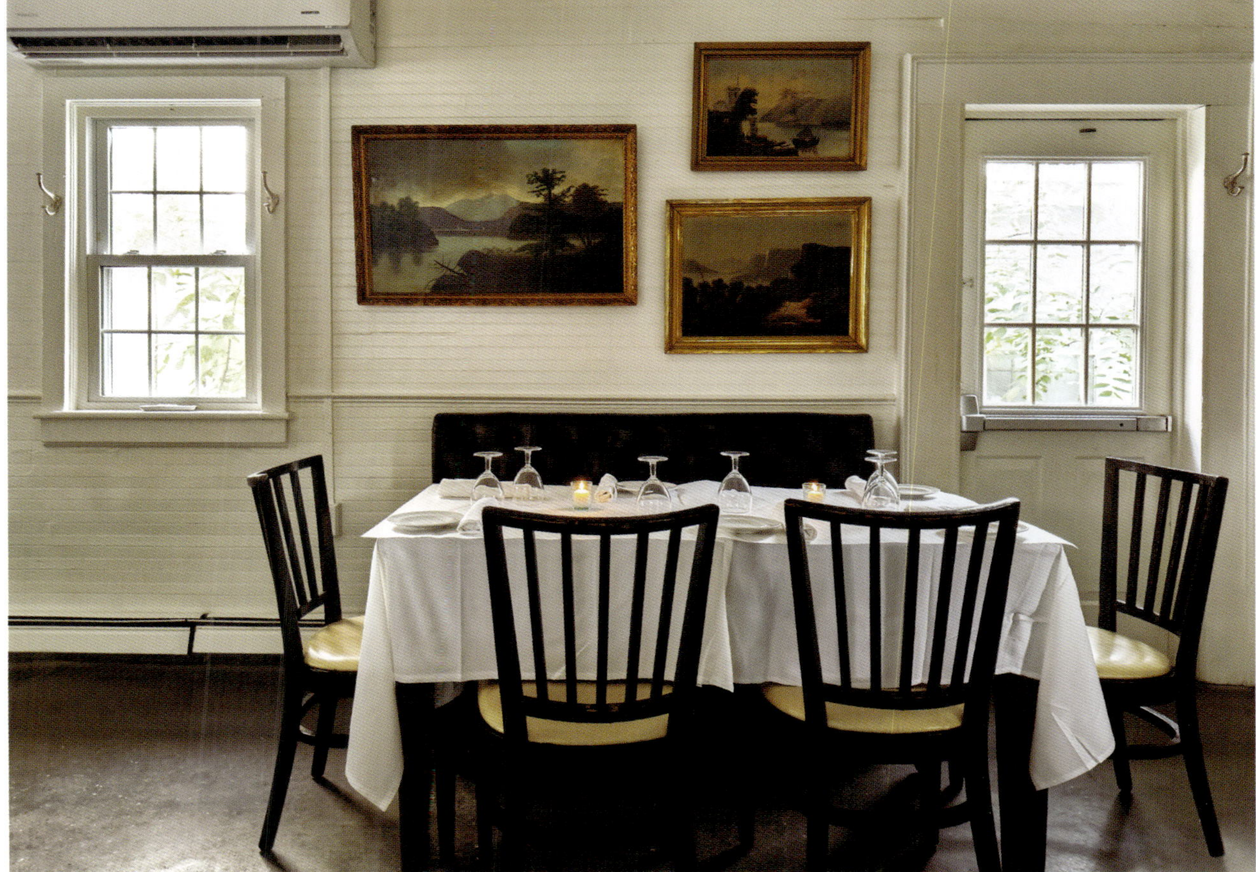

Silver Brothers Distillery

Old Chatham, New York

Matt Driessen moved home to start a new business. After years of being away from Chatham—going to college, living and working in New York City, and visiting his family upstate on weekends—Matt and his wife, Kim, along with their twin sons decided to take the leap and start something fresh. After extensive research, they bought a farm just before the COVID pandemic and started preparing to make American single malt and rye whiskeys.

In recent years, field-to-glass distilleries have been cropping up in the Hudson Valley and Catskills. Not far from Old Chatham, in Valatie, Golden Harvest, a family orchard, makes a line of brandies and liquors under the brand Harvest Spirits, including an apple jack distilled from the fruits from their family's farm. Matt and Kim have also taken a hyperlocal approach to making Silver Brothers Distillery's whiskey and rye. The grain they use is grown on their farm and their neighbors' farms, where they lease additional land.

The farm they purchased has quite a history. At one time, it was the location of a Relais & Château restaurant—one of the first farm-to-table restaurants in America. When the restaurant closed, the farm was adapted for sheep. The Old Chatham Sheepherding Company produces high-quality sheep's milk–based cheese. The Clarks, who started the company, were here for more than twenty years, before the business was sold and the flock moved to the Finger Lakes District. The farm and its beautiful red barns, one of which was moved from the Shaker settlement

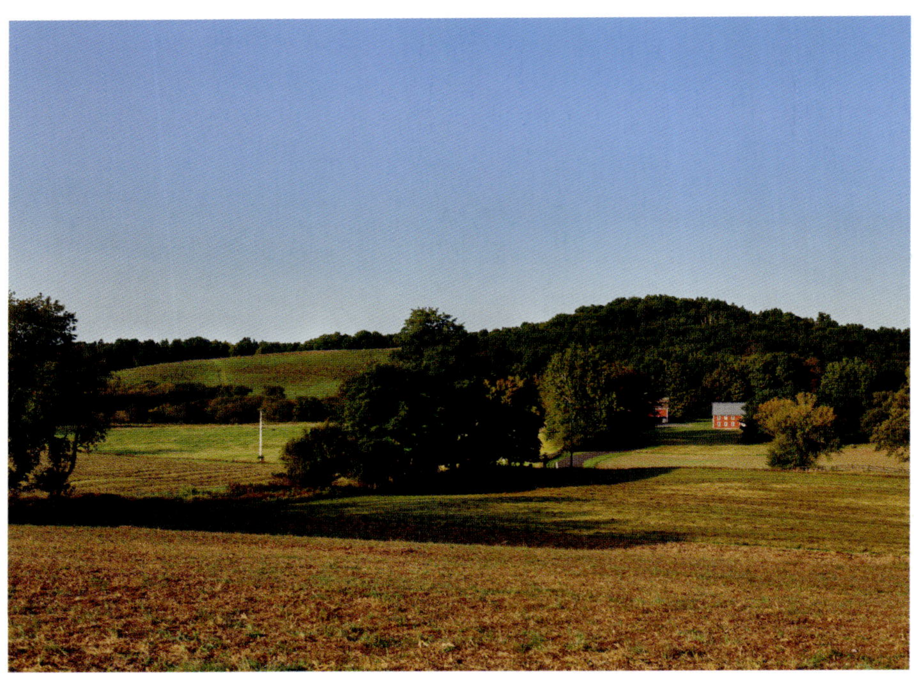

above
The Silver Brothers Distillery's three-hundred-acre farm viewed from a hilltop field. The expansive estate produces rye and barley for whiskey.

opposite, top
The entire distilling process is under one roof of the repurposed barns, including the tasting room.

opposite, bottom
A previous owner moved the barn from the Shaker settlement in Watervliet. Each slate tile on the roof was numbered as the barn was disassembled and then put back in place.

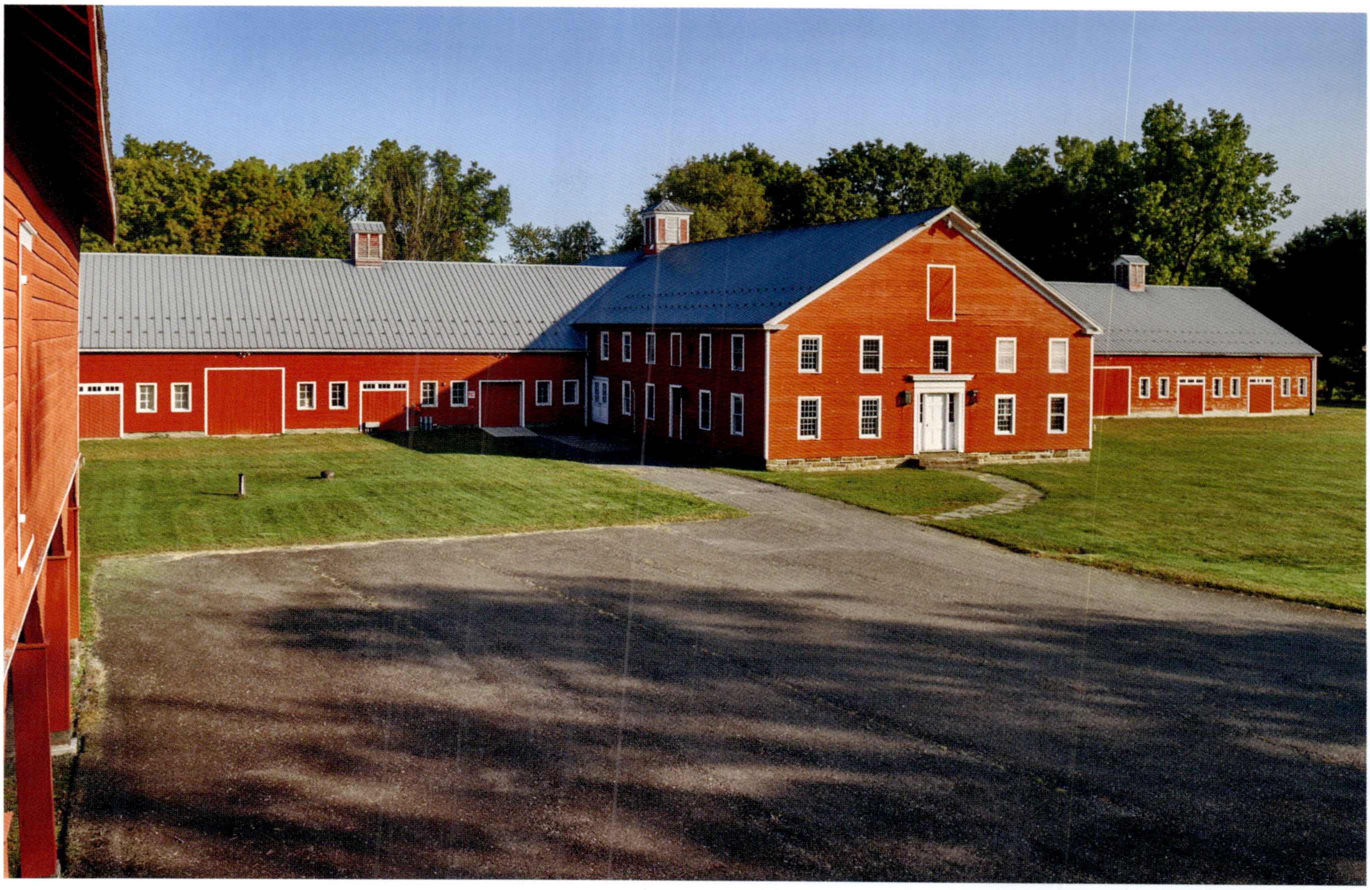

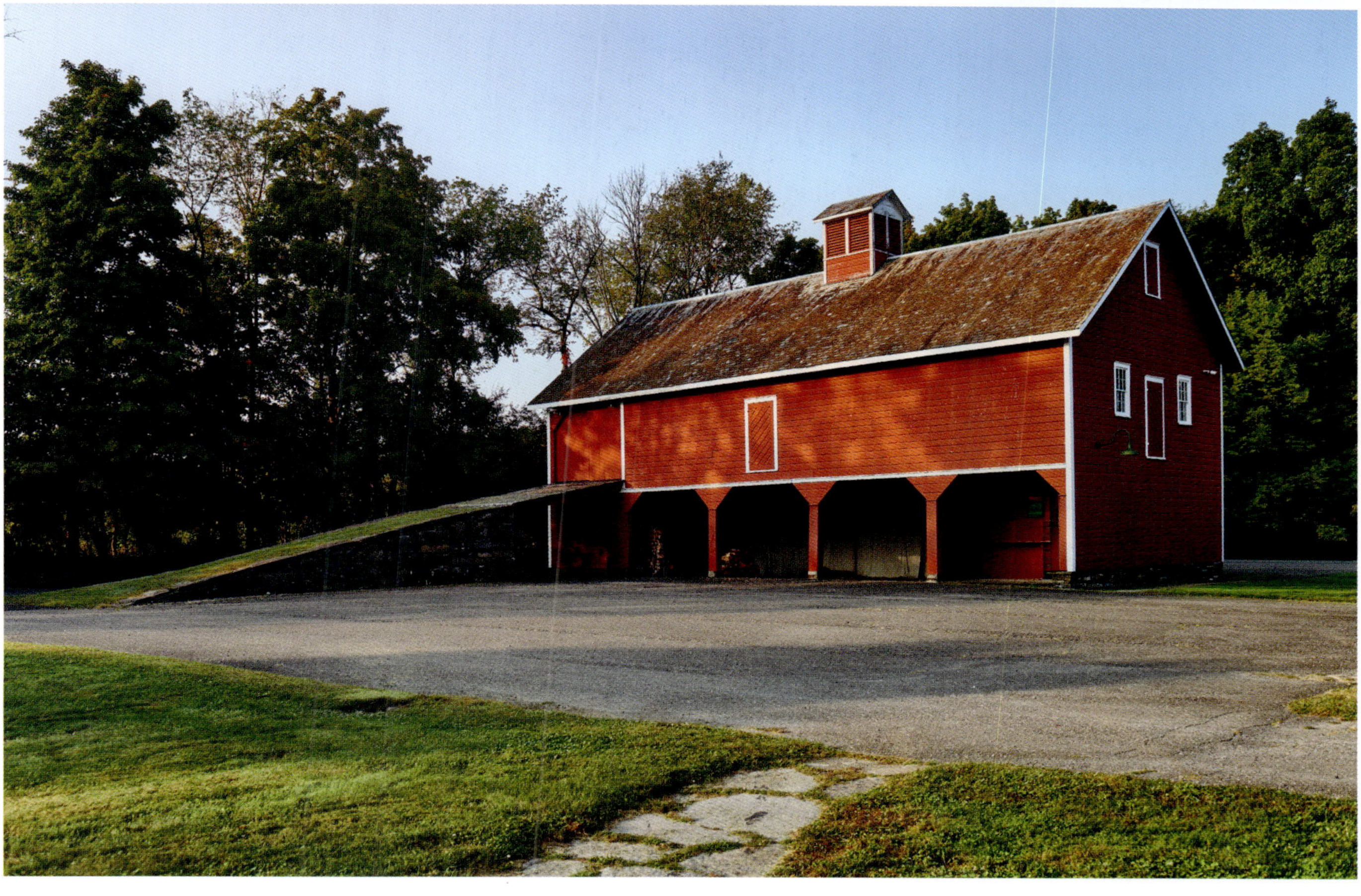

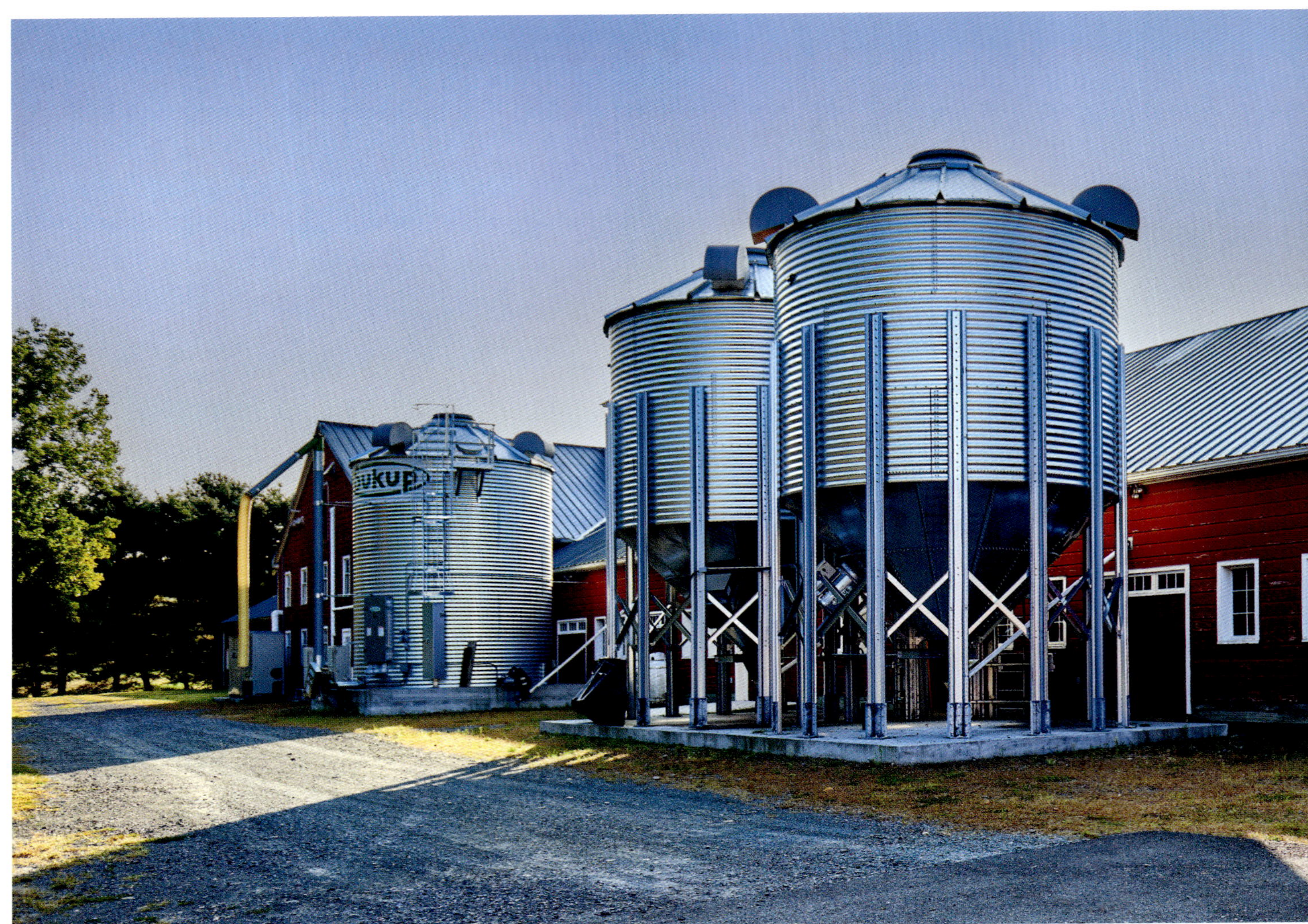

at Watervliet, slate roof and all, have been adapted again. The long sheep barn has been refitted with rooms to store grain, a water storage system, two giant copper stills, and a barrel room.

The redesigned tasting room will be ready to host the public in 2025, open just in time for Matt and Kim's first whiskeys, which are part of the Empire Rye whiskey program, unique to New York State. All the grain and the process must be completed in New York State. Silver Brothers Distillery's goal is to produce 100 percent of their grain on the farm. For the moment, a sweet mellow aroma wafts through the buildings—a scent of drinks to come.

above
The grain storage bins stand alongside the barn.

opposite, top
The previous owner used the barns to house the sheep. Imagine a long aisle that went the length of the building with sheep in open pens on either side. The distillery design divided the building into sections according to the whiskey-making process. Malted grains are stored near the entry of this section.

opposite, bottom
Grain is harvested from the farm and processed on the farm.

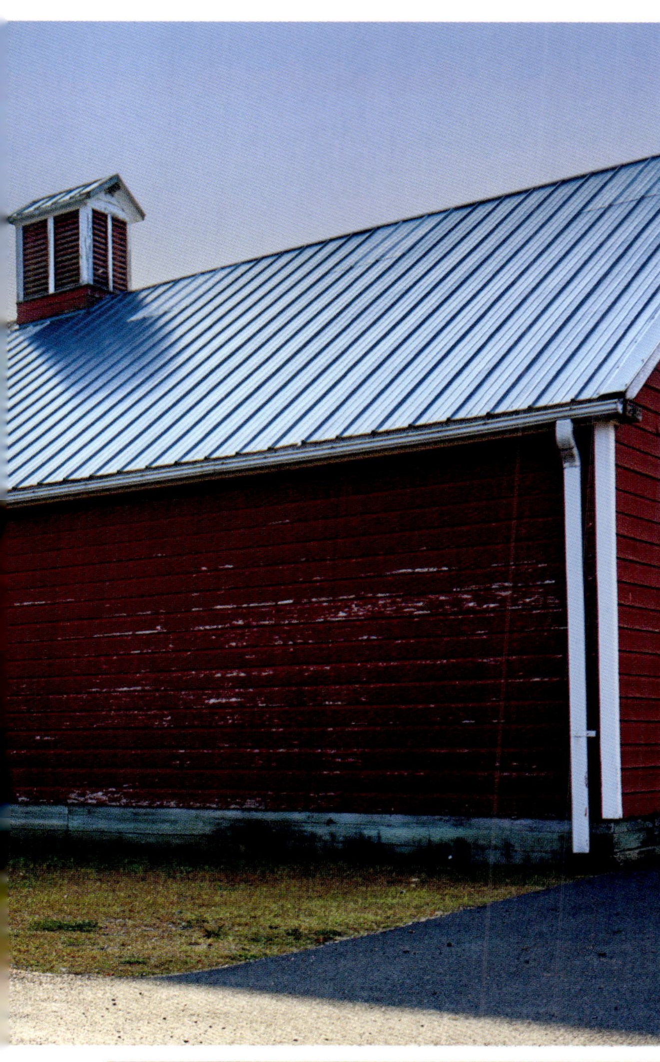

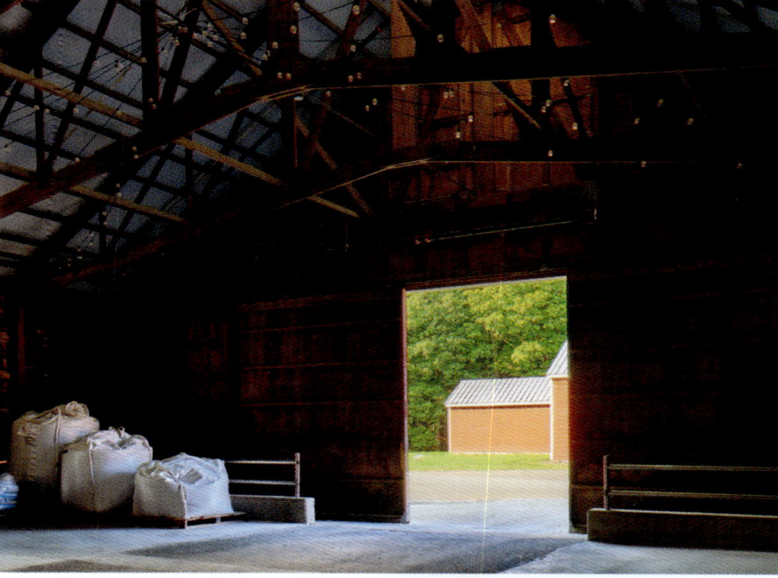

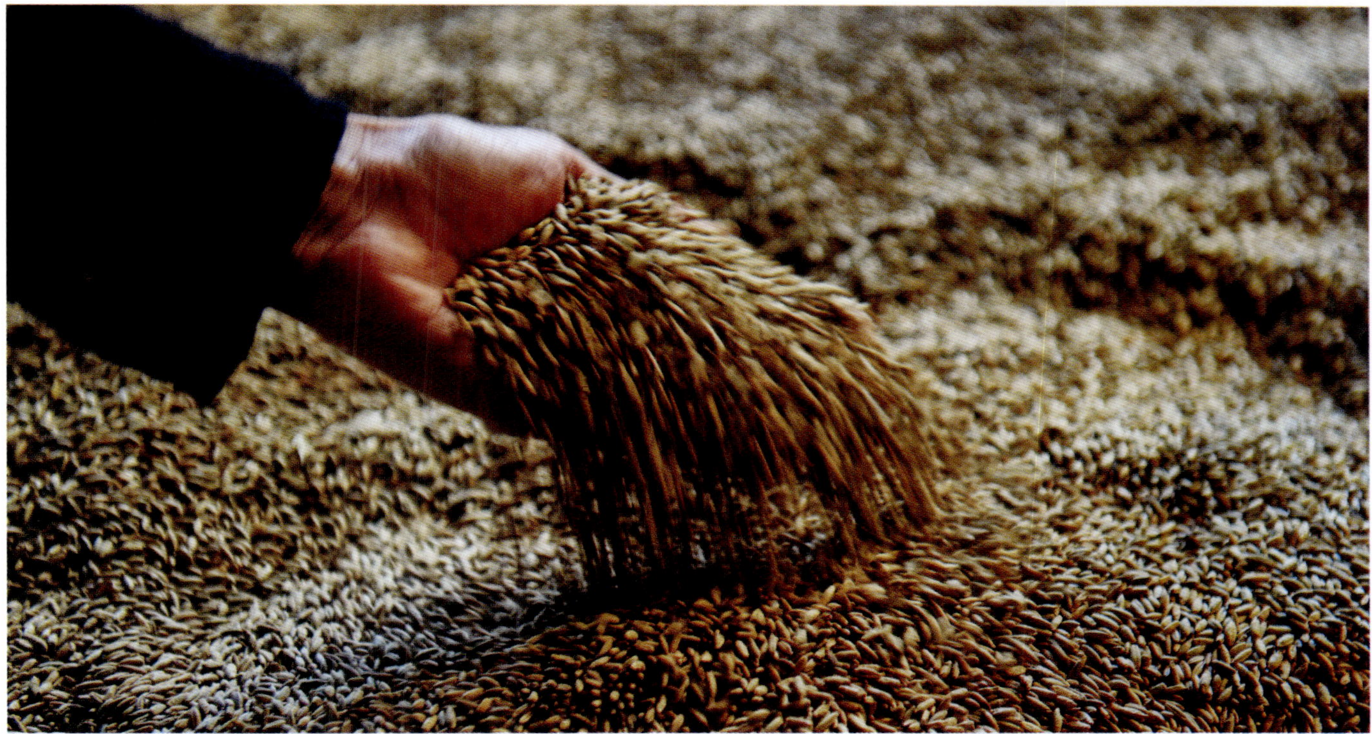

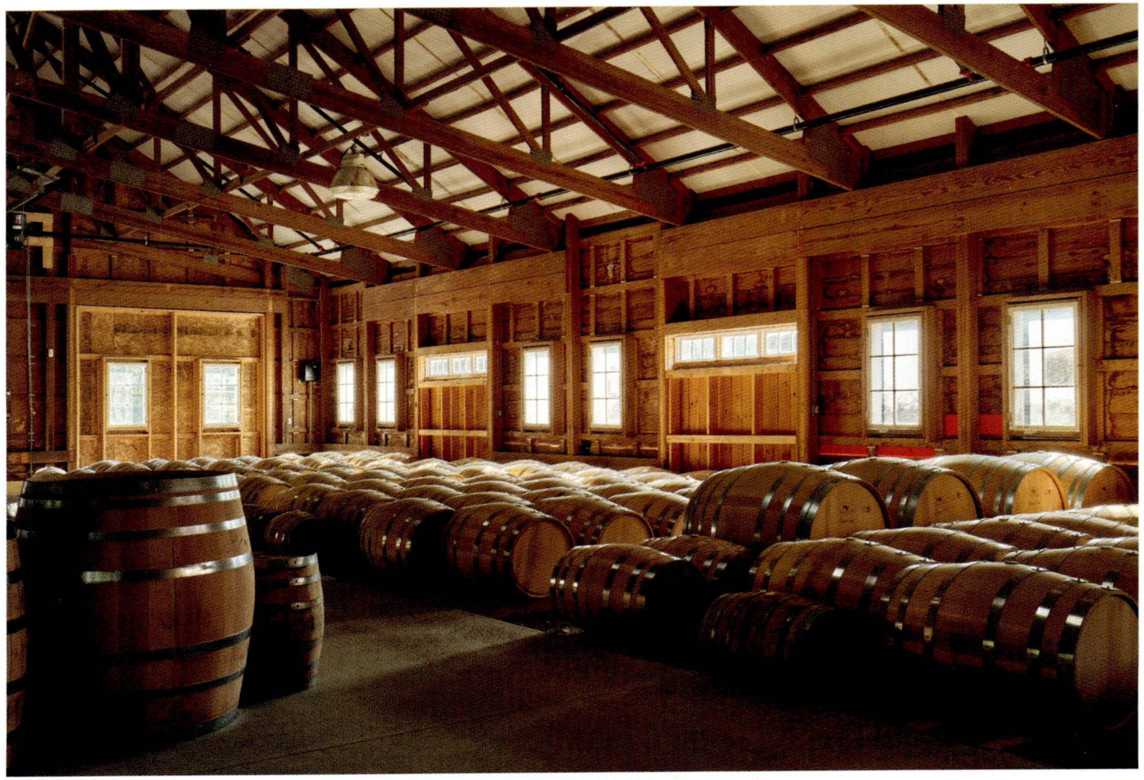

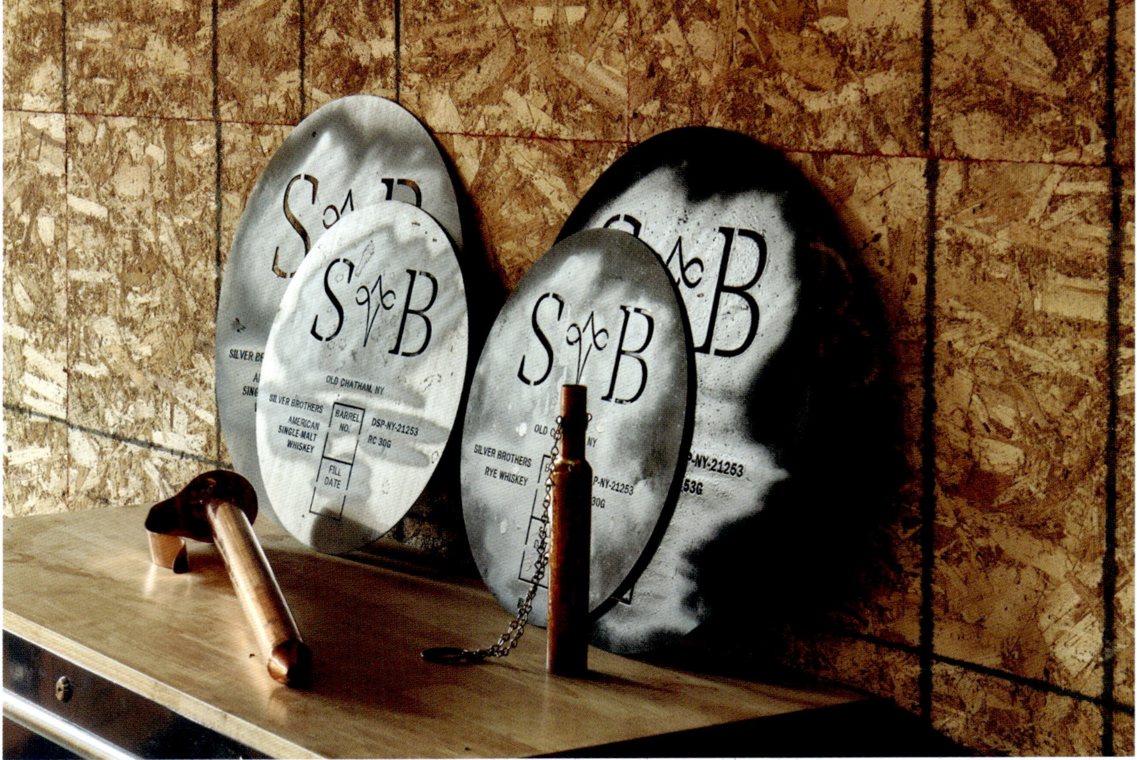

top
Barrels are purchased from a cooperage near Albany. The barrels are charred on the inside, which influences the flavor. The spirits will remain in the barrels for three years.

bottom
The Silver Brothers brand mark is applied to the barrels of whiskey with a barrel stencil. Other tools are used for testing and tasting the whiskey, and a mallet is used to close the barrels.

opposite
The copper stills were made in Louisville, Kentucky, by Vendome Copper & Brass Works. The spirit is at its most neutral pure point at this stage of the process.

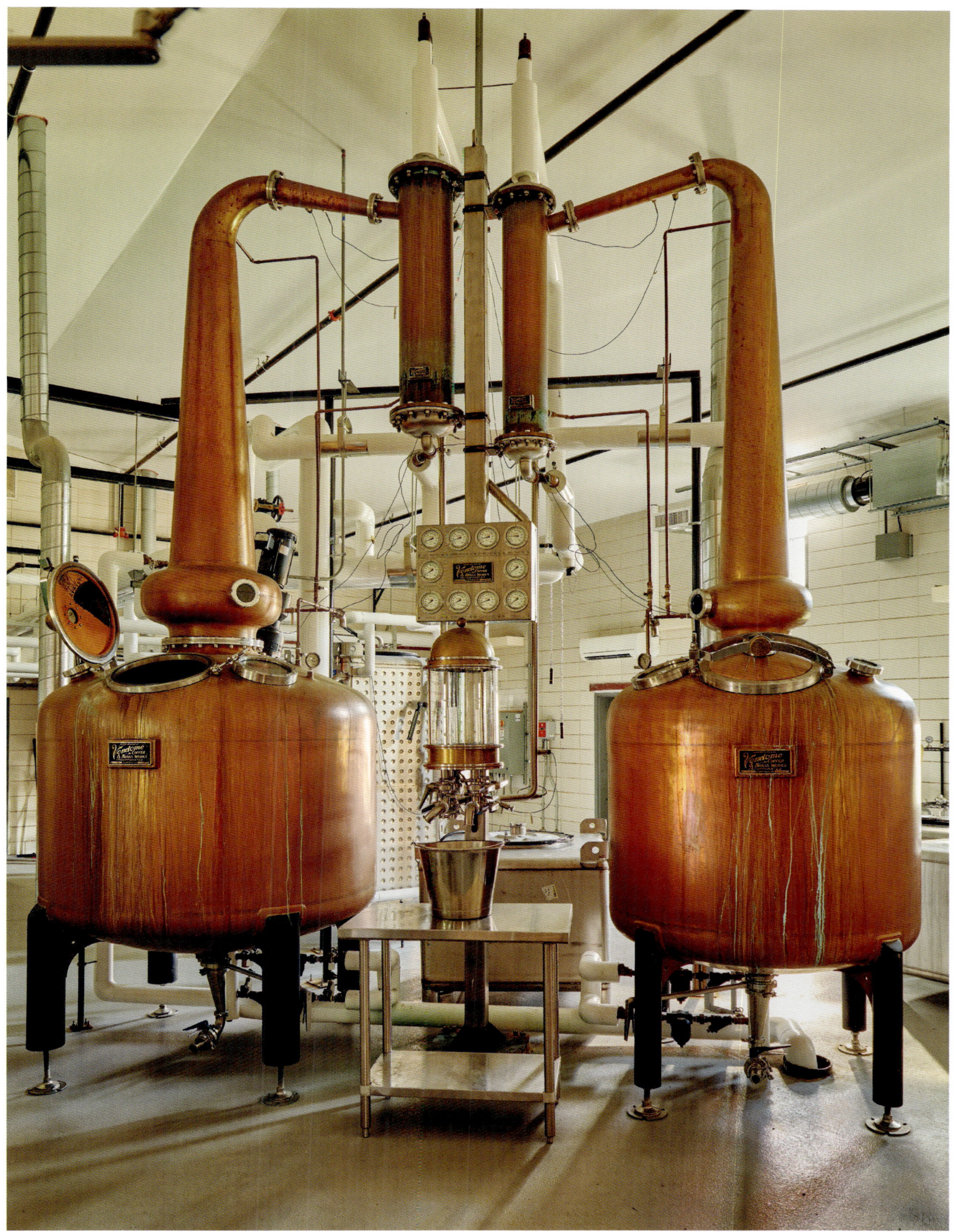

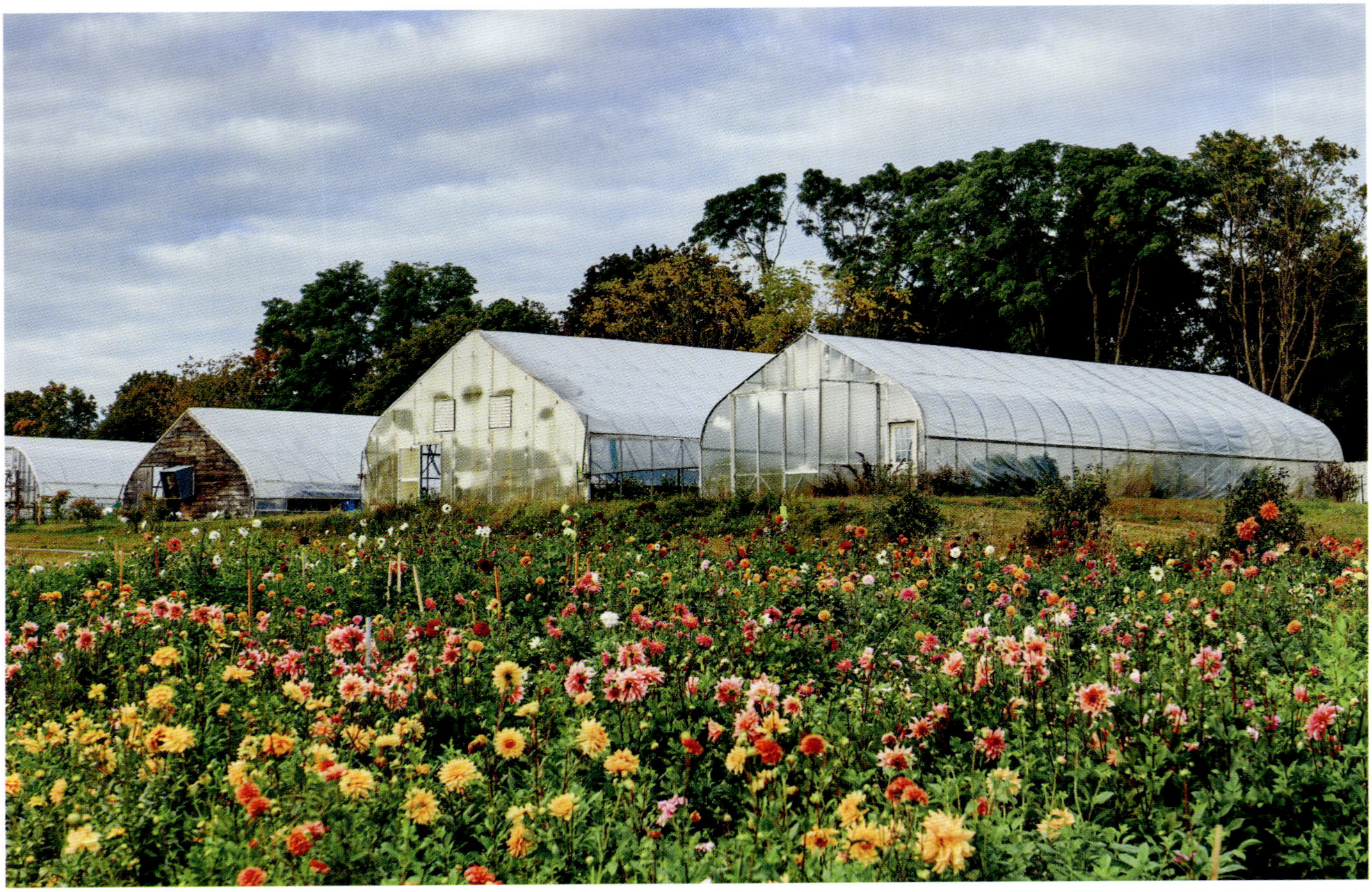

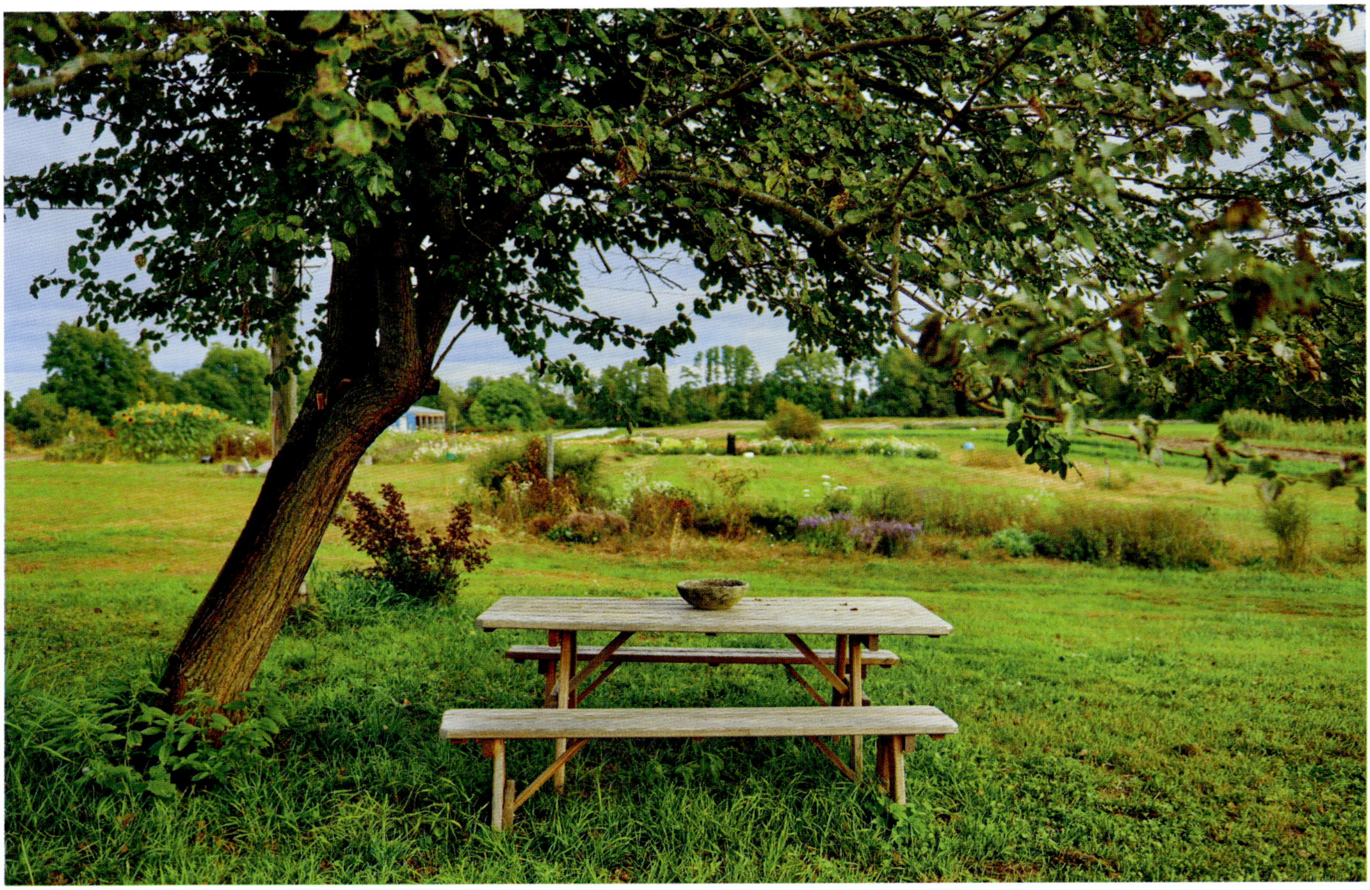

Damsel Garden

Stuyvesant, New York

Walking through the flower fields with Denise Pizzini, her enthusiasm is obvious. She moves slowly through the rows of flowers planted on her "just shy" of eighty-two acres farm. She lifts the drooping heads of dahlias, marveling over the size, shape, and color of each one. She starts to gather a bouquet; perhaps she will include these flowers in one of the sixty bouquets she takes to the Kinderhook farmers market on Saturdays.

Flowers are a big deal upstate. Some commercial farmers supply New York City's flower market. Others, like Damsel Garden, service the local community. Denise sells 100 percent of her flowers within Columbia County. Many of the flower farm owners, like the two sisters who run Cedar Farm Wholesale in Ghent, Marilyn Cederoth and Kate Swift, came over to meet Denise and offer her advice when she got started. Joe Gilbert from the Chatham Berry Farm also visited and made some suggestions.

Denise is a New Yorker. She grew up in New York City and built a life around urban farming. She went to work with schoolchildren, showing them how to grow plants. She and her husband, Evan Jahn, were both "West Siders"

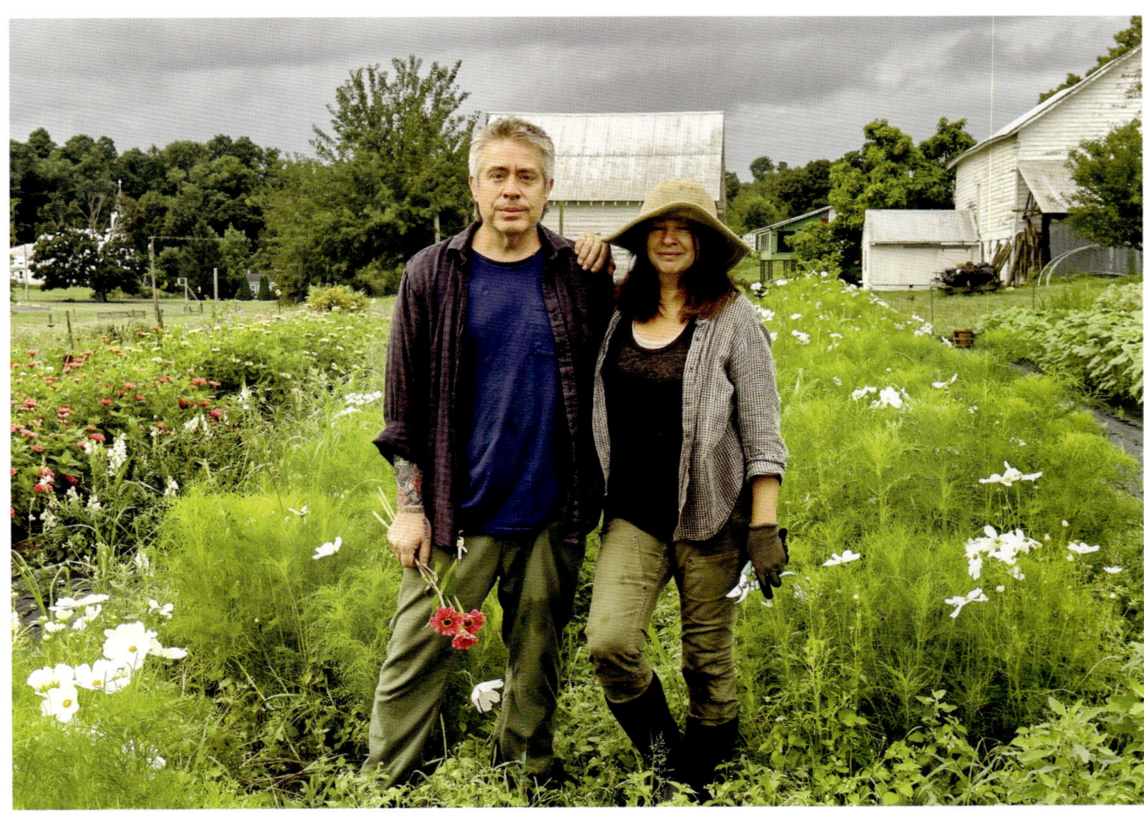

opposite, top
Looking through Denise Pizzini's fields of dahlias toward the five greenhouses.

opposite, bottom
A picnic table under a tree overlooks the flower fields before the dahlias bloomed.

above
Denise Pizzini and Evan Jahn on their flower farm in Stuyvesant, New York.

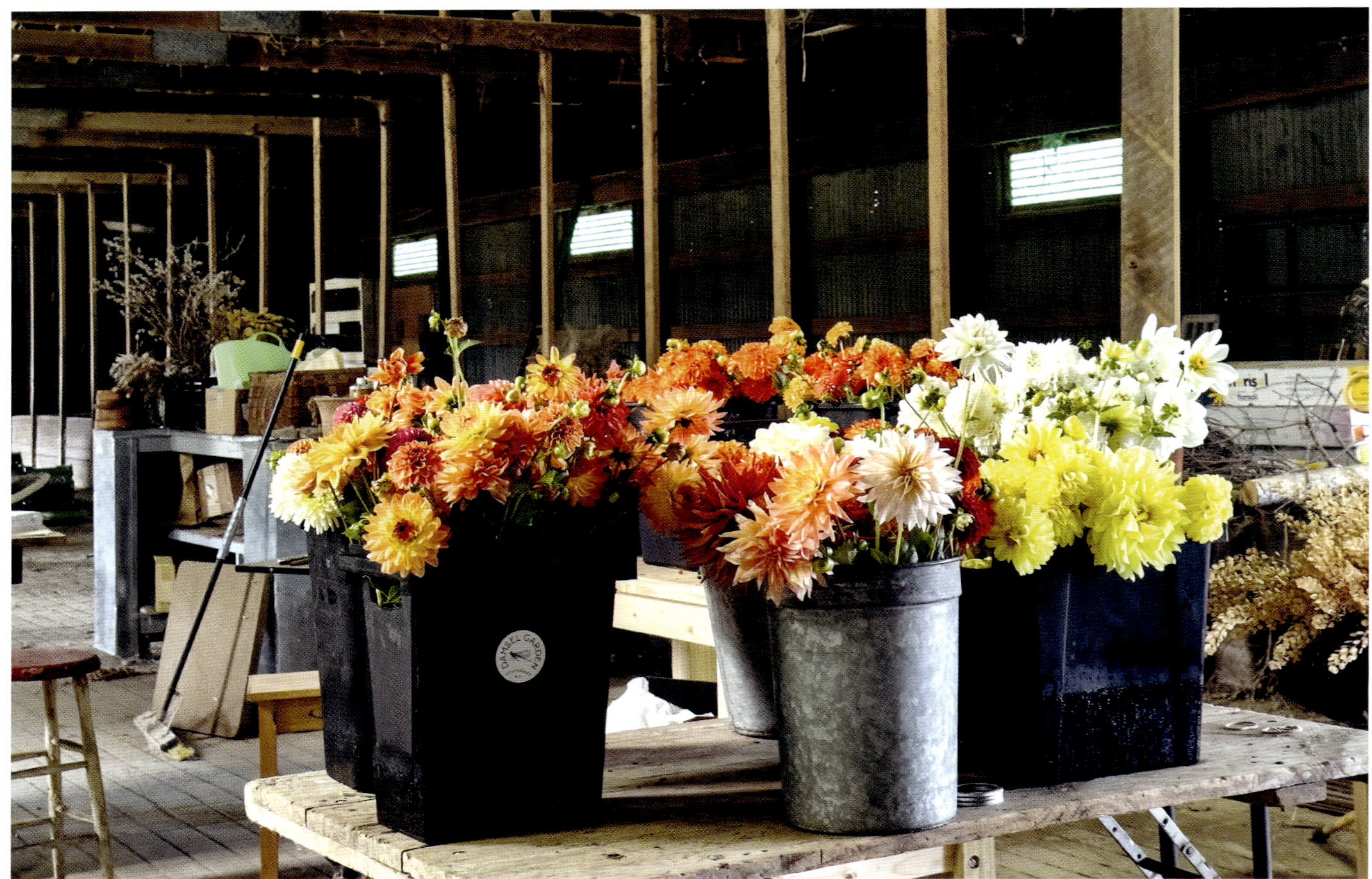

in Manhattan when they moved upstate in 2002. But she didn't start her flower farm until 2017. She relishes the time outside, working the land. Over the years she has had helpers, and friends and family pitch in, but most days she's by herself. However, during the COVID pandemic when Evan was able to work remotely, he too began working in the fields during his off hours.

Denise believes in and implements no-till and low-till methods of caring for and using the land. Her planting processes are regenerative. She doesn't want to wreck the soil with pesticides. She's reusing and cutting back on plastics at the farm. Waste is composted in piles. To keep things going, Denise leases land for a neighbor's Hereford cows, which came from England and are used in oxen teams and for pets. Some land is leased for strawberries. Her goal, she shares, is to "be in a business that makes people happy."

above
Buckets of bouquets are ready to go to the Kinderhook flower market. Denise uses a mile of twine a year wrapping bouquets for market. One of the barns is fitted with a cold room to keep flowers fresh.

opposite, top
As the leaves are starting to change in the trees that border the farm, the dahlias are reaching their peak. Denise plans and organizes how and which flowers are planted in which field or greenhouse. In the spring, she sells shares in a tulip CSA.

opposite, bottom left
Dahlias from Damsel Gardens.

opposite, bottom right
Dahlias are in full bloom in September in upstate New York, including a red variety.

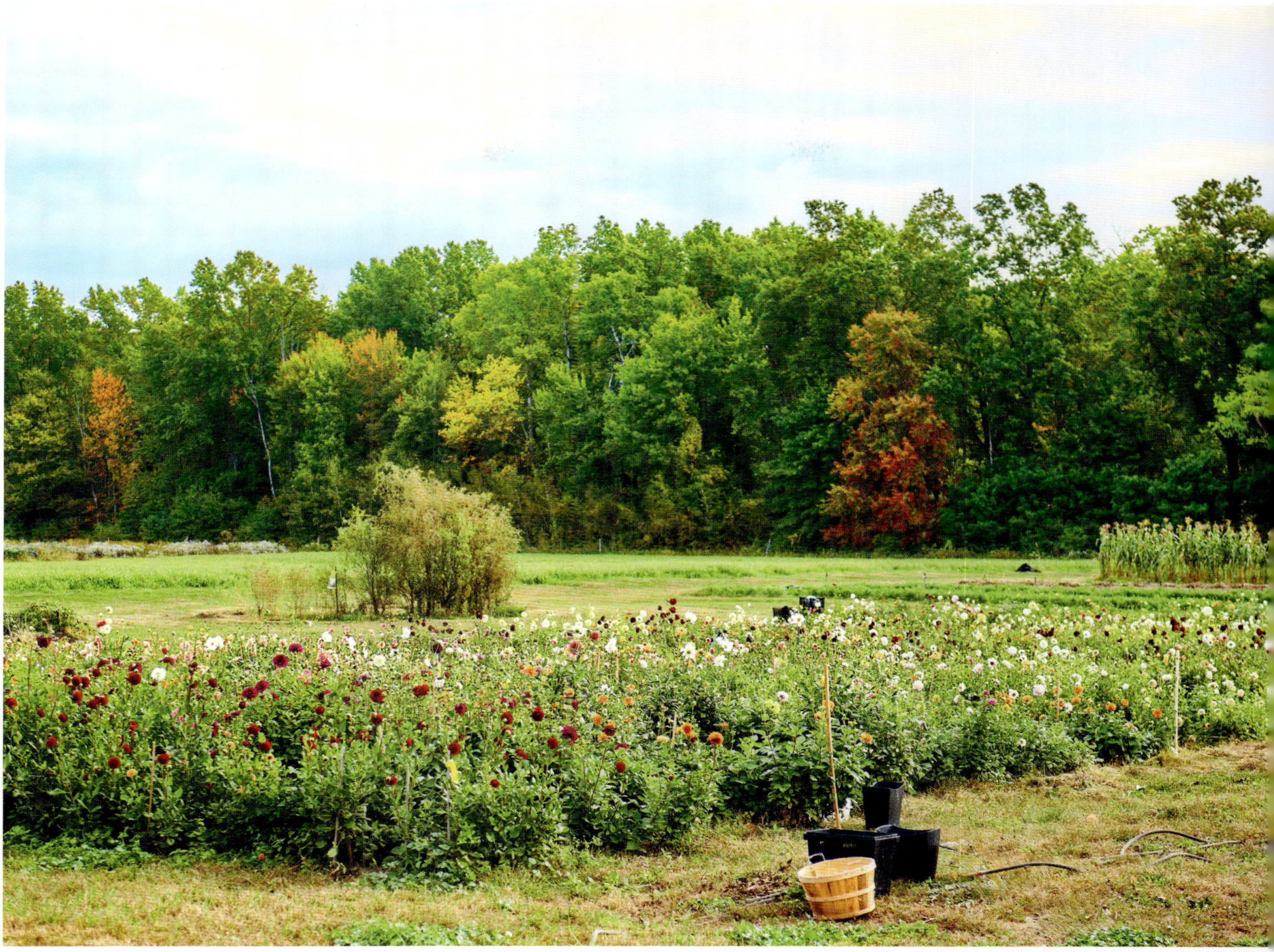

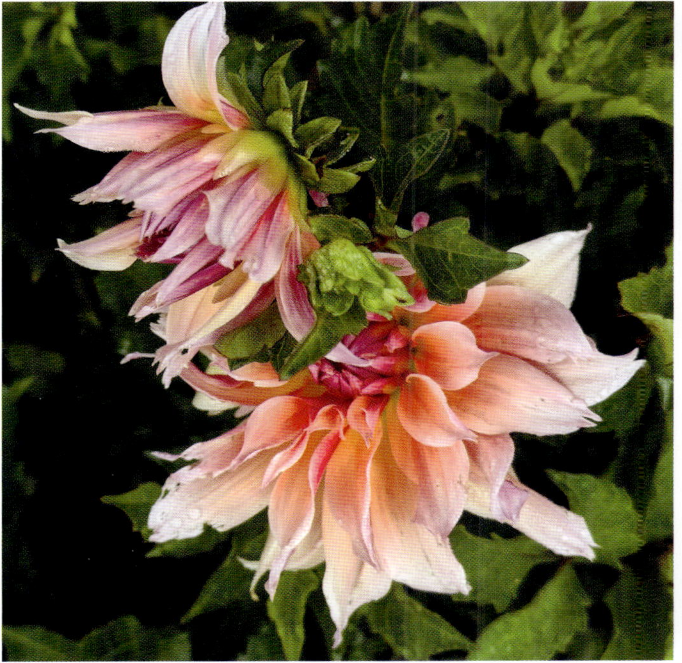

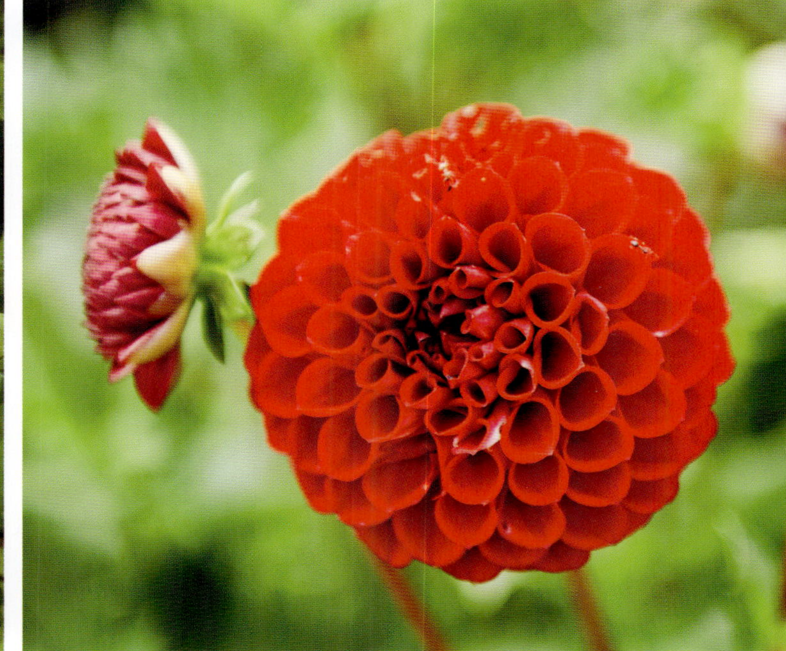

Cafe Mutton

Hudson, New York

Cafe Mutton is located on the corner of a busy street and a quiet street in Hudson, New York. It is that combination of slow and fast that makes sense, especially after you take a bite of anything you order in chef/owner Shaina Loew-Banayan's restaurant. Take, for instance, a recent radicchio salad: artfully arranged dark pinkish and off-white leaves of two different kinds of the bitter Italian lettuce arrive on a vintage plate. The impulse is to devour the whole dish at once. But that's not possible. Covered in a creamy dressing, with cool cucumbers, chives, and breadcrumbs toasted in butter, each bite has a savory crunch that must be eaten slowly. And when you do slow down, you start to look around the tiny place that's filled with mismatched antique-looking furnishings. Two of the main window walls look directly out on the street.

About five years ago, Shaina stopped in Hudson, New York, while passing through on a trip back to New York City. They and their partner felt welcome in the town and decided to make the move upstate. After years of working in some of New York City's best restaurants, they weren't thinking about opening their own place but just getting a job. Shaina found one at the Bartlett House, a local bakery in Ghent about twenty minutes northeast of Hudson. After two years there, a friend mentioned that a space in Hudson was available for sublet. They stopped by to look at the corner shop, which had a previous life as an auto parts store.

They took the space in February and opened their restaurant in May 2021, just as people were starting to eat inside after the pandemic. A reporter from the *Times Union* wrote a glowing review. Food author and former restaurant critic Ruth Reichl gave a mention on her Instagram. Then in June 2022, *Bon Appétit* wrote about the restaurant and the *New York Times* added it to "Our 50 Favorite Restaurants of 2022." Lines started to form around the corner. Shaina served bowls of cereal to those waiting.

Shaina describes their goal as a desire "to make honest food with spirit behind it." They place an emphasis on meat in their dishes. There are other small independent restaurants on the Columbia Street block, including Lil' Deb's Oasis and the Bodega Aguila Real. Shaina says they are happy to be part of the growing scene.

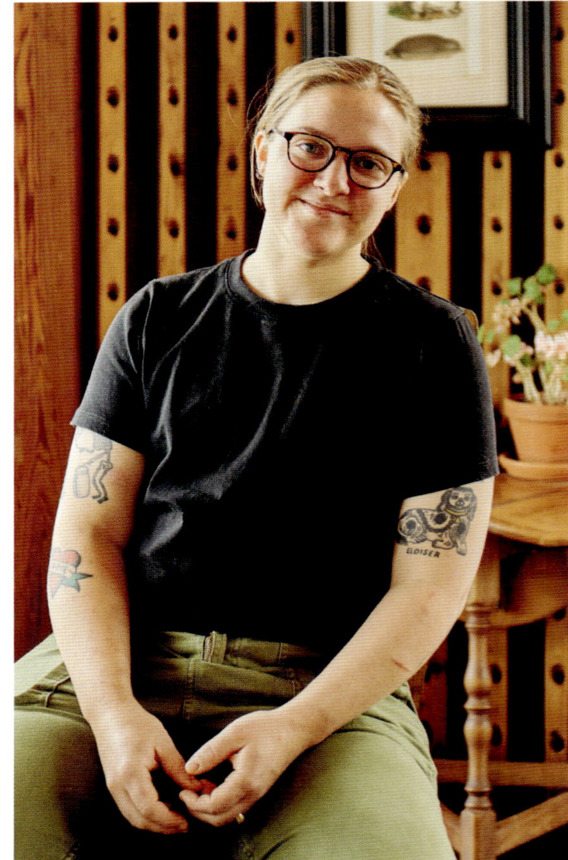

right
The chef/owner of Cafe Mutton, Shaina Loew-Banayan.

opposite
Cafe Mutton is in a former auto parts store on one of Hudson's main streets. The storefront display platform is used for seating inside.

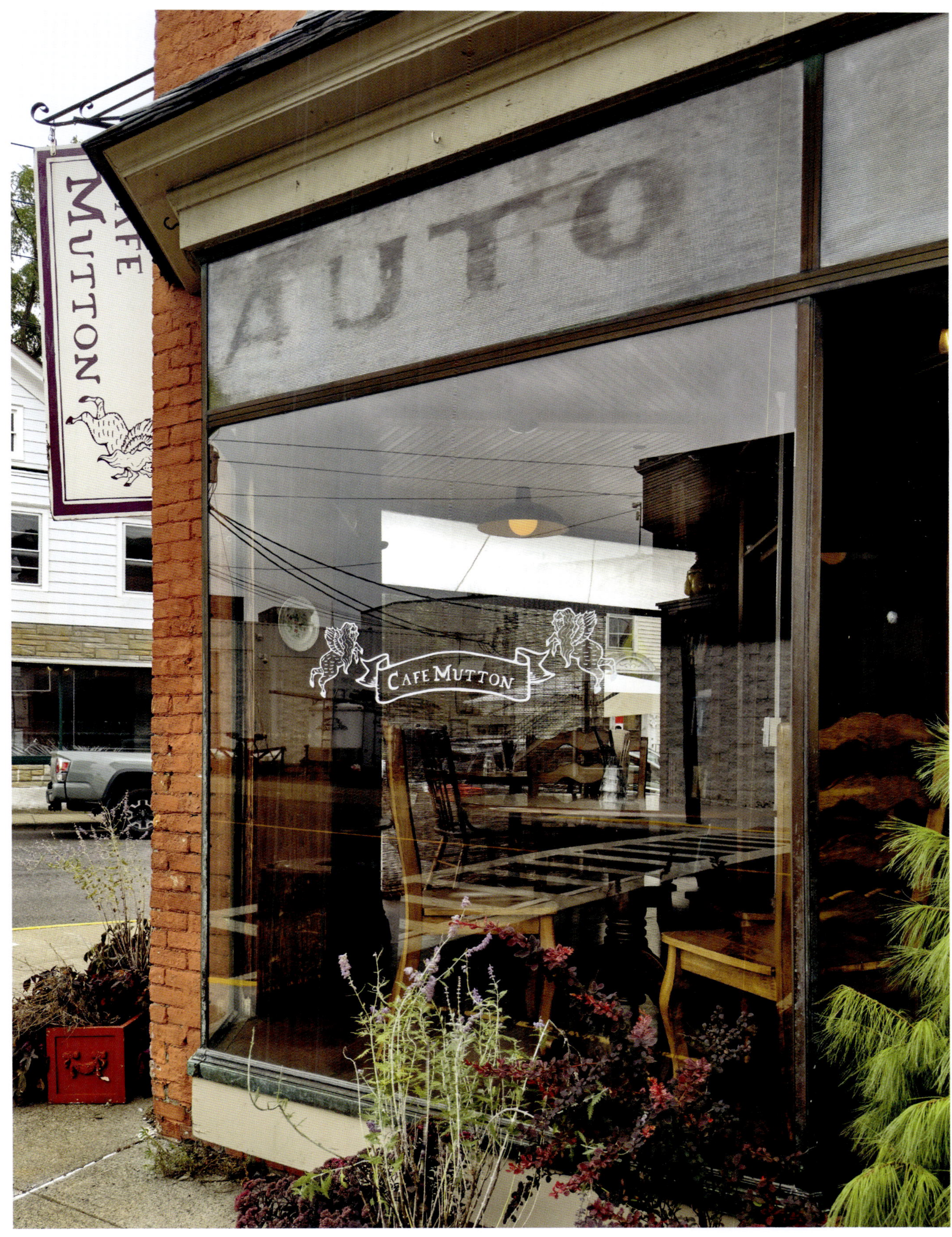
MUTTON
AUTO
CAFE MUTTON

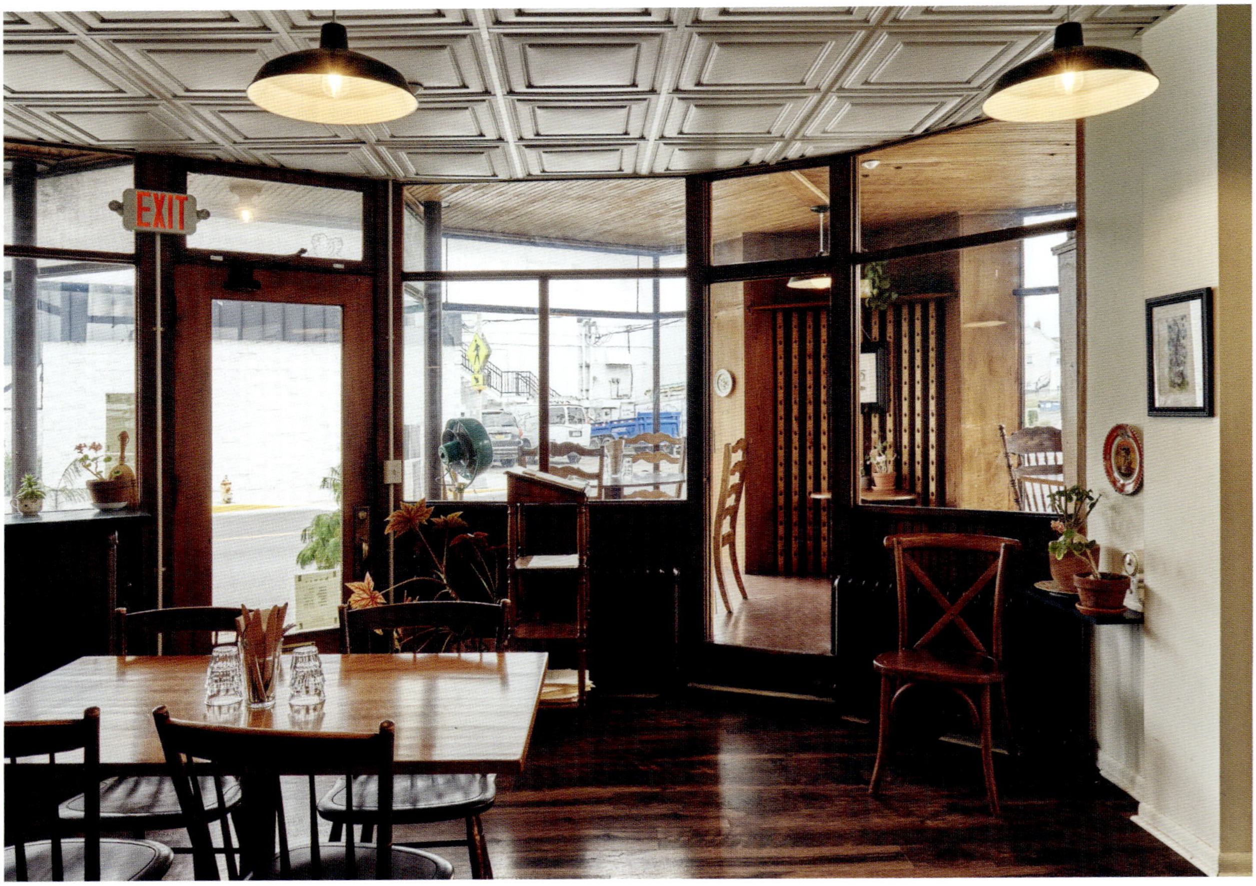

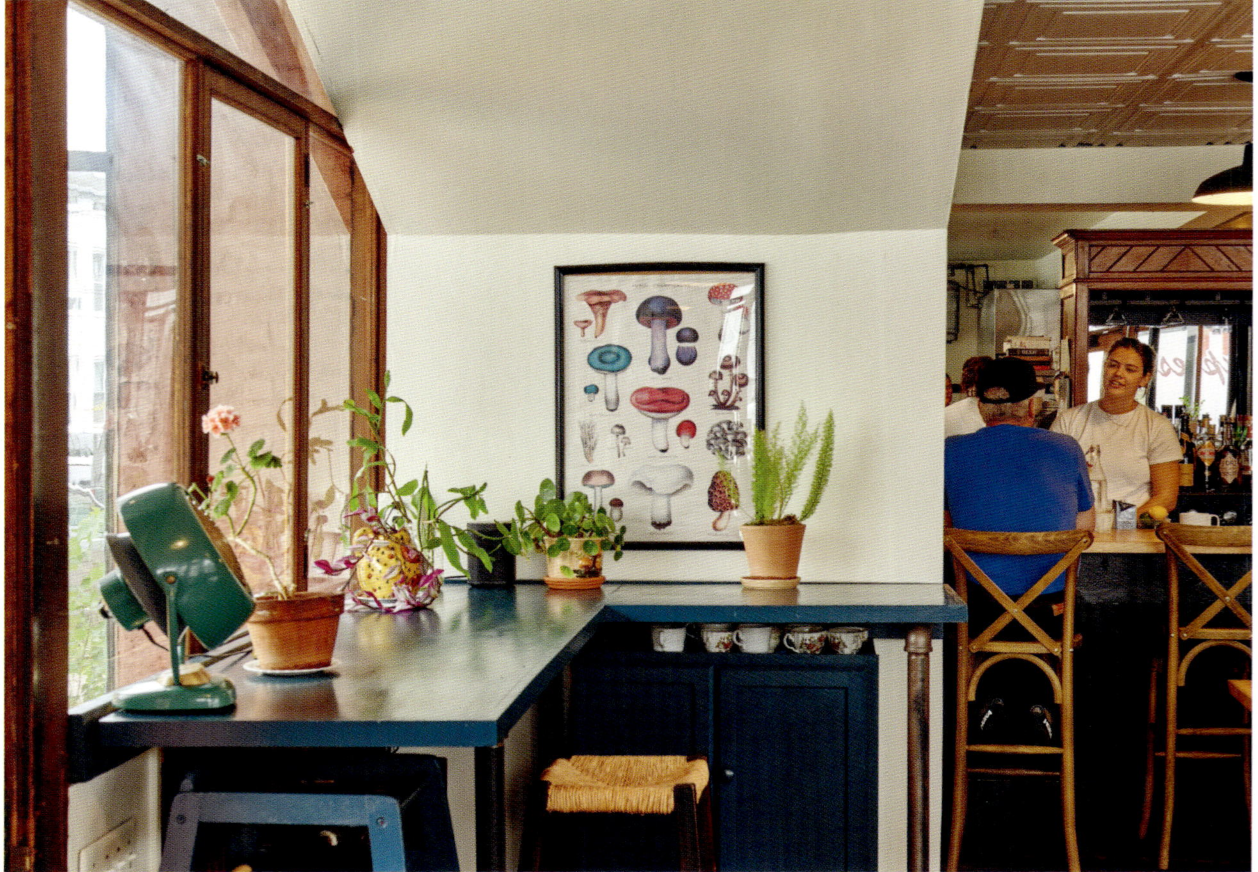

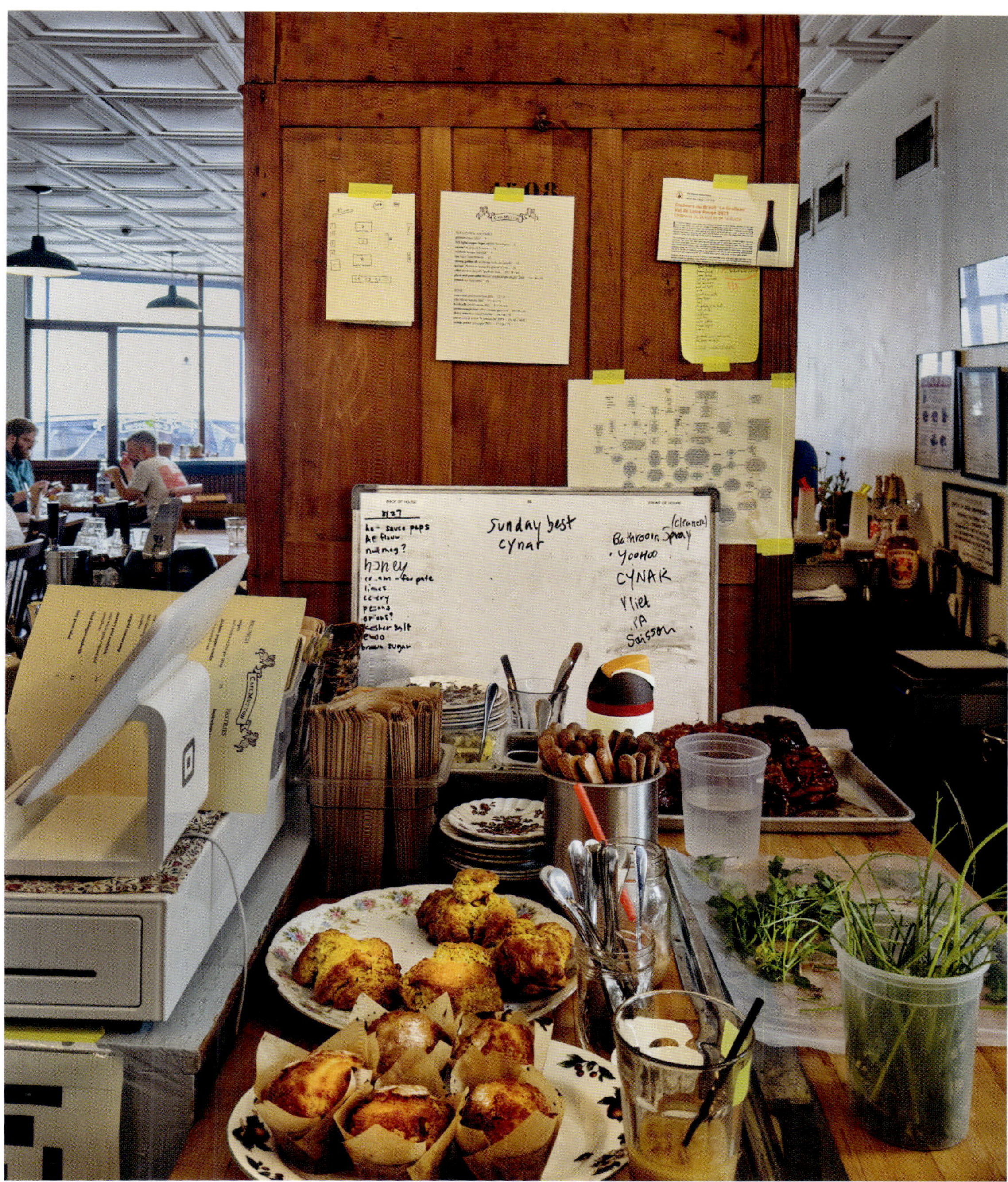

opposite, top
Out front, the restaurant has several options for seating. One is in the front window. A raised platform and a wall of windows create a separate, more intimate space.

opposite, bottom
A corner counter and one near the kitchen create additional seating in the modest restaurant.

above
Behind the scenes, the kitchen is a busy hub. Baked goods are prepared for breakfast service. A cabinet acts as a room divider between the kitchen and the front counter.

Bread Alone

Boiceville, New York

Nels Leader grew up upstate. His family made the move up from New York City in the 1980s when he was four. His parents worked in the New York City restaurant world—his father, Dan Leader, as a chef and his mother, Lynne Gilson, in the front of house. While traveling in France as a culinary student, Dan toured French bakeries. He decided to use that knowledge to make organic bread in the Catskills town of Boiceville, where there was more room to spread out. Dan brought over Frenchman and oven mason Andre Lefort to build two traditional wood-fired ovens at their then new bakery. Those ovens are still in use at the original site.

Over time, the business evolved: Dan retired, Sharon Burns-Leader remains the co-owner of the bakery, and Nels is now the CEO. Nels has built upon the values and principles he learned from his parents of protecting the environment, using the best organic ingredients, and creating a supportive management system within the company. Bread Alone added solar arrays to both their renovated bakery in Boiceville and the new production bakery in Kingston. The company's goal is to become carbon neutral by 2030. In fact, the Boiceville location is a net-zero facility. Nels is also leading the company toward an employee-ownership future. All their breads have had and continue to have organic status from the beginning of organic certification in the United States in 2002.

In 2024, they expanded to add an outdoor pizza oven in Boiceville. The pizza pies pulled from the nine-hundred-degree oven rival those made in Naples, Italy: thin, pliable crust, a tangy tomato sauce, and creamy mozzarella cheese plus a list of other toppings. At the opening, a steady stream of customers lined up to order. As Sharon said then, "In making bread, you have to feed your starter for it to grow." At Bread Alone, Nels, Sharon, and their teams are doing just that, riffing off the original idea of making great bread and being "earth conscious" while growing their business.

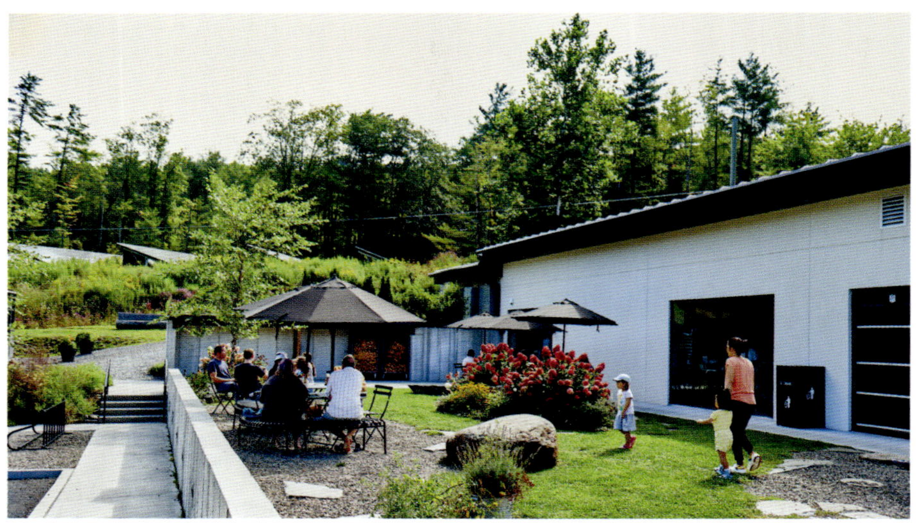

above
A view of the side garden's green space and a glimpse of the solar array in the background.

opposite, top
The 2022 renovation of the original Bread Alone bakery, nestled in the Catskill Mountains, included a 350-kilowatt solar array and an expanded terrace for outdoor dining.

opposite, bottom
The front terrace is next to the bakery's retail shop. On Sundays, the customer mix is New Yorkers headed back to the City after the weekend and locals relaxing on the patio. Dogs are welcome outside.

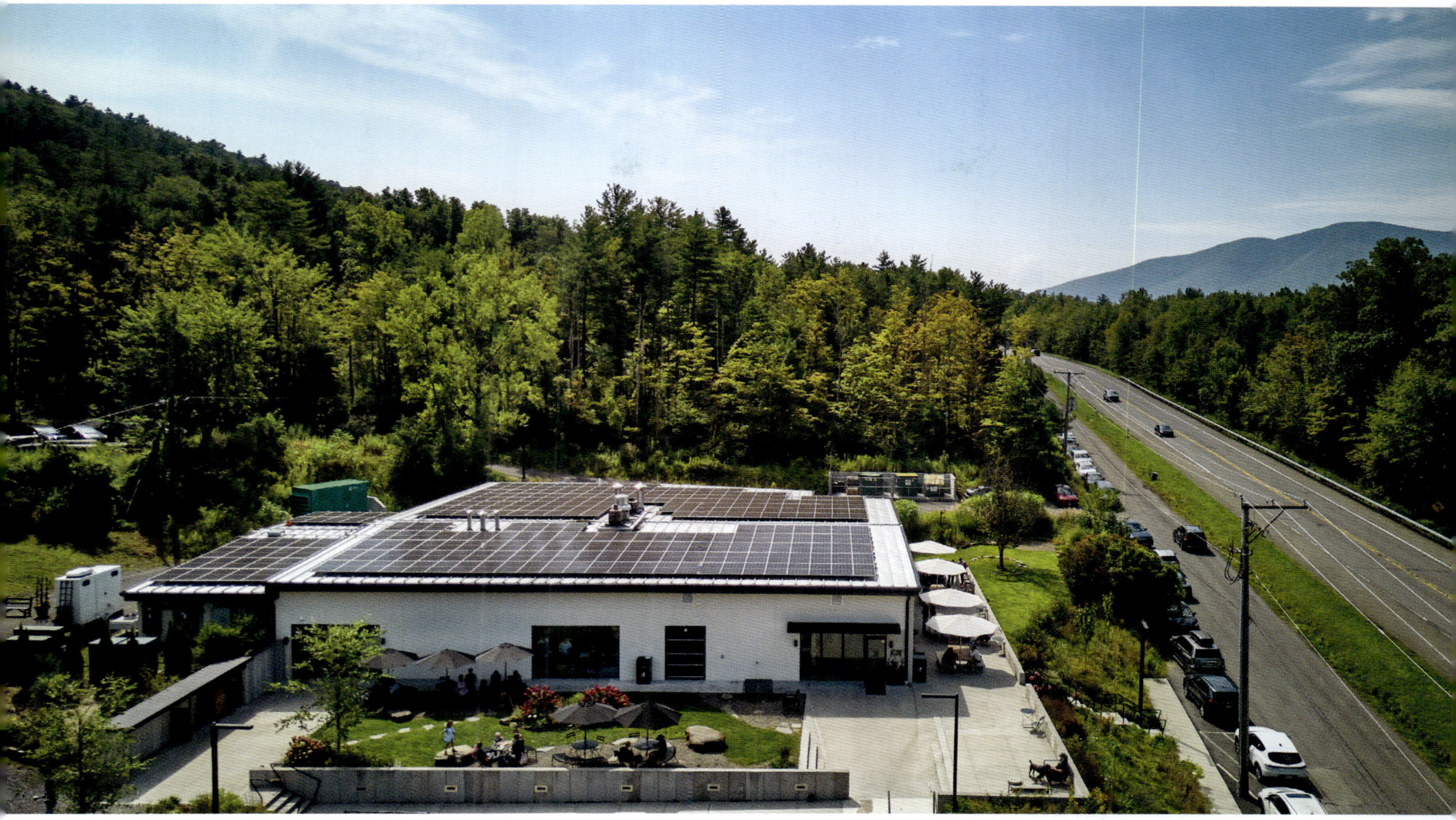

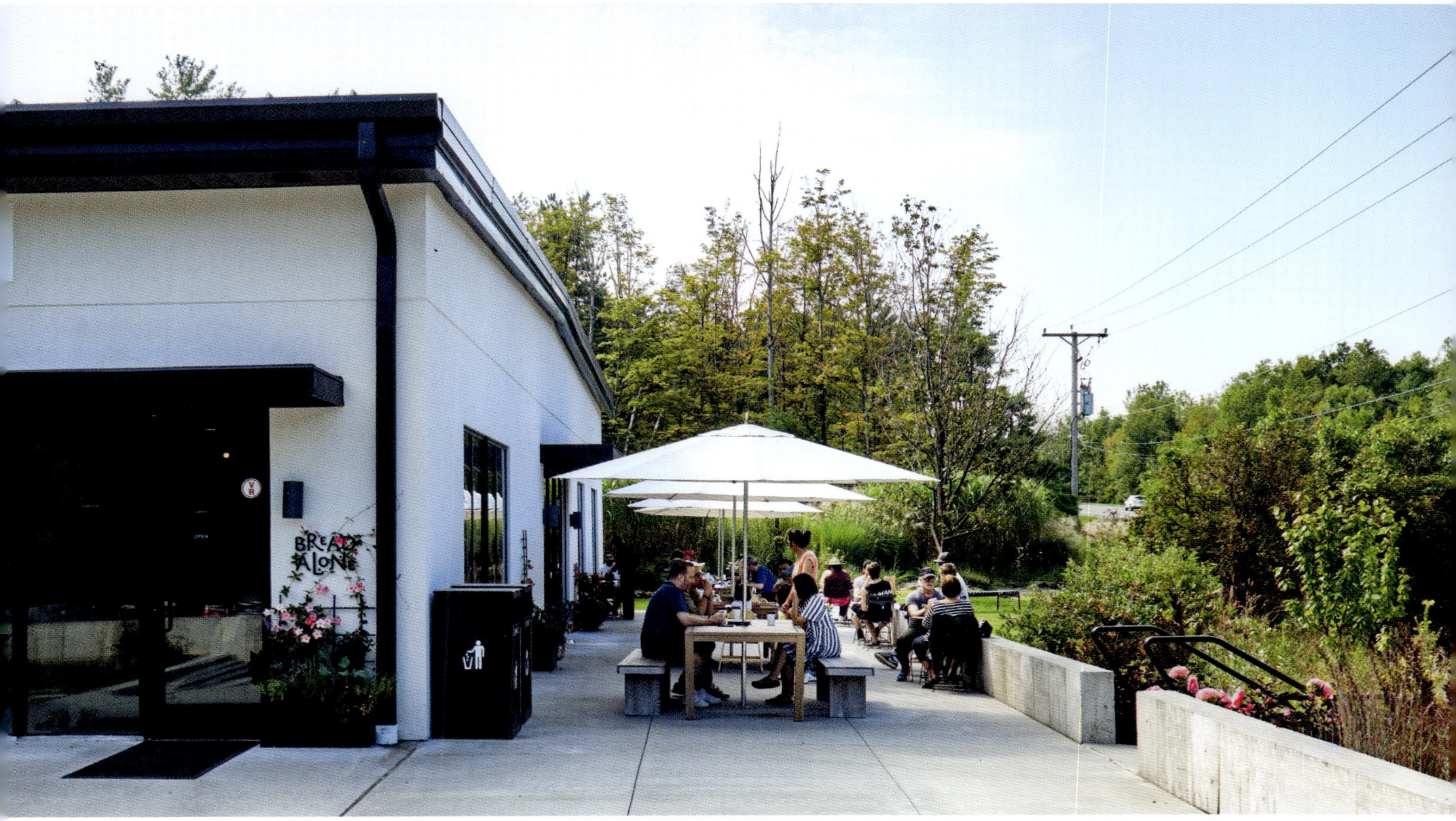

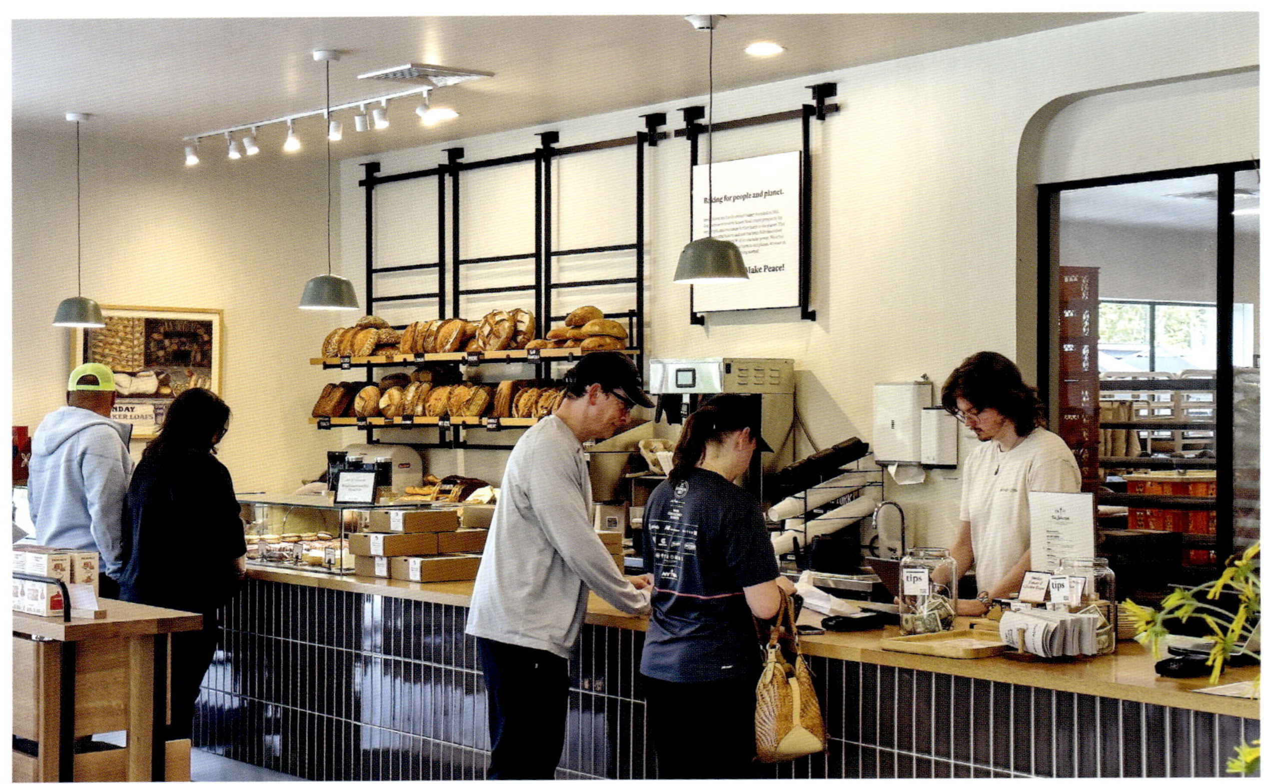

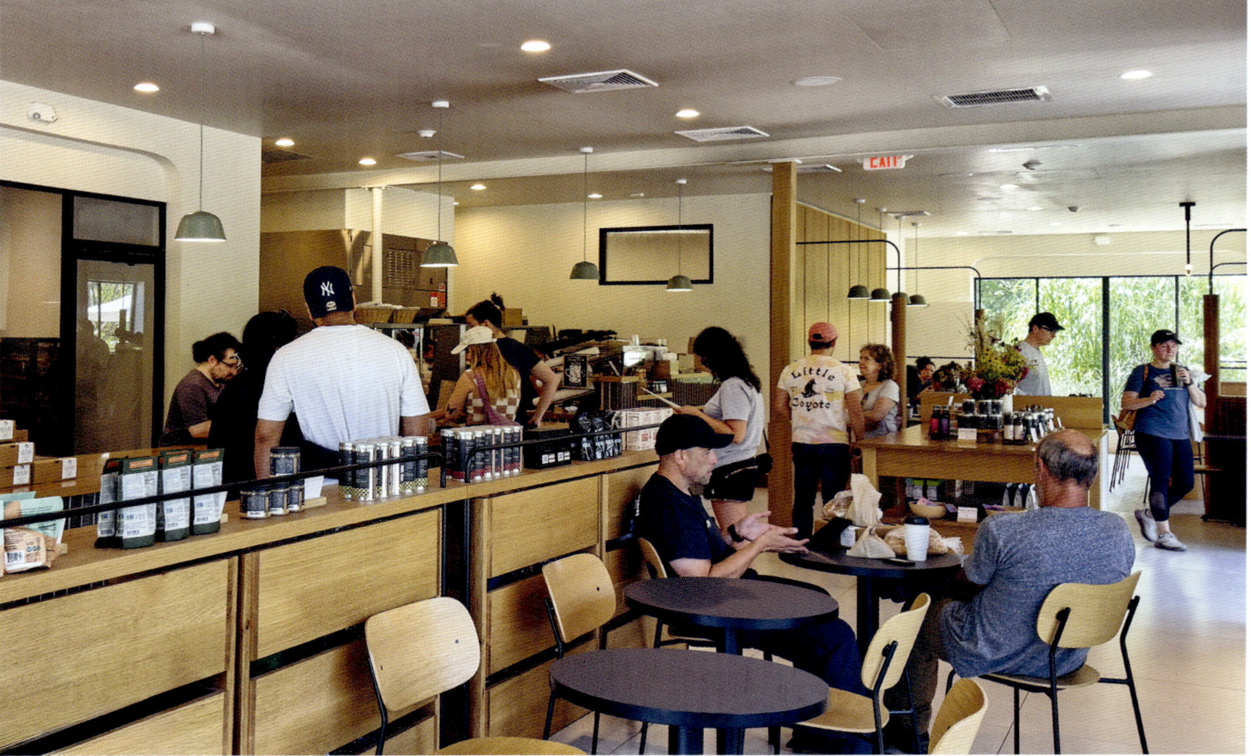

The interior of the bakery café is modern and bright, with big picture windows bringing in natural light in front and on either side. Patrons can sit inside or out. A variety of breads and pastries are on offer.

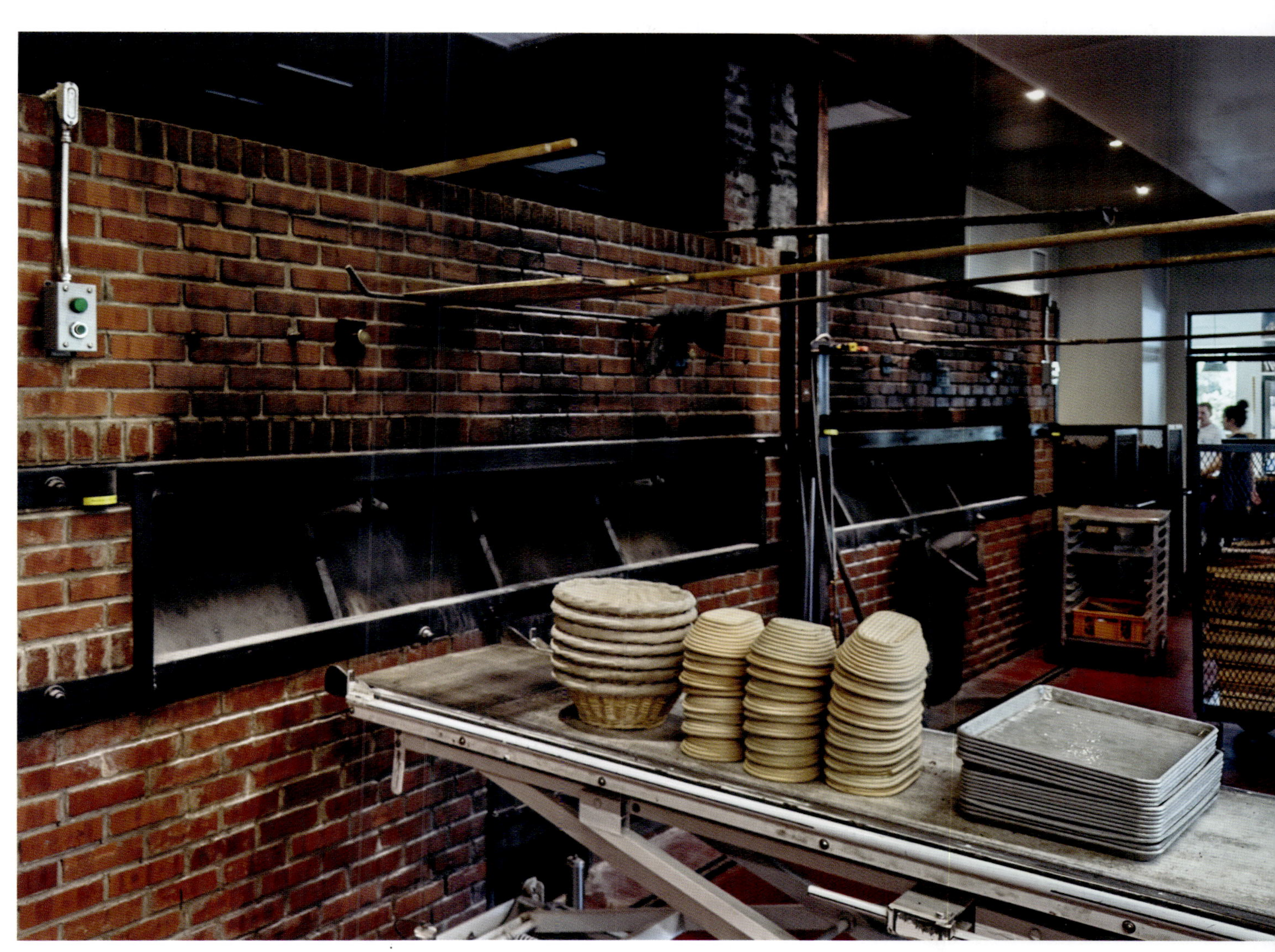

The original Lefort ovens were built on-site using local brick on the outside and French brick inside.

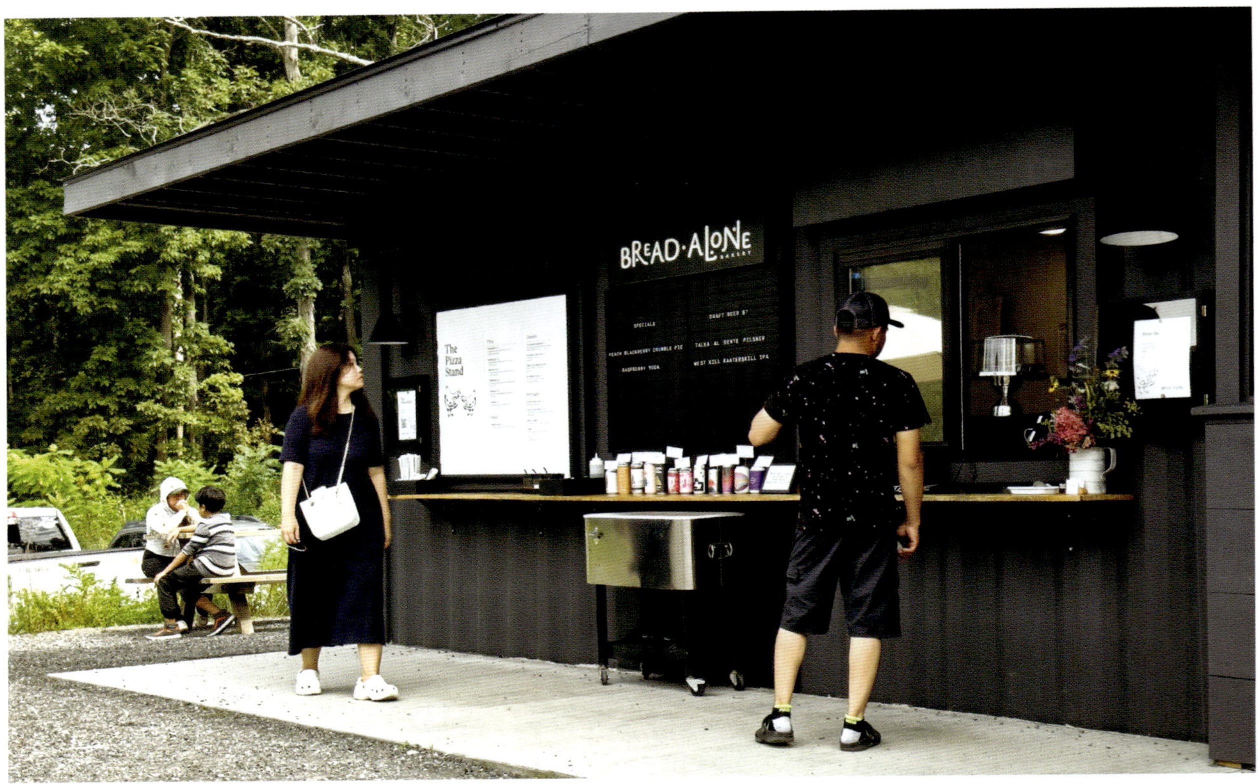

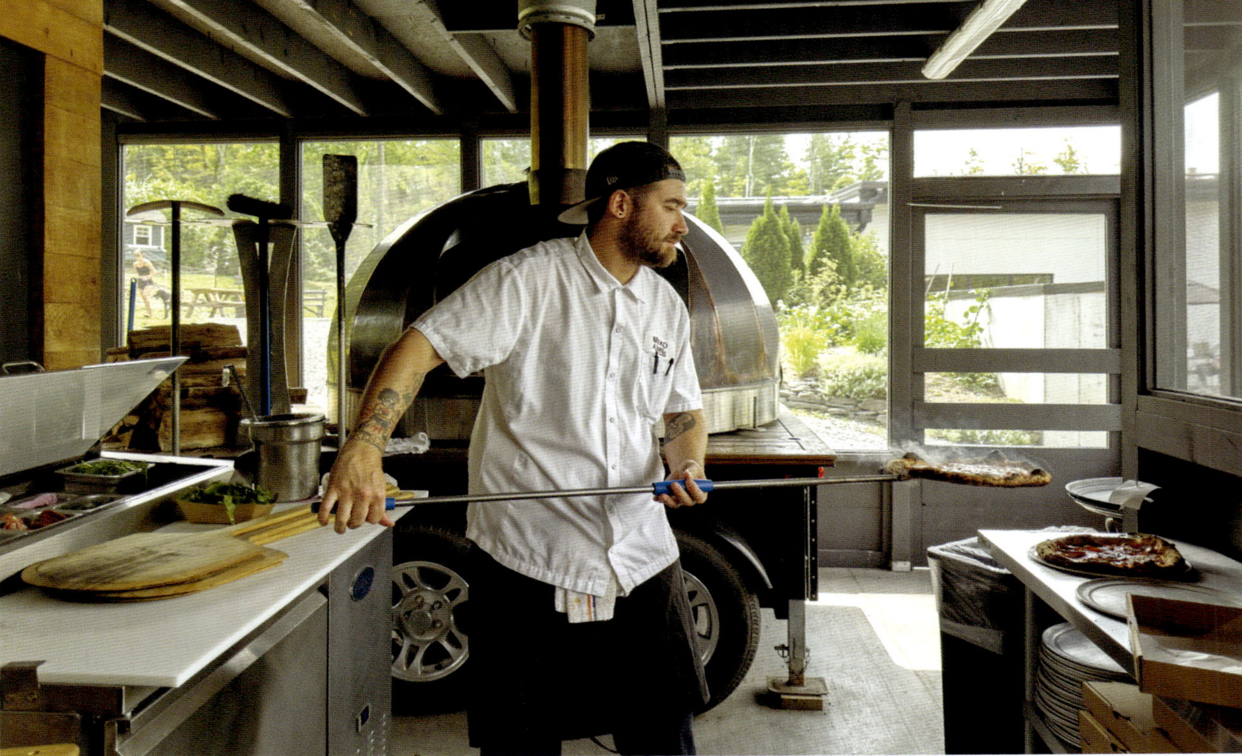

top
The Bread Alone pizza stand at the launch weekend in August 2024.

bottom
Blessing Schuman-Strange brings out steaming hot pizza pies from the new on-site woodburning oven.

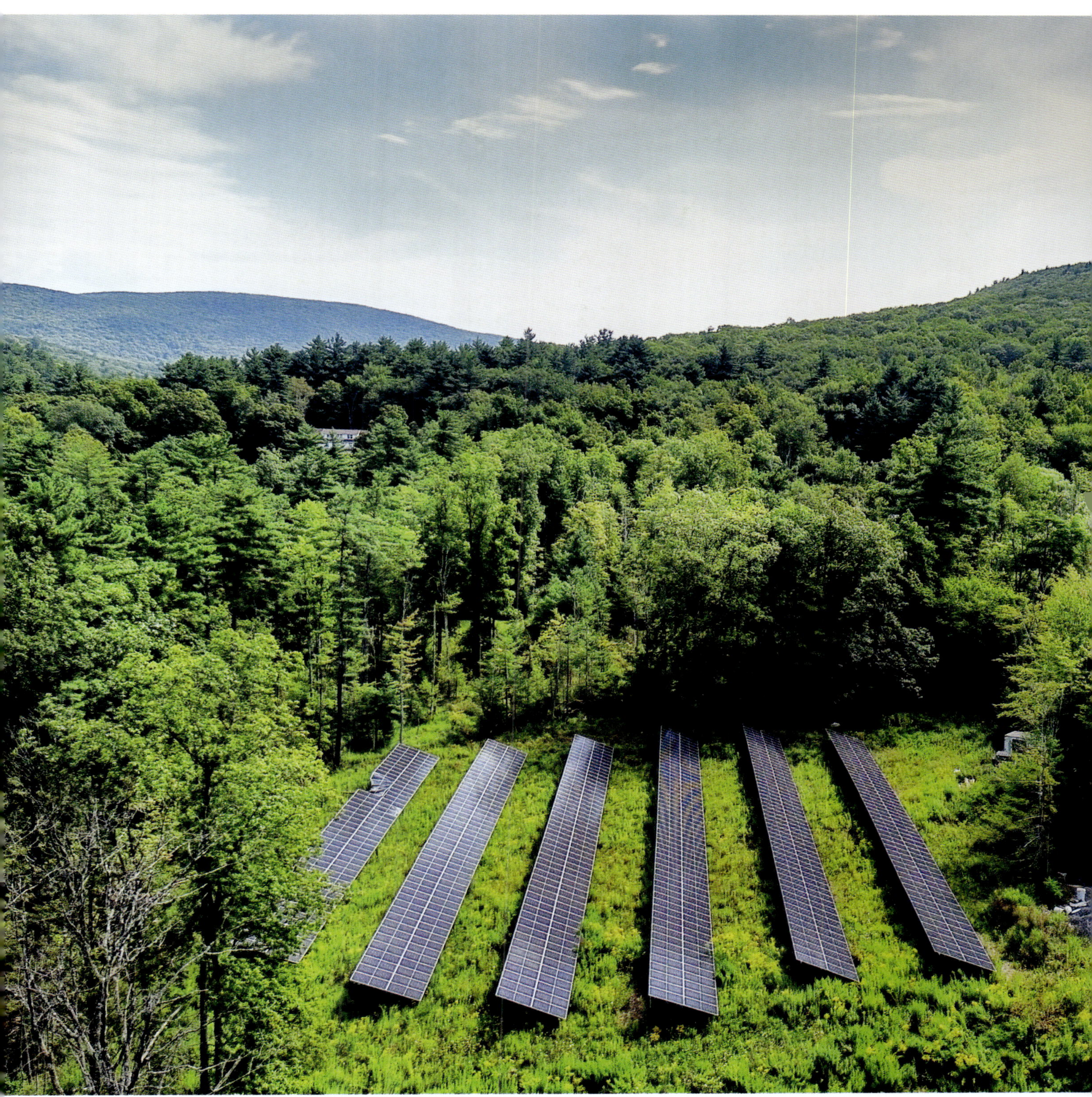

These solar panels produce enough electricity to run the bakery in Boiceville, New York, and help make the bakery carbon neutral.

S&S Farm Brewery

Nassau, New York

When is a brewery not about the beer? When the place—a 140-acre family farm—is about community. That feeling of "a giant family picnic" is what the owners of S&S Farm Brewery are hoping to create. Judging from the number of people gathered on Friday and Saturday nights, the plan is working. Families and friends come to hang out, listen to music, order from the food trucks, and drink handcrafted beer.

Owner of the brewery and fifth-generation farmer Matt Sanford knows which beers are most popular because he loads and empties the kegs himself. He sees and literally feels what sells and what doesn't by picking up empty kegs. That's how he tailors the "menu" of flavors. Self-described as more of a "cook" than a connoisseur or master brewer, Matt grew up milking cows in that same barn when it was his family's dairy. Before that (in this case, prior to 1960), his grandfather had an egg route in Albany about thirty minutes north of Nassau. The farm shifted from eggs to dairy, eventually owning a herd of a hundred cows. Because the price of milk didn't change from the 1960s to the 1990s, as expenses continued to mount, those cows were sold.

In 2003, Matt and his brothers and sisters decided to pivot to a brewery, beef cows, and community. At first, the siblings grew their own organic grains to use in the beers. Matt raised the money to renovate the milking barn into a taproom through a Kickstarter campaign. These days, Matt and his wife, Shaina, run the brewery with the help of friends and family. Their kids, now six and two, are the sixth generation of Sanfords on the same land. Here, looking west over the fields to the Catskill Mountains and east to the silhouettes of the Berkshire range, there is space for everyone to come together.

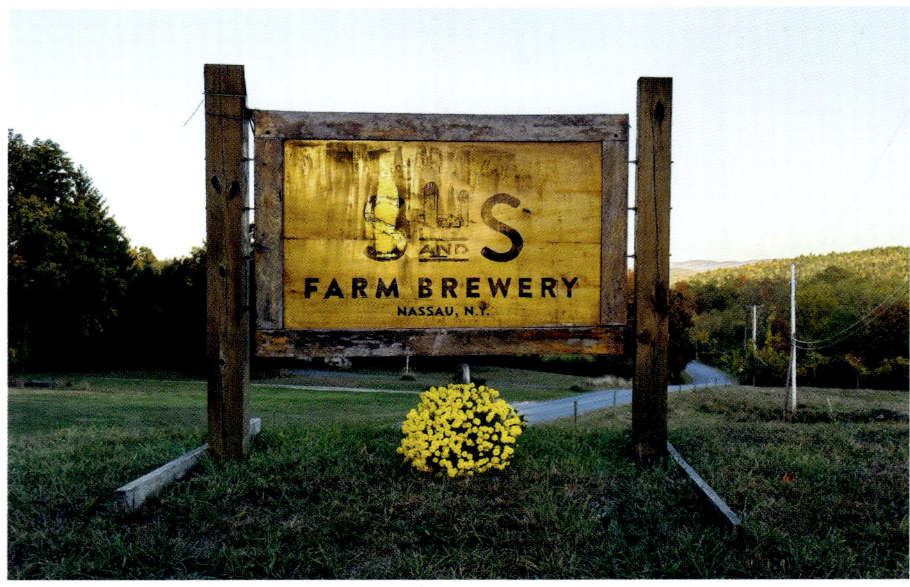

above and opposite, bottom
Signs from the farm's past as a dairy farm are still present at the brewery.

opposite, top
The entrance to the S&S Farm Brewery is through the doors of an old milking barn.

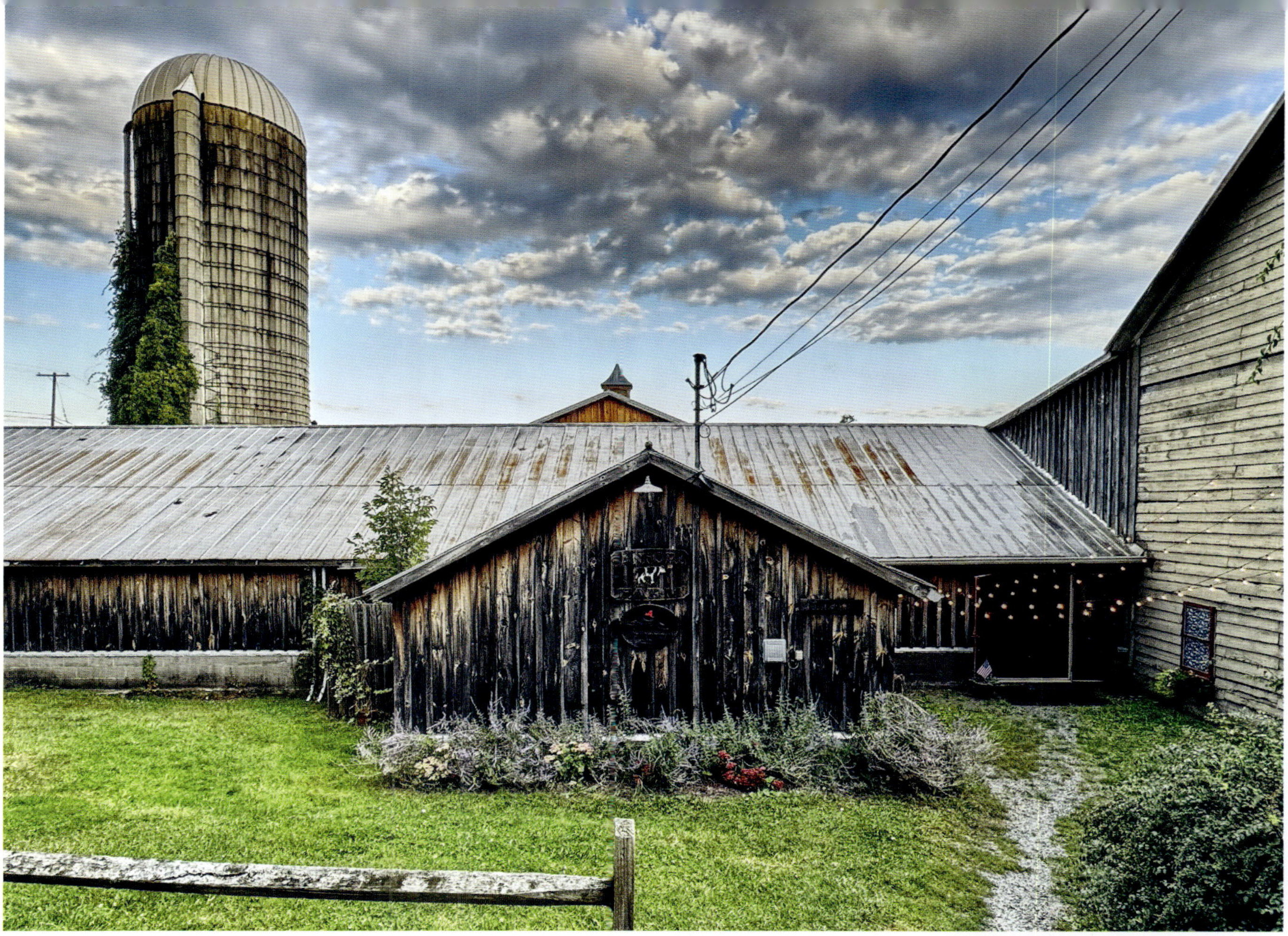

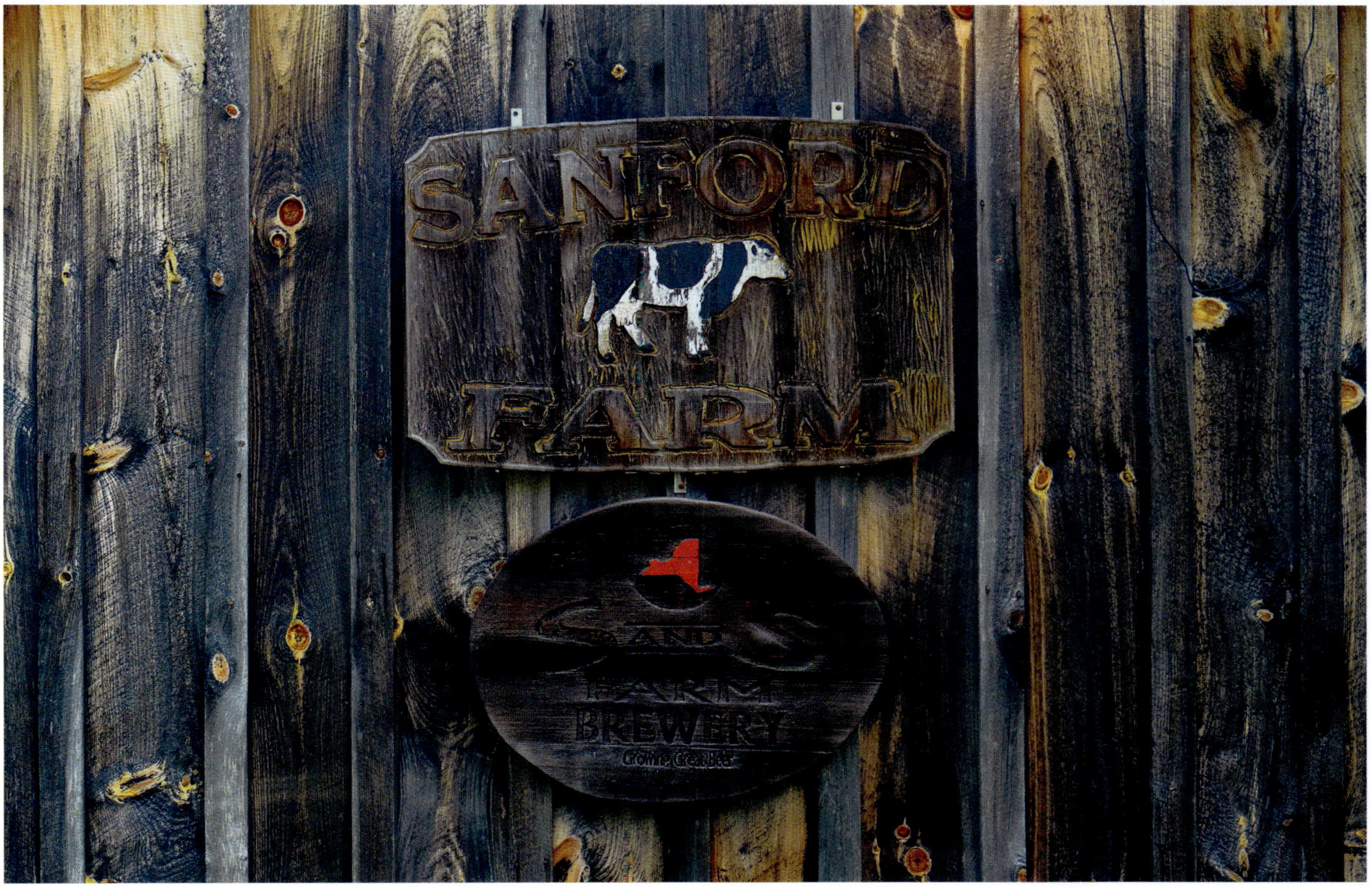
SANFORD
FARM
FARM
BREWERY

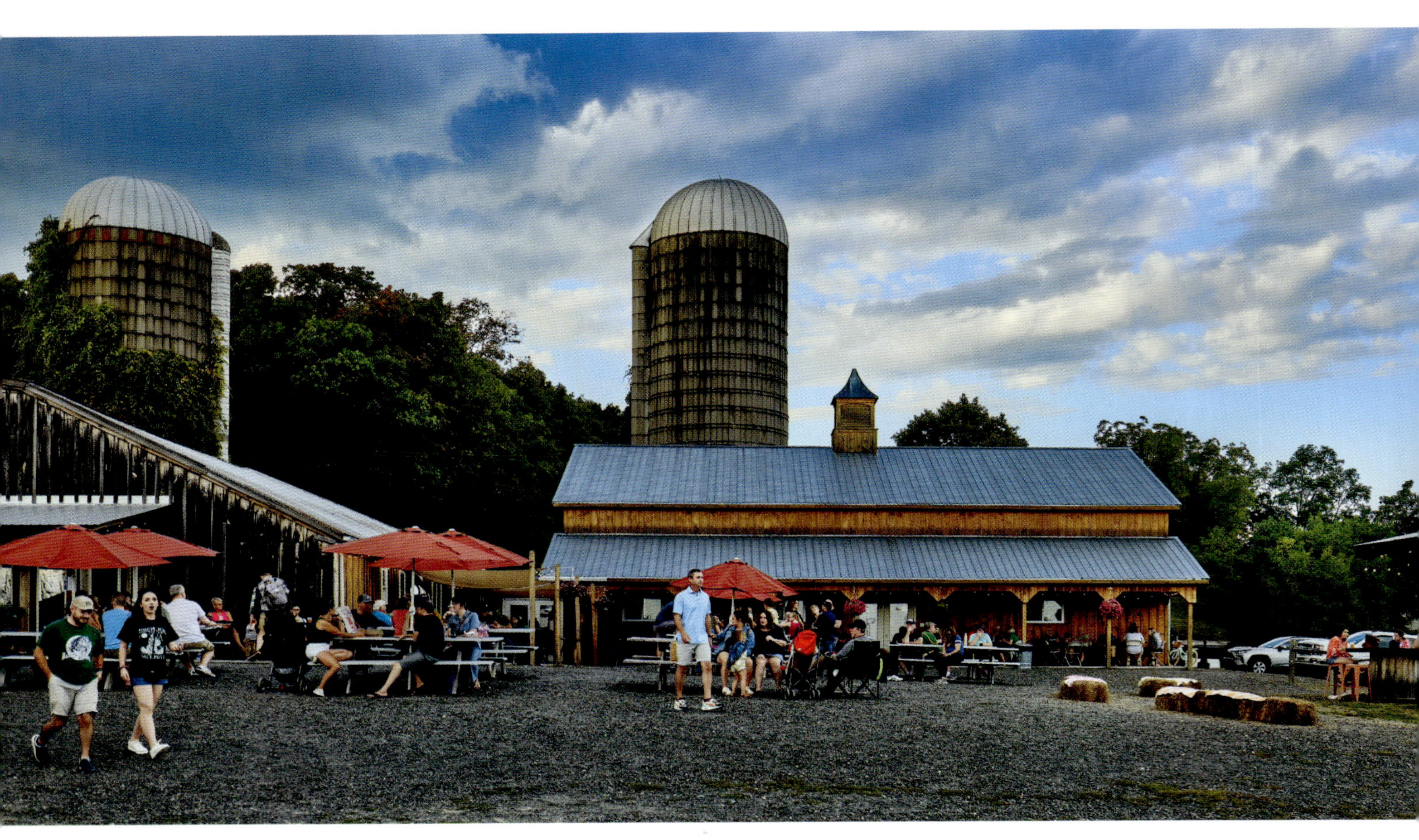

On Fridays and Saturdays, locals and visitors to the area come to hang out around the barns of the old dairy farm.

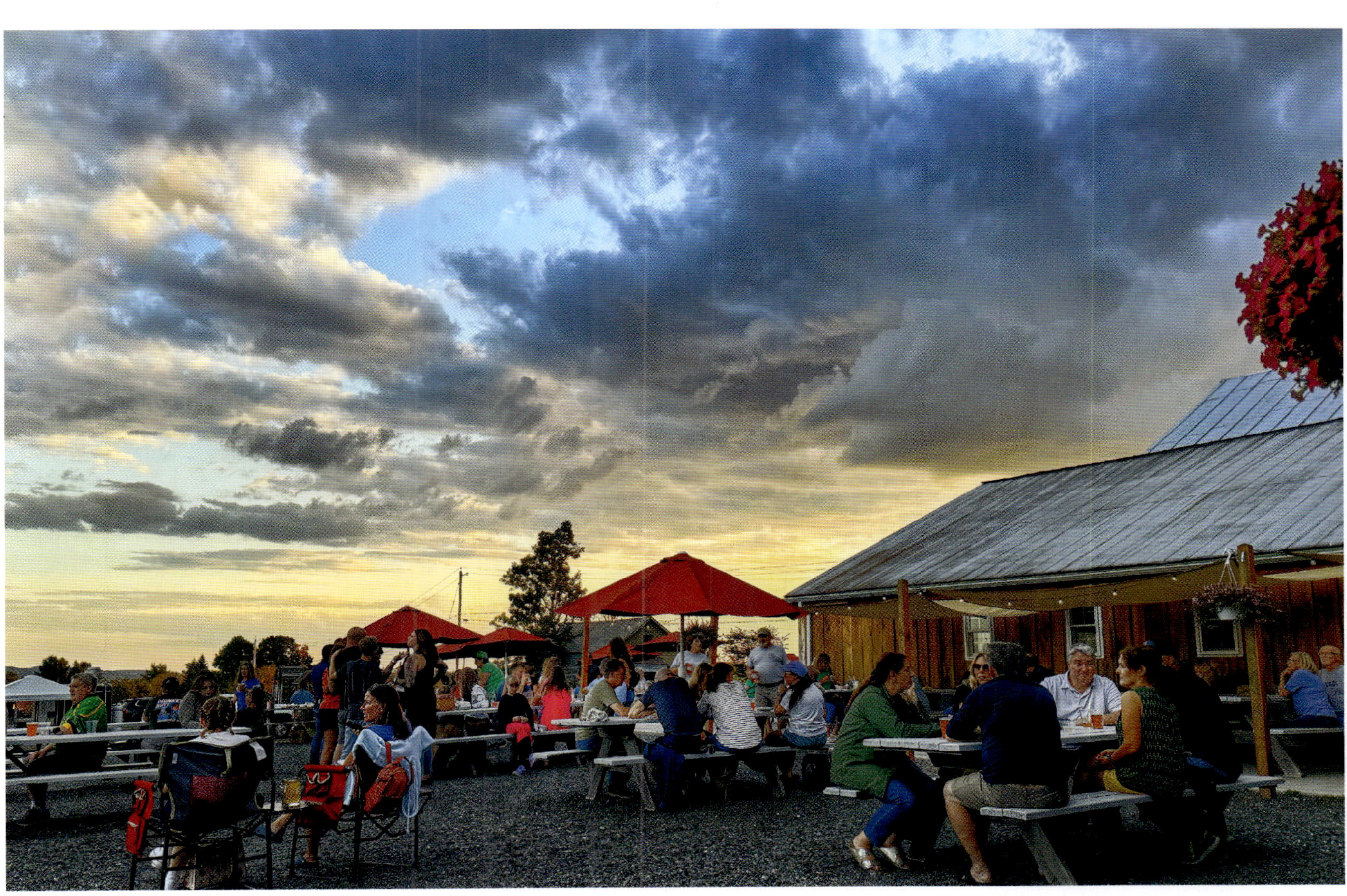

above
Picnic and other tables, some with umbrellas, are placed around the outside of the old barn and silos. A couple of food trucks sell basic fare.

overleaf
There is a designated playground where kids swing, slide, and run around under their family's supervision. The farm buildings, along with the beer, make for a relaxing atmosphere.

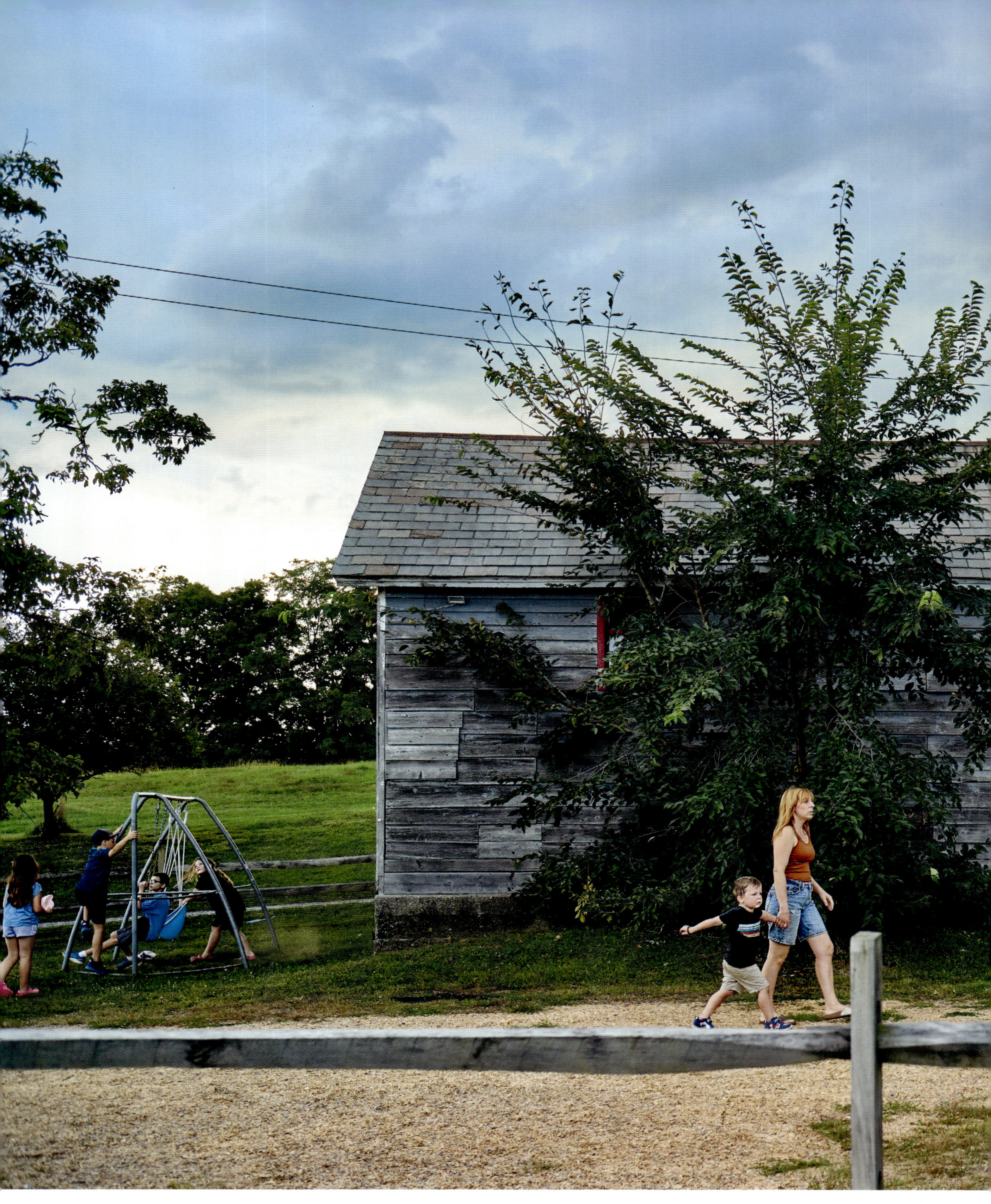

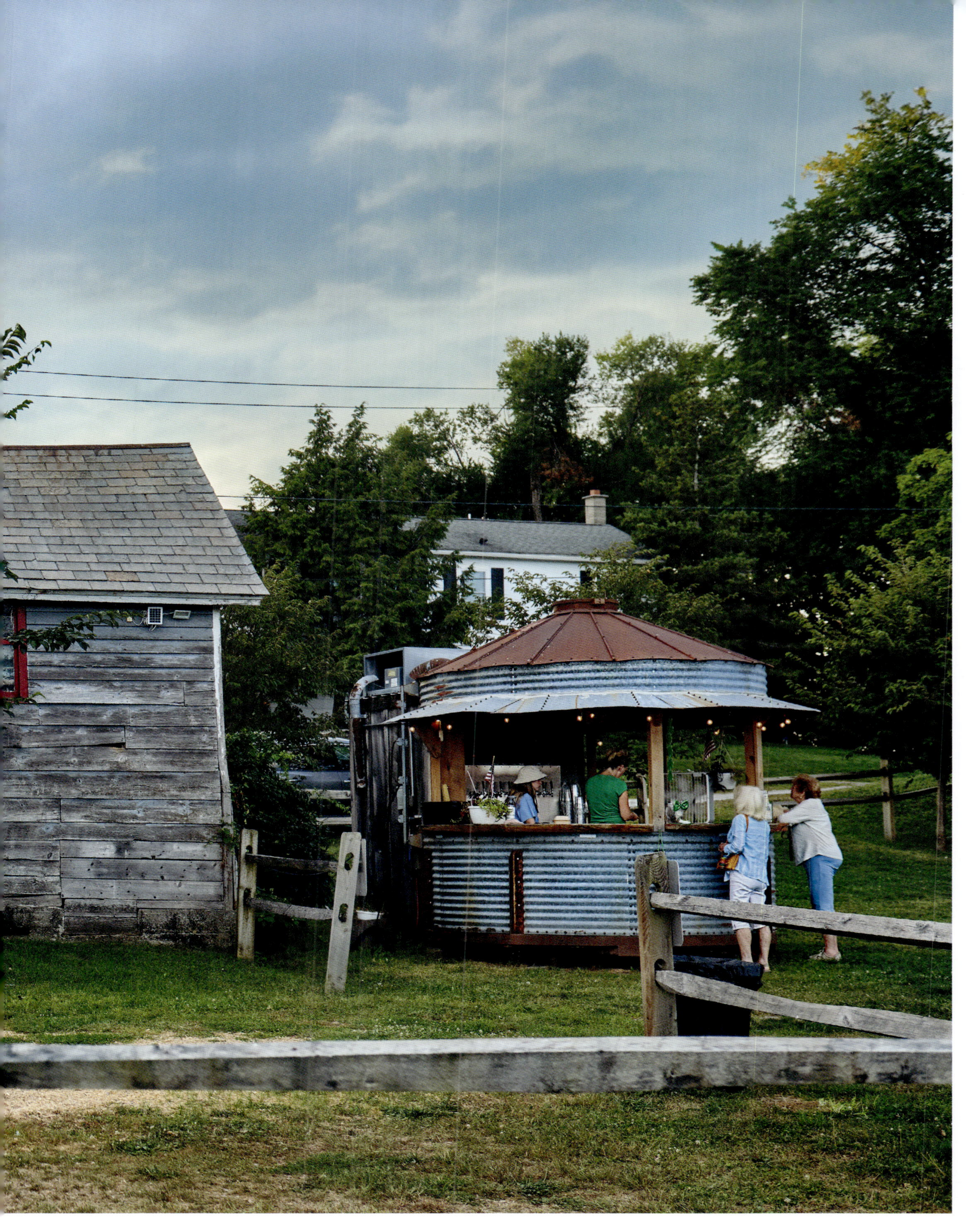

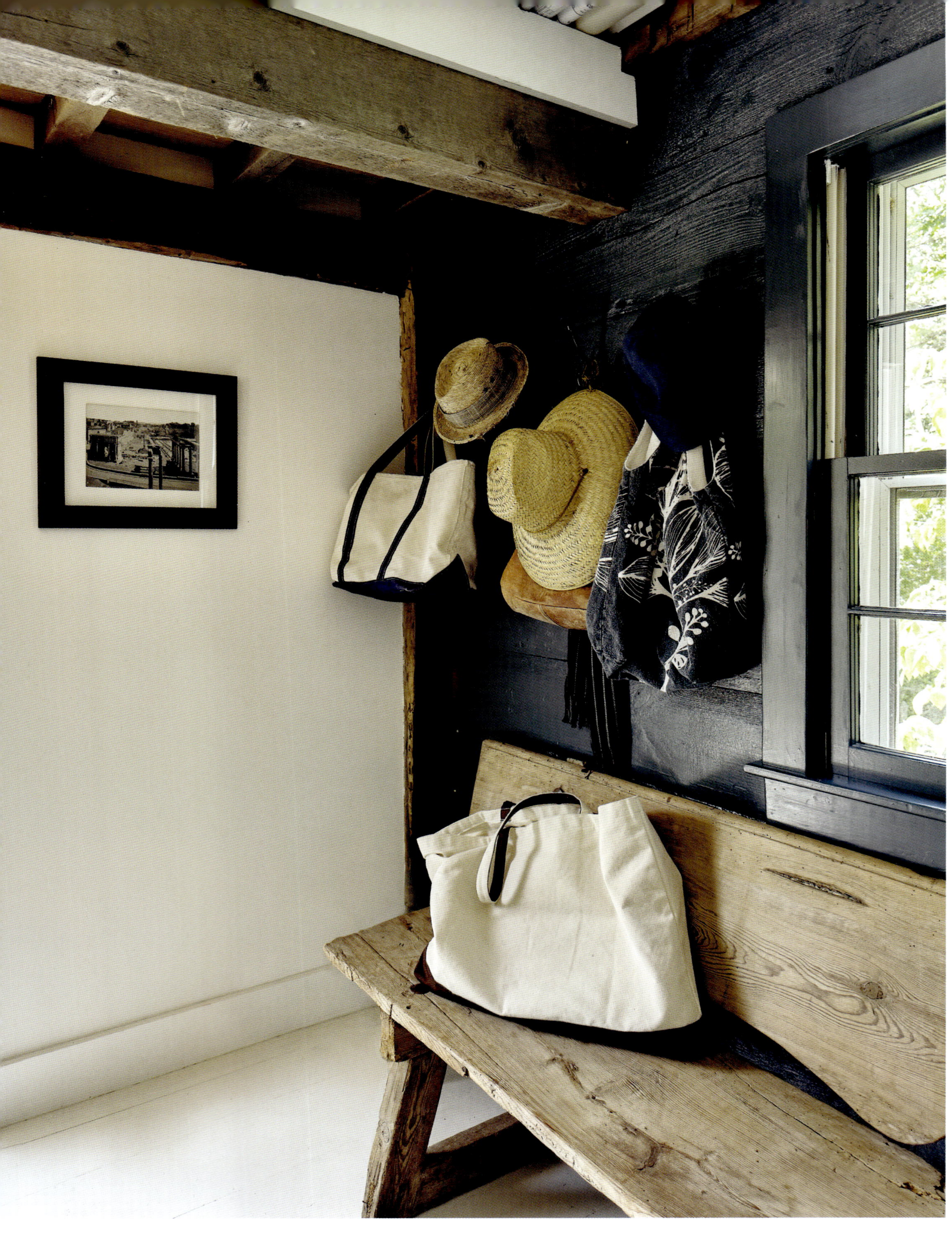

ACKNOWLEDGMENTS

In 2020, our friend and neighbor, writer and publisher Kevin Lippert, came to us to discuss the possibility of working on a book together. The three of us could see the changes happening in upstate New York and wanted to document all these new places and ideas. We set out to scout projects. But soon, COVID-19 restrictions shut down our travels. Around that same time, Kevin's cancer, which had been in remission for over ten years, returned. Kevin died in 2022. We decided to put the idea of the book on hold, but it was Kevin who started us on this journey, and we are grateful.

Three years later, a meeting with Jennifer Thompson reignited the project. The timing was perfect. There were even more places to visit and cover. This book is the result of our work with Jennifer, who provided advice, time, and enthusiasm, without which this book would not have happened. Thank you, Jennifer.

The crack smart team at PA Press, including design director Paul Wagner, managing editor Sara Stemen, and copy editor Karen Levy, was also a pleasure to collaborate with.

We would especially like to thank all those featured in the book, including homeowners, business owners, architects, and artists. Thank you for welcoming us into your business or home—even though we would sometimes arrive unannounced—and for allowing us to tell your story and show your artworks. It has been our honor to get to know you. You have inspired us.

Special thanks to our longtime upstate friends Warren and Lenny Collins and downstate friends Beth O'Neill and Chris McVoy, Barbara Hogenson, and Jeffrey Couchman, who made suggestions on the places to include and provided connections to the people to meet.

Thank you to Ann Sublett for contributing her insightful foreword and for her suggestions on places to investigate.

And to our families, who gave (and continue to give) us love, encouragement, and support all along.

Michel Arnaud & Jane Creech

BIBLIOGRAPHY

Books

Boyle, Robert. *The Hudson River: A Natural and Unnatural History*. W. W. Norton, 1969.

Casscles, Stephen J. *Grapes of the Hudson Valley, and Other Cool Climate Regions of the United States and Canada* (2nd ed.). Flint Mine, 2023.

Morgan, William. *A Simpler Way of Life: Old Farmhouses of New York & New England*. Norfleet, 2013.

Oliver, Bobbie. *Bobbie Oliver/Found Objects*. With an essay by Nancy Princenthal. High Noon Gallery/Jared Linge, 2024.

Przystup, Lisa. *Upstate: Living Spaces with Space to Live*. Monacelli, 2020.

Silverman, Stephen M., and Raphael D. Silver. *The Catskills: Its History and How It Changed America*. Alfred A. Knopf, 2015.

Sokol, David. *Hudson Modern: Residential Landscapes*. Monacelli, 2018.

Articles

Boughton, Kathryn. "Mill Gets New Lease on Life as an Emerging Arts Space." *CT Insider*, July 1, 2009.

Curley, Jane. "The Onteora Club." *The Magazine Antiques*, February 18, 2022.

Davis, Jennifer. "The Haudenosaunee Confederacy and the Constitution." Library of Congress Blogs, September 21, 2023.

Faber, Harold. "Sunday Outing; For Book Lovers, Paradise in a Rural Setting." *New York Times*, December 29, 1991.

Gardner, Ralph, Jr. "Our Local Flower Fairy." WAMC Northeast Public Radio, May 22, 2021.

Halligan, Laura. "Beer Buddies Milk Family's Farming Heritage to Breath Life into New Business, Old Property." *Troy Record*, July 21, 2021.

Hodson, Janice. *Martin Van Buren National Historic Site Historic Furnishings Report Addendum, Part 1: Historical Data Section with Implementation Options*, 2019.

Kazakina, Katya. "A Former School in Upstate New York Is Now a Sprawling Arts Venue." Artnet.com, July 8, 2024.

Kohan, Carol E. *Historic Furnishings Report for Linenwald. U.S. Department of the Interior/National Parks Service Harpers Ferry Center*, 1986.

Kolko, Jed, Emily Badger, and Quoctrung Bui. "How the Pandemic Did and Didn't Change Where Americans Move." *New York Times*, April 19, 2021.

Kristijansdottir, Thorunn. "The Copake Hillsdale Farmers Market Is Not Your Average Farmers Market." *Mainstreet Magazine*, February 2023.

Larson, Jamie. "Why Does Everyone Love the Berry Farm in Chatham?" *Rural Intelligence*, January 22, 2018.

Lee, Denny. "Check In/Check Out: The Roxbury." *New York Times*, January 2, 2005.

"Omi International Art Center Grows Greener." Inhabitat.com, November 22, 2008.

Palaia, Franc. "Artist Brings Garden Street Mural Back to Life." *Poughkeepsie Journa*l, August 3, 2016 (updated August 8, 2016).

Schuetz, Annemarie. "Home as a Gift from the Past." *River Reporter*, March 12, 2019.

Sheets, Hilarie. "Foreland, an Art Complex with Big Ambitions, Grows in Catskill." *New York Times*, June 30, 2022.

Smith, Roberta. "Art in Review: Jim Ziviv/Burning Relic." *New York Times*, February 2, 2021.

van Straaten, Laura. "An Abandoned School Becomes a Canvas for Art Galleries." *New York Times*, May 8, 2024.

Yelavich, Susan. "Coal, Steel, Rubber, Leather." *Nest: Warp & Woof*, Winter 2002–2003.

Websites

Art Omi | artomi.org

Lindenwald, Martin Van Buren National Historic Site | vanburenpapers.org | zuber.fr/en/scenic-wallpapers/hunting-landscape

'T' Space/The Steven Myron Holl Foundation Archive | stevenholl.com

The Campus | nxthvn.com | thecampusupstate.com

The Iroquois Museum | projectilepoints.net | iroquoismuseum.org

The Rock Valley Schoolhouse | therockvalleyschoolhouse.com

Troy Waterfront Farmers Market | troymarket.org

Watervliet Shaker Settlement, Church Family Site | virtual.shakerheritage.org

ARTWORK INDEX

Credits are alphabetized by artist's name:
Name: *title* (year), page number

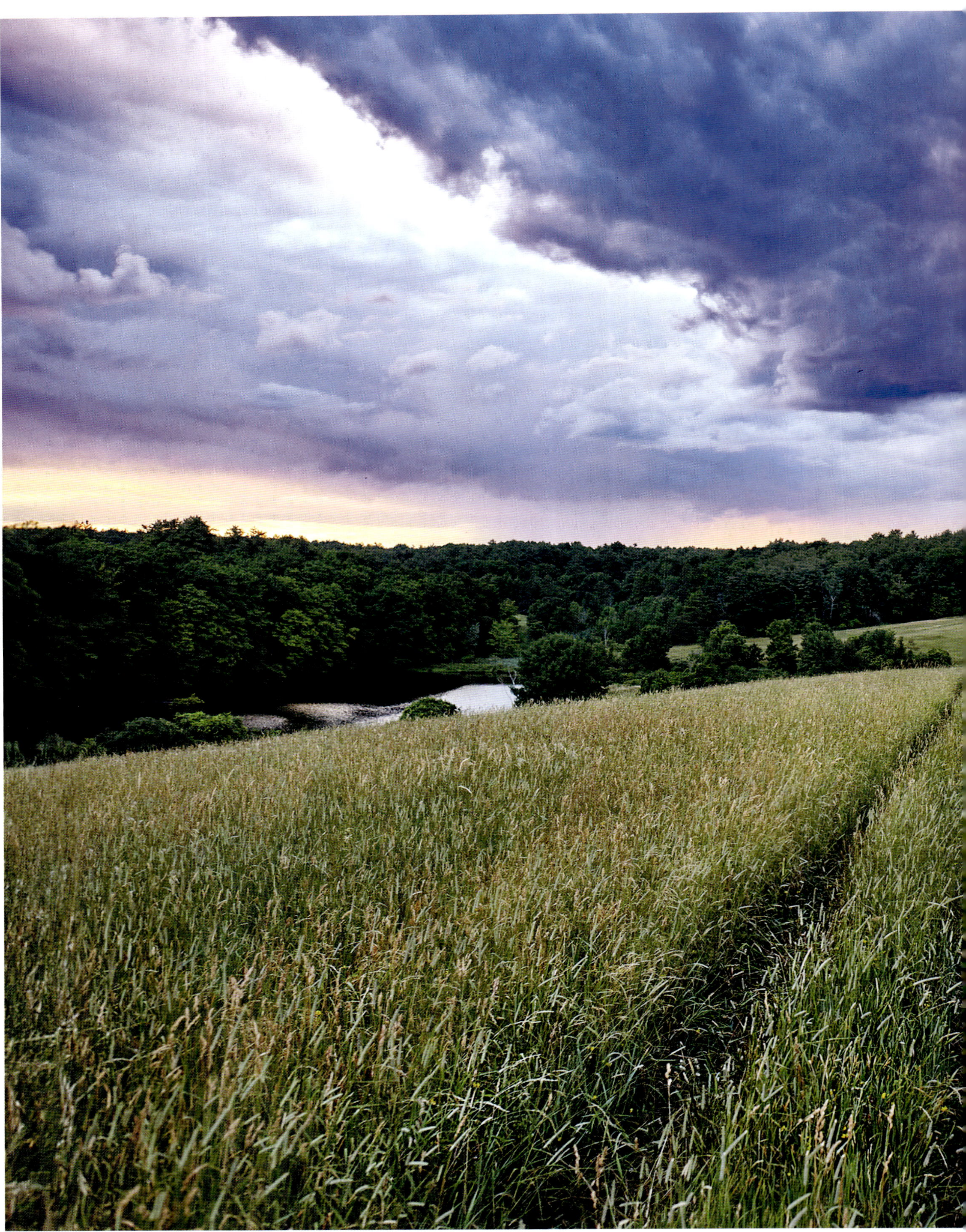

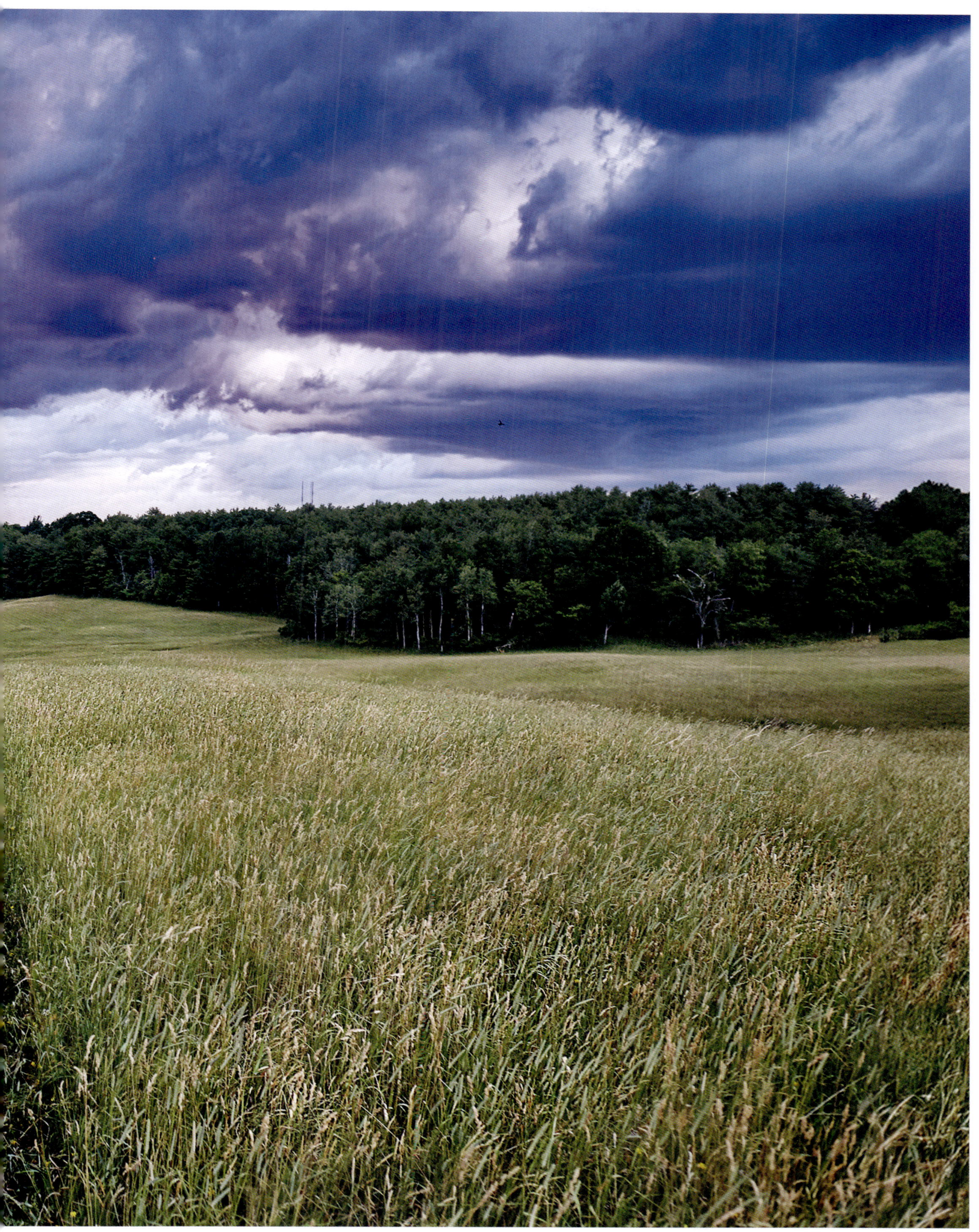

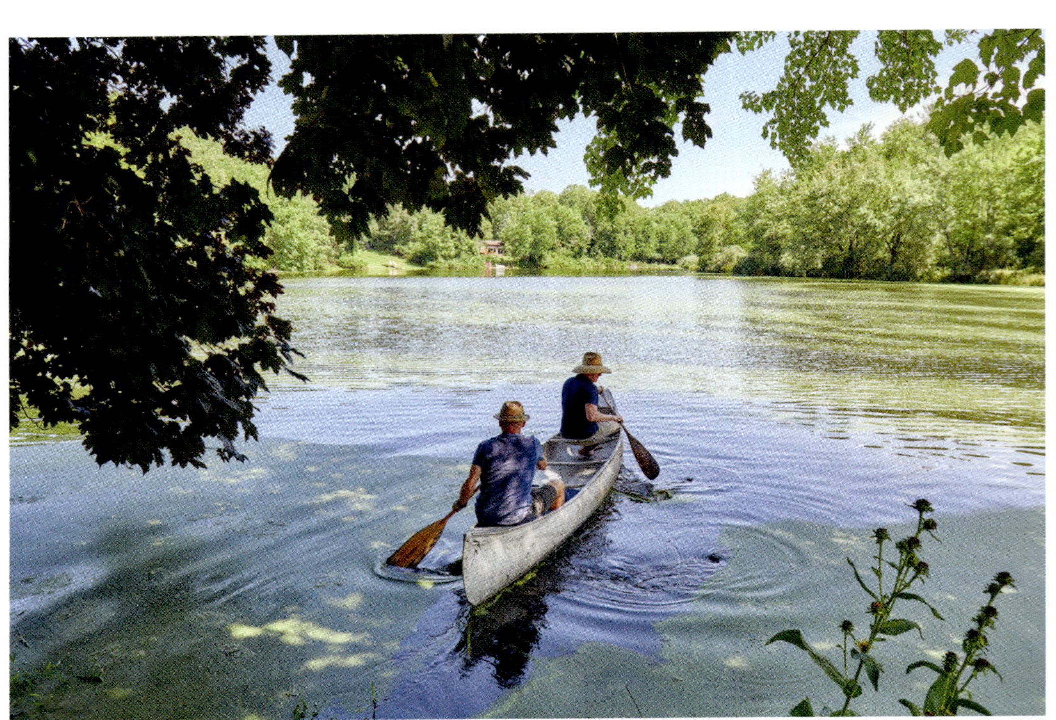